D1460459

Word 2000:
The Complete Reference

Word 2000:
The Complete Reference

Peter Weverka
David A. Reid

Osborne/**McGraw-Hill**

Berkeley   New York   St. Louis   San Francisco
Auckland   Bogotá   Hamburg   London   Madrid
Mexico City   Milan   Montreal   New Delhi   Panama City
Paris   São Paulo   Singapore   Sydney
Tokyo   Toronto

Osborne/**McGraw-Hill**
2600 Tenth Street
Berkeley, California 94710
U.S.A.

For information on translations or book distributors outside the U.S.A., or to arrange bulk purchase discounts for sales promotions, premiums, or fund-raisers, please contact Osborne/**McGraw-Hill** at the above address.

Word 2000: The Complete Reference

234567890 DOC DOC 90198765432109

ISBN 0-07-211969-1

Publisher
Brandon A. Nordin

Associate Publisher and Editor-in-Chief
Scott Rogers

Acquisitions Editor
Joanne Cuthbertson

Project Editor
Betsy Manini

Editorial Assistant
Stephane Thomas

Technical Editor
Eric Ray

Copy Editor
Claire Splan

Proofreader
Rhonda Holmes

Indexer
Rebecca Plunkett

Computer Designers
Michele Zmijewski
Roberta Steele
Gary Corrigan

Illustrators
Brian Wells
Beth Young

Series Design
Peter F. Hancik

For Sofia

About the Authors

Peter Weverka is the author of 18 computer books, including *Office 2000 for Busy People*, *Microsoft Office 97: The Complete Reference*, and *Word 2000 for Dummies Quick Reference*. He has edited 80 computer books on various topics, and his articles and stories have appeared in *Harper's* and *Spy*.

David A. Reid is a Web site developer, consultant, and corporate trainer. He teaches classes in the Internet, Web site development, and program development for community colleges and corporations. His Berkeley-based company, CyberGuild.com, provides information design services to many Bay Area clients.

Contents at a Glance

Part VII   Appendixes

Contents

Part I

Learning the Ropes

Part II

Formatting Text and Pages

Part III

Professional-Looking Documents with Word 2000

Part VI

Getting More Out of Word 2000

Acknowledgments

This book owes a lot to many hard-working people at the offices of Osborne/McGraw-Hill in Berkeley, California. I would especially like to thank Acquisitions Editor Joanne Cuthbertson for giving me the opportunity to write this book and for suggesting how to make this book a better one.

Two people at Osborne worked long hours on my book and took an interest in it above and beyond the call of duty. I am very grateful to Betsy Manini for overseeing the production of this book and for thoughtfully considering the thousand and one decisions that a project editor has to make. I would also like to thank the hawk-eyed Claire Splan, this book's copyeditor, for doing such an exemplary job.

Thanks, of course, go to Stephane Thomas for her cheerful disposition and skill at juggling manuscripts to make sure that every one of them land in the right place.

David Reid, my co-author, wrote Chapters 16 and 17 and lent his Web expertise in two or three other places as well, and I was glad to have David along for the ride. I must also thank M'Kail Iapoce for writing the sample documents on the CD and for showing me how to slam-dunk.

Technical editor Eric Ray dogged me every step of the way to make sure that all the instructions in this book are indeed correct, and I thank him for his work. I would also like to thank Rebecca Plunkett for her excellent index.

These people at the offices of Osborne/McGraw-Hill went the extra mile for this book, and I am grateful to all of them: Designers Roberta Steele, Michele Zmijewski, Michelle Galicia, Jean Butterfield, Ann Sellers, Gary Corrigan, and Jani Beckwith; Graphics Illustrators Brian Wells, Robert Hansen, and Beth Young; Technical Operator Peter F. Hancik; and Proofreader Rhonda Holmes.

Finally, I would like to thank my family—Sofia, Henry, and Addie—for accommodating my vampire-like writing schedule and eerie demeanor at daybreak.

Peter Weverka
San Francisco
February, 1999

Introduction

This book presents instructions for completing every task that can be undertaken in Word 2000. This book is your key to understanding how Word 2000 works and how you can use the program to the best advantage. Whether you don't know how to complete a task or you want to learn a better way, look to the pages of this book. Here you will discover how to make Word 2000 work for you instead of the other way around.

How This Book Differs from Other Books About Word 2000

You are holding in your hands a first of its kind—a computer book designed to make learning Word 2000 as easy and comfortable as possible. This book is decidedly different from other books about Word for the following reasons.

A TASK-ORIENTED APPROACH Most computer books describe how to use the software, but this book explains how to complete tasks. I assume you came to this book because you want to know how to *do* something—print form letters, run text in columns, generate an index. You came to the right place.

Information in this book is presented by topic, not according to where it is found on the Word menus. Nothing infuriates me more in a Word book than an exhaustive table that describes, for example, all the options on the Save tab in the Options dialog box (choose Tools | Options to get there). Just because all those options are found in the same place doesn't mean they have a lot in common or should be described in the same place in a book. No, the options on the Save tab pertain to many different tasks. In this book, you will find a description of each Save tab option in the appropriate place—as part of the instructions for completing a task.

ACCESSIBILITY OF INFORMATION   This book is a reference, and that means readers have to be able to find instructions quickly. To that end, the editors and I took great pains to make sure that the material in this book is well organized. You are invited to turn to a chapter, thumb through the pages, and find out by reading the headings which strategies are available for completing a task. The descriptive headings help you find information quickly. The bulleted and numbered lists make following instructions simpler. The tables make options easier to understand. I want you to be able to look down the page and see in a heading or list the name of the topic that concerns you. Computer books are famous for their long, dreary, ponderous paragraphs, but if you look for a long, dreary, ponderous paragraph in this book you will look in vain. You don't have to slog through a morass of commentary to find the information you need in this book.

TOP TEN LISTS   At the end of most chapters in this book is a Top Ten List—a list of ten tips, tricks, or problem-solving techniques. Rather than distribute these valuable nuggets of knowledge throughout a chapter, I put them all at the end so you can find them easily. Be sure to look at the end of the chapters to find out strategies for doing it well, doing it right, and doing it quickly.

PRACTICE DOCUMENTS   The CD that comes with this book includes 60 practice documents. Open the practice documents to get hands-on experience with Word. Where a practice document is available, I include a Learn by Example icon and a description of the document in the text. Appendix D explains how to access the practice documents on the CD and perhaps copy them to your computer.

LEARN BY EXAMPLE
Look for Learn by Example icons like this one. The icons tell you when a practice document is available on the CD.

ANNOTATED FIGURES   Most of the figures (not the illustrations) in this book are annotated. They are thoroughly annotated, in fact. A savvy Word user can simply look at the figures to find out how to complete tasks.

EASY-TO-UNDERSTAND SCREEN SHOTS   Look closely at the screen shots in this book and you will see that all of them show only what you need to see to understand a Word feature. When instructions refer to one part of the screen, only that part of the screen is shown. In most computer books, you see the entire Word screen whether you need to see the whole screen or a corner of it. I took great care to make sure that the figures and illustrations in this book serve to help you understand Word and know how to make the best use of the program.

INSTRUCTIONS FOR "UNDOING IT"   Every computer book tells you how to do tasks, but when you complete a task at the computer, half the time you discover that you shouldn't have completed it. In other words, you want to undo what you just did. In this book, wherever instructions for completing a task are given, instructions for undoing it follow. You are entitled to change your mind, and if you change your mind about doing a task for which I give instructions, all you have to do is follow the instructions for "undoing it."

CROSS-REFERENCES   This book is filled to the brim with cross-references. Word 2000 is even more complicated than its predecessor, and most features are linked to other features. You have to know about styles to create a Web page. You have to know about bookmarks to insert a cross-reference. Most books refer you vaguely to another chapter, but the cross-references in this book point to specific headings in other chapters. In this book, you know by name exactly where to go to get the background information you need to complete a task.

IN-DEPTH GLOSSARY   A definition of every computing term readers might conceivably stumble over is found in the Glossary. If you don't know a term, look for it there. The Glossary at the back of this book is quite long and wanted to be a dictionary, but smoking stunted its growth.

What's in This Book, Anyway?

This book is organized to help you find the information you need quickly. Your best bet for finding instructions is to turn to the table of contents or index, but you are also invited to turn the pages at leisure. Find a chapter whose topic interests you and thumb through its pages—you will discover tips and tricks you didn't know before.

The topics in this book are too numerous to describe in an introduction, but here are the bare outlines of what you will find in Parts I through VII:

- **Part I: Learning the Ropes**   Shows how to create, open, and edit documents. You also discover how to use the Help program and print documents.

- **Part II: Formatting Text and Pages**   Demonstrates how to take advantage of speed techniques for using Word. You learn how to format text, paragraphs, pages, and documents. You also find out how to handle lists and proof your work.

- **Part III: Professional-Looking Documents with Word 2000**   Takes you beyond simple layouts. You find out how to handle and create styles, develop your own templates, and embellish documents with artwork and text boxes. Part III also gives instructions for creating newsletters and brochures. This part of the book offers the most comprehensive coverage of the Drawing tools found in any computer book.

- **Part IV: Developing Web Pages with Word 2000**   Describes the many tools for creating Web pages. You see how to create a Web site composed of many Web pages and link the pages with hyperlinks. You also discover how to lay out Web pages and all the organizing principles that you need to know to successfully post a page on the Internet.

- **Part V: Using Word 2000 at the Office**   Explores the many features that help when writing reports, manuals, and scholarly papers, including tables of contents, indexes, and cross-references. You learn the many ways that Word tools can help you collaborate with others. You find out how to generate form letters and labels as well.

- **Part VI: Getting More Out of Word 2000**   Explains how to manage documents and customize the program. Included is a chapter about creating online documents with Word.

- **Part VII: Appendixes**   Includes four appendixes and a glossary that explain how to install Word and how to take advantage of the opportunities this book presents for getting a MOUS certificate.

Help for MOUS Exam Candidates

The Microsoft Office User Specialist (MOUS) program is a program whereby candidates can be certified to use Word 2000. Appendix B describes in detail how MOUS candidates can use this book and the tests on the CD to prepare for the MOUS exams. However, this book is by no means strictly for MOUS exam candidates. This book is for everybody who toils happily or unhappily in Word 2000.

What's on the Companion CD

Appendix D describes in detail what is on the companion CD. The CD offers a test to help candidates prepare for the Microsoft Office User Specialist (MOUS) exams. Also on the CD are 60 practice documents you can use to help hone your skills with Word 2000. Appendix D explains how to copy the practice documents to your computer or open them from the CD.

Conventions Used in This Book

To make this book more useful and a pleasure to read, I joined heads with the publisher to create several conventions. Following are descriptions of the conventions in this book.

Icons

To alert you to an important bit of advice, a shortcut, or a pitfall, you see a Note, Tip, or Caution icon and a few important words in the text.

Notes refer you to other parts of the book, offer background information, and occasionally define terms.

Tips give you shortcuts and handy pieces of advice to make you a better user of Word 2000. Take a tip from me and read the Tips carefully.

When you see a Caution, prick up your ears. Cautions appear when you have to make a crucial choice or when you are about to undertake something you might regret later.

Besides Notes, Tips, and Cautions, you also see Learn by Example icons in this book.

LEARN BY EXAMPLE
The Learn by Example icon tells you when a practice document is available that you can use to try out a Word 2000 feature. Appendix D explains how to access the practice documents.

Sidebars

From time to time you will find sidebars in this book. Sidebars present information that is tangential to the main discussion. Sidebars appear in boxes—boxes like this one.

Command Names

In this book, the | symbol is used in menu command sequences. For example, you can choose File | New to open a new Word document. The | is just a shorthand way of saying, "Choose New from the File menu." "Choose Tools | Language | Thesaurus" is a shorthand way of saying, "Open the Tools menu, choose the Language command, and choose Thesaurus from the Language submenu."

I Wouldn't Mind Hearing from You

Every tip, trick, and problem-solving technique I know of for working in Word 2000 is found on the pages of this book. This book is comprehensive. It explores every nook and cranny of Word. However, if you can't find a solution to a problem in this book, you may e-mail me at peter_weverka@msn.com. Please put the words "Complete Reference Word 2000" in the subject heading of the message so that I know what your message pertains to. I will do my best to answer your question notwithstanding my busy schedule and natural inclination to be lazy.

The
Complete
Reference

Part I

Learning the Ropes

1

The
Complete
Reference

Word
2000

Chapter 1

Getting Acquainted
with Word 2000

In this chapter, you'll learn a handful of things that you will do nearly every time you run Word 2000. This chapter explains the ins and outs of starting and closing Word and opening and closing documents. It describes the various parts of the Word screen and how to manipulate the toolbars and ruler. In this chapter there are numerous shortcuts for opening files and managing files better. My Word, there is a lot of good stuff in this chapter!

Fast Ways to Start Word 2000

It goes without saying, but you can't begin writing a masterpiece on your word processor until you start Word 2000. The standard way to start Word is to click the Start button and choose Programs | Microsoft Word, as shown in Figure 1-1. Everybody, or nearly everybody, knows how to start a program the standard way. The following pages explain how to open a document and Word at the same time, start Word with a shortcut icon, or start Word whenever you turn on your computer.

Note
A file you create with Word is called a document. For practical purposes, "file" and "document" mean the same thing when you are working in Microsoft Word.

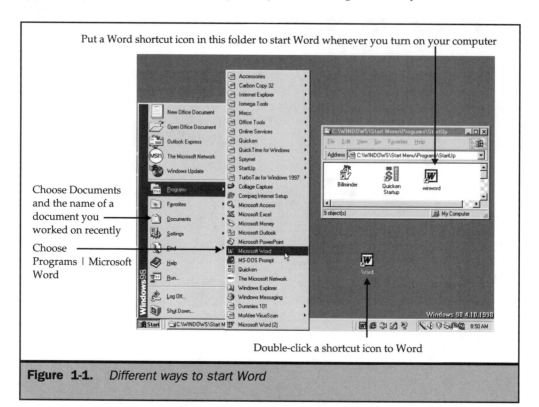

Figure 1-1. *Different ways to start Word*

Opening a Document and Word at the Same Time

Clicking the Start button and choosing Programs | Microsoft Word to start Word takes but a second, but suppose you are speed demon. In that case, you can open a Word document and start Word at the same time with one of these techniques:

- **Windows Documents Menu**   Click the Start button, choose Documents, and click the name of a Word document on the Documents menu. This menu lists the last 15 files you opened.

- **My Documents Folder**   Click the Start button and choose Documents | My Documents. The My Computer program opens and you see the contents of the My Documents folder. Double-click a document icon in this folder. "Opening and Closing Documents," later in this chapter, explains the My Documents folder.

- **Document in My Computer or Windows Explorer**   Open My Computer or Windows Explorer, find the folder that the document you want to open is located in, and double-click the document. My Computer and Windows Explorer are file-management programs that come with Windows.

Starting Word with a Shortcut Icon

Perhaps the fastest way to start Word is to create a *shortcut icon* (see Figure 1-1). After you create a Word shortcut icon, it sits on the Windows desktop where you can double-click it and start Word instantly. Probably one or two shortcut icons are on your

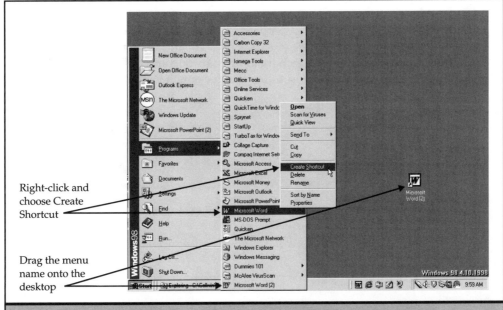

Right-click and choose Create Shortcut

Drag the menu name onto the desktop

Figure 1-2.   *Users of Windows 98 can create a shortcut icon for Word by right-clicking Microsoft Word and choosing Create Shortcut*

desktop already. To find one, look for an icon with an arrow in the lower-left corner. Users running Windows 98 on their computers can create a shortcut icon simply by right-clicking a program name on a menu; users of Windows 95 have to burrow into the files on their computers to create a shortcut icon. Read on.

Creating a Word Shortcut Icon in Windows 98

Follow these steps to create a shortcut icon for Word if you are running Windows 98:

1. Click the Start button, choose Programs, and right-click Microsoft Word on the Programs menu. As shown in Figure 1-2, a shortcut menu appears.

2. Choose Create Shortcut on the menu. As shown in Figure 1-2, a new name appears at the bottom of the Programs menu: Microsoft Word (2).

3. Drag Microsoft Word (2) onto the desktop. That's right—simply click the name, hold down the mouse button, and drag the menu name off the menu. A Word shortcut icon appears on the desktop.

4. Right-click the Word shortcut icon, choose Rename, type **Word**, and press ENTER.

Starting Word from the Quick Launch Toolbar

Users whose machines run Windows 98 can also start Word by clicking its shortcut icon on the Quick Launch toolbar, the toolbar located on the right side of the Taskbar. Wherever your work takes you, you can see the Quick Launch toolbar and click its shortcut icons to open programs. To put a Word shortcut icon on the Quick Launch toolbar, create a Word shortcut for the desktop and then copy the shortcut icon onto the Quick Launch toolbar. To do so, hold down the CTRL key, and drag the Word shortcut icon onto the Quick Launch toolbar:

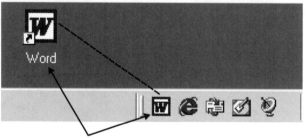

Hold down the CTRL key and drag a Word shortcut icon onto the Quick Launch toolbar to copy it there

Creating a Word Shortcut Icon in Windows 95

Follow these steps to create a shortcut icon for Word if your computer runs Windows 95:

1. As shown in Figure 1-3, start Windows Explorer or My Computer and open the C:\Program Files\Microsoft Office\Office folder.

2. Find the winword file. You have to scroll to the end of the files to find it.

3. Choose View | Details to switch to Details view.

4. Right-click the winword file and choose Create Shortcut from the shortcut menu. A shortcut icon and the words "Shortcut to winword" appear at the end of the file list. If necessary, scroll to the end of the list to see it.

Caution   *Make sure you right-click the winword application file, not the TUW file. You can tell which is which by glancing at the Type column (in Details view), which lists file types.*

5. Drag the shortcut icon out of the window and onto the desktop. If necessary, click the Restore button in the upper-right corner of the My Computer or Windows Explorer window to shrink the window onscreen before you start dragging.

6. Right-click the shortcut icon and choose Rename.

7. Type **Word** or another descriptive name and press the ENTER key.

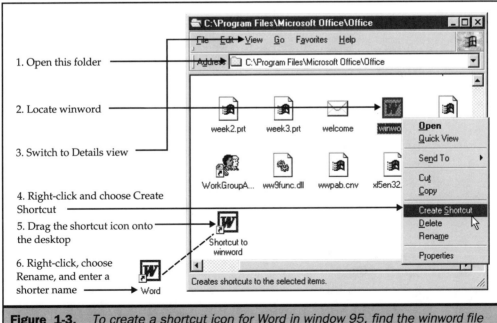

Figure 1-3.   *To create a shortcut icon for Word in window 95, find the winword file in the C:\Program Files\Microsoft Office\Office folder*

Making Word Start When You Turn on Your Computer

Instead of going to the trouble of starting Word each time you sit at your desk, you can kill two birds with one stone and make Word start automatically whenever you turn on your computer. To do so, put a shortcut to Word in the C:\Windows\Start Menu\Programs\StartUp folder. Windows offers a special set of commands for doing just that.

 The fastest way to make Word start automatically is to simply make a Word shortcut icon and copy it in the C:\Windows\Start Menu\Programs\StartUp folder (see Figure 1-1).

Follow these steps to start Word whenever you turn on your computer:

1. Click the Start button and choose Settings | Taskbar & Start Menu.
2. Click the Start Menu Programs tab in the Taskbar Properties dialog box.
3. Click the Add button. You'll see the Create Shortcut dialog box.
4. Type **"C:\Program Files\Microsoft Office\Office\winword.exe"** in the Command Line text box, as shown in Figure 1-4. You can also click the Browse button and locate the winword file in the Browse dialog box. You will find it in the C:\Program Files\Microsoft Office\Office folder.
5. Click the Next button. You will see the Select Program Folder dialog box.

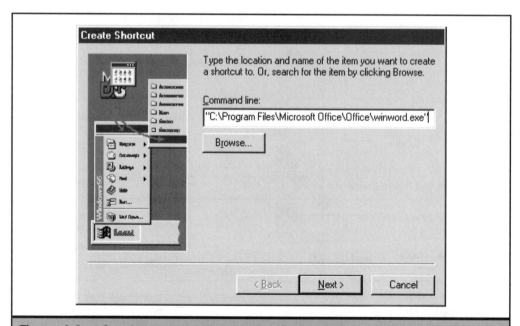

Figure 1-4. *Creating a shortcut icon to Word so the program opens automatically when you turn on the computer*

6. Click the StartUp folder and click Next. You have to scroll to the bottom of the dialog box to find the StartUp folder.

7. Type **Word** in the Select a Title dialog box and then click the Finish button.

If you decide against opening Word automatically when you start your computer, remove the Word shortcut icon from the C:\Windows\Start Menu\Programs\StartUp folder. To do so, open that folder in My Computer or Windows Explorer, right-click the shortcut icon, choose Delete from the shortcut menu, and click Yes when you are asked if you really want to delete the shortcut.

Finding Your Way Around the Screen

Learning your way around a new computer program is like the first day of junior high school—it's intimidating. Your palms sweat. You feel agitated. To keep you from being intimidated, the following pages explain what the different parts of the Word 2000 screen are, how to read the status bar at the bottom of the screen, and how to handle the ruler and toolbars.

The Different Parts of the Screen

Figure 1-5 shows the different parts of the Word screen. Fold down the corner of this page so you can return here if screen terminology confuses you. Here are brief descriptions of the parts of the screen:

- **Title Bar**   The stripe along the top of the screen. It lists the document's name.
- **Window Buttons**   These buttons are for shrinking, enlarging, and closing the window that you are working in. See "Working in Two Places or Documents at Once" in Chapter 6.
- **Main Menu**   The menus you can open and choose commands from. "A Word about Menu Commands," later in this chapter, explains Word's new truncated menus.
- **Document Close Button**   Click this button when you want to quit working on a document.
- **Document Window**   Where you process words but not cheese.
- **Standard and Formatting Toolbars**   The two most important toolbars in Word. Click a button on a toolbar to give a command.
- **Ruler**   Helps show where items are laid out on the page.
- **Split Box**   For dividing the screen in two so you can work in more than one place in the same document. See "Working in Two Places or Documents at Once" in Chapter 6.

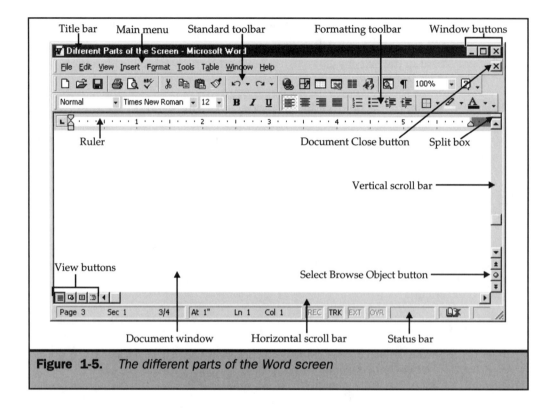

Figure 1-5. *The different parts of the Word screen*

■ **Scroll Bars** For moving up and down and side to side onscreen. The scroll bar along the right side of the screen is called the *vertical scroll bar*; the one along the bottom is the *horizontal scroll bar*.

■ **Select Browse Object Buttons** Click the round button and you'll see a menu for moving to different places in a document. Click the arrows to move from place to place. See "Using the Select Browse Object Button to Get Around" in Chapter 2.

■ **View Buttons** Changes your view of a document. Some views are better than others for doing different tasks. See "Getting a Better View of Your Work" in Chapter 2.

■ **Status Bar** Shows what page the cursor is in, which section it is in, and where it is on the page and in the document.

Reading the Status Bar

Glance at the Status bar along the bottom of the screen when you want to know where the cursor is in a document. In this illustration, for example, the Status bar tells you that the cursor is

■ On page 22; in section 2; and on page 22 of a 32-page document.

■ At a position 1.7 inches from the top of the page; on the fifth line; and in a position 4 spaces, characters, or tab spaces from the left margin. Don't let the letters "Col" on the Status bar fool you—the Col designation has nothing to do with columns, but with the location of the cursor onscreen.

Those four ghostly-looking sets of letters on the right side of the Status bar are buttons. Double-click REC to record a macro; TRK to track revisions to documents; EXT to select text; and OVR to overwrite, or cover, characters that are already there as you type in new characters. What are the empty boxes on the right side of the Status bar for? Those are storefronts that have yet to be rented.

If you are desperate for space onscreen, you can remove the Status bar, horizontal scroll bar, and vertical scrollbar. To do so, choose Tools | Options, click the View tab in the Options dialog box, and uncheck the Status Bar, Horizontal Scroll Bar, and Vertical Scroll Bar check boxes.

Displaying and Removing the Ruler

As shown in Figure 1-6, use the ruler when you are laying out a page and you want to see where text falls and pictures lie. The gray areas on either side of the ruler show where the left and right margins are. By dragging indent markers on the ruler, you can indent text. Besides the horizontal ruler along the top of the document window, a vertical ruler appears along the left side in Print Layout view (choose View | Print Layout to switch to Print Layout view).

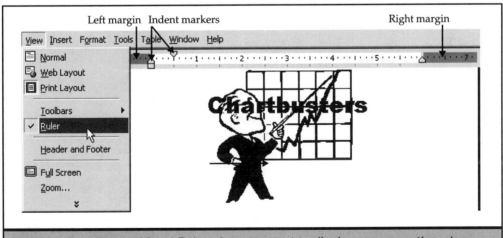

Figure 1-6.   *Choose View | Ruler when you want to display or remove the ruler*

Throughout this book I describe different ways to use the ruler. For now, you need to know that displaying the ruler isn't always necessary. When you want more room onscreen or you are writing and you want to focus on the words, you might as well remove the ruler. To remove or display the ruler, choose View | Ruler.

When the ruler isn't displayed, you can still make it appear briefly by sliding the pointer to the top of the window where the ruler normally is.

Changing the Ruler Measurements

Back in 1974, President Gerald Ford set the goal of converting the United States to the metric system by the year 1981. Twenty-five years later, standard measurements are still the norm, but that doesn't mean you can't display millimeters or centimeters on the ruler if you are metric-minded. You can display points or picas as well (the Glossary describes what they are).

To change the unit of measurement on the ruler, choose Tools | Options and click the General tab in the Options dialog box. Then make a choice from the Measurement Units drop-down menu. Here are five rulers, one for each option—Inches, Centimeters, Millimeters, Points, and Picas—on the Measurement Units drop-down menu:

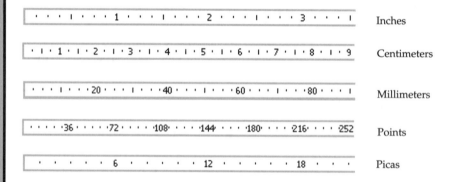

By the way, when you choose a new unit of measurement for the ruler, you also change the unit of measurement in all the dialog boxes in which measurements are entered. For example, the Paragraph dialog box (choose Format | Paragraph to get there) offers text boxes for indenting paragraphs. If you choose centimeters instead of inches as the unit of measurement, the Paragraph dialog box asks for centimeter instead of inch measurements when you indent text.

Getting to Know the Toolbars

A *toolbar* is an assortment of buttons for completing tasks. Two toolbars appear onscreen when you start Word—the Standard toolbar and the Formatting toolbar—but those are by no means the only toolbars. Word offers more than 20 toolbars, and you can create your own as well (a subject of Chapter 23). Click a button on a toolbar instead of choosing a command and you can usually get things done faster.

Throughout this book, I explain when to display various toolbars and click different buttons. These pages are devoted to manipulating toolbars. The next few pages explain how to learn what toolbar buttons do, display and hide toolbars, and arrange toolbars onscreen. You also learn about a strange but highly useful variation on the toolbar—the floating toolbar.

Finding Out What Buttons Do

To find out what clicking a button on a toolbar does, gently slide the mouse pointer over the button. You'll see the button's name, which gives some idea of its purpose, and a keyboard shortcut as well if there is a keyboard equivalent to clicking the button. Another way to find out what a button does is to press SHIFT-F1 (or choose Help | What's This?), click a button, and read the button's name and description:

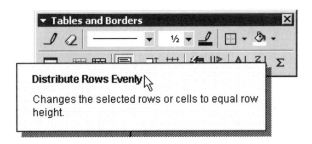

If toolbar button names don't appear when you move the pointer over them, choose View | Toolbars | Customize, click the Options tab in the Customize dialog box, and check the Show ScreenTips On Toolbars check box. Click the Show Shortcut Keys In ScreenTips check box to see the shortcut key equivalent of clicking buttons when you move the mouse pointer over buttons.

Displaying and Hiding Toolbars

I suggest that you get used to hiding and displaying toolbars. Keeping a toolbar onscreen when you no longer need it wastes screen space. And displaying or hiding a toolbar takes but a second. Word offers two ways to display or hide a toolbar:

■ Choose View | Toolbars and click the name of the toolbar on the submenu.

■ Right-click a toolbar or the menu bar and select the name of the toolbar on the shortcut menu, as shown in Figure 1-7.

The Drawing toolbar and Tables and Borders toolbar get special treatment. To hide or display them, click the Drawing button or Tables and Borders button on the Standard toolbar.

Arranging Toolbars Onscreen

Toolbars are "anchored" to the top or bottom of the screen when you display them. However, as Figure 1-7 shows, you can move a toolbar away from the top or bottom of the screen. You can change its shape, too. Tuck a toolbar in the corner of the screen to

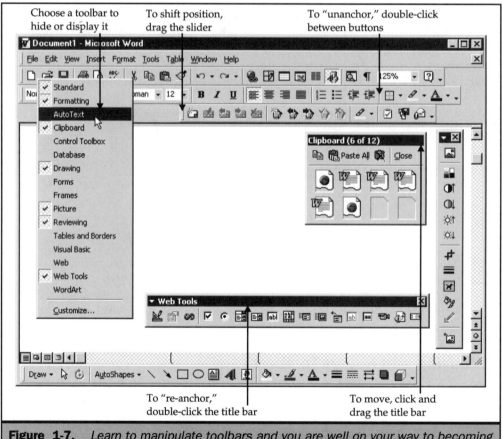

Figure 1-7.   *Learn to manipulate toolbars and you are well on your way to becoming a speedy user of Word*

move it out of the way but still be able to click its buttons. Here are instructions for manipulating toolbars:

- ■ **"Unanchoring"** To move a toolbar away from its homeport at the top or bottom of the screen, move the pointer to the left side of the toolbar, and, when you see the four-headed arrow, click, and start dragging. Soon the toolbar appears in the middle of the screen and you can see its title bar, the stripe along the top with the toolbar's name on it.

- ■ **Shifting** On the left side of toolbars is a slider. Drag the slider to move an anchored toolbar from side to side.

- ■ **Moving** Drag the title bar to move a toolbar onscreen.

- ■ **Changing Shape** Gently move the mouse pointer over the perimeter of the toolbar. When you see the double arrows, click and drag.

- ■ **"Re-anchoring"** Double-click the title bar to move a toolbar back to its home port at the top or bottom of the screen.

The Strange Case of the Floating Toolbar

Notice the stripe at the top of the Order submenu in the illustration shown here. As the tip in the illustration says, you can drag the stripe to make the Order menu float:

Drag the stripe…   …to access commands on a floating toolbar

In the illustration are three floating toolbars: Text Wrapping, Order, and Rotate or Flip. Throughout this book, I will show you why the buttons on floating toolbars are so valuable. For now, all you need to know is that a stripe at the top of a submenu means you can turn the submenu into a floating toolbar by dragging it. Commands on floating toolbars are much easier to get at than commands on submenus.

All About Documents

Word 2000 files are called "documents," a highfalutin name if there ever was one. A document is nothing more than a file you create with Word. This section explains everything you need to know about documents: how to create new ones, save and name them, open and close them, and delete and rename them. Along the way, you will learn what templates are and how you can use templates to create fancy layouts without having to go to any trouble whatsoever.

Creating a New Document

When you start Word, you also create a brand-new document. As a glance at the title bar shows, the document is called "Document1" until you save and give it a name. To create a document on your own, you can either create another normal document like the one you see when you start Word or create a document with the help of a template or wizard.

Figure 1-8 shows a document that was created with the Contemporary Letter template. A *template* is a set of styles, or formats. When you create a document with a template, your document is laid out and decorated for you. All you have to do is enter the text. A *wizard* is similar to a template in that you also get a laid-out, formatted

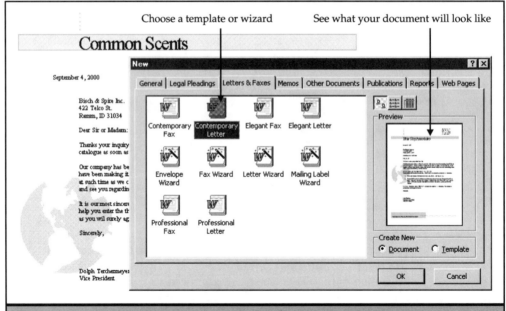

Figure 1-8.   *Creating a document with a template or wizard saves you the trouble of laying out and designing the document on your own*

document. To create a document with a wizard, however, you answer questions in dialog boxes about how you want to lay out the document before Word creates it.

If you want any degree of sophistication in a document, create it with a template or wizard. You'll save time that way and impress others with your desktop-publishing prowess.

Follow these steps to create a new document:

- **Normal Document**   Click the New button on the Standard toolbar or press CTRL-N. You can also choose File | New and double-click the Blank Document icon in the New dialog box.

- **Template or Wizard Document**   Choose File | New to open the New dialog box shown in Figure 1-8. Then click a tab—Legal Pleadings, Letters & Faxes, and so on—and click a template or wizard icon. The Preview box shows what your document will look like. Click OK to create your document. In the case of a wizard, answer the questions as they are presented in dialog boxes.

Note   *When you create a normal document by clicking the New button or pressing CTRL-N, you also create a document with a template—the Normal template. Unlike the other templates, however, Normal is a bare-bones template with only a few formats. Chapter 12 takes up the subject of templates, including how to create your own. For now, all you need to know is that every Word document is based on a template, either the Normal template or another, more sophisticated one.*

Writing a Résumé with the Résumé Wizard

These days, when people change occupations and personalities frequently, everybody needs at least one résumé. The schizophrenic author of this book, for example, maintains four résumés: one each as Writer, Editor, Tech Writer, and Consultant. Because writing, designing, and especially laying out résumés is a monumental task, Word offers the Résumé Wizard. The wizard helps you choose what to put on your résumé and does the layout work for you. After the wizard does its work, all you have to do is fill in the text.

Follow these steps to create a résumé with the Résumé Wizard:

1. Choose File | New and click the Other Documents tab in the New dialog box.

2. Select the Résumé Wizard icon and click OK. You see the first Résumé Wizard dialog box.

3. Click the Next button. The next dialog box asks if you want a Professional, Contemporary, or Elegant résumé:

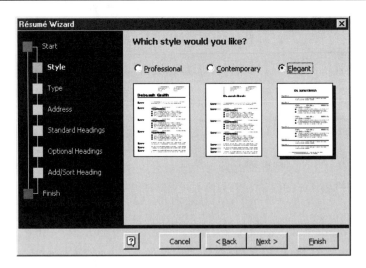

4. Peer at the three sample résumés, select Professional, Contemporary, or Elegant, and click Next.

5. In the next dialog box, choose the option that best describes the type of résumé you want—Entry-level, Chronological, Functional, or Professional—and click Next. The four types of résumé are only different insofar as the headings they offer (you choose headings in step 7). In layout and appearance, they hardly differ at all.

6. Enter the particulars about yourself—your name, address, phone, and so on—and click Next. The information you enter will appear on your résumé.

7. Click check boxes to choose the headings you want for your résumé and then click Next. In effect, you are choosing what to put on your résumé when you choose headings. Only choose the headings under which you can or want to provide information. For example, click the Awards Received check box if you want your résumé to show awards you have won.

8. If you want, repeat step 7 to put more headings on your résumé, and then click Next. Remember, however, that employers see many résumés when they post a job notice. A short, concise, to-the-point résumé is often better than a long one that takes many minutes to read.

9. Arrange the résumé headings. To do so, click a résumé heading in the dialog box and then click the Move Up or Move Down button to move the heading and the information you will provide higher or lower on your résumé. For example, to make Work Experience the first heading on your résumé, click Work Experience and then start clicking the Move Up button.

You can also add a heading by entering it in the text box and clicking the Add button.

10. Click Next and then click Finish to close the Résumé Wizard. You see an empty résumé with brackets that show where to enter text of your own. Notice, however, that only one piece of boilerplate text appears under each heading. For example, space for describing only one job appears below the "Work Experience" or "Professional Experience" heading. Before you start entering your own text, you need to make copies of boilerplate text. In other words, you need to make one copy of the job description boilerplate text for each job you care to list on your résumé. Chapter 3 describes copying text in detail. Following are quick instructions for doing it.

11. Move the pointer to the left of the boilerplate text and click once to select the text. The text is highlighted:

12. Click the Copy button on the Standard toolbar or press CTRL-C to copy the text.

13. Click the Paste button as many times as necessary, once for each job you want to describe, or the educational institutions you attended, for example. You get several more boilerplate entries:

WORK EXPERIENCE

19xx - 19xx	[Company/Institution Name]	[City, State]
[Job Title]		
• [Details of position, award, or achievement.]		

19xx - 19xx	[Company/Institution Name]	[City, State]
[Job Title]		
• [Details of position, award, or achievement.]		

14. Throughout your résumé, click between the brackets and start describing yourself, your work experiences, and your numerous talents and abilities. Save your résumé when you are done.

Saving and Naming Documents

Soon after you create a new document, be sure to save it. And save your document from time to time as you work on it as well. Until you save your work, it rests in the computer's electronic memory (RAM), a precarious location. If a power outage occurs, your computer crashes, or someone trips over the computer's power cord, you lose all the work you did since the last time you saved your document. Make it a habit to save files every ten minutes or so or when you complete an important task.

To save a document:

- Click the Save button.
- Press CTRL-S.
- Choose File | Save.

 Chapter 22 explains how to save a document under a new name, save a document for use in an earlier version of Word or another word processor, save different versions of the same document, and other file-saving esoterica.

The first time you save a document, Word opens the Save As dialog box shown in Figure 1-9 and invites you to give the document a name and choose the folder in which

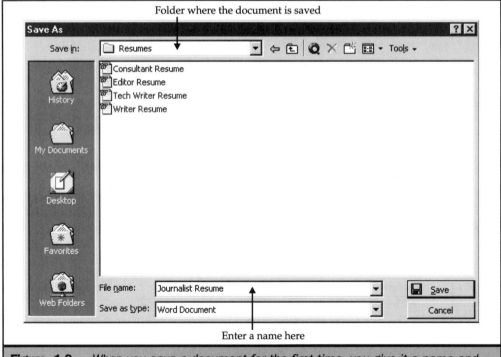

Figure 1-9.   *When you save a document for the first time, you give it a name and choose where to save it in the Save As dialog box*

to store it. As explained in "Ten Techniques for Managing Files Better" at the end of this chapter, creating a folder for each project you are working on and saving documents in those folders saves time because you always know where to find a document when you want to open it. When you save a document, be sure to save it where you can find it again.

"Opening and Closing Documents," the next part of this chapter, explains the tools you can use to locate folders in the Save As or Open dialog box.

Make sure the name of the folder where you want to store your document shows in the Save In box. Then enter a name for your document and click the Save button. Document names can be 255 characters long and can include spaces, but cannot include these characters: / ? : * " < > and |.

Opening Documents

Word and Windows offer many shortcuts for opening documents. To open a document, you can either take the standard route or take advantage of the numerous ways to open documents quickly. Better read on.

The Slow, Standard Way to Open a Document

If you can't open a file by any other means, you have to resort to the Open dialog box:

1. Click the Open button, choose File | Open, or press CTRL-O. You see the Open dialog box shown in Figure 1-10.
   If you've opened a document already, the dialog box opens to the folder where the last document you opened is kept. Otherwise, the dialog box opens to the My Documents folder. You can tell which folder you are looking at by glancing at the folder name in the Look In text box.

2. Find the folder in which the document you want to open is located. The Open dialog box offers these tools to help you do so:

   ■ **Look In Drop-Down Menu**   To look for folders or documents on a different drive or disk (3 1/2 Floppy [A:] or [C:], for example), click the down arrow to open the Look In drop-down menu and select a drive.

   ■ **Back Button**   Click the Back button to revisit folders you saw before in the course of your search. In other words, click this button to backtrack.

   ■ **Up One Level Button**   Moves up the folder hierarchy to show the contents of the folder one level above the one you are looking at.

   ■ **Views Drop-Down Menu**   Lets you display folder contents differently in the Open dialog box. Click the down arrow and select a new view (see Figure 1-10).

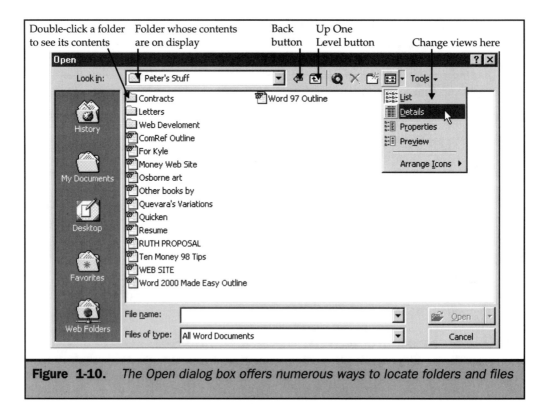

Figure 1-10. *The Open dialog box offers numerous ways to locate folders and files*

- ■ **Folders** Double-click a folder to see its contents in the Open dialog box. For example, double-clicking the Contracts folder in Figure 1-10 displays the files in that folder.

Note *The next part of this chapter, "Fast Ways to Open a Document," explains what the buttons in the Open dialog box do.*

3. Keep searching until the document you want to open appears in the Open dialog box.

4. Either double-click the document or select it and click the Open button.

Tip *To find out what is in a document without having to open it, right-click the document icon and choose Quick View on the shortcut menu. The document appears in the Quick View screen. To open the document from there without having to return to the Open dialog box, choose File | Open File for Editing in the Quick View screen.*

Fast Ways to Open a Document

Next, the shortcuts. If you can use one of the following techniques to open a document, go for it! Here are speedy techniques for opening documents.

WINDOWS DOCUMENTS MENU   The Windows Documents menu lists the last 15 files you opened. If the Word document you want to open is one of the lucky 15, click the Start button, choose Documents, and click the name of the document to open it.

FILE MENU   Names of the last four documents you opened are listed on the bottom of the File menu. Perhaps the document you want to open is listed there. To find out, open the File menu. Then click a document name if indeed you see the document you want to open.

You can make more than four document names appear at the bottom of the File menu. To do so, choose Tools | Options and click the General tab in the Options dialog box. Then enter a number greater than 4 in the Recently Used File List text box. I suggest making eight or more document names appear on the File menu. Why not? You save time opening files that way.

FAVORITES FOLDER   Put a shortcut to the documents and folders you use often in the Favorites folder. That way, you can get to your favorite documents and folders quickly. As shown in Figure 1-11, Word offers a special command in the Open dialog box

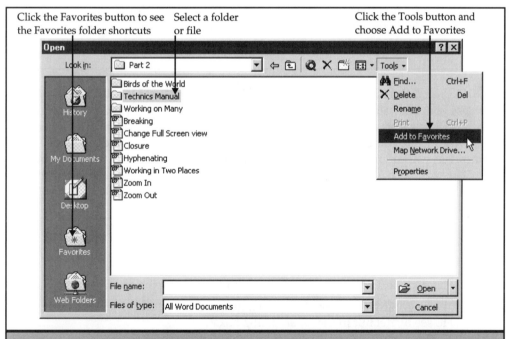

Figure 1-11.   *Put a shortcut to your favorite folders and documents in the Favorites folder. To open a document or see the contents of a folder, just click the Favorites button in the Open dialog box and double-click a shortcut icon*

for creating Favorites folder shortcuts. After you have created the shortcut, all you have to do to open a folder or document is click the Favorites button in the Open dialog box to open the Favorites folder and then double-click a document or folder name.

Follow these steps to put a shortcut to a folder or document in the Favorites folder:

1. Choose File | Open to see the Open dialog box.

2. Find the folder or document that needs a shortcut and click to select it.

3. Click the Tools button and choose Add to Favorites on the drop-down menu.

4. Click the Favorites button. Do you see your folder or document? All you have to do to open it now is double-click it.

MY DOCUMENTS FOLDER   One way to open files quickly is to keep the documents on which you are currently working in the My Documents folder where you can get at them. That way, all you have to do to open a document is choose File | Open, click the My Documents button in the Open dialog box to see the contents of the My Documents folder, and double-click a document name. When you finish with a document and don't need to open it often, move it from the My Documents folder to a permanent home.

HISTORY FOLDER   The Open dialog box also offers the History button. Click it and you'll see an exhaustive list of the last hundred or so files you opened with Office programs. Double-click a file to open it.

Choosing a New Default Folder for Storing Documents

Unless you tell it otherwise, Word assumes that you want to keep documents in the My Documents folder. The first time you try to open a file after you start Word, you will see the contents of the My Documents folder in the Open dialog box. However, you can make another folder appear by default in the Open dialog box. Perhaps you keep the documents you use most often in another folder and you want to see it by default when you choose File | Open. Follow these steps to tell Word which folder to display by default in the Open dialog box:

1. Choose Tools | Options to open the Options dialog box.

2. Click the File Locations tab.

3. Under File Types, click Documents, and then click the Modify button.

4. In the Modify Location dialog box, find and select the folder that you want to see by default in the Open dialog box.

5. Click OK. The location and name of the folder you chose appears in the Location column of Options dialog box.

6. Click the Close button.

SHORTCUT ICON   Create shortcut icons to the documents you open very, very often and put the shortcut icons on the desktop. That way, you can open documents quickly by double-clicking their shortcut icons on the Windows desktop. Or, if you are in the Open dialog box, you can click the Desktop button and then double-click a shortcut icon.

To create a shortcut icon to a document, choose File | Open and find the file you want to create a shortcut to in the Open dialog box. Then right-click the file, choose Send To on the shortcut menu, and choose Desktop As Shortcut on the submenu.

Closing a Document

Closing a document is certainly easier than opening one. To close a document, save your file and then choose File | Close or click the Close button (the *X*) in the upper-right corner of the document window. Be sure to click the document window's Close button, not Word's Close button, or else you will close Word as well as your document.

If you forget to save a file before you close it, a dialog box asks if you want to save the changes you recently made to the document. Click the Yes button, or click No if you made changes but regret making them. The next time you open the document, the changes you regret making won't show. Instead, you will see an earlier version of the document, the one that you saved on-disk before you made the changes you so regret.

    Sometimes closing a document without saving the changes you made to it is worthwhile. Suppose you make a bunch of editorial mistakes and want to start over. To do so, close the file without saving the changes you made. The next time you open the file, you will see the version that you had before you made all those mistakes.

Deleting and Renaming Documents

Deleting and renaming documents is easier to do in My Computer and Windows Explorer, the Windows programs that handle files, but you can delete and rename documents in Word. To do so, choose File | Open as though you were opening the document you want to rename or delete, locate the document in the Open dialog box, and follow these instructions:

- **Renaming**   Right-click the document and choose Rename from the shortcut menu. Then type a new name and press ENTER.

- **Deleting**   Right-click the document and choose Delete from the shortcut menu. Then click Yes when Word asks if you really want to delete the file. To delete several documents at once, CTRL-click each one, then right-click one of the files and choose Delete.

 If you regret deleting a document, you can resuscitate it. Go to the Windows desktop and double-click the Recycle Bin icon. The Recycle Bin opens with a list of the files you deleted. Click the one you regret deleting and choose File | Restore in the Recycle Bin.

A Word About Menu Commands

Word 2000 has adopted a new way of offering menu commands. To make choosing commands simpler, only commands that you chose recently appear on menus. Don't worry if you pull down a menu but don't see the command you want—you haven't chosen the command lately, that's all. Click the double arrows at the bottom of the menu to make all the commands appear, and then click the one you want:

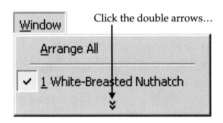
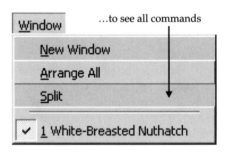

 If you don't like how Word offers menu commands and you want to see all the commands at once, choose View | Toolbars | Customize. Then click the Options tab in the Customize dialog box and uncheck the Menus Show Recently Used Commands First check box.

Exiting Word 2000

Word 2000 offers no less than four ways to shut down the program:

- Click the Close button (the *X*) in the upper-right corner of the Word screen.
- Choose File | Exit.

- Press ALT-F4.
- Double-click the Control menu icon, the *W* in the upper-left corner of the screen next to the name of the document you are working on.

Be sure to save your documents before closing Word. Anyhow, if you forget to do that, a dialog box appears and asks if you want to save your work before you shut down Word.

Exam | MOUS Exam Objectives Explored in Chapter 1

Objective	Heading	Practice File
Use templates to create a new document	"Creating a New Document"	
Locating and opening an existing document	"Opening Documents"	
Use Save	"Saving and Naming Documents"	
Create a new document using a wizard	"Creating a New Document"	

Ten Techniques for Managing Files Better

You can save a lot of time and grief by managing files well. Here are ten tips for managing files so that you never lose them and you can access them quickly.

1. CREATE FOLDERS AND SUBFOLDERS FOR NEW PROJECTS.   As soon as you begin a new project, create a folder or perhaps a folder and subfolders to store the documents you will create. While you're at it, name the folder after the project. By keeping documents that pertain to the same project in the same place, you make it easier to find and open documents.

The easiest and probably the best way to create new folders is to do so with My Computer or Windows Explorer in the Windows operating system. However, you can follow these steps to create a folder without leaving Word:

1. Choose File | Open to see the Open dialog box.

2. In the dialog box, find and select the folder that you want your new folder to be subordinate to. See "Opening a Document" earlier in this chapter if you need help finding your way around the Open dialog box.

3. Click the Create New Folder button. You see the New Folder dialog box.

4. Enter a descriptive name for the folder and click OK. Your new folder appears in the Look In box.

5. Click Cancel to close the Open dialog box.

2. KEEP ALL YOUR PERSONAL FILES IN ONE PLACE.   Many people mistakenly believe that documents created with Word have to be stored deep in the folder hierarchy where the Word program files are. Nothing could be further from the truth. You can store the Word files you create yourself anywhere you want. And you should store them in a convenient place where you can access them easily.

This user keeps all her documents in a folder at the top of the C drive called "AAA My Stuff." The letters *AAA* ensure that the folder will be the first in the list of folders in the Open dialog box. Devise a strategy like this one for storing your work on disk where you can find it quickly.

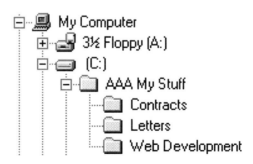

3. KNOW WHICH DOCUMENTS NEED BACKING UP—AND BACK THEM UP.

Be sure to back up important documents. *Backing up* means to make a second copy of a document, put it on a floppy disk or zip disk, and store the disk in a safe place where nothing can harm it. Not all documents need to be backed up, but if losing a document would cause undo grief or require too much time to restore, back it up. Unless you back up important files, you are doomed if your computer breaks down, your computer is stolen, or your computer is ruined by a virus. See "Backing Up Your Work" in Chapter 22.

4. PERIODICALLY DELETE DOCUMENTS YOU NO LONGER NEED.   Finding the
document you want to open is difficult when the folder in which you are looking is crowded with documents. To prevent overcrowding, periodically delete the documents you no longer need. See "Deleting and Renaming Documents" earlier in this chapter.

5. ARCHIVE DOCUMENTS YOU DON'T USE OFTEN.   Another way to prevent
overcrowding in folders is to archive documents. *Archive* means to store documents in a special folder meant for documents that you need but don't need very often. By keeping documents in an archive folder, you prevent them from crowding the folders you go to often.

6. KEEP CURRENT DOCUMENTS IN THE MY DOCUMENTS FOLDER.   As
explained in "Fast Ways to Open a Document" earlier in this chapter, you can open documents quickly by keeping current documents in the My Documents folder. All you have to do to see the contents of this folder is click the My Documents button in the Open dialog box. When you finish working on a document, move it from the My Documents folder to a more permanent folder.

7. PUT SHORTCUTS TO IMPORTANT FOLDERS IN THE MY FAVORITES
FOLDER.   "Fast Ways to Open a Document" also explained that you can open
documents quickly by putting shortcuts to the folders that hold them in the My Favorites folder. Click the My Favorites button in the Open dialog box to see and double-click the shortcuts in the Favorites folder.

8. OPEN DOCUMENTS QUICKLY FROM THE FILE MENU.   At the bottom of
the File menu is a list of the last four documents you opened. Opening the File menu and clicking the name of a document is perhaps the fastest way to open a document in Word. And you can list more than four documents on the File menu: Choose Tools | Options, click the General tab in the Options dialog box, and enter a number larger than 4 in the Recently Used File List text box. I highly recommend putting more than four document names on the File menu. My File menu lists eight documents.

9. USE THE WINDOWS DOCUMENTS MENU TO OPEN DOCUMENTS QUICKLY.
As explained in "Opening a Document and Word at the Same Time" at the start of this chapter, you can open Word and a document in one swoop by clicking the Start button,

choosing Documents, and clicking a document name. The Windows Documents menu lists the last 15 files you opened, be they Word documents or other files.

10. DECIDE HOW TO SAVE DOCUMENTS. On the Save tab of the Options dialog box (choose Tools | Options to get there), Word offers several options for saving documents, saving documents quickly, and recovering documents in the event of a computer crash. "Strategies for Saving Documents" in Chapter 22 explains what these options are. Sooner or later, decide on a strategy for saving documents and backup copies of documents in Word.

The
Complete
Reference

Word 2000

Chapter 2

Writing and Editing
a Document

This chapter explains everything you need to know to write the first draft of your masterpiece. It describes how to enter and edit text, get quickly from place to place in a document, and change views. Along the way, you'll find out many excellent shortcuts for getting your work done quickly and thoroughly.

Entering the Text

To type a document, you wiggle your fingers over the keyboard. That's all there is to it, although Word 2000 provides a few shortcuts to help you along the way. In the following pages, you find out how to fix mistakes, enter foreign characters and symbols, enter capital letters quickly, and start a new paragraph, line, or page. Readers new to word processing who were born before 1973 are encouraged to read the following section of this book. All others may skip ahead to "Typing Text and Erasing Mistakes."

Note   *In Chapter 6, "Ways to Enter Text Quickly" offers more techniques for entering text in a hurry.*

Word Processing Advice for People Born Before 1973

If you were born before 1973, you are old enough to remember the pop-top can, curb-feelers, 8-track tapes, and the typewriter. Chances are, in fact, you learned how to type on a typewriter, and that means you have to unlearn two or three habits:

- Do not press the ENTER key to end one line and start another. Word starts a new line for you when you come to the end of a line. Only press the ENTER key to begin a new paragraph.

- Do not press the SPACEBAR to move text around or align text. For example, don't press the SPACEBAR to move a heading to the center of a page. Word has special tools for aligning and centering text.

- Do not press the ENTER key over and over again to move to the next page. Simply press CTRL-ENTER to start a new, blank page.

- Do not rest your hands on the keyboard.

Typing Text and Erasing Mistakes

When you type, text appears at the *insertion point,* the blinking vertical line shown in Figure 2-1. Suppose you want to enter a word or two in the middle of a sentence. To move the insertion point elsewhere, either press arrow keys or move the *text cursor* (the large egotistical I) to a new location and click. To move it onscreen, roll your mouse across your desk.

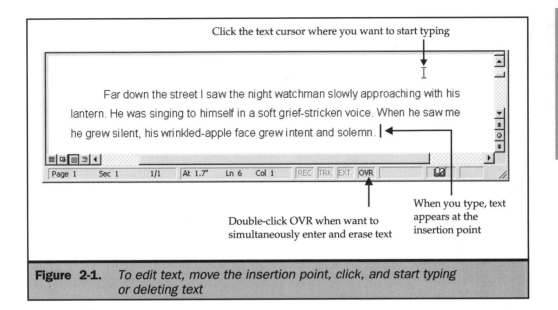

Figure 2-1.   *To edit text, move the insertion point, click, and start typing or deleting text*

When you type, text that is already there moves to the right to accommodate the new text. However, you can type over text that is already there by double-clicking the OVR button on the Status bar, as shown in Figure 2-1. Double-click OVR when you want to simultaneously enter and erase text—and be sure to double-click OVR again to go back to inserting text, not overtyping it.

Everybody makes typing errors. To erase an error, click to move the insertion point to the left or right of the error, and then press the BACKSPACE key to erase the character to the left of the insertion point or the DELETE key to erase the character to the right of the insertion point. In Chapter 3, "Deleting Chunks of Text" explains how you can select text—a word, a paragraph, several paragraphs, or even a whole document—and erase it all at once by pressing the DELETE key. Meanwhile, for people who like keyboard shortcuts, here are the keyboard techniques for erasing text:

Pressing	Deletes
BACKSPACE	The character to the left of insertion point
DELETE	The character to the right of the insertion point
CTRL-BACKSPACE	The word to the left of the insertion point
CTRL-DELETE	The word to the right of the insertion point

Suppose you are editing a document and you realize, to your dismay, that the last edit you made was done incorrectly. If the edit was made in the middle of a document, finding the error can be difficult. To locate the last three places where you entered or edited text, press SHIFT-F5 once, twice, or three times.

UPPERCASE to lowercase and Back Again

"Case" refers to whether letters are capitalized or not. In the old days when type was set by hand, typesetters kept capital letters in the upper tray, which is why these letters are called *uppercase* letters, and they kept *lowercase* letters in—you guessed it—the lower tray.

Everybody knows that you hold down the SHIFT key and press a letter on the keyboard to enter an uppercase letter. And everybody knows that you press the CAPS LOCK key to enter many uppercase letters at once. What most people don't know is that Word offers a keyboard shortcut for changing letters from upper- to lowercase and vice versa. Select text and keep pressing SHIFT-F3 to change words to sentence case, lowercase, uppercase, or title case. Or choose Format | Change Case and make a selection in the Change Case dialog box, as shown in Figure 2-2.

Figure 2-2 demonstrates what the choices are. Some choices are suitable for headings, others for plain text. The tOGGLE cASE option is for correcting text that you entered accidentally while CAPS LOCK was turned on. Pressing SHIFT-F3 to change the case of letters is one of the best shortcuts I know of in Word.

You can also press CTRL-SHIFT-A to capitalize letters directly without seeing them in title case, lowercase, or sentence case.

Option	Example
Sentence case	Ours is not to choose, say i
lowercase	ours is not to choose, say i
UPPERCASE	OURS IS NOT TO CHOOSE, SAY I
Title Case	Ours Is Not To Choose, Say I
tOGGLE cASE	oURS iS nOT tO cHOOSE, sAY i

Change Case   ? ✕
- ⦿ Sentence case.
- ○ lowercase
- ○ UPPERCASE
- ○ Title Case
- ○ tOGGLE cASE

OK   Cancel

Figure 2-2. *To change the case of text, select it and keep pressing SHIFT-F3, or choose Format | Change Case and choose an option in the Change Case dialog box*

Entering Symbols and Foreign Characters

Don't panic if you need to enter an umlaut, a grave accent, or a cedilla in a document, because you can do it by way of one of the shortcut keys shown in Table 2-1 or the Symbol dialog box shown in Figure 2-3. And Word offers other means of entering symbols and foreign characters as well.

The Symbol dialog box offers symbols as well as foreign characters. To enter one, place the insertion point where you want the symbol to stand in your document and follow these steps:

1. Choose Insert | Symbol to open the Symbol dialog box.

2. Choose a font and subset, if necessary, from the drop-down menus.

3. Click a symbol or foreign character to get a better look at it.

4. Click the Insert button to enter the symbol and click Close to close the dialog box.

To Enter*	Type This...	...and Then This
à, è, ì, ò, *or* ù	CTRL-'	a, e, i, o, *or* u
á, é, í, ó, ú, *or* ý	CTRL-'	a, e, i, o, u, *or* y
â, ê, î, ô, *or* û	CTRL-SHIFT-^	a, e, i, o, *or* u
ä, ë, ï, ö, ü, *or* ÿ	CTRL-SHIFT-:	a, e, i, o, u, *or* y
ñ *or* õ	CTRL-SHIFT-~	n *or* o
å	CTRL-SHIFT-@	a
æ	CTRL-SHIFT-&	a
ç	CTRL-,	c
ø	CTRL-/	o
Œ	CTRL-SHIFT-&	o
ß	CTRL-SHIFT-&	s
¿ *or* ¡	ALT-CTRL-SHIFT	? *or* !

* This table only lists lowercase foreign characters, but you can enter uppercase characters by substituting the lowercase characters in column three for uppercase characters.

Table 2-1. *Keyboard Shortcuts for Entering Foreign Characters*

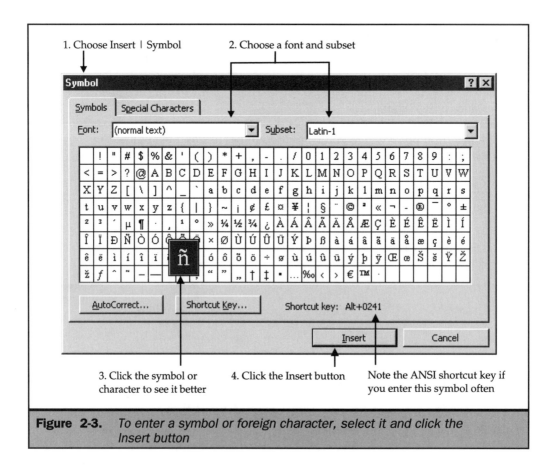

Figure 2-3. *To enter a symbol or foreign character, select it and click the Insert button*

The Symbol dialog box (see Figure 2-3) also offers these amenities:

- **AutoCorrect Button** Choose a symbol and click this button to devise an AutoCorrect shortcut for entering the symbol you chose. See "Entering Text and Graphics Quickly with the AutoCorrect Command" in Chapter 6.

- **Shortcut Key Button** Choose a symbol you enter often and click this button to create a shortcut key for entering it (if the shortcut key isn't already listed in Table 2-1). See "Designating Your Own Keyboard Shortcuts" in Chapter 23.

The ANSI Keyboard Shortcuts for Entering Foreign Characters

In Figure 2-3, notice the shortcut key ALT + 0241 in the bottom of the Symbol dialog box. You can also enter symbols and foreign characters by pressing these ANSI (American National Standards Institute) keyboard shortcuts. If you are a translator who often has to enter foreign characters, learn the characters' ANSI keyboard shortcuts from the Symbol dialog box and try your hand at entering characters the ANSI way. To enter an ANSI character, make sure NUM LOCK is turned on (and press the NUM LOCK key if it isn't), hold down the ALT key, and enter the numbers by way of the numeric keypad. You can't enter the numbers by pressing the numbered keys on the keyboard itself.

Starting a New Paragraph, Line, or Page

Press the ENTER key to start a new paragraph. Suppose, however, that you want to start a new line, or *break a line,* without starting a new paragraph. For example, consider the heading in Figure 2-4 and the lines of text below the heading. The first heading is top-heavy, so I broke it after the word "Sucker" to make the heading easier to read. In the lines of text, I broke the second line after the word "Kiwanis" to make the words break more evenly along the right margin. To break a line, click where you want the break to occur and press SHIFT-ENTER.

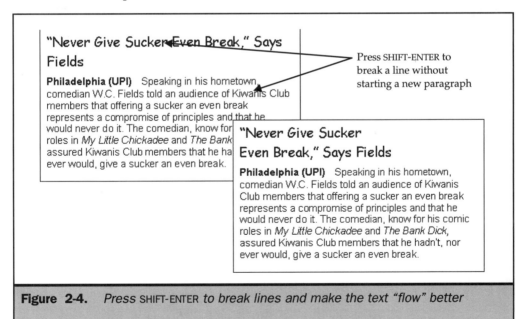

Figure 2-4. *Press* SHIFT-ENTER *to break lines and make the text "flow" better*

"Viewing the Hidden Format Symbols" later in this chapter explains how to find out where line breaks are. To delete a line break, click the Show/Hide ¶ button and backspace over the line break symbol.

When you come to the bottom of one page, Word starts a new page for you, but if you want to start a new page immediately, press CTRL-ENTER. You can also start a new page by choosing Insert | Break and selecting the Page Break option in the Break dialog box. Break the page after you enter the text on a title page, for example. Whatever you do, don't press ENTER over and over to reach the bottom of a page.

Recognizing a page break in Normal view is easy because the words "Page Break" and a dotted line appear onscreen. In Print Layout view, however, page breaks look exactly like the page breaks that Word introduces when you reach the end of a page: you see the bottom of one page and the top of the next. To erase a page break, switch to Normal view, click the words "Page Break," and press the DELETE key. Later in this chapter, "Getting a Better View of Your Work" will explain the different views.

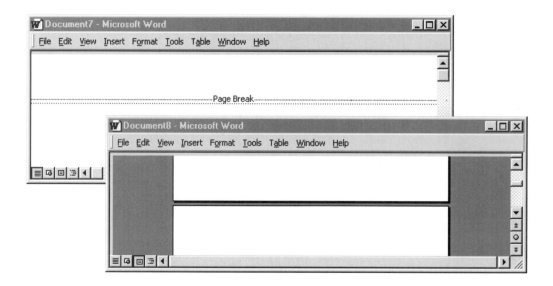

How Word Handles Paragraphs

All the formatting—the indentations, character fonts, and formats—are carried to the next paragraph when you press ENTER. When you start formatting paragraphs, you will learn how critical paragraphs are to formatting. In Word, formatting commands affect the paragraph that the cursor is in, or, if you selected several paragraphs, formatting commands affect the paragraphs you selected. A heading, single line of text, and blank line and are all considered paragraphs. In Word, a paragraph is simply what you put onscreen before you press the ENTER key.

Tricks for Editing Text

Following are some tried-and-true techniques for editing faster and better. On these pages, you find out how to take some of the drudgery out of repetitive work, fix errors, fit text on the screen, and view format symbols so you can tell why text lies where it does on the page.

Repeating a Command or Text Entry

Repeat is my favorite command. For especially repetitive word-processing tasks—and there are many—see if you can make the Repeat command do the work for you. To give the Repeat command, press F4, choose Edit | Repeat, or press CTRL-Y. This command repeats the last command or keyboard entry you made.

Suppose you have to indent twelve different paragraphs throughout a document. Instead of attacking the twelve paragraphs one at a time and repeating the burdensome indentation command, indent the first paragraph. Then put your left index finger on the F4 key, click the next paragraph that needs indenting, and press F4. The paragraph is indented—not only that, you can rest assured that it and the remaining ten paragraphs will be indented the same way. Suppose you have to type "I will not talk in class" one hundred times. Using the Repeat command, you only have to type it once and press F4 ninety-nine times.

In Chapter 6, "Entering Text and Graphics Quickly with the AutoCorrect Command" explains another way to quickly enter your address, company name, or other item you have to enter often.

Undoing a Mistake—and Redoing What You Undid

Suppose you give a command or enter text and realize immediately that you shouldn't have done that. Don't despair—you can undo your mistake by clicking the Undo button, pressing CTRL-Z, or choosing Edit | Undo. The Undo command reverses your last action, whatever it happened to be. And if you regret undoing your last action, you can "redo" it by clicking the Redo button. The Redo command is an antidote to the Undo command—it redoes what you undid.

Not only can you undo your most recent editorial change or command with the Undo command, you can undo as many as your last 99 actions. To undo a mistake you made some time ago, click the down arrow beside the Undo button. You'll see a drop-down menu of your last six actions, but you can scroll down the list and see as many as 99. When you have found the action you want to undo, click it on the drop-down menu:

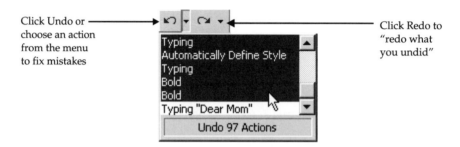

Click Undo or choose an action from the menu to fix mistakes

Click Redo to "redo what you undid"

When you close a document, all records of the edits you made are lost. The Undo menu is emptied out. Sorry, you can't undo an edit you made the last time you opened your document.

The only drawback to choosing an action on the Undo drop-down menu is that you also undo all the actions that took place before it. For example, if you undo the 97th action on the list, you undo the 96 before it, too. Besides the Undo command, another way to fix monstrous errors is to close the document and click No when Word asks if you want to save the changes you made. As long as you didn't save your document after you made the monstrous error, the error won't be in your document when you reopen it.

"Wrapping" Text So It Stays Onscreen

As you write the first draft of a document, work in Normal view and Outline view. In those views, you can exclude the fancy stuff and concentrate on the words. In Normal view and Outline view, however, the text is prone to stray off the right side of the screen, as shown in Figure 2-5, but you can prevent that from happening by choosing the Wrap To Window option in the Options dialog box. In Figure 2-5, text strays outside the window in the first document, but in the second it wraps to, or stays inside, the window so you can see and work on it.

Text that doesn't "wrap"

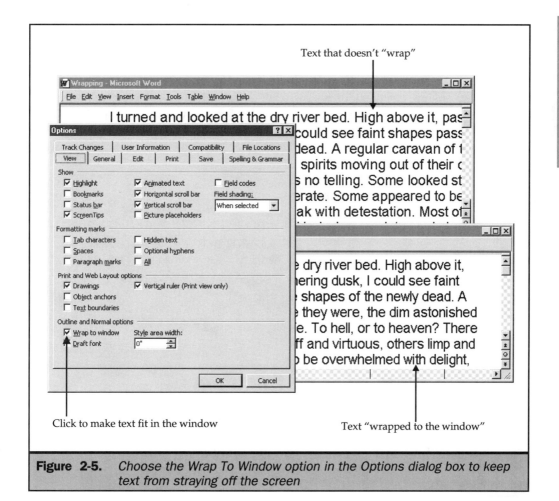

Click to make text fit in the window

Text "wrapped to the window"

Figure 2-5.   *Choose the Wrap To Window option in the Options dialog box to keep text from straying off the screen*

To make text stay inside the window in Normal view and Outline view, choose Tools | Options, click the View tab in the Options dialog box, and check the Wrap To Window check box, as shown in Figure 2-5

Caution   *Wrapping text inside the window gives an unrealistic picture of where lines end on the page. When you are laying out text or working on tables, be sure to turn off the Wrap To Window mechanism or else do your work in Print Layout view or Web Layout view. Those views show precisely where lines break on the page.*

Viewing the Hidden Format Symbols

Sometimes it pays to see the hidden format symbols when you are editing and laying out a document. The symbols show where lines break, where tab spaces are, where one paragraph starts and another ends, and whether two spaces instead of one appear between words. To see the hidden format symbols, click the Show/Hide ¶ button. Click the button again to hide the symbols. This illustration shows what the hidden symbols are, how to enter them, and what they look like onscreen:

Symbol	Name	How to Enter
↵	Line break	Press SHIFT-ENTER
¶	Paragraph	Press ENTER
·	Space	Press SPACEBAR
→	Tab	Press TAB

→ The·show·features·an·all-↵
star·cast·and·is·sure·to·be·a·hit.·
Already·ticket·sales·are·brisk·↵
and·the·Orpheum·box·office·is·
predicting·a·blockbuster·of·a·
show·¶

Moving Around in Long Documents

Documents have a habit of getting longer, and as they do, getting from place to place within them gets harder and harder. This section explains the numerous ways to go here and there in documents. You can press keys, use the scroll bar, use the Document Map, place bookmarks in documents, or click the Select Object Browse button. Pick your poison. You will discover one or two favorite techniques after you have experimented a bit.

In a pinch, you can also use the Find command to get around. Press CTRL-F or choose Edit | Find, enter a target word in the Find and Replace dialog box, and click the Find Next button. In Chapter 6, "Finding and Replacing Text and Other Things" explains the nuances of the Find command.

Keyboard Techniques for Getting Around

Even if, like me, you are a fan of the mouse and prefer clicking the scroll bar to get around, one or two keyboard shortcuts are worth using. I especially like CTRL-HOME, which moves the insertion point to the top of the document, and CTRL-END, which moves it to the bottom. Table 2-2 lists the keyboard shortcuts that are indispensable to everyone.

To Move Here	Press
Top of document	CTRL-HOME
Bottom of document	CTRL-END
Up one screen	PAGE UP
Down one screen	PAGE DOWN
Start of paragraph	CTRL-↑
End of paragraph	CTRL-↓
Start of line	HOME
End of line	END

Table 2-2. *Essential Keyboard Shortcuts for Moving Around*

Scroll Bar Methods for Getting Around

For the mouse-inclined, the best way to go here and there in a document is to use the scroll bars. Figure 2-6 shows how the scroll bars work. Use the vertical scroll bar on the right side of the window to move backward and forward in a document. When you drag the scroll box on the vertical scroll bar, you see which page you are scrolling to. And if you assigned heading styles to the headings in your document, you also see heading names.

 By scrolling, you don't move the insertion point—all you do is put a different page onscreen. To move the insertion point to the page to which you've scrolled, click on the page.

Using the Select Browse Object Button to Get Around

In the lower-right corner of the Word screen is an obscure but very useful button called Select Browse Object. Why the ugly name? Because computer people are very fond of the word "object," by which they mean just about anything, and the word "browse," by which they mean "to go to." Click the Select Browse Object button and you see 12

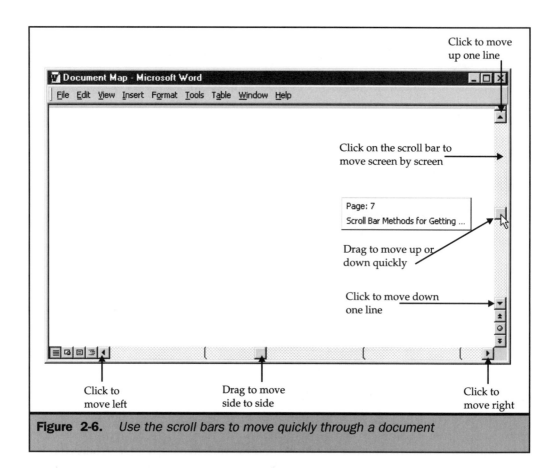

Click to move
up one line

Click on the scroll bar to
move screen by screen

Page: 7
Scroll Bar Methods for Getting ...

Drag to move up or
down quickly

Click to move down
one line

Click to
move left

Drag to move
side to side

Click to
move right

Figure 2-6.   *Use the scroll bars to move quickly through a document*

"Browse By" buttons. Click a button to go immediately to the thing whose button you
clicked—the next heading, graphic, table, or whatever.

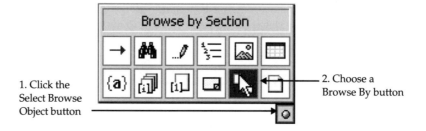

1. Click the
Select Browse
Object button

2. Choose a
Browse By button

EXAMPLES

*To test-drive the different ways of getting around in a document, open the 2-1 Navigate
document on the CD that comes with this book.*

What makes the Select Browse Object so useful is that you can skip merrily from object to object after you click a Browse By button. After you click a button, the double arrows on either side of the Select Browse Object turn blue. To go to the previous or next heading, graphic, table, or whatever, click one of the blue double arrows (or press CTRL-PAGE UP or CTRL-PAGE DOWN).

When the double arrows on either side of the Select Browse Object button are black, clicking the double arrows takes you to the previous or next page. Choose the Browse By Page button to turn the double arrows blue again and be able to click the double arrows to skip from page to page.

Going from Place to Place with the Go To Command

Yet another way to get from place to place is to use the Go To command. The Go To command works much like the Select Browse Object button. After you choose the item you want to "go to," the double arrows on either side of the Select Browse Object button turn blue, and you can click the blue double arrows to go to the item you chose without having to open a dialog box.

To use the Go To command, choose Edit | Go To, press CTRL-G, or double-click the left side of the Status bar. You'll see the Go To tab of the Find and Replace dialog box. Choose what you are seeking in the Go To What box and then do either of the following:

■ Click the Previous or Next button to go to the previous or next instance of the thing you chose.

■ Make an entry or a choice in the Enter box and click the Go To button. The Enter box changes names, depending on what you chose in the Go To What box.

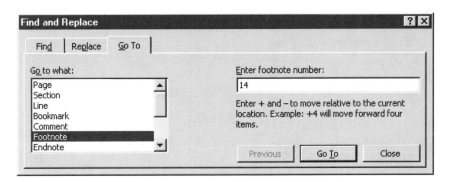

To try the Go To command, open the 2-2 Go To practice document on the CD.

Bookmarks for Getting Around

One of the fastest ways to get from place to place is to mark the places in your document that you will return to time and time again with a bookmark. When you want to return to an important place, all you have to do is choose Insert | Bookmark, double-click a bookmark name in the Bookmark dialog box, and click Cancel. True to the craft, the mystery writer whose bookmarks are shown in Figure 2-7 wrote the end of the story first and used bookmarks to jump back and forth between the beginning and end to make all the clues fit.

Besides bookmarking a place, you can also select text and bookmark the text you selected. Bookmark a lengthy table, for example, and you'll be able to select it merely by choosing its bookmark instead of going to the trouble of using the selection commands. As "Indexing a Document" in Chapter 18 explains, you have to bookmark a text selection to include a page range ("California, economy 92–97") in an index entry. Bookmarks are also used to make hyperlinks between two places on the same Web page.

Choose Insert | Bookmark (or press CTRL-SHIFT-F5) and do the following in the Bookmark dialog box to create bookmarks or go to them in a document:

- **Create a Bookmark**   Make sure the insertion point or text selection is where you want the bookmark to be before you choose Insert | Bookmark. In the Bookmark dialog box, enter a name in the Bookmark Name text box and click the Add button or press ENTER.

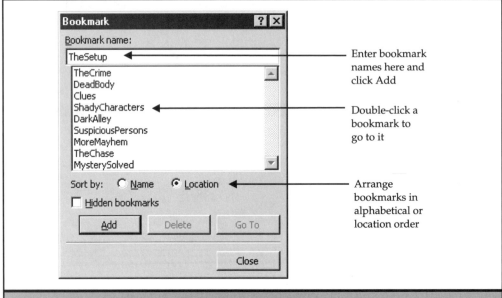

Figure 2-7.   *Bookmark important places in long documents and be able to go to those places very, very quickly*

- **Go to a Bookmark**   Double-click a bookmark name in the Bookmark dialog box. To find names, use the scroll bar if necessary. You can also choose a Sort By option to arrange the names in alphabetical or location order.

 Bookmark names cannot include blank spaces. The first character must be a letter, not a number.

Using the Document Map to Get Around

Last but not least, you can use the document map to jump from heading to heading in a document. To use the document map, however, you must have assigned heading styles—Heading 1, Heading 2, and so on—to the headings in your document. By clicking the Document Map button or choosing View I Document Map, you can see the names of headings in the document map on the left side of the screen, as shown in Figure 2-8. To move to a heading, all you have to do is click its name in the document map.

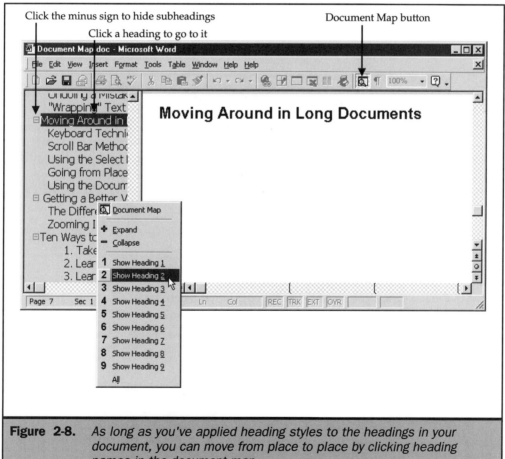

Figure 2-8.   *As long as you've applied heading styles to the headings in your document, you can move from place to place by clicking heading names in the document map*

Note *Chapter 12 explains styles, why they are so useful, and how you can apply them from the Style menu on the Formatting toolbar.*

To help you find the headings you want to go to, the document map offers these amenities:

■ **Read Headings**   Place the pointer over a heading to be able to read it in its entirety. You can also drag the bar that separates the document map from the document to the left or right to make the document map narrower or wider.

■ **Choose Which Outline Levels You Want to See**   Right-click the document map and choose an outline level option to tell Word which headings to display. See "Choosing an Outline Level for Paragraphs" in Chapter 8 to learn more about outline levels.

■ **See or Hide Subheadings**   Click the minus sign next to a heading to remove its subheadings from the document map and make more headings appear on screen. Click the plus sign next to a heading to see its subheadings.

Getting a Better View of Your Work

Wherever you go in Word 2000, make sure you get a good view. The program offers four different ways to view documents, plus two more if you count Print Preview and Full Screen as views. Depending on the task at hand, some views are better than others. Throughout this book, I mention which view is best for doing which task. For now, these pages explain the different views, how to change views, and how to zoom in and zoom out to keep yourself from going blind at the computer screen.

Changing Your View of a Document

Figure 2-9 shows the six ways to view documents. To change views, click a View button in the lower-left corner of the screen or choose a command from the View menu. In the case of Print Preview, choose File | Print Preview or click the Print Preview button on the Standard toolbar to see it.

Figure 2-9. *The six ways to view a document (clockwise from upper-left): Normal view, Web Layout view, Outline view, Full Screen view, Print Preview, and Print Layout view*

Here are brief descriptions of the six possible views of a document and when to use them:

Normal	For writing first drafts and basic editing. In Normal view, you can focus on writing. Sophisticated layouts, including graphics and columns, do not appear in this view.
Web Layout	For laying out Web pages to be displayed online. Color backgrounds only appear in this view. By switching to Web Layout view, you can see what Web pages will look like online in the Internet Explorer Web browser (choose File | Web Page Preview to see what I mean—the pages in Word and Internet Explorer look the same).
Print Layout	For laying out documents. In this view, you can see where graphics, columns, and the pages begin and end. Headers and footers also appear, however faintly, in Print Layout view.
Outline	For organizing papers and reports. In Outline view, you can move headings (and the text underneath them) around quite easily. See "Organizing Your Work with Outlines" in Chapter 19.
Print Preview	For seeing what entire pages look like. Use this view to see the big picture and find out whether documents are laid out correctly. See "Previewing a Document Before You Print It" in Chapter 5.
Full Screen	For focusing on the task at hand. In this view, the toolbars, menu bar, Status bar—everything, in fact—is removed from the screen except the page you are working on. Full Screen view gives the best idea of what a document will look like after you print it. To give commands, either use keyboard shortcuts, right-click to see shortcut menus, or slide the mouse pointer to the top of the screen to make the menu bar appear. You can also right-click the menu bar and choose a toolbar name to display a toolbar onscreen. Press ESC or click Close Full Screen to leave Full Screen view.

Zooming In and Zooming Out

No matter which view you are in—Normal, Web Layout, Print Layout, or Outline—you can zoom in or zoom out to make the onscreen page look larger or smaller. Zoom in when you are proofreading to get a better look at the letters; zoom out to shrink pages and see whether they were laid out correctly.

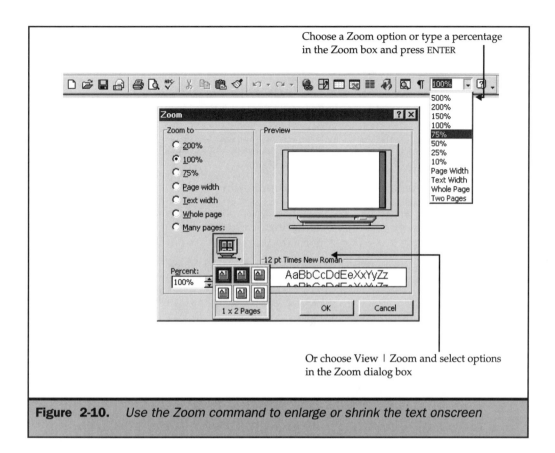

Choose a Zoom option or type a percentage
in the Zoom box and press ENTER

Or choose View | Zoom and select options
in the Zoom dialog box

Figure 2-10.   *Use the Zoom command to enlarge or shrink the text onscreen*

As Figure 12-10 shows, Word offers two ways of zooming—with the Zoom menu
on the Standard toolbar or the Zoom dialog box. To open the Zoom dialog box, choose
View | Zoom. The Zoom settings are:

- **By Percentage**   Either choose a percentage or enter one of your own. At 100%,
  the letters and page are the same size they will be when you print them; below
  100%, they are smaller; above 100%, they are bigger. To choose your own
  percent setting, enter it in the Zoom text box and press the ENTER key.

- **By Width**   Makes the widest line of text or the entire page fit snugly across
  the screen.

- **By Page**   Fits one, two, or several pages on the screen. In the Zoom dialog box,
  click the down arrow beside the computer monitor and choose how many
  pages to display, as shown in Figure 2-10.

Exam ┃ MOUS Exam Objectives Explored in Chapter 2

Objective	Heading	Practice File
Use the Overtype mode	"Typing Text and Erasing Mistakes"	
Insert page breaks	"Starting a New Paragraph, Line, or Page"	
Use the Undo, Redo, and Repeat command	"Tricks for Editing Text"	
Insert symbols	"Entering Symbols and Foreign Characters"	
Use Go To to locate specific elements in a document	"Going from Place to Place with the Go To Command"	2-2 Go To
Navigate through a document	"Moving Around in Long Documents"	2-1 Navigate
Use bookmarks*	"Bookmarks for Getting Around"	2-3 Bookmarks

* Denotes an Expert exam objective.

Ten Ways to Edit Faster

Half the time you spend at the keyboard is spent editing, but I want you to spend a fourth of the time, not half the time. To that end, here are ten editing techniques that every Word user should know.

1. TAKE CARE OF THE TEXT FIRST, THEN DO THE LAYOUT WORK. Write the first draft of a document before you attempt to lay out the pages or text. Editing text after it has been squeezed into columns, rammed into text boxes, or pressed into tables is difficult. Write the clean copy first and you will spare yourself the trouble of having to edit with one hand tied behind your back.

2. LEARN THE TECHNIQUES TO SELECT, COPY, AND MOVE TEXT. Much of editing requires copying and moving text. And as the next chapter explains, you can't copy or move text until you select it. Therefore, knowing all the shortcuts for selecting, copying, and moving text is worthwhile. Well worthwhile, in fact. Chapter 3 explains selecting, copying, and moving text.

3. MAKE USE OF THE UNDO AND REPEAT COMMANDS. In "Tricks for Editing Text," earlier in this chapter, I explained how valuable the Undo and Repeat commands are. Instead of cursing when you make a mistake, click the Undo button to redeem it. And opportunities to use the Repeat command are many. After a while, you'll start to recognize them and you'll get used to using the Repeat command to cut down on the amount of work you have to do.

4. LEARN THE CAPITALIZATION KEYPRESS. Few things are easier than selecting text and pressing SHIFT-F3. That's all it takes to correct a capitalization error, as this chapter explained.

5. TAKE ADVANTAGE OF THE WINDOW MENU COMMANDS. As "Working in Two Places or Documents at Once" in Chapter 6 explains, the New Window and Split commands on the Window menu can be very useful when you are editing a document. Choose the New Window command to simultaneously work in two different places in a document without having to scroll between the two places. Choose the Split command to put two parts of the same document on screen at the same time.

6. CHOOSE A GOOD VIEW AND ZOOM SETTING. Get used to switching views and choosing new zoom settings. Depending on the task at hand, some views and zoom settings are better than others. Fortunately, between the convenient View buttons and just-as-convenient Zoom drop-down menu, getting a better view is easy.

7. LEARN HOW TO MOVE QUICKLY THROUGH DOCUMENTS.   In this chapter, "Moving Around in Long Documents" offers several techniques for getting around quickly: keyboard shortcuts, the scroll bar, the Select Browse Object button, the Go To Command, bookmarking, and the document map. Explore all the techniques to find the ones that work best for you.

8. FOR FIRST DRAFTS, CHOOSE A FONT THAT IS EASY TO READ.   In Chapter 7, "Changing the Way Characters Look on the Page" explains how to change fonts. A *font* is a typeface style. When you write the first draft, choose a font that is easy on the eyes. Most people prefer the Courier New, Times Roman, or Arial font.

9. "WRAP" TEXT SO IT STAYS ONSCREEN.   If, like me, you treasure your eyesight and you like to gaze at large letters onscreen, you will run into the problem of not being able to see all the text because the letters are too large and get pushed off screen. You can solve this problem by "wrapping" text to the screen, as explained in the section "Wrapping Text So It Stays Onscreen," in this chapter.

10. LEARN HOW TO USE THE AUTOTEXT AND AUTOCORRECT COMMANDS. Some words and names get typed over and over again—your name and address, for example. And if you work in, say, a scientific field, you might have to type long scientific names all day long. To spare yourself from having to do that, you can let the AutoText and AutoCorrect commands do the work for you. See "Ways to Enter Text Quickly" in Chapter 6.

The
Complete
Reference

Word
2000

Chapter 3

Copying, Moving, and Deleting Text

This short but important chapter describes the many techniques for selecting, deleting, copying, and moving text. I'm afraid you will find an inordinate number of "tips" in this chapter because there are so many shortcuts for selecting, deleting, copying, and moving text. Learn the many shortcuts and techniques and you will considerably cut down the time that you spend editing.

Selecting Blocks of Text

Many word-processing tasks require you to select text first. Before you can delete text, you have to select it. Before you can move or copy text, you have to select it. You can't change fonts or font sizes until you select the text first. To make selecting text easy, Word 2000 offers nearly a dozen ways to do it. These pages explain how to select text with the mouse and how to do it with precision by double-clicking the EXT button on the Status bar.

Note *"Selecting Objects So You Can Manipulate Them" in Chapter 13 explains how to select clip art images, graphics, text boxes, autoshapes, and other so-called objects.*

Basic Mouse Techniques for Selecting Text

Table 3-1 describes the nearly dozen ways to select text with the mouse. The trick to selecting more than one word or several words at a time is to click (or double-click) in the margin to the left of the words and do so when the mouse pointer is pointing to the right, not the left. In this illustration, I selected an entire paragraph by double-clicking to its left, and the selected text is highlighted on screen. Don't click or double-click until the pointer points to the right, as it does in this illustration:

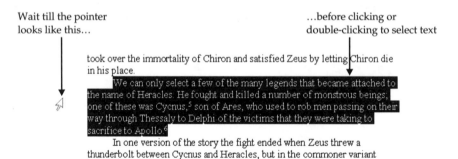

Wait till the pointer looks like this…

…before clicking or double-clicking to select text

took over the immortality of Chiron and satisfied Zeus by letting Chiron die in his place.
We can only select a few of the many legends that became attached to the name of Heracles. He fought and killed a number of monstrous beings; one of these was Cycnus,[5] son of Ares, who used to rob men passing on their way through Thessaly to Delphi of the victims that they were taking to sacrifice to Apollo.[6]
In one version of the story the fight ended when Zeus threw a thunderbolt between Cycnus and Heracles, but in the commoner variant

The program selects one word at a time when you drag over words to select them. Some people find that a bother. If you are good with the mouse and used to selecting text, you can tell Word not to jump ahead and select entire words when you drag over

To Select This	Do This
A word	Double-click the word.
A few words	Drag over the words.
A line	Click to the left of the line.*
Several lines	Drag up or down to the left of the lines.*
A sentence	Hold down the CTRL key and click in the sentence.
A paragraph	Double-click to the left of the paragraph* (or triple-click inside the paragraph).
A block of text	Click at the start of the text you want to select, hold down the SHIFT key, and click at the end of the text.
Several paragraphs	Double-click to the left of a paragraph and then drag up or down.*
A table	Choose Table │ Select or hold down the ALT key and double-click in the table.
The whole document	Press CTRL-A or choose Edit │ Select All (or triple-click to the left of the text*).

* Make sure the pointer points to the right before clicking, double-clicking, or triple-clicking to the left of the text.

Table 3-1.   *Techniques for Selecting Text*

them. To do so, choose Tools │ Options, click the Edit tab in the Options dialog box, and uncheck the box called When Selecting, Automatically Select Entire Word.

Selecting Blocks of Text with Precision

Word offers a special technique for selecting large or unwieldy blocks of text with precision. Suppose you want to select everything from the middle of page 2 to the middle of page 4, including a table and graphic on page 3. In that case, the selection

What Happens to Formats When You Copy Text

When you select text for the purpose of copying it, whether you select the paragraph format symbol at the end of the paragraph determines whether you copy the paragraph's formats as well as the text. Besides marking the end of a paragraph, the all-important paragraph format symbol holds the formatting for the paragraph. As a general rule, clicking or double-clicking to the left of the text selects the paragraph symbol as well as the text itself. Press the Show/Hide ¶ button to see the format symbols. "Viewing the Hidden Format Symbols" in Chapter 2 explains what the symbols are.

In·this·paragraph,·the·paragraph·formatting·symbol·has·been·selected.¶

techniques in Table 3-1 won't do any good, because they are designed for selecting units of text—a line, a paragraph, and so on. However, you can select a large or unwieldy block of text by following these steps:

1. Click at the start or end of the text you want to select.
2. Either double-click the EXT button on the Status bar or press F8. The dark letters EXT on the Status bar tell you that you can start selecting text:

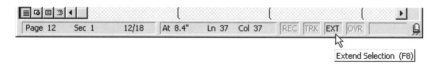

Extend Selection (F8)

3. Scroll to or move to the other end of the text that you want to select and click. The text is highlighted to show it has been selected.

All the keyboard shortcuts for moving around in documents also work for selecting text after you press F8 or double-click EXT. For example, press CTRL-HOME to select all text to the beginning of the document. See "Keyboard Techniques for Getting Around" in Chapter 2 for a list of keyboard shortcuts.

As long as EXT is highlighted on the Status bar, you can click elsewhere in your document to change the size of the text block you selected. Perhaps you didn't select enough text; click again to select more words and letters. But after you give a command—you change fonts or copy the block of text, for example—EXT is no longer highlighted on the Status bar and you can't click elsewhere to select more text or less text.

Press ESC or double-click EXT on the Status bar if a bunch of highlighted text is onscreen but you don't want to do anything with it. Pressing ESC or double-clicking EXT tells Word that you want to quit trying to select text.

 To select successively larger blocks of text, click in the text and start pressing F8. The second click selects a word, the third a sentence, the fourth a paragraph, the fifth a section, and the sixth the entire document.

Deleting Chunks of Text

Deleting chunks of text is simple as long as you know how to select text. To delete chunks of text, all you have to do is select the text and press the DELETE key (or choose Edit | Clear). Remember: The Undo button is ready and waiting to be clicked in case you accidentally delete the wrong text.

Chapter 1 explained how to press DELETE or BACKSPACE to delete one character at a time. Here are a couple of keyboard shortcuts for deleting one word at a time:

- ■ **CTRL-BACKSPACE**   Deletes the word to the left of the insertion point.
- ■ **CTRL-DELETE**   Deletes the word to the right of the insertion point.

 You can delete text without pressing the DELETE key. After you select the text you want to delete, start typing. The words you selected are replaced instantly by the words you type.

Moving and Copying Text

In my opinion, one of the best things going in Word 2000 is being able to copy and move text. A paragraph from the company report, with a few changes, can be included in a letter. The summary paragraph at the end of an academic paper can be moved to the start of the paper and be made into the introduction. Copying and moving text are valuable word-processing tasks, so knowing the different techniques for copying and moving text is worthwhile.

On the following pages are numerous tip and tricks for moving and copying text quickly. Here are instructions for copying and moving with the Clipboard, dragging to copy and move, and assembling "scraps" from different documents in a single document.

LEARN BY EXAMPLE
Open the 3-1 Copying and Moving practice document on the CD if you want to try
your hand with the various techniques for copying and moving text. The sample file
contains a lot of text that you can copy and move—or delete, for that matter.

Copying and Moving Text with the Clipboard

Copy and move text with the Clipboard when you want to copy or move text long
distances or to other documents. The *Clipboard* is a sort of electronic holding tank for
storing text. The last 12 items you cut or copied are stored on the Clipboard. Follow
these steps to move or copy text with the Clipboard:

1. Select the text you want to move or copy.

2. Move or copy the text to the Clipboard:

    ■ **Moving**   Choose Edit | Cut, press CTRL-X, click the Cut button, or
    right-click the text and choose Cut from the shortcut menu. The text is
    removed from the document.

    ■ **Copying**   Choose Edit | Copy, press CTRL-C, click the Copy button, or
    right-click and choose Copy. You can also click the Copy button on the
    Clipboard toolbar.

3. Open a second document, if necessary, and click where you want to move or
copy the text.

4. Paste the text in your document:

    ■ **Item You Just Cut or Copied**   Choose Edit | Paste, press CTRL-V, click the
    Paste button, or right-click and choose Paste.

    ■ **Item You Cut or Copied Earlier**   Display the Clipboard toolbar if it isn't
    already onscreen by right-clicking a toolbar and choosing Clipboard from
    the shortcut menu. Then slide the pointer over the scraps to read the first
    few words of each one, find the item you want to paste, and click the item:

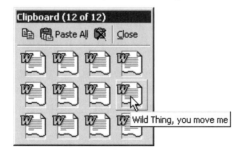

Saving What Is on the Clipboard in a File

You can see the last item that was copied or cut to the Clipboard and even save the contents of the Clipboard in a file. To do so, click the Start button and choose Programs | Accessories | System Tools | Clipboard Viewer. The Clipboard Viewer window appears and you see what is on the Clipboard, as shown in the illustration (you might have to choose Display | Text or Display | Picture to see anything). To save the contents of the Clipboard in a file, choose File | Save As, choose a folder and enter a name for the file, and click OK in the Save As dialog box.

Choose File | Save As to save
the Clipboard contents in a file

Suppose you want to strip the fancy formatting from text or a table when you copy or move it to a new location. To do so, choose Edit | Paste Special instead of Edit | Paste. In the Paste Special dialog box, choose Unformatted Text and click OK.

Tip   *When you move or copy text to a new location, Word inserts a blank space on either side of the text. The blank spaces are meant to keep words from running together, but some people find the blank space annoying. If the extra blank spaces bother you, you can tell Word to stop inserting them when you move or copy text. Choose Tools | Options, click the Edit tab in the Options dialog box, and uncheck the Use Smart Cut And Paste check box.*

Copying and Moving Text Short Distances with Drag-and-Drop

The most convenient way to move or copy text short distances is to use the drag-and-drop method. By "short distances" I mean two places in the same document when you can see both places onscreen. You can also drag text from one open window to another. Follow these steps to copy or move text with the drag-and-drop method:

1. Make sure both the text you want to copy or move and the place to which you will copy or move it appear onscreen.

2. Select the text.

3. As shown in Figure 3-1, either move or copy the text. As you move or copy the text, a vertical line shows where the text will go and a box appears below the pointer. If you are copying the text, a small cross appears in the box.

   - **Moving** Drag the text where you want to move it.
   - **Copying** Hold down the CTRL key as you drag the text where you want to copy it.

As if there aren't enough copying and moving techniques to remember, you can also drag the text while holding down the right mouse button. Release the right mouse button when the text is where you want to move or copy it. You see a shortcut menu. Click either Move Here or Copy Here to move or copy the text:

> Look at the pyramid on the dollar bill! On your very own dollar you can see it!
>
> One has to realize that these things have very deep ramifications. Look at your own Supreme Court with the lady with the blind eye! Look at the Book o[Move Here   ] where they got it from – from the Druids to here, from the Egyptian [Copy Here   ]
> Link Here
> Create Hyperlink Here
>
> Cancel

Another way to move text is to do it in Outline view. In Chapter 19, "Moving Headings—and Text—in a Document" explains how you can move headings and the text below headings backward and forward in a document very quickly in Outline view.

Two More Techniques for Copying and Moving Text

Because this book has the word *complete* in its title and it endeavors to cover every nook and cranny of Word, here are two more techniques for copying and moving text. The text is not stored on the Clipboard with these techniques:

- **Copying** Select the text and press SHIFT-F2. The Status bar asks, "Copy to where?" Click where you want to copy the text and press ENTER. This technique does not work for copying text to another document.

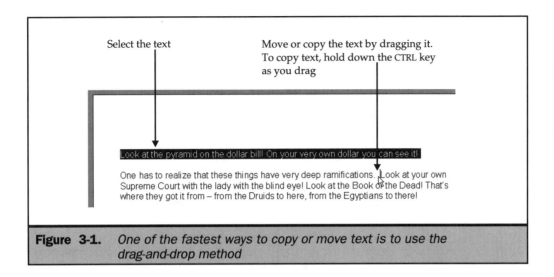

Select the text

Move or copy the text by dragging it.
To copy text, hold down the CTRL key
as you drag

Look at the pyramid on the dollar bill! On your very own dollar you can see it!

One has to realize that these things have very deep ramifications. Look at your own
Supreme Court with the lady with the blind eye! Look at the Book of the Dead! That's
where they got it from — from the Druids to here, from the Egyptians to there!

Figure 3-1.   *One of the fastest ways to copy or move text is to use the drag-and-drop method*

- **Moving a Paragraph at a Time**   Click a paragraph you want to move and then press ALT-SHIFT-↑ or ALT-SHIFT-↓ as many times as necessary to move the paragraph up or down the page.

Assembling Text from Many Different Places in One Place

The Clipboard toolbar holds the last 12 items you cut or copied. To assemble text from 12 or fewer different places, cut or copy the text, place the insertion point where you want to assemble it, and click the Paste All button on the Clipboard toolbar. Text is pasted in the order in which it was cut or copied to the Clipboard.

The Clipboard is fine for handling 12 or fewer items. What if you want to assemble text from many different documents and paste it in one place? To do that, either use the Spike or paste the scraps onto the desktop and then reassemble them. Keep reading.

Using the Spike to Move Text from Many Different Places

The *Spike,* a sort of supersonic Clipboard, can hold as many items as you want it to hold. Use the Spike to move text and graphics from many different places to a single place. When you empty the Spike, the items you moved are deposited in the order in which you cut them from a document or documents.

To use the Spike, one by one select each text or graphic you want to move and press CTRL-F3. Then click the insertion point where you want to dump the material and do either of the following:

- **Paste and Clear the Contents of the Spike**   Press CTRL-SHIFT-F3 to paste the contents of the Spike in a document. Go this route to empty the Spike of its contents.

■ **Copy What Is on the Spike So You Can Paste It Again**   Choose Insert |
AutoText | AutoText, click the AutoText tab in the AutoCorrect dialog box,
click the word "Spike" in the Enter AutoText Entries Here box, and click the
Insert button. The contents of the Spike are pasted in your document. With this
technique, the contents of the Spike remain intact so you can paste them again.

Copying and Moving Text with the "Scraps" Method

Figure 3-2 shows how the "scraps" method works. To start, you select text and drag it
onto the Windows desktop. To copy the text, simply drag it out of the Word window;
to move the text, hold down the SHIFT key while you drag. After text arrives on the
desktop it takes the form of a scrap, as shown in Figure 3-2. When you have assembled
all the scraps on the desktop, you can drag them one by one into another document.

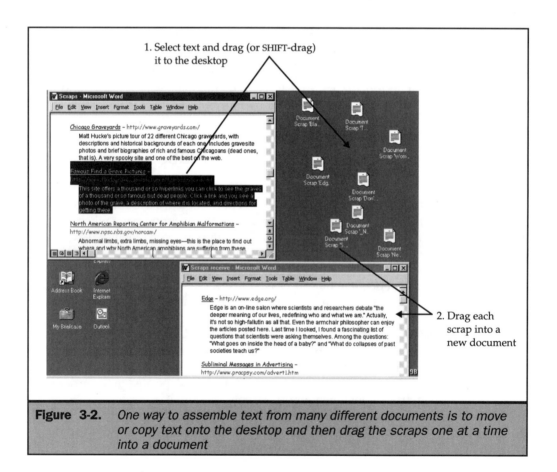

Figure 3-2.   *One way to assemble text from many different documents is to move
or copy text onto the desktop and then drag the scraps one at a time
into a document*

Before you can copy or move text with the scraps method, however, you have to lay the groundwork:

- Shrink the Word window as shown in Figure 3-2 to make room onscreen to put scraps. To do so, click the Restore button, if necessary, and then reshape the window ("Changing the Size and Position of Windows" in Chapter 6 explains how).

- Turn off AutoArrange. The Windows AutoArrange option makes desktop icons line up in strict military fashion on the left side of the screen. But you want text scraps to float on the right side of the screen where you can see them. To turn off AutoArrange, if that is necessary, right-click a blank spot on the desktop, choose Arrange Icons, and uncheck the AutoArrange option on the submenu.

Scraps remain on the desktop after you drag them into a new document. To keep scraps from littering the desktop, hold down the CTRL key and click each scrap to select it. Then right-click a scrap, choose Delete from the shortcut menu, and choose Yes when Word asks if you really want to delete the scraps.

Copying Documents

Copying text isn't enough? You want to copy an entire document? It can be done. Word offers commands for inserting one document into another, opening a second copy of a document, and copying an entire document to the Clipboard:

- **Inserting One Document into Another**   You can recycle documents by inserting one into another. Perhaps the essay about Thomas Jefferson, with a change here and there, can be put to use in the term paper about Colonial America. To insert one document into another, choose Insert | File to open the Insert File dialog box. Then find and select the document you want to insert and click the Insert button.

- **Copying a Document to the Clipboard**   To copy an entire document to the Clipboard, choose File | Open and find the name of the document you want to copy in the Open dialog box. Then right-click the name of the document and choose Copy from the shortcut menu. Click the Cancel button to close the Open dialog box.

- **Opening a Second Copy of a Document**   Choose File | Open and, in the Open dialog box, find the name of the document you want to copy. Then right-click the document's name and choose Open As Copy from the shortcut menu, as shown in Figure 3-3. A new document called "Copy of" followed by the name of the original document appears onscreen.

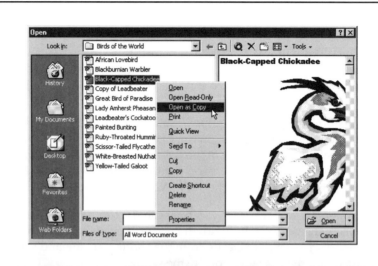

Figure 3-3. Choose File | Open, right-click a document name, and choose Open As Copy to copy a document. Choose Copy to place a copy of the document on the Clipboard

Note *"Saving (and Opening) Different Versions of a Document" in Chapter 22 explains how, as you work on a document, you can retain copies of it in various stages of completion. Chapter 22 also explains how to save a document so it can be opened in another word processor or an earlier version of Word.*

Linking Documents So That Text Is Copied Automatically

Besides conventional ways of copying text, you can also link documents so that changes made to text in the source of the copy are made automatically to the copy as well. The ability to update copies this way is called *Object Linking and Embedding* (OLE). A telephone list that is updated regularly, for example, can be linked to other documents so that changes made to the master telephone list are made automatically to all documents that include the telephone list. And you can even establish links to data in a program other than Word. These pages explain how to establish an OLE link so copies can be made automatically, as well as how to update and alter a link.

Caution *OLE links are broken when documents are renamed or moved to different folders. If you are disciplined and can plan ahead, make OLE links between documents. But linking documents is more trouble than it's worth if you often move or rename documents. Very carefully create or choose folders for storing linked documents so you don't have to move them.*

Establishing the Link

For the purposes of linking documents, the original document from which the copy is made is called the *server*. Its cousin, which gets updated when the copied text in the server document changes, is called the *client*. A link is actually a field code in the client document that tells the client document where the server document is located. The code lists the path from the client document to the server document and tells what kind of link to make, in this case an OLE link:

{ LINK Word.Document.8 "C:\\Zudstuff\\Word Made Easy\\Chap03\\Server.doc" "OLE_LINK2" \a \r }

Follow these steps to establish a link so that copied text in the client document is updated when text in the server document changes:

1. Open the server document with the text that you will copy to the client document.

2. Select and copy the text (choose Edit | Copy, press CTRL-C, or click the Copy button).

3. Open or switch to the client document and click where you want the copy to go.

4. Choose Edit | Paste Special. You see the Paste Special dialog box:

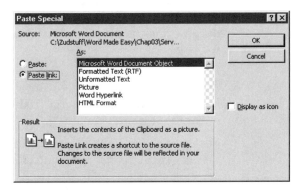

5. Click the Paste Link option button.

6. In the As box, choose how you want to paste the copy in the client document. Table 3-2 explains what the options are.

7. Click OK.

Note *You can tell where a link is located because it is highlighted onscreen when you click it. Don't edit the highlighted text—your edits will be erased the next time the link is updated. "All about Fields" in Chapter 24 explains how to keep fields like those created when you establish a link from being highlighted onscreen and how to display field codes instead of data.*

Paste Link Option	How the Copy Is Made
Object	The data is pasted in Word as an object (Chapter 13 explains objects and how to manipulate them). As such, you can drag it to different places onscreen or wrap text around it. (This option changes names, depending on where the copied material came from. For example, the option is called Excel Worksheet Object if the link is being made to an Excel worksheet.) This option requires the most memory.
Formatted Text (RTF)	Data retains text formats—boldfacing, shading, backgrounds, and color—from the server document when it is pasted in the client document.
Unformatted Text	Formats are stripped from the data when it is pasted in the client document. Choose this option to copy raw data from the server document and format the data as you please.
Picture	Copies the data as a picture. A picture is an object, so you can move the picture onscreen or wrap text around it, for example. However, this option requires half the memory of the Object option. Use it to copy graphics and other data-intensive images to the client document without making the client document grow too large.
Word Hyperlink	Pastes the text in the form of a hyperlink (the text is blue and the pointer changes into a hand when it is moved over the pasted text). Clicking the hyperlink opens the server document.
HTML Format	Text is pasted in HTML format. Select this option if the client document is an online HTML file.

Table 3-2.   *Options for Linking Data in the Server Document to the Client Document*

Updating a Link

Unless you change the default settings, links are updated automatically and the text in the client document is updated from the server document under these circumstances:

■ When you make editorial changes in the server document and save the document.

■ When you open the client document. (If the copy isn't updated automatically when you open the client document, choose Tools | Options, click the General tab in the options dialog box, and check the Update Automatic Links At Open check box.)

Tip   *While you are working in the client document, you can open the server document and perhaps make changes there. To do so, right-click the copied text in the server document, choose Linked Document Object, and choose either Edit Link or Open Link on the submenu. If you choose Edit Link, the changes you make in the server document are made instantly in the client document. If you choose Open Link and make changes in the server document, you have to save the server document before the changes show up in the client.*

However, you can decide for yourself how and when changes made in the server document show up in the client document. To do so, open the client document and choose Edit | Links. As shown in Figure 3-4, the Links dialog box appears. This dialog box lists all the links in the client document and gives you opportunities for updating links and deciding how links should be updated.

Unlike automatic links, manual links are updated only when you tell Word to update them. To change an automatic link to a manual link, select a link in the Links dialog box and click the Manual option button. To update the manual links in the client document, choose Edit | Links to open the Links dialog box, select the link you want to update (or CTRL-click to select several links), and click the Update Now button.

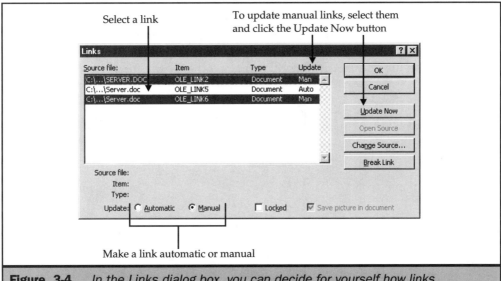

Figure 3-4.   *In the Links dialog box, you can decide for yourself how links are updated*

To make sure all links are updated before you print the client document, choose Tools | Options, click the Print tab in the Options dialog box, and check the Update Fields check box.

Breaking, Locking, and Unlocking Links

The Links dialog box (see Figure 3-4) offers many options for handling links. Select a link and do one of the following to break it, lock it, or unlock it:

- **Breaking Links** Break a link when you want the copied material to stay the same no matter what happens to the source material in the server document. To break a link, click the Break Link button. After you break the link, you can't re-establish it.

- **Locking and Unlocking Links** Lock a link to make the copied material stay the same and not be updated from the server document. To lock a link, check the Locked check box. Unlike the Break Link option, however, a locked link keeps its relationship with the server document. You can still update the link by unchecking the Locked check box.

- **Reestablishing a Link When the Server Document Has Changed Locations** Reestablish a link when you move the server document to a different folder, rendering its link to the client document invalid. To reestablish a link, click the Change Source button, find and select the server document in the Change Source dialog box, and click the Open button.

- **Opening the Server Document** Click the Open Source button to open the server document and perhaps edit the original data there. (You can also open the server document by right-clicking the link, choosing Linked Document Object on the shortcut menu, and then choosing Open Link.)

Exam | MOUS Exam Objectives Explored in Chapter 3

Objective	Heading	Practice File
Insert and move text	"Moving and Copying Text"	3-1 Copying and Moving
Cut, Copy, Paste, and Paste Special using the Office Clipboard	"Copying and Moving Text with the Clipboard" and "Linking Documents so that Text Is Copied Automatically"	

Ten Ways to Prevent Eyestrain

People who spend many working hours in front of a computer screen owe it to themselves to look after their health. Computers are dangerous to the lower back, the wrists, and the eyes—especially the eyes. Here are ten Windows and Word 2000 techniques to help prevent eyestrain.

 Some of the techniques listed here only work in Windows 98, not Windows 95. If you want to try a technique but you can't on your computer, blame it on Windows 95, not me.

1. KEEP THE MONITOR IN THE PROPER LIGHT.   Glare on a monitor screen causes eyestrain. Keep the monitor out of direct light to reduce glare and use an adjustable light to illuminate whatever it is you are working with besides your computer and monitor. If you are using a laptop, put the monitor in direct light. Laptops are sidelit or backlit, and they work better in full lighting.

2. PLAY WITH THE KNOBS ON THE MONITOR.   Those funny knobs on the monitor can be useful indeed. Twist them, turn them, and experiment until you find a look that is comfortable for your eyes.

3. OPT FOR A SMALLER SCREEN RESOLUTION.   With a smaller screen resolution, or area, everything looks bigger, although things can get cramped, too. To get a smaller resolution, right-click on the Windows desktop and choose Properties. In the Display Properties dialog box, click the Settings tab. Then drag the Screen area slider to the left, so the setting reads 640 by 480 pixels, and click OK. Try this setting on for size.

4. PUT LARGE ICONS ON THE DESKTOP AND IN FOLDERS.   To make the icons on the Windows desktop and in folders larger, right-click on the desktop and choose Properties. In the Display Properties dialog box, click the Effects tab, check the Use Large Icons check box, and click OK.

5. MAKE THE ICONS ON THE START MENU LARGER.   To make the icons on the Start menu larger, right-click the Taskbar and choose Properties. Then, in the Taskbar Properties dialog box, uncheck the Show Small Icons In Start menu check box, and click OK.

6. USE LARGE DISPLAY FONTS.   Large display fonts make menu choices and icon names easier to read. To see if you like them, right-click the Windows desktop and choose Properties to open the Display Properties dialog box, and click the Settings tab. Then click the Advanced button. On the Font Size drop-down menu, choose Large Fonts. Windows says that the large fonts can only take effect after you restart the computer. Restart the computer and see how you like large fonts.

7. MAKE THE MOUSE POINTERS LARGER. Another way to make your eyes last longer is to make the mouse pointers larger. Click the Start button and choose Settings | Control Panel. Then double-click the Mouse icon, click the Pointers tab in the Mouse Properties dialog box, and choose Windows Standard (extra large) or Windows Standard (large) from the Scheme drop-down menu.

8. FOR LAPTOP USERS: USE MOUSE POINTER TRAILS. Pointer trails can help laptop users find the mouse pointer onscreen. To tell Windows to display pointer trails, click the Start button and choose Settings | Control Panel. Then double-click the Mouse icon, click the Motion tab, and check the Show Pointer Trails check box in the Mouse Properties dialog box.

9. USE A BLUE BACKGROUND AND WHITE TEXT As a drastic measure, you can see if you like seeing a blue background on the screen and white text. In Word, choose Tools | Options, and click the General tab in the Options dialog box. Then check the Blue Background, White Text check box and click OK.

10. GAZE AT THE HORIZON. Every so often, leave your desk, step to the window, part the curtains, and stare. Stare at the most faraway point you can see. Stare and dream. Then blink a few times and marvel at how good the world looks when you're not staring at a computer screen.

Chapter 4

Getting the Help You Need

As soul singers say, "Everybody needs a little help sometime, baby." This chapter explains how to seek help for using Word 2000. Here you will find instructions for using the Help programs as well as looking to outside sources such as the Internet. Personally, I think the best way to get help with Word is to look in the Index or Table of Contents of this book, find the topic you need help with, and turn to the page that the Index or Table of Contents refers to.

Surveying the Ways to Get Help

Before you start flailing your arms and screaming for help, consider your options, all of which are described in the pages that follow:

■ **Office Assistant**   This cartoon character offers advice, some of it unwanted.

■ **Help Program**   The Help program is the surest but slowest way to seek help.

■ **What's This? Command**   You can choose the What's This? command and click on a part of the screen or a dialog box option to find out what it is or does.

■ **WordPerfect Help**   Word 2000 offers a special Help program for people who have quit WordPerfect and embraced Word.

■ **By Telephone**   You can call Microsoft and get help that way.

■ **On the Internet**   This chapter explains how to get help on the Internet from Microsoft and from other sources.

The Office Assistant and What You Can Do About It

As you must have noticed by now, an animated figure called the Office Assistant appears onscreen from time to time whether you like it or not. Type **Dear Jane:** and press the ENTER key, for example, and the Office Assistant leaps onscreen. "It looks like you're writing a letter," the Assistant says. "Would you like help?" Close a document without saving the changes you made to it and the Office Assistant rears its ugly head again. "Do you want to save the changes you made?" the Assistant asks.

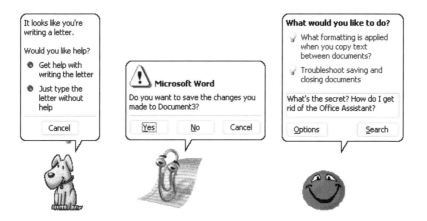

The Office Assistant is programmed like the Lone Ranger to appear out of the blue when you need help or assistance. But assistance with writing a letter? In my experience, the Office Assistant is more of a nuisance than anything else, so the following pages explain how to keep the Office Assistant from appearing as well as how to seek help with the Office Assistant. You will also find instructions for fine-tuning the Office Assistant so you can make it work your way, including how to choose which animated figure appears when you call on the Office Assistant for help.

To temporarily remove the Office Assistant from the screen, choose Help | Hide the Office Assistant, or right-click the Office Assistant and choose Hide from the shortcut menu. You can also shove the Office Assistant out of the way by dragging it to a corner of the screen.

Seeking Help with the Office Assistant

Follow these steps to find instructions for doing a task with the Office Assistant:

1. Press F1, click the Microsoft Word Help button, or choose Help | Show the Office Assistant. The Office Assistant appears onscreen.

2. Click the Office Assistant. As shown in Figure 4-1, a bubble caption appears with a "What would you like to do?" list of topics. At the bottom of the list is a box for entering a topic of your own. Word notes which activities you have performed lately and lists topics that have to do with those activities.

3. If the topic for which you need help is listed, double-click the topic. You might have to click See More at the bottom of the list to see all the topics. If your topic isn't listed, enter a topic name in the box, click the Search button, examine the new list of topics, and double-click a topic.

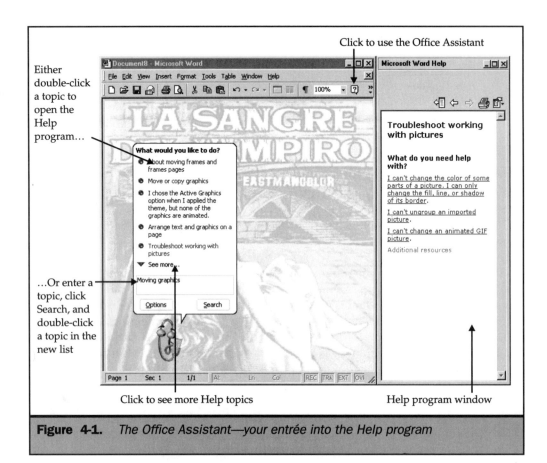

Click to use the Office Assistant

Either double-click a topic to open the Help program...

...Or enter a topic, click Search, and double-click a topic in the new list

Click to see more Help topics

Help program window

Figure 4-1. *The Office Assistant—your entrée into the Help program*

The Help program opens on the right side of the screen. See "Using the Word 2000 Help Program" later in this chapter to learn how to rummage for advice in the Help program.

Note *The last topic in the bubble caption is called "None of the above, look for more help on the Web." Double-click that topic to start your Web browser and visit a Microsoft Web site where, theoretically, your question will be answered.*

Getting Rid of the Office Assistant

To my way of thinking, the Office Assistant is nothing but a hurdle you have to leap over to get to the Help program. After you press F1, click the Microsoft Word Help button, or choose Help | Microsoft Word Help, and the Office Assistant appears. Then you double-click a topic, wait for the Help program window to appear, and hope that the right Help screen or right set of questions appears in the Help window.

How would you like to bypass the Office Assistant and go straight to the Help program when you press F1 or click the Microsoft Word Help button? It can be done. For that matter, you can keep the Office Assistant from appearing at all. Follow these steps to retire the Office Assistant and keep it from bothering you again:

1. Press F1 or click the Microsoft Word Help button to make the Office Assistant appear onscreen.

2. Click the Options button in the bubble caption above the Office Assistant, or, if you don't see the bubble caption, right-click the Office Assistant and choose Options from the shortcut menu. You'll see the Options tab of the Office Assistant dialog box.

3. Uncheck the Use The Office Assistant check box and click OK.

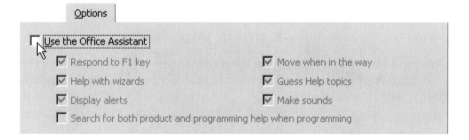

The next time you press F1, click the Microsoft Word Help button, or choose Help | Microsoft Word Help, the Help program opens right away. Suppose you miss the Office Assistant and you want the lovable animated figure to start distracting you again. To breathe life back into the Office Assistant, choose Help | Show the Office Assistant. The Office Assistant appears and you are back where you started.

Fine-Tuning the Office Assistant

Instead of ditching the Office Assistant altogether, you can visit the Options tab of the Office Assistant dialog box and fiddle with the options to make the thing work better. To do so, click the Microsoft Word Help button or press F1 to see the Office Assistant, and then click the Options button in the bubble caption (right-click and choose Options if you don't see the bubble caption). The Office Assistant dialog box appears.

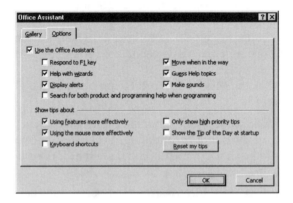

Changes made to the Office Assistant settings apply to all the Office 2000 programs, not just Word.

Check or uncheck these options to make the Office Assistant work your way:

- **Respond To** F1 **Key**   This option opens the Office Assistant instead of the Help program when you press F1. Uncheck this box if you want to go straight to the Help program by pressing F1.

- **Help With Wizards**   When you use a wizard to create a Web page or document, for example, the Office Assistant occasionally jumps aboard to offer advice. Uncheck this box if you find that annoying.

- **Display Alerts**   Alerts are timely messages like the one that appears if you try to close a file without saving the changes you made to it. Uncheck this check box to make alerts appear in message boxes instead of the Office Assistant's bubble caption.

- **Search For Both Product And Programming Help When Programming**   This option offers help advice for Word as well as Visual Basic when you are programming with Visual Basic.

- **Move When In The Way**   With this option enabled, the Office Assistant moves to the other side of the screen when you work beside its present location. Leave the check mark here.

- **Guess Help Topics**   This option makes Help topics appear in the bubble caption when you click the Office Assistant.

- **Make Sounds**   As you may have noticed, some Office Assistants are noisy. Uncheck this option to shut them up.

A tiny light bulb appears on the Microsoft Word Help button when the Assistant wants to offer you a tip. The light bulb appears above the Office Assistant as well. The options at the bottom of the Office Assistant dialog box pertain to tips, both the light bulb variety and the kind you can see when you start Word.

- **Light Bulb Tips**   Check the first four boxes—Using Features Effectively, Using the Mouse More Effectively, Keyboard Shortcuts, and Only Show High Priority Tips—to tell Word how often you want the light bulb to appear and what kind of tips you want to see, if any.

- **Startup Tips**   Click the Show The Tip Of The Day At Startup check box to make the Office Assistant appear and offer a tip whenever you start Word. The Reset My Tips button is for telling Word to start at the beginning of the list of tips it shows you when you start the program.

Choosing an Office Assistant Animated Figure

Because the word "complete" appears in the title of this book, I am obliged to tell you how to choose an animated figure for the Office Assistant. You have eight choices, including a bug-eyed paperclip rendition of Jimmy Durante and Einstein himself (what's he doing here?). To choose a new animated figure for the Office Assistant:

1. Press F1 or click the Microsoft Word Help button to display the Office Assistant.

2. Right-click the Office Assistant and select the Choose Assistant option on the shortcut menu. You'll see the Gallery tab of the Office Assistant dialog box.

3. Click the Next or Back button to examine the different choices.

4. Click OK when you have found the Office Assistant you want.

Using the Word 2000 Help Program

The Help program is a program unto itself and is completely separate from Word 2000. The program appears in a window on the right side of the screen so you can refer to help instructions as you do your work (see Figure 4-1). Read on to find out how to open the Help program, find the instructions you need, and handle the Help window.

Starting and Closing the Help Program

Earlier in this chapter, "Seeking Help with the Office Assistant" explains how to open the Help program by way of the Office Assistant. Unless you tinker with default settings, the only way to start the Help program is to invoke the Office Assistant first. However, "Getting Rid of the Office Assistant" and "Fine-Tuning the Office Assistant," also found earlier in this chapter, explain two strategies for opening the Help program without having to see the Office Assistant first. If you're serious about using the Help program, I suggest learning how to bypass the Office Assistant by reading the earlier sections in this chapter.

Tip   *Another way to open the Help program without seeing the Office Assistant first is to place the Contents and Index command on the Help menu. "Setting Up Your Own Menus" in Chapter 23 explains how to put commands on the Word menus and create menus of your own. After you put the Contents and Index command on the menu, you can choose Help | Contents and Index to open the Help program.*

The Help program window is like any program window. Click its Minimize button to shrink it to nothing. Click its Maximize button to make it fill the screen. To close the Help program, click the Close button (the X) in the upper-right corner of the Help program window.

Going Here and There in the Help Program

The Help program is like a massive Web site. Besides visiting the Contents tab, Answer Wizard tab, and Index tab to find instructions (they are explained shortly), you can simply click hyperlinks to get from Help screen to Help screen and hope that your search leads to the right set of instructions. As shown in Figure 4-2, hyperlinks are underlined and appear in blue or violet—blue if you haven't clicked a hyperlink or violet if you've clicked it already and been to the Help screen to which the hyperlink leads. You can tell where hyperlinks are because the pointer turns into a gloved hand when you move it over a hyperlink.

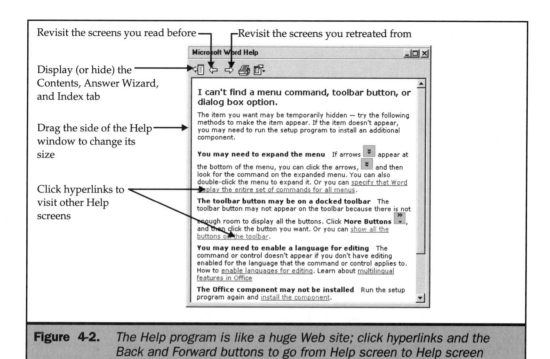

Figure 4-2.   *The Help program is like a huge Web site; click hyperlinks and the Back and Forward buttons to go from Help screen to Help screen*

While you are gazing at the Help program window and clicking hyperlink after hyperlink, take advantage of these amenities to help find the instructions you need:

- **Show/Hide Button**   Click the Show button to see the three tabs—Contents, Answer Wizard, and Index—and turn your search for help in another direction (see "The Three Ways to Look for Help," later in this chapter). After you click the Show button, it changes names and becomes the Hide button. Click the Hide button to remove the three tabs and focus on the instructions on the Help screen.

- **Back and Forward Buttons**   The Help program remembers all the instruction screens you visit in the course of a search. Click the Back button to revisit a help screen; click the Forward button to move ahead to a screen from which you retreated.

- **Print Button**   Click the Print button to print Help instructions and be able to refer to them later.

Tip   *To make the Help program window wider or narrower, move the mouse pointer over the left border of the window. When you see the double-headed arrows, click and start dragging.*

The Three Ways to Look for Help

When the Help window opens, you will see a Help screen with instructions for doing this, that, or the other thing. But suppose the Help screen doesn't present the instructions you need. In that case, click the Show button at the top of the Help program window to enlarge the window. You'll see three tabs—Contents, Answer Wizard, and Index—for turning your search for help in another direction. Use the Contents tab like the table of contents in a book to find instructions, the Answer Wizard tab to query the Help program, and the Index tab to search the Help files for instructions.

Starting from the Contents Tab

As shown in Figure 4-3, the Contents tab offers a list of topics similar to a table of contents in a book. Follow these steps to find help on the Contents tab:

1. Scour the list of topics until you find the one you are looking for. The topics are listed in alphabetical order.

2. When you've found the topic that interests you, either double-click its book icon or click the plus sign beside its name. The book "opens" and you'll see subtopics, each with a question mark icon beside its name.

3. Click the question mark beside the name of the subtopic that interests you. Instructions pertaining to the topic appear on the right side of the screen.

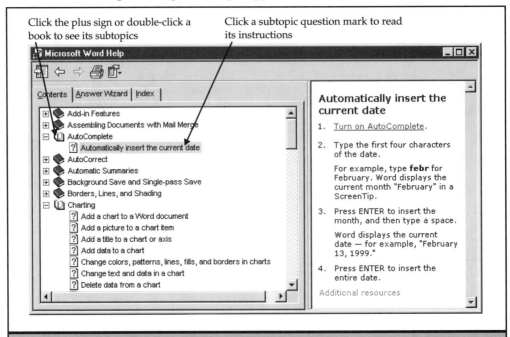

Figure 4-3. *The Help program's Contents tab works like the table of contents in a book*

By the way, you can click the minus sign next to a book to close the book and keep its subtopics from cluttering the Help window.

Asking Questions of the Answer Wizard

The Answer Wizard works exactly like the Office Assistant. In fact, the Answer Wizard is the Office Assistant in disguise. Enter the topic for which you need assistance in the box that asks, "What would you like to do?" The box instructs you to "Type your question here and then click Search," but you don't have to type a question. Just enter one or two or three words that describe the topic for which you need instructions.

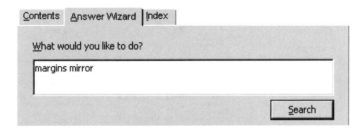

After you click the Search button, a list of topics appears. Click the topic you need help with and read the instructions on the right side of the Help program window.

Searching by Keyword on the Index Tab

Searching for instructions on the Index tab is like searching the Internet. To search, you enter *keywords*—words that describe what you want to know. Follow these steps to search for Help program instructions on the Index tab:

1. In box 1, type a keyword that describes the topic you want to know about. As shown in Figure 4-4, the list of words in box 2 scrolls to the word you entered. You must enter one of the keywords listed in box 2 to conduct the search.

2. Press the SPACEBAR or the ENTER key. As shown in Figure 4-4, a list of Help topics appears in box 3. These are topics whose instructions mention the keyword you entered in step 1. The top of box 3 says how many Help topics were found.

   At this point, you can either scroll through the list of Help topics in box 3 and click a topic to read its instructions on the right side of the program window, or you can enter another keyword to decrease the number of topics in box 3 and thereby narrow the search to fewer topics.

3. After waiting a sufficient amount of time for all the topics in box 3 to appear, type another keyword in box 1 and press the SPACEBAR or the ENTER key. The list of topics in box 3 is narrowed, as shown in Figure 4-4. Now only topics whose instructions mention both keywords appear.

4. Click a topic in box 3 to see its instructions on the right side of the Help program window.

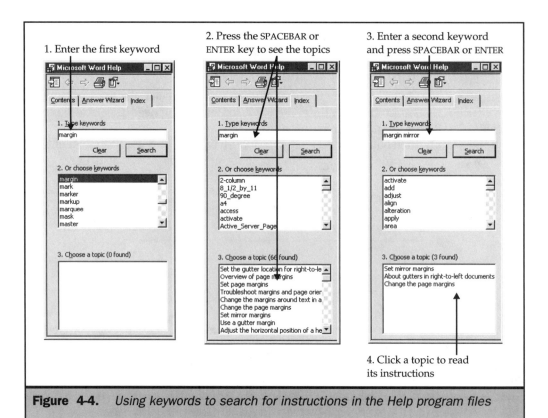

Figure 4-4. *Using keywords to search for instructions in the Help program files*

Of course, you can enter as many keywords as you want, but the list in box 3 shrinks pretty quickly, and I've never had to enter more than two.

  Be sure to click the Clear button before you conduct a new search. Clicking the Clear button empties box 3 of topics so you can start all over.

The What's This? Button for Finding Out What's What

With the idea that the fastest way to find out anything is to ask, Word offers the What's This? command. Choose Help | What's This? or press SHIFT-F1 and the pointer changes into an arrow with a question mark beside it. Click the quizzical pointer on the thing you want to know more about and you'll see either a box with an explanation or a box

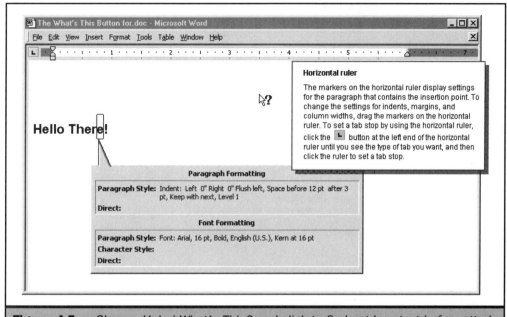

Figure 4-5.   *Choose Help | What's This? and click to find out how text is formatted (left) or what something on the screen is (right)*

with rudimentary instructions for completing a task. When you click text, you get a description of how the text was formatted, as shown in Figure 4-5.

    If you're a fan of keyboard shortcuts, you can arrange it so that Word lists keyboard shortcuts as well as button names when you move the pointer over buttons. Choose Tools | Customize, click the Options tab in the Customize dialog box, and check the Show Shortcut Keys In ScreenTips check box.

Learning What Dialog Box Options Are

In the upper-right corner of most dialog boxes is a question mark. Click the question mark and then click a dialog box option, text box, check box, or spinner box to find out what you are supposed to do with or enter in the thing you clicked. Some dialog box options are hard to decipher. Get used to clicking the question mark in dialog boxes to find out what's what.

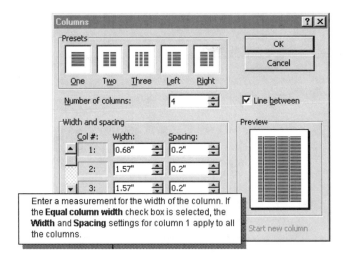

Enter a measurement for the width of the column. If the **Equal column width** check box is selected, the **Width** and **Spacing** settings for column 1 apply to all the columns.

Help for WordPerfect Turncoats

As part of its plan to entice WordPerfect users, Word 2000 offers a special Help program for people who have made the switch to Word from WordPerfect. To check it out, choose Help | WordPerfect Help or double-click the WPH button on the Status bar (WPH stands for WordPerfect Help). You will see a Help window with topics that concern WordPerfect users. By the way, you can't get help for using WordPerfect unless the Help For WordPerfect Users check box in the Options dialog box has been checked off. To get to the Options dialog box, choose Tools | Options, click the General tab, and check the Help For WordPerfect Users check box.

A WordPerfect User's Lament: "Where Are the Reveal Codes?"

Reveal codes are to WordPerfect what water is to Niagara Falls. In WordPerfect, you press F11 and reveal codes show precisely how text is formatted. Most WordPerfect users love their reveal codes. When they switch to Word, the first question they ask is, "Where are the reveal codes?"

Sorry, but there are none. To see how text is formatted, look at the text, the rulers, the Font menu, and the Style menu. If you are desperate, you can always press SHIFT-F1 or choose Help | What's This? and click text to find out how it is formatted (see Figure 4-5). However, you'll soon learn to live without reveal codes. After a while, you will learn to tell by looking at how text is formatted. You'll learn to stand on your own two feet and not look at reveal codes when you want to know what is on the screen.

Converts from WordPerfect who prefer the WordPerfect keypresses for getting from place to place in a document can use the WordPerfect keypresses in Microsoft Word. Choose Tools | Options, click the General tab in the Options dialog box, and check the Navigation Keys For WordPerfect Users check box.

Detecting and Repairing Word 2000 Installation Errors

Use the Help | Detect and Repair command to make sure that Word program files are intact. Files are sometimes overwritten or replaced when you install new software. And sometimes files get damaged. The Help | Detect and Repair command checks the health of Word program files and replaces files if that proves necessary.

The Help | Detect and Repair command takes a good 30 minutes to run. Don't detect and repair if you are in a hurry.

Follow these steps to run the Help | Detect and Repair command:

1. Shut down all programs—if any are open—and put the Word 2000 or Office 2000 CD in the CD drive on your computer.

2. Choose Help | Detect and Repair.

3. Click the Start button in the Detect and Repair dialog box.

Getting Technical Support from Microsoft

Besides getting help from Microsoft on the Internet (see the next section in this chapter), you can also use that ancient device, the telephone, to seek help:

- **Technical Support**   Call 425/462-9673 to speak to a Microsoft technician. The cost for this service is a whopping $35 per call if your copy of Word came preinstalled on your computer. If you bought your copy of Word over the counter, the call is free. Hours are 6 A.M. to 6 P.M. Pacific Standard Time.

- **Fast Tips Service**   Call 800/936-4100 and negotiate the torturous automated phone system to get answers to common questions. You can also order a catalog of articles about Word and request articles from the catalog from this telephone number. Automated telephone numbers, like rust, never sleep, so you can call this number any time of day.

You can also e-mail a request for help to Microsoft. In the Subject line of the message, enter the topic for which you need help. Send the message to **mshelp@microsoft.com**.

Seeking Help from Microsoft on the Internet

Table 4-1 describes the different ways to go on the Internet and get help for using Word from the Microsoft Corporation.

*Be sure to visit the Word Home Page (**www.microsoft.com/word/**) from time to time. Inevitably, bugs appear in software programs. The Word Home Page describes Word 2000 bugs and offers repair files, called* patches, *that you can download to your computer to fix the bugs.*

Web Site	What You Will Find There
Contact Microsoft	Tell Microsoft what you think of Word and how Word could be improved. Address: **register.microsoft.com/regwiz/regwiz.asp**
Microsoft Home Page	The official storefront of the Mighty Microsoft Corporation. Address: **home.microsoft.com**
Office Home Page	Information about Office 2000, Word's older brother. You can also go here by choosing Help | Office on the Web. Address: **www.microsoft.com/office/default.htm**
Support Page	For getting information about how to use Word. Search for and download "KnowledgeBase" articles from this site. Address: **support.microsoft.com/support/**
Word Home Page	Offers patches and other software fixes for Word. Address: **www.microsoft.com/word/**

Table 4-1. *Ways to Seek Help from Microsoft on the Internet*

 # MOUS Exam Objectives Explored in Chapter 4

Objective	Heading	Practice File
Use the Office Assistant	"The Office Assistant and What You Can Do About It"	

Ten Places on the Internet to Get Help with Word 2000

Microsoft isn't the only place on the Internet that offers advice for using Microsoft Word 2000. A lot of people want to get into the act. Following is a list of ten Web sites where you can seek help for using Word.

 The Web site addresses listed here were valid as of winter 1999. Web sites, however, come and go. If you can't locate a site listed here, try using an Internet search engine to find more current addresses.

1. AMERICA ONLINE'S HELP DESK   Starting here, you can find support channels that pertain to Microsoft Word. For AOL subscribers only. Keyword: **Help Desk**.

2. BAARNS MICROSOFT OFFICE RESOURCE CENTER   Offers FAQ (frequently asked questions) files about Word and the other Office 2000 programs. The last time I looked, there was a useful list of all the features that are new to Word. Address: **www.baarns.com**.

3. BUG NET   Bug Net is the self-proclaimed "world's leading supplier of PC bug fixes." Click the Search button, enter **Word 2000** in the Search For text box, and see how many, how various, and how disagreeable the bugs are in Word. Address: **www.bugnet.com**.

4. DEJA NEWS   Deja News is a service for locating *newsgroups*, the places on the Web where people post and exchange opinions, information, and drivel. To find Word newsgroups, click the Computers link on the home page, the Software link on the next page, the Word Processing link on the next page, and then the Microsoft Word link. You'll see a list of newsgroups. Click one to visit it. The last time I looked, Deja News listed about 30 newsgroups pertaining to Word.

 Don't believe everything you read in a newsgroup. Sometimes opinions aren't as authoritative as they are ear splitting. What's more, if you post a message on a newsgroup, you leave your e-mail message there. Junk e-mail companies often "mine" addresses from newsgroups.

5. KNOWHOW ON THE WEB ON-LINE GUIDE: WORD FOR WINDOWS   Here you will find several "KnowHow Guides" about advanced Word features such as heading numbering and fields. Former users of WordPerfect, be sure to check out "For WordPerfect Escapees: How Word Formats Text" (**www.knowhow.com/wwfmt1a.htm**), which explains why you can get along just fine without WordPerfect's famous reveal codes. Address: **www.knowhow.com**.

6. TECHSTATION   Go to this site when you need technical support and you want to find the Web address of a software or computer manufacturer. The site lists the Web addresses of thousands of manufacturers. Address: **www.techstation.com/index2.htm**.

7. WOODY'S OFFICE PORTAL   Woody Leonhard, the "Woody" of this Web site, is a bit of a gasbag, and some of his opinions concerning Word fall on the near side of shrill, but you can find the occasional good word of advice by clicking the Office Tips, Bug Alerts, and Fixes link at this site. Woody offers a free weekly newsletter for Word and Office power users. Address: **www.wopr.com**.

8. WORDINFO   Say the creators of this site: "Our mission is simple: To help Microsoft Word users create attractive, well-written documents as painlessly as possible." This site includes a good list of links to other sites that pertain to Word and a list of online magazine articles as well. Address: **www.wordinfo.com**.

9. WORD TUTORIALS   A neat little site that offers online tutorials for using Word. I'm not sure if these tutorials will be updated for Word 2000. The Chart Wizard and Equation Editor tutorial are especially good, which is good news indeed, since these features were not updated for Word 2000 anyway. Address: **www.cant.ac.uk/title/word.htm**.

10. ZD HELP   From this site, run by Ziff-Davis, publisher of *PC Magazine* and other glossy computer tomes, you can search for articles about Word. This site is a very useful resource, although I should warn you that the *PC Magazine* set is in love with computers and sometimes the authors gush when they should clarify. Address: **www.zdnet.com/zdhelp**.

The
Complete
Reference

Word
2000

Chapter 5

All About Printing

In spite of predictions to the contrary, the paperless office is still a pipe dream. The day when Johnny is at his computer, totally digitized and communicating with his colleagues without having to commit anything to paper, has yet to materialize. Johnny still has to print letters, contracts, prospectuses, and other material. As for Jane, she can hardly go a day without printing reports, legal briefs, and brochures. The office is still awash in paper, and all Jane and Johnny can do for consolation is try their best to recycle.

This chapter explains everything you need to know to print documents in Word 2000. You will learn how to acquaint Word with your printer, preview documents so you can see what they look like before you print them, and make small editorial changes on the Preview screen. This chapter explains the numerous ways to print documents and how to print different parts of a document—the odd pages, a section, or a handful of pages in the middle. In this chapter you will also find instructions for printing envelopes and labels. At the end, for the weary and frustrated, are instructions for solving printer problems.

Introducing Word 2000 to Your Printer

Word 2000 and your printer need to be on speaking terms before you can print documents flawlessly. These pages explain how to make the introduction. Read on to find out how to tell Word which printer you will use (if your computer is connected to more than one printer) and which paper tray you want to get paper from when you print documents (if your printer has more than one paper tray).

Telling Word Which Printer You Will Use

If you can send a file to more than one printer, perhaps a color printer and a black-and-white job, you need to tell Word which printer you will print your file on. Do this long before you actually print your file. In fact, choose the printer shortly after you create your document. Different printers have different capabilities, and Word changes layouts, however slightly, to accommodate the printer on which you will print your file. Therefore, Word needs to know which printer you intend to use.

Follow these steps to tell Word on which printer you will print your document:

1. Choose File | Print (or press CTRL-P). You'll see the Print dialog box, the top of which is shown in this illustration:

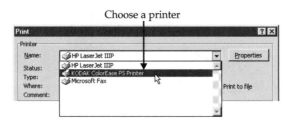

LEARNING THE ROPES

2. Open the Name drop-down list and choose a printer.

3. Click OK.

Telling Word Which Paper Tray to Use

Some people are fortunate enough to have two paper trays in their printers. Perhaps you are one of those lucky people and you keep 8.5 × 11-inch paper in the upper tray and legal-size or color paper in the lower tray. If your printer has two trays, printing on different kinds of paper is easier for you, but you also have to tell Word from which tray to get the paper when you print a document.

Word offers a two-pronged strategy for choosing a paper tray. As shown in Figure 5-1, you can go to the Printer Properties dialog box to choose a default paper tray, the paper tray where Word goes first to get paper for printing documents. You can also go to the Page Setup dialog box to tell Word to print certain documents or certain pages with paper from a tray other than the default tray.

Choosing the Default Paper Tray

The default paper tray is Word's first choice for printing documents. Unless you tell Word otherwise, paper is taken from the default tray. For the default tray, choose the tray with the paper on which you will print most often. To choose the default paper tray:

1. Choose File | Print and select a printer, if necessary, in the Print dialog box.

2. Click the Properties button and choose a default tray from the Paper Source drop-down list in the Printer Properties dialog box (see Figure 5-1).

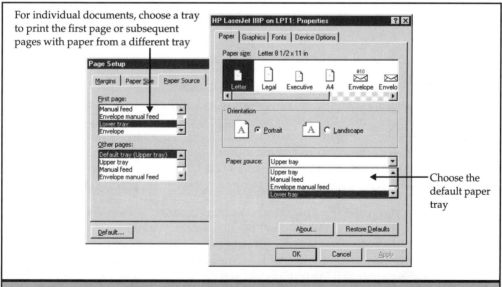

Figure 5-1.   *Choose the default paper tray in the Printer Properties dialog box (left). To override the default paper tray setting, go to the Page Setup dialog*

Telling Word to Print from a Tray Other Than the Default Tray

Occasionally you have to go against the default choice and print certain pages or even a whole document with paper in a tray that isn't the default. Word offers options for printing all pages or just the first page of a document or section, perhaps a letterhead page, with paper from a different tray. Follow these steps to tell Word to get paper from a tray other than the default tray where you normally get paper:

1. Click in a section if you want to print a particular section on different paper; otherwise, it doesn't matter where you start.

2. Choose File | Page Setup to open the Page Setup dialog box.

3. Click the Paper Source tab (see Figure 5-1).

4. Choose a tray:

   - **Different Paper for the First Page**   From the First Page list, choose a tray other than the default tray to print the first page of a document or section on different paper. If you want to print the first page of a section on different paper, choose This Section in the Apply To drop-down list.

   - **Different Paper for All the Pages**   Choose a tray from the Other Pages drop-down list to print all the pages in the document or section (except perhaps the first page) on different paper. Be sure to choose This Section in the Apply To drop-down list to print the pages in a section differently.

5. Click OK.

In order to include paper of a different size in a document and be able to print on it, you have to create a new section for the different-size paper. See "Section Breaks for Changing Layouts" in Chapter 9.

Precautions to Avoid Printing Problems

Printing problems are like soccer goals. As any soccer mom can tell you, the goalie gets the blame when the other team scores, but the problem is usually caused upfield by poor defending on the part of the fullbacks. Similarly, printing problems get noticed when documents are printed, but the origin of most printing problems can be traced to faulty decision-making on the part of the person who created the document. To keep printing errors to a minimum, take these precautions:

- **Fix the Margins Early On**   When the margins are too wide, text doesn't fall in the right places and lines don't break correctly. Moreover, if you change margin sizes after you are well into a project, you are asking for it. Text is indented from the margins, not from the edge of the page, so changing the margins changes all the text indents and can create a mess. Decide on the size of the margins early on to avoid line-break and other layout problems.

- **Know What Paper Size the Document Was Made For**   Make sure you know which size paper you are printing on. If you are trying to print a document that you got from a foreigner, chances are the document was formatted for paper other than the standard 8.5 × 11 that North Americans love so well. Chances are, too, that your margins and other layout settings are askew. See "Ten Printing Problems and How to Solve Them" at the end of this chapter (see item number 2) to learn how to format an A4 210 × 297 mm document for an American printer.

- **Tell Word Which Printer You Intend to Use**   As you make layout settings, Word takes note of which printer you intend to use and adjusts the layout settings accordingly. Therefore, if your are lucky enough or wealthy enough to have two printers, you should tell Word right away which printer you intend to print your document on. See "Telling Word Which Printer You Will Use" earlier in this chapter.

- **Use TrueType Fonts**   Some printers cannot print all the fonts whose names appear on the Font menu. However, all printers can print TrueType fonts, the fonts with "*TT*" next to their names on the Font menu. To make sure letters look the same onscreen as they will look when you print them, stick to TrueType fonts.

Previewing a Document Before You Print It

Before you print a document, examine it closely to see if a last-minute error needs correcting. That way, you will save yourself from printing two, three, or twenty pages before you realize that the document needs more work. Word offers a special screen for previewing documents. These pages explain how to preview documents before you print them and make layout changes in the Print Preview window.

LEARN BY EXAMPLE
Open the 5-1 Preview document on the companion CD if you would like to experiment with the tools in the Print Preview window.

Examining a Document in the Print Preview Window

As "Getting a Better View of Your Work" in Chapter 2 explains, the Print Preview window is a great place to see what documents will look like on the printed page. And the window also offers a number of tools for finding and fixing errors. To see a document in the Print Preview window, either click the Print Preview button on the Standard toolbar or choose File | Print Preview. The Print Preview window appears, as shown in Figure 5-2.

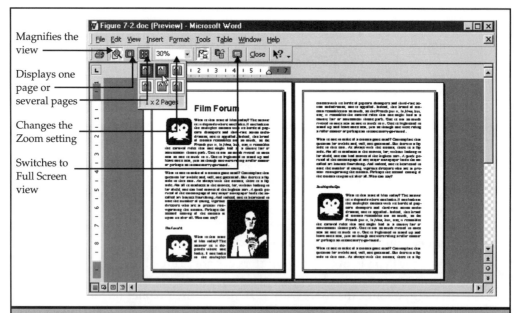

Magnifies the view

Displays one page or several pages

Changes the Zoom setting

Switches to Full Screen view

Figure 5-2. *Examine documents on the Print Preview window to get a better look at your work and to catch errors before you commit them to paper*

On the Print Preview toolbar are buttons and menus for examining documents, fixing errors, and printing. Here are instructions for examining a document in the Print Preview window (the next part of this chapter explains how to make editorial and layout changes):

- **Looking Closely at Part of a Document** If part of a document looks odd and needs investigating, examine it with the Magnifier. If necessary, click the Magnifier button so it is "pressed down," and then move the pointer onto the part of the document you want to examine. When the pointer changes to a magnifying glass with a cross inside it, click your document. The document is enlarged to its real size—that is, to 100 percent—so you can read it. To shrink the document onscreen, click it a second time.

- **Enlarging the Pages** To make pages look larger, either change the Zoom setting or click the Full Screen button. "Getting a Better View of Your Work" in Chapter 2 explains the Zoom menu and Full Screen view.

- **Hiding and Displaying the Rulers** Click the View Ruler button to hide or display the rulers. You need to see the rulers if you want to adjust margin sizes or indentations in the Print Preview window.

- **Viewing One or Several Pages** Click the Multiple Pages button and drag the pointer to tell Word how many pages to display. To display a single page, click the One Page button.

To get from page to page, press CTRL-PAGE UP or CTRL-PAGE DOWN, or else click the Previous Page or Next Page button (the double arrows) in the lower-right corner of the Print Preview window.

You can only examine one page with the Magnifier. Which page is that? The page where the cursor was when you clicked the Print Preview button to see your document on the Preview screen. If you're the kind of person who likes to examine pages with the Magnifier, make sure the cursor is on the page you most want to examine when you give the Print Preview command.

Making Editorial and Layout Changes in Print Preview

You can make editorial changes, change the size of margins, or indent text in the Print Preview window (see Figure 5-2), although doing any kind of work in the window can be difficult, because text is hard to read and pages are hard to examine when two or more appear. Before you attempt to edit a document in the Print Preview window, click the Magnifier button, if necessary, to turn off the Magnifier, and click the One Page button, if more than one page is shown, to display only one page. Then do the following:

- **Editorial Changes**   Click where you want to enter or erase text, and go to it. Remember: You can use the Zoom menu to enlarge the text. See "Zooming In and Zooming Out" in Chapter 2.

- **Changing the Size of Margins**   Drag the Left Margin, Right Margin, Top Margin, or Bottom Margin marker on the rulers, as shown in Figure 5-3. The pointer changes to a double-headed arrow when you move it over a marker. Click the View Ruler button if you don't see the rulers. Changes to the margins affect the entire document or, if the document has been divided into sections, the section that the cursor is in. See "Setting the Margins" in Chapter 9 to learn more about margins.

- **Indenting Text**   Drag an indent marker on the ruler—Left Indent, Right Indent, or First Line Indent—to change indents in the paragraph that the cursor is in. To indent several paragraphs at once, drag the pointer onscreen to select them before you start dragging the indent markers. "Indenting Text on the Page" in Chapter 8 explains the indent markers.

Unless you are working on a one-page document—an announcement or invitation, for example—don't change margin settings in the Print Preview window. Margin settings affect many different paragraphs, far more than can be seen well in the Print Preview window, so changing margins in the window can have unforeseen consequences.

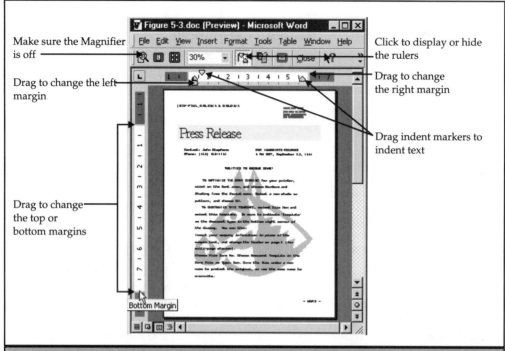

Make sure the Magnifier is off

Drag to change the left margin

Drag to change the top or bottom margins

Click to display or hide the rulers

Drag to change the right margin

Drag indent markers to indent text

Figure 5-3. *You can indent text and change margin settings in the Print Preview window*

Printing Documents

How do you print a document in Word? Let me count the ways. You can "quick-print" a document, print parts of documents, print many copies, print on both sides of the paper, print to a file, print an outline, or cancel a print job before you waste five or ten pages. Better start reading.

Making Faxes, Letters, and Résumés Fit on One Page

It's strange how faxes, résumés, and business letters always stray onto the second page. No matter how hard you try to fit them on a single page, one or two lines always creep onto page 2. To keep this from happening, Word offers a button on the Print Preview toolbar called Shrink to Fit. Click this button and Word endeavors to shrink your document. To do so, it reduces font sizes, margins sizes, and line spacing ever so slightly.

After you shrink a document, examine it to see whether it shrunk too much in the wash. You can do so by clicking parts of the document with the Magnifier. If you don't like the shrunken document, choose Edit | Undo (or press CTRL-Z) to get the old document back.

LEARN BY EXAMPLE
Open and print the 5-2 Print sample document on the companion CD to try out the
different ways of printing documents.

"Quick Printing" Documents

To print a document in its entirety, open it and either click the Print button on the
Standard toolbar or choose File | Print and immediately click OK in the Print dialog box.
Try this technique to print a document or several documents without opening them first:

1. Choose File | Open (or press CTRL-O) to see the Open dialog box.

2. Find and open the folder with the document or documents you want to print.

3. CTRL-click the names of documents that need to be printed. In other words, hold
   down the CTRL key and click the names.

4. Right-click a document you selected and choose Print from the shortcut menu,
   as shown in Figure 5-4.

5. Click Cancel or press ESC to close the Open dialog box.

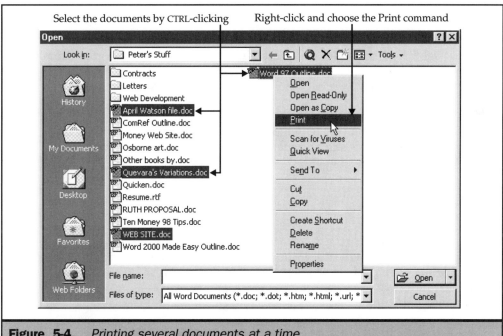

Figure 5-4. *Printing several documents at a time*

Dragging to Print a Document

The fastest way to print a document is to create a shortcut icon to your printer, open My Computer or Windows Explorer, find the document you want to print, and drag its icon over the printer shortcut icon, as shown here:

In My Computer or Windows Explorer, find and click the document you want to print

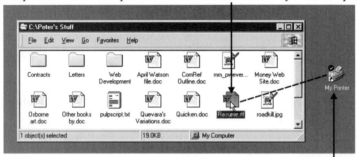

Drag the document over the printer shortcut icon

Follow these steps to create a shortcut icon for your printer:

1. Click the Start button and choose Settings | Printers. You'll see the contents of the Printers folder in the My Computer window. In this folder are icons for each printer that is installed on your system.

2. Right-click the printer you print with and choose Create Shortcut from the menu. A message box tells you that Windows can't place the shortcut icon in the folder but you can place it on the Windows desktop.

3. Click Yes in the message box to place the shortcut icon on the desktop.

4. Find your new shortcut on the Windows desktop, right-click it, choose Rename from the shortcut menu, and type a descriptive name for the printer shortcut icon.

Printing Parts or Copies of a Document

When you want to print part of a document, print more than one copy, print thumbnail pages, or print to a file, choose File | Print (or press CTRL-P). You'll see the Print dialog box shown in Figure 5-5. This dialog box offers numerous options for printing this, that, and the other thing, as the following pages so eloquently demonstrate.

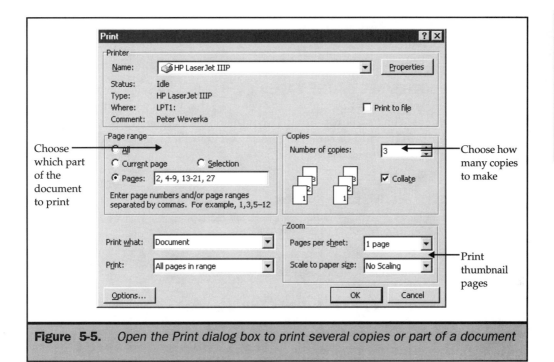

Choose which part of the document to print

Choose how many copies to make

Print thumbnail pages

Figure 5-5. *Open the Print dialog box to print several copies or part of a document*

Printing Particular Pages or Text

Herewith are instructions for printing a single page, several pages, parts of pages, even and odd pages, and document sections.

PRINTING A PAGE OR RANGE OF PAGES Click the Current Page option button to print the page that the cursor is on. To print certain pages only, enter their page numbers in the Pages text box. You can print a range of pages by entering hyphens between the page numbers, and even enter commas and hyphens to print several different pages or page ranges. For example, the following entry in the Pages text box tells Word to print page 4, 7 through 10, 13, 15, and 18 through 21:

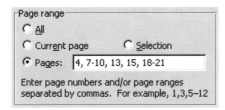

PRINTING PART OF A PAGE   To print part of a page, select it before choosing File | Print to open the Print dialog box. Then click the Selection option button and click OK.

PRINTING ON BOTH SIDES OF·THE PAPER   To print on both sides of the paper, print the odd pages first, then turn the pages over, feed them into your printer, and print the even pages. The Print drop-down list at the bottom of the Print dialog box offers options for printing odd or even pages. Choose Odd Pages or Even Pages from the Print drop-down list and click OK:

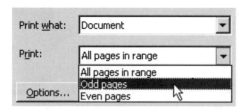

PRINTING SECTIONS AND PAGES IN SECTIONS   When a document has been divided into sections, you can print it the usual way by entering page numbers and page ranges, or you can print documents a section at a time:

- **Printing Whole Sections**   Choose File | Print to open the Print dialog box, and enter an **s** and then the section number in the Pages text box. For example, entering **s4** tells Word to print section 4; entering **s4-s6** tells Word to print sections 4 through 6.

- **Printing Pages in Sections**   In the Print text box, enter a **p**, a page number, and then an **s** and the section number. For example, entering **p8s6** in the Pages text box tells Word to print page 8 in section 6. Entering **p1s6-p4s6** tells Word to print pages 1 through 4 in section 6.

Printing Copies of Documents

To print more than one copy of a document, enter a number in the Number of Copies text box. Normally, pages are collated when you print more than one copy. For example, three three-page documents come out of the printer like so: 1-2-3, 1-2-3, 1-2-3. But if you uncheck the Collate check box, the pages arrive this way: 1-1-1, 2-2-2, 3-3-3.

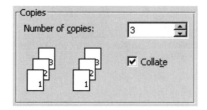

If for whatever reason you need to print a file backward, you can do it. Click the Options button in the Print dialog box (see Figure 5-5). Then, in the next Print dialog box, check the Reverse Print Order check box.

Printing Thumbnail Pages

One way to review a document to make sure all is well is to print thumbnail copies of the pages. Follow these steps to print thumbnail copies of all the pages in a document:

1. Choose File | Print or press CTRL-P to open the Print dialog box (see Figure 5-5).

2. Under Zoom in the lower-right corner of the Print dialog box, open the Scale To Paper Size drop-down list and select the size paper you will print on.

3. From the Pages Per Sheet drop-down list, choose how many thumbnail pages to print on each piece of paper and click OK:

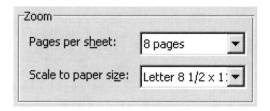

To print thumbnail copies of some of the pages in a document, select them. Then choose File | Print, click the Selection option button under Page Range in the Print dialog box, and choose a Pages Per Sheet and Scale to Paper Size option, and click OK.

Printing an Outline

As "Organizing Your Work with Outlines" in Chapter 19 explains, you can see in Outline view whether your manual, treatise, or report is well organized, and if it isn't well organized, you can rearrange the headings and the text below headings in Outline view. What Chapter 19 doesn't say is that you can print an outline.

See "Getting the Right View of Your Outline" in Chapter 19 to learn the different ways to display a document in Outline view.

When you click the Print button in Outline view, Word prints whatever is displayed onscreen. If only first-level headings are displayed, they are printed; if all the headings appear, all the headings are printed. Use the buttons on the Outline toolbar to display the parts of the Outline that you want to print and then give the Print command to print your outline. Remember: You can click the Show Formatting button on the Outline toolbar to display fonts in headings.

Canceling and Postponing Print Jobs

Suppose you give the command to print a document or a bunch of documents but then realize that one or two documents shouldn't be printed or one needs to be printed before the rest. You can control how documents are printed by following these steps:

1. Either double-click the Printer icon next to the clock on the right side of the Taskbar, or click the Start button, choose Settings | Printers, and double-click the icon of the printer you are using to print the documents. You see a Printer window similar to the one in Figure 5-6. Documents in the window are shown in the order they will be printed.

2. Do the following to postpone or stop printing a document:

   - **Stop Printing a Document**   Click the document and choose Document | Cancel Printing. The document is removed from the list.

   - **Stop Printing All Documents**   Choose Printer | Purge Print Documents.

   - **Postpone Printing a Document**   Click a document and choose Document | Pause Printing. The words "Paused - Printing" appear in the Status column (see Figure 5-6) and the document is not printed. To print it, click it and choose Document | Pause Printing again.

Separator Pages for Keeping Your Printed Material Separate from Others'

In a crowded office in which many people share the same printer, digging into a stack of printed material to find your printed pages is a hassle. However, you can make finding your pages easier by creating a *separator page,* a page that appears between each printed document in a stack of printed documents. Separator pages announce the name of the printed document, who printed it, and when it was printed. Follow these steps to create a separator page and make finding your documents easier:

1. Click the Start button and choose Settings | Printers. The contents of the Printers folder appear in a My Computer window.

2. Right-click the icon of the printer with which you print your files and choose Properties from the shortcut menu. You'll see the Properties dialog box.

3. Click the General tab, if necessary.

4. From the Separator Page drop-down list, choose Simple to print a plain-text separator page, or Full to print a page with large type and the words "Separator Page" across the top.

5. Click OK.

Next time you print a document, you will be able to find it by looking for your separator page.

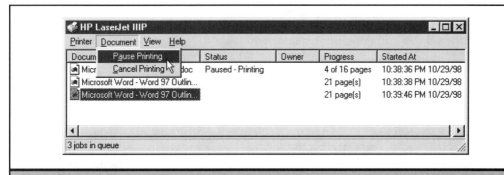

Figure 5-6.   *In the Printer window, you can keep documents from being printed or postpone printing a document*

Printing Addresses and Return Addresses on Envelopes

Word processors have made it very easy to enter and edit text, but in my humble opinion handwriting an address on an envelope is easier than printing an address on an envelope. Envelopes sometimes get stuck in printers. And setting up a printer so it can print envelopes can be difficult. Still, printing addresses on envelopes has one advantage: delivery point bar codes and facing identification marks appear on the envelope to help the postal service deliver your letter faster:

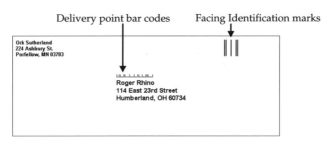

Tip   *One way to get around the problem of putting addresses on envelopes is to print an address label and paste it on the envelope. The next part of this chapter explains how to print address labels. If you send a lot of letters to clients and customers, try using window envelopes to get around the problem of printing addresses.*

Follow these steps to print an address and return address on an envelope:

1. Open the document with the letter you want to send and select the recipient's name and address. If you didn't type the recipient's name and address in the letter, go straight to step 2.

2. Choose Tools | Envelopes and Labels. As shown in Figure 5-7, you will see the Envelopes and Labels dialog box.

3. Enter the recipient's address in the Delivery Address box if the address isn't listed already. You can click the Address Book button to get the recipient's name from the Outlook address list or click the down arrow beside the button and choose the name of someone to whom you recently addressed a letter.

4. If no name or address or the wrong name or address appears in the Return Address box, enter the correct name and address. Or check the Omit check box to keep a name and address from appearing on the envelope.

Tip *Word gets the name and address in the Return Address box from the User Information tab in the Options dialog box. Make sure your name and address appear on this tab. To get to the User Information tab and enter your name and address there, choose Tools | Options and click the User Information tab in the Options dialog box.*

5. Feed an envelope to your printer and click the Print button.

   The envelope in the lower-right corner of the Envelopes and Labels dialog box shows how to feed envelopes to your printer. Keep reading if your envelope

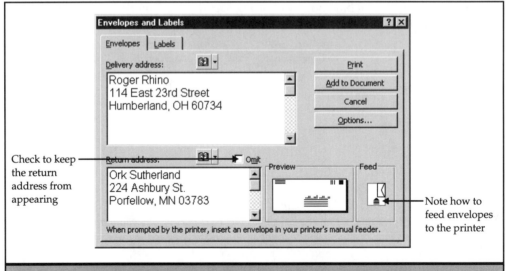

Figure 5-7.   *The delivery address and return address in the Envelopes and Labels dialog box are printed on the envelope*

didn't print correctly, you want to print on an envelope other than the standard $4\frac{3}{4} \times 11$-inch legal envelope, or you want to tinker with fonts.

With a little bit of luck, your envelope prints correctly and all is well after you click the Print button in the Envelopes and Labels dialog box. But maybe you need to tinker a bit, in which case you should follow these instructions:

- **Making the Envelope Part of the Document**   Click the Add To Document button if your printer has two trays and you can devote one tray to envelopes. When you click the button, the envelope becomes page 1 of the document. Choose File | Page Setup, click the Paper Source tab in the Page Setup dialog box, and, on the First Page drop-down list, choose Upper Tray or Lower Tray to tell Word which tray holds envelopes.

- **Printing on a Different-Size Envelope**   To tell Word which size envelope to print on, click the Options button in the Envelopes and Labels dialog box. Then, in the Envelope Options dialog box shown in Figure 5-8, choose an envelope from the Envelope Size drop-down list.

- **Changing Fonts**   Click the Options button in the Envelopes and Labels dialog box and, in the Envelope Options dialog box (see Figure 5-8), click a Font button and then choose a new font. You can also change the position of the addresses on the envelope by playing with the From Left and From Top options.

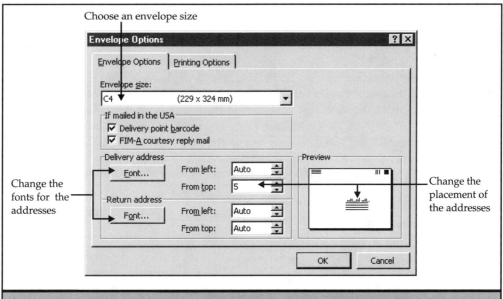

Figure 5-8.   *Go to the Envelope Options dialog box to print on a different-size letter, change fonts, or tell Word how envelopes are fed to the printer*

■ **Telling Word How Your Printer Accepts Envelopes**   As long as Word knows
what kind of printer you have (see "Introducing Word 2000 to Your Printer" at
the start of this chapter), the program probably knows how envelopes are fed to
your printer. But if you try to print an address and it comes out on the wrong part
of the envelope, visit the Printing Options tab of the Envelope Options dialog box
and click an option or options to tell Word how your printer accepts envelopes:

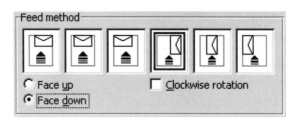

LEARN BY EXAMPLE
*Open the 5-3 Envelopes practice document on the companion CD if you would like
practice in printing addresses on envelopes.*

Decorating an Envelope with a Graphic or Logo

For a professional look, you can place a logo or clip art image on an envelope. To
do so, click the Add To Document button in the Envelopes and Labels dialog box
(see Figure 5-7) to make the envelope page 1 of the document. Then go to page 1
and place a clip art image or logo there (Chapter 13 explains how to handle
graphics). For that matter, you can make your return address and logo or graphic
an AutoText entry to make entering return addresses and graphics on envelopes
very, very easy (see "Creating and Inserting AutoText Entries" in Chapter 6).

   To print the address, place an envelope in the printer tray and click the Print
button in the Envelopes and Labels dialog box. After Word prints the address on
the envelope, put paper in the tray to commence printing the rest of the letter.

Printing a Single Label or Sheet of Labels with the Same Address

Printing on envelopes, as you know if you read the past few pages, is a hassle. You may as well print labels and paste labels on the letters you want to send. You can save time that way. Before you print labels, take note of what brand labels you have and what size your labels are. Word needs that information to print labels.

Note   *See "Printing Labels for Mass-Mailings" in Chapter 20 if you want to print labels addressed to many different people.*

Follow these steps to print a single label or a sheet of labels with the same address:

1. Select the name and address for the label if it is in a document you are working on; otherwise, go straight to step 2.

2. Choose Tools | Envelopes and Labels and click the Labels tab in the Envelopes and Labels dialog box. Figure 5-9 shows the Labels tab.

3. Enter an address in the Address box, if necessary.

4. Glance at the label brand in the lower-right corner of the dialog box, and if the brand and label size shown there aren't what you intend to use, click the

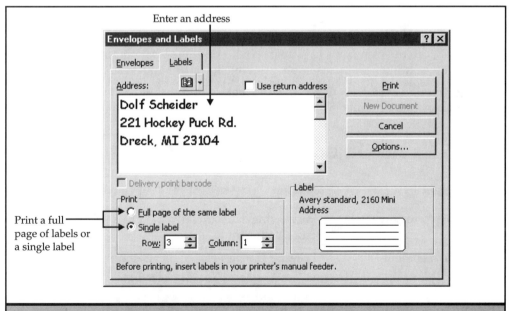

Figure 5-9.   *In the Envelopes and Labels dialog box, describe the label you will print on and tell Word whether you are printing a single label or a sheet of labels*

Options button. In the Label Options dialog box, choose options from the Label Products and Product Number drop-down lists to describe the labels you will print on. The Label Information box clearly shows what size label you are choosing. Click OK to return to the Envelopes and Labels dialog box.

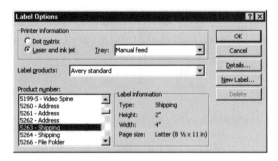

If you can't find your label brand, choose Other on the Label Products drop-down list and try to find a product number that matches the labels you have. If you are desperate, you can click the New Label button and describe your labels in the New Custom dialog box.

5. Under Print, click the Full Page option or the Single Label option. Enter the row and column where the label is if you chose the Single Label option.

6. Print your label or labels:

■ **Full Page of the Same Label**   Click the New Document button. You will see your labels in a Word document. Save and name the document so you can use it over and over again to print labels. To print the labels, insert a sheet of labels in the printer and then simply print the document you created.

■ **Single Label**   Insert the sheet of labels in your printer and click the Print button to print the label.

Exam MOUS Exam Objectives Explored in Chapter 5

Objective	Heading	Practice File
Use print preview	"Previewing a Document Before You Print It"	5-1 Preview
Print a document	"Printing Documents"	5-2 Print
Prepare and print envelopes and labels	"Printing Addresses and Return Addresses on Envelopes"	5-3 Envelopes

Ten Printing Problems and How to Solve Them

Few things are more frustrating than not being able to print a document. To keep you from gnashing your teeth or tearing your hair out, here are ten common printing problems and the steps you can take to solve them.

1. NOTHING HAPPENS WHEN I TRY TO PRINT.   Not being able to print anything is the most common printing problem of all. Usually, the problem can be fixed by plugging in the printer, turning on the printer, or making sure that the computer is indeed connected to the printer.

2. THE MARGINS AND LINE BREAKS ON MY PAGES ARE ALL GOOFY.   Either your margins are too wide or you are printing on the wrong size paper. If you inherited your document from a European, Latin American, African, Asian, or Australian, choose File | Page Setup, click the Paper Size tab in the Page Setup dialog box, and look in the Paper Size box to see what kind of paper Word wants to print on. If the Paper Size box says "A4 210 × 297 mm," you are dealing with a foreign paper size standard. Click Cancel in the Page Setup dialog box and follow these steps to solve the problem:

1. Choose Tools | Options to open the Options dialog box.
2. Click the Print tab.
3. Check the Allow A4/Letter Paper Resizing check box, if it is not already checked, and click OK.
4. Print your document.

   Don't choose a new paper size in the Paper Size dialog box to solve the problem of handling a foreign paper size standard. Doing so can cause margin settings and other page layout elements to go haywire.

3. I'M HAVING TROUBLE PRINTING A LONG DOCUMENT THAT I DIVIDED INTO SECTIONS.   Printing documents that have been divided into sections is problematic, especially if each section has its own numbering scheme. For example, if pages in the first section are not numbered, perhaps because a table of contents or title page is found in the first section, and page numbering begins at the start of section 2, knowing what page you are looking at and which pages to print can be difficult. The Status bar tells you that you are on page 8, for example, because you are on the eighth page in the document, but the header on page 8 tells you that you are on page 5, because you are on the fifth page in section 2.

To solve the problem of printing a document that has been divided into sections, print the sections one at a time. See "Printing Parts or Copies of a Document," earlier in this chapter, to learn how to print sections.

4. MY FONTS DON'T LOOK RIGHT.   Your document includes fonts that your printer can't reproduce. Replace the fonts that didn't come out right with TrueType fonts. These fonts, which have the letters "TT" next to their names on the Font menu, look the same onscreen and on paper when they are printed.

5. MY GRAPHICS AREN'T BEING PRINTED.   Your machine could be running low on memory. Try shutting down, restarting your computer, and printing again. If that doesn't work, investigate these possibilities:

- Choose File | Print and click the Options button in the Print dialog box. In the second Print dialog box, make sure that the Drawing Objects check box is selected.

- Also in the second Print dialog box, make sure that the Draft Output check box is _not_ selected. Checking the Draft Output option tells Word to print documents with very few formats. The option is for working with documents in the proofreading stage. Graphics are not printed as part of draft output.

- Choose Tools | Options and click the View tab in the Options dialog box. On the tab, make sure the Picture Placeholders option is _not_ selected. This option prints empty boxes where graphics should be so that documents can print faster.

6. A BLANK PAGE IS PRINTED AT THE END OF MY DOCUMENT.   This one is easy to solve. The blank page gets printed because you left a few blank paragraphs at the end of your document. Press CTRL-END to go to the end of the document, click the Show/Hide ¶ button to see the paragraph formatting symbols (¶), and delete the symbols.

7. MY HEADERS AND FOOTERS DIDN'T COME OUT RIGHT.   If your headers and footers don't fit on the page, there isn't enough room in the margin for the header or footer or else the header or footer lies in a nonprinting part of the page. To make more room for headers and footer, choose File | Page Setup, click the Margins tab in the Page Setup dialog box, and enlarge the top and bottom margin. Increase the From Edge distances as well to make sure headers and footers aren't being pushed into the nonprinting part of the page.

8. WORD WON'T LET ME CHOOSE THE FILE | PRINT COMMAND.   If the File | Print is grayed out on your computer and you can't choose the command, your computer doesn't know that it is attached to a printer. Re-install the printer.

9. I CAN'T PRINT PAGE BORDERS.   Most printers cannot print text or graphics that are too close to the edge of the page. By definition, borders fall close to the edge of the page, which is why your printer can't handle them. Follow these steps to solve the problem:

1. Choose Format | Borders and Shading. You'll see the Borders and Shading dialog box.

2. Click the Page Border tab.

3. Click the Options button to open the Border and Shading Options dialog box.

4. Under Margin, enter larger point sizes in the Top, Bottom, Left, and Right boxes to move the borders further from the edge of the page.

5. Click OK twice.

10. MY PRINTER PRINTS TOO SLOWLY.   Welcome to the club! Unfortunately, how fast a printer can do its job depends mostly on how fast it can process requests to print documents. However, if you are growing very impatient with your printer, you can take this drastic measure to increase its speed: Disable background printing.

"Printing in the background" means that Word can print files while you do other tasks—format a document or type text, for example. By disabling the background printing mechanism, you tell Word to devote all its resources to printing, and consequently documents get printed faster. The drawback, however, is that you can do nothing else with the computer while your documents are being printed. Until the printer spits out the last page, you have to twiddle your thumbs. You can't format a document or enter text.

Follow these steps if you want to take the drastic measure of turning off the background printing mechanism:

1. Choose Tools | Options.

2. Click the Print tab in the Options dialog box.

3. Uncheck the Background Printing check box and click OK.

> **Tip**   *To make pages with many graphics on them print faster, you can print placeholders instead of graphics. Choose Tools | Options, click the View tab in the Options dialog box, and check the Picture Placeholders check box. When the time comes to print the final draft of the document, open the Options dialog box and uncheck the Picture Placeholders option so that graphics are printed.*

The Complete Reference

Word 2000

Part II

Formatting Text and Pages

The
Complete
Reference

Word 2000

Chapter 6

Speed Techniques
for Using Word 2000

This chapter is dedicated to the proposition that there is a faster way. In this chapter, you will learn how to do things fast. I want you to be done with your work at lunchtime and catch the afternoon matinee. I want you to run back to the office when the movie is over and arrive in a sweat so that everyone thinks you had to hurry to get it done, when really you just had to hurry back from the movie theater.

In this chapter, you'll learn how to work with several documents at once, work in two places in the same document, and rearrange windows onscreen. You will also discover techniques for searching for and replacing text. The Search and Replace commands are very powerful. This chapter delves into a handful of ways to enter text quickly, including the AutoText and AutoCorrect mechanisms. Finally, you'll learn ten tried-and-true techniques for working faster in Word 2000.

Chapter 23 offers more techniques for working faster. Believe me, creating toolbars for your favorite commands, rearranging the Word menus, creating new menus, and designating your own keyboard shortcuts can save lots of time, and it's a lot easier than most people think.

Working in Two Places or Documents at Once

Who wouldn't like to be in two places at once? In Word 2000, you can be in two documents or two places in the same document at the same time. These pages explain how to split the screen so that you can see two different places in the same document and open a second window on a document so you can work in two places at once. You will also find instructions here for working on several documents and manipulating the windows that Word documents appear in.

Splitting the Screen

Figure 6-1 shows a screen that has been split across the middle. Notice the scroll bars on each half of the screen. By using the scroll bars or pressing keyboard shortcuts, you can go wherever you please on either side of the screen. Splitting the screen is invaluable when you want to refer to one part of a document while you work on another part. And you can copy or move text with the drag-and-drop method by dragging the text across the divide from one side of the screen to another.

Do the following to split the screen:

1. Choose Window | Split. The pointer changes to a double-headed arrow and a line appears across the middle of the screen.

2. Move the pointer up or down onscreen to adjust the position of the line and click when the line is where you want the screen to be split. If the ruler is on display, a second ruler appears across the middle of the screen.

Drag the line across the middle of the screen to adjust the split and give more room to the top or bottom portion of the screen. Click in one side or the other to move the cursor there.

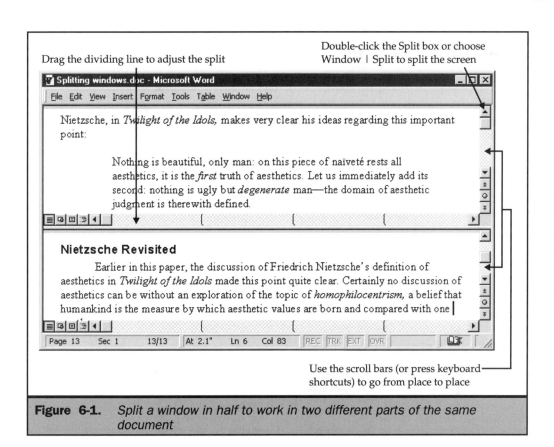

Figure 6-1.   *Split a window in half to work in two different parts of the same document*

   The fastest way to split the screen is to double-click the Split box, the tiny box at the top of the vertical scroll bar. You can tell when you have moved the pointer over the Split box because it changes into double arrows.

When you get tired of the schizophrenic split-screen arrangement, do either of the following to unsplit the screen:

- Choose Window | Remove Split.
- Double-click the dividing line between the screen halves.

Opening Two or More Windows on the Same Document

Besides splitting the screen, another way to be two places at once is to open a second window on the same document. For that matter, you can open a third, fourth, or fifth

Viewing the Same Page Two Different Ways

Another advantage of splitting the screen is being able to view the same document in different ways. In this illustration, the top half of the screen appears in Outline view and the bottom half is in Print Layout view. Besides changing views on either side of the dividing line, you can change Zoom settings. Being able to view the same document in two different ways is mighty convenient, as this illustration shows:

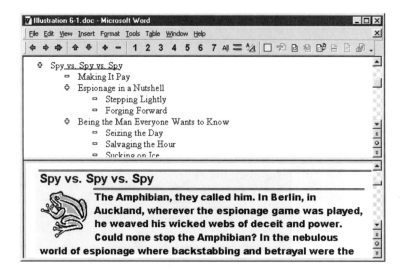

window—you can open as many new windows as you want. In this illustration, I have opened five windows on the same document. The Window menu lists the five different windows, and to go from one place to another in my document, I have only to click a button on the Taskbar or make a choice on the Window menu:

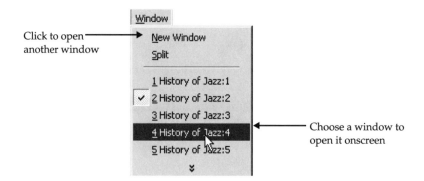

Click to open another window

Choose a window to open it onscreen

Follow these instructions to work with more than one window:

- **Opening a New Window**   Choose Window | New Window.
- **Going from Window to Window**   Open the Window menu and choose another window, click a button on the Taskbar, or keep pressing CTRL-F6 until your window appears onscreen.
- **Closing a Window**   Click the Close button (the X) in the upper-right corner of the window or press ALT-F.

Working on Several Documents at Once

Yes, you can work on several Word documents at once. The names of documents that are open appear on buttons on the Taskbar and in alphabetical order on the Window menu. To start working on a different document, either click its button on the Taskbar or open the Window menu and click its name. You can also keep pressing CTRL-F6 until the document you are looking for appears onscreen.

The active document

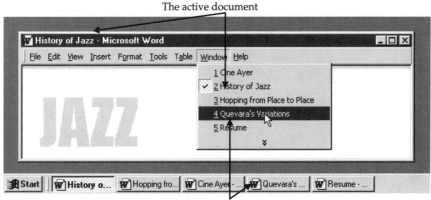

Choose a name on the Window menu or click a
Taskbar button to switch documents

   To tell which document you are working on, glance at the name on the title bar. On the Window menu, a check mark appears beside the active document, the one in which you are currently working.

Changing the Size and Position of Windows

Windows are so important that Microsoft named an operating system after them. (Microsoft thought of naming the operating system "Buttons," since many buttons appear in the Windows operating system, but "Buttons" sounded too much like a kitten or clown's name and, besides, the name "Windows" appeals to voyeurs.) If you can learn how to manipulate the windows that Word documents appear in, you can work much, much faster. Read on to learn how to minimize and maximize windows, arrange windows onscreen, move windows, and change the size of windows.

Minimizing, Maximizing, and Closing Windows

When you open a Word document, it appears in its own window and fills the entire screen. However, you can *minimize* the window to remove a document from the screen without closing it, and when you want to see the document again, you can *maximize* its window. Minimizing, maximizing, and closing windows is accomplished with the three square buttons in the upper-right corner of windows—the Minimize, Maximize (or Restore), and Close button. Table 6-1 explains what the window buttons do.

Changing the Shape and Position of Windows

Sometimes minimizing and maximizing windows is not enough and you have to change a window's size and position on your own. Use these techniques to move and change the size of windows:

■ **Moving a Window** As shown in Figure 6-2, click the window's title bar and start dragging. When the window is where you want it to be, release the mouse button.

Button	Button Name	What It Does
	Minimize	Collapses the window and makes it disappear. However, clicking this button does not close a document. To see a window after it has been minimized, click its button on the Taskbar.
	Restore	Shrinks the window to the size it was before you maximized it last time. After you click the Restore button, it changes names (and appearances) and becomes the Maximize button. You can also double-click the title bar to restore a window.
	Maximize	Enlarges the window to full-screen size. After you click the Maximize button, it changes names (and appearances) and becomes the Restore button. You can also double-click the title bar to maximize a window.
	Close	Closes the document.

Table 6-1. *The Window Buttons*

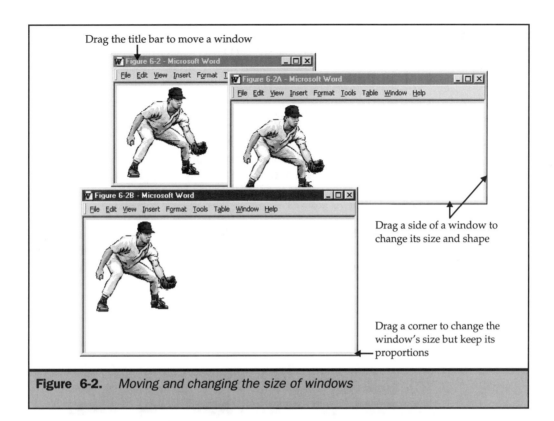

Figure 6-2.   *Moving and changing the size of windows*

■ **Changing a Window's Size**   Move the mouse pointer over a border of the window and start dragging when the pointer changes into double-arrows. Release the mouse button when the window is the right size.

Tip   *Drag a corner of a window to change its size but keep its proportions.*

Finding and Replacing Text and Other Things

The Find and Replace commands in Word 2000 are two of the most powerful commands in the program. Use them wisely and you can quickly find passages in documents, correct mistakes *en masse,* change words and phrases throughout a document, and reformat a document without having to visit all the pages that need reformatting. To give you an idea how powerful these commands are, suppose you wrote an 800-page Russian novel and realized on page 799 that the main character's name should be Oblomov, not Oblonsky. Using the Find and Replace command, you could change all *Oblonsky*s to *Oblomov*s throughout the document in about ten seconds.

Another way to find items in a Word document—a footnote, endnote, field, graphic, comment, section, table, bookmark, or heading—is to take advantage of the Select Browse Object button or the Edit | Go To command. See "Using the Select Browse Object Button to Get Around" and "Going from Place to Place with the Go To Command" in Chapter 2.

Find Basics: Searching for Text

When you conduct a search with the Edit | Find command, Word starts searching where the cursor is, searches to the end of the document, and then searches from the beginning of the document to the place where the search began. You can search part of a document by selecting it before you give the Edit | Find command.

Follow these steps to search for a word, name, or phrase in a document:

1. Press CTRL-F, choose Edit | Find, or click the Select Browse Object button and choose Find on the menu. You'll see the Find and Replace dialog box shown in Figure 6-3. (In the figure, I clicked the More button so you can see all the Find options.)

2. Type the word or phrase that you seek in the Find What box.

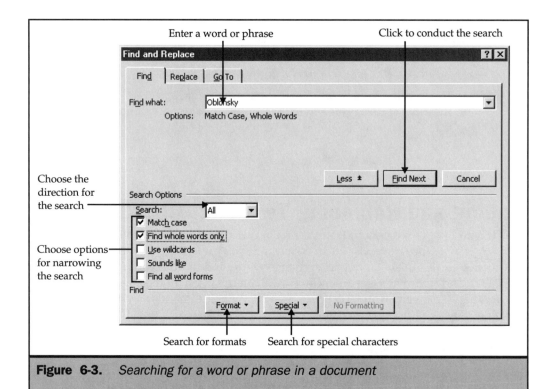

Figure 6-3. *Searching for a word or phrase in a document*

Tip *On the Find What drop-down list are the words and phrases, if any, that you looked for since you started Word. Open the list and make a choice to repeat a search you made earlier.*

3. Click the More button if you want to see and take advantage of the advanced search options (they are explained shortly).

4. Click the Find Next button. If Word finds the text, it is highlighted onscreen. You can click outside the Find and Replace dialog box and edit the text.

5. Either click Find Next again to keep searching or click the Cancel button to close the Find and Replace dialog box.

Tip *You can leave the Find and Replace dialog box onscreen while you edit a document, but an easier way to handle searches is to close the dialog box and click the double-arrows in the lower-right corner of the screen to go from search item to search item. After you give the Find command, the double arrows turn blue. Click a blue double arrow (or press CTRL-PAGE up or CTRL-PAGE down) to conduct a search without having to see the bulky Find and Replace dialog box.*

The Find and Replace dialog box offers numerous options for making searches faster and more accurate. Use these options or a combination of these options to find exactly what you are looking for:

■ **Search**   Tells Word in which direction to search: All searches the entire document; Up searches from the cursor position to the start of the document; Down searches from the cursor position to the end of the document.

Caution *When you search with the Up or Down option, Word does not look at these items in the course of the search: headers, footers, comments, footnotes, and endnotes. With the All option, however, Word searches in every nook and cranny of the document.*

■ **Match Case**   Finds words with upper- and lowercase letters that exactly match those of the word or phrase in the Find What box. For example, a search for **Bow** finds "Bow" but not "bow" or "BOW."

■ **Find Whole Words Only**   Finds the word in the Find What box, but ignores the word if it is part of another word. For example, a search for **bow** finds "bow" but not "bows," "elbow," "bowler," or "rainbow." Unless you are looking for a proper name or other one-of-a-kind word, be sure to check this option. Your search will go faster and be more accurate.

■ **Use Wildcards**   Check this check box, click the Special button, and choose a search operator to use wildcards in searches. See "Searching for Formats and Special Characters," the next topic in this chapter.

■ **Sounds Like**   Searches for words that sound like the word in the Find What box. For example, a search for **bow** also finds "beau;" a search for "metal" also finds "medal," "middle," and "muddle."

■ **Find All Word Forms**   Takes into account plurals, verb endings, and tenses in searches. For example, a search for **bow** also finds "bows," "bowed," and "bowing."

As you choose search options, they are listed below the Find What text box. Be sure to double-check the list before you click the Find Next button to start searching:

Fi**n**d what:	Paradise	▼
Options:	Search Up, Match Case, Whole Words	

LEARN BY EXAMPLE
Open the 6-1 Find and Replace document on the companion CD if you would like to test-drive the Find and Replace options.

Searching for Formats and Special Characters

By way of the Format and Special buttons at the bottom of the Find and Replace dialog box, you can conduct searches for formats and what Word calls "special characters"—paragraph marks, tab characters, page breaks, and the like. These pages explain how to search for formats and special characters.

Searching for Formats and Text That Was Formatted a Certain Way

Suppose you want to find a certain kind of formatting in your document, perhaps because it needs changing, or you want to find text that was formatted a certain way. Press CTRL-F (or choose Edit | Find) to open the Find and Replace dialog box and follow these steps to find formats or formatted text:

1. Enter the text in the Find What box if you are looking for text that was formatted a certain way (go straight to step 2 if you are merely searching for a format).

2. Click the Format button. As shown in Figure 6-4, you will see a menu with seven format types on it.

3. Choose a format type—Font, Paragraph, Tabs, Language, Frame, Style, or Highlight. The Find dialog box opens, as shown in Figure 6-4, so you can describe the format you are looking for. Which dialog box you see depends on which format command you chose. In Figure 6-4, I chose the Font command, so the Find Font dialog box appears. The Find dialog boxes are identical to the dialog boxes that are used to create the different formats.

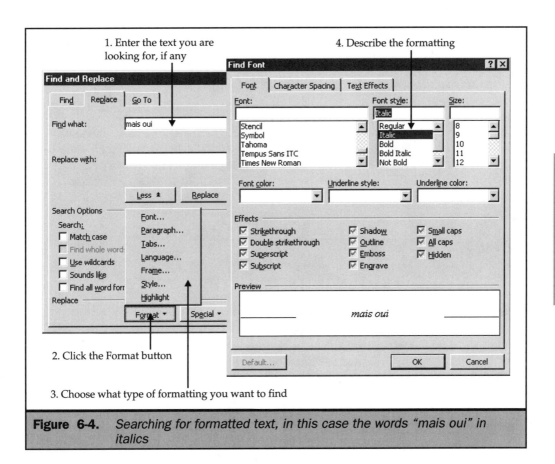

1. Enter the text you are looking for, if any

4. Describe the formatting

2. Click the Format button

3. Choose what type of formatting you want to find

Figure 6-4. *Searching for formatted text, in this case the words "mais oui" in italics*

4. In the dialog box, choose options to describe the format. In Figure 6-4, I am looking for italicized text, so Italic has been chosen in the Font Style box. Look in the Preview box to see what your choices amount to in real terms.

5. Click OK to close the Find dialog box. In the Find and Replace dialog box, the word "Format" and a description of the formats you are looking for appears below the Find What text box:

Find what:

Format: Style: Body Text Indent, French

6. Click Find Next to conduct the search.

Be sure to click the No Formatting button in the Find and Replace dialog box when you are finished looking for formats and you want to search for plain text again or start all over and search for another type of format. Clicking the No Formatting button tells Word that you no longer want to look for formats or you want to search for a different set of formats.

By the way, you can search for formats for which there are keyboard shortcuts without clicking the Format button in the Find and Replace dialog box (see Figure 6-4). To do so, click to move the cursor into the Find What text box and then type a keyboard shortcut. In this illustration, I pressed CTRL-B (Bold), CTRL-I (Italic), and CTRL-E (Centered):

Fi<u>n</u>d what:		▼
Format:	Font: Bold, Italic, Centered	

Searching for Special Characters

Table 6-2 describes the special characters you can look for in Word documents. To look for the special characters listed in Table 6-2, either enter the character directly into the Find What text box, or, as shown in Figure 6-5, click the Special button in the Find and Replace dialog box and choose a special character from the menu. Be sure to enter lowercase letters. For example, you must enter ^n, not ^N, to look for a column break.

 Before you search for special characters, click the Show/Hide ¶ button. That way, you will see the special characters—also known as the hidden format symbols—onscreen when Word finds them. See "Tricks for Editing Text" in Chapter 1 if you need to know how the hidden format symbols work.

If you are creative, you can find many uses for the special characters. For example, the easiest way to find section breaks, column breaks, and manual line breaks in a document is to enter ^b, ^n, or ^ |, respectively, in the Find What text box and start searching. By combining special characters with text, you can make search operations more productive. Consider how special characters and text are used in this illustration. This search operation finds all paragraphs that begin with a tab space and the word "This."

Fi<u>n</u>d what:	^p^tThis	▼
Options:	Match Case	

To Find/Replace	Enter
Manual Formats That Users Insert	
Column break	^n
Line break (↵)	^|
Page break	^m
Paragraph break (¶)	^p
Section break[1]	^b
Tab space (→)	^t
Hyphens, Dashes, and Spaces	
Em dash (—)	^+
En dash (–)	^=
Nonbreaking hyphen	^~
Optional hyphen	^-
White space (one or more blank spaces)	^w
Characters and Symbols	
Foreign character	You can type foreign characters in the Find What and Replace With text boxes (see Table 2-1 in Chapter 2).
ANSI and ASCII characters and symbols	^*nnnn*, where *nnnn* is the four-digit code (see Chapter 2).
Clipboard contents[2]	^c
Contents of the Find What box[2]	^&
Elements of Reports and Scholarly Papers	
Comment mark[1]	^a
Endnote mark[1]	^e
Footnote mark[1]	^f
Graphic[1]	^g

[1] For use in search operations; can only be entered in the Find What text box

[2] For use in replace operations; can only be entered in the Replace With text box

Table 6-2. *Searching and Replacing with Special Characters, Format Characters, and Foreign Characters*

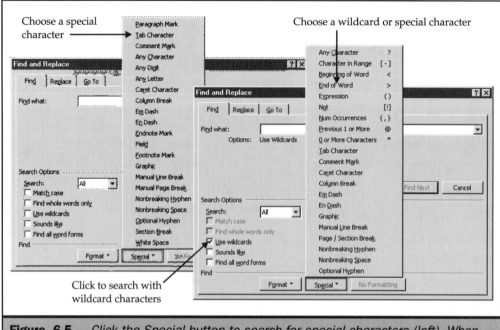

Figure 6-5. *Click the Special button to search for special characters (left). When you check the Use Wildcards check box, a handful of wildcard choices appears on the Special menu (right)*

Special characters are especially useful in find-and-replace operations (a subject you will learn about shortly). This find-and-replace operation finds all double hyphens in a document and replaces them with em dashes:

Find what: | --
Replace with: | ^+

Using Wildcard Operators to Refine Searches

A *wildcard operator* is a character that represents characters in a search expression. Wildcards aren't for everybody, since using them requires a certain amount of expertise, but once you know how to use them, wildcards can be very valuable in searches and macros. Table 6-3 explains the wildcard operators you can use in searches.

Operator	What It Finds	Example
?	Any single character	**b?t** finds "bat," "bet," "bit," and "but."
*	Zero or more characters	**t*o** finds "to," "two," and "tattoo."
[*xyz*]	A specific character, *x*, *y*, or *z*	**t[aeiou]pper** finds "tapper," "tipper," and "topper."
[*x-z*]	A range of characters, *x* through *z*	**[1-4]000** finds "1000," "2000," "3000," and "4000," but not "5000."
[!*xy*]	Not the specific character or characters, *xy*	**p[!io]t** finds "pat" and "pet," but not "pit" or "pot."
<	Characters at the beginning of words	**<info** finds "information," "infomaniac," and "infomercial."
>	Characters at the end of words	**ese>** finds "these," "journalese," and "legalese."
@	One or more instances of the previous character	**sho@t** finds "shot" and "shoot."
{*n*}	Exactly *n* instances of the previous character	**sho{2}t** finds "shoot" but not "shot."
{*n,*}	At least *n* instances of the previous character	**^p{3,}** finds three or more paragraph breaks in a row, but not a single paragraph break or two paragraph breaks in a row.
{*n,m*}	From *n* to *m* instances of the previous character	**10{2,4}** finds "100," "1000," and "10000," but not "10" or "100000."

Table 6-3. *Wildcard Search Operators*

FORMATING TEXT AND PAGES

Check the Use Wildcards check box in the Find and Replace dialog box to use wildcard operators in searches. To enter a wildcard operator in the Find What text box, either type it yourself or click the Special button and choose a wildcard from the top of the menu (refer to Figure 6-5).

Tip *To search for an asterisk (*), question mark (?), or other character that serves as a wildcard search operator, place a backslash before it in the Find What text box. For example, /*{2,} tells Word to look for two or more asterisks in a row.*

Conducting a Find-and-Replace Operation

Conducting a find-and-replace operation is the spitting image of conducting a find operation. Figure 6-6 shows the Replace tab in the Find and Replace dialog box, the place where you tell Word what to find and what to replace. Do the options and buttons look familiar? They do if you read the past several pages about searching, because the settings on the Replace tab are the same as those on the Find tab, except the Replace tab offers a Replace and Replace All button.

Caution *Be sure to save your file before you conduct a find-and-replace operation. You never know what the powerful Replace command will do. If the command makes a hash of your file but you saved it first, you can close your file without saving the changes. Next time you open the file, you will see the original copy—the one you had before the Replace command mutilated it.*

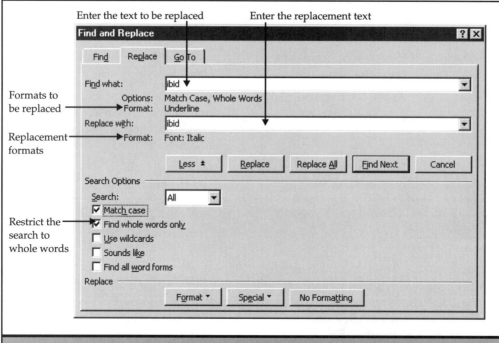

Figure 6-6.   *Use the powerful Replace command to find and replace text, formats, and special characters*

The next few pages explain the nuances of finding and replacing text, formats, and special characters. Follow these basic steps to conduct a find-and-replace operation:

1. Choose Edit | Replace, press CTRL-H, or click the Replace tab in the Find and Replace dialog box. The Replace tab of the Find and Replace dialog box appears (see Figure 6-6).

Tip   *The key to a successful find-and-replace operation is making sure you find exactly what you want to find and replace. One way to make sure you find the right text or formatting is to start by choosing Edit | Find (or press CTRL-F). Choose options on the Find tab in the Find and Replace dialog box (see Figure 6-3) and click the Find Next button. If Word scrolls to precisely the text or formatting you wanted to find, you're in business. Click the Replace tab in the Find and Replace dialog box. On that tab, the Find What options and text are already entered. All you have to do is enter the Replace With options and text.*

2. If necessary, click the More button to see the advanced search options, the Format button, the Special button, and the No Formatting button.

3. Enter the text, formats, or special characters you are searching for in the Find What text box.

Note   *If necessary, click the No Formatting button if you searched for formats before and formats are still listed below the Find What or Replace With text box. Clicking the No Formatting button tells Word to strip the formats from the Find and Replace dialog box so you can search for new formats.*

4. Enter the replacement text, formats, or special characters in the Replace With text box.

5. Click the Find Next button. If Word finds the text, formats, or special characters that you seek, the text, formats, or special characters are highlighted in the document.

6. Click the Find Next, Replace, or Replace All button:

   - **Find Next**   Bypasses the text, format, or special character that has been found and does not replace it with what is in the Replace With text box.

   - **Replace**   Makes the replacement. What is in the Replace With text box is entered in the document and Word scrolls to the next instance of the thing you want to find and replace. Click the Replace button to review each occasion in which Word wants to make a replacement.

   - **Replace All**   Makes all replacements throughout the document immediately.

FORMATTING TEXT
AND PAGES

Only click the Replace All button if you are very, very confident that the thing Word has found is the thing you want to replace throughout the document. If you click Replace All but regret doing so, click the Undo button to undo all the replacements.

Replacing Text with Text

To replace text with text, choose Edit | Replace to open the Find and Replace dialog box, enter the word or words you want to find in the Find What text box and the replacement word or words in the Replace With text box. Following are a couple of things to know about replacing text with text.

BE SURE TO CHECK THE FIND WHOLE WORDS ONLY CHECK BOX.   The Find Whole Words Only check box tells Word to look for whole words, not character strings. Forgetting to select the check box can have disastrous consequences in a find-and-replace operation that involves words. To see why, suppose you are editing a sexist author who insists on using "man" where "humankind" or "humanity" would be more appropriate. To solve the problem, you run a find-and-replace operation like this one:

Fi_n_d what:	man	▼
Replace with:	humanity	▼

If you forget to check the Find Whole Words Only check box, your search will find the letters "man" wherever they are found and replace them with the letters "humanity." A sentence like "Man, the manifest measure of all things, the talisman of nature, wears the mantle of God," is turned into "Humanity, the humanityifest measure of all things, the talishumanity of nature, wears the humanitytle of God."

FIND-AND-REPLACE OPERATIONS TAKE ACCOUNT OF UPPER- AND LOWERCASE LETTERS.   Don't worry about case when you conduct a find- and-replace operation. If a word you want to replace happens to appear at the start of a sentence and is capitalized, its replacement word will be capitalized as well. However, if you want to change the case of a word or words in a document, you can do so by entering different upper- or lowercase letters in the Replace With text box, as shown here:

Fi<u>n</u>d what:	nearly dead poets society	▼

Replace w<u>i</u>th:	Nearly Dead Poets Society	▼

YOU CAN REPLACE FORMATTED TEXT WITH FORMATTED TEXT.   By entering text in the Find What and Replace With dialog boxes, and by choosing formats for the Find What text and Replace With text (read the next part of this chapter), you can replace formatted text with formatted text. For example, this find-and-replace operation searches for a company name that has been formatted a certain way and replaces it with a different company name with an entirely different format:

Fi<u>n</u>d what:	Johnathon Freeman Technology, Inc.	▼
Format:	Font: Impact, 16 pt, Font color: Auto	

Replace w<u>i</u>th:	Cyberinfo Management, Inc.	▼
Format:	Font: Haettenschweiler, 16 pt, Bold, Font color...	

Replacing Formats with Formats

One of the fastest ways to reformat a document is to search for one kind of format and replace it with another. Earlier in this chapter, "Searching for Formats and Special Characters" explains how you can click the Format button in the Find and Replace dialog box to search for formats in documents. The procedure for entering a replacement format is the same (see Figure 6-5)—click the Format button, choose a format from the pop-up menu, and describe the format in the Replace dialog box.

This find-and replace operation looks for 16-point text that has been formatted in Tahoma font and changes it to 18-point text formatted in Comic Sans MS font:

Fi<u>n</u>d what:		▼
Format:	Font: Tahoma, 16 pt	

Replace w<u>i</u>th:		▼
Format:	Font: Comic Sans MS, 18 pt	

FORMATTING TEXT AND PAGES

The Two "Replace With" Special Characters

If you look closely at Table 6-2, which describes the special characters you can use in find and find-and-replace operations, you may notice that two special characters can't be entered in the Find What text box and are strictly for use as replacement text: ^c, which places the Clipboard contents in the Replace With text box, and ^&, which places what is in the Find What text box in the Replace With text box.

Use the Clipboard contents special character (^c) to insert large blocks of text in documents or to insert text that has been formatted in various ways:

- **Large Blocks of Text**   Entering a lot of text in the Replace With box is difficult, so if you have to do that, enter the text in Word and copy it to the Clipboard (by pressing CTRL-C or choosing Edit | Copy). Then choose Edit | Replace, enter the text you want to search for in the Find What box, and enter ^c in the Replace With box to make the large block of text the replacement text.

- **Text with Different Formats**   As you know, you can click the Format button in the Find and Replace dialog box to search for formats and replace one format with another. Suppose, however, that the replacement text includes more than one format. For example, if a company changed its motto from "We do it better" to "We *really* do it better," you couldn't find-and-replace the motto by clicking the Format button, because only one word in the new motto is italicized, and the Format commands apply to all the words in the Find What and Replace With text boxes. To solve this problem, you could copy the new motto—italicized word and all—to the Clipboard and enter ^c in the Replace With box.

Fi_n_d what:	We do it better	▼
Replace wi_th_:	^c	▼

Use the contents of the Find What box special character (^&) to enter whatever is in the Find What box in the Replace With box as well. This special character is really just a means of making sure that text is replaced correctly. In the find-and-replace operation shown here, for example, *Esq.* is being attached to the name McClannahan Skejellifetti throughout a long document. Because the name is so hard to type, you would run a risk of misspelling it by typing it in the Replace With box. If you spelled the name incorrectly, you would introduce errors throughout the document. Rather than do that, you can enter the ^& special character and be absolutely certain that the text you find is also used in the replacement text:

| Find what: | McClannahan Skejellifetti |
| Replace with: | ^&, Esq. |

Note   *"Finding and Replacing Styles" in Chapter 12 explains how to reapply styles throughout a document with the Edit | Find and Replace command.*

Finding and Replacing with the Special Characters

Finding and replacing with the special characters can be very helpful for cleaning up a document. To enter special characters in the Replace With text box, either enter them yourself or click the Special button and choose them from the menu. Earlier in this chapter, Table 6-2 describes the special characters and "Searching for Formats and Special Characters" describes how they work.

In this illustration, the paragraph break special character (^p) and white space special character (^w) are used in a find-and-replace operation to strip blank spaces from the ends of paragraphs:

| Find what: | ^w^p |
| Replace with: | ^p |

Here, the paragraph break special character (^p) and tab character (^t) are used to strip tab-space indents from the first line of paragraphs:

| Find what: | ^p^t^p |
| Replace with: | ^p^p |

Ways to Enter Text Quickly

This section presents two nifty techniques for entering text and graphics quickly: AutoText and AutoCorrect. As well as entering text and graphics, the AutoCorrect mechanism corrects typos on the fly. Addresses, letterheads, boilerplate text of all shapes and sizes—anything that you have to enter frequently—is a candidate for an AutoText or AutoCorrect entry. These pages explain the AutoText and AutoCorrect mechanisms.

Creating and Inserting AutoText Entries

An *AutoText entry* is a word, a few words, or a graphic that you can enter merely by making a selection from a menu. To see how the AutoText entries work, choose Insert | AutoText | Salutation | Dear Sir or Madam:. The salutation "Dear Sir or Madam:" is entered immediately in your document.

Word provides a dozen or two AutoText entries on seven submenus and you can create your own AutoText entries as well. As shown in Figure 6-7, the submenus are Attention Line, Closing, Header/Footer, and so on. AutoText entries that you create yourself are placed on the Normal submenu. These pages explain how to insert, create, and manage AutoText entries.

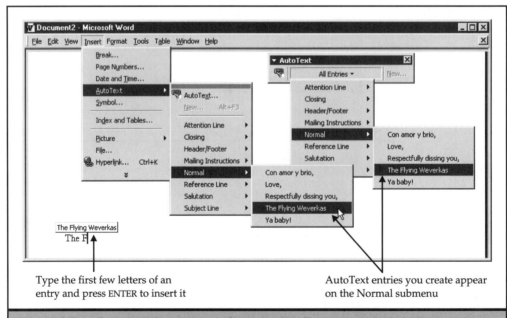

Type the first few letters of an entry and press ENTER to insert it

AutoText entries you create appear on the Normal submenu

Figure 6-7. *Type it (left), choose it from the AutoText submenu (middle), or choose it from the AutoText toolbar (right)*

LEARN BY EXAMPLE
Open the 6-2 AutoText entries document on the companion CD if you want some practical experience with AutoText entries.

Inserting an AutoText Entry in a Document

Carefully place the cursor where you want to insert the AutoText and insert it with one of these techniques:

- Choose Insert | AutoText, a submenu name, and the name of an AutoText entry (see Figure 6-7).

- Open the AutoText toolbar, click the All Entries button, choose a submenu, and click the name of the AutoText entry (see Figure 6-7).

- Type the name of the AutoText entry and press F3.

- Type the first few letters of the AutoText entry, and when you see the complete entry in the bubble, press ENTER:

The Flying Weverkas

Everyone knows that the world's best circus is The F

Some people find the AutoText bubbles annoying. If you are one of those people, you can keep them from appearing by choosing Insert | AutoText | AutoText and unchecking the Show AutoComplete Tip For AutoText And Dates check box on the AutoText tab of the AutoCorrect dialog box.

For times when you can't remember which AutoText entry is which, you can also insert an AutoText entry you created yourself by choosing Insert | AutoText | AutoText or clicking the AutoText button on the AutoText toolbar. On the AutoText tab of the AutoCorrect dialog box, click an AutoText entry's name. The Preview box shows what the entry looks like. Click the Insert button to enter it in the document.

Creating Your Own AutoText Entries

The name "AutoText" is a little misleading because you can create an AutoText entry for graphics as well as text. In fact, you can create an AutoText entry for anything whatsoever that can be selected in a Word document. Follow these steps to create an AutoText entry:

1. Select the text or graphic that you want to enter in a hurry.

Select a blank space on one side of the text if you are selecting text. That way, the AutoText entry will fit nicely in the middle of a sentence when you insert it there.

2. Choose Insert | AutoText | New, click the New button on the AutoText toolbar, or press ALT-F3. You will see the tiny Create AutoText dialog box. If you selected text in step 1, the text appears in the dialog box:

3. Enter a name for the AutoText entry, if necessary. Enter a short and to-the-point name so you you'll be able to enter your AutoText entry with the F3 keyboard shortcut (typing the entry's name and pressing F3).

4. Click OK to close the Create AutoText dialog box.

AutoText entries you create are available to all Word templates. However, if you want an entry to be available only in the Normal template or another template you are working in, choose Insert | AutoText | AutoText to open the AutoText tab of the AutoCorrect dialog box. Then click the AutoText entry you created, open the Look In drop-down list, and choose a template.

Deleting, Renaming, and Editing AutoText Entries

Go to the AutoText tab of the AutoCorrect dialog box to delete, rename, or edit an AutoText Entry. To get there, either choose Insert | AutoText | AutoText or click the AutoText button on the AutoText toolbar. You'll see the dialog box shown in Figure 6-8.

Follow these instructions to delete, rename, or edit an AutoText entry:

■ **Deleting**   Select the entry and click the Delete button in the AutoCorrect dialog box.

■ **Renaming**   Insert the entry, select it, and choose Insert | AutoText | AutoText. In the AutoCorrect dialog box, enter a new name in the Enter AutoText Entries Here text box and click the Add button. Then select the old name and click the Delete button.

■ **Editing**   Insert the AutoText entry, edit it, and select it. Then open the AutoCorrect dialog box, enter the entry's name in the Enter AutoText Entries Here text box, and click the Add button. Word asks if you want to redefine the AutoText entry. Click Yes.

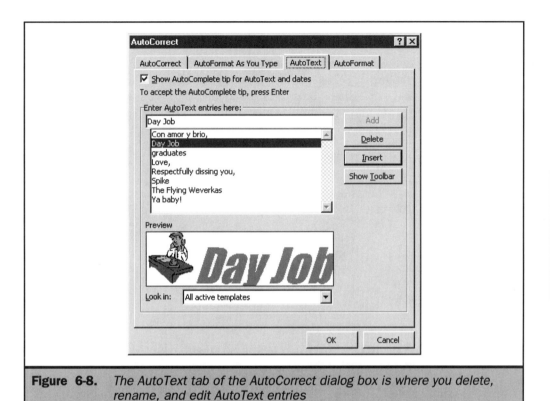

Figure 6-8.   *The AutoText tab of the AutoCorrect dialog box is where you delete, rename, and edit AutoText entries*

Entering Text and Graphics Quickly with the AutoCorrect Command

The AutoCorrect command was invented to help correct typing errors, but with a little cunning you can also use it to insert text and graphics quickly. To see how AutoCorrect works, choose Tools | AutoCorrect. You see the AutoCorrect dialog box shown in Figure 6-9. In the Replace column on the AutoCorrect tab are hundreds of common typing errors that Word corrects automatically. The program corrects the errors by entering text in the With column whenever you mistakenly type the letters in the Replace column.

"Correcting Typos with the AutoCorrect Command" in Chapter 11 explains how AutoCorrect can help you fix the typing errors you frequently make.

To make AutoCorrect work as a means of entering text or a graphic, you tell Word to enter the text or graphic whenever you type three or four specific characters. In Figure 6-9, for example, Word is being instructed to insert a graphic and the words "Day Job"

Quickly Entering the Date and Time

On the subject of entering text quickly, nothing could be faster than entering the date or time with the Insert | Date and Time command. Choose the command and you see the Date and Time dialog box. Click a date format, time format, or date-and-time format to enter the date or time in your document:

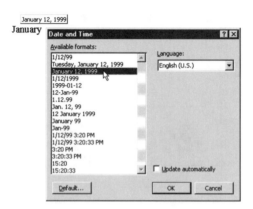

The Date and Time dialog box also offers these amenities:

- **Default Button**   Choose a format and click this button to change the default date or time—the date or time that appears in the bubble box as you type. When you see the bubble, you can press ENTER to insert the date or time without having to type the whole enchilada.

- **Update Automatically Check Box**   Check this check box to enter a date or time field—a date or time entry that always stays up to date with the clock in your computer. To make the date or time field show the current date or time, select the field and press F9. To make sure printed documents list the date or time they were printed, choose Tools | Options, click the Print tab in the Options dialog box, and check the Update Fields check box.

whenever I enter the characters **/dayj** (and press the SPACEBAR) in a document. Follow these steps to use AutoCorrect to enter text, a graphic, or text and a graphic:

1. Enter the text, graphic, or text and graphic in a document and select it. Format the text if you want the AutoCorrect mechanism to insert formatted text.

2. Choose Tools | AutoCorrect. The AutoCorrect dialog box appears (see Figure 6-9). The item you selected in step 1 appears in the With box.

3. In the Replace text box, enter the three or four characters that will trigger the AutoCorrect mechanism and make it enter your text or graphic.

Enter text to trigger the AutoCorrect mechanism

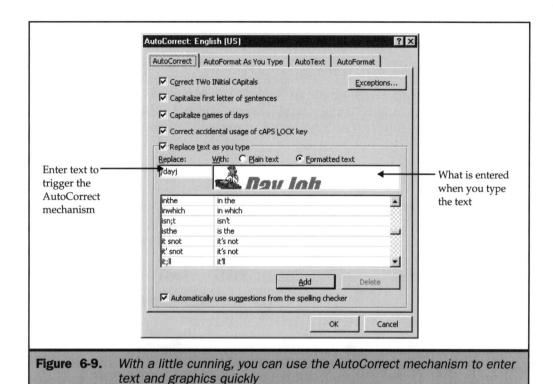

What is entered when you type the text

Figure 6-9.   *With a little cunning, you can use the AutoCorrect mechanism to enter text and graphics quickly*

Caution   *Don't enter a word in the Replace box or characters that you might really type someday. If you do, the AutoCorrect mechanism might kick in when you least expect it. Enter three or four characters that never appear together. And start all AutoCorrect entries with a slash (/). You might forget which characters trigger the AutoText entry or decide to delete your AutoCorrect entry someday. By starting it with a slash, you can find it easily in the AutoCorrect dialog box at the top of the Replace list.*

4. Click the Formatted Text option button if you want a text entry to keep its formatting when it is inserted in a document.

5. Click the Add button and click OK to close the AutoCorrect dialog box.

Test your AutoCorrect entry by typing the Replace text you entered in step 3 and pressing the SPACEBAR. AutoCorrect doesn't do its work until you press the SPACEBAR. To delete an AutoCorrect entry, open the AutoCorrect dialog box, select the entry, and click the Delete button.

Making Your Own Letterhead

Why spend money on stationary when you can make your own letterhead with the AutoText or AutoCorrect command? You can even include the date—a date that stays current, no matter when you print letters—in the letterhead (see "Quickly Entering the Date and Time" earlier in this chapter). Being able to enter a fancy letterhead with the AutoText or AutoCorrect command beats having to enter text and a graphic whenever you begin a letter:

MOUS Exam Objectives Explored in Chapter 6

Objective	Heading	Practice File
Insert the date and time	"Quickly Entering the Date and Time"	
Find and replace text	"Finding and Replacing Text and Other Things"	6-1 Find and Replace
Create and apply frequently used text	"Ways to Enter Text Quickly"	6-2 AutoText Entries
Use find and replace with formats, special characters, and nonprinting elements	"Conducting a Find-and-Replace operation"	

Ten Ways to Work Faster in Word 2000

Following are ten suggestions for working faster in Word 2000. Being a speed demon myself, I am very interested in how tasks can be done faster, and you will find tips and tricks throughout this book for working faster. These ten tips, however, represent the ten best ways to get it done—or get it over with, depending on your point of view—in Microsoft Word.

1. LEARN TO USE STYLES.   Nothing makes formatting easier than using styles. A *style* is a collection of commands and formats that have been bundled under one name. By using styles, you free yourself from having to visit and revisit numerous dialog boxes whenever you want to change the formatting of a paragraph. Chapter 12 is devoted to learning about styles.

2. USE A TEMPLATE OR WIZARD IF YOU CAN.   Why waste time formatting a document when you can create it with one of Word's templates or wizards? Your document is laid out for you when you create a document with a template. All you have to do is enter the text. "Creating a New Document" in Chapter 1 explains how to create a document with a Word template. You can create your own templates as well. See "Building Your Own Templates" in Chapter 12.

3. TAKE ADVANTAGE OF THE AUTOTEXT AND AUTOCORRECT COMMANDS. This chapter describes the very speedy AutoText and AutoCorrect commands and how you can use them to enter addresses and other kinds of boilerplate text that has to be entered frequently. You can also stick a graphic in a document very easily with the AutoText or AutoCorrect command. I suggest learning how to use these valuable commands forthwith.

4. LEARN ALL THE WAYS TO OPEN DOCUMENTS QUICKLY.   The Open dialog box offers many ways to open documents. And you can open documents from the Windows Document menu or Favorites menu as well. "Opening Documents" in Chapter 1 explains the numerous ways to open documents. Learn them all or at least a handful of good ones and you can get your work done faster.

5. MOVE AND COPY TEXT WITH THE DRAG-AND-DROP METHOD.   If you can manage it, the fastest way to copy or move text is to drag and drop it. However, dragging and dropping takes practice, since you have to be good with the mouse to drag and drop. I suggest taking the time to learn to drag and drop and using the method to copy and move text whenever you can. "Copying and Moving Text Short Distances with Drag and Drop" in Chapter 3 explains the drag-and-drop method.

   Don't confuse the drag-and-drop method of copying or moving text with the drop-and-drag method of hunting deer. The two are completely different and have nothing in common.

6. GET IN THE HABIT OF RIGHT-CLICKING TO SELECT MENU COMMANDS.

You can tell who the experienced word processors are because they rely on shortcut menus more than they do toolbar buttons and menu commands. Chances are you can right-click whatever you happen to be working on and see, on a shortcut menu, the command you need. Check it out. Get in the habit of right-clicking to access commands faster.

7. CREATE A TOOLBAR WITH YOUR FAVORITE BUTTONS ON IT.   Creating a

toolbar is much, much easier than most Word users know. In fact, it's downright simple. You can create a toolbar for your favorite commands or remove the buttons you never use from toolbars. See "Creating Your Own Toolbars—or Modifying Word 2000's" in Chapter 23.

8. USE THE REPEAT COMMAND AS OFTEN AS YOU POSSIBLY CAN.   You'll

find that the Edit | Repeat command (pressing F4) may be the most valuable of all. You can make the command do repetitive tasks for you. Instead of choosing the same style over and over again from the unwieldy Style menu, for example, you can select the style once and then give the Repeat command many times to reformat several paragraphs. See "Repeating a Command or Text Entry" in Chapter 2.

9. REMEMBER THE UNDO COMMAND WHEN YOU MAKE A MISTAKE.   Word

invented the Undo button and Undo command for the mistake-prone—I should know, I'm one of them. "Undoing a Mistake—and Redoing What You Undid" in Chapter 2 explains the Undo command in detail. Suffice it to say you can click the Undo button on the Standard toolbar to correct a mistake as soon as you make it or open the Undo menu and choose an action to undo several different mistakes at once.

10. LEARN A TASK'S KEYBOARD SHORTCUT—OR CREATE YOUR OWN

KEYBOARD SHORTCUT.   Especially if you are a laptop user and you have to rely on

keyboard shortcuts, you owe it to yourself to learn keyboard shortcuts for the commands you often use. One way to do that is to make keyboard shortcuts appear next to button names when you move the pointer over a button. After you click the button a few times, you will learn its keyboard shortcut and start relying on it. Follow these steps to make the keyboard shortcuts appear when you move the pointer over a toolbar button:

1. Choose View | Toolbars | Customize.
2. Click the Options tab in the Customize dialog box.
3. Check the Show Shortcut Keys In ScreenTips check box:

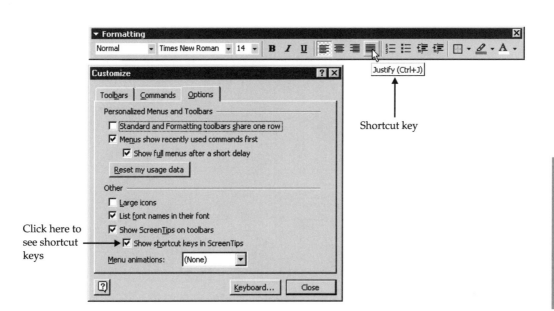

FORMATTING TEXT
AND PAGES

Note   *"Customizing the Menus, Toolbars, and Keyboard Shortcuts" in Chapter 23 explains how to create your own keyboard shortcuts.*

The Complete Reference

Chapter 7

Formatting Text on the Page

This and the next two chapters are hereby dedicated to Oscar Wilde, who said, "Appearances are everything." A well-formatted document says a lot about how much thought and effort was put into the work. Appearances count in word processing. In this chapter, you will discover how to make text look "just so" on the page.

This chapter explains how to change the look of characters, draw borders around paragraphs, and place a shaded background behind a paragraph. You'll also learn all the subtleties of punctuation—how to handle hyphens, dashes, and quotation marks, for example. This chapter describes WordArt, a feature for bending, spindling, and mutilating text, as well as how to make "hanging headings" and do other strange things to headings in documents.

Changing the Way Characters Look on the Page

The first part of this chapter explores the various and sundry ways to decorate text. You'll learn how to change fonts and font sizes, boldface and underline text, and experiment with text effects. You will also learn to do to text what Ted Turner and his crayons did to classic black-and-white movies: colorize it. I suggest reading the following pages with a pencil in hand so you can underline the numerous shortcuts, tips, and tricks.

Whatever you want to do to decorate text can be done by way of the Font dialog box shown in Figure 7-1. And you can decorate text several ways at once in the Font dialog box. In Figure 7-1, I've chosen the Impact font, the Italic font style, a font size of 42 points, an underline, and the Shadow text effect. The Preview box shows the cumulative effect of all my choices so I know what the text will look like when I return to my document.

You will be hearing a lot about the Font dialog box in the next few pages. To open this dialog box:

- Choose Format | Font.
- Right-click and choose Font from the shortcut menu.
- Press CTRL-D.

By the way, you can choose text formats before you type text or after you've typed it. To apply formats to text you have typed already, select the text and choose a text format command. Otherwise, choose the text formats and start typing—your letters will appear in the text formats you chose.

Tip	*As Chapter 12 explains, a style is a collection of commands that have been assembled under one name. A character style can include font, font size, text effect, font color, and language settings. To save time and heartache, create a character style if you find yourself giving the same text-formatting commands over and over and over again.*

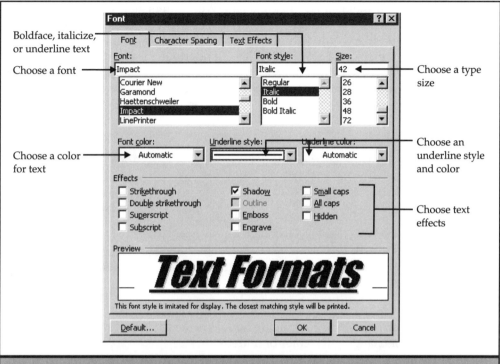

Figure 7-1. *The Font dialog box is the be-all and end-all as far as changing the appearance of text is concerned*

Boldfacing, Italicizing, and Underlining Text

Probably the three most common character formats are boldface, italics, and underlines. To boldface, italicize, or underline text, go to the Font dialog box and choose an option from the Font Style and Underline Style lists (see Figure 7-1); click the Bold, Italic, or Underline button on the Formatting toolbar; or press CTRL-B, CTRL-I, or CTRL-U, respectively.

> **Boldface text appears in a heavier type so it looks darker and stands out on the page. When readers see a page, their eyes travel first to the boldface words, which is why headings are almost always boldfaced.**
>
> *Italicized letters slant upward and to the right. Foreign words and expressions are usually set in italics. Conventional wisdom says to italicize words for emphasis, but only one or two words should be italicized at a time. Otherwise, you get the impression that the author is screaming at you!*
>
> <u>Underlines are also used for emphasis. Like boldface text, readers' eyes travel first to underlined text. I have noticed that a lot of junk mail solicitations include underlined words where italics might be used. Why's that?</u>

Why anyone needs them all I don't know, but Word offers no less than 17 different ways to underline letters. Press CTRL-U to underline text, as you know already; press CTRL-SHIFT-W to underline words only; or press CTRL-SHIFT-D to double underline text. And when you have exhausted all possibilities of underlining text with keyboard shortcuts, choose Format | Font to open the Font dialog box (see Figure 7-1) and make a choice from the Underline Style drop-down list. For what it's worth, here are the 17 ways to underline text:

One little piggy went to market.
Two little piggies went to market.
Three little piggies went to market.
Four little piggies went to market.
Five little piggies went to market.
Six little piggies went to market.
Seven little piggies went to market.
Eight little piggies went to market.
Nine little piggies went to market.

Ten little piggies went to market.
Eleven little piggies went to market.
Twelve little piggies went to market.
Thirteen little piggies went to market.
Fourteen little piggies went to market.
Fifteen little piggies went to market.
Sixteen little piggies went to market.
Seventeen little piggies went to market.

To add wealth to riches, the Font dialog box also offers a drop-down list called Underline Color for changing the color of underlines.

TrueType Fonts for Making Sure Fonts Are Printed Correctly

Choose TrueType fonts if you intend to print your documents. TrueType fonts look the same onscreen as they do when printed. You can tell a TrueType font because the letters "TT" appear beside its name on the Font menu on the Formatting toolbar. Choose TrueType fonts and you will never be surprised by strange text formats when you print a document.

By the way, if you share Word documents with others and you want to be absolutely sure that your document prints the same on your computer and theirs, choose Tools | Options, click the Save tab in the Options dialog box, and check the Embed TrueType Fonts check box. Doing so saves the fonts in the document along with the document itself. No matter where your document is printed, the fonts that are installed on your computer need not be installed on other computers for the document to be printed correctly.

The drawback: Embedding TrueType fonts in a document makes it grow in size exponentially. You might have trouble fitting your document on a floppy disk. Sending it over a network or the Internet could take an age.

EXAMPLES

LEARN BY EXAMPLE
Open the 7-1 Boldface, Italics, Underlines practice document on the CD to get first-hand experience with boldface, italicized, and underlined text.

Choosing a Font and Font Size for Text

A *font* is a typeface design of a particular type. Usually, headings and text are in different fonts. It may or may not interest you to know that the headings in this book are in 18-, 16-, 14-, and 11-point ITC Franklin Gothic Demi font and the text is in 10-point Palatino font. Font size is measured in *points*; a point is 1/72 of an inch. The larger the point size, the larger the letters. At 72 points, text is one inch high. Most people prefer to read type between 10 and 14 points high; headings are usually larger.

Tip

To start all over and remove all font and text formatting from text, select the text and press CTRL-SPACEBAR. Pressing CTRL-SPACEBAR also removes any character styles that were applied to the text.

Choosing a Font

Follow these instructions to choose a new font for text:

- **Font Menu on the Formatting Toolbar**   Click the down arrow to open the Font menu and then click a font name. As Figure 7-2 shows, you can tell what fonts look like by studying their names on the Font menu. You might have to scroll down the list to find the font you are looking for. Fonts you chose in the course of your work appear at the top of the Font menu in case you want to choose them again.

  If yours is a long list of fonts and you know the name of the font you need, try clicking in the Font menu box and typing the first one or two letters of the font's name. The list scrolls to the font whose name you started to enter.

  Laptop users: You can also press CTRL-SHIFT-F and start pressing the ↓ key. The names of fonts appear one after the other in the Font menu box. When the name of the font you want appears, press ENTER.

- **Font Dialog Box**   Choose Format | Font or press CTRL-D to open the Font dialog box (see Figure 7-1). Then choose a font from the Font list, glance at the Preview box to see what your font looks like, and click OK.

Note

Is your Font menu loaded down with too many fonts? Appendix A explains how to uninstall fonts and thereby remove font names from the Font menu.

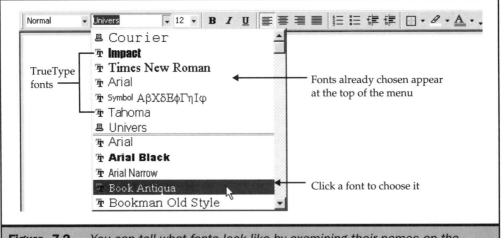

Figure 7-2. You can tell what fonts look like by examining their names on the Font menu

Choosing Your Default Font

What's your favorite font? Which font do you find easiest to work in? You can make your favorite font and font size the *default font*, the one that Word uses to begin with when you create a new document based on a particular template. However, be careful about changing the default font in a template other than Normal. In most templates, the majority of styles are based on the default font, so if you change the default font, you change styles throughout a document, often with dire consequences. See "The Two Ways to Create a Style" in Chapter 12.

Follow these steps to choose a new default font:

1. Open a document in the template in which you want to change the default font. For example, click the New Blank Document button to open a document in the Normal template; choose File | New and double-click a template in the New dialog box to change a template's default font. Most Word documents are based on the Normal template.

2. Choose Format | Font (or press CTRL-D) to open the Font dialog box.

3. Choose a font and font size.

4. Click the Default button. Word asks if you really want to change the default font. Note which template is listed in the message box:

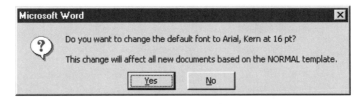

5. Click Yes in the message box.

When you change the default font in a template other than Normal and close the document, a message box asks if you want to save your changes to the template. Click Yes if you really want to go through with it.

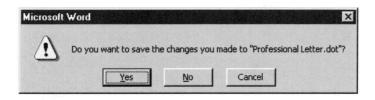

LEARN BY EXAMPLE
Open the 7-2 Fonts practice document on the CD if you want to see different fonts and try your hand at changing fonts and font sizes.

Changing the Font Size

Follow these instructions to change the size of letters:

- **Font Size Menu on the Formatting Toolbar**   As shown in Figure 7-3, click the down arrow to open the Font Size menu and choose a point size. To choose a point size that isn't on the menu, click in the Font Size menu box, enter a point size, and press the ENTER key. (Laptop users: Press CTRL-SHIFT-P to move the cursor into the Font Size menu box. Then either press the ↓ key until you see the point size you want or enter the point size you want, and then press the ENTER key.)

- **Size List in the Font Dialog Box**   Choose Format | Font or press CTRL-D to open the Font dialog box (see Figure 7-1). Then either choose a point size from the Size list or enter a point size in the Size box, glance at the Preview box to see how large the letters will be, and click OK.

- **Pressing CTRL-SHIFT-> or CTRL-SHIFT-<**   Press either key to increase or decrease the point size by the next interval on the Font Size menu on the Formatting toolbar. Watch the Font Size menu or your text and note how the text changes size. This is an excellent technique when you want to "eyeball it" and you don't care to fool with the Font Size menu or Font dialog box

- **Pressing CTRL-] or CTRL-[**   Press either key to increase or decrease the point size by 1 point. Use this technique to make subtle changes to the font size of letters.

Tip   *Use the CTRL-] or CTRL-[shortcut keys when you are dealing with fonts of different sizes and you want to change the size of all the letters at once but still retain their size differences relative to one another.*

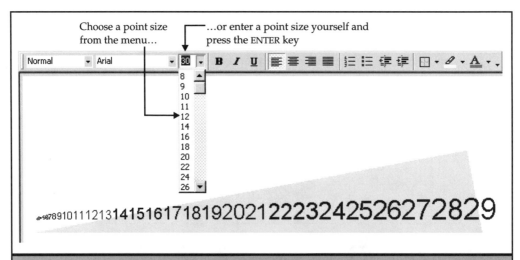

Choose a point size from the menu...

...or enter a point size yourself and press the ENTER key

Figure 7-3. *Changing the font size from the Font Size menu on the Formatting toolbar*

Finding Out How Text Has Been Formatted

In a complicated document with many formats, sometimes it is hard to tell which formats have been applied to text. To find out how text is formatted, click the text and glance at the Font menu and Font Size menu. While you're at it, see if the Bold, Italic, and Underline buttons on the Formatting toolbar are pressed down. These clues tell you which font and font size are in use and whether text has been boldfaced, italicized, or underlined.

To learn even more about formats, choose Help | What's This? (or press SHIFT-F1) and click the text. A gray box tells you in no uncertain terms which styles, fonts, font sizes, indents, and character styles have been assigned to the text you clicked:

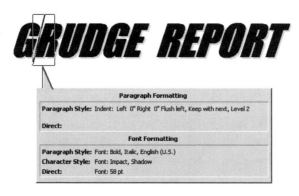

Changing the Color of Text

People with color printers can take advantage of the fact by printing text in color. The Font dialog box (see Figure 7-1) offers a Font Color drop-down list for choosing colors, but the easiest way to do it is to select the text and choose a color from the Font Color menu on the Formatting toolbar. What's more, the Font Color menu is a "floater," so you can drag it off the toolbar and start clicking buttons until the text you selected looks just right. See "The Strange Case of the Floating Toolbar" in Chapter 1 if your Font Color menu sinks instead of floating like the one in this illustration:

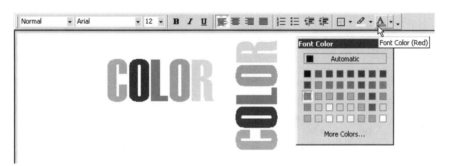

Two commands come in especially handy when you are changing fonts and font sizes: Edit | Repeat and Edit | Find and Replace. Change fonts once, and all you have to do to change them elsewhere in the same way is keep selecting text and pressing F4 (the Repeat command shortcut key). As well as replacing words and phrases, the Find and Replace command is good for replacing formats, including fonts and font sizes. See "Repeating a Command or Text Entry" in Chapter 2 and "Conducting a Find-and-Replace Operation" in Chapter 6.

Playing with Word's "Text Effects"

Dead center in the Font dialog box (choose Format | Font to get there) are the Effects options. These options have various uses, some utilitarian and some strictly for yucks. They are described on the following pages.

LEARN BY EXAMPLE
Open the 7-3 Text Effects document on the practice CD if you want to see examples of, and experiment with, the different text effects.

STRIKETHROUGH AND DOUBLE STRIKETHROUGH Strikethrough is used to show where passages have been struck from a contract or other important document. Double strikethrough, for all I know, is used to shows where passages have been struck out forcefully. Click the Strikethrough or Double Strikethrough check box to draw lines through text:

~~Upon orders from above, this text is hereby struck from our contract.~~
~~And, look here I say, this text is hereby struck out twice as hard.~~

Note *If you see strikethrough text colored red, blue, or another color, you are very likely looking at revised text, not strikethrough text. Word offers a Track Changes feature whereby deleted text is not removed from the page but struck out instead. See "Keeping Track of Revisions to Documents" in Chapter 19.*

SUPERSCRIPT AND SUBSCRIPT A superscripted letter or number is one that has been raised in the text. Superscript is used in mathematical and scientific formulas, in ordinal numbers (1st, 2nd, 3rd), and to mark footnotes (but if you need to enter footnotes, use Word's Insert | Footnote command, which is explained in Chapter 18). In the theory of relativity, the 2 is superscripted: $E = mc^2$.

Tip *Word enters ordinal numbers in superscript automatically. If you prefer to write ordinal numbers that are not superscripted, choose Tools | AutoCorrect, click the AutoFormat As You Type tab in the AutoCorrect dialog box, and uncheck the Ordinals (1st) With Superscript check box.*

A subscripted letter has been lowered in the text. In this chemistry equation, the 2 has been lowered to show that two atoms of hydrogen are needed along with one atom of oxygen to form a molecule of water: H_2O.

To superscript or subscript a number or letter, select it and do the following:

- **Superscript** Check the Superscript check box in the Font dialog box (choose Format | Font or press CTRL-D to get there) or press CTRL-SHIFT-=.

- **Subscript** Check the Subscript check box or press CTRL-=.

SHADOW The Shadow check box in the Font dialog box is for use in desktop publishing to make headlines cast a faint shadow on the page. To make the Shadow option work, however, you have to choose a heavy font so the characters are wide enough to cast a shadow:

The Shadow Knows

OUTLINE   The Outline option presents letters in outline form. This option, like Shadow, Emboss, and Engrave, is for use in desktop publishing. To use it successfully, the letters have to be heavy enough and tall enough to be seen as outlines:

Outline the Possibilities

EMBOSS AND ENGRAVE   Clicking the Emboss or Engrave check box turns the text white. Embossed text looks as though it has been raised from the paper; engraved text is meant to look as though it has been chiseled into the paper like words on a gravestone. With either option, be sure to choose a *serif font*, a font like the Times Roman font shown here with short, ornamental strokes called *serifs* on the ends of letters. The serifs help make the embossing or engraving stand out.

Embassy Boss

Engraved and Buried

> **Note**   *Hidden text is used for critiquing others' work and communicating secretly across interstate boundaries. It does not appear on the page unless you click the Show/Hide¶ button. See "Making Notes with Hidden Text" in Chapter 19.*

SMALL CAPS   A *small cap* is a small capital letter. Table 7-1 describes the uses that conventional publishers make of small capital letters. In this book, you may have noticed, small caps are used to describe keys on the keyboard ("press CTRL-SHIFT-K"). In newspapers, small capital letters are often used in the dateline at the start of the article ("KEY WEST, FLA. NOV 8 (UPI)"). To enter a small cap, type the letter in lowercase, select it, and do either of the following.

- Open the Font dialog box, and check the Small Caps check box (or open the Font dialog box first, check the Small Caps check box, close the dialog box, and then start typing).

- Press CTRL-SHIFT-K.

Caution *Be sure to type lowercase letters in order to create small caps. Type an uppercase letter and Word refuses to turn it into a small cap. Not all fonts can produce small capital letters.*

Small Cap	Meaning	Explanation	Example
A.M.	*ante meridian*	Before noon	4:00 A.M.
P.M.	*post meridian*	Afternoon	5:30 P.M.
A.D.	*anno Domini*	In the year of the Lord	A.D. 1066*
A.H.	*anno Hebraico; also anno Hegirae*	In the Hebrew year; in the year of (Mohammed's) Hegira (i.e., his flight from Mecca in A.D. 622)	A.H.1378*
A.U.C.	*ab urbe condita*	From the founding of the city (i.e., Rome, in 753 B.C.)	2753 A.U.C.
B.C.	"before Christ"	Before the birth of Jesus Christ	540 B.C.
B.C.E.	"before the common era"	Religiously neutral equivalent to B.C.	540 B.C.E.
B.P.	"before the present"	Before the present year	1 B.P.
C.E.	"of the common era"	Religiously neutral equivalent to A.D.	1066 C.E.

* The small cap abbreviations A.D. and A.H. precede the year.

Table 7-1. *Conventional Uses for Small Capital Letters*

Putting Borders, Shading, and Color on Paragraphs

Word 2000 offers a command for putting borders around paragraphs and color or gray shades behind paragraphs. Before you know anything about the Format | Borders and Shading command, however, you should know that the command is not necessarily the best way to draw lines around paragraphs or put color or a gray shade behind them.

Figure 7-4 shows a document in which borders and gray shades have been placed on several paragraphs with the Format | Borders and Shading command. Notice what is wrong with the borders and gray shades in the figure:

- **Borders and Shades Don't Line Up**   With the Format | Borders and Shading command, borders are drawn along the left and right margin, unless the paragraph is indented, in which case the borders are drawn at the indentation. In Figure 7-4, several paragraphs are indented, so the left and right borderlines don't line up and you get an ugly, blocky-looking couple of pages. Without digging around in the Border and Shading Options dialog box (I'll show you how), you can't decide for yourself where the borders lie or how much of the page to fill with color or a gray shade.

- **No Border at Page Break**   The last paragraph breaks across two pages, so no borderline appears along the bottom of the first page or the top of the second.

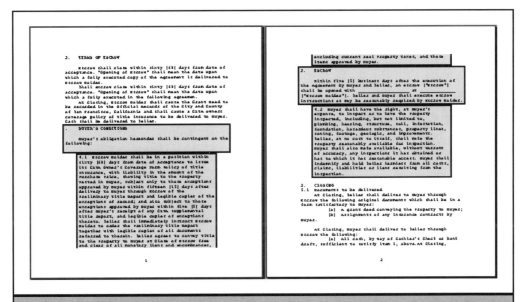

Figure 7-4.   *With the Format | Borders and Shading command, borders are placed on the margin or where paragraphs are indented. You can also use text boxes or the Rectangle button on the Drawing toolbar for borders and shading*

What is the Format | Borders and Shading command good for, seeing that you can't decide where the borders fall or keep a paragraph with borders and shading from breaking across the bottom of a page? The command *is* good for putting borders, shading, and color on a single paragraph. And, as shown in this illustration, you can use it to draw borderlines across the top and bottom of paragraphs:

> It is only shallow people who do not judge by appearances. The true mystery of the world is the visible, not the invisible. — Oscar Wilde

 You can also draw borders along the sides of the page. See "Decorating a Page with a Border" in Chapter 9.

Putting Borderlines Around a Paragraph

To put borders around a paragraph, start by clicking the paragraph. Then follow these instructions:

- **Simple Lines**   As shown in Figure 7-5, go to the Formatting toolbar and click the down arrow next to the Border button to open the Border menu. Then click a Border button or click two or three buttons to put borders on two or three sides of the paragraph.

- **Box, Shadow, 3-D, and Custom Borders**   Choose Format | Borders and Shading and click the Borders tab in the Borders and Shading dialog box,

Alternatives to the Format | Borders and Shading Command

Consider these alternatives to the Format | Borders and Shading command before you draw borders around a paragraph or place a gray shade or color behind it:

- **Text Boxes**   A *text box* is a box in which you can enter text. Text boxes can be shaded, filled with color, and given borders. You can move them wherever you want on the page. Text boxes do not break across pages—they slide to the next page if they are pushed too close to the bottom of the previous one. See "Putting a Text Box on the Page" in Chapter 13.

- **Rectangles**   Click the Rectangle button on the Drawing toolbar to draw a rectangle onscreen. You can fill a rectangle with color or a gray shade, put borders on it, and make text show through it. See "Drawing Lines and Shapes" in Chapter 13.

For fancy borders, go to the
Borders and Shading dialog box

Click a Border button to put a
simple border on a paragraph

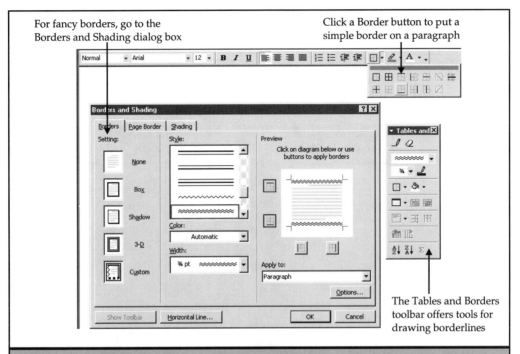

The Tables and Borders
toolbar offers tools for
drawing borderlines

Figure 7-5. *The Borders and Shading dialog box offers many options for drawing borders, and you can also use the Border buttons or the Tables and Borders toolbar*

shown in Figure 7-5, to draw fancy borders. Click a Setting button—Box, Shadow, 3-D, and so on—to create an unusual border. From the Style, Color, and Width drop-down lists, choose what the lines will look like. Under Preview, either click the buttons or click sides of the square to tell Word on which sides of the paragraph to draw borderlines.

■ **Tables and Borders Toolbar**   Display the Tables and Borders toolbar, as shown in Figure 7-5. The Line Style, Line Width, and Border Color menus offer the same kinds of lines and colors as the Borders and Shading dialog box. Click the down arrow to open the Border menu and click one or more Border buttons.

Removing borderlines is a lot easier than drawing them. Click anywhere inside the border, click the down arrow beside the Borders button on the Formatting toolbar, and click the No Border button to remove all the borders. To remove one or two of them, click buttons that are "pressed down" on the Border drop-down menu.

Note *You can control how close text comes to the border around a paragraph. To do so, choose Format | Borders and Shading, click the Borders tab, and click the Options button. In the Border and Shading Options dialog box, change the measurements in the Top, Bottom, Left, and Right boxes to move text closer or further away from the borders.*

FORMATTING TEXT
AND PAGES

Shading or Coloring a Paragraph

To shade or put a color background on a paragraph, click it and display the Tables and Borders toolbar. Then click the down arrow to open the Shading Color menu and choose a color or gray shade. That's all there is to it. If you decide to remove the color or shading, open the Shading Color menu again and choose No Fill from the top of the menu.

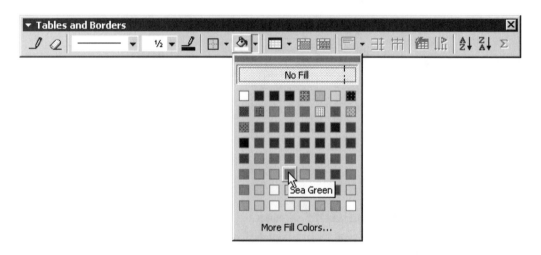

LEARN BY EXAMPLE
The 7-5 Shades practice document on the CD offers splendid examples of paragraphs that have been shaded. Open the document to try your hand at shading paragraphs.

Exciting Ways to Format Heading Text

Everybody knows that heading text is larger than other text and that headings are boldfaced. Do you want headings that really stand out? These pages explain how to make jazzy headings that get readers' attention. Read on to learn about WordArt (a means of stretching and teasing words into different shapes), and hanging heads (headings that hang into the margin). You will also learn how to raise and lower letters from the baseline and fix letter-spacing problems in headings.

WordArt for Bending, Spindling, and Mutilating Text

A *WordArt image* is a word or two that has been stretched, crumpled, or squeezed into an odd shape. Figure 7-6 shows the WordArt Gallery, where WordArt images are made, and an example of a WordArt image. After you insert a WordArt image, you can fool with the buttons on the WordArt toolbar and torture the word or phrase even further. Read on.

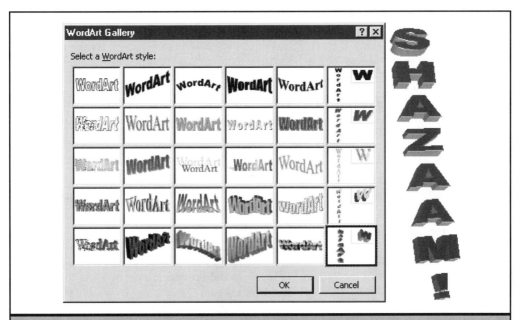

Figure 7-6. *To create a WordArt image like the one shown here, start by selecting a style in the WordArt Gallery*

Creating a WordArt Image

Follow these steps to insert a WordArt image in a document:

1. Click on the page where you want the WordArt image to go and either choose Insert | Picture | WordArt or click the Insert WordArt button on the Drawing toolbar. You'll see the WordArt Gallery dialog box shown in Figure 7-6.

2. Select a WordArt style and click OK. Don't worry about selecting the right style—you can choose a different one later on. You see the Edit WordArt Text dialog box.

3. Enter the text for the image, choose a font and font size, and boldface or italicize the letters if you want. As I will explain shortly, returning to the Edit WordArt Text dialog box later is easy, so don't worry about choosing the right font and font size.

4. Click OK.

Note

The next section in this chapter explains how to change the appearance of words in a WordArt image. See "Manipulating Art, Text Boxes, Shapes, and Other So-Called Objects" in Chapter 13 to learn how to move a WordArt image on the page or wrap text around it. A WordArt image, like clip art and text boxes, is an object. As far as Word is concerned, the same commands apply to WordArt images, text boxes, and clip art when it comes to manipulating objects.

FORMATTING TEXT
AND PAGES

Editing a WordArt Image

Usually, you have to wrestle with a WordArt image before it comes out right. By clicking buttons on the WordArt toolbar, you can win the wrestling match. Display the WordArt toolbar (choose View | Toolbars | WordArt), click the image, and start wrestling.

CHANGING THE TEXT, FONT, AND FONT SIZE   To change the text or font of an image, click the Edit Text button on the WordArt toolbar or double-click the image. You'll see the Edit WordArt Text dialog box that you used to create your image. Type new words, choose a new font or font size, and click OK.

CHANGING THE STYLE OF THE IMAGE   You don't like the WordArt style you chose when you created the image? You can choose a new one by clicking the WordArt Gallery button on the WordArt toolbar. In the WordArt Gallery dialog box (see Figure 7-6), select a new style and click OK.

CHANGING THE COLOR OF LETTERS   Click the Format WordArt button and choose new colors on the Colors and Lines tab of the Format dialog box. As the following illustration shows, the dialog box offers two Color drop-down lists if your WordArt image has two colors. Experiment with the Fill Color list and the Line Color list until your WordArt image is just so. Increase or decrease the weight of lines to make the letters in the image thicker or spindlier.

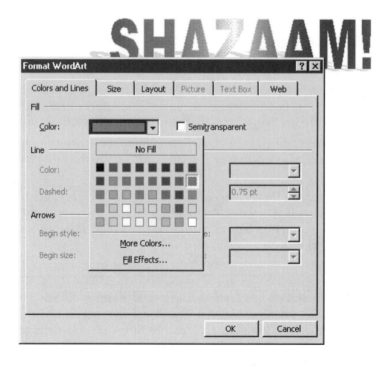

STRETCHING AND SKEWING IMAGES   To change the shape of an image, do one or all three of the following:

- Click and drag the yellow diamond to stretch or scrunch the image.
- Drag a white selection handle.
- Click the WordArt Shape button on the WordArt toolbar and choose a new shape from the menu.

     Click the WordArt Vertical Text button on the WordArt toolbar to flip an image so that letters appear one below the other, like the word "Crack" in this illustration.

ROTATING AN IMAGE   To turn an image on its back or side, click the Free Rotate button on the WordArt or Drawing toolbar. Green selection handles appear on the corners of the image. Click and drag a handle to rotate the image and make it perform somersaults.

PLAYING WITH THE LETTERS   The final three buttons on the WordArt toolbar are for fooling with the letters in the image:

- **WordArt Same Letter Heights**   Click this button to make all the letters, upper- and/or lowercase, the same height.
- **WordArt Alignment**   To begin with, WordArt images are centered, but you can click this button and make a choice from the drop-down list to change that.

The Stretch Justify option stretches the letters so they fill the frame that the WordArt image resides in; the Letter Justify option puts enough space between letters so the letters fill the frame; and the Word Justify option puts spaces between words so that the words fill the frame.

■ **WordArt Character Spacing**   Click this button and choose an option from the drop-down list to make the letters looser or tighter.

To make WordArt images look especially strange, try clicking the Shadow or 3-D button on the Drawing toolbar and choosing a Shadow setting or 3-D setting for your WordArt image. You could amuse yourself for hours this way.

Raising and Lowering Letters from the Baseline

Contrary to what tennis players and referees know, the *baseline* is the imaginary line that letters sit on in a line of text. Word offers commands for raising and lowering letters from the baseline. These commands are supposed to be for adjusting the distance that superscripted letters are raised above and subscripted letters are lowered below the baseline, but you can also use them to good effect in headings. In this wacky-looking heading, for example, letters are raised and lowered from the baseline and different fonts are used. A heading like this is sure to attract readers' attention.

Follow these steps to raise or lower letters from the baseline:

1. Select the letter or letters that you want to raise or lower.
2. Choose Format | Font.
3. Click the Character Spacing tab in the Font dialog box.
4. From the Position drop-down list, choose Raised or Lowered.
5. In the By box beside the Position box, enter how many points above or below the baseline you want to raise or lower the letters.
6. Click OK.

Raising and lowering letters from the baseline is one of those tasks wherein the Repeat command comes in especially handy. After you've raised or lowered one letter from the baseline, select another and press F4 or choose Edit | Repeat Font Formatting to raise or lower the other letter as well.

Making Headings Fit Across Pages and Columns

Suppose you want a heading to fit across an entire page or column but the heading only goes partway across or, worse yet, it breaks onto another line. In Figure 7-7, for example, the heading on the left side of the first set of headings breaks onto another line. How can you fix that? Meanwhile, the heading on the right does not stretch across the column. Suppose you want it to fit across the column. The Font dialog box offers commands for shrinking and stretching headings in cases like these.

Follow these steps to make a heading fit snugly atop a page or column:

1. Select the heading.

2. Choose Format | Font.

3. Click the Character Spacing tab in the Font dialog box.

4. Enter a percentage in the Scale box by clicking an arrow or typing a number. Numbers above 100% stretch headings; number below 100% shrink them. Look in the Preview box to see how much you are stretching or shrinking your heading.

5. Click OK.

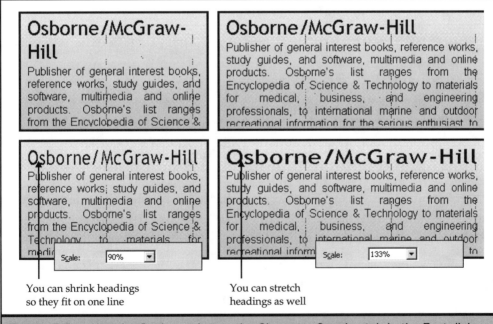

You can shrink headings so they fit on one line

You can stretch headings as well

Figure 7-7. *Use the Scale setting on the Character Spacing tab in the Font dialog box to shrink or stretch headings so they fit across pages or columns*

FORMATTING TEXT AND PAGES

Note *See "Starting a New Paragraph, Line, or Page " in Chapter 2 to learn how to deliberately break a heading across two lines (hint: press SHIFT-ENTER).*

Kerning to Fix Spacing Problems in Headings

Occasionally when you increase the size of letters for a heading, certain letter pairs stand too far apart. The letter pairs "YO," "WA," "AV," "Tw," and "To" are notorious in this regard. In the first heading in this illustration, notice how far apart the "YO," "WA," and "AV" letter pairs are. I fixed this problem in the second heading by kerning the letter pairs. *Kerning* means to push two letters closer together or farther apart in order to make words easier to read. You can only kern TrueType fonts and Adobe Type Manager fonts.

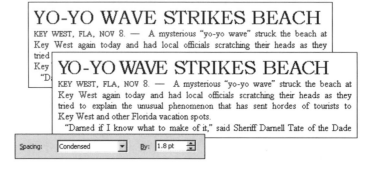

Follow these steps to kern a pair of letters in a word to make a heading easier to read:

1. Select the letter pair in the heading.

2. Choose Format | Font.

3. Click the Character Spacing tab in the Font dialog box.

4. On the Spacing drop-down list, choose Condensed to draw the letters closer together or Expanded to push them further apart.

5. In the By box, click the up or down arrow as many times as necessary to tell Word by how many points to move the letters. Watch the Preview box to see how close or far apart your letter pair will be.

6. Click OK.

While you are visiting the Character Spacing tab in the Font dialog box, you can check the Kerning For Fonts check box and enter a point size measurement in the Points And Above text box to tell Word to automatically kern letter pairs above a certain font size.

Creating a "Hanging Heading"

A so-called *hanging heading* is one that appears to hang, or stick, into the left margin of the page. Look at the heading directly above this paragraph to see what a hanging heading is. Notice how the first few letters of the word "Creating" stick into the left margin. Hanging headings work very nicely in reference books like this one because they permit readers to look up headings quickly. The headings hang in the margin, which makes finding them easier.

Here are two strategies for creating hanging headings in documents:

- **Indent the Text Below Headings**   By indenting the text below headings, you make headings appear to hang in the margin.

- **Use a Negative Left Indent for the Heading**   Create a negative indent for the heading so it sticks in the margin, as shown in the following illustration. To do so, either drag the Left Indent marker on the ruler into the left margin or open the Paragraph dialog box (choose Format | Paragraph) and enter a negative number in the Left text box under Indentation. See "Indenting Text on the Page" in Chapter 8 to learn all the indenting details. If you go this route, be sure to make the left margin wider to account for hanging headings. See "Setting the Margins" in Chapter 9.

Negative indent

Finding the Instructions You Need

Many argue that finding information is easier in a book in which the headings hang in the left margin. Suppose a reader goes to the table of contents, finds a chapter that he or she is interested in, and decides to take a closer look at the chapter. Upon arriving at the chapter, the reader skims the pages, reading heading after heading after heading. If the headings "hang," the reader can find and read them faster. Hanging headings, you see, stick in the margin where you can't miss 'em.

Tip   *Hanging headings are a prefect candidate for a style. If you want to use hanging headings in your report or manual, see Chapter 12 to learn how to create a style for them. Or, create a style to indent the text in the document and make the headings above the text appear to hang in the left margin.*

FORMATTING TEXT AND PAGES

Handling Hyphens, Dashes, and Other Punctuation

The next several pages take on what many people consider the dreariest topic in the human lexicon: punctuation. Before you start yawning, however, consider the fact that hyphenating words makes text fit better on the page. In narrow columns, hyphenating is a must, since only by hyphenating can you squeeze all the words in. As for em dashes, en dashes, ellipses, and the other esoterica you will find on the following pages, read on only if you are interested in creating professional documents that meet the high standards of magazine and book publishers.

LEARN BY EXAMPLE

Open the 7-4 Hyphenating practice document on the CD if you want some practical experience with hyphenating text.

Hyphenating Text

Hyphenating text isn't always necessary. Hyphenated text is harder to read, which is why the words in this book, for example, are not hyphenated. Only hyphenate when you have to squeeze text into narrow columns, you are dealing with justified text and you have to pack more letters on each line to keep empty spaces from appearing in lines, or a word is simply crying out to be hyphenated. The beauty of hyphenating in Word is that the hyphens only appear where words break at the end of lines. When a hyphenated word gets shunted to the next line, the hyphens disappear.

Note   *Don't confuse hyphens with two similar-looking punctuation marks: the em dash and en dash. Dashes are used to indicate inclusive numbers or to introduce a new thought in the middle of the sentence—know what I mean? Later in this chapter, "Handling Dashes, Quotation Marks, Ellipses, and Other Tricky Punctuation" explains dashes.*

Word offers no less than three strategies for hyphenating words. These strategies are explained in the pages that follow and are outlined here:

- **Automatic Hyphenation**   Word hyphenates the entire document for you. With this technique, you have to hyphenate the entire document at once (although you can mark paragraphs beforehand and tell Word not to hyphenate them). If you change your mind about hyphenating, however, removing all the automatic hyphens is simple.

- **Manual Hyphenation**   Word suggests putting hyphens in various words and you say Yes or No to each suggestion. The only way to remove hyphens that were entered manually is to delete them one at a time, which can be time-consuming if you change your mind about hyphenating a document.

■ **Optional Hyphens** If a single word is crying out to be hyphenated, you can enter an *optional hyphen*—a hyphen that breaks the word but disappears if the word doesn't break across two lines.

Don't enter a plain hyphen to solve a line-break problem. If the word you hyphenated gets pushed to the next line, the hyphen will remain. Use an optional hyphen instead, since optional hyphens only appear when words break at the end of lines.

Inserting an Optional Hyphen on Your Own

Even in a document that you don't intend to hyphenate, occasionally a word begs for a hyphen. In this illustration, the word "tintinnabulation" (it means "a jingling or tinkling sound") needs to be hyphenated to keep the large empty space from appearing below it on the second line. Optional hyphens only appear when words break on the line; the rest of the time they stay hidden.

> As she strolled, she heard the tintinnabulation of the bells in distant and dreadful Minneapolis, and she sighed.

> As she strolled, she heard the tintinnabulation of the bells in distant and dreadful Minneapolis, and she sighed.

To insert an optional hyphen:

1. Click where you want the hyphen to appear.

2. Press CTRL-hyphen or choose Insert | Symbol, click the Special Characters tab in the Symbol dialog box, click the Insert button, and click Close.

As you know, optional hyphens don't appear unless they break words on the right sides of lines, but if you want to see them, choose Tools | Options, click the View tab in the Options dialog box, and check the Optional Hyphens check box. You can also search for optional hyphens in documents by choosing Edit | Find, clicking the Special button in the Find and Replace dialog box, and choosing Optional Hyphen. Boy, this book *is* a complete reference, isn't it?

Hyphenating Words Automatically

Follow these steps to make Word hyphenate your entire document automatically:

1. Choose Tools | Language | Hyphenation.

2. In the Hyphenation dialog box, click the Automatically Hyphenate Document check box:

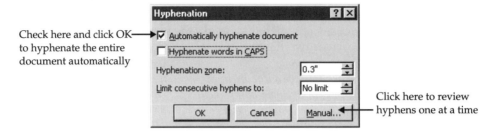

Check here and click OK to hyphenate the entire document automatically

Click here to review hyphens one at a time

3. Uncheck Hyphenate Words in CAPS if you don't care to hyphenate words in uppercase.

4. The Hyphenation Zone text box is for hyphenating left-aligned text. The *hyphenation zone* is the maximum amount of space that Word permits on the right side of lines. A large zone makes for fewer hyphens, since Word allows more white space, but allows more gaps to appear on the right side of lines. A narrow zone makes for more hyphens and breaks lines more often. However, seeing many hyphens down the side of a column or page is a little disconcerting.

5. In book publishing, the convention is not to allow more than two consecutive hyphens in a row, so enter **2** in the Limit Consecutive Hyphens To box if you are bookish.

6. Click OK.

To "unhyphenate" a document you hyphenated automatically, choose Tools | Language | Hyphenation, uncheck the Automatically Hyphenate Document check box, and click OK.

Keeping Text from Being Hyphenated

As a rule, headings are not hyphenated. Neither are indented paragraphs where quotations are found. To keep Word from hyphenating parts of a document, select them and choose Format | Paragraph, click the Line and Page Breaks tab in the Paragraph dialog box, and check the Don't Hyphenate check box. If you devise a style for headings, be sure to visit the Page Break tab and check the Don't Hyphenate box. Styles are explained in Chapter 12.

Manually Hyphenating Words

Follow these steps to pick and choose where words are hyphenated:

1. Click where you want to start hyphenating and choose Tools | Language | Hyphenation. You will see the Hyphenation dialog box.

2. Change the Hyphenation Zone and Limit Consecutive Hyphens To settings if you so desire (the previous set of instructions explains how to do so).

3. Click the Manual button. The Manual Hyphenation dialog box appears and you see a blinking cursor where Word suggests putting a hyphen:

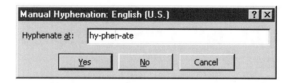

4. Click Yes or No, and keep clicking Yes or No until Word informs you that "Hyphenation is complete."

Nonbreaking Hyphens and Nonbreaking Spaces

Some hyphenated compound words and verbs that include a hyphen are hard to read when they break on the right side of a line. Consider the illustration shown here. Words such as *e-mail* and *yo-yo* are jarring when they break across two lines.

> It's about time you showed a little self-
> restraint. Your very disturbing habit of e-
> mailing me all the time about the Vice-
> President's fixation with that comic strip X-
> Men is making me buggy. You're just a yo-
> yo.

To keep these words from breaking, press CTRL-SHIFT-hyphen to enter a *nonbreaking hyphen* where normally you would enter a hyphen (you can also choose Insert | Symbol, click the Special Characters tab, and choose Nonbreaking Hyphen). Even where nonbreaking hyphens appear at the end of a line, Word does not shunt the second word to the next line.

Certain kinds of compound phrases should stay on the same line, too. Consider the ones shown in this illustration. Lines should not break after an ampersand (&), for example, or before a number if the number is attached to something else (Act 1, Psalm 22).

> I understand from my sources that Sen.
> Jones intends to write the book for Harper &
> Row. But just surely as Act 2 follows Act
> 1, and as surely as Psalm 23 follows Psalm
> 22, you can bet that the senator will forget.

> To keep compounds like these from breaking at the end of a line, press CTRL-SHIFT-SPACEBAR to enter a *nonbreaking space* where normally you would press the SPACEBAR to enter a space. You can also choose Insert | Symbol, click the Special Characters tab in the Symbol dialog box, and choose Nonbreaking Space.

Handling Dashes, Quotation Marks, Ellipses, and Other Tricky Punctuation

The last part of this longwinded chapter takes on a couple of mundane subjects. Read on to learn how to enter em and en dashes, em and en spaces, smart quotes or straight quotes, ellipses, and accent marks over capital letters in French words.

Entering Em and En Dashes

What most people know as the "dash" is really two types of punctuation mark, the *em dash* and the *en dash*. The em dash, which is the width of the letter "M," is used to show an abrupt change of thought in a sentence. The en dash indicates inclusive numbers. It is also used instead of a hyphen in a compound adjective if one or both parts of the adjectives consists of two words ("San Francisco–Seattle shuttle"). Not surprisingly, the en dash is the width of the letter "N." Note the use of en dashes on the left side of this illustration and em dashes on the right side.

1941–1945	"Would you—could you—with a goat?"
John Doe (1958–)	The patient—he had suffered all night—finally succumbed.
Exodus 16:11–16:18	She completed the job—a job well done.
pp. 54–58	The four boys—Jim, Tad, Bill, and Donny—finally arrived.
July–August 1863	Picasso, Matisse—they are the 20th Century masters.
New York–Caracas flight	"What the—?" gasped Lt. Jones.

Follow these instructions to insert dashes:

- **En Dash (–)**   Press CTRL-minus key on the numeric keypad or choose Insert | Symbol and select En Dash on the Special Characters tab of the Symbol dialog box.

- **Em Dash (—)**   Press ALT-CTRL-minus key on the numeric keypad or choose Insert | Symbol, click the Special Characters tab in the Symbol dialog box, and select Em Dash. You can also press two hyphens in a row (—) to enter an em dash. As soon as you press the SPACEBAR, Word inserts the em dash for you.

Tip *If you prefer to mark em dashes in your manuscript with two hyphens (—) instead of an em dash (—), you can tell Word to let the two hyphens stand when you enter them. To do so, choose Tools | AutoCorrect, click the AutoFormat As You Type tab in the AutoCorrect dialog box, and uncheck the Symbol Characters (—) With Symbols (—) check box.*

Besides em and en dashes, you can enter em and en spaces. Em and en spaces, like em and en dashes, are the width of an "M" or "N." Em spaces are used in this book, for example, to separate the boldfaced part of an item in a bulleted list from the rest of the item. Choose Insert | Symbol, click the Special Characters tab, and choose Em Space or En Space to insert an em or en space.

Choosing Which Kind of Quotation Mark You Want

Unless you change the default settings, Word inserts "smart" quotation marks when you press the single quote (') or double quote (") key on the keyboard. A smart quote is one that curls, either to the left if it appears at the start of a word or phrase in quotations, or to the right if it appears after the word or phrase. You can, however, enter straight-up quotation marks that don't curl. This illustration shows the difference between smart quotation marks and straight quotation marks.

> "These are 'smart' quotation marks," he said.
> "These are 'dumb' quotation marks," she said.

If you prefer straight quotes to smart quotes, follow these steps to enter straight quotes:

1. Choose Tools | AutoCorrect.
2. Click the AutoFormat As You Type tab in the AutoCorrect dialog box.
3. Uncheck the "Straight Quotes" With "Smart Quotes" check box.
4. Click OK.

Suppose you opted for straight quotes but you need to insert a single smart quote (a curly quote) in a document. In that case, choose Insert | Symbol, click the Special Characters tab in the Symbol dialog box, choose a quote option (Single Opening, Single Closing, Double Opening, or Double Closing), and click the Insert button. Take note of the shortcut keys in the dialog box and use the shortcut keys if you find yourself having to enter curly quotes often.

FORMATTING TEXT AND PAGES

Handling Ellipses and Accents on Uppercase Letters

Finally, to end this chapter with a whimper and not a bang, here are two more slices of punctuation esoterica:

- **Ellipses (...)** When you type three periods in a row to enter an ellipsis, Word automatically spreads the periods out a bit to make the ellipsis easier to see on the page. If for some reason you don't want Word to do that, choose Tools | AutoCorrect, click the AutoCorrect tab in the dialog box that appears, click the ellipsis (...) in the Replace list, and click the Delete button.

- **Accents on Uppercase Letters** Word does not print accent marks over uppercase letters in French words. *Quel damage!* If you want the accent marks to appear, choose Tools | Options, click the Edit tab in the Options dialog box, and check the Allow Accented Uppercase In French check box.

Exam | MOUS Exam Objectives Explored in Chapter 7

Objective	Heading	Practice File
Apply font formats (Bold and Italic)	"Boldfacing, Italicizing, and Underlining Text"	7-1 Boldface, Italics, Underlines
Apply character effects (superscript, subscript, strikethrough, small caps, and outline)	"Playing with Word's Text Effects"	7-3 Text Effects
Select and change font and font size (automatically and manually)	"Choosing a Font and Font Size for Text"	7-2 Fonts
Use hyphenation	"Hyphenating Text"	7-4 Hyphenating
Apply paragraph and section shading	"Putting Borders, Shading, and Color on Paragraphs"	7-5 Shades
Use non-breaking spaces*	"Non-breaking Hyphens and Non-breaking Spaces"	

* Denotes an Expert exam objective.

The
Complete
Reference

Word 2000

Chapter 8

Aligning
and Controlling Text

The last chapter looked into the question of how to format text on the page. In this chapter, you will lean away from the page a bit and examine the question of how to format paragraphs. You'll learn how to arrange text on the page by aligning, centering, or justifying it, and how to manage hanging indents and other indentation tricks. This chapter takes on the difficult matter of handling tab stops in a document. You will also learn how to adjust the space between lines and paragraphs and how to make sure that paragraphs stay on the same page. First, however, a little background…

Everything You Need to Know about Formatting Paragraphs

Before you start giving paragraph-formatting commands, you need to know how Word 2000 handles paragraphs, the essential element of a Word document. The following pages explain what Word thinks a paragraph is, which commands pertain to paragraphs, the Golden Rules of paragraph formatting, and how to tell how or whether a paragraph has been formatted.

What Paragraphs Mean to Formatting

Back in English class, your teacher probably told you that a paragraph is a part of a longer composition that presents one idea, or, in the case of dialogue, the words of one speaker. And your teacher was right, too. But in Microsoft Word a paragraph is much less than that. In Word, a paragraph is simply what you put onscreen before you press the ENTER key.

A blank line is considered a paragraph. So are 40 rambling Faulkneresque sentences without a paragraph break. So is a heading.

Knowing what a paragraph is in Word is especially important when you are formatting paragraphs because the formatting commands apply to entire paragraphs, not to words or lines of text. And you can change the formatting of several paragraphs at once by selecting them before you give a paragraph-formatting command.

Giving Commands from the Paragraph Dialog Box and Formatting Toolbar

Apart from pressing shortcut keys, the chief means of formatting paragraphs are the Paragraph dialog box and the Formatting toolbar, both of which are shown in Figure 8-1. The options in the Paragraph dialog box and the buttons on the Formatting toolbar are explained throughout this chapter. Do either of the following to open the Paragraph dialog box:

- Choose Format | Paragraph.
- Right-click and choose Paragraph from the shortcut menu.

In the Paragraph dialog box, you can give many paragraph-formatting commands at once. The dialog box offers commands for aligning text, assigning outline levels to text, indenting text, changing the line spacing, and controlling where text breaks across pages. On the other hand, it's hard to beat the Formatting toolbar for formatting paragraphs. All you have to do is click a button or two and see what happens.

Tip   *"Changing the Ruler Measurements" in Chapter 1 explains how to change the unit of measurement on the ruler. When you choose a new unit of measurement, the unit of measure also changes in the Paragraph dialog box and other dialog boxes where measurements are entered. If you prefer centimeters, millimeters, points, or picas to inches, choose Tools | Options, click the General tab in the Options dialog box, and choose a new unit of measurement.*

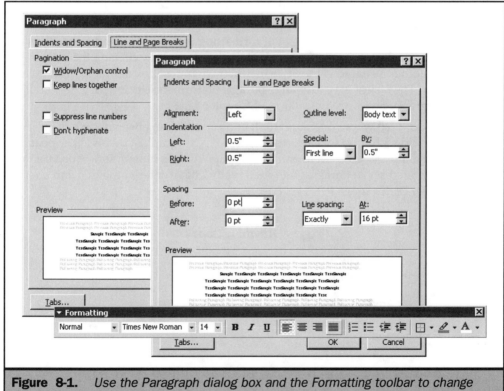

Figure 8-1.   *Use the Paragraph dialog box and the Formatting toolbar to change paragraph formats*

The Golden Rules of Paragraph Formatting

Remember these Golden Rules of paragraph formatting:

- When you press the ENTER key, all formats from the paragraph you finished entering are carried to the next paragraph.

- To change the formatting of a paragraph, all you have to do is click it and give a formatting command. Because paragraph-formatting commands apply to entire paragraphs, you don't have to select an entire paragraph as you do, for example, to change the font of all the letters in a paragraph.

- To change the formatting of adjacent paragraphs, you can select part of each one instead of all of them at once. In fact, as shown in Figure 8-2, you can simply swipe the pointer over a part of each paragraph to select part of each and then give a paragraph-formatting command. Your command will work on all the paragraphs. In Figure 8-2, the three middle paragraphs—a quotation from a book—have been justified and indented from the left and right margins. If you notice, only part of each paragraph was selected before I changed paragraph formats, yet all three paragraphs have been reformatted *in toto*.

- Each paragraph is assigned a set of formatting commands called a *style*. You can tell which style has been assigned to a paragraph by clicking the paragraph and reading the name in the Style menu, the leftmost box on the Formatting toolbar. The fastest way to change paragraph formats is to assign a new style to a paragraph. Styles are the subject of Chapter 12.

- If you can't tell where one paragraph ends and the next begins, click the Show/Hide ¶ button (or press CTRL-SHIFT-*). Paragraph symbols (¶) appear where you pressed ENTER to end a paragraph. In this illustration, Word thinks I have entered seven paragraphs, when really I have entered the title and chorus of a Cole Porter song:

> *Anything·Goes¶*
> ¶
> In·olden·days·a·glimpse·of·stocking¶
> Was·looked·on·as·something·shocking¶
> But·now,·God·knows,¶
> Anything·goes.¶
> ¶

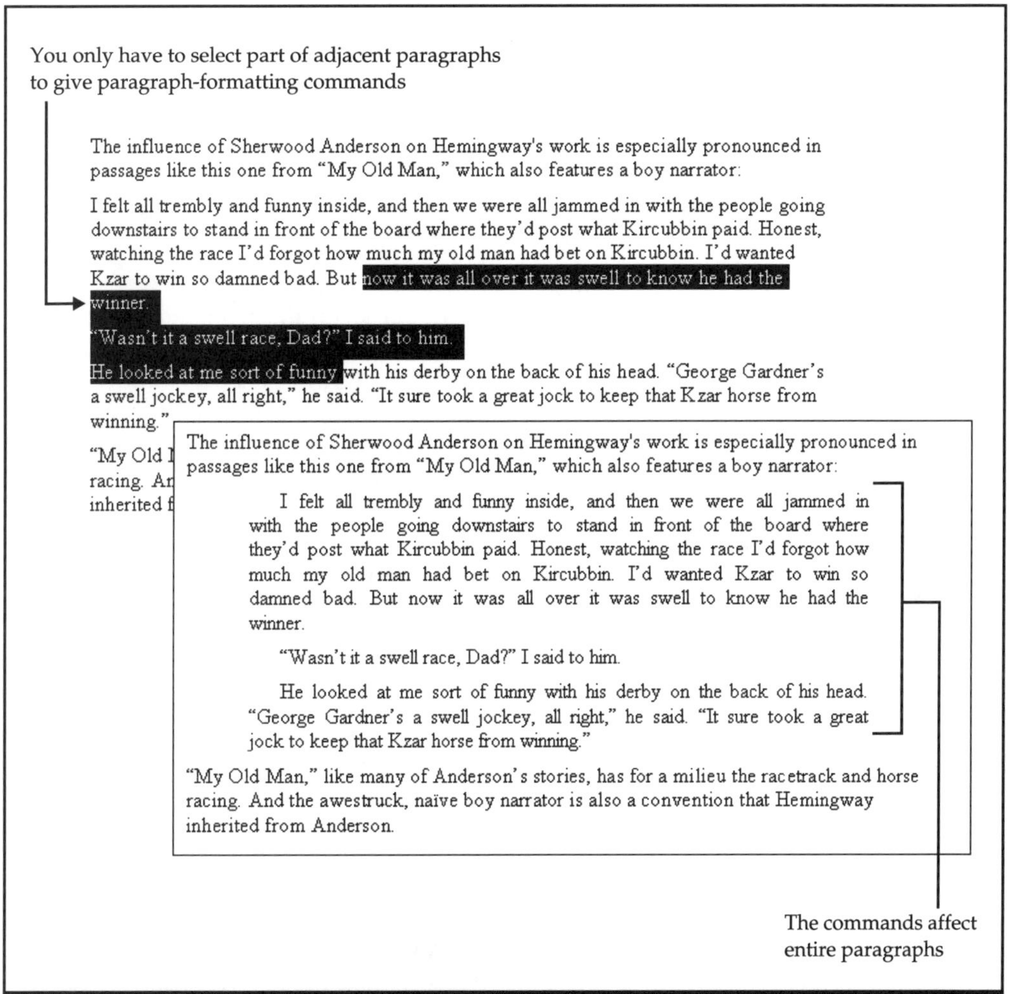

You only have to select part of adjacent paragraphs
to give paragraph-formatting commands

The influence of Sherwood Anderson on Hemingway's work is especially pronounced in
passages like this one from "My Old Man," which also features a boy narrator:

I felt all trembly and funny inside, and then we were all jammed in with the people going
downstairs to stand in front of the board where they'd post what Kircubbin paid. Honest,
watching the race I'd forgot how much my old man had bet on Kircubbin. I'd wanted
Kzar to win so damned bad. But now it was all over it was swell to know he had the
winner.

"Wasn't it a swell race, Dad?" I said to him.

He looked at me sort of funny with his derby on the back of his head. "George Gardner's
a swell jockey, all right," he said. "It sure took a great jock to keep that Kzar horse from
winning."

"My Old M
racing. An
inherited f

The influence of Sherwood Anderson on Hemingway's work is especially pronounced in
passages like this one from "My Old Man," which also features a boy narrator:

I felt all trembly and funny inside, and then we were all jammed in
with the people going downstairs to stand in front of the board where
they'd post what Kircubbin paid. Honest, watching the race I'd forgot how
much my old man had bet on Kircubbin. I'd wanted Kzar to win so
damned bad. But now it was all over it was swell to know he had the
winner.

"Wasn't it a swell race, Dad?" I said to him.

He looked at me sort of funny with his derby on the back of his head.
"George Gardner's a swell jockey, all right," he said. "It sure took a great
jock to keep that Kzar horse from winning."

"My Old Man," like many of Anderson's stories, has for a milieu the racetrack and horse
racing. And the awestruck, naïve boy narrator is also a convention that Hemingway
inherited from Anderson.

The commands affect
entire paragraphs

Figure 8-2.   *Paragraph-formatting commands affect entire paragraphs, so you only
have to click a paragraph or select part of several paragraphs to
change their formats*

Note   *See "Viewing the Hidden Format Symbols" in Chapter 2 to learn what all the hidden
format symbols are.*

Learning How a Paragraph Was Formatted

Sometimes you have to discern how a paragraph was formatted in order to decide whether it needs reformatting. Click the paragraph in question and look for these clues to see which formats are at work:

- **Alignment** Look at the Alignment buttons on the Formatting toolbar. Whichever is pressed down—Align Left, Center, Align Right, or Justify— tells you how the paragraph is aligned.

- **Indent Marks on the Ruler** The indent marks on the ruler show whether the first line of the paragraph was indented and if the paragraph was indented from the left and right margins. Later in this chapter, "Indenting Text on the Page" explains how to read the indent markers. Choose View | Ruler to see the ruler, if necessary.

- **Style Menu** The Style menu tells you which style was assigned to the paragraph.

If these clues still don't tell you what you want to know, choose Help | What's This? (or press SHIFT-F1) and click the paragraph. A gray box appears. Look in the top half of the box under "Paragraph Formatting" to learn more than you need to know about your paragraph.

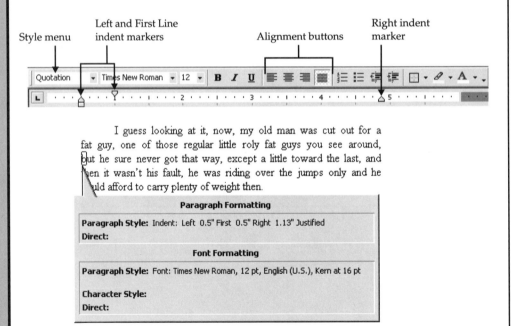

Arranging Text on the Page

Now that you know the details of paragraph formatting, you can get down to work. These pages explain how to align, center, and justify text on the page. You will also learn how to indent text from the left and right margins, indent the first line of paragraphs, and create a hanging indent.

Aligning, Centering, and Justifying Text

Figure 8-3 demonstrates the four ways that you can align text on the page. You are invited to try out the different ways of aligning text. By using more than one alignment on the same page, you can create interesting effects. To align text, select it if necessary and then do the following:

- **Formatting Toolbar**   Click an Alignment button on the Formatting toolbar: Align Left, Center, Align Right, or Justify.

- **Keyboard Shortcut**   Press a keyboard shortcut: CTRL-L (align left), CTRL-E (center), CTRL-R (align right), or CTRL-J (justify).

- **Paragraph Dialog Box**   Choose Format | Paragraph. In the Paragraph dialog box on the Indents and Spacing tab (see Figure 8-1), open the Alignment menu and choose Left, Centered, Right, or Justified.

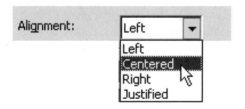

Notice that two of the four alignment methods produce what typesetters call a *ragged edge*—a paragraph in which words do not line up flush on the left or right side. Ragged text is thought to be easier to read and is why the text in the book you are reading, for example, has a ragged right edge. Justify text in formal documents or when you want to squeeze words into columns. Remember: Left-aligned text with a ragged right edge is considered easiest for reading.

FORMATTING TEXT
AND PAGES

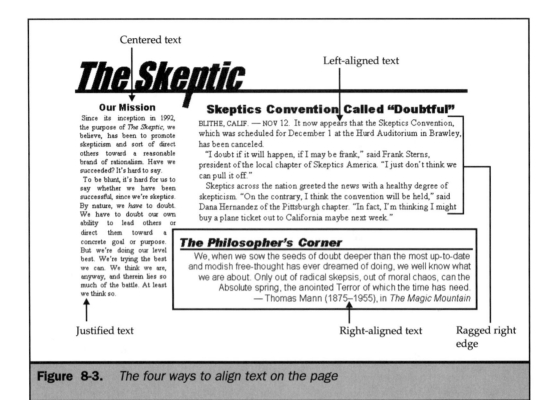

Figure 8-3.   *The four ways to align text on the page*

Note   *When text is indented and you give an alignment command, the text is aligned with respect to the indent marks—not the left and right margin, the left and right sides of the column, or the left and right sides of the text box. Unless you are centering text, aligning text that has been indented doesn't pose a problem. But if you click the Center button to center text and the paragraph you are working in is not indented by the same amount on the left and right side, the text will not appear to be centered. You might have to change the indents to make the centered text land squarely across the top of the page, column, or text box.*

LEARN BY EXAMPLE
Open the 8-1 Aligning practice document on the CD that comes with this book if you would like some practical experience with aligning text.

Indenting Text on the Page

By indenting text, you make a paragraph or paragraphs stand out on the page. Figure 8-4 shows the different ways to indent text in a Word document. In the figure, everything

FORMATTING TEXT AND PAGES

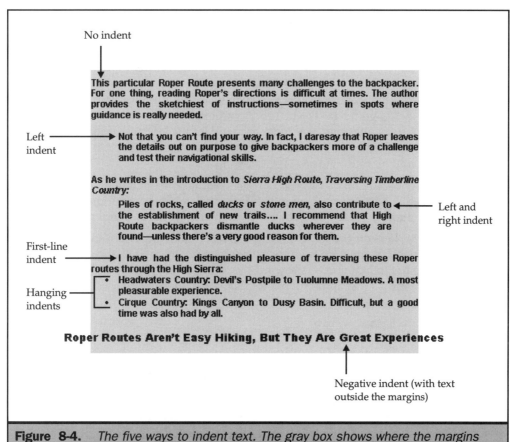

No indent

This particular Roper Route presents many challenges to the backpacker. For one thing, reading Roper's directions is difficult at times. The author provides the sketchiest of instructions—sometimes in spots where guidance is really needed.

Left indent

Not that you can't find your way. In fact, I daresay that Roper leaves the details out on purpose to give backpackers more of a challenge and test their navigational skills.

As he writes in the introduction to *Sierra High Route, Traversing Timberline Country:*

Piles of rocks, called *ducks* or *stone men*, also contribute to the establishment of new trails…. I recommend that High Route backpackers dismantle ducks wherever they are found—unless there's a very good reason for them.

Left and right indent

First-line indent

I have had the distinguished pleasure of traversing these Roper routes through the High Sierra:

Hanging indents

- Headwaters Country: Devil's Postpile to Tuolumne Meadows. A most pleasurable experience.
- Cirque Country: Kings Canyon to Dusy Basin. Difficult, but a good time was also had by all.

Roper Routes Aren't Easy Hiking, But They Are Great Experiences

Negative indent (with text outside the margins)

Figure 8-4. *The five ways to indent text. The gray box shows where the margins start and end. Text is indented with respect to the left and right margins*

outside the gray box is in the margin. As you can see, text is indented with respect to the left and right margins, not the sides of the page. A .5-inch indent, for example, places text 1.5 inches from the edge of the page if the left and right margins are 1 inch wide.

Word offers two ways to indent text—make that three ways. You can drag indent markers on the ruler, choose Format | Paragraph and tinker with the Indentation settings in the Paragraph dialog box (see Figure 8-1), or click the Increase Indent or Decrease Indent button on the Formatting toolbar.

EXAMPLES

LEARN BY EXAMPLE

Open the 8-2 Indenting practice file on the CD if you would like to try out the different ways to indent text.

Indenting Text from the Left and Right Margins

To indent text from the left and right margins, choose your weapon:

- **Increase Indent and Decrease Indent Buttons (Left Indent Only)**   Click the Increase Indent button (or press CTRL-M) to indent the paragraph rightward by one tab stop (tab stops are set at half-inch intervals, but you can change tab-stop settings, as "Aligning Text with Tab Stops" explains later in this chapter). Click the button as many times as you want to indent the left side of the paragraph. To move the paragraph toward the left margin and "unindent" it, click the Decrease Indent button (or press CTRL-SHIFT-M).

- **Paragraph Dialog Box**   Choose Format | Paragraph or right-click and choose Paragraph. Under Indentation in the dialog box, enter measurements in the Left and Right boxes. Watch the Preview box to see how far you indent text.

- **Indent Markers on the Ruler**   Drag the Left Indent and Right Indent markers on the ruler. The gray areas on the ruler show where the left and right margins are. Drag the Indent markers toward the center of the page to indent text. Choose View | Ruler if the ruler isn't displayed onscreen.

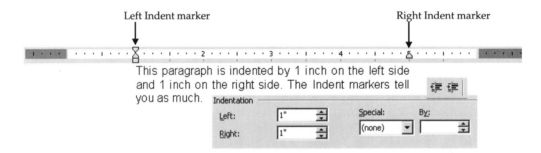

Indenting the First Line of a Paragraph or Paragraphs

A first-line indent moves the first line of the paragraph away from the left margin and saves you the trouble of pressing the TAB key to indent the first line. To indent the first line of paragraphs:

- **Using the Paragraph Dialog Box**   Choose Format | Paragraph or right-click and choose Paragraph. Under Indentation, open the Special menu and choose First Line. Then enter a measurement in the By box to tell Word how far to indent first lines.

- **Using the First Line Indent Marker on the Ruler**   Drag the First Line Indent marker to the right. You can also click the box on the left side of the ruler as many time as necessary to see the First Line Indent marker and then click on the ruler where you want the first line to be indented.

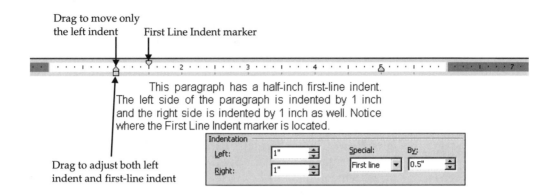

Drag to move only the left indent

First Line Indent marker

This paragraph has a half-inch first-line indent. The left side of the paragraph is indented by 1 inch and the right side is indented by 1 inch as well. Notice where the First Line Indent marker is located.

Drag to adjust both left indent and first-line indent

Tip   *After you move the First Line Indent marker, changing the left margin becomes slightly problematic. Drag the square at the base of the Left Indent marker to simultaneously adjust both the left margin and the first-line indent. Drag the triangle at the top of the Left Indent marker to adjust the left margin but leave the first-line indent where it stands.*

Creating a Hanging Indent

A *hanging indent* is the opposite of a first-line indent. Instead of the first line being shorter than subsequent lines in the paragraph, the first line is longer because subsequent lines are indented by one tab stop. Because the first line is longer, it appears to jut into the margin, which accounts for the name "hanging indent." A hanging indent is also known as an *outdent*.

Use hanging indents in lists when you want the first word or two in each list item to stand out. Word creates hanging indents for you when you click the Numbering or Bullets button on the Formatting toolbar to create a numbered or bulleted list. Notice where the First Line Indent marker is in this illustration and how the bullets stick out in the list:

- Mary, the lonely country lass who dared to make her dreams come true in the Silicon Valley.
- Tom, "Mr. Ambition" to his friends, who struck out to become a millionaire software developer but who, alas, struck out.
- Jimmy, the tireless programmer, who loved them all and bore a terrible, ill-fated secret.

Do the following to create a list in which each item begins with a hanging indent:

1. Enter the text for the list.

2. In each line in the list, press TAB after the part of the list that you want to "stick out." For the list in Figure 8-5, for example, I pressed the TAB key after the names Mary, Tom, and Jimmy. When you create a hanging indent, you indent the second and subsequent lines in paragraphs by one tab stop. By pressing TAB after the part of the list that is to stick out, you indent part of the first line so that it will line up with the second and subsequent lines.

3. Select the list and do either of the following:

   ■ **Paragraph Dialog Box**   Choose Format | Paragraph or right-click and choose Paragraph. Under Indentation, open the Special menu and choose Hanging. Then enter a measurement in the By box to tell Word how far to indent the second and subsequent lines in the paragraph or paragraphs. Be sure to check the Preview box to make sure the hanging indent is wide enough.

   ■ **Hanging Indent Marker on the Ruler**   Drag the Hanging Indent marker—the triangle directly above the Left Indent marker—toward the right. You can also click the box on the left side of the ruler as many times as necessary to see the Hanging Indent marker and then click on the ruler where you want subsequent lines in the paragraph to be indented.

   ■ **Shortcut Keys**   Press CTRL-T to create the hanging indent and then adjust it by dragging the Hanging Indent marker. You can also press CTRL-SHIFT-T to move the secondary lines to the previous tab stop.

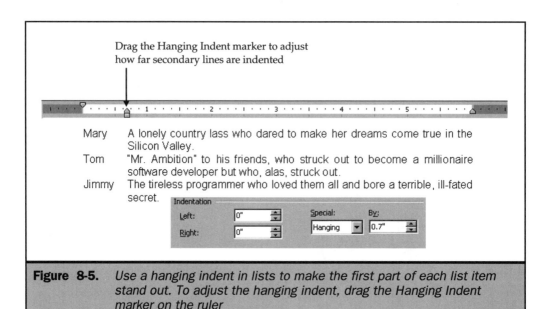

Figure 8-5.   *Use a hanging indent in lists to make the first part of each list item stand out. To adjust the hanging indent, drag the Hanging Indent marker on the ruler*

Tip   *A layout like the one in Figure 8-5 is far easier to achieve by creating a table than by creating hanging indents (Chapter 14 explains tables). What's more, if you want to adjust how far bulleted and numbered lists are indented, don't fool with the hanging indent commands. Word offers special dialog boxes for adjusting Bulleted and Numbered lists. See "Adjusting How Far Bullets and Numbers Are Indented" in Chapter 10.*

Negative Indents for Making Headlines Fit on One Line

One way to make headings fit on one line, or make them really stand out, is to create a negative indent and allow the heading to trespass on the left and right margin. However, if you find yourself fooling with negative indents throughout a document, chances are you need to make the margins narrower. Follow these steps to create a negative indent:

- **Paragraph Dialog Box**   Choose Format | Paragraph or right-click and choose Paragraph. Under Indentation, enter a negative number in the Left and Right boxes. The numbers indicate how far to let text drift into the left and right margins.

- **Hanging Indent Marker on the Ruler**   Drag the Left Indent marker and Right Indent marker into the gray areas of the ruler. The gray areas show where the margins are. Notice where the Left Indent and Right Indent markers are in this illustration.

Read these and other tales of Silicon Valley romance from the HEARTSICK PRESS!

Note   *"Making Headings Fit Across Pages and Columns" in Chapter 7 explains another way to make headings fit on one line—shrinking them.*

Choosing an Outline Level for Paragraphs

As shown in Figure 8-6, the outline level assigned to a paragraph matters in Outline view, in the Document Map, and in tables of contents. Word offers nine levels as well as Body Text, the lowest level on the totem pole. Headings are given outline level assignments automatically, the idea being that everyone wants to see headings in the Document Map, Outline view, and tables of contents. A heading assigned the Heading 1 style from the Style menu, for example, is assigned outline level 1. What about captions, sidebar titles, table headings, and other unusual elements? Do you want to see them in the Document Map, Outline view, and tables of contents?

Note   *Outline levels are primarily for use with styles. When you create a new style, be sure to assign it an outline level so that Word knows how to handle it in Outline view, in the Document Map, and in tables of contents. Chapter 12 explains how to create styles and also how to modify styles in case you want to give a style a different outline level.*

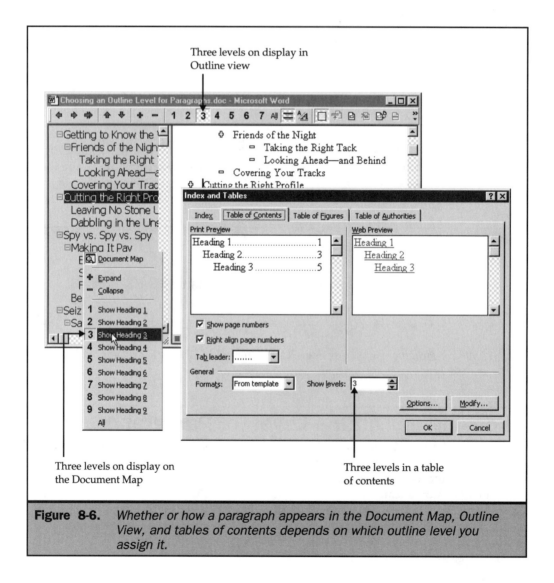

Figure 8-6.   *Whether or how a paragraph appears in the Document Map, Outline View, and tables of contents depends on which outline level you assign it.*

Follow these steps to assign an outline level to a paragraph or paragraph style:

1. Choose Format | Paragraph or right-click and choose Paragraph from the shortcut menu. You'll see the Paragraph dialog box (see Figure 8-1).

2. Open the Outline Level menu and choose an option.

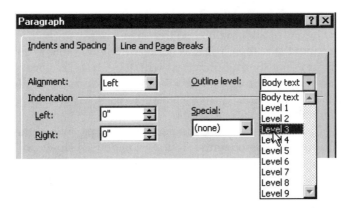

By choosing an outline level from the Outline Level menu in the Paragraph dialog box, you can tell Word whether—or how—to make a paragraph appear in Outline view, the Document Map, and tables of contents:

- **Outline View**   Click a Show Heading button (1 through 7) to display or not display text to which you've assigned outline levels 1 through 7. See "Organizing Your Work with Outlines" in Chapter 19.

- **Document Map**   Right-click the Document Map and choose a Show Heading option to tell Word which outline levels to display. See "Using the Document Map to Get Around" in Chapter 2.

- **Tables of Contents**   Open the Index and Tables dialog box and enter a number in the Show Levels text box to tell Word which outline levels to include in the table of contents. See "Generating a Table of Contents" in Chapter 18.

Aligning Text with Tab Stops

A *tab stop* is a position on the page against or around which text is aligned. In a new document, tab stops are set at half-inch intervals and are left-aligned. However, Word offers five different kinds of tab stops and four tab-stop alignments. Use the tabs to align text in different ways—or else skip tab stops and use the Table commands instead. These pages explain why Table commands are usually superior to tab stops, the different kinds of tab stops, how to set tabs with the ruler and the Tabs dialog box, and how to create a leader with options in the Tabs dialog box.

LEARN BY EXAMPLE
Open the 8-3 Setting Tabs sample document on the CD if you would like to test-drive
the different ways to align text with tab settings.

Why You Should Use the Table Commands Instead of Tabs

Tab stops are a means of aligning text on the page, but not *the* means. Before you know anything about tab stops, you should know that aligning text in table columns is far, far easier than aligning text with tab stops. Tabs are really a throwback to the days of the typewriter when you needed tabs to align text. You don't need tab stops anymore. The only reason to use them is to align numbers along a decimal point or to enter a leader.

To see why Table commands are superior to tab stops, look at this illustration. The top half shows text aligned with tab stops; the bottom shows the same text in a table. When these documents are printed, they will look exactly alike (the gridlines in the table are for formatting purposes only and do not appear when tables are printed). The difference between the two is that it took me, the Word expert, five minutes to enter and align the data with tab stops; it took me only a minute to create the table and enter the data.

Left Tab	Center Tab	Right Tab
February	February	February
Aug.	Aug.	Aug.
1234	1234	1234
$45.95	$45.95	$45.95
43,928.13	43,928.13	43,928.13

Left Aligned	Center Aligned	Right Aligned
February	February	February
Aug.	Aug.	Aug.
1234	1234	1234
$45.95	$45.95	$45.95
43,928.13	43,928.13	43,928.13

Moreover, if I need to edit the data or realign it, I can do so far more easily in the table:

- To add another column of figures to the tabbed data, I'd have to drag three different tab stops on the ruler, press the TAB key several times to make room for another column, pray that everything lines up correctly, and enter the numbers. In the table all I would have to do is choose an Insert Column command and start entering numbers.

- To indent the tabbed data, I must drag three tab stops sideways on the ruler and hope for the best. In the table, I would simply choose Table | Properties and give an indent command. I can indent the table from the left margin or right margin, or I can center the table on the page.

- To change the alignment of the tabbed data, I'd have to remove one tab stop on the ruler and very carefully enter another in its place. In the table, I'd simply click an alignment button. Moreover, the Tables and Borders toolbar offers nine ways to align data, not three.

Chapter 14 is devoted to the subject of tables. If you came to this chapter because you want to align data on the page, I strongly suggest turning to Chapter 14 before going any further.

The Five Kinds of Tab Stops

Figure 8-7 shows the five kinds of tab stops. They work similarly to the Alignment buttons on the Formatting toolbar, except for the Decimal tab, which aligns text along a decimal point or period, and the Bar tab, which draws a line down the page. Use the Bar tab to distinguish one set of figures from another, as was done on the right side of Figure 8-7, where someone's bar tab has been recorded. You can tell which tab stops are in effect by glancing at the tab stop markers on the ruler. Notice the six tab stop markers in Figure 8-7.

By default, tab stops are left-aligned and are set at half-inch intervals. Until or if you change the tab settings, pressing the TAB key moves the cursor by a half-inch to the next tab stop—a left-aligned tab stop.

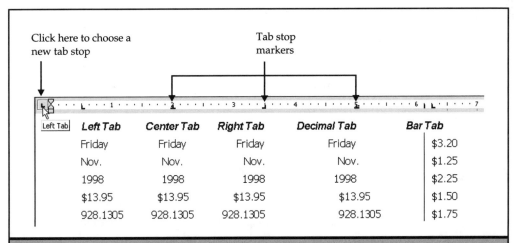

Figure 8-7.   *The five kinds of tab stops. You can tell which tab stops are in effect by looking on the ruler*

Sometimes it is hard to tell where the TAB key was pressed and text was moved to the next tab stop. To find out, click the Shows/Hide ¶ button (or press CTRL-*) to see the format symbols. "Viewing the Hidden Format Symbols" in Chapter 2 explains what all the symbols are.

Changing the Tab Settings

Continuing a theme that has been developing throughout this chapter, you can change tab settings in two different ways: using a dialog box or the ruler. Choose View | Ruler if the ruler isn't onscreen and you want to use it to change tab settings. As for the Tabs dialog box, using it to change tab settings is kind of difficult, since you can't see, on the page, where you are creating your tab stops. But you can use the dialog box to draw leaders between tab stops.

Tab settings belong to the paragraphs in which they are found. When you press ENTER and start typing a new paragraph, you carry tab settings from one paragraph to the next. Before you change tab settings, make sure the cursor is in the right paragraph—the one for which you want to change the settings. Make sure as well that you have selected the paragraphs whose tab settings you want to change if you want to change settings in several paragraphs.

Changing Tab Settings with the Ruler

Follow these instructions to change the tab settings with the ruler:

1. Click the box on the left side of the ruler as many times as necessary to see the symbol of the kind of tab stop you want.

2. Click on the ruler where you want the tab stop to be. The symbol on the ruler tells you which kind of tab stop you created.

You can put as many tab stops on the ruler as you want this way. When you place a new tab stop on the ruler, all default tab stops to the left of the one you created are removed. You can tell where default tab stops are by leaning into the computer monitor, squinting, and looking for the tiny gray lines on the ruler's bottom stripe. On this ruler, a left tab stop is located at the 1-inch mark and a right tab stop is located at the 3-inch mark. The default, left-aligned tab stops located to the right of the 3-inch tab stop are still intact.

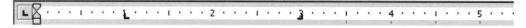

Changing Tab Settings with the Tabs Dialog Box

Follow these steps to change tab settings with the Tabs dialog box:

1. Choose Format | Tabs (you can also click the Tabs button in the Paragraph dialog box). You will see the Tabs dialog box shown in Figure 8-8.

2. Enter a position for the first new tab stop in the Tab Stop Position box.

3. Choose an Alignment option to declare the kind of tab you want.

4. Click the Set button.

5. Repeat steps 2 through 4 to create other tab stops and click OK.

To remove a tab stop, select it in the Tab Stop Position list and click the Clear button. Click the Clear All button to remove all the tab stops if you get tangled up and need to start over.

Adjusting and Removing Tab Stops

Select paragraphs if necessary and follow these instructions to adjust or remove tab stops:

- **Adjusting Tab Stop Positions** On the ruler, drag the tab marker left or right. Text that is aligned to the tab stop moves as well. In the Tabs dialog box (see Figure 8-8), delete the tab stop by selecting it and clicking the Clear button, and then enter a new tab stop position.

- **Removing Tab Stops** Drag the tab marker off the ruler. In the Tabs dialog box, select the tab stop and click the Clear button. When you remove a tab stop, text that is aligned to that tab stop is aligned to the next tab stop on the ruler instead.

LEARN BY EXAMPLE
The 8-4 Creating Leaders practice file on the CD offers leaders that you can play with if you want to experiment with tab stops and leaders.

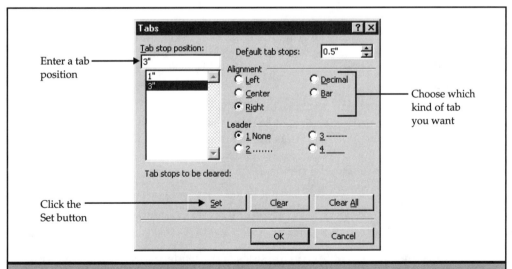

Figure 8-8. *Besides using the ruler, you can set tabs inside the Tabs dialog box*

Using Tab Stops to Create a Leader

A *leader* is a series of identical characters, usually periods, which lead the reader's eye from one place on the page to another. In tables of contents, leaders are often used to connect table of contents entries to the page numbers they refer to. ("Generating a Table of Contents" in Chapter 18 explains how you can fashion a table of contents, with leaders, from headings in a document.) Leaders look very elegant and are the best reason to fool with tab settings. In this illustration, dashed-line, underline, and period leaders are used in playbills so you can see which actor plays which role in Tennessee Williams' *A Streetcar Named Desire*:

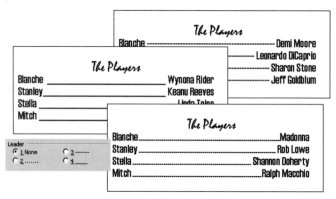

Follow these steps to create a leader:

1. Choose Format | Tabs to open the Tabs dialog box (see Figure 8-8).

2. Enter the first tab position by entering a measurement in the Tab Stop Position box, clicking an Alignment option button, and clicking the Set button. The first tab position determines how far the items on the left side of the list (the role names in the previous illustration) are indented from the left margin.

3. Enter the second tab position, but this time click an option button under Leader before you click the Set button. The choices are periods, dashes, or underlines (the None option is for removing leaders). Leaders appear between tab stops. When you set leader tabs, attach the leader to the second tab stop—the one on the right side of the periods, dashes, or underlines.

4. Click OK to close the Tabs dialog box.

5. Enter the text. When you press the TAB key after entering the text at the first tab stop, the periods, dashes, or underlines appear.

To adjust the position of text on the sides of the leader, select the text and drag tab markers on the ruler. Choose View | Ruler to display the ruler.

Adjusting the Space Between Lines and Paragraphs

This section has to do with space—not outer space, but the amount of space between lines of text and between different paragraphs. No longer do you have to tremble for fear that a professor or supervisor will tell you to double-space it or single-space it. Changing the amount of space between lines is simply a matter of choosing options in the Paragraph dialog box. Adjusting the amount of space between paragraphs is also easy, but the task isn't one to undertake lightly, either.

LEARN BY EXAMPLE
Open the 8-5 Line Spacing practice document on the CD to try your hand with the different line-spacing commands.

Adjusting the Space Between Lines

Unless you tell Word to measure the distance between lines in points, the amount of space between lines is measured in lines. In a single-spaced paragraph in which a 12-point font is used, for example, lines are slightly more than 12 points apart. Word throws in a bit of extra space to keep the low-slung letters, called *descenders,* on one line ("y" and "g," for example) from touching high-and-mighty letters, called *ascenders,* on the following line ("h" and "k"). In a double-spaced paragraph in which a 12-point font is used, lines are exactly 24 points apart.

However, when Word encounters a tall character, superscripted character, subscripted character, handful of words in a larger font, or a formula that is too tall to fit between lines, the program automatically puts more space between lines to accommodate the tall characters. It does that unless you change the line-spacing settings and tell Word to place a specific amount of space between lines with the Exactly option in the Paragraph dialog box.

If you're in a hurry to change the amount of space between lines, try one of these shortcuts: press CTRL-1 for single-spacing, CTRL-5 for 1.5-line spacing, or CTRL-2 for double-spacing.

Now that you've been briefed, follow these steps to change the amount of space between lines of type:

1. Either click in a single paragraph or select part of several paragraphs whose line spacing you want to change.

2. Choose Format | Paragraph or right-click and choose Paragraph from the shortcut menu. The Paragraph dialog box appears (see Figure 8-1).

3. Open the Line Spacing menu and choose one of the options described in Table 8-1. Keep your eye on the Preview box to see what your choices mean in real terms.

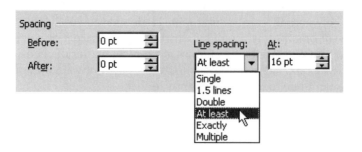

Option	Places This Much Space Between Lines
Single-spacing	The amount of space in the font, plus a bit more to accommodate ascending and descending letters. Word increases the amount of space to accommodate tall characters.
1.5-spacing	One-and-a-half times the font size. Spacing is increased to accommodate tall characters.
Double-spacing	Two times the font size, with spacing increased to accommodate tall characters.
At Least	The amount of space, in points, that you enter in the At box. Line spacing is increased to accommodate tall characters.
Exactly	The amount of space, in points, that you enter in the At box. Space between lines is *not* increased to accommodate tall characters with this option. Characters taller than the Exactly amount get their heads chopped off.
Multiple	Three, four, or another multiple of the font size. Enter the multiple in the At box. For example, entering **3** when a 12-point font is in use places 36 points between lines. However, Word increases the line spacing to accommodate tall characters.

Table 8-1.   *Line-Spacing Options in the Paragraph Dialog Box*

4. If you chose At Least, Exactly, or Multiple in step 3, enter a number in the At box:

- ■ **At Least**   In points, enter the amount of space you want to appear between lines.

- ■ **Exactly**   In points, enter the exact amount of space you want to appear between lines. (Word does not under any circumstances change the amount of space between lines with the Exactly option.)

- ■ **Multiple**   Enter a line-spacing multiple, such as 3 for triple-spacing or 4 for quadruple-spacing.

5. Click OK.

*Besides single-, 1.5-, and double-spacing, you can place other line multiples between lines of type. For example, choose Multiple and enter **1.75** in the At box to place one and three-quarters lines between lines of type.*

Adjusting the Space Between Paragraphs

Rather than pressing ENTER to put a blank line between paragraphs, you can open the Paragraph dialog box (see Figure 8-1) and enter a point-size measurement in the Before or After text box. The Before and After options, adjuncts to the line-spacing commands, place a specific amount of space before and after paragraphs.

Truth be told, the Before and After options are for use with styles (a subject of Chapter 12). When you create a style, you can tell Word to always follow a paragraph in a certain style with a paragraph in another style. For example, a paragraph in the Chapter Title style might always be followed by a paragraph in the Chapter Intro style. When you know that paragraphs assigned to one type of style will always follow paragraphs assigned to another style, you can confidently put space before and after paragraphs. But if you use the Before and After styles indiscriminately, you can end up with large blank spaces between paragraphs. Suppose you call for one paragraph to be followed by 12 points of empty space and the next paragraph to be preceded by 12 points of empty space. You end up with 24 points of empty space—a gaping hole—between paragraphs.

Note   *Word ignores space tacked to the top of a paragraph with the Before option if the paragraph falls at the top of a page. However, if the paragraph is the first in a document or the first in a section, the Before space is acknowledged and it appears above the paragraph. Press CTRL-0 (zero) to remove a line's worth of space before a paragraph.*

Follow these steps to make a specific amount of space precede or follow a paragraph or paragraphs assigned to a style:

1. Choose Format | Paragraph or right-click and choose Paragraph from the shortcut menu. The Paragraph dialog box appears (see Figure 8-1).

2. Under Spacing, make an entry in the Before box to tell Word how many points of empty space to put before the paragraph.

3. Make an entry in the After box to tell Word how much empty space to put below the paragraph, and click OK. Be sure to watch the Preview box, since it shows better than anything what your choices do to the space before and after paragraphs.

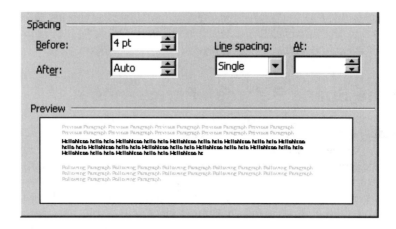

Click the down arrow once in the Before or After text box to choose the Auto option. The Auto option enters one blank line between paragraphs in whatever the line-spacing choice happens to be. For example, if the Line Spacing menu calls for double-spacing between paragraphs and you choose Auto in the After box, two blank lines appear after the paragraph.

Controlling Where Text Falls on the Page

The Line and Page Breaks tab in the Paragraph dialog box (see Figure 8-1) offers commands for controlling where text falls on the page. These commands are useful for making sure that lines of text and paragraphs that should be on the same page stay on the same page. A bulleted or numbered list with only three items, for example, is easier to read when all three items are on the same page. A heading that stands by itself at the bottom of a page without any text below it is an embarrassment that should be avoided.

Follow these steps to go to the Line and Page Breaks tab of the Paragraph dialog box and give commands for controlling where text falls on the page:

1. Choose Format | Paragraph or right-click and choose Paragraph from the shortcut menu.

2. Click the Line and Page Breaks tab in the Paragraph dialog box.

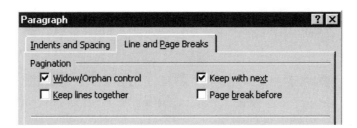

Keeping Lines and Paragraphs Together on a Page

As you know, text creeps up and down pages when you edit a document. Enter a new paragraph at the start of a document and all the text below gets pushed into a new position. Snip a paragraph out of the middle of page 1 and text on subsequent pages creeps upward. One of the side effects of editing is that sometimes page breaks occur in awkward places after text is added to or removed from a document. The shaded paragraph that looked fine when you entered it in the middle of a page gets broken across two pages. A figure gets separated from its caption, so that the figure is on the bottom of one page and the caption is on the top of the next.

To make sure paragraphs and lines stay on the same page, you can use the Keep With Next and Keep Lines Together commands in the Paragraph dialog box:

- **Keep With Next**   Makes sure a paragraph and at least the first line of the paragraph below it appear on the same page. This command is especially valuable for headings, since a heading should not appear by itself at the bottom of a page but should be followed by at least one line of text.

  To keep a page break from occurring between two paragraphs, click the topmost paragraph of the two you want to keep together, choose Format | Paragraph, click the Line and Page Breaks tab, and check the Keep With Next check box.

- **Keep Lines Together**   Tells Word not to break a paragraph (or more than one paragraph if you select more than one) across two pages. Use this command to keep short lists and announcements on the same page.

  To keep a page break from interfering with one or more paragraphs, click theparagraph or select all of them if you are dealing with more than one, choose

Format | Paragraph, click the Line and Page Breaks tab, and check the Keep Lines Together check box.

> **Caution** *When you choose the Keep Lines Together command, Word usually has to push the entire paragraph or all the paragraphs to the top of the next page to keep text together. Consequently, a huge blank space can appear at the bottom of the page from which the paragraph or paragraphs were pushed. Before choosing the Keep Lines Together command, see whether using a text box might do the job better. Text boxes are not broken across pages. They can be locked to one place on the page. And you can make text flow around the sides of a text box. See "Putting a Text Box on the Page" in Chapter 13.*

Making Sure Text Appears at the Top of a Page

Certain kinds of paragraphs beg to appear at the top of pages. A chapter title, for example, belongs at the top of a page. So might a figure or a table. Follow these steps to make sure a paragraph appears at the top of a page:

1. Click the paragraph.
2. Choose Format | Paragraph or right-click and choose Paragraph.
3. Click the Line and Page Breaks tab in the Paragraph dialog box.
4. Check the Page Break Before check box and click OK.

Be careful about using the Page Break Before command. Word usually has to end one page in the middle in order to make a paragraph appear at the top of the next page, so the command has a habit of introducing half-empty pages in documents.

> **Note** *If you came here to learn how to make chapter titles appear on the top of pages, be sure to investigate sections before you go any further. As "Section Breaks for Changing Layouts" in Chapter 9 explains, you can also begin a chapter on a new page by introducing a section break.*

Preventing Widows and Orphans

The Widow/Orphan Control check box in the Paragraph dialog box is checked for you. Don't uncheck it except under unusual circumstances (keep reading to see what those circumstances are). The command prevents what typesetters call *widows* and *orphans* from appearing in documents:

■ **Widow**   A single line, the last in a paragraph, that appears by itself at the top of a page. Especially on a page where empty space appears between paragraphs, a widow sticks out like a sore thumb. To prevent widows, Word automatically places at least two lines of a paragraph at the top of the page when a paragraph breaks across pages.

- **Orphan**   A single line, the first in a paragraph, that appears by itself at the bottom of a page. Orphans are also considered eyesores. Not only that, they are thought to cheat readers, since the reader doesn't know that a single line on the bottom of a page isn't a paragraph unto itself until he or she turns the page and finds no paragraph on the following page. To prevent orphans, Word puts the first two lines of paragraphs at the bottom of the page when paragraphs break across two pages.

And suppose a paragraph is only three lines long? How does Word prevent a widow or orphan from occurring, seeing that the program can't place two lines at the bottom of one page and two lines at the top of the next? In a three-line paragraph, all three lines are moved to the top of the next page—and therein lies the only reason why you would uncheck the Widow/Orphan Control check box.

If you are using a very large font and your paragraph is three-lines long, moving all three lines to the next page to prevent a widow or orphan from occurring creates a big empty space at the bottom of the first page. Uncheck the Widow/Orphan Control box to prevent the empty space from occurring. With large fonts, a widow or orphan isn't an eyesore, since the letters take up so much space at the top or bottom of the page.

Click and Type to Make Formatting Easier (Sort of)

Word 2000 offers a special feature called *click and type* that is supposed to help you format text, graphics, and tables quickly. Click and type is one of those "I'll do the thinking for you" features. To see how it works, open a blank document and move the pointer around the screen. As you do so, notice how alignment symbols appear to the side of the pointer. If you double-click and start typing when the Align Right symbol appears, for example, your text is right-aligned. Double-click in the middle of a blank page and you can type a centered title whether you want one or not.

Double-click and start typing in a blank area of a document to use click and type. Like most of Word 's features that do the thinking for you, click and type is more trouble than it is worth (at least in my opinion). However, you are invited to keep your eyes pealed for symbols beside the pointer. When you see a symbol that happens to show the kind of formatting you want, double-click and start typing to take advantage of the click and type feature.

Note   *If you don't see formatting symbols on the side of the cursor when you move it to a blank area of a document, click and type has not been activated. To activate the feature, choose Tools | Options, click the Edit tab in the Options dialog box, and check the Enable Click and Type check box.*

FORMATTING TEXT AND PAGES

Exam | MOUS Exam Objectives Explored in Chapter 8

Objective	Heading	Practice File
Align text in paragraphs (Center, Left, Right, and Justified)	"Aligning, Centering, and Justifying Text"	8-1 Aligning
Use indent options (Left, Right, First Line, and Hanging Indent)	"Indenting Text on the Page"	8-2 Indenting
Use the Tabs command	"Changing the Tab Settings"	8-3 Setting Tabs
Set tabs with leaders	"Using Tab Stops to Create a Leader"	8-4 Creating Leaders
Set character, line, and paragraph spacing options	"Adjusting the Space Between Lines"	8-5 Line Spacing
Use click and type	"Click and Type to Make Formatting Easier (Sort of)"	

Ten Ways to Format Paragraphs Faster

Formatting paragraphs does not rank high on the list of fun things to do. To make the irksome task go faster, here are ten tidbits of advice to help you along.

1. USE STYLES TO FORMAT PARAGRAPHS.   A style is a bunch of different paragraph-formatting commands that have been bundled under one name. To keep from having to choose numerous formatting commands, you can simply construct a new style with the formatting commands you want and choose the style from the Style menu to apply the formats. That's all there is to it. Chapter 12 explains styles.

2. LEARN THE WAYS TO SELECT TEXT.   Being able to select text quickly and in a variety of ways helps a lot when you are formatting text. "Selecting Blocks of Text" in Chapter 3 explains the numerous ways to select text. Experiment with a half-dozen text-selection techniques, find the four or five you like best, and make them part of your repertoire as you format paragraphs.

3. UNDERSTAND WHAT PARAGRAPHS ARE IN WORD.   "What Paragraphs Mean to Formatting" near the start of this chapter explains that to Word, a paragraph is simply that appears onscreen before you press the ENTER key. A heading, a blank line, as well as what is normally considered a paragraph are all paragraphs in Word. Make sure you understand what paragraphs are before you start formatting paragraphs.

4. USE THE FIND AND REPLACE COMMAND TO REPLACE FORMATS.   Did you know that you can replace paragraph formats with the Edit | Replace command? Follow these steps to do so:

1. Click the Save button (or press CTRL-S) to save your document.

    Always save your document before a find-and-replace operation. That way, if finding and replacing turns your document into guacamole, you can close the document without saving the changes you made to it, reopen the document, and get the original back.

2. Choose Edit | Replace (or press CTRL-H). You'll see the Replace tab of the Find and Replace dialog box.

3. Click the More button to see all of the find-and-replace options.

4. Click the Format button and choose Paragraph from the pop-up menu. You'll see the Find Paragraph dialog box. Not coincidentally, it looks like—and offers the same options as—the Paragraph dialog box.

5. By choosing options in the Find Paragraph dialog box, describe the paragraph formats that need replacing; then click OK. Back in the Find and Replace dialog box, a description of the paragraph formats you want to replace appears under the Find What box.

6. Click in the Replace With box.

7. Click the Format button and choose Paragraph from the pop-up menu. You see will the now familiar Replace Paragraph dialog box.

8. Carefully enter the paragraph formats that you want to replace the formats you entered in the Find Paragraph dialog box; then click OK.

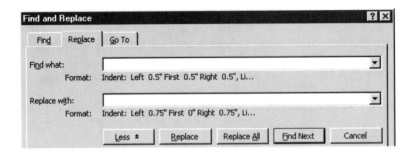

9. Click the Find Next button. If Word finds a paragraph whose paragraph formatting matches the description under the Find What box, the paragraph is highlighted onscreen.

10. Click the Replace button to change the paragraph's formats. Word scrolls to the next paragraph that matches your description.

11. Click the Replace button again or else click the Replace All button to change paragraph formats throughout your document without reviewing them one at a time.

Next time you choose Edit | Find or Edit | Replace, the Find and Replace dialog box will list the formats you entered. To look for plain text instead of formats, click the No Formatting button. "Finding and Replacing Text and Other Things" in Chapter 6 explains everything a mortal would care to know about the Edit | Replace command.

5. LEARN ALL THE WAYS TO GET FROM PLACE TO PLACE QUICKLY.   When you are formatting documents, you need to know how to get from place to place quickly. When you are doing anything whatsoever in Word, you need to know how to get there fast. See "Moving Around in Long Documents" in Chapter 2.

6. USE THE REPEAT COMMAND WHEN YOU FORMAT PARAGRAPHS.   The Repeat command comes in especially handy when you are formatting paragraphs. After you format one paragraph in the Paragraph dialog box, all you have to do is click another and press F4 or choose Edit | Repeat Paragraph Formatting to format another paragraph the same way. The Repeat command repeats the last command you gave, whatever it happened to be.

7. KNOW THE REMOVE FORMAT SHORTCUT.   Word offers a special keyboard shortcut—CTRL-Q—for stripping a paragraph of all formats except the ones that belong to the style that was assigned to the paragraph. On occasion, the average Word user goes overboard with paragraph formats and wants to return to the original, bare-bones paragraph formatting. On those occasions, press CTRL-Q.

8. LEARN HOW TO CREATE NUMBERED AND BULLETED LISTS AUTOMATICALLY.   Earlier in this chapter, "Indenting Text on the Page" explained how to create a hanging indent, a paragraph whose first line appears to hang into the left margin. Word creates hanging indents automatically when you click the Numbering or Bullets button on the Formatting toolbar. Chapter 10 explains how to create numbered and bulleted lists.

9. USE TABLES INSTEAD OF TABS.   As "Why You Should Use the Table Commands Instead of Tabs " pointed out so vehemently earlier in this chapter, aligning text with tab stops is a monumental waste of time when the task can be done so much faster with commands on the Table menu. Tabs are really a holdover from the typewriter. Except for creating leaders, you are wasting your time by using the Format | Tabs command.

10. CREATE DOCUMENTS WITH THE WORD TEMPLATES.   You can save time that would otherwise be spent formatting paragraphs by creating documents with templates. In a template, the paragraphs are already formatted, so you don't have to do the work of designing formats yourself. See "Creating a New Document" in Chapter 1.

The Complete Reference

Word 2000

Chapter 9

Framing and Laying Out the Pages

The last chapter looked at how to lay out text on the page, and the one before that took on the subject of formatting text. In this chapter, you'll discover how to format pages. A well-laid-out page says a lot about how much time and thought was put into a document. This chapter presents tips, tricks, and techniques for making pages look just right.

In this chapter, you will learn how to change the size of page margins, and, just as importantly, when to change the margins. This chapter describes what section breaks are and when to introduce a section break, how to create headers and footers for all occasions, and how to number pages. You'll learn how to change the orientation of pages, print on paper of various sizes, decorate a page with a border, and align text on the page with respect to the top and bottom of the page. At the end of this chapter is a list of ten tasks to complete first when you start a complex document.

Setting the Margins

Margins are the empty spaces that appear along the sides of the page. Figure 9-1 shows where the left, right, top, and bottom margins are. Notice the header and footer in Figure 9-1. Headers and footers fall, respectively, in the top and bottom margins. And you can put graphics, text boxes, and page numbers in the margins as well. Margins serve to frame the text and make it easier to read.

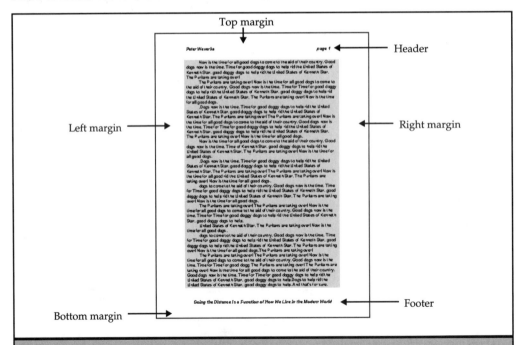

Figure 9-1.   *One of your first tasks when you open a new document is to decide on the size of the margins*

If you came here to indent text, you came to the wrong place. See "Indenting Text on the Page" in Chapter 8. Text is indented from the margins. Don't change margin settings to indent text.

When you start a new document, give a moment's thought to the margins. Changing the size of margins after you have entered the text, clip art, graphics, and whatnot can be disastrous. Text is indented from the left and right margins. Pages break on the bottom margin. If you change margin settings, indents and page breaks change for good or bad throughout your document. By setting the margins carefully from the beginning, you can rest assured that text will land on the page where you want it to land.

Word offers two ways to change the size of margins. Besides explaining the two ways, these pages explain how to create mirror margins for double-sided pages, adjust margins to make room for binding, and change the default margins that are in effect when you create a new document by clicking the New button or pressing CTRL-N.

 "Creating a Side Heading or Margin Note" in Chapter 15 explains how you can create a side heading or put artwork in the margins of a document.

LEARN BY EXAMPLE
Open the 9-1 Margins practice file on the CD if you want to test the different ways of changing margin sizes.

The Two Ways to Change Margin Sizes

Change the size of margins either by going to the Page Setup dialog box or by dragging the margin markers on the rulers. The Page Setup dialog box offers many more options for changing margin sizes. Only use the margin markers on the rulers to make last-minute adjustments to one-page documents such as announcements and invitations.

 In order to change margin settings in the middle of a document, you have to create a new section. In fact, Word creates a new section for you if you change margin settings in the middle of a document. Later in this chapter, "Section Breaks for Changing Layouts" explains what sections are.

Changing Margin Sizes in the Page Layout Dialog Box

Follow these steps to change margin settings by way of the Page Setup dialog box:

1. Place the cursor in the section whose margins you want to change; if you want to change margin settings throughout a document, it doesn't matter where the cursor is.

2. Either double-click the ruler or choose File | Page Setup. You'll see the Page Setup dialog box.

3. Click the Margins tab, as shown in Figure 9-2.

4. In the Top, Bottom, Left, and Right boxes, enter margin measurements. You can see what your measurements mean in real terms by glancing at the sample page in the Preview box.

5. In the Header and Footer boxes, enter measurements to tell Word how close to put the header and footer to the top or bottom of the page. The smaller the measurement in these boxes, the closer headers and footers will be to the page edge. Be careful not to enter too large or small a measurement. A large measurement pushes headers and footers too close to the text on the page; a small measurement moves them perilously close to the page edge, where your printer might not be able to print them.

6. Click OK.

Tip *If you prefer to work with a unit of measurement other than inches in the Page Setup dialog box, you can do so. Choose Tools | Options, click the General tab in the Options dialog box, and choose Centimeters, Millimeters, Points, or Picas from the Measurement Units menu.*

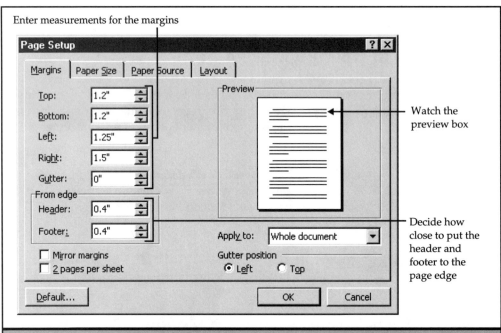

Figure 9-2.   *The Preview box shows roughly what the margins will look like after you enter margin measurements*

Changing Margin Sizes with the Rulers

The other way to change margin sizes is to drag markers on the rulers. Only use the ruler method to make slight adjustments to a one- or maybe a two-page document. Adjusting the margins across page after page by dragging markers on the rulers is an invitation to trouble, since you can't see all the pages whose margins are being changed. Follow these steps to change the size of margins with the rulers:

1. Switch to Print Layout view or Print Preview view. "Getting a Better View of Your Work" in Chapter 2 explains how to change views of a document.

2. Choose View | Ruler if the rulers aren't showing on your screen. If you still can't see the vertical ruler on the left side of the screen after choosing View | Ruler, choose Tools | Options, click the View tab in the Options dialog box, and check the Vertical Ruler (Print View Only) check box.

3. Change the size of margins by dragging the margin markers:

■ **Left or Right Margin** Move the pointer over the ruler along the top of the screen, to the left or right side where the ruler changes from gray to white. When the pointer changes into double arrows, click and drag to adjust the size of the margin.

In 1785 French draperies were fuller but remained symmetrical. It was still fashionable to soften the architecture with fabric. Pelmets were softened with swags and could be enlivened with a decoration of tapestry sometimes applied in a separate rosette in the center of the pelmet.

■ **Top or Bottom Margin** Move the pointer to the ruler along the left side of the screen, to the point at the top or bottom where the ruler changes color. Then click and drag when the pointer changes into double arrows.

Notice how, when you drag a Right or Left margin marker, all indent markers on the ruler move as well. There is your irrefutable proof that text is indented from the margins, not from the page edge.

Adjusting Margins for Bound Documents

When documents are bound with fat plastic bindings, the bindings eat into the page margins. To accommodate bindings and make them part of your calculations when you decide what size to make the margins, Word provides the Gutter box in the Page Setup dialog box (see Figure 9-2). In a bound document, the *gutter* is the part of the paper that the binding eats into.

To see how bindings will effect the layout of a document's pages, choose
File | Page Setup, click the Margins tab in the Page Setup dialog box, and click the up
arrow in the Gutter box. As you do so, bindings appear on the sample page in the
Preview box. Changing the gutter size doesn't do anything to margin sizes, but it does
give you a sense of how wide or narrow to make the margins. After you have found
the right gutter size, you can change the margins to accommodate bindings.

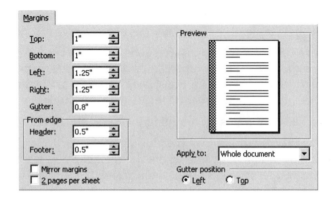

You can also bind pages from the top instead of the side. To do so, click the Top
option button under Gutter Position in the Page Setup dialog box and start clicking the
up arrow in the Gutter box. Bindings at the top of pages can interfere with headers.
You might increase the distance between the header and the top of the page by adding
a quarter inch or so to the measurement in the Header box.

"Mirror Margins" for Bound, Two-Sided Pages

When the pages of a document are bound together, readers see two pages at a time
instead of one. Take the book you are reading at this very moment, for example. You
can see two pages, this one and its opposite. In typesetter's terms, you can see a *page
spread* like the one in Figure 9-3. Even-numbered pages appear on the left side of the
page spread; odd-numbered pages appear on the right side.

In a bound document with text on both sides of the pages, the terms "left margin"
and "right margin" are meaningless. What matters instead is in the *inside margin*, the
margin in the middle of the page spread next to the bindings, and the *outside margin*,
the margin on the outside of the page spread that isn't affected by the bindings. The
inside margin has to absorb the bindings. Especially if the document is a thick one
that requires fat plastic bindings, words can get lost in bindings if the inside margin
is too narrow.

Follow these steps to adjust the inside and outside margins to accommodate
bindings in a two-sided Word document that you intend to bind:

1. Choose File | Page Setup.

2. Click the Margins tab in the Page Setup dialog box.

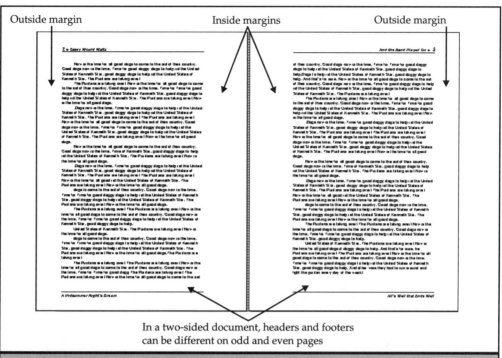

Figure 9-3. *In bound documents with text on both sides of the paper, adjust the size of the inside margin to accommodate bindings*

3. Check the Mirror Margins check box. When you do so, the Left box for changing the size of the left margin changes names—it becomes the Inside box. The Right box also changes names and becomes the Outside box.

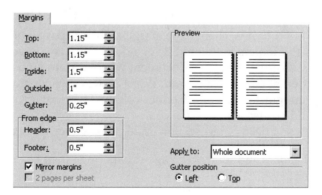

4. Click the up arrow in the Gutter box and watch bindings appear on the sample page in the Preview box.

5. Enter measurements in the Inside box and Outside box to adjust the size of the inside and outside margins (see Figure 9-3).

6. Click OK.

 As shown in Figure 9-3, the custom in books and two-sided, bound documents is to put a different header and footer on odd- and even-numbered pages. See "Headers and Footers for Different Pages and Sections," later in this chapter.

Choosing Page Setup Default Settings

Click the New Blank Document button or press CTRL-N to open a new document and Word gives you a generic 8.5 by 11-inch document with these margin settings:

- Top and bottom margin: 1 inch
- Left and right margin: 1.25 inches
- Header and footer from edge of page: .5 inch

Suppose you want to change these margin settings so that you get margins that you like whenever you open a new document. To do so, choose File | Page Setup, enter your favorite margin settings in the Page Setup dialog box, and click the Default button. A message box appears and tells you what you knew already—that the new settings will go into effect whenever you open a new document based on the Normal template. Click Yes in the message box. The Normal template is the standard template that is used to create documents when you click the New Blank Document button or press CTRL-N.

Section Breaks for Changing Layouts

In order to put text in columns, change the margins, change page-numbering schemes, or change headers and footers in the middle of a document, you have to create a new section. A *section* is a formal break in a document where certain kinds of formats are introduced or a different paper size is used. Word 2000 is very touchy about sections. If you try to change margin settings or introduce columns without creating a section, Word takes over and creates a section for you.

To be thorough, you need a new section under these circumstances:

- Changing headers and footers or page-numbering schemes in headers and footers
- Inserting newspaper-style columns
- Changing the orientation of pages (from portrait to landscape or vice versa)
- Changing margin sizes

- Changing page alignments with respect to the top and bottom margin
- Using endnotes instead of footnotes or vice versa
- Printing on different-size paper in the middle of a document
- Changing paper sources during printing (changing the printer tray in which paper or envelopes are kept)

You can tell if a document has been divided into sections and which section the cursor is in by glancing at the Status bar along the bottom of the screen. Next to the page number are the letters "Sec" followed by the section the cursor is in:

LEARN BY EXAMPLE
The 9-2 Sections practice document on the CD is a document that has been divided into sections. Open the practice document to see how sections work.

Follow these steps to introduce a section break in a document:

1. Choose Insert | Break. You'll see the Break dialog box shown in Figure 9-4.

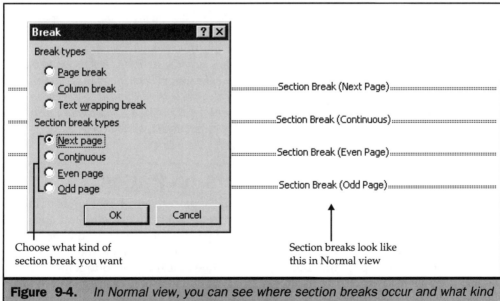

Choose what kind of section break you want

Section breaks look like this in Normal view

Figure 9-4. *In Normal view, you can see where section breaks occur and what kind of break you are dealing with*

FORMATTING TEXT AND PAGES

2. Under Section Break Types, choose which kind of section break you want:

- **Next Page** Introduces a section break and a page break to start a new section immediately on the next page.

- **Continuous** Introduces the section break starting in the middle of the page. Choose Continuous, for example, to put text in columns in the middle of a page.

- **Even Page** Creates the section break on the next even-numbered page.

- **Odd Page** Creates the break on the next odd-numbered page. In conventional publishing, a new chapter always begins on an odd page. Choose this kind of section break when headers and footers change from chapter to chapter and you want to start a new chapter in your document on an odd-numbered page.

3. Click OK. If you are in Normal view, dotted lines and the words "Section Break" followed by the kind of break you chose appear onscreen.

The best way to delete a section break or be sure where section breaks are located for that matter is to switch to Normal view. As Figure 9-4 shows, you can see where the break starts and even what kind of section break you are dealing with in Normal view. In Print Layout view, Outline view, and Web Layout view, you have to click the Show/Hide ¶ button to see the dotted lines, the word "Section Break," and the variety of section break.

To delete a section break, click it and then press the DELETE key.

Tip *You can copy a section break, paste it elsewhere, and in so doing create a new section with the same formats as another section. All the formats in a section are recorded in the section break that follows it, much the same way that paragraph formats are stored in the paragraph symbol at the end of each paragraph. To copy a section's formats, go to the end of the section, click in the left margin beside the section break to select it, and click the Copy button. Then scroll to the tail-end of the part of the document you want to copy the formats to, click there, and click the Paste button. By doing so, you create a new section with the same formats as the section whose section break you copied.*

Putting Headers and Footers on Pages

A *header* is a line of text in the top margin of the page that tells readers what is in the document. In the book you are reading, for example, headers on the left-hand page list the title of the book and headers on the right-hand page list the chapter number and chapter title. In Word documents, headers often list the author's name, the title of the work, and sometimes a page number. A *footer* is a line of text in the bottom margin. Footers do what headers do, except they do it along the bottom of the page instead of the top.

These pages explain everything a body cares or needs to know about headers and footers. You'll learn how to enter headers and footers and how to take advantage of the buttons on the Header and Footer toolbar as you enter a header or footer. These pages explain how to include page numbers in headers and footers, as well as dates, times, and other document information that can be updated automatically. Read on to find out how to change the header or footer in the middle of a document, remove a header or footer from the first page of a document or section, and create different headers for odd-numbered and even-numbered pages. You will also learn how to draw a line beneath a header or above a footer to help separate headers and footers from the main text.

Earlier in this chapter, "The Two Ways to Change Margin Sizes" explains how to tell Word how close to place a header or footer to the top or bottom edge of the page.

LEARN BY EXAMPLE

The 9-3 Header and Footer practice document on the CD has headers and footers in different sections. Open the sample document to see how headers and footers can be used in different sections to good effect.

Entering a Header or Footer

Entering a header or footer in a document is simple enough. After you get to the Header or Footer box, all you have to do is start typing. Follow these steps:

1. Choose View | Header and Footer. You'll see the Header and Footer toolbar, and, on the top of the page, the Header box:

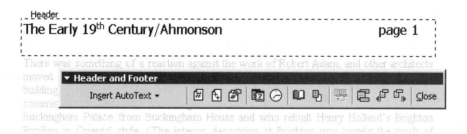

2. Type the header. As you do so, you can call on most of Word 2000's formatting commands. Boldface or italicize the header, for example. Click an Align button on the Formatting toolbar to center text or align it with the left or right margin. You can even include a clip art image in a header or footer.

3. Click the Switch Between Header and Footer button on the toolbar to enter a footer. You'll see the Footer box along the bottom of the page. Click the Switch Between Header and Footer button to go back and forth between the header and footer.

4. Enter the text of the footer. Again, you can call upon most of Word's formatting commands to decorate the footer.

5. Click the Close button on the Header and Footer toolbar to return to the document proper.

To edit a header or footer, choose View | Header and Footer to open the Header box, and go to it. If necessary, click the Switch Between Header and Footer button on the Header and Footer toolbar to get to the Footer box.

After you enter a header and footer, it appears, however faintly, at the top and bottom of pages in Print Layout view. To edit a header or footer in that view, simply double-click the header or footer. You'll see the Header or Footer box without having to choose View | Header and Footer.

The Buttons on the Header and Footer Toolbar

In the Introduction of this book, I promised not to include exhaustive lists of toolbar buttons or dialog box options. I said that such lists are useless for the most part because wading through an exhaustive list of buttons or option names in hopes of finding the one button or option that will do the trick is a waste of time. I promised a book that shows how to complete tasks, not a description of the Word 2000 software. I said I would describe toolbar buttons and dialog box options along the way only insofar as they are needed to complete a task.

However, because every rule requires an exception, following are descriptions of the buttons on the Header and Footer toolbar. These buttons are hard to figure out at first. And most of the buttons on the Header and Footer toolbar do not have equivalents on the command menus. A quick survey of the buttons will help you understand all the things you can do with headers and footers.

■ **Insert AutoText** Opens a drop-down list so you can include document information—the filename or author's name, for example—in a header or footer. You can also include your own AutoText entries. See "Creating and Inserting AutoText Entries" in Chapter 6 to learn what AutoText entries are.

Insert AutoText ▾

■ **Insert Page Number** Puts the page number in the header or footer. Page numbers are updated automatically. See "Numbering the Pages" later in this chapter.

FORMATTING TEXT
AND PAGES

■ **Insert Number of Pages** Lists the total number of pages in the document. The number is updated automatically. By typing **page**, clicking the Insert Page Number button, typing **of**, and clicking this button, you can include an up-to-date report on the page number and number of pages in the document in a header and footer.

■ **Format Page Number** Opens the Page Number Format dialog box so you can change page-numbering schemes. See "Numbering the Pages" later in this chapter.

■ **Insert Date** Lists the date the document was opened. When you print the document, it lists the date it was printed.

■ **Insert Time** Lists the time the document was opened, or, when you print the document, the time it was printed.

By the way, the date and time appear in the default date and time format, whatever it happens to be, when you click the Insert Date or Insert Time button. To enter the date or time in a different format, choose Insert | Date and Time, select a date or time format in the Date and Time dialog box, and click OK. "Quickly Entering the Date and Time" in Chapter 6 explains how to change the default date and time formats. *Hint:* Click the Default button in the Date and Time dialog box.

■ **Page Setup** Opens the Layout tab of the Page Setup dialog box so you can make different headers and footers for odd and even pages, change the header or footer on the first page of a document or section, or draw lines below or above headers and footers. See "Numbering the Pages" and "Drawing a Line Below a Header or Above a Footer," later in this chapter.

■ **Show/Hide Document Text**   Hides or shows the text in the document so you can see what it looks like in relation to the header or footer text.

■ **Same as Previous**   Allows you to create different headers or footers for different sections in a document or make the headers and footers in one section the same as the those in the previous section. See "Headers and Footers for Different Pages and Sections," later in this chapter.

■ **Switch Between Header and Footer**   Shows the Header box at the top of the page or the Footer box at the bottom so you can enter or edit a header or footer.

■ **Show Previous**   Shows the header or footer in the previous section of a document that has been divided into sections. Click this button to see what the previous section's header or footer is.

■ **Show Next**   Shows the header or footer in the next section.

■ **Close**   Closes the Header and Footer toolbar.

Numbering the Pages

Page numbers are probably the most common items found in headers and footers. Everybody wants to know what page they are currently reading. Everybody wants the sense of accomplishment that comes from glancing at the page number and finding out that they are on page 10 or 23 or 57. Read on to find out how to put simple page numbers in headers and footers, change the page-numbering scheme so that pages are numbered with Roman numerals or letters, make chapter numbers part of the page number, and put page numbers in the left or right margin instead of the header or footer.

Later in this chapter, "Headers and Footers for Different Pages and Sections" describes how to remove the page number from the first page of a document but keep pages numbers on subsequent pages.

The Quick, No-Frills Way to Number Pages

As you know if you've read the last page or two, you can click the Insert Page Number button on the Header and Footer toolbar (or press ALT-SHIFT-P) to insert the page number in a header or footer. Word offers a second, no-frills way to enter page numbers: the Insert | Page Numbers command. This command places a page number and nothing more in the header or footer. You get to decide where in the header or footer the page number goes.

Choose Insert | Page Numbers if all you want is a simple number on each page. However, if you intend to include headers or footers in your document, enter page numbers in the header or footer. A page number entered with the Insert | Page Numbers command does not fit beside text entered in a header or footer. The Insert | Page Numbers and View | Header and Footer commands do not work harmoniously.

Follow these steps to place a simple page number in the header or footer:

1. Choose Insert | Page Numbers. You will see the Page Numbers dialog box shown in Figure 9-5.

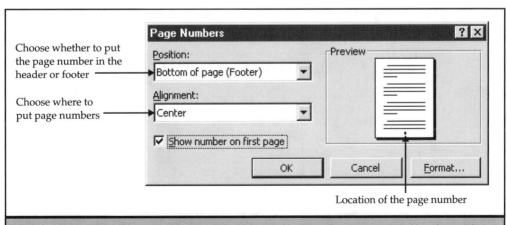

Figure 9-5. *Besides clicking the Insert Page Number button on the Header and Footer toolbar, you can insert page numbers with the Insert | Page Numbers command*

2. From the Position menu, choose whether to place the page number in the header or footer.

3. From the Alignment menu, choose to place the page number on the left side, middle, or right side of the header or footer; or, in the case of two-sided documents that will be bound, choose Inside to place page numbers near the binding (not recommended) or Outside to place them away from the binding. The sample page in the Preview box shows precisely where your page numbers will land.

4. Click OK.

As shown in Figure 9-6, page numbers entered with the Insert | Page Numbers command appear in frames. A *frame*, like a text box, is a container for text. Frames are kind of problematic, because when you delete page numbers, change their font, or change their position, you have to select either the text inside the frame or the frame itself.

To remove page numbers, change their fonts, or adjust their position on the page, start by going to the Header box or Footer box where the page number is: Either double-click the page number in Print Layout view, or choose View | Header and Footer to see the Header box. (If necessary, click the Switch Between Header and Footer button on the toolbar to see the page number in the Footer box.) Then follow these instructions:

■ **Deleting Page Numbers**   Click the page number to make its frame appear, and then gently move the pointer over the frame border. When you see the four-headed arrow, click again. Eight black selection handles appear on the frame to show it has been selected (see Figure 9-6). Click the DELETE button.

■ **Changing the Font of Page Numbers**   Click the page number to see the frame, and then carefully drag the mouse over the page number to select it. With the page number highlighted and selected (see Figure 9-6), choose a new font and font size from the Font and Font Size menus on the Formatting toolbar. If you

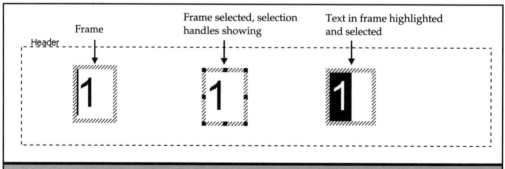

Figure 9-6.   *Page numbers appear in frames when you insert them with the Insert | Page Numbers command*

need to enlarge the frame, select it and move the mouse pointer over a corner. When you see the double-headed arrow, click and start dragging.

■ **Adjusting the Page Number Position**   Click the page number to see its frame, and then gently move the pointer over the frame border. When you see the four-headed arrow, click and drag the frame to a new position in the Header or Footer box.

Note

Page numbers are field codes. If you see field codes such as {PAGE} or {NUMPAGES} in the Header or Footer box instead of bona fide page numbers, you or someone else told Word to display field codes instead of field code results. To remedy the problem, choose Tools | Options, click the View tab in the Options dialog box, and uncheck the Field Codes check box. Chapter 23 explains fields.

Changing the Page-Numbering Scheme

The Arabic number system has been in use in Western culture since the thirteenth century, but that doesn't mean you can't forsake Arabic numerals and number pages as the Romans used to when Word VI came out in A.D. 6. Besides Roman numerals, you can number pages from A to Z with letters. Follow these steps to change the page-numbering scheme:

1. Either click the Format Page Number button on the Header and Footer toolbar (choose View | Header and Footer to see the toolbar) or click the Format button in the Page Numbers dialog box (choose Insert | Page Numbers to see the dialog box). The Page Number Format dialog box shown in Figure 9-7 appears.

2. From the Number Format menu, choose a page-numbering scheme.

3. Click OK.

Including Chapter Numbers in Page Numbers

In manuals and scholarly papers, the chapter number is sometimes made part of the page number. For example, the pages in Chapter 1 are numbered 1-1, 1-2, 1-3, and so on; the pages in Chapter 2 are numbered 2-1, 2-2, 2-3, and so on. The idea behind numbering pages this way is that including the chapter number in the page number helps readers find the material they are looking for.

You must do the following to your document in order to make the chapter number part of the page number:

■ Divide the document into sections so that each section comprises one chapter. Be sure to start each new break on an odd page (by choosing Odd Page in the Break dialog box). See "Section Breaks for Changing Layouts," earlier in this chapter.

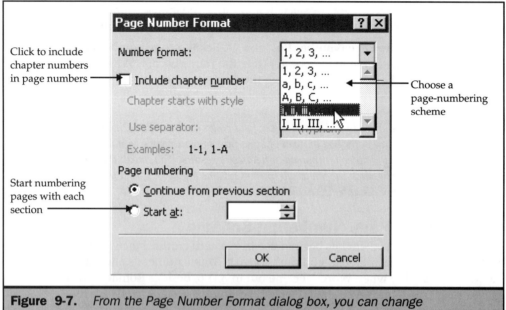

Click to include
chapter numbers
in page numbers

Choose a
page-numbering
scheme

Start numbering
pages with each
section

Figure 9-7. *From the Page Number Format dialog box, you can change page-numbering schemes, put chapter numbers in page numbers, and start numbering pages a new in a section*

■ Tell Word to start numbering each section beginning with page 1. See "Headers and Footers for Different Pages and Sections," later in this chapter (specifically, see "Numbering Pages Section by Section" under that heading).

■ Use the Format | Bullets and Numbering command to assign chapter numbers to the headings throughout your document. Be sure to assign chapter numbers and not outline numbers and letters. The chapter number schemes are found on the bottom half of the Outline Numbered tab in the Bullets and Numbering dialog box. See "Numbering the Headings and Chapters in a Document" in Chapter 10.

■ Make sure that each section begins with a heading assigned the same Heading 1 style and that subsequent headings in the section are assigned subordinate styles. Chapter 12 explains how to assign and modify styles. Word gets the chapter number part of the page number from headings assigned the Heading 1 style, so if more than one heading in a chapter is assigned the Heading 1 style, the page-numbering scheme will go awry in the middle of the chapter. For example, pages in Chapter 2 would be numbered 2-1, 2-2, 3-3, 3-4 if a second heading assigned the Heading 1 style appeared on page 3.

After the ground has been tilled and you are ready to include chapter numbers in page numbers, visit the first page of each section and do the following:

1. Either double-click the header or footer in Page Layout view or choose View | Header and Footer to see the Header or Footer box (click the Switch Between Header and Footer button on the Formatting toolbar, if necessary, to see the Footer box).

2. Click where you want the page number to appear. If a page number has already been entered, select it by dragging the pointer across it.

3. Click the Format Page Number button on the Header and Footer toolbar. The Page Number Format dialog box appears.

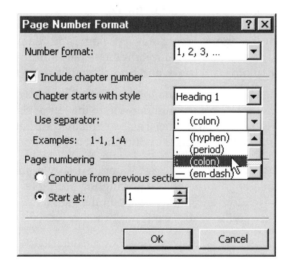

4. Check the Include Chapter Number check box.

5. In the Use Separator menu, choose a punctuation mark to separate the chapter number from the page number.

6. Click the Start At option button to make 1 appear in the Start At box.

7. Click OK.

Headers and Footers for Different Pages and Sections

The same header and footer does not have to appear on every page of a document. You can change headers and footer in the middle of a document, keep headers and footers from appearing on page 1, create different headers and footers for odd-numbered and even-numbered pages, and number pages starting with 1 in each section of a document that has been divided into sections. Better read on.

FORMATTING TEXT
AND PAGES

Putting Page Numbers in the Left or Right Margin

The top and bottom margins aren't the only places you can put page numbers. You can also put them in the left or right margin. A page number in the left or right margin looks kind of elegant and is a good way to impress your impressionable friends. Word offers two strategies for putting page numbers in the margin:

- Create a text box for the page number, drag the text box into the left or right margin, click in the text box, and click the Insert Page Number button on the Header and Footer toolbar (or press ALT-SHIFT-P). To do this successfully, however, you have to choose View Header and Footer and insert the text box while the Header box or Footer box is showing. Technically, the text box is part of the header or footer, even though it has been dragged into the left or right margin. Because the text box is part of the header or footer, it appears on every page, and the page number inside it is updated as you add pages to or remove pages from the document. Chapter 13 explains text boxes and how to manipulate them.

- Insert the page number with the Insert | Page Numbers command and then drag the frame that the page number is in to the left or right margin. As "The Quick, No-Frills Way to Number Pages" explained earlier in this chapter, you can move a frame by clicking and dragging it to a new position.

In Print Layout view, you can see page numbers that you moved to the left or right margin. To edit a page number that is dangling out there, either double-click it or choose View | Headers and Footers to open the Header or Footer box where the page number is lodged, and then start hacking away.

2

12:30 — Luncheon

"Lovely Italy's Magliano Region"
Mr. Ickles Bowdoin

"Whither the Whooping Crane"
Prof. Bertron Rainder

1:30 — Seminars

"In Search of the Birdwatcher's Paradise"
Prof. Harlin Quatley

Changing Headers and Footers in the Middle of a Document

In order to introduce a new header or footer in the middle of a document, you have to create a new section where you want the new header and footer to start appearing. (Earlier in this chapter, "Section Breaks for Changing Layouts" explains how to insert a section break.) Word assumes that you want to keep the same header and footer throughout, and it runs the headers and footers from the previous section into the new section as well.

Follow these steps to introduce a new header or footer after you have created a new section:

1. Choose View | Header and Footer (and click the Switch Between Header and Footer button if you want to enter a new footer). The Header or Footer box tells you which section you are in and informs you that the header or footer in this section is the same as that in the previous section. Notice as well that the Same as Previous button on the Header and Footer toolbar is pressed down.

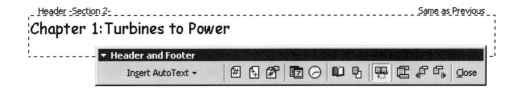

2. Click the Same as Previous button to disconnect the header and footer in the section you are in from the header and footer in the previous section. Now the Header or Footer box no longer reads "Same as Previous."

3. Delete the header or footer from the previous section and enter a new header or footer.

4. Click the Close button on the Header and Footer toolbar.

 On the Header and Footer toolbar are buttons called Show Previous and Show Next. You can click these buttons to read and perhaps change the header or footer in the next or previous section in your document.

Removing or Changing Headers and Footers on Page 1

Usually, a header and footer does not appear on the first page, or title page, of a document. Sometimes the header and footer are different on the first page. Follow these steps to remove or change the header and footer on the first page of a document or the first page of a section in a document:

1. Put the cursor in the section if you want to change the header and footer on its first page; it doesn't matter where the cursor is if you want to change the header and footer on the first page of a document.

2. Choose File | Page Setup or click the Page Setup button on the Header and Footer toolbar. You'll see the Page Setup dialog box.

3. Click the Layout tab, if necessary. Figure 9-8 shows the Layout tab.

4. Check the Different First Page check box.

5. In the Apply To menu, choose This Section to change the header and footer on the first page of the section, or Whole Document to change the first page of your document.

6. Click OK. No header or footer appears on the first page and the Header or Footer box reads, "First Page Header (or Footer)."

7. Enter a new header or footer if your purpose is to change the header or footer, not remove it.

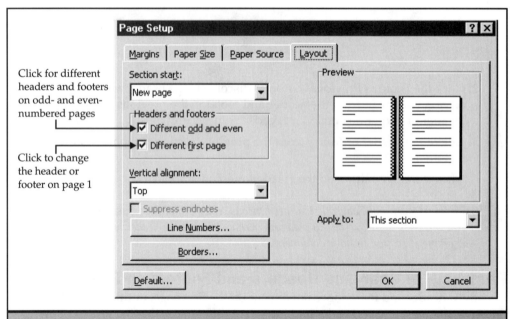

Figure 9-8.   *The Layout tab of the Page Setup dialog box is where you tell Word to put different headers and footers on different pages*

You can click the Show Next button on the Header and Footer toolbar to leap from the first page header or footer to the header or footer on the following page. Click the Show Previous button to return to the first page.

Headers and Footers for Odd- and Even-Numbered Pages

Earlier in this chapter, "'Mirror Margins for Bound, Two-Sided Pages" explained how readers see two pages instead of one when documents are bound and printed on both sides of the paper. Instead of a single page, readers see a page spread, with the odd-numbered page on the left and the even-numbered page on the right.

Usually, a different header and footer appear on either side of the page spread when a book or document is printed on both sides of the paper. In the book you are reading, for example, headers on even-numbered pages on the left side of the page spread list the title of this book; headers on odd-numbered pages on the right side of the page spread list which chapter you are reading. In two-sided documents, even-numbered pages always appear on the left side of the page spread and odd-numbered pages appear on the right side—they do, at least, if the document is printed and bound correctly.

If you opted for "mirror margins" because you intend to print your document on both sides of the paper and bind it, you owe it to yourself to create different headers and footers for odd- and even-numbered pages. Do it even if the text in headers and footers is the same on odd- and even-numbered pages to keep text from getting too close to the binding where it is hard to read. In the following document, for example, the text in the headers is the same, but I created a left-aligned header for even-numbered pages and a right-aligned header for odd-numbered pages to keep the headers from falling in the gutter, the place where the binding eats into pages.

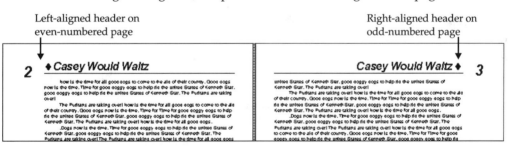

LEARN BY EXAMPLE

The 9-5 Odd and Even Headers practice document on the CD that comes with this book demonstrates how you can make different headers and footers appear on odd-and even-numbered pages.

Follow these steps to create different headers and footers for odd- and even-numbered pages:

1. Choose File | Page Setup or click the Page Setup button on the Header and Footer toolbar. You will see the Page Setup dialog box.

2. Click the Layout tab, if necessary (see Figure 9-8).

3. Check the Different Odd And Even Check box.

4. Click OK.

5. In your document, visit an odd-numbered page and enter headers and footers there; do the same on an even-numbered page.

Remember to right-align headers and footers on odd-numbered pages to keep headers and footers on those pages away from the bindings. To right-align text, click the Align Right button on the Formatting toolbar.

Numbering Pages Section by Section

Word offers a command for numbering pages starting at the beginning of a section. Use this command, for example, if your document begins with a title page, table of contents, preface, or other "front matter" material. Usually, front matter material is numbered in Roman numerals (as it is in this book), whereas the rest of the document is numbered, beginning with the first chapter or first heading, in Arabic numerals. If yours is a long document with a table of contents and other front matter, create a section for the front matter and start numbering pages anew in Arabic numerals where the document really begins, in section 2.

Follow these steps to number the pages of a section beginning with 1 (or a, A, I, i, I—whatever numbering scheme you choose):

1. Place the cursor in the section you want to start numbering at page 1.

2. Either click the Format Page Number button on the Header and Footer toolbar (choose View | Header and Footer to see the toolbar) or click the Format button in the Page Numbers dialog box (choose Insert | Page Numbers to see the dialog box). The Page Number Format dialog box appears (see Figure 9-7).

3. Under Page Numbering, click the Start At option button. The number 1 (or a, A, i, or I) appears in the text box.

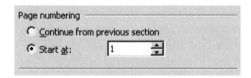

4. Click OK.

Drawing a Line Below a Header or Above a Footer

One of the easiest ways to spruce up a document is to draw a line below headers and above footers. The line separates the header or footer from the main text in the document. In Word, you can choose from many different lines, as this illustration shows:

The Necessity of Decorating Headers   1

Headers and You   4

Footing the Bill   3

Staying on a Good Footing   6

Follow these steps to place a line—that is, a border line—below a header or above a footer:

1. Either double-click a header or footer in Print Layout view or choose View | Header and Footer to see your header. If you want to draw a line above a footer, click the Switch Between Header and Footer button on the Header and Footer toolbar.

2. Choose Format | Borders and Shading and click the Borders tab in the Borders and Shading dialog box, if necessary.

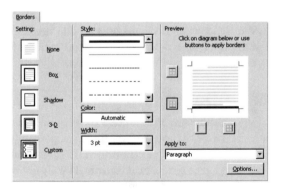

3. Under Setting, click the Box option (the None option is for removing page borders).

4. On the Style menu, find and click the kind of line you want. The lines get more exotic the further you travel down the menu.

5. Choose a width for the line from the Width drop-down menu.

6. Make sure Paragraph is selected in the Apply To menu.

7. Make a line appear below the header or above the footer by clicking in the Preview box:

   ■ **Below a Header**   Click the bottom of the box to make a line appear, or else click the button with the line along the bottom.

   ■ **Above a Footer**   Click the top of the box, or else click the button with the line long the top.

8. Click OK.

You can click the Options button in the Borders and Shading dialog box and enter measurements in the Border and Shading Options dialog box if you want to be specific about how close the line can come to the header or footer.

Pages throughout a document are numbered consecutively. When you start numbering a section at page 1, the following sections are renumbered. If your document has many sections and you want each to be numbered starting at 1, visit each section and give the command to number it starting with 1.

Changing the Size and Orientation of Pages

One of the surest ways to make a document stand out is to print it on unusual-size paper or change orientation and print the document in landscape view instead of portrait view. A 'zine printed on oblong paper or a chapbook printed on half-size pages sticks out in a crowd. Read on to find out how to change the orientation of a page, print on unusual-size paper, and print pages so you can cut them in half and make a chapbook.

Creating a Landscape Document

A *landscape* document is wider than it is long, like a painting of a landscape. Most documents, like the pages of the book you are reading, are printed in the *portrait* style, with the short sides of the page on the top and bottom. Figure 9-9 demonstrates the difference between portrait and landscape orientation. The figure shows the same page—more or less—in portrait and landscape style.

Note   *To change the orientation of one or two pages in the middle of a document, you have to create a new section for the pages. See "Section Breaks for Changing Layouts" earlier in this chapter.*

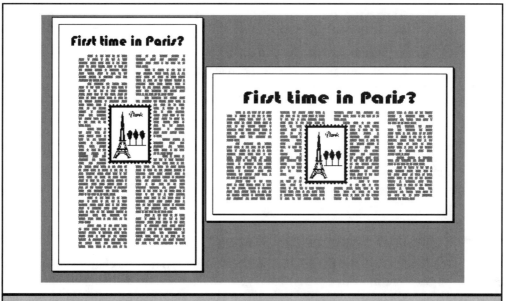

Figure 9-9.   *A portrait-style document (left) and a landscape-style document (right)*

Follow these steps to change the orientation of the pages in a document:

1. Choose File | Page Setup to open the Page Setup dialog box.
2. Click the Paper Size tab.
3. Click the Landscape option button.
4. If you are changing the orientation of pages in a section, choose This Section from the Apply To menu.
5. Click OK.

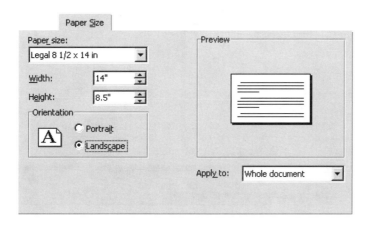

Printing a Document on Legal- or Unusual-Size Paper

As long as your printer can handle it, you can print on unusual-size paper. Does legal-size paper (8.5 × 14 inches) count as unusual? Well, you can print pages on legal-size paper, too, as well as the A4 European standard (210 × 297 millimeters). To tell Word what size paper you want to print on:

1. Choose File | Page Setup.
2. Click the Paper Size tab in the Page Setup dialog box.
3. Either choose a size from the Paper Size menu or choose the Custom Size option and then enter the dimension of the paper you want to print on in the Width and Height text box.
4. Click OK.

Printing Half-Size Chapbook Pages

A *chapbook* is a book that is published on half-size pages. To make a chapbook, you print the pages on normal-size paper. Then you cut the pages in half with a paper-cutter and staple them together. Not so long ago, printing pages for a chapbook was a monumental chore because you had to figure out for yourself where to divide the text in the middle of each page to make sure nothing got lost when you cut the pages in half.

However, creating half-size paper for chapbooks has become a lot easier, since Word offers a command for dividing the pages in half. As Figure 9-10 shows, Word

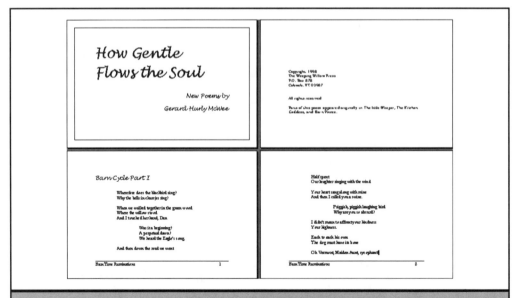

Figure 9-10. *As you work with half-size chapbook pages, Word shows you where they will break after you cut them in half*

runs the text from half-page to half-page and treats each page as though it had already been cut in half. You can include page numbers, headers, and footers on the half-pages. All you have to do is cut the pages in half and staple them together after they are printed. In Print Layout view and Print Preview view, you can see where the half-pages will to be divided when you cut them in half.

To create chapbook pages, choose File | Page Setup and click the Margins tab in the Page Setup dialog box. Then click the 2 Pages Per Sheet button and click OK.

Decorating a Page with a Border

A border around a page is mighty handsome. And page borders tell readers that the page is an important one. Often the title page of a document has a page border around it. Certificates, menus, and invitations all deserve page borders. You can place borders on all four sides of the page, or on three sides, two sides, or one side. Word offers many kinds of page borders. You can even put artwork around the sides of the page. This illustration shows examples of page borders.

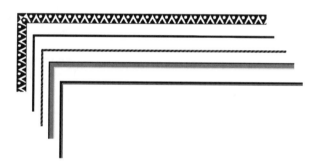

You're ready to go if you want to put borders around the first page in a document or section. But if you want to put borders around a certain page or certain pages in the middle of a document, create a section for that page or those pages (see "Section Breaks for Changing Layouts" earlier in this chapter). Word offers commands for putting borders around all the pages in the document, an entire section, the first page in a section, and all pages in a section except the first page.

Caution   *Putting page borders on pages with headers and footers is not recommended because the page borders usually run too close to the header and footer. Besides, on a page without borders, it is easy to see that the header and footer are in the margin, but on a page with borders, the header and footer appear to be part of the main text. Remove the header and footer from the first page of a document or section before you put borders on a first page. Earlier in this chapter, "Headers and Footers for Different Pages and Sections" explains how to remove headers and footers from first pages.*

Follow these steps to put a border around pages:

1. Click in the section whose first page or subsequent pages you want to place borders on. If your document is not divided into sections, where the cursor is doesn't matter.

2. Choose Format | Borders and Shading to open the Borders and Shading dialog box. If you happen to be in the Page Setup dialog box (choose File | Page Setup or click the Page Setup button on the Header and Footer toolbar to get there), you can also click the Borders button on the Layout tab.

3. Click the Page Border tab, as shown in Figure 9-11. Be prepared to wrestle with the options on the Page Border tab. The Preview box shows what your page borders will look like as you choose a setting, style, color, and line width.

4. Under Setting, choose which kind of border you want. The None option is for removing borders. The Custom option is for drawing different borderlines on different sides of the page.

5. On the Style menu, choose what kind of line you want.

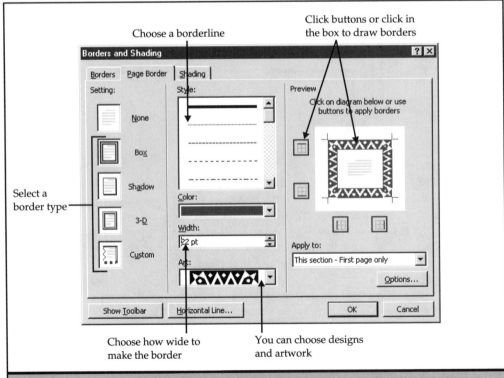

Figure 9-11. *You can be quite the artist when it comes to drawing borders around the edge of a page*

6. From the Art menu, you can choose a design instead of a line.

7. If you so desire, choose a color for borderlines from the Color menu. The Automatic option removes colors.

8. In the Width menu, enter a point-size setting to tell Word how fat to make the borderlines or artwork.

9. Either click the Border buttons or click on the sides of the Preview box to draw the borders on the sides of the sample page.

10. Choose an Apply To option to tell Word on which pages to put borders. Choose This Section – First Page Only to put the borders around the first page of a document even if it isn't divided into sections.

11. Click OK.

To remove borders from a page, choose Format | Borders and Shading, click the Page Border tab, choose the None setting, and click OK.

Certain kinds of printers can't print text that falls too close to the edge of the page. If your printer is one of them, click the Options button on the Page Border tab (see Figure 9-11). In the Border and Shading Options dialog box, increase the measurements in the Top, Bottom, Left, and Right text boxes to move page borders further away from the edge of the page.

LEARN BY EXAMPLE
Open the 9-6 Borders document on the CD to see an example of a document in which different page borders are used.

Aligning Text with Respect to the Top and Bottom of the Page

For title pages and other marquee pages in a document, Word offers commands for aligning text with respect to the top and bottom of the page. Figure 9-12 shows the four ways to align text on a page. You can align text in these ways:

- **Top-Aligned**   Pushes text to the top of the page. Normally, text on pages is top-aligned.

- **Centered**   Centers the text so that the same amount of empty space appears above and below the text.

- **Justified**   Spreads the text evenly across the length of the page.

- **Bottom-Aligned**   Pushes text to the bottom of the page.

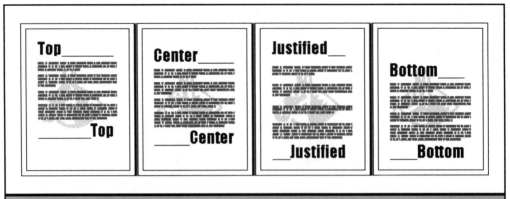

Figure 9-12. *The four ways to align text with respect to the top and bottom of the page: Top, Center, Justified, and Bottom*

 Word doesn't offer a means of realigning the first page of a document or section but not the other pages. To center, justify, or bottom-align a page, you must create a section for it. See "Section Breaks for Changing Layouts" earlier in this chapter.

Follow these steps to align a page with respect to the top and bottom margin:

1. Put the cursor in the page you want to realign. Unless you want to re-align all the pages in the document, you should have created a section for the page.

2. Choose File | Page Setup.

3. Click the Layout tab in the Page Setup dialog box.

4. In the Apply To menu, choose This Section.

5. Choose an option from the Vertical Alignment menu and click OK.

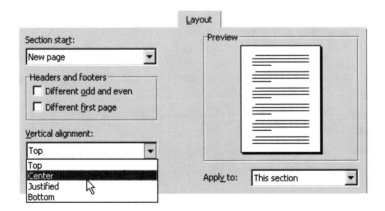

LEARN BY EXAMPLE
The 9-7 Page Align practice document on the CD shows the four different ways that text can be aligned with respect to the top and bottom margin.

Exam | MOUS Exam Objectives Explored in Chapter 9

Objective	Heading	Practice File
Set margins	"Setting the Margins"	9-1 Margins
Create sections with formatting that differs from other sections	"Section Breaks for Changing Layouts"	9-2 Sections
Create and modify headers and footers	"Entering a Header or Footer"	9-3 Header and Footer
Insert page numbers	"Numbering the Pages"	9-3 Header and Footer
Format first page different from subsequent pages*	"Headers and Footers for Different Pages and Sections"	9-4 First Page Header
Create and modify pages borders*	"Decorating a Page with a Border"	9-6 Borders
Set page orientation	"Creating a Landscape Document"	
Align text vertically	"Aligning Text with Respect to the Top and Bottom of the Page"	9-7 Page Align

* Denotes an Expert exam objective.

FORMATTING TEXT
AND PAGES

Ten Tasks to Do Right Away When You Start a Complex Document

You can spare yourself heartache and perhaps a headache by doing these important tasks straightaway when you start work on a complex document such as a long report, manual, or white paper.

1. SEE IF YOU CAN USE ONE OF WORD'S TEMPLATES.   Half the work of formatting a document is done already if you create it with a template. Choose File | New, click the Publications or Reports tab in the New dialog box, and see if you can find a template to help you on your way. The Publications tab offers templates called Manual and Thesis, and the Reports tab presents three different report templates. Check 'em out.

2. DECIDE HOW MANY STYLES YOU NEED—AND CREATE THE STYLES. Chapter 12 explains how you can save hours and hours of formatting time by thoughtfully creating the styles you need for a document. Choosing styles from the Style menu on the Formatting toolbar is by far the easiest way to format a document. Especially if others will work on the complex document you are creating, nail down the styles from the start and tell others to use your styles, not invent their own, as they format the document.

3. USE THE OUTLINE FEATURE TO DRAW AN OUTLINE.   For long documents, the Outline feature is invaluable. You can use it to stay organized, see how the different parts of a document fit together, promote and demote headings, and even get quickly from place to place. If your document needs organizing, you can move headings and subheadings from one place to another. Chapter 19 explains how the Outline feature works.

4. CREATE THE SECTIONS YOU NEED—IF YOU NEED SECTIONS.   Dividing a document into sections after it has been written is hard because you have to go through the business of disconnecting each section from the previous one when you enter the headers and footers. Create sections from the get-go if you happen to know that your document requires sections. You'll save time that way.

5. SET THE MARGINS.   Changing margins after a document has been written and formatted is asking for trouble. All indentations are made from the left and right margin, so if you change margin settings, indentations change as well. And pages break in unexpected places. Give a moment's consideration to margins as soon as you create a new document.

6. CREATE THE HEADERS AND FOOTERS.   The purpose of a header or footer is to tell the reader what he or she is reading. Headers and footers can also help writers by showing them what they are supposed to write. If you enter the headers and footers early on, you will never get lost in a document. All you have to do is look at the header and footer to see where you are and what you are supposed to be writing.

7. DECIDE HOW TO NUMBER THE PAGES.   As "Putting Headers and Footers on Pages" in this chapter pointed out, there are about 15 different ways to number the pages in a Word document. You can opt for no-frills page numbers by putting the numbers in frames. You can start numbering pages anew in each section. You can remove page numbers from the first page of a section or document. You can choose among different numbering schemes. Decide how to number the pages early on, while you are entering the headers and footers, to get this irksome chore out of the way.

8. CHOOSE A PAPER SIZE AND ORIENTATION.   Like margin sizes, page size and orientation settings should be made from the start. Changing the page size or orientation after you have written and formatted a document causes nothing but trouble because lines break in new places and you have to do much of the formatting all over again. "Changing the Size and Orientation of Pages" in this chapter explains how to choose a page size and orientation.

9. TURN OFF BACKGROUND PAGINATION.   "Background pagination" is a feature whereby Word redraws page breaks as you edit text. In other words, when you remove a paragraph or add a paragraph, all page breaks in the document are redrawn. Redrawing the page breaks is fine and dandy except when you are working on a very long document with graphics, charts, and other memory-hungry items. Redrawing pages around those items can take a long time. You have to twiddle your thumbs while Word draws the page breaks.

To turn off the background pagination, choose Tools | Options, click the General tab, and uncheck the Background Pagination check box. Be sure to turn the feature back on again when you are finished editing and you want to see where the page breaks will occur in your document.

10. CREATE A MASTER DOCUMENT—MAYBE.   The Master Document feature takes outlines a step further and lets you create a master document—a document made of subdocuments that you can bring in or out of the master document at will. Chapter 19 explains master documents, their pitfalls, and how you can use them to stay organized in really big jobs if you have enough foresight and cunning.

The
Complete
Reference

Word
2000

Chapter 10

Handling Lists
and Numbered Items

This chapter looks at lists and numbered items. What is a word-processed document without a list or two? It's like an emperor without any clothes on. This chapter explains how to alphabetize a list, make bulleted and numbered lists, and give the chapters and appendixes numbers so that you can use the numbers in page-numbering schemes, for example. You will also learn how to get address data from an e-mail program and save it in a Word document.

Numbered and bulleted lists can be as simple or complex as you want them to be. Word offers a bunch of different ways to format lists, but if you are in a hurry or you don't care whether your Word documents look like everyone else's, you may as well take advantage of the Numbering and Bullets button on the Formatting toolbar. Click either of those buttons to get a generic numbered or bulleted list. Nonconformists and people with nothing else to do, however, can try their hand and at making a fancy list. This chapter covers that topic, too.

"Numbering the Lines in a Document" in Chapter 21 explains that particular aspect of numbering in Word 2000. Chapter 21 also describes how to number the paragraphs in a document.

Alphabetizing and Sorting Lists

Alphabetizing a list, especially a long one, is one of those tasks that make most people wince. Besides the tediousness of it, deciding whether certain words come before or after others can be difficult. In a list of cities, for example, which comes first, San Jose, California or San José, Costa Rica? What does the accented "e" do to alphabetical order? And how do you account for blank spaces? Does Sandia or San Diego come first in a list?

Fortunately for you, Word 2000 offers the Table | Sort command for alphabetizing and sorting lists. As demonstrated in Figure 10-1, *sorting* means to arrange text alphabetically from A to Z (or Z to A), numbers in order from smallest to largest (or largest to smallest), and dates in order from past to future (or future to past). When you use the Table | Sort command, Word makes all the little decisions about alphabetizing or sorting for you. Best of all, Word rearranges the list in the right order, so you don't have to cut and paste names, dates, or numbers to put the list in order.

The Table | Sort command is meant for sorting data in tables, but you can use it on plain lists as long as the list entries are entered the same way. For example, if you are alphabetizing a list by last name, make sure each entry starts with a last name. If by accident an entry reads "John Smith" instead of "Smith, John," Word places John Smith with the J's although he belongs with the S's. Before you sort a list, read it over to make sure the entries were made correctly and consistently.

Follow these steps to sort a list:

1. Select the list.

2. Choose Table | Sort. The Sort Text dialog box appears (see Figure 10-1).

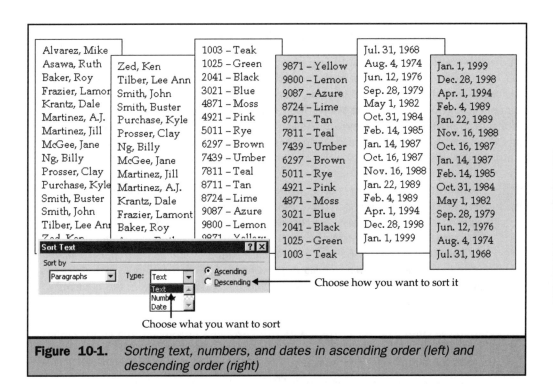

Figure 10-1.   *Sorting text, numbers, and dates in ascending order (left) and
descending order (right)*

3. In the Type drop-down list, make sure the correct data type—Text, Number, or
   Date—appears, and choose the right data type if necessary.

4. Click the Ascending or Descending option button:

   ■ **Ascending**   Arranges text from A to Z, numbers from smallest to largest,
     and dates from earliest in time to latest in time.

   ■ **Descending**   Arranges text from Z to A, numbers from largest to smallest,
     and dates from latest in time to earliest.

5. Click OK.

*The Then By options in the Sort Text dialog box are for use with tables. See "Sorting, or
Reordering, a Table" in Chapter 14.*

LEARN BY EXAMPLE
*Open the 10-1 Sort practice file on the CD that comes with this book to try out the
different ways of sorting lists.*

Saving Address Data in a Word Document

On the subject of lists, how would you like to save the list of addresses, e-mail addresses, and phone numbers in the e-mail program you use in a Word document? You could tack the list to a bulletin board and refer to it when you want to call someone. Or you could use the Word document as a means of backing up the address information in your e-mail program. As long as your e-mail program has a File | Export command, you can save the addresses and phone numbers you cherish in a Word document.

Note   *The instructions presented here for saving address data from an e-mail program in a Word document are specific to two e-mail programs: Outlook 2000 and Outlook Express 5. However, the basic instructions for exporting address data from an e-mail program are the same no matter which e-mail program you use. If you don't have Outlook 2000 or Outlook Express 5, see if the e-mail program you use offers commands for saving address data in a comma- or tab-separated file. Very likely it does. After you have saved the data in a comma- or tab-separated file, skip to step 8 in the following instruction list.*

Follow these steps to save address data from an e-mail program in a Word table:

1. Open the e-mail program you use.
2. Choose the File | Export command. Where this command is located, and what it is named, varies from program to program.
   - **In Outlook** Choose File | Import and Export, choose Export to a File in the Import and Export Wizard dialog box, and click Next.
   - **In Outlook Express** Choose File | Export | Address Book.
3. In the dialog box that asks how you want to export your address file, choose Comma Separated or Tab Separated. Figure 10-2 shows a comma- and tab-separated file. In a comma-separated file, each person's information—name, phone number, e-mail address, and so on—is separated by a comma. In a tab-separated file, each piece of information is separated from the next by a tab stop. Either way, turning a comma- or tab-separated file into a Word table is easy.
4. Click the Next button (in Outlook 2000) or the Export button (in Outlook Express).
   - **In Outlook Only** Choose the address book from which to export the data—Contacts or Personal—and click the Next button.
5. Choose where to store the address data and what to name it.
   - **In Outlook** In the Export to a File dialog box, click the Browse button. In the Browse dialog box, find and select the folder where you will store the address list data. Then enter a name for the data file in the File Name text box and click OK. Click Next in the Export to a File dialog box.

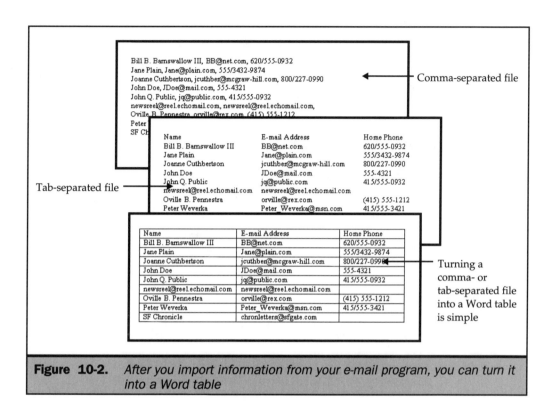

Figure 10-2. *After you import information from your e-mail program, you can turn it into a Word table*

■ **In Outlook Express**   In the CSV Export dialog box, click the Browse button to open the Save As dialog box and tell Word in which folder to store the address data file. Enter a name for the file in the File Name text box, and click the Save button. Click Next in the CSV dialog box.

6. Decide how much of your address data to save and place in a Word document. How much address data you include in the address file depends on what you want to use the file for. In this step, you decide which information is important enough to include in the file.

Caution *Storing all the address data creates a very, very large file—one too large to be of any use in a Word document. Only include all the data in the address file if your intention is to create a backup file for the addresses in your e-mail program.*

■ **In Outlook**   In the Export to a File dialog box, click the Finish button to keep and back up all the address data. To only place some of the data in the file, click the Map Custom Fields button. You will see the Map Custom Fields dialog box shown in Figure 10-3. To remove data from the file, drag

FORMATTING TEXT AND PAGES

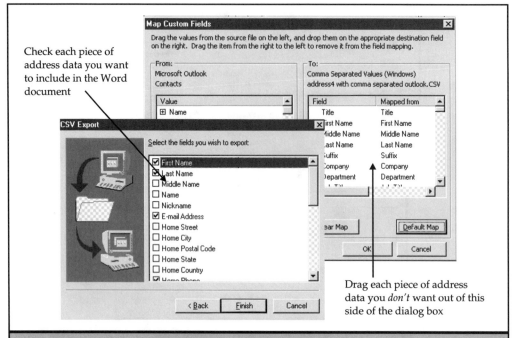

Check each piece of address data you want to include in the Word document

Map Custom Fields

Drag the values from the source file on the left, and drop them on the appropriate destination field on the right. Drag the item from the right to the left to remove it from the field mapping.

From:
Microsoft Outlook
Contacts

To:
Comma Separated Values (Windows)
address4 with comma separated outlook.CSV

Value		Field	Mapped from
⊞ Name		Title	Title
		First Name	First Name
		Middle Name	Middle Name
		Last Name	Last Name
		Suffix	Suffix
		Company	Company
		Department	Department

CSV Export

Select the fields you wish to export:

- ☑ First Name
- ☑ Last Name
- ☐ Middle Name
- ☐ Name
- ☐ Nickname
- ☑ E-mail Address
- ☐ Home Street
- ☐ Home City
- ☐ Home Postal Code
- ☐ Home State
- ☐ Home Country
- ☑ Home Phone

Clear Map   Default Map

OK   Cancel

< Back   Finish   Cancel

Drag each piece of address data you *don't* want out of this side of the dialog box

Figure 10-3.   *Choosing which parts of the address file to put in the Word document in Outlook 2000 (above) and Outlook Express 5 (below)*

names out of the Field column on the right side of the dialog box and drop them in the left side of the dialog box—that's right, drag them from the right side of the dialog box to the left. As you do so, the list of fields on the right side gets pared down. In Figure 10-3, for example, only four pieces of information from the address file will appear in the Word document. When you have pared the list to only the data you want for reference purposes, click OK to return to the Export to File dialog box.

■ **In Outlook Express**   In the CSV Export dialog box shown in Figure 10-3, click the Finish button right away if you want to keep all the data for backup purposes. To be choosy about which data to include in the address file, uncheck boxes. A check next to a box means that you want to include the data in the address file.

7. Click the Finish button.

Now that you have created and saved the tab-separated or comma-separated file, either put it away for safekeeping if you created it for backup purposes, or do the following to place the data in a Word document and turn the data into a table you can refer to.

8. In Word, open a new document and choose Insert | File.

9. In the Insert File dialog box, find the tab- or comma-separated file that you named and saved in step 5, click the file's name, and click the Insert button.

10. In the File Conversion dialog box, click the Plain Text option button and click OK. Your address information, looking much like confetti, appears in the Word document.

11. Press CTRL-A or choose Edit | Select All to select all the data in the document.

12. Choose Table | Convert | Text to Table. You will see the Convert Text to Table dialog box.

13. Under Separate Text At on the bottom of the dialog box, click the Tabs option button if your address file is a tab-separated file, or the Commas option button if your file is comma-separated, and click OK. The data appears in a Word table.

14. Save your new Word document.

Chapter 14 explains how to format a table, if that proves necessary or if you want to cut a column or two or row or two out of the table.

The Bare-Bones Basics: Bulleted and Numbered Lists

Look no further if you are new to Word and you want to know how to make a bulleted or numbered list the conventional way. As I mentioned at the start of this chapter, making a bulleted or numbered list is simple if you use the generic numbers and bullets that Word provides. Throughout this chapter, I will explain how to twist, tweak, and torture bulleted and numbered lists to make them your own. For now, here are the basics of creating a bulleted or numbered list according to Word's specifications. You will also find instructions here for telling Word not to generate numbered and bulleted lists automatically.

LEARN BY EXAMPLE
Open the 10-2 Bullets and Numbers practice file on the CD if you want to try your hand at working with bulleted and numbered lists.

Making a Generic Bulleted List

In typesetting terms, a *bullet* is a black, filled-in circle or other character that marks an item on a list. As Figure 10-4 shows, bulleted lists are useful when you want to present the reader with alternatives or present a list in which the items are not ranked in any order. Follow these steps to create a bulleted list:

1. Click the Bullets button on the Formatting toolbar. The standard round bullet appears.

 Note   *If you don't see the standard bullet character when you click the Bullets button, you or someone else has been tinkering with the bullet character settings. Later in this chapter, "Changing Bullets and Numbering Schemes" explains how to mark bulleted lists with different characters and how to start using the standard bullet character again.*

2. Type the first entry in the list and click ENTER. A bullet appears on the next line as well.

3. Type the next and subsequent entries.

4. Either backspace over the last bullet or press the ENTER key twice to end the list and keep bullets from appearing at the start of each line.

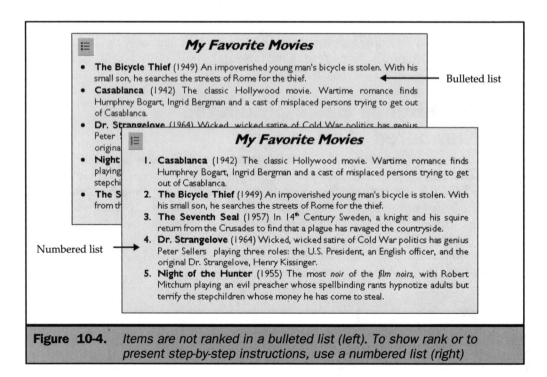

Figure 10-4.   *Items are not ranked in a bulleted list (left). To show rank or to present step-by-step instructions, use a numbered list (right)*

The easiest way to create a bulleted list is to type it first without clicking the Bullets button. Type all the list entries, select them, and then click the Bullets button.

Making a Generic Numbered List

Numbered lists are invaluable in manuals and books like this one for presenting step-by-step instructions. You can also rank the items in a list by making the list a numbered list (see Figure 10-4). Lists are numbered sequentially. When you remove an item from a list or stick a new item in the middle of the list, Word renumbers the list for you.

Follow these steps to create a generic numbered list:

1. Click the Numbering button on the Formatting toolbar. You will see the number 1.

2. Type the first entry in the list and press ENTER. The number 2 appears on the next line.

3. Type the rest of the list.

4. To end the list and prevent Word from putting numbers at the start of lines, either press BACKSPACE to remove the last number or press ENTER twice.

Numbering a list after you've typed it makes typing the list a little easier. Try typing the list entries, selecting the list, and clicking the Numbering button to create a numbered list.

Preventing Word from Generating Numbered and Bulleted Lists Automatically

Word numbers lists automatically when you type **1.** (or **A.**, **a.**, **I.**, or **i.**), press the SPACEBAR or the TAB key, type a line, and press ENTER. Do that and the number 2 (or B, b, II, or ii) followed by a period appears on the next line. Similarly, the program creates a bulleted list automatically if you start a line with an asterisk (*) or one of several other characters or character combinations ("Using Symbols and Pictures for Bullets," later in this chapter, describes them all), press the SPACEBAR or TAB key, type a line, and press ENTER.

Many Word users, however, think that automatic numbered and bulleted lists are a nuisance. These users would like to create lists on their own without the invisible hand of Word butting in. Follow these steps if automatic numbered and bulleted lists annoy you and you want to keep Word from creating lists automatically:

1. Choose Tools | AutoCorrect.

2. Click the AutoFormat As You Type tab in the AutoCorrect dialog box.

FORMATTING TEXT AND PAGES

3. Uncheck the Automatic Bulleted Lists and Automatic Numbered Lists
check boxes and click OK.

AutoFormat As You Type

Apply as you type
☐ Headings   ☐ Automatic bulleted lists
☑ Borders   ☐ Automatic numbered lists
☑ Tables

Removing the Bullets or Numbers from a List

Removing the bullets or numbers from a list is quite simple:

1. Select the list.

2. Click the Bullets or Numbering button. The bullets or numbers are removed
instantly and you are left with several paragraphs where a list used to be.

The other way to remove bullets or numbers is to select the list, choose Format |
Bullets and Numbering, and click the None button in the Bullets and Numbering
dialog box.

*To turn a numbered list into a bulleted list or a bulleted list into a numbered list, select
the list and click the Numbering button or Bullets button on the Formatting toolbar.*

Resuming and Restarting Lists

Suppose you write a numbered or bulleted list, stop the list at the fourth entry, type a
paragraph or two of commentary, and decide to resume the list. In the case of a
bulleted list, resuming the list is easy. All you have to do is click the Bullets button on
the Formatting toolbar and start typing. But resuming a numbered list is more
complicated. If you stopped the list at step 4 and want to resume it later at step 5, for
example, you have to tell Word to pick up the list at step 5.

Follow these steps to resume a numbered list:

1. Either click where you want to resume the list or, if you have already typed the
next entry or entries in the list, select the next entry or entries.

2. Click the Numbering button on the Formatting toolbar. Word numbers the list
beginning with 1. Now tell Word to resume numbering the list.

3. Either right-click and choose Bullets and Numbering from the shortcut menu or choose Format | Bullets and Numbering. You will see the Numbered tab of the Bullets and Numbering dialog box.

4. Under List Numbering, click the Continue Previous List option button and click OK.

Once in a while you may attempt to start a numbered list and Word will mistakenly think you want to resume a list. When that happens, the numbered list you want to start at 1 starts at 3, 4, 5, or another number. To remedy the problem, choose Format | Bullets and Numbers and click the Restart Numbering button in the Bullets and Numbering dialog box.

Another Way to Interrupt and Resume Numbered Lists

Another way to interrupt a numbered list with a paragraph or two of commentary is to press SHIFT-ENTER instead of ENTER after you type a list entry. As you know if you read "Starting a New Paragraph, Line, or Page" in Chapter 2, pressing SHIFT-ENTER tells Word to break a line without starting a new paragraph. When you press SHIFT-ENTER at the end of a numbered line, the next line is not numbered because it is officially part of the previous line. Instead of getting a number, the line following the numbered line is indented.

Press SHIFT-ENTER, not ENTER, to keep the next line from being numbered

3. Vigorously swing the baseball bat around, "cracking your wrists" as you do so, and continue with the follow through.
As the bat swings round the body, the hips move parallel to home plate in a swivel-like motion
Moreover, bodyweight is transferred from the back leg to the front leg as the bat travels its course.

4. Transfer the weight of the bat from the arm farthest from the pitcher to the arm closest to the pitcher.

Keep pressing SHIFT-ENTER to end paragraphs until you reach what you want to be the next numbered line. When you get there, press ENTER. The next line is numbered.

FORMATTING TEXT AND PAGES

Fancy Formats for Bulleted and Numbered Lists

Word makes it fairly easy to do fancy things to lists. As shown in Figure 10-5, you can start by choosing Format | Bullets and Numbering to open the Bullets and Numbering dialog box and choosing a different bullet character or numbering scheme. And if you are daring and want to get very fancy, you can click the Customize button in the Bullets and Numbering dialog box, visit the Customize dialog box, and really go to town. These pages explain how to choose a new numbering scheme for numbered lists, change the look of bullets and numbers, and change the indentation and alignment of bulleted and numbered lists. First, however, a word about what happens in the Bullets and Numbering dialog box when you do fancy things to lists...

Tip
If you go to the trouble to create a new format for a bulleted or numbered list, you might as well create a style for your new format. After you create the style, you can copy the bulleted or numbered list format to other documents and templates and use it there. What's more, applying a style is the fastest way to reformat a bulleted or numbered list. Instead of visiting the Bullets and Numbering dialog box, all you have to do is choose your bulleted or numbered list style from the Style menu on the Formatting toolbar. Chapter 12 explains styles and how to copy them from document to document and template to template.

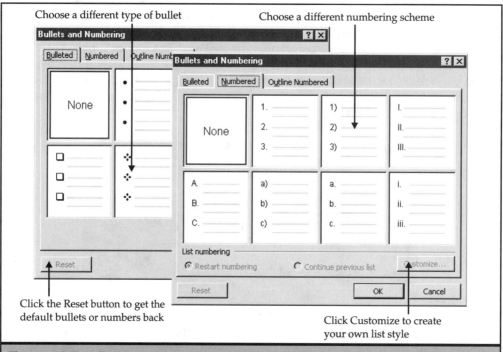

Figure 10-5. *To create fancy bulleted and numbered lists, start by choosing Format | Bullets and Numbering to visit the Bullets and Numbering dialog box*

What Changing List Formats Does to the Bullets and Numbering Dialog Box

After you create a new format for a bulleted or numbered list, your new format appears as a choice in the Bullets and Numbering dialog box (see Figure 10-5). This card shark, for example, created formats in which clubs, diamonds, hearts, and spades are used as bullet characters. Now the Bulleted tab of the Bullets and Numbering dialog box offers the four bulleted list formats that she created:

Being able to choose a fancy format you created yourself in the Bullets and Numbering dialog box is convenient. All you have to do to apply your fancy format to a list is choose it in the dialog box. In fact, after you have applied the fancy format, you can apply it again simply by clicking the Numbering or Bullets button on the Formatting toolbar. Clicking the Numbering or Bullets button applies the last numbering or bulleted list format that you selected in the Bullets and Numbering dialog box, whatever that format happened to be.

As convenient as choosing fancy formats in the Bullets and Numbering dialog box is, however, sooner or later you might want the original bullets and numbers back. To make one of the default bullets and numbers shown in Figure 10-5 appear again in the Bullets and Numbering dialog box, select a format and click the Reset button. A message box asks if you want to "reset this gallery position to the default setting?" Click Yes.

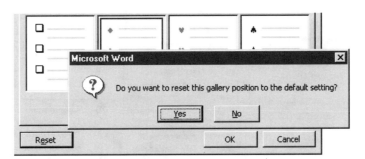

By the way, if you try to click the Reset button but you can't because it is grayed out, you are dealing with a default format already. You can't change it back because, to paraphrase James Brown, "it is what it is."

Choosing a New Numbering Scheme

As Figure 10-6 shows, Word offers a bunch of different ways to number lists. The program also gives you the opportunity to decide for yourself which character comes after the letter or number—a period, for example, or a parenthesis or hyphen. Follow these steps to choose a numbering scheme for a list:

1. Choose Format | Bullets and Numbering to open the Bullets and Numbering dialog box (see Figure 10-5).

2. Click the Numbered tab, if necessary.

3. Choose a numbering scheme, if the scheme you want appears on the Numbers tab, and click OK.

To choose a scheme that doesn't appear on the Numbers tab, or to select a punctuation character for your numbered list, click the numbering scheme in the Bullets and Numbering dialog box that most resembles the scheme you want, and then click the Customize button. You will see the Customize Numbered List dialog box. Follow these instructions and click OK twice to fashion a numbering scheme:

■ **Number Format** In the Number Format text box, enter the character that you want to appear after the number or letter. Enter a hyphen, for example, or a bracket (]). Or else delete the character after the number to remove punctuation from numbers.

■ **Number Style** Choose a numbering method from the drop-down list.

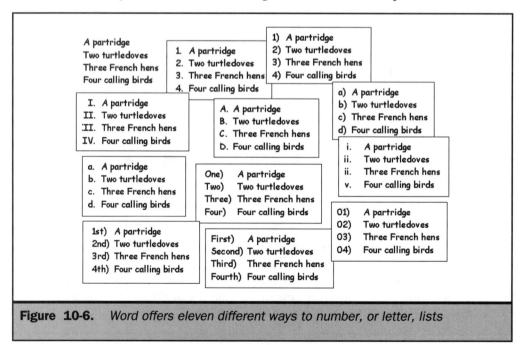

Figure 10-6. *Word offers eleven different ways to number, or letter, lists*

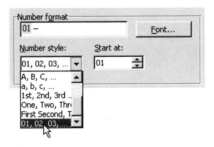

 After you choose or fashion a new numbering scheme, all you have to do to apply it a second time is click the Numbering button on the Formatting toolbar. Clicking this button applies the numbering format you last chose, whatever that format happens to be.

Using Symbols and Pictures for Bullets

The black, filled-in circle seems to be everyone's first choice for a bullet symbol, but that doesn't mean you can't stray from the herd and use another symbol to decorate your bulleted lists. Every character in the Symbol dialog box can be used to mark entries in a bulleted list. And you can also use bullets from the ClipArt dialog box and even use clip art images for bullets. Better read on.

Choosing a Bullet Symbol of Your Own

Follow these steps to choose a symbol for bulleted lists that is different from the black, filled-in circle that you normally get when you click the Bullets button on the Formatting toolbar:

1. Choose Format | Bullets and Numbering to open the Bullets and Numbering dialog box.
2. Click the Bulleted tab, if necessary.
3. Choose a new bullet style and click OK.

Note After you choose a new bullet, it becomes the default bullet that gets entered when you click the Bullets button on the Formatting toolbar.

John	• John	○ John	▪ John
Paul	• Paul	○ Paul	▪ Paul
George	• George	○ George	▪ George
Ringo	• Ringo	○ Ringo	▪ Ringo

❑ John	❖ John	➢ John	✓ John
❑ Paul	❖ Paul	➢ Paul	✓ Paul
❑ George	❖ George	➢ George	✓ George
❑ Ringo	❖ Ringo	➢ Ringo	✓ Ringo

As the previous illustration shows, the seven bullets in the Bullets and Numbering dialog box are pretty, but they are by no means the only symbols you can use in bulleted lists. Any symbol in the Symbol dialog box can be made a symbol in a bulleted list. Follow these steps to mark a bulleted list with an exotic symbol:

1. Choose Format | Bullets and Numbering.

2. Choose any bullet choice on the Bulleted tab in the Bullets and Numbering dialog box.

3. Click the Customize button. As shown in Figure 10-7, you will see the Customize Bulleted List dialog box, which lists symbols you've chosen for bulleted lists. If the symbol you want is one of the six in the dialog box, select it and click OK.

4. Click the Bullet button to open the Symbol dialog box.

5. Find and select a symbol. You'll find a lot of good ones in the Wingdings font. "Entering Symbols and Foreign Characters" in Chapter 2 explains the Symbol dialog box in detail.

6. Click OK twice to return to your document and see your new bullet in all its glory.

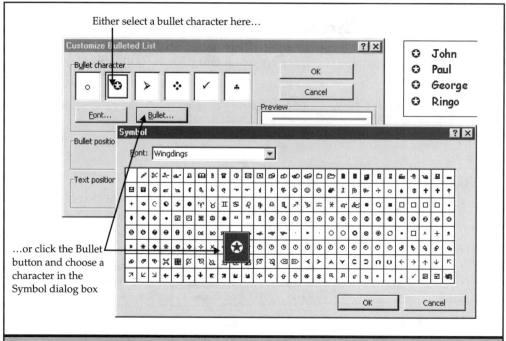

Figure 10-7. *You can use any symbol in the Symbol dialog box to mark entries in a bulleted list*

Keyboard Shortcuts for Entering Bullet Symbols

Besides entering bullet symbols by way of the Bullets and Numbering dialog box, you can enter them by typing keyboard shortcuts. To do so, type the character or characters shown in the left-hand column of the following illustration, press the SPACEBAR or the TAB key, write the first entry on the list, and press ENTER. In place of the character or characters you typed, Word enters the bullet symbol shown in the illustration. See "Preventing Word from Generating Numbered and Bulleted Lists Automatically" earlier in this chapter if you prefer that Word not generate bulleted lists like the ones shown here.

*	•	• Minneapolis, the largest city in Minnesota • St. Paul, the capital of Minnesota
-	-	- Hibbing, birthplace of Kevin McHale - Duluth, birthplace of Blanche McPhee
--	■	■ Meeker County, home of Land O' Lakes Butter ■ Rochester, home of the Mayo Clinic
>	➤	➤ Hastings, gravesite of Plantina Chaffee Hayford ➤ Hastings, birthplace of Maude Hayford
->	→	→ Boundary Waters Canoe Area, recreational paradise → 55 persons per square mile population density
=>	⇨	⇨ The Sioux once roamed Minnesota ⇨ The Chippewa (Ojibway) roamed the state, too

Tip *Click the Picture button on the Bulleted tab in the Bullets and Numbering dialog box to open the Web Bullets & Buttons tab of the Insert ClipArt dialog box. There you will find many colorful symbols that you can use to decorate bulleted lists. Click the symbol you want and then click the Insert Clip button to attach the symbol to your list.*

Using a Clip Art Image as a Bullet

To get really fancy, you can use a clip art image as a bullet in a bulleted list, as shown in Figure 10-8. I warn you, however, that the text in the list has to be fairly large in order for this neat layout trick to work. How large does the text have to be? The author of this book spent the last 40 minutes trying in vain to find a formula. Suffice it to say, the text has to be nearly the same size as the clip art image, and if you shrink the clip art image too far, Word refuses to use it as a bullet symbol.

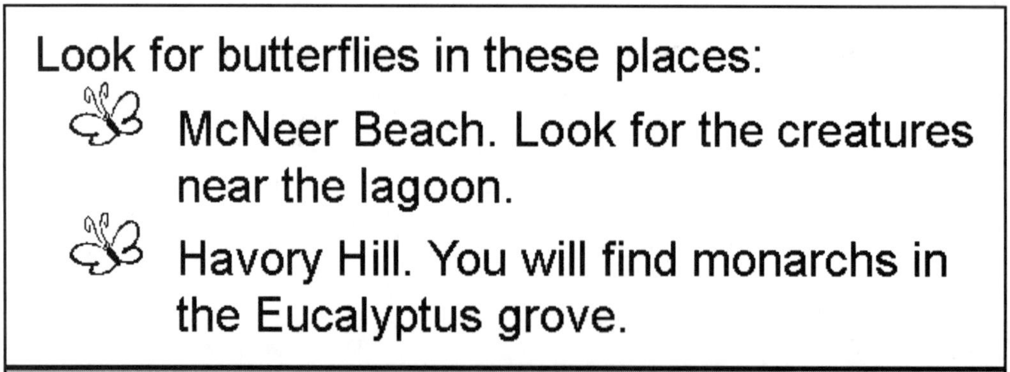

Look for butterflies in these places:

 McNeer Beach. Look for the creatures near the lagoon.

 Havory Hill. You will find monarchs in the Eucalyptus grove.

Figure 10-8. *You can use clip art images to mark entries in a bulleted list. Word does the formatting for you and places the image at the beginning of each line*

Follow the following steps to use a clip art image as a bullet in a bulleted list.

1. Insert the clip art image and shrink it a bit or a lot, depending on its size. Chapter 13 explains how to insert a clip art image, move it, and change its size.

2. With the cursor to the right of the clip art image, press the SPACEBAR or TAB key.

3. Type the first entry in the bulleted list and press ENTER. Word formats the clip art image as a bullet and places a second clip art image on the next line.

4. Type the rest of your list. Press ENTER twice to end it.

Very likely, you will have to adjust the size of the clip art image before Word recognizes it as a bullet and formats the list for you.

In "Adjusting How Far Bullets and Numbers Are Indented," explained later in this chapter, Word offers commands in the Customize Numbered List and Customize Bulleted List dialog boxes for indenting lists. However, those commands don't work on lists in which clip art images are used as bullets. To make the second line and subsequent lines in each bullet entry stay to the right of the clip art image, drag the Hanging Indent marker on the ruler to the right. See "Indenting Text on the Page" in Chapter 8 to learn about hanging indents and how to change indents with the markers on the ruler.

Changing the Font, Font Size, and Color of Numbers and Bullets

Unless you give instructions otherwise, bullets and numbers are the same font size as the text in the rest of the list; numbers appear in the same font as well. As this illustration shows, however, a few larger-than-life bullets or numbers perched on the side of a list looks elegant. In numbered lists, you can make the numbers stand out even more by giving them a different font as well as a different font size. You can even give bullets or numbers a different color.

✿ The fringed swags over poles combined with paired curtains caught back in the distinctive, slightly ballooned shape were typical of the period.

✿ Upholstered furniture played an important part in Regency interiors.

✿ Block-printed, scenic wallpapers from France were popular.

1) The fringed swags over poles combined with paired curtains caught back in the distinctive, slightly ballooned shape were typical of the period.

2) Upholstered furniture played an important part in Regency interiors.

3) Block-printed, scenic wallpapers from France were popular.

Follow these steps to change the font, font size, and color of the bullets or numbers in a list:

1. Select the list if you have already written it. Be sure to select the entire list. If you select part of it, Word thinks you want to change the font and font size of the list entries, not the numbers or bullets.

2. Choose Format | Bullets and Numbering to open the Bullets and Numbering dialog box (see Figure 10-5).

3. As necessary, click the Bulleted or Numbers tab.

4. Select a bullet or numbering style and click the Customize button. As shown in Figure 10-9, you will see the Customize Bulleted List dialog box or the Customize Numbered List dialog box.

5. Click the Font button. You'll see the Font dialog box.

6. Choose a new font size and perhaps a different color. For numbers, choose a new font and perhaps a font style as well. "Choosing a Font and Font Size for Text" in Chapter 7 explains the ins and outs of the Font dialog box.

7. Click OK to return to the Customize dialog box.

8. If you chose a large font size, you probably have to adjust the Indent At and Aligned At measurements to make the entries in the list line up correctly. The next section in this chapter explains how to indent lists. Keep your eye on the Preview box. It shows how text lines up in the list.

9. Click OK twice to return to your document and see what your bullets or numbers look like.

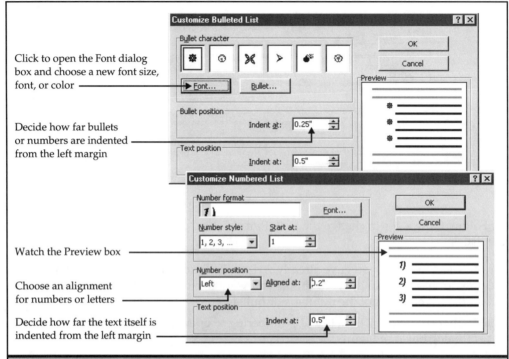

Click to open the Font dialog box and choose a new font size, font, or color

Decide how far bullets or numbers are indented from the left margin

Watch the Preview box

Choose an alignment for numbers or letters

Decide how far the text itself is indented from the left margin

Figure 10-9. *In the Customize Bulleted List and Customize Numbered List dialog boxes, you can create your own style of bulleted and numbered lists*

Adjusting How Far Bullets and Numbers Are Indented

Continuing the crusade to deviate from the standard bulleted or numbered list, you can also change the distance that list entries are indented from the left margin. In a standard bulleted or numbered list, the number or bullet is indented from the left margin by .2 inch, and the text in the list is indented from the left margin by .45 inch. However, you can change that by following these steps:

1. Choose Format | Bullets and Numbering to open the Bullets and Numbering dialog box, and then click either the Bulleted or Numbered tab.

2. Click the bullet or numbering style whose indentation you want to change, and click the Customize button. The Customize Bulleted List or Customize Numbered List dialog box appears (see Figure 10-9).

3. Under Bullet Position or Number Position, click the arrows in the Indent At or Aligned At box to change the distance by which the bullets or numbers in the list are indented from the left margin.

Bullet position
Indent at: 0.5"

Number position
Left   Aligned at: 0.2"

Text position
Indent at: 0.6"

Text position
Indent at: 0.55"

4. Under Text Position, click the arrows to change the distance that the text in the list is indented from the left margin. Watch the Preview box as you change the settings—the box shows where the bullets or numbers and text will appear in relation to the left margin.

5. Click OK twice to return to your document.

 To indent an entire list by one tab stop from the left margin, select the list and click the Increase Indent button on the Formatting toolbar. You can also right-click and choose Increase Indent from the shortcut menu.

Choosing an Alignment for the Numbers in Lists

In the two default numbering schemes in which plain Arabic numbers are used, the numbers are left-aligned. In other words, the numbers in lists are aligned under the first, or left-hand, character. In lists that do not reach double-digits, left-aligned numbers are not a problem, but left-aligned numbers look odd when lists go beyond the number 10 because the text entries come too close to the numbers, as shown in this illustration.

Maids a-milking
Ladies dancing
Swans a-swimming
Lords a-leaping
Drummers drumming

8. Maids a-milking
9. Ladies dancing
10. Swans a-swimming
11. Lords a-leaping
12. Drummers drumming

8) Maids a-milking
9) Ladies dancing
10) Swans a-swimming
11) Lords a-leaping
12) Drummers drumming

You can, however, right-align or center-align the numbers in a list to solve the problem of text running too close to the numbers. For that matter, you can left-align, right-align, or center-align the numbers and letters in any list for the sheer aesthetic enjoyment of it or to amuse yourself on a rainy day. Follow these steps:

1. Select the list if you have already entered it and choose Format | Bullets and Numbering.

2. Click the Customize button on the Numbered tab in the Bullets and Numbering dialog box. The Customize Numbered List dialog box appears (see Figure 10-9).

FORMATTING TEXT AND PAGES

3. Under Number Position, choose Left, Centered, or Right from the drop-down list; adjust the Aligned At and Indent At measurements, if necessary; and click OK twice to return to your document.

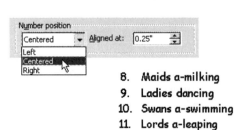

8) Maids a-milking
9) Ladies dancing
10) Swans a-swimming
11) Lords a-leaping
12) Drummers drumming

8. Maids a-milking
9. Ladies dancing
10. Swans a-swimming
11. Lords a-leaping
12. Drummers drumming

Making Sublists or Nested Lists

A *sublist*, also known as a *nested list*, is a list that is found inside another list. At the top of Figure 10-10 is a common type of sublist, a bulleted sublist inside a numbered list. The numbered sublist on the right side of Figure 10-10 is not as common. Still, you see numbered sublists inside of numbered lists from time to time.

Creating a bulleted sublist is simple: Type the entire list without regard for sublists, and click the Numbering or Bullets button to make the entire list a bulleted

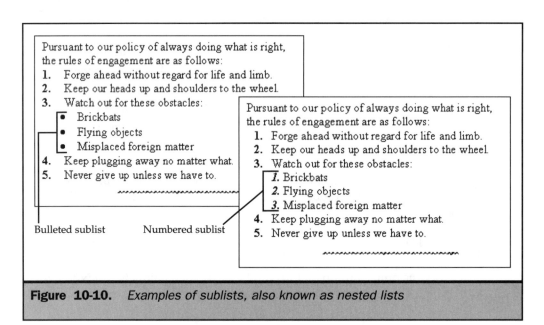

Figure 10-10. *Examples of sublists, also known as nested lists*

or numbered list. Then select the items that you want for the sublist and do either of the following:

- **Bulleted Sublist Inside a Numbered List** Click the Bullets button. The list is renumbered and the items you selected are given bullets. If you want, click the Increase Indent button to indent the bulleted sublist or else choose Format | Bullets and Numbering to format the sublist.

- **Bulleted Sublist Inside a Bulleted List** Click the Increase Indent button to indent the sublist and set it apart from the bulleted list. Word assigns a new bullet character to the sublist entries. Choose Format | Bullets and Numbering if you want to change the bullet character or indentation of the sublist.

To create a numbered sublist, type the entire list and click the Bullets or Numbering button to make the list a bulleted or numbered list. Then select the items for the numbered sublist and do the following:

- **Numbered Sublist Inside a Bulleted List** Click the Numbering button on the Formatting toolbar. That's all there is to it, unless you want to click the Increase Indent button or choose Format | Bullets and Numbering to set the sublist apart somehow.

- **Numbered Sublist Inside a Numbered List** Click the Increase Indent button on the Formatting toolbar to indent the list and make it a sublist. Word assigns a new numbering scheme to the items in the sublist. If you want, choose Format | Bullets and Numbering to choose a different numbering scheme or to format the sublist. However, do not choose the same numbering scheme as you chose for the numbered list. If you do, Word does not indent the sublist and you can hardly distinguish it from the numbered list.

Figure 10-11 shows another kind of sublist—a series of numbered clauses inside a paragraph. Normally in a list like this, you have to retype the numbers if you add or remove a numbered item. For this list, however, I used the ListNum field to enter the numbers automatically. When I remove or add a clause, Word renumbers the list. Because I used a field code to number the list, I can choose a new numbering scheme for all the clauses instantaneously without having to retype anything.

Field codes are explained in detail in Chapter 23. For now, here are basic instructions for numbering items in the same paragraph with the ListNum field code:

1. Type all the text for the paragraph, excluding the numbers and then click in the paragraph where the first number is to appear.

2. Choose Insert | Field, click the Numbering category in the Field dialog box, and click the ListNum field name, as shown in Figure 10-11.

3. Click OK. A number appears in the document.

4. Click the number to select it.

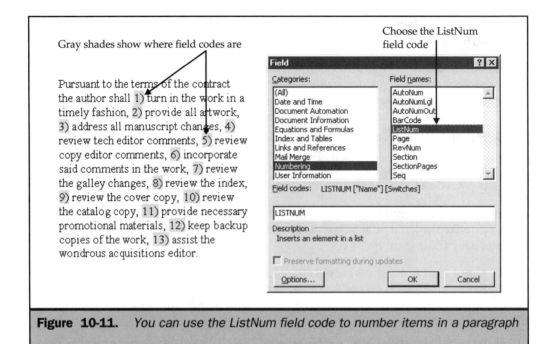

Figure 10-11.   *You can use the ListNum field code to number items in a paragraph*

5. Start clicking the Increase Indent or Decrease Indent button until you see the number scheme you want. As you click the buttons, the following number schemes appear: 1), a), i), (1), (a), (i), 1., a., and i.

6. Click to the right of the number and press the SPACEBAR to enter an empty space.

7. Select the number and empty space and copy them to the Clipboard (press CTRL-C or click the Copy button).

8. Click where the next number is to go and click the Paste button or press CTRL-V. The next number in the sequence appears.

9. Click where the third number is to go and press F4 or choose Edit | Repeat Paste.

10. Repeat step 9 until all the numbers are entered.

You might have to select the paragraph and choose a new font, font size, or style to format the text and numbers the same way. Don't worry about the gray shades. Gray shades show where field code results are located. They don't appear on the page when you print a document. Select the first number in the paragraph and start clicking the Decrease Indent or Increase Indent button if you decide to choose a different numbering scheme.

Numbering the Headings and Chapters in a Document

In formal documents, scholarly papers, and legal briefs, headings are sometimes numbered so that commentary and cross-references can refer to headings by number as well as by name. Numbering the headings has other advantages, too. For example, you can include chapter numbers in page numbers if you number the chapters in your document.

The commands for numbering the headings in a document are found in the Bullets and Numbering dialog box. Word renumbers headings automatically if you delete a heading or add a new one. To use the heading-numbering commands, however, you must have assigned heading styles to the headings in your document (Chapter 12 describes styles).

Choosing a Heading-Numbering Scheme

Figure 10-12 shows, in Outline view, the four ways to number the headings in a document. Notice in some heading-number schemes that words—"Article," "Section," "Chapter"—as well as numbers and letters are attached to headings. One scheme is strictly for numbering the chapters in a document. In that scheme, Heading 1 headings are given the prefix "Chapter 1," "Chapter 2," and so on, but other headings are not numbered or lettered.

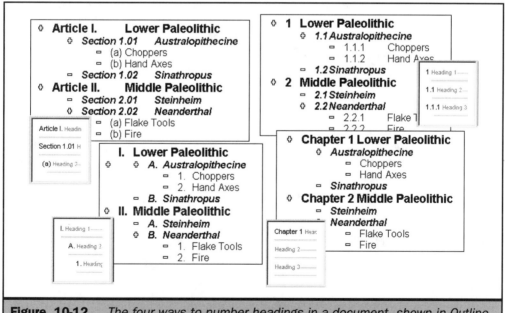

Figure 10-12. *The four ways to number headings in a document, shown in Outline view. You can also devise your own heading-numbering schemes*

Before you number headings, understand that only headings assigned the Heading 1 through Heading 9 style are given heading numbers, unless you devise a numbering scheme of your own or modify one of Word's numbering schemes. What's more, headings are numbered throughout the document. You can't number some headings but not others because choosing a heading-numbering scheme also changes heading styles, so all headings assigned a certain style are assigned a heading number as well. After you number headings, the heading styles on the Style menu change to show how headings are numbered. From now on when you choose a heading style, you will also number the heading.

 The Outline Numbered tab in the Bullets and Numbering dialog box offers a command called None for removing numbers from headings. The command works fine in that it does remove heading numbers, except it doesn't undo the style modifications you make when you number headings. After you remove heading numbers, numbers continue to appear on the Style menu, and when you assign a heading style to a paragraph, heading numbers appear whether you like it or not. The moral: Numbering headings radically changes heading styles, so decide carefully whether you want to number the headings. As a practical matter, you can't remove heading numbers without going back and modifying all the heading styles to remove the heading numbers.

Follow these steps to number all the headings in a document:

1. Switch to Outline view by clicking the Outline View button in the lower-left corner of the screen. In Outline view, you can see headings more easily. Click a Show Heading button on the Outlining toolbar to see only the headings in the document. Chapter 19 explains how to work in Outline view.

2. Choose Format | Bullets and Numbering.

3. As shown in Figure 10-13, click the Outline Numbered tab.

4. Choose one of the four heading number options in the bottom half of the dialog box (the ones with the word "heading" on them).

5. Click OK.

If I were you, I would scroll through the document, look at the headings, and see if you like them. Click the Undo button if you regret numbering the headings. By clicking Undo, you remove the numbers and also restore the heading styles to what

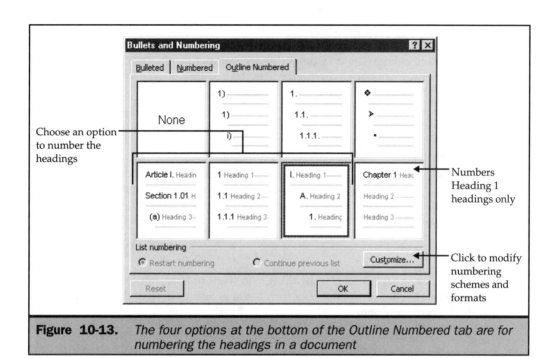

Choose an option to number the headings

Numbers Heading 1 headings only

Click to modify numbering schemes and formats

Figure 10-13. *The four options at the bottom of the Outline Numbered tab are for numbering the headings in a document*

they were before you numbered the headings. In other words, you get numberless heading styles again.

All the headings in the document are numbered to begin with. Follow these instructions in Outline view if you want to number only a handful of headings, start numbering anew, or pick up the numbering sequence where you left off:

- **Removing Numbers from Headings**   Select the headings whose numbers you want to remove and click the Numbering button on the Formatting toolbar.

- **Restarting the Numbers**   Click the heading that you want to be first in the new numbering sequence (you can't select several headings, since Word doesn't allow it) and choose Format | Bullets and Numbers. Select the numbering scheme you are using on the Outline Numbered tab, click the Restart Numbering option button, and click OK. Headings below the one you selected are renumbered.

- **Resuming the Numbers**   Click the heading that you want to number and choose Format | Bullets and Numbering (you can't select several headings). On the Outline Numbered tab, one option does not begin with 1 or I., but with the next heading number in the sequence. Click that option, make sure the Continue Previous List option button is selected already, and click OK. Click another heading and press F4 or choose Edit | Repeat Bullets and Numbering to number other headings as well.

Altering a Numbering Scheme

Perhaps you want to change the way headings are numbered, change the punctuation of numbering schemes, or change the distance that a heading is indented. Personally, I think Word is wrong to put a blank space after the chapter number where a colon (:) and a blank space would do the job better. Maybe you want to include a style in the numbering scheme apart from the heading styles that Word includes.

To alter a numbering scheme or be able to number paragraphs marked with styles other than heading styles, choose Format | Bullets and Numbering, select the scheme you want to alter in the Bullets and Numbering dialog box (see Figure 10-13), and click the Customize button. You will see the unduly complicated Customize Outline Numbered List dialog box shown in Figure 10-14. Following are explanations of the options in the dialog box. Watch the Number Format box and Preview box as you construct your number format. Those boxes show exactly what your choices will do to heading numbers.

- ■ **Level**   Choose which level of heading you want to alter. For example, choose 3 if you want to change the number formats of headings assigned the Heading 3 style in your document.

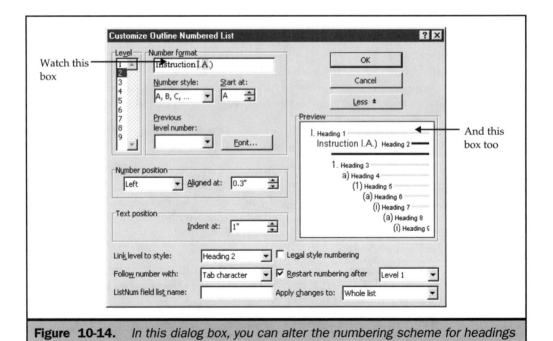

Figure 10-14.   *In this dialog box, you can alter the numbering scheme for headings*

- **Number Format**   Enter a word—**Section**, **Title**, or **Instruction**, for example—before the number or letter, if you want to label headings as well as number them. Enter a punctuation mark—a colon, hyphen, or blank space, for example—after the number or letter if you so desire.

- **Number Style**   Choose how you want to number the headings on this level.

- **Start At**   Choose a number or letter other than 1, I, i, A, a, if for some reason you want heading numbers not to start at the beginning.

- **Previous Level Number**   For levels 2 through 9, enter a number here if you want numbers from previous levels to be part of the number in the level you are working on. For example, if the level 1 number is *I* and the level 2 number is *A*, the first second-level heading will be number I.A, as shown in Figure 10-14. Choose level numbers from the drop-down list. The number appears in the Number Format box after you select it.

- **Font Button**   Click this button to open the Font dialog box and choose a new font or font size for your heading number and perhaps heading label as well.

- **Number Position**   Change the alignment of the numbers. The choices are left-aligned, center-aligned, or right-aligned.

- **Aligned At**   Adjust the distance between the heading number and the left margin.

- **Indent At**   Adjust the distance between the heading number and the start of the text in the heading. You can also do this by entering a space in the Number Format text box or making a choice in the Follow Number With drop-down list.

Click the More button to see and negotiate these options:

- **Link Level to Style**   Choose a different style if you want it to be numbered instead of the heading style shown on the menu. For example, you could choose Subtitle or Subhead or another style you created for headings in your document.

- **Legal Style Numbering**   Changes Roman numerals throughout a numbering scheme to their Arabic numeral equivalents.

- **Follow Number With**   If you didn't enter a blank space after the number in the Number Format text box, you can choose Space from the drop-down list or else choose Tab to enter a tab space between the number and the heading text.

- **Restart Numbering After**   Uncheck this check box on the outside chance that you do not want to restart the numbers after a certain level heading. For example, suppose you want third-level headings to continue incrementing throughout the chapter and not be reset to number 1 after another, higher-level heading. In that case, uncheck this checkbox.

- **ListNum Field List Name**   If you intend to write detailed lists with ListNum field codes, enter the word or two that introduces those lists (this option is for numbering paragraphs, not headings).
- **Apply Changes To**   Make sure Whole Document appears here.

Suppose you modify a heading-numbering scheme but realize to your dismay that you want one of Word's original schemes back. To get it back, open the Bullets and Numbering dialog box, select the scheme you altered, and click the Reset button. Then click Yes when Word asks if you want the default setting.

If you go to the significant trouble of modifying a heading-numbering scheme, be sure to save it as a style. That way, you can use it in other documents and templates. Chapter 12 explains styles.

MOUS Exam Objectives Explored in Chapter 10

Objective	Heading	Practice File
Sort lists*	"Alphabetizing and Sorting Lists"	10-1 Sort
Add bullets and numbering	"The Bare-Bones Basics: Bulleted and Numbered Lists"	10-2 Bullets and Numbers
Create an outline-style numbered list	"Numbering the Headings and Chapters in a Document"	

* Denotes an Expert exam objective.

The Complete Reference

Chapter 11

Proofing Your Work

I was going to call this chapter "Foolproofing Your Work," but that seemed kind of presumptuous, since keeping every error from slipping into a document is impossible. Still, you can do a good job of proofing your work and eliminating errors by using the tools that Word provides for that purpose. This chapter describes those tools. Read on to find out how to correct typos and capitalization errors with the AutoCorrect command, correct spelling and grammatical errors, and improve your writing by taking advantage of the Thesaurus. You will also find instructions in this chapter for handling text that was written in a foreign language.

Correcting Typos with the AutoCorrect Command

You may have noticed that the invisible hand of Word 2000 corrects certain misspellings and typos as you make them. For example, try typing "accomodate" with one "m"—Word corrects the misspelling and inserts the second "m" for you. Try typing "perminent" with an "i" instead of an "a"—the invisible hand of Word corrects the misspelling and you get "permanent." While you're at it, type a colon and a close parenthesis :)—you get a smiley face.

Word corrects common spelling errors and turns punctuation marks into symbols as part of its AutoCorrect feature. To see which typos are corrected and which punctuation marks are turned into symbols, choose Tools | AutoCorrect. You will see the AutoCorrect dialog box shown in Figure 11-1. Scroll down the Replace list in the middle of the dialog box to see the list of words and typos that are auto-corrected.

As good as the AutoCorrect feature is, you can make it even better. And you can also add the typos and misspellings you often make to the list of words that are corrected automatically. These pages explain how to do that and also how to fix capitalization errors. If for some reason you don't want Word to hide in the background and correct typos or misspellings automatically, uncheck the Replace Text As You Type check box in the AutoCorrect dialog box (see Figure 11-1).

 "Entering Text and Graphics Quickly with the AutoCorrect Command" in Chapter 6 explains how you can use the AutoCorrect command as a means of entering boilerplate text and graphics.

Telling Word Which Typos and Misspellings to Correct

No doubt you make the same typing errors and spelling errors time and time again. The author of this book cannot type the word "chapter" without spelling it "chatper." Several years ago, a Vice President of the United States named Dan Quayle made headlines when he read from a mistyped card that spelled "potato" with an "e" on the end: "potatoe." To save time and to keep from looking foolish, you can add typos like "chatper" and misspellings like "potatoe" to the list of words that are corrected automatically.

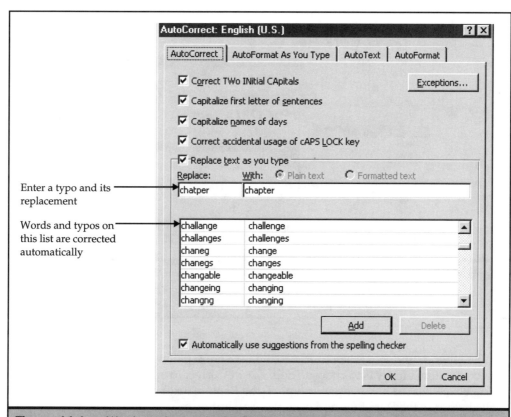

Enter a typo and its replacement

Words and typos on this list are corrected automatically

Figure 11-1. *Words and typos in the Replace column are replaced automatically with the words in the With column*

The fastest and surest way to add misspellings and typos to the list is to do it while you are spell-checking a document. In Figure 11-2, the misspelling "Chatper" and its replacement "Chapter" are being added to the Replace With list in the AutoCorrect dialog box (see Figure 11-1). During a spell-check, add words to the list with these techniques:

- **By Choosing AutoCorrect on the Shortcut Menu**   Word draws squiggly red lines underneath words that are misspelled. Right-click a misspelling if you want to add it to the list of errors that are corrected automatically, choose AutoCorrect from the shortcut menu, and select the word that is to replace the typo or misspelling on the submenu.

- **By Choosing AutoCorrect in the Spelling and Grammar Dialog Box**   In the Spelling and Grammar dialog box, select the word that is to replace the typo or misspelling in the Suggestions list. Then click the AutoCorrect button. Later in this chapter, "Correcting Your Spelling Errors" explains all the options in the Spelling and Grammar dialog box.

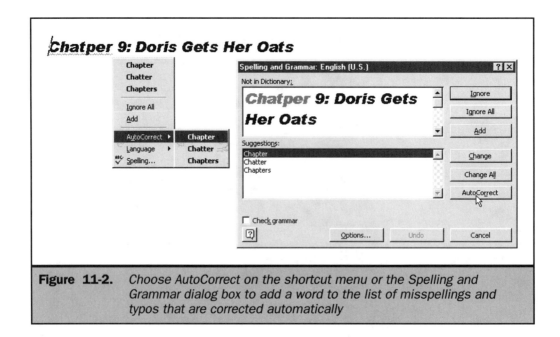

Figure 11-2.   *Choose AutoCorrect on the shortcut menu or the Spelling and Grammar dialog box to add a word to the list of misspellings and typos that are corrected automatically*

The other, roundabout way to add to the list of misspellings and typos that are corrected automatically is to choose Tools | AutoCorrect to open the AutoCorrect dialog box, enter the misspelling or typo in the Replace text box, enter the correctly spelled word in the With box, and click the Add button.

You can remove misspellings and typos from the list of words that are corrected automatically. Perhaps you are working on a novel with gritty realistic dialogue and you want "should of," "themself," and other such words to stay in the text without being corrected. To remove a word from the list of corrected words, select it in the AutoCorrect dialog box, and click the Delete button. Then backspace over the word and its replacement in the Replace and With text boxes.

Preventing Capitalization Errors with AutoCorrect

At the top of the AutoCorrect dialog box (choose Tools | AutoCorrect to get there) are four check boxes whose job is to prevent capitalization errors. These options do their jobs very well, sometimes to a fault:

- **Correct TWo INitial CApitals**   Prevents two capital letters from appearing in a row at the start of a word with more than two letters. Only the first letter is capitalized. This option is for people who can't lift their little fingers from the SHIFT key fast enough after typing the first capital letter at the start of a word.

- **Capitalize first letter of sentences**   Makes sure that the first letter in a sentence is capitalized.

Don't forget the Capitalize first letter of sentences option when you enter computer code or other text that doesn't need to be capitalized. Unchecking the option can be very helpful on such occasions.

■ **Capitalize names of days**   Makes sure the names of the days of the week are capitalized.

■ **Correct accidental usage of cAPS LOCK key**   Changes capital letters to lowercase letters if you press the SHIFT key to start a sentence while Caps Lock is on. The idea here is that if you press down the SHIFT key while Caps Lock is on, you don't know that Caps Lock is on, since you don't need to hold down the SHIFT key to enter capital letters. Word turns the first letter into a capital letter and the following letters into lowercase letters and turns Caps Lock off.

Making Exceptions to the AutoCorrect Capitalization Controls

Except when certain abbreviations are used in sentences, you have to type the rare name that starts with two uppercase letters, or you want to enter an acronym that happens to be listed in the AutoCorrect dialog box, the AutoCorrect capitalization settings work fine. For those rare occasions when they don't work, click the Exceptions button in the AutoCorrect dialog box shown in the following illustration.

Click to handle abbreviations, two
capital letters in a row, and acronyms

AutoCorrect

☑ Correct TWo INitial CApitals   Exceptions...

☑ Capitalize first letter of sentences

☑ Capitalize names of days

☑ Correct accidental usage of cAPS LOCK key

You'll see the AutoCorrect Exceptions dialog box. By making entries in the First Letter, INitial CAps, and Other Corrections tabs, you can eat your cake and have it too. In other words, you can continue to use AutoCorrect to correct typos and misspellings except under certain circumstances:

■ **First Letter Tab**   When Word encounters an abbreviation that is listed on the First Letter tab, it allows the word following the abbreviation to start with a lowercase letter. However, if the abbreviation is not listed, Word assumes that the period at the end of the abbreviation marks the end of a sentence, so the program begins the next word incorrectly with a capital letter. If Word persists in capitalizing a word after an abbreviation you use, solve the problem by entering the abbreviation on the First Letter tab so that Word can recognize it as an abbreviation.

- **INitial CAps Tab**   Newfangled company names sometimes start with two capital letters: QUest Data Inc., DIgital DIngbats, Inc. Enter such names on the INitial CAps tab to keep Word from lowercasing the second capital letter.

- **Other Corrections Tab**   Enter acronyms that also happen to be listed in the AutoCorrect dialog box to keep Word from correcting acronyms. An *acronym* is a word in all capital letters that is formed from the initial letters of other words.

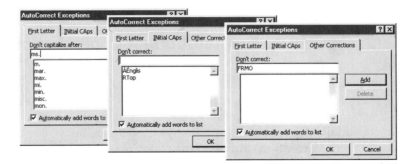

As long as the Automatically Add Words To List check boxes are selected in the AutoCorrect Exceptions dialog box, Word adds abbreviations, words with two initial capital letters, and acronyms to the Exceptions lists when you press the BACKSPACE key to reverse a correction Word made automatically. For example, suppose you enter **TEchnics Inc.**, Word changes "TEchnics" to "Technics," but then you BACKSPACE over the "echnics" and type the company name again: **TEchnics**. By doing so, you add "TEchnics" to the list of words on the INitial CAps tab that are not auto-corrected.

Note   *A word is not added the list if you correct it by clicking the Undo button after Word auto-corrects it.*

Correcting Your Spelling Errors

Word 2000 keeps a dictionary in its hip pocket. The program consults the dictionary as you enter text and draws lines in red underneath words that are misspelled and words that were entered twice in a row. To correct misspellings, you can either address them one at a time or start the spell-checker and proof many pages or an entire document at once. You can even create a dictionary of your own with the jargon and slang peculiar to your way of life and have Word check the spelling of jargon and slang. Better read on.

Don't trust the smell-checker to be accurate all of the time. It doesn't really locate misspelled words—it locates words that are not in its dictionary. For example, if you write, "Nero diddled while Rome burned," the spell-checker will not catch the error. Nero fiddled *while Rome burned, but because "diddle" is a legitimate word in the spelling dictionary, the spell-checker overlooks the misspelling. The moral: Proofread your documents carefully and don't rely on the spell-checker to catch all your smelling errors.*

LEARN BY EXAMPLE
Open the 11-1 Spelling document on the companion CD if you want some practical experience with spell-checking a document.

Correcting Misspellings One at a Time

With the one-at-a-time method of spell-checking a document, you right-click each word that is underlined in red and choose a correct spelling from the shortcut menu. (If you don't see any suggestions for correct spellings, choose Tools | Options, click the Spelling & Grammar tab in the Options dialog box, check the Always Suggest Corrections check box, and click OK.) When you choose a word from the shortcut menu, it replaces the misspelling that you right-clicked. Click the Delete Repeated Word option to erase a duplicated word you entered accidentally.

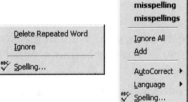

If you aren't sure but vaguely remember how to spell a word, you can use wildcards and the spell-checker to find out how to spell it. Enter the asterisk (*) or the question mark (?) wildcard in place of the letters or letter you aren't sure of and run the spell-checker on the word. This trick works especially well with place names. For example, entering **Timbuk*** *finds the correct spelling of the ancient kingdom where the great Sundiata Keita ruled—Timbuktu.*

Getting Rid of the Squiggly Red Lines

More than a few users of Word think that the squiggly red lines that appear under misspelled words are annoying. To keep those lines from appearing, choose Tools | Options, click the Spelling & Grammar tab in the Options dialog box, and check the Hide Spelling Errors In This Document check box.

Even with the red lines gone, you can do a quick spell-check of a word that you suspect has been misspelled. To do so, select the word (by double-clicking it) and do one of the following:

- Double-click the book icon on the right side of the Status bar. A short list of alternative spellings appears if the word was misspelled. Click a word on the list to enter it in place of the misspelling.

- Either press F7 or choose Tools | Spelling and Grammar. The Spelling and Grammar dialog box appears if the word has indeed been misspelled. Click a word in the Suggestions box and then click the Change button.

Spell-Checking an Entire Document or Text Selection

Instead of correcting misspellings one at a time, you can spell-check a document or part of a document and address misspellings one after the other. To spell-check part of a document, select the part you want to spell-check. Start the spell-check by pressing F7, choosing Tools | Spelling and Grammar, or right-clicking a misspelled word and choosing Spelling from the shortcut menu. You'll see the Spelling and Grammar dialog box shown in Figure 11-3. Misspellings are highlighted in the document and appear in bright red in the Not In Dictionary box.

Table 11-1 describes all the buttons in the Spelling and Grammar dialog box. As Word encounters misspellings, do one of the following to correct them:

- Select the correct spelling in the Suggestions box and click the Change button.

- Delete the misspelled word in the Not In Dictionary box (by pressing DELETE or BACKSPACE), type the correct spelling in the Not In Dictionary box, and click the Change button.

- Click outside the Spelling and Grammar dialog box, correct the misspelled word in the document, and click the Resume button in the Spelling and Grammar dialog box (the Resume button appears where the Ignore button used to be).

Tip   *Grammatical errors appear in green in the Spelling and Grammar dialog box. To ignore grammatical errors for the time being and focus on misspellings, uncheck the Check Grammar check box. Later in this chapter, "Correcting Grammatical Errors" explains how to address grammatical errors in a document.*

Misspelled word

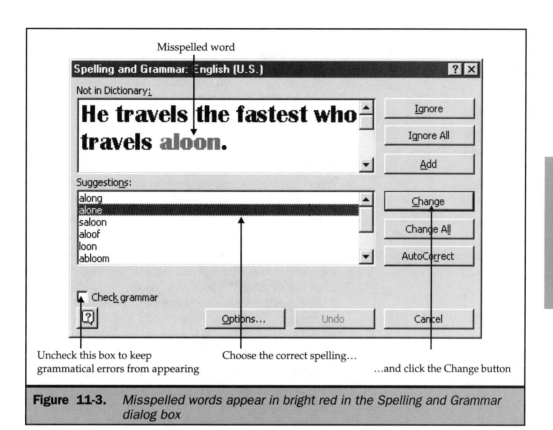

Spelling and Grammar: English (U.S.)   ? ☒

Not in Dictionary:

He travels the fastest who
travels aloon.

[Ignore]

[Ignore All]

[Add]

Suggestions:

along
alone
saloon
aloof
loon
abloom

[Change]

[Change All]

[AutoCorrect]

☐ Check grammar

[?]   [Options...]   [Undo]   [Cancel]

Uncheck this box to keep
grammatical errors from appearing

Choose the correct spelling...

...and click the Change button

FORMATTING TEXT AND PAGES

Figure 11-3.   *Misspelled words appear in bright red in the Spelling and Grammar dialog box*

Button	What It Does
Ignore	Ignores this instance of the misspelling but stops on it again if the same misspelling appears later in the document.
Ignore All	Ignores the misspelling throughout the document. If you click this button but regret doing so, click the Recheck Document button on the Spelling & Grammar tab of the Options dialog box to stop ignoring the misspelling. Choose Tools	Options and click the Spelling & Grammar tab to see the Recheck Document button.

Table 11-1.   *Buttons for Correcting Spelling Errors in the Spelling and Grammar Dialog Box*

Button	What It Does
Add	Adds the misspelling to a spelling dictionary so that Word never stops on it again. By clicking the Add button, you tell Word that the misspelling is a legitimate word or name.
Change/Delete	Enters the highlighted word in the Suggestions box in the document where the misspelling used to be. When the same word appears twice in a row, the Delete button appears where the Change button was. Click the Delete button to delete the second word in the pair.
Change All/Delete All	Replaces all instances of the misspelled word with the word that is highlighted in the Suggestions box. Click the Change All button to correct a misspelling that occurs throughout a document. When two words appear in a row, this button is called Delete All. Click the Delete All button to delete the second word in the pair throughout your document.
AutoCorrect	Adds the spelling correction to the list of words that are corrected automatically. See "Correcting Typos with the AutoCorrect Command," earlier in this chapter.
Options	Opens the Spelling & Grammar tab of the Options dialog box so you can tell Word how to spell-check your document.
Undo	Reverses your previous action in the Spelling and Grammar dialog box. You can keep clicking Undo to reverse more than one action.

Table 11-1.   *Buttons for Correcting Spelling Errors in the Spelling and Grammar Dialog Box* (continued)

In spell-checks, Word presumes that words in uppercase are acronyms, so the program ignores those words. It also ignores words with numbers in them and Internet and file addresses. However, you can spell-check those items as well by clicking the Options button in the Spelling and Grammar dialog box (see Figure 11-3) or choosing Tools | Options and clicking the Spelling & Grammar tab in the Options dialog box.

On the Spelling & Grammar tab are three Ignore check boxes. Uncheck them to spell-check uppercase words, words with numbers, and Internet and file addresses.

Spelling & Grammar
Spelling
☑ Check spelling as you type
☐ Hide spelling errors in this document
☑ Always suggest corrections
☐ Suggest from main dictionary only
☑ Ignore words in UPPERCASE
☑ Ignore words with numbers
☑ Ignore Internet and file addresses

FORMATTING
TEXT AND PAGES

Spell-Checking Text in Foreign Languages

Spanish and French dictionaries are included in the version of Word that is sold in the United States. That means you can spell-check Spanish and French words. And you can spell-check words in other languages, too, as long as you installed proofing tools for those languages by way of the Microsoft Proofing Tools Kit. Later in this chapter, "Working with Text Written in a Foreign Language" explains how to mark foreign text in a document so that you can spell-check it. After the foreign text has been marked, you can spell-check it the same way that you spell-check English text.

Employing Other Dictionaries to Help with Spell-Checking

To find spelling errors, Word compares each word on the page to the words in its main dictionary and a second dictionary called Custom.dic. If a word you type is not found in either dictionary, the program considers the word a misspelling. The main dictionary lists all known words in the English language. The Custom.dic dictionary lists words, proper names, and technical jargon that you deemed legitimate when you clicked the Add button in the course of a spell-check. In this illustration, for example, the word "gangsta" is being added to the Custom.dic dictionary. Never again will the spell-checker pause over this hybrid of the word "gangster" because I am adding it to the Custom.dic dictionary.

Taking the Rap for Gangsta Rap

Gangster
Gangsters
Ignore All
Add
AutoCorrect ▶
Language ▶
Spelling...

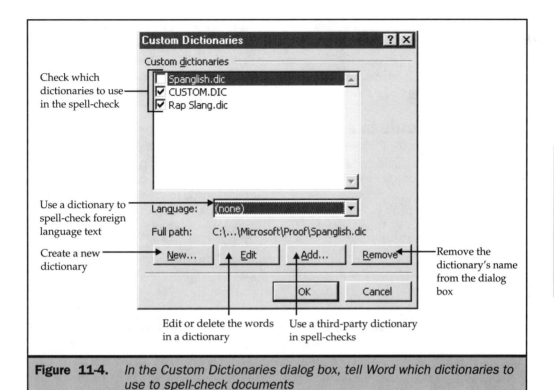

Check which
dictionaries to use
in the spell-check

Use a dictionary to
spell-check foreign
language text

Create a new
dictionary

Remove the
dictionary's name
from the dialog
box

Edit or delete the words
in a dictionary

Use a third-party dictionary
in spell-checks

Figure 11-4.   *In the Custom Dictionaries dialog box, tell Word which dictionaries to
use to spell-check documents*

Note   *From Word's standpoint, a dictionary is merely a list of words, one word per line, which
has been spelled correctly and saved as a .dic (dictionary) file. You can acquire
dictionary files for use with Word from Microsoft and from professional associations.*

Follow these steps to create a new spelling dictionary or tell Word that you want to
use a secondary dictionary to check the spelling of words:

- **Create a New Spelling Dictionary**   Click the New button in the Custom
  Dictionaries dialog box (see Figure 11-4). In the Create Custom Dictionary
  dialog box, enter a name for your new dictionary and click the Save button. See
  "Editing the Words a Dictionary," later in this chapter, to learn how to enter
  terms in your new spelling dictionary.

- **Use a Secondary Dictionary**   Make note of where the dictionary file is located
  on your computer. It doesn't have to be in the C:\Windows\Application
  Data\Microsoft\Proof folder along with the other dictionaries for Word to use
  it. Click the Add button in the Custom Dictionaries dialog box (see Figure 11-4)
  to use a dictionary that you acquired elsewhere. The Add Custom Dictionary
  dialog box appears. Locate the dictionary on your computer, select it, and click
  OK. Its name appears in the Custom Dictionaries dialog box.

Select a dictionary and click the Remove button to remove its name from the Custom Dictionaries dialog box. Removing a name in no way, shape, or form deletes the dictionary. You can click the Add button to place the dictionary's name in the dialog box again and use it for spell-checking. Only ten dictionaries total can appear in the Custom Dictionaries box.

Editing the Words in a Dictionary

To edit the words in the Custom.dic dictionary or any other dictionary, select it in the Custom Dictionaries dialog box (see Figure 11-4), click the Edit button, and click OK when Word warns you that you effectively stop spell-checking documents when you edit words in a dictionary. You will see the list of the words in the dictionary. Delete words, enter new words, or change the spelling of words. Make sure that each word appears on its own line. When you are done editing, save the dictionary file.

After you edit a dictionary, Word turns off the spell-checking mechanism. To turn it on, choose Tools | Options, click the Spelling & Grammar tab in the Options dialog box, and check the Check Spelling As You Type check box.

Telling Word Which Dictionaries to Use in a Spell-Check

Word checks for misspellings against the words in the main dictionary and each dictionary whose name is checked off in the Custom Dictionaries dialog box (see Figure 11-4). To make use of a dictionary in spell-checks, click the check box beside its name; uncheck the boxes beside the names of dictionaries you don't need.

On the Spelling & Grammar tab of the Options dialog box is a check box called Suggest From Main Dictionary Only; click it to exclude all secondary dictionaries, Custom.dic included, from spell-checks. Choose Tools | Options and click the Spelling & Grammar tab in the Options dialog box to see and check this option.

Correcting Grammatical Errors

Much of what constitutes good grammar is, like beauty, in the eye of the beholder. Still, you can do your best to repair grammatical errors by getting the assistance of the grammar-checker. The grammar-checker identifies grammatical errors, explains what the errors are, and gives you the opportunity to correct the errors. These pages explain how to check for and repair grammatical errors, tell Word how scrupulously to look for errors, and turn off the grammar-checker.

LEARN BY EXAMPLE
Open the 11-2 Grammar practice document on the companion CD to try out the grammar-checker.

Checking a Document for Grammatical Errors

By now you must have noticed the green lines that appear underneath words from time to time. (If you don't see the green lines, choose Tools | Options, click the Spelling & Grammar tab in the Options dialog box, check the Check Grammar As You Type check box, and make sure that no check mark appears in the Hide Grammatical Errors In This Document check box.) The green lines appear where Word thinks it has encountered a grammatical error.

Figure 11-5 shows the two ways to correct grammatical errors. You can correct them one at a time by right-clicking and choosing a correction from the shortcut menu, or you can open the Spelling and Grammar dialog box and correct grammatical errors one after the other throughout a document.

FORMATTING TEXT AND PAGES

Tip *Click the Microsoft Word Help button in the lower-left corner of the Spelling and Grammar dialog box to get an explanation of a grammatical error from the Office Assistant. You can also right-click a grammatical error and choose About This Sentence from the shortcut menu to read why Word thinks your sentence is grammatically incorrect. You will also find brief descriptions of the grammatical errors in the top of the Spelling and Grammar dialog box.*

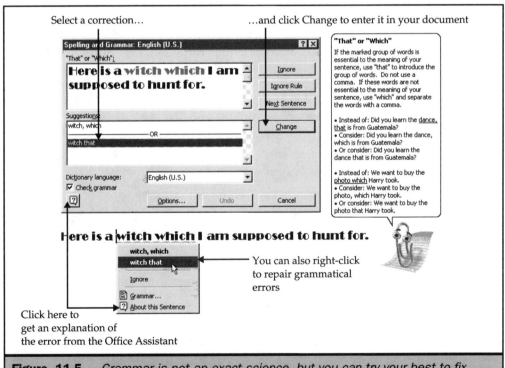

Figure 11-5. *Grammar is not an exact science, but you can try your best to fix grammatical errors with the grammar-checker*

Press F7 or choose Tools | Spelling and Grammar to correct grammatical errors in the Spelling and Grammar dialog box. Sentences in which grammatical errors appear are highlighted in the document. The grammatical errors themselves appear in bright green in the box at the top of the dialog box (along with spelling errors, which are red). Table 11-2 describes the buttons in the Spelling and Grammar dialog box for correcting grammatical errors. When Word encounters an error, take one of these actions to correct it:

- Select a correction in the Suggestions box and click the Change button.

- Delete the misspelled word or words in the top of the dialog box, enter a correction, and click the Next Sentence button.

- Click outside the Spelling and Grammar dialog box, correct the grammatical error in the document, and click the Resume button (you will find it where the Ignore button used to be).

Button	What It Does
Ignore	Ignores the breach of grammar and proceeds to the next grammatical error.
Ignore Rule	Tells Word to ignore, throughout the document, the kind of grammatical error that is listed at the top of the Spelling and Grammar dialog box. For example, if the top of the dialog box reads "Passive Voice," all passive-voice errors are disregarded.
Next Sentence	Tells Word to move on to the next sentence. Click this button after you repair a grammatical error by editing words inside the Spelling and Grammar dialog box.
Change	Corrects the grammatical error by entering the highlighted word, phrase, or sentence in the Suggestions box in the document.
Options	Opens the Spelling & Grammar tab of the Options dialog box so you can tell Word how to check for grammatical errors in your document.
Undo	Reverses your previous action in the Spelling and Grammar dialog box. You can keep clicking Undo to reverse more than one action.

Table 11-2. *Buttons for Correcting Grammatical Errors in the Spelling and Grammar Dialog Box*

Strategies for Handling the Grammar-Checker

The grammar-checker isn't for everybody. Some people think that the green lines that the grammar-checker draws underneath grammatical errors are annoying. And if you have any degree of confidence in your writing, you probably don't need the grammar-checker. What's more, the grammar-checker occasionally offers up a ridiculous suggestion for correcting what it thinks is an error. This famous line from *Hamlet*, for example, would not make any sense if Shakespeare had corrected it with his grammar-checker.

Neither a borrower nor a lender be.

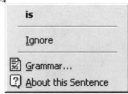

Choose Tools | Options, click the Spelling & Grammar tab in the Options dialog box, and take note of the check boxes under the word "Grammar." By checking or unchecking these boxes, you can impair the grammar-checker or make it work better:

- **Turn the Grammar-Checker Off**   Uncheck the Check Grammar As You Type check box to turn off the grammar-checker altogether.

- **Keep the Green Lines from Appearing**   Check the Hide Grammatical Errors In This Document check box. With this strategy, the green lines don't appear, but Word still looks out for grammatical errors. When you press F7 or choose Tools | Spelling and Grammar, the grammatical errors appear in the Spelling and Grammar dialog box (see Figure 11-5). You can also find grammatical errors by double-clicking the book icon on the Status bar.

- **Only Handle Spelling Errors in the Spelling and Grammar Dialog Box**   Uncheck the Check Grammar With Spelling check box if you want to keep grammatical errors from appearing in the Spelling and Grammar dialog box. You can still correct grammatical errors by right-clicking.

Grammar

☑ Check grammar as you type
☑ Hide grammatical errors in this document
☑ Check grammar with spelling
☐ Show readability statistics

Writing style:
Standard ▼

Settings...

Recheck Document

Telling Word How to Check for Grammatical Errors

Not all documents are alike, so Word gives you a means of deciding how thoroughly and rigidly to check for grammatical errors. After all, a letter to Aunt Enid does not have to be as grammatically up to snuff as a letter to a bank examining board or a clemency plea addressed to the governor of Texas. Read on to learn how to change the standards by which good grammar is measured and choose for yourself what the rules of good grammar are.

Choosing a Standard for Judging Grammar

Follow these steps to tell Word what kind of document you are working on and therefore how carefully to grammar-check a document:

1. Choose Tools | Options and click the Spelling & Grammar tab in the Options dialog box. You can also get to the Spelling & Grammar tab by clicking the Options button in the Spelling and Grammar dialog box (see Figure 11-5)

2. From the Writing Style drop-down list, choose an option that describes your document and click OK. The Custom option is for describing a writing style apart from Standard, Casual, Formal, or Technical.

   - **Casual**   The most relaxed of the four. Doesn't even catch double negatives.
   - **Standard**   The default style. Catches common grammatical errors but doesn't address style issues such as wordiness and the use of clichés and colloquialisms.
   - **Formal**   The most rigid of the styles. Checks for all grammatical errors and all style errors except gender-specific words and the use of the first person.
   - **Technical**   For use in scientific papers and technical manuals. Permits jargon and passive sentences but not the use of the first person.

Choose an option from the Writing Style drop-down list and click the Settings button to open the Grammar Settings dialog box and see which grammatical rules apply to each style. Table 11-3 describes the Grammar and Style options in the Grammar Settings dialog box.

Option	What It Checks For
Require	
Comma Required Before Last List Item	A comma before the word "and" or "or" when more than two nouns are strung together ("no, yes, or maybe," not "no, yes or maybe"). The options are Always, Never, and Don't Check.

Table 11-3.   *Grammatical Rules Used in Grammar-Checking*

Option	What It Checks For
Punctuation Required with Quotes	Whether punctuation marks such as commas and periods appear inside or outside quotation marks. In American usage, punctuation marks always appear inside quotation marks. (He was "inconvenienced.") In British usage, punctuation marks sometimes appear outside quotation marks. (He was "inconvenienced".) The options are Inside, Outside, and Don't Check.
Spaces Required Between Sentences	Whether one or two blank spaces appear after the periods at the end of sentences. The options are 1, 2, and Don't Check.
Grammar	
Capitalization	Capitalization errors in proper names ("Ms. gonzales") and titles ("president Wilson").
Common Confused Words	Words that are often used mistakenly ("towards" instead of "toward") and words that sound alike but have different meanings ("flea" and "flee").
Hyphenated and Compound Words	Words that are hyphenated mistakenly ("pre-historic") and words that should be hyphenated but aren't ("self restraint").
Misused Words	Misuse of superlatives and comparatives such as "like," "nor," and "whom."
Negation	Use of double negatives ("You don't have no reason to do that").
Numbers	The digits 1 through 10, which are often spelled out ("one," "ten").
Passive Sentences	Sentences in the passive voice ("He was tackled by me").
Possessives and Plurals	Misuse of possessives and plurals as regards the use of the apostrophe (') ("Janes' car," "the peoples' voice").
Punctuation	Incorrect use of commas, periods, colons, and question marks.
Relative Clauses	Incorrect use of relative clauses ("which" for "that," "that's" for "whose").

Table 11-3. *Grammatical Rules Used in Grammar-Checking* (continued)

Option	What It Checks For
Sentence Structure	Sentence fragments, run-on sentences, and sentences with too many conjunctions (that is, too many "ands" and "ors").
Subject-Verb Agreement	Subjects and verbs that do not agree ("The country are big," "Dogs is tired").
Verb and Noun Phrase	Incorrect verb tenses ("they will smiled"), number disagreement errors ("three peach"), and the misuse of "a" and "an" ("a important time").
Style	
Clichés	Shopworn phrases ("each and every," "one and all").
Colloquialisms	Words and phrases that belong in conversation, not writing ("how come," "awfully nice").
Contractions	Use of contractions that could be spelled out ("won't," "could've," "hadn't").
Gender-Specific Words	Words with the letters "man" that might also refer to women ("chairman," "workmanlike").
Jargon	Words peculiar to a trade or technical profession. The program is very vague about what these words are, rendering this option useless.
Sentence Length	Sentences longer than 90 words.
Sentences Beginning with And, But, and Hopefully	Sentences that begin with these three words.*
Successive Nouns	More than three nouns in a row ("The countryside market development fund is healthy").
Successive Prepositional Phrases	Three or more prepositions in a row ("The neighborhood on the hill in the city by the sea").
Unclear Phrasing	Sentences with referents that are hard to locate ("All of the racers did not finish the race" instead of "Not all the racers finished the race").

* There is nothing wrong with starting a sentence with "And" or "But." Strange that "Hopefully" is lumped with the other two words, because "hopefully," a dangling modifier, is grammatically wrong and should not be used under any circumstances, much less the start of a sentence.

Table 11-3. *Grammatical Rules Used in Grammar-Checking* (continued)

Option	What It Checks For
Use of First Person	Use of the word "I" and "me," which is considered a *faux pas* in technical writing ("I must be right").
Wordiness	Excessive use of modifiers ("necessarily," "certainly") and overuse of adverbs.
Word in Split Infinitives	Two words used to split an infinitive ("They want to very thoroughly complete the job").

Table 11-3.   *Grammatical Rules Used in Grammar-Checking* (continued)

Deciding for Yourself What the Rules of Good Grammar Are

Depending on which writing style is in use, some of the grammar rules described in Table 11-3 are enforced and some are not enforced. Follow these steps to tell Word which grammar rules to use during a grammar-check:

1. Go to the Spelling & Grammar tab of the Options dialog box. To get there, either choose Tools | Options and click the Spelling & Grammar tab, or, starting from the Spelling and Grammar dialog box (see Figure 11-5), click the Options button.

2. If necessary, choose an option from the Writing Style drop-down list to modify a set of grammar rules; to impose an entirely new set of rules, choose Custom from the drop-down list.

3. Click the Settings button. You see the Grammar Settings dialog box shown in Figure 11-6.

4. Choose options from the Require drop-down menus and check off boxes next to the rules that you want to apply. Table 11-3 describes these options.

5. Click OK twice to return to your document.

   Click the Reset All button in the Grammar Settings dialog box if you get in a tangle and want the original set of Casual, Standard, Formal, or Technical grammatical rules to apply.

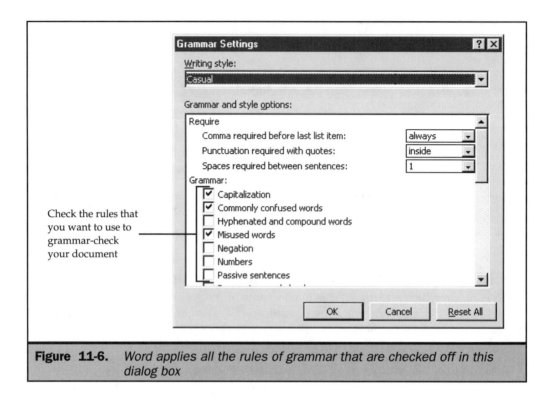

Check the rules that you want to use to grammar-check your document

Figure 11-6.   *Word applies all the rules of grammar that are checked off in this dialog box*

Checking Out Your Readability Statistics

For what it's worth, and I don't think it's worth a lot, you can obtain "readability statistics" that describe how easy or difficult reading a document is. Readability statistics include the average number of sentences per paragraph and what percentage of sentences in a document were written in the passive voice. You can also find out where your document stands on two scales, both of which take account of the average number of syllables per word and the average number of words per sentence:

- **Flesch Reading Ease Scale**   On a scale of 100, how easy it is to read a document. A score of 60 to 70 is considered average.

- **Flesch-Kincaid Grade Level**   At what grade level a document was written. Seventh to eighth grade is considered average.

To obtain these statistics of dubious value, check the Show Readability Statistics check box on the Spelling & Grammar tab of the Options dialog box before you grammar-check your entire document. To get to the Spelling & Grammar tab, click the Options button in the Spelling and Grammar dialog box (see Figure 11-5).

As an experiment, I obtained readability statistics for Martin Luther King's much acclaimed "I Have a Dream" speech, one of the finest examples of oratory in the English language. The results of my experiment (shown in the following illustration) would have us believe that Dr. King's speech barely passed the Flesch Reading Ease test and that it was written at a ninth-grade reading level. From my experiment we can conclude that the average number of syllables per word and the average number of words per sentence do not amount to a useful indicator of the power or clarity of anyone's writing.

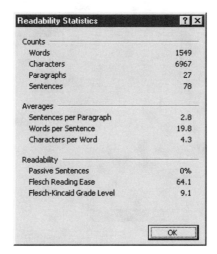

Finding the Right Word with the Thesaurus

Choosing the right word is so important in writing that Microsoft included a thesaurus with its word processor. As you endeavor to describe your thoughts, use the Thesaurus to find *synonyms*—words that have the same or a similar meaning. Do either of the following to find a synonym for a word:

- Right-click the word, choose Synonyms on the shortcut menu, and choose a synonym from the shortcut menu, as shown in Figure 11-7.

- Click the word and press SHIFT-F7 or choose Tools | Language | Thesaurus to open the Thesaurus dialog box shown in Figure 11-7. You can also open the dialog box by right-clicking and choosing Thesaurus on the Synonyms submenu. Open the Thesaurus dialog box when you want to conduct an intensive search for a synonym.

Use these boxes and buttons in the Thesaurus dialog box to find the synonym you so desperately seek:

- **Looked Up**   Lists the words you investigated in your search for a synonym. Choose a word from the drop-down list to backtrack.

- **Meanings**   Lists variations of the word you are looking up, including different word forms. Click a word to steer the search in a different direction.

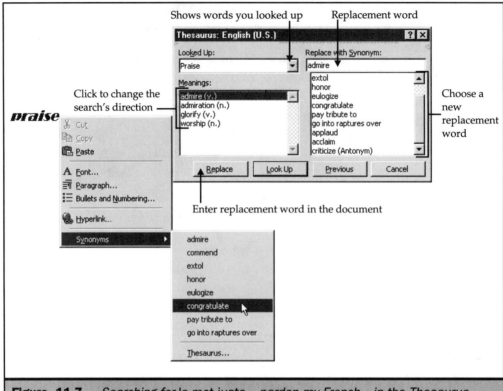

Figure 11-7.   *Searching for* le mot juste—*pardon my French—in the Thesaurus dialog box*

- **Replace With Synonym**   Lists what the program thinks is the best synonym for the word in the Looked Up box. Click a word in the box below to make it the replacement word—the word that goes in your document when you click the Replace button. You can type your own replacement word in this box.

- **Replace Button**   Enters the word in the Replace With Synonym box in the document. Click this button when your search is done.

- **Look Up Button**   Tells the program to find synonyms for the word in the Replace With Synonym box. Click to see a new batch of synonyms.

- **Previous Button**   Lists synonyms for the last word you investigated. Click this button to backtrack.

Tip   *If you can't quite remember a word but you know its antonym (its opposite), enter its antonym in the Replace With Synonym text box and click the Look Up button. With any luck, the Replace With Synonym list shows the word you are looking for—the antonym of the antonym you entered. In Figure 11-7, for example, the antonym "criticize" appears in the Replace With Synonym list. If you were looking for a word that means the opposite of "praise," you could look up "praise" in the Thesaurus dialog box, look for an antonym of "praise," and find the word "criticize" that way.*

Working with Text Written in a Foreign Language

The version of Word 2000 that is sold and distributed in the United States comes with a Spanish and French dictionary as well as an English one. That means you can spell-check and grammar-check words in Spanish and French. To spell- and grammar-check text written in Uzbek, Estonian, Afrikaans, and other languages apart from English, Spanish, and French, you have to obtain the Microsoft Proofing Tools Kit. Call Microsoft at 425/462-9673 to obtain the kit, or else visit the Office Home Page (**www.microsoft.com/office/default.htm**) to learn more about the kit and buy a copy online.

Microsoft's literature claims that Word can "detect" a language other than English when you enter text in another language. Without being asked, Microsoft says, the program can bring to bear its proofing tools on the other language. Before you can work in a foreign language, however, you have to tell Word which language or languages besides English you intend to use. Read on.

The Status bar lists which language the cursor is in if your document includes more than one language that Word recognizes. Look at the box directly to the right of the OVR button on the Status bar to see which language you are dealing with.

Telling Word Which Languages You Will Use

Follow these steps to inform Word that you will use a language or languages besides English in your documents:

1. Close all programs, if any are open.

2. Click the Start button and choose Programs | Office Tools | Microsoft Office Language Settings. You will see the Microsoft Office Language Settings dialog box.

3. On the Enabled Languages tab, check the boxes next to the names of languages you intend to use in your work.

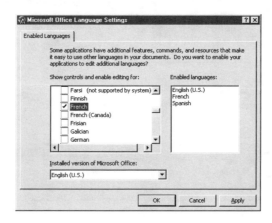

4. Click OK.

5. Click Yes when Word warns you that you must restart your computer for the language settings to take effect.

   You must have installed the Microsoft Proofing Tools Kit to spell-check and grammar-check words written in languages besides English, French, and Spanish.

Telling Word When You Are Using a Foreign Language

As I mentioned earlier, Microsoft boasts that its software can "automatically detect" when a language besides English is in use. How does the software do it? In the first place, Word knows which languages to look for, since you told it which languages you will use in the Microsoft Office Language Settings dialog box. As for determining which language is on the page, "Word uses special language algorithms and statistics to analyze the letter combinations in every sentence," says a Help program screen. Huh? Sounds dubious to me. To be on the safe side, I suggest marking foreign language text in your documents as well as telling the program to "detect" the foreign words. After you mark the text as foreign language text, Word can spell-check and grammar-check it with the proper dictionaries.

Follow these steps to tell Word to keep a lookout for foreign languages and to mark text so Word knows in which language it was written:

1. Select the text that you wrote in a foreign language.

2. Choose Tools | Language | Set Language. You'll see the Language dialog box shown in Figure 11-8.

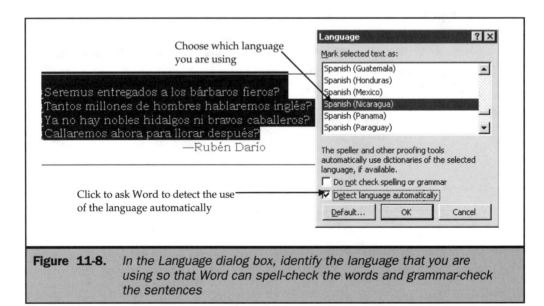

Figure 11-8.   *In the Language dialog box, identify the language that you are using so that Word can spell-check the words and grammar-check the sentences*

3. In the Mark Selected Text As list box, find the language and select it.

4. Check the Detect Language Automatically check box if you want Word to try on its own to find out when you are using the language.

5. Click OK.

Besides foreign languages, the Language dialog box offers varieties of the English language, including U.K. English, Canadian English, and Australian English. Choose a different type of English if you want to pass yourself off as a Brit, Canadian, or Australian, for example.

After you have chosen a language in the Mark Selected Text As list box, you can mark text in documents by right-clicking: Select the text, right-click it, choose Language, and choose a language from the submenu.

Create a character style for other languages. That way, you can simply select the foreign language text and choose a style from the Style menu to mark the text as foreign. Hint: Click the Format button in the New Style dialog box and choose Language. Chapter 12 explains character styles.

Exam MOUS Exam Objectives Explored in Chapter 11

Objective	Heading	Practice File
Use the Spelling feature	"Correcting Your Spelling Errors"	11-1 Spelling
Use the Thesaurus feature	"Finding the Right Words with the Thesaurus"	
Use the Grammar feature	"Correcting Grammatical Errors"	11-2 Grammar

* Denotes an Expert exam objective.

FORMATTING
TEXT AND PAGES

The Complete Reference

Word 2000

Part III

Professional-Looking Documents with Word 2000

Keeping Words from Being Spell-Checked

Spell-checking address lists, lines of computer code, and foreign languages for which Microsoft doesn't offer foreign-language dictionaries is a thorough waste of time. Follow these steps to tell the spell-checker to ignore text in a document:

1. Select the text.

2. Choose Tools | Language | Set Language. You'll see the Language dialog box.

3. Check the Do Not Check Spelling Or Grammar check box and click OK.

Create a character style for text that need not be spell-checked. That way, you can simply apply the style to the text instead of having to select it and choose the Tools | Language | Set Language command. *Hint:* Click the Format button in the New Style dialog box and choose Language. Chapter 12 explains styles.

Besides the Custom.dic dictionary, you can employ other dictionaries to help with spell-checking. People who work in specialized professions such as law or medicine can also use legal dictionaries and medical dictionaries to spell-check their work. You can create dictionaries of your own for slang words, colloquialisms, or special projects. Before you start spell-checking, you can tell Word which dictionaries to use. And you can edit dictionaries as well. All this magic is done by way of the Custom Dictionaries dialog box shown in Figure 11-4. Do either of the following to open this dialog box:

■ Press F7 or choose Tools | Spelling and Grammar to open the Spelling and Grammar dialog box, and then click the Options button. In the Spelling & Grammar dialog box, click the Dictionaries button.

■ Choose Tools | Options, click the Spelling & Grammar tab in the Options dialog box, and click the Dictionaries button.

Using Secondary Dictionaries for Spell-Checking

People who work in law offices, research facilities, and medical facilities type hundreds of arcane terms each day, none of which are in the main dictionary. One way to make sure that arcane terms are spelled correctly is to create or acquire a dictionary of legal, scientific, or medical terms and use it for spell-checking purposes.

The Complete Reference

Word 2000

Chapter 12

Styles for Consistent

and Easy Formatting

Welcome to what may be the most important chapter in this book. A *style* is a collection of commands and formats that have been bundled under one name. By using styles, you free yourself from having to visit and revisit numerous dialog boxes whenever you want to change the formatting of a paragraph. Styles save a lot of time. When you want to reformat a paragraph or text, you simply choose a style name from the Style drop-down menu. The paragraph or text is reformatted instantly. What's more, you can rest assured that all parts of the document that were assigned the same style are laid out and look the same. By using styles, you make sure that various parts of your document are consistent with one another and that your documents have a professional look.

Read on if styles interest you—and they should if you intend to do any serious work whatsoever in Microsoft Word. Styles can save a ridiculous amount of time that you would otherwise spend formatting and wrestling with text. And many Word features rely on styles. You can't create a table of contents or use the Document Map unless each heading in your document was assigned a heading style. Nor can you take advantage of Outline view and the commands on the Outline toolbar. And you can't cross-reference headings or number the headings in a document. To create a table of figures or illustrations, you must have tagged their captions with the Caption style.

The advantages of using styles are many. Do yourself a big favor by learning how to work with and apply styles. This chapter explains how to create a style of your own, apply a style, and modify a style. You will also learn the subtle and not so subtle ways to manage styles, how to copy styles between documents and templates, and how to create a template for styles that you've created. At the end of this chapter is a list of ten style problems and how to solve them.

Styles: An Overview

Most people break into a yawn or a cold sweat when they hear the word "styles." But styles are essential in Word and are worth taking the trouble to learn. To help you get going, this section presents a brief overview of styles. Later, I describe all the things you can do with styles in detail.

UNIFORMITY OF STYLES   By using styles, you make sure that the various parts of your document present a uniform appearance and are consistent with one another. All headings assigned the Heading 1 style look the same. Paragraphs assigned the Quotation style look alike, as shown in Figure 12-1. If you change your mind about a style's appearance, all you have to do is redefine it. The new, redefined style is applied instantly throughout your document. Paragraphs and text that were assigned the style are reformatted. You don't have to do the reformatting yourself by going from paragraph to paragraph and choosing commands.

Styles are especially important in the business world. A company makes a good impression on customers and clients when its letters, faxes, and invoices present a uniform appearance. You can make sure your company's correspondence presents a

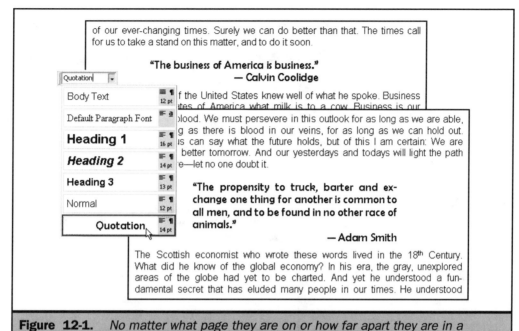

of our ever-changing times. Surely we can do better than that. The times call for us to take a stand on this matter, and to do it soon.

"The business of America is business."
— Calvin Coolidge

f the United States knew well of what he spoke. Business

tes of America what milk is to a cow. Business is our

blood. We must persevere in this outlook for as long as we are able,

g as there is blood in our veins, for as long as we can hold out.

is can say what the future holds, but of this I am certain: We are

better tomorrow. And our yesterdays and todays will light the path

e—let no one doubt it.

"The propensity to truck, barter and ex-change one thing for another is common to all men, and to be found in no other race of animals."
— Adam Smith

The Scottish economist who wrote these words lived in the 18th Century. What did he know of the global economy? In his era, the gray, unexplored areas of the globe had yet to be charted. And yet he understood a fundamental secret that has eluded many people in our times. He understood

Quotation

Body Text	12 pt
Default Paragraph Font	
Heading 1	16 pt
Heading 2	14 pt
Heading 3	13 pt
Normal	12 pt
Quotation	14 pt

Figure 12-1.   *No matter what page they are on or how far apart they are in a document, paragraphs assigned the same style—the Quotation style, in this case—look alike*

PROFESSIONAL-LOOKING DOCUMENTS WITH WORD 2000

uniform appearance by creating styles for use in letters, faxes, and invoices and saving the styles in templates that employees can use when they create documents. Creating styles for company correspondence also saves time because employees can choose styles from the Style menu as they create documents instead of formatting the text themselves.

STYLES AND TEMPLATES   A *template* is a special kind of file that is used as the starting point for creating other files. All Word documents are created from templates. When you click the New Blank Document button or press CTRL-N to create a new document, Word uses the Normal template to create your file, but when you choose File | New to create a new document, you can choose among many exotic templates in the New dialog box.

Each template comes with a collection of styles that you can use to format documents. Figure 12-2, for example, shows a document that was created with the Elegant Report template. In the figure, the Style menu is open and you can see the many styles that are available in documents created with the Elegant Report template. These are styles that the document in Figure 12-2 inherited from the template with which it was created.

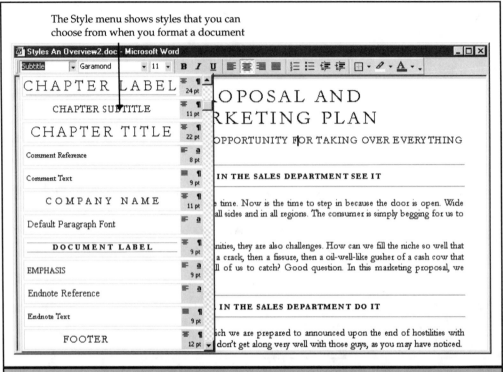

Figure 12-2.   *Each document is created from a template. As such, each document comes with many predefined styles that you can use for formatting*

However, the styles that a document inherits from a template are not the only ones you can use for formatting. You can also create your own styles. And if a style you create happens to be one you want to use again, you can add your new style to a template. That way, the style you created will be available when you create other documents with the template. You can even create a template of your own with styles that you know and love.

PARAGRAPH STYLES AND CHARACTER STYLES   Word offers two kinds of styles, *paragraph styles* and *character styles*. By far, the majority of styles are paragraph styles. Character styles apply to text you select, whereas paragraph styles apply to entire paragraphs, including the text:

- Paragraph styles format paragraphs—they indent them, align them, and change their line spacing, for example. A paragraph style, like a character style, can include font and font size settings.

- Character styles are for hard-to-lay-out text such as small capital letters, for combinations of font and font size commands that are too troublesome to apply in conventional ways, and for foreign words that you want the spell-checker and grammar-checker to proof. Before you assign a character style, select text in the document. Character styles apply to selected text, not to all the text in a paragraph.

You can tell by glancing at the style names on the Style menu which are paragraphs styles and which are character styles. Paragraph styles are marked with the paragraph symbol (¶); character styles are marked with the letter "a."

Applying Styles in a Document

Word 2000 offers a bunch of different techniques for applying styles. Some of the techniques fall in the esoteric category and are not used very often, but knowing about them doesn't hurt a bit. Read on to find out how to apply styles one at a time and how to get Word's help in applying many styles at once.

In most cases, the style from the previous paragraph is carried to the new one automatically when you press ENTER to start a new paragraph. After heading styles and certain other kinds of styles, however, Word applies a different style to the new paragraph. Later in this chapter, "Creating Your Own Styles" explains the benefits of making one style automatically follow another and how you can make a style follow another style automatically.

LEARN BY EXAMPLE
Open the 12-1 Apply Styles practice document on the companion CD to get some practical experience with apply styles.

Applying Styles One at a Time

The fastest and best way to apply a style is to do so from the Style menu on the Formatting toolbar, but you can also apply a style by way of the Style dialog box, one or two keyboard shortcuts, and the Format Painter. For that matter, sometimes Word applies styles on its own. Better read on.

The Repeat command comes in especially handy when you apply styles to paragraphs. Apply a style to a paragraph, click another paragraph or select other paragraphs to which you want to apply the style, and press F4 or choose Edit | Repeat Style.

PROFESSIONAL-LOOKING DOCUMENTS WITH WORD 2000

Applying a Style by Way of the Style Menu

Follow these steps to apply a style from the Style drop-down menu:

1. Place the insertion point in the paragraph whose style you want to change or select several paragraphs to apply a style to them. To apply a character style, select the text.

2. Open the Style drop-down menu on the Formatting toolbar and choose a style.

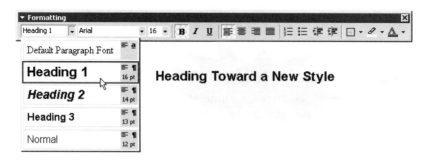

Heading Toward a New Style

Keyboard fans can choose styles from the Style menu by pressing CTRL-SHIFT-S. Pressing that key combination moves the cursor into the Style menu. Either press the ↓ key repeatedly until the name of the style you want appears in the Style menu box, or press ALT-↓ to make the Style menu drop and then press the ↓ key until you land on the style you want to apply. Press ENTER when the name of the style you want to apply appears in the Style menu box, or press the first letter of the style's name to go straight to styles whose names begin with the letter you pressed.

Reading the Style Menu

You can tell a lot about styles by studying the names on the Style menu. Names appear in the font that they apply to the text. Look at the boxes to the right of the names and you can find out the following:

- How text is aligned—left-aligned, right-aligned, centered, or justified. The alignment symbols on the Style menu look like the Alignment buttons on the Formatting toolbar.

- Whether the style is a paragraph or a character style. Paragraph styles show the ¶ symbol; character styles are marked by an underlined letter "a̲."

- The font size of the text, which is listed in points.

Applying a Style from the Style Dialog Box

Another way to apply a style is to visit the Style dialog box and select it there. The Preview boxes in the Style dialog box give a fair idea of what paragraphs will look like after you apply a style to them. Follow these steps to apply a style from the Style dialog box:

1. Click the paragraph whose style you want to change or select several paragraphs to apply a style to them. To apply a character style, select the text.

2. Choose Format | Style. You'll see the Style dialog box shown in Figure 12-3.

   In the Style list, paragraph symbols (¶) appear beside the names of paragraph styles; character styles are marked with the letter "a." If the paragraph or paragraphs to which you will apply your style have been marked with both a paragraph and character style, a small triangle appears next to a character style on the list (note the Default Paragraph Font style in Figure 12-3).

3. If necessary, choose an option from the List drop-down menu—Styles in Use, All Styles, or User-Defined Styles—to find the style you need on the list.

4. Choose a style on the Styles list and click the Apply button.

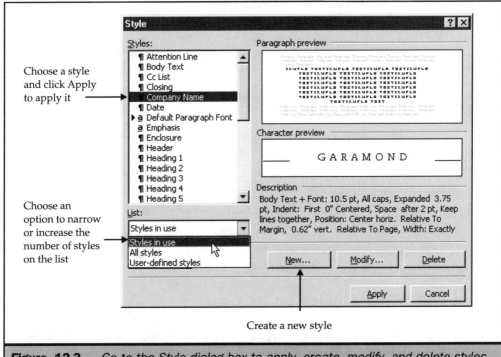

Figure 12-3.   *Go to the Style dialog box to apply, create, modify, and delete styles*

Keyboard Shortcuts for Applying Styles

For people who can type faster than they can click the mouse, here are some keyboard shortcuts for applying styles:

Apply This Style	By Pressing
Normal	CTRL-SHIFT-N
Heading	ALT-CTRL-1
Heading 2	ALT-CTRL-2
Heading 3	ALT-CTRL-3
Next higher heading	ALT-SHIFT-→
Next lower heading	ALT-SHIFT-←

"Designating Your Own Keyboard Shortcuts" in Chapter 23 explains how you can invent a keyboard shortcut of your own for applying a style.

Applying Styles with the Format Painter

Yet another way to apply styles one at a time is to use a peculiar tool on the Standard toolbar called the Format Painter. Use the Format Painter as you would the Repeat command to copy paragraph styles from paragraph to paragraph. Follow these steps to use the Format Painter to copy paragraph styles:

1. Click a paragraph whose style you want to copy elsewhere.
2. Double-click the Format Painter button on the Standard toolbar. The button is located to the right of the Paste button. After you double-click, the pointer turns into a paintbrush.
3. Click a paragraph to apply a style to it. To apply a style to more than one paragraph, drag the pointer over more than one paragraph.
4. Press ESC or click the Format Painter button when you are done copying paragraph styles.

Keyboard fans press CTRL-SHIFT-C, then click the paragraph or select parts of paragraphs to which you will copy the paragraph style, and press CTRL-SHIFT-V.

Styles That Word Applies on Its Own

Word applies certain styles automatically when you enter headers and footers and choose certain commands from the Insert menu. Don't be surprised when the Style

Seeing Which Styles Are in Use

Sometimes distinguishing one style from another is hard to do when you are working on a complex document. And if the Style menu is loaded down with a number of styles, remembering which style is which can be doubly hard. To help make style choices in complex documents, Word offers a special option in the Options dialog box called Style Area Width. When this option is turned on, style names appear on the screen to the left of the text. Of course, you can also choose the Help | What's This? command and click a paragraph to see precisely what a style does to the text (see "The What's This? Button for Finding Out What's What" in Chapter 4).

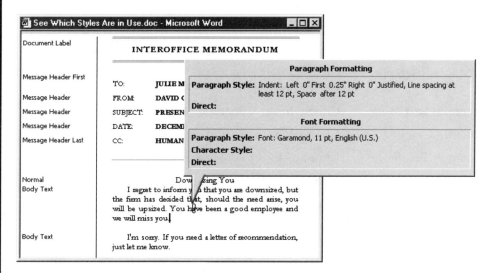

To see style names on the left side of the document window, follow these steps:

1. Choose Tools | Options to open the Options dialog box.
2. Click the View tab.
3. Under Outline and Normal Options at the bottom of the dialog box, enter .5 or .7 inches in the Style Area Width box and click OK.

You can only see the style names in Normal view and Outline view. To remove the style names, revisit the Options dialog box and shrink the style area to .0 inches. By the way, you can print descriptions of all the styles in a document. Choose File | Print, open the Print What drop-down menu in the Print dialog box, choose Styles, and click OK.

menu gets loaded down with the names of styles that you didn't apply yourself. Table 12-1 lists styles that Word applies automatically. These styles start appearing on the Style menu after you choose the commands listed in the table.

Tip   *Hold down the SHIFT key and click the down arrow in the Style menu on the Formatting toolbar to make the menu display all the styles that are available in a document.*

Style Name	Style Applied When You
Comment Reference*	Choose Insert I Comment. Marks the comment reference in the text.
Comment Text	Choose Insert I Comment and enter a comment.
Caption	Choose Insert I Caption and enter a caption.
Endnote Reference	Choose Insert I Footnote and enter an endnote. Marks the endnote reference.
Endnote Text	Choose Insert I Footnote and enter an endnote.
Footer	Choose View I Header and Footer and enter a footer.
Footnote Reference*	Choose I Insert Footnote. Marks the footnote reference.
Footnote Text	Choose Insert I Footnote.
Header	Choose View I Header and Footer and enter a header.
Index 1–9	Choose Insert I Index and Tables and generate an index.
Page Number*	Click the Insert Page Number button on the Header and Footer toolbar.
Table of Authorities	Choose Insert I Index and Tables and generate a table of authorities.
Table of Figures	Choose Insert I Index and Tables and generate a table of figures.
TOA Heading	Choose Insert I Index and Tables and generate a table of authorities.
TOC 1–9	Choose Insert I Index and Tables and generate a table of contents.

* Character style, not a paragraph style

Table 12-1.   *Styles That Word Applies Automatically*

Applying Styles *En Masse* with the Templates and Add-Ins Command

Occasionally you'll make a mistake and create a document with the wrong template. Or you'll get a document from someone else and realize to your dismay that the person who gave you the document created it with the wrong template. For such occasions, Word offers the Tools | Templates and Add-Ins command. This command rips a document from its original template and gives it to a new template.

To be specific, the Tools | Templates and Add-Ins command does and doesn't do the following to a document:

- Paragraphs assigned to a style whose name is found in the original template and the new template are reformatted. For example, if the original template includes a style called Body Text and the new template also has a style called Body Text, paragraphs assigned the Body Text style are reformatted according to the rules of the new template.

- Nothing happens to paragraphs assigned to a style whose name is not found in the new template. A paragraph tagged with the Quotation style, for example, looks the same under the new template if the new template doesn't include the Quotation style.

Note
Usually, you have to assign a new style to paragraphs that didn't change or else modify a style to make paragraphs that didn't change fit the new, revamped document. Later in this chapter, "Finding and Replacing Styles" explains how you can use the Find and Replace command to exchange one style for another. "Modifying a Style" explains how to modify a style.

- Margin settings and page-orientation settings stay the same.
- The macros and AutoText entries from the original template do not make the transition. Instead, you get the macros and AutoText entries from the new template.

Caution
Create a backup copy or second copy of a document before you attach it to a new template. You can't click the Undo button if you change your mind about which template belongs to which document. If attaching a new template makes hash of your document, you can use the backup copy.

Follow these steps to attach a new template to a document and in so doing apply new styles throughout:

1. Choose Tools | Templates and Add-Ins. You see the Templates and Add-ins dialog box shown in Figure 12-4. The Document Template box lists the template to which the document is currently attached.

PROFESSIONAL-LOOKING
DOCUMENTS WITH
WORD 2000

Template that is or will be
attached to the document

Click here to apply styles
from the new template

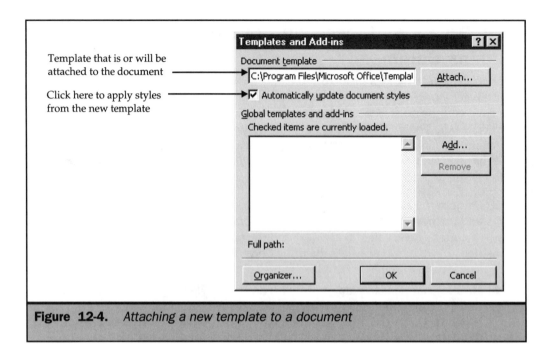

Figure 12-4.   *Attaching a new template to a document*

2. Click the Attach button. You'll see the Attach Template dialog box. In this dialog box, you'll find the template that you want to impose on your file. Word templates are located either in the C:\Program Files\Microsoft Office\ Templates folder and its subfolders or the C:\Windows\Application Data\Microsoft\Templates folder and its subfolders.

3. Find and select the template you want, and click the Open button. You will return to the Templates and Add-ins dialog box, where the name of the template you chose appears in the Document Template box.

Caution   *The original template and new template must be similar for the Tools | Templates and Add-Ins command to work. Changing a report to a letter or a letter to a report, for example, can turn a perfectly good document into guacamole.*

4. Click the Automatically Update Document Styles check box. Doing so tells Word to apply the styles from the new template to your document.

5. Click OK.

Tip   *When you clicked the Attach button to attach a new template to a file, did the Attach Template dialog box open to the right folder? If it didn't, choose Tools | Options and click the File Locations tab in the Options dialog box. Then, under File Types, choose User Templates and click the Modify button. In the Modify Location dialog box, find the folder in which your templates are located and click OK.*

Using the Style Gallery to Change Templates

As long as the template you want to impose on a document is one of Word's and not a template you created yourself, you can attach a new template to a document by visiting the Style Gallery. Follow these steps:

1. Choose Format | Theme to open the Theme dialog box.
2. Click the Style Gallery button. You will see the Style Gallery dialog box.

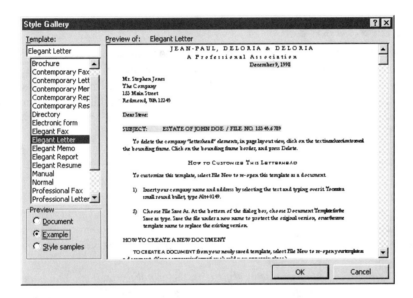

3. In the Template list, click the name of the Word template that you want to attach to your document. You can click the Example option button to see a sample document that shows what the template does to text or the Style Samples option button to see samples of the different styles found in the template.
4. Click OK. Styles from the new template are imposed on your document and it looks brand new.

Creating Your Own Styles

You are hereby invited to create a new style whenever you format a paragraph or text and suspect that sometime in the future you will have to format a paragraph or text the same way. By creating a style, you only have to format the paragraph or text once. After that, you can simply choose an option from the Style menu when the time comes to format.

What's more, you can copy styles from document to document or template to template. So the time you take to create a style can pay many dividends in the future. I know someone who has a whole library of Word styles and makes a living by recycling them. My friend designs Word templates for companies. Her clients don't know it, but most of her templates are stitched together from styles she created for projects she did years ago. (Later in this chapter, "Building Your Own Templates" explains how to bundle styles into a template.)

These pages explain how to create a style, redefine a style, copy styles from document to document, and find and replace styles. Better read on.

The Two Ways to Create a Style

Word offers two ways to create a style: the prototype method and the from-the-ground-up method. With the prototype method, you create a model paragraph for your new style. Then you tell Word to format paragraphs according to the specifications of the model paragraph. The advantage of the prototype method is that you can tell precisely how your new style formats paragraphs. You can tell because the prototype paragraph shows you.

The from-the-ground-up method takes longer, and you can't see what the style looks like onscreen, but you can do a more thorough job of creating a style this way. With the from-the-ground-up method, you visit different dialog boxes—the same dialog boxes you visit to format a paragraph—and pick and choose formats for your style. Moreover, this method offers some amenities that you can't get with the prototype method. For example, you can tell Word to update the style automatically as you make formatting changes and add the style to the template you are working in.

Sorry, you can't create a character style with the prototype method. You have to choose Format | Style and create it from the ground up in the New Style dialog box. "Styles: An Overview" at the start of this chapter explains the difference between character styles and paragraph styles.

Creating a Style from a Model Paragraph

Start with a model paragraph to create a style with the prototype method. Indent the paragraph, align the paragraph, change the line spacing—do to your model paragraph what you want your style to do to text when your style is applied to text. Then follow these steps to create the style:

1. Click in the paragraph.

2. Click inside the Style menu box. The words in the Style menu box are highlighted.

Click in the Style menu box, type a style name, and press ENTER

"I sound my barbaric yawp over the roofs of the world."
— Walt Whitman

3. Type a name for the new style and press ENTER.

Styles names can be 253 characters long, but choose a short, descriptive name. For that matter, choose a name that doesn't stretch the Style menu out of shape when you open it from the Formatting toolbar.

One drawback of creating a style with the prototype method is that the style is based on the style that was in effect when you clicked inside the Style menu box to type a name. If the "based on" style changes, so does the style you created. See "Basing One Style on Another Style," later in this chapter, to learn about the pitfalls of basing one style on another.

Creating a Style from the Ground Up

To create a style from the ground up, follow these steps:

1. Click the paragraph or heading for which you want to create a new paragraph style, or select the text for which you want to create a character style.
2. Choose Format | Style to open the Style dialog box (see Figure 12-3).
3. Click the New button. You see the New Style dialog box shown in Figure 12-5.
4. Enter a name in the Name box. The style name you enter will appear on the Style drop-down list. Names can be 253 characters long, but choose a short, descriptive name that will fit on the Style menu on the Formatting toolbar.
5. Choose Character in the Style Type drop-down list to create a character style; choose Paragraph to create a paragraph style.
6. Click the Format button. You see a pop-up menu of formatting choices for defining your style. Table 12-2 describes the options on the Format menu.

7. Choose an option from the Format pop-up menu to open a dialog box and give formatting commands. For example, choosing Font opens the Font dialog box.

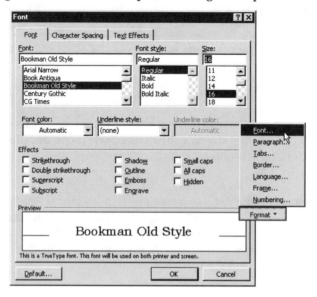

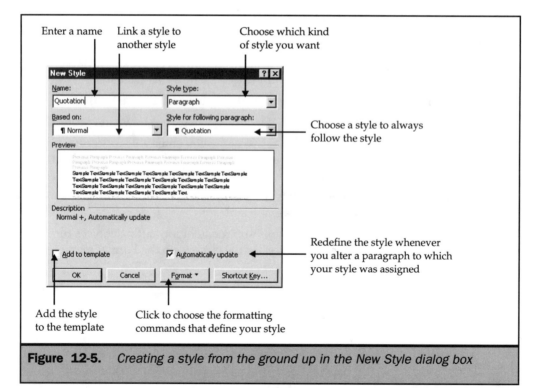

Figure 12-5. *Creating a style from the ground up in the New Style dialog box*

Format Button Option	Defines These Formats
Font	Fonts, font styles, font sizes, font color, underlining, text effects, character spacing, kerning, animation. *Menu equivalent:* Format I Font.
Paragraph*	Text alignment, outline level, indentation, before- and after-paragraph spacing, line spacing, widow and orphan control, pagination instructions, suppressing hyphenation, suppressing line numbers. *Menu equivalent:* Format I Paragraph.
Tabs*	Tab stop settings, leader settings. *Menu equivalent:* Format I Tabs.
Border	Borderlines for paragraphs, shading for paragraphs. *Menu equivalent:* Format I Borders and Shading.
Language	Language for proofing documents. *Menu equivalent:* Tools I Language I Set Language.
Frame*	Text wrapping around frames, frame size, horizontal and vertical position. *Menu equivalent:* Format I Frame (not to be confused with the Format I Frames command).
Numbering*	Bulleted lists, numbered lists, outline numbers, and heading numbers. *Menu equivalent:* Format I Bullets and Numbering.

*For creating paragraph styles only; the rest of the commands are for paragraph styles and character styles.

Table 12-2.   *Format Commands for Building Styles*

Note   *The Paragraph, Tabs, Frame, and Numbering options on the Format pop-up menu are not available if you are creating a character style. Those options are for creating paragraph styles.*

8. In the dialog box that appears, choose formatting options for the new style and then click OK. The dialog boxes that appear are the same ones that appear if you choose the Format menu and Tools menu commands listed in Table 12-1.

9. Repeat steps 7 and 8 as many times as necessary to create the style. You can visit as many dialog boxes as you want and make your style as complex as it needs to be.

10. The other options in the New Style dialog box are optional. Choose them as you see fit:

- **Based On** See "Basing One Style on Another," the next section in this chapter, to learn the ins and outs of building one style atop another.

- **Style For Following Paragraph** Choose a style from the drop-down list if the style you are creating is always to be followed by an existing style. For example, a style called Chapter Head might always be followed by one called Chapter Intro. Someone who applies the style you are creating and presses ENTER finds the style you choose here on the next line of the document. Choosing a style for the following paragraph saves time when you enter text and helps make sure that styles are applied correctly.

- **Add To Template** Click this check box if you want to add the style you are creating to the template with which you created the document you are working on. Unless this box is checked, new styles are available only in the document for which they were created. Click this box to save the style in the document *and* in the template. Anyone who creates a file with the template can draw upon the style you create if this box is checked.

- **Automatically Update** Check this box to be able to modify the style simply by reformatting a paragraph to which the style has been applied. For example, indent a paragraph and all other paragraphs that were assigned the style are indented accordingly. Checking this box tells Word to redefine the style automatically whenever you format a single paragraph that was assigned the style.

Tip *Click the Shortcut Key button if you care to create a shortcut key for applying the style. The Customize Keyboard dialog box appears. See "Designating Your Own Keyboard Shortcuts" in Chapter 23.*

11. Click OK to close the New Style dialog box.

12. Click Apply to apply the style you created to the paragraph or text you selected in step 1.

Copying Styles from Document to Document

All you have to do copy a style from one document to another is copy a paragraph to which you've assigned the style from the first document to the second. Copying styles this way works fine as long as you copy an entire paragraph (including the paragraph symbol at the end). You can delete the text after you copy the paragraph. Although the text has been deleted, the style you copied to the second document remains and is available on the Style menu.

Basing One Style on Another Style

When you create a style from a prototype paragraph, your new style is "based on" the style that was assigned to the prototype paragraph to begin with. For example, suppose a paragraph is assigned the Normal style when you fashion it into a prototype paragraph. After you create a style from the paragraph, your new style is "based on" the Normal style. Similarly, you can choose a "based on" style in the New Style dialog box (see Figure 12-5) when you create a style from the ground up.

The "based on" terminology that Word uses to describe the relationship between two styles is kind of misleading. Really, the new style isn't so much "based on" as it is "linked to" the other style, because when the "based on" style changes, so does the new style. For example, if you change the font in the Normal style, fonts change in all styles based on the Normal file as well. Change the line spacing or alignment of paragraphs in the Body Text style, and all styles that are based on the Body Text style change.

Unexpected changes brought about because someone modified the "based on" style are a chief cause of style problems. Therefore, you should be careful which "based on" style you choose. Choose one that isn't likely to be changed. Or choose the No Style option, the one at the top of the Based On menu in the New Style dialog box (later in this chapter, "Modifying a Style" explains how to change the particulars of a style, including which style it is based on). The point is to choose a "based on" style that won't wreak havoc on other styles if it is changed.

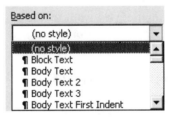

To be fair to the "based on" idea, however, basing one style on another can be a powerful way to make sure that the different parts of a document are consistent with one another. To see why, suppose you are designing a menu with many different elements—a title, subtitles ("Breakfast," "Lunch"), and descriptions of fare. As you tinker with your design, you intend to experiment with many different font sizes and text alignments. Throughout the menu, however, all styles will share the same font. To make sure they share the same font, you create a Menu Font style and base all other styles on Menu Font. That way, if you change the font in the Menu Font style, fonts in all the other styles change as well and you can rest assured that the same font appears in all parts of the menu.

You can't copy a style from one document to another if the style you are copying has the same name as a style in the document to which the copy is being made. To copy a style, its name must be different from all the style names in the document that is receiving the copy. Rename the style being copied, if necessary.

Later in this chapter, "Assembling Styles from Different Templates" describes how you can use the Organizer to copy styles from one document to another. The same techniques for assembling styles for a template work for copying styles between documents.

Finding and Replacing Styles

Sometimes when you change templates or copy text from another document, you discover paragraphs throughout a document that have the wrong style assignment. One way to fix this problem is to use the Find and Replace command to replace one style with another. The Find and Replace dialog box offers a special option for doing just that.

"Finding and Replacing Text and Other Things" in Chapter 6 explains the Find and Replace command in gruesome detail.

Follow these steps to find and replace a style throughout a document and thereby assign the right style to paragraphs:

1. Select part of your document if you want to find and replace styles on a handful of pages; to find and replace styles throughout, start at the top of the document.
2. Choose Edit | Find and Replace or press CTRL-F.
3. Click the More button to see all the options in the Find and Replace dialog box, as shown in Figure 12-6.
4. Make sure you are looking at the Find tab, and then click the Format button and choose Style from the pop-up menu.
5. In the Find Style dialog box (see Figure 12-6), locate the style that needs replacing, select it, and click OK. The name of the style you selected appears next to the word "Format" under the Find What box (see Figure 12-6).
6. Click the Find Next button. Word scrolls to the first instance of the style you choose and selects the paragraph to which it was assigned. Examine the paragraph to make sure that Word has found the style that needs replacing.
7. Click the Replace tab in the Find and Replace dialog box (see Figure 12-6).
8. Click in the Replace With text box.
9. Click the Format button and choose Style from the pop-up menu.

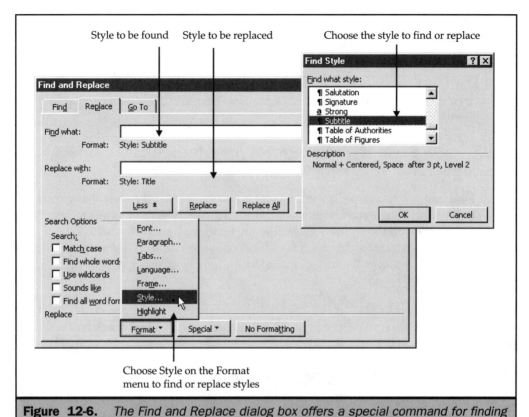

Style to be found   Style to be replaced   Choose the style to find or replace

Choose Style on the Format
menu to find or replace styles

Figure 12-6.   *The Find and Replace dialog box offers a special command for finding and replacing styles*

10. In the poorly named Find Style dialog box, select the style that will *replace* the style you chose in step 5, and click OK. On the Replace tab, the name of the replacement style appears next to the word "Format" under the Replace With text box.

11. Either click the Replace All button to replace all styles without reviewing them first, or click the Replace button and examine each paragraph before you assign the replacement style to it.

Modifying a Style

So a paragraph or text doesn't look quite right when you assign a style to it? You can fix that by modifying the style. Modifying styles is similar to creating them in that you can do it by example or by visiting the Modify Style dialog box, which looks and works much like the New Style dialog box. After you modify a style, paragraphs and text throughout your document are modified, too. Modifying a style is the fastest way to reformat a document.

LEARN BY EXAMPLE

Open the 12-2 Edit Styles document on the companion CD if you want to try your hand at editing a style or two.

Modifying a Style with the Prototype Method

Follow these steps to modify a style with the prototype method:

1. Find and reformat a paragraph to which you've applied the style that you want to redefine. When you are finished modifying the style, paragraphs to which you've applied the style will look like the paragraph you reformatted. To modify a character style, select a word to which you assigned the style.

2. Click in the Style menu box on the Formatting toolbar. The letters of the style name are highlighted.

3. Press the ENTER key. You see the Modify Style dialog box.

4. Make sure the Update The Style To Reflect Recent Changes? check box is checked and click OK.

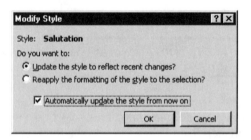

Check the Automatically Update The Style From Now On? check box if you want all paragraphs in the document that are assigned the style to be reformatted whenever you reformat a single paragraph that was assigned the style. Checking this box is the equivalent to checking the Automatically Update check box in the New Style dialog box (see Figure 12-5).

Modifying a Style in the Modify Style Dialog Box

The other way to modify a style is to visit the Modify Style dialog box. This technique offers the same advantages as creating a style in the New Style dialog box. You can add the style to the template with which the document was created, for example, or choose a new "based on" style. Follow these steps to redefine a style from the Modify Style dialog box:

1. Click a paragraph whose style you want to redefine, or select a word or two if you are modifying a character style.

2. Choose Format | Style.

3. In the Style dialog box, click the Modify button. You will see the Modify Style dialog box shown in Figure 12-7. Does this dialog box look familiar? The options in this dialog box are identical to those in the New Style dialog box (see Figure 12-5) with one exception: You can't choose between a Paragraph or Character style on the Style Type drop-down menu. Your choice of style types, I'm afraid, is set in stone and can't be altered.

4. Modify the style in the Modify Style dialog box. Use the same techniques you use when creating a style (see "The Two Ways to Create a Style," earlier in this chapter).

5. Click OK.

6. Click the Apply button to apply the new formats to all paragraphs or text in the document that were assigned the style you modified.

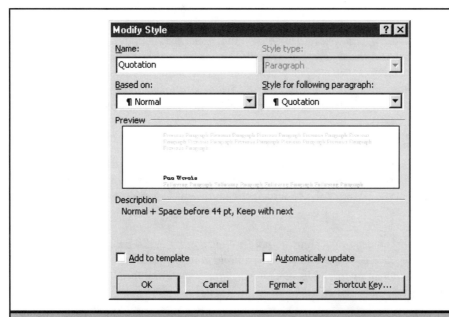

Figure 12-7.   *The Modify Style dialog box is nearly identical to the New Style dialog box. The options and choices are nearly identical as well*

Renaming and Deleting Styles

Sometimes you have to rename a style in order to copy it to another document. As "Copying Styles from Document to Document" explained earlier in this chapter, you can't copy a style from one document to another if a style in the receiving document has the same name as the style being copied. As for deleting styles, you might as well delete a style from a document if you don't need it to keep the Style menu list from growing too long.

Renaming a Style

Follow these steps to rename a style:

1. Choose Format | Style to open the Style dialog box.
2. In the Styles list, select the style you want to rename (choose an option from the List drop-down menu if you can't see your style).
3. Click the Modify button to open the Modify dialog box (see Figure 12-7).
4. Enter a new name for the style in the Name box.
5. Click OK and then Apply.

Paragraph or character style assignments throughout the document are given the new name.

Tip   *If you're in a hurry, and I mean a big hurry, to rename a style, click a paragraph to which you assigned the style, click in the Style menu box on the Formatting toolbar, type a new name, and press ENTER. The problem with renaming styles this way is that the style's old name remains on the Style menu to cause confusion and woe. Better to change names in the Modify Style dialog box to keep old names from crowding the Style menu.*

Deleting a Style

You can't delete the built-in styles that come with every Word document (Normal and the Heading styles, for example), but you can delete styles you fashioned yourself. After you delete a style, paragraphs to which the style was assigned are assigned the Normal style.

Caution   *Think twice before deleting a style. If another style you created is based on the style you want to delete, deleting the style can cause untold damage. What's more, you can't tell by looking how many paragraphs in a long document were assigned a style, so there is no telling what deleting it will do.*

Follow these steps to delete a style:

1. Choose Format | Style to open the Style dialog box.

2. Open the List drop-down menu and choose User-Defined Styles. Only the styles you created yourself can be deleted.

3. In the Styles list, click the style you want to delete.

4. Click the Delete button. Word asks if you really want to delete the style.

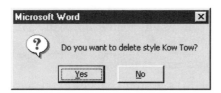

5. Click Yes and then click Close to close the Style dialog box.

Building Your Own Templates

After you create a template, you can use it as a launching pad for creating other documents. All Word documents are created from templates, as you know if you ever chose File | New and created a document in the New dialog box. Each template comes with many predefined styles. In these pages, you learn how to create templates of your own. Read on to find out how to create a template from a prototype document and assemble styles from different templates to create a new template.

Creating a Template from a Prototype Document

One way to create a template is to make one from a document you have been working on. With this technique, you choose File | Save As to save the document as a template, open the template, and delete the text. After you delete the text, the styles you created remain in the template. Later, you can create a Word document from your new template and make use of all the styles you so carefully created.

Follow these steps to create a template from a prototype document:

1. With the document open and staring you in the face, choose File | Save As. The Save As dialog box appears.

2. Click the Save As Type drop-down list and choose Document Template. You see the Templates folder in the Save In list at the top of the dialog box. In the dialog box are the names of templates that appear on the General tab of

the Open dialog box when you choose File | New to open a new document. You also see folder names—Legal Pleadings, Letters & Faxes, and so on. Not coincidentally, these are the names of tabs in the New dialog box. If you want to keep your template on a tab in the New dialog box besides the General tab, double-click the folder representing the template tab where you want to store your new template.

3. Type a descriptive name for your template in the File Name box. Template names must observe all the Windows file-naming conventions.

4. Click the Save button to complete the operation and close the Save As dialog box. The document you see onscreen is not really a document—it's a template file.

5. Delete all the text in the template file.

6. Click the Save button to save your changes to the template.

7. Choose File | Close to close the template.

As this illustration shows, templates you store in the Templates folder appear beside the Blank Document template on the General tab of the New dialog box. Here, I created a template called Personal Template and stored it in the Templates folder. To create a document with this template, I choose File | New, click the Personal Template template on the General tab of the New dialog box, and click OK.

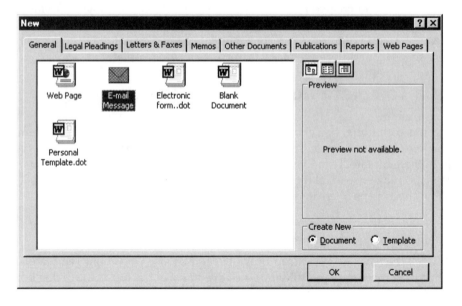

Setting the Default File Location for Workgroup Templates

If you are using Word in an office and your machine is attached to a network workgroup, you can share templates over the network with other members of the workgroup. To do so, however, you have to tell your computer where the templates are located by following these steps:

1. Choose Tools | Options.
2. Click the File Locations tab in the Options dialog box.
3. Under File Types, select Workgroup Templates, and then click the Modify button. You will see the Modify Location dialog box.
4. Find the folder on your network where the workgroup templates are located. You might have to ask the network administrator or someone in the know where that sacred place is.
5. Click OK and then click OK again in the Options dialog box.

Assembling Styles from Different Templates

Another way to create a template is to assemble styles from other templates and documents. Word offers a special gizmo called the Organizer for assembling styles from various places. Besides passing styles from template to template, you can also pass macros, AutoText entries, and toolbars with the Organizer. A template is a repository for macros, AutoText entries, and custom-made toolbars as well as styles.

To create a template with the Organizer, start either by opening a template to which you want to add styles or creating a brand-new template. Then you open the Organizer and start copying styles (and macros, AutoText entries, and toolbars, if you so desire) from other templates and documents to the template you opened or created.

Follow these steps to copy styles from templates and documents to a template:

1. Open the template that you want to copy styles to or create a new template:

- **Open an Existing Template**   Choose File | Open. In the Open dialog box, click the Files Of Type drop-down list, choose Document Templates, and locate the folder with the template to which you want to copy styles. You can find Word templates in the C:\Program Files\Microsoft Office\Templates folder and its subfolders, or the C:\Windows\Application Data\Microsoft\Templates folder and its subfolders. When you have found the template, click it and then click the Open button. Click Enable Macros if Word asks how to open the template.

Tip *A fast way to open a template is to open Windows Explorer or My Computer, go to C:\Program Files\Microsoft Office\Templates or C:\Windows\Application Data\Microsoft\Templates folder, and double-click the template to open it.*

■ **Create a New Template**   Choose File | New. Under Create New in the New dialog box, click the Template option button, and then click OK. When the new template opens, click the Save button and save and name your new template. (The previous section in this chapter, "Creating a Template from a Prototype Document," gives instructions for saving a template in the Templates folder where you can find it easily.)

2. Choose Format | Style. You'll see the Style dialog box.

3. Click the Organizer button. The Organizer dialog box shown in Figure 12-8 appears. Click the Styles tab, if necessary, to see the styles.

    The Organizer dialog box is kind of confusing at first. When you open it, the Organizer is set up to copy styles (and AutoText entries and macros) to the Normal template. However, you can change that with a few clicks, as the next few steps demonstrate.

4. Click the Close File button on the right side of the dialog box. When you do so, the button changes its name to Open File.

5. Click the Open File button. The Open dialog box appears.

6. Find the template or document you want to copy styles from. Remember: You can find Word templates in the C:\Program Files\Microsoft Office\Templates folder and its subfolders, or the C:\Windows\Application Data\Microsoft\Templates folder and its subfolders. However, if you want to copy styles from a template you created yourself, go to the folder where you saved the template.

7. Click the name of the template or document from which you want to copy styles and click Open. The styles in the template or document appear in the box on the right side of the Organizer dialog box.

8. On the right side of the Organizer dialog box, click the name of a style you want to copy to the template or document on the left side of the dialog box. As soon as you click, the Copy button arrows point to the left instead of the right. Now you can start copying styles.

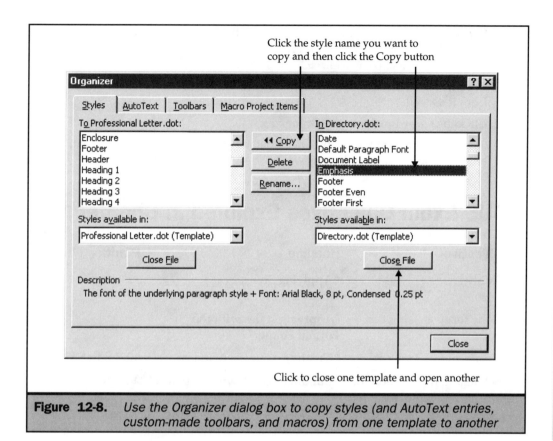

Click the style name you want to
copy and then click the Copy button

Click to close one template and open another

Figure 12-8. *Use the Organizer dialog box to copy styles (and AutoText entries, custom-made toolbars, and macros) from one template to another*

Tip   *Notice the description of the style at the bottom of the Organizer dialog box. If you have any doubts about which style you are copying, read the description.*

9. Click the Copy button to copy the style from the template or document on the right side of the Organizer dialog box to the template on the left side. Names of styles that you copy appear in the left side of the dialog box.

Caution   *If you try to copy a style with the same name from one template to another, Word warns you that you will delete the style in the template to which the copy is made. To keep from losing a style in the "copied to" template, rename the style. To do so, click its name and click the Rename button in the Organizer dialog box. Then type a new name in the Rename dialog box and click OK.*

PROFESSIONAL-LOOKING DOCUMENTS WITH WORD 2000

10. Repeat steps 8 and 9 to copy more styles to the template or document on the left side of the dialog box. While you're at it, you can copy AutoText entries, toolbars, and macros as well.

11. Repeat steps 4 through 8 to open another document or template and copy styles from it as well.

12. Click the Close button in the Organizer.

13. Save your template when you have finished copying styles (or AutoText entries, macros, and toolbars as well).

Exam MOUS Exam Objectives Explored in Chapter 12

Objective	Heading	Practice File
Apply styles	"Applying Styles in a Document"	12-1 Apply Styles
Copy formats using the Format Painter	"Applying styles with the Format Painter"	
Create and edit styles*	"Creating Your Own Styles"	12-2 Edit Styles
Set default file location for workgroup templates*	"Building Your Own Templates"	

* Denotes an Expert exam objective.

Ten Style Problems and How to Solve Them

Especially when you copy text from other documents or work on documents that you've received from other people, styles can be problematic. Sometimes Word 2000 changes style assignments without being asked to. Sometimes style formats get changed right under your nose and you can't do anything about it. Sometimes perfectly normal lines of
text turn into headings. Here are ten common style problems and explanations for solving them.

1. MY STYLES KEEP CHANGING ON ME.   It could be that your styles are supposed to change on you and you don't know it. As long as the Automatically Update check box is selected in the Modify Style dialog box, formats throughout a document change whenever you make a change to a single paragraph. Indent a paragraph that has been assigned the Quotation style, for example, and all paragraphs in the document to which that style was assigned are changed accordingly.

To keep formats from being changed, go to the Modify Style dialog box and tell Word not to update a style automatically whenever you make formatting changes to a paragraph. See "Modifying a Style," earlier in this chapter.

2. MY STYLES STILL KEEP CHANGING ON ME.   You could have a "based on" problem. One style can be based on another, and if the "based on" style changes, all styles to which it is linked change as well. As I pointed out earlier in this chapter in "Basing One Style on Another Style," a style isn't so much based on another style as linked to it.

This problem is not easy to solve and may require some detective work. Did you change a style lately—a style that other styles are based upon? Pinpoint a style that has changed, open the Modify Style dialog box, and see whether the style is based on another. If the problem turns out to be that you changed a style, change it back. Otherwise, choose a new "based on" style for the styles that keep changing on you. See "Modifying a Style," earlier in this chapter.

3. MOST OF MY STYLES CHANGED ON ME.   When this happens, you can bet that somebody fooled with the template that your document is attached to. Changing styles in a template is a risky business and must be done with caution. Either restore the template to its pristine original state or attach your document to another template to which it is more suitable. See "Applying Styles *En Masse* with the Templates and Add-Ins Command."

 To sever the tie between a document and the template with which it was created, choose Tools | Templates and Add-Ins and uncheck the Automatically Update Document Styles check box. As long as no check mark is in that check box, a document's styles remain the same no matter what happens to the template with which it was created.

4. WORD ISN'T UPDATING MY STYLES AUTOMATICALLY AFTER I MAKE A FORMAT CHANGE.   Being able to modify a style automatically merely by formatting a paragraph to which a style has been applied is a powerful way to update styles. However, styles are not updated automatically unless you tell Word to do so. "Modifying a Style," earlier in this chapter, explains how to design a style that is updated automatically. Here's a quick way make a style "automatically updateable":

1. Click a paragraph to which the style was assigned and change the formatting.

2. Click in the Style menu. The style's name is highlighted in the menu.

3. Press ENTER. You will see the Modify Style dialog box.

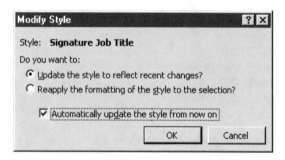

4. Check the Automatically Update The Style From Now On check box and click OK.

5. WHEN I COPY TEXT TO ANOTHER DOCUMENT, MY STYLES DON'T HOLD UP.   You can't copy text from one document to another and keep your style formats if the style you are copying has the same name as a style that is in the document to which the copy is being made. For example, if both documents have styles called Body Text but the Body Text formats are different, the copied text adopts the formats of the Body Text style in the document to which it is copied. To copy text assigned a particular style and keep the formatting, the style's name must be different from all the style names in the document that is receiving the copy. Change the style's name before you copy the text if you want the text to retain its formatting when it lands in the other document. See "Renaming a Style," earlier in this chapter.

By the way, if you copy styles from one document to another with the Organizer, the style that is being copied takes precedence over the style that is already there when two styles have the same name. See "Assembling Styles from Different Templates," earlier in this chapter.

6. SOMETIMES I GET A NEW STYLE WHEN I PRESS ENTER.   Some styles—heading styles, for example—are designed so that a new style is assigned to the next line. Press ENTER after typing a Heading 1 heading and the next line is usually assigned either the Normal style or the Body Text style.

Automatically assigning a new style to the following paragraph is supposed to be a convenience. Instead of having to choose a style from the Style menu, the style you need is ready and waiting. Obviously, a different style needs to follow a heading style because two headings cannot appear one after the other.

However, sometimes template designers mistakenly design a style so that a different style follows one style when really no style should follow it. Sometimes the same style should carry to the next paragraph when you press ENTER. See "Modifying a Style," earlier in this chapter, to learn how to modify a style so that no style follows it. *Hint:* In the Modify Style dialog box, open the Style For Following Paragraph drop-down list and choose the name of the style you are modifying, not the name of a different style.

7. WORD KEEPS ASSIGNING HEADING STYLES TO MY PARAGRAPHS.   Don't worry—it happens in the best of families. You type a line of text, press ENTER twice, and get a heading whether you like it or not. The heading appears because Word assigns a heading style to any line of text that begins with a capital letter, is not followed by a punctuation mark, and is followed by a blank line. Follow these steps to tell Word to stop turning innocent lines of text into headings:

1. Choose Tools | AutoCorrect.
2. Click the AutoFormat As You Type tab in the AutoCorrect dialog box.
3. Under Apply As You Type, uncheck the Headings check box and click OK.

8. WORD KEEPS ASSIGNING STYLES WITHOUT MY PERMISSION.   Sometimes, like a thing that goes bump in the night, Word assigns a paragraph style to text when you least expect it. For example, try this exercise to see how Word assigns styles automatically:

1. Click the New button to start a new document.
2. Type **In the Beginning** in boldface letters and click the Center button on the Formatting toolbar.
3. Press ENTER twice.
4. Click the words "In the Beginning" and glance at the Style menu on the Formatting toolbar. Word has assigned a style called "Title" to the words you typed.

Word follows various rules for assigning styles automatically. Many people like to merrily type along and let Word handle style assignments, but others resent Word's interference and prefer to assign styles on their own. Follow these steps to prevent Word from assigning styles automatically:

1. Choose Tools | AutoCorrect to open the AutoCorrect dialog box.
2. Click the AutoFormat As You Type tab.
3. Uncheck the Define Styles Based On Your Formatting check box and click OK.

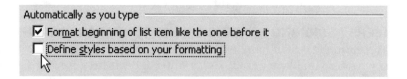

Note *Earlier in this chapter, Table 12-1 lists the styles that Word applies automatically when you choose commands on the Insert and View menus.*

9. TWO OF MY PARAGRAPHS LOOK DIFFERENT EVEN THOUGH I APPLIED THE SAME STYLE TO EACH.

You probably formatted some of the text by conventional means—by boldfacing it, for example, or indenting it. When you format text or a paragraph to which you applied a style, your formats take precedence over the style's. Try one of these keyboard shortcuts to strip formats from a paragraph or text so that only style formats remain:

- Press CTRL-Q to remove all formats from a paragraph.
- Press CTRL-SPACEBAR to remove formats from characters. Be sure to select the characters first.

10. NOT ALL STYLES APPEAR IN THE STYLE DIALOG BOX.

Maybe not. But you can make them appear by opening the List drop-down menu and choosing All Styles. To see all the styles on the Formatting toolbar's Style menu, hold down the SHIFT key and click the down arrow. All the styles will appear on the drop-down menu.

Chapter 13

Embellishing Documents with Artwork and Text Boxes

This chapter is meant to bring out the artist in you. Here, you will learn the many ways to decorate a document with artwork and text boxes. You will be pleasantly surprised to find that dropping a clip art image or text box in a document is easy. Word offers other kinds of art as well. The problems start when you try to make your clip art image, text box, or piece of artwork fit on the page.

The first half of this chapter is devoted to the different kinds artwork you can place on the page, text boxes included. You will find instructions for inserting clip art images, graphics, watermarks, and text boxes in a document. You'll also learn how to draw lines and shapes with the tools on the Drawing toolbar. The second half of the chapter explains how to manipulate images, shapes, text boxes, and other so-called objects. The commands for selecting, positioning, changing the size of, applying borders to, filling, overlapping, and wrapping text around objects such as clip art images, shapes, and text boxes are the same no matter which kind of object you are dealing with.

"WordArt for Bending, Spindling, and Mutilating Text" in Chapter 7 explains how to decorate documents with WordArt images—words that have been stretched, crumpled, or squeezed into odd shapes.

Handling Graphics and Clip Art in Documents

Surely the easiest way to spruce up a document is to include a clip art image or two. Putting clip art images in documents is ridiculously easy. And Word 2000 comes with the Microsoft Clip Gallery, a collection of 500 or so clip art images, so it's not as if you have to search far and wide to find clip art. You can even go on the Internet, rummage for clip art, and insert it directly into a document.

These pages explain how to insert a clip art image or graphic in a document, whether you obtained the image from the Microsoft Clip Gallery or elsewhere. You will also learn how to cut off part of an image, change its brightness and contrast, and turn a color image into a grayscale or black-and-white image.

Getting Images from Microsoft's Clip Gallery

As a proud user of Word 2000, you can take advantage of the numerous clip art images in the Microsoft Clip Gallery. These pages explain how to insert a clip art image from the gallery, search for the right image, and organize and manage clip art images so that you can find them again when you need them. You'll also find out how to store your own clip art images in the Clip Gallery.

Be sure to put the Office 2000 or Word 2000 CD in your computer before you go fishing for clip art images in the Microsoft Clip Gallery. Unless you loaded the images on your computer when you installed Word—a bad idea if there ever was one, since clip art images take up a lot of disk space—Word gets the images from the CD.

Figure 13-1 demonstrates two ways to search for clip art in the Clip Gallery—by typing a keyword in the Search for Clips text box or clicking on a category. Follow these basic steps to find and insert a clip art image in a document:

1. Choose Insert | Picture | Clip Art or click the Insert Clip Art button on the Drawing toolbar. You will see the Microsoft Clip Gallery dialog box shown in Figure 13-1. In the dialog box are 51 categories that you can search.

2. Either scroll to and click a category to search for images or enter a search word in the Search For Clips text box and press ENTER. Clip art images appear in the dialog box where the category names used to be.

3. Click an image you want to use. A drop-down menu with four buttons appears.

4. Click the Insert Clip button to insert the image in your file. If you would like to get a better look at the image before you insert it, click the Preview Clip

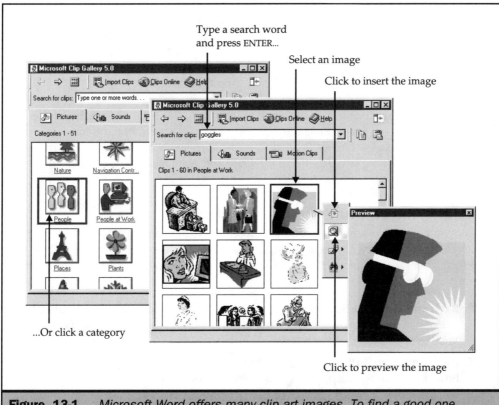

Figure 13-1.   *Microsoft Word offers many clip art images. To find a good one, either type a search word or click a category in the Microsoft Clip Gallery dialog box*

button. As shown in Figure 13-1, the Preview box shows an enlarged picture of your image.

5. Click the Close button (the X) in the upper-right corner of the Clip Gallery dialog box to close the dialog box, leave the dialog box open to insert more images, or click the Minimize button to land the Clip Gallery on the Taskbar where you can click its button if you need it again.

When you first insert an image, it arrives as an inline graphic and can't be moved elsewhere. To fix that, display the Picture toolbar, click the Text Wrapping button, and choose Behind Text or In Front Of Text. "Manipulating Art, Text Boxes, Shapes, and Other So-Called Objects" in the second half of this chapter explains everything you need to know about moving images and changing their size.

Tip   *Click the Change to Small Window button (or press CTRL-SHIFT-<) to make the Clip Gallery dialog box small enough to fit on the side of the screen. You can leave it there while you work. The Change to Small Window button is located below the Maximize button in the dialog box. To enlarge the dialog box again, click the Change to Full Window button (or press CTRL-SHIFT->).*

Searching for an Image in the Clip Gallery

Usually you have to rummage inside the Clip Gallery to find the right clip art image. Besides clicking category names and entering search words in the Search For Clips text box, Word offers these tools in the Clip Gallery dialog box to help you find the image you need:

- **Back and Forward Buttons**   These buttons work like the Back and Forward buttons in a Web browser. Click them to revisit and relocate categories you saw before.

- **All Categories Button**   Click this button to see the categories again, no matter how deep into the Clip Gallery your search takes you.

- **Search for Clips Drop-Down Menu**   Besides typing a search word in this text box, you can click the down arrow and see a list of words you entered before. Click a word to enter it in the text box.

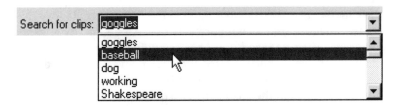

■ **Find Similar Clips Button**   Find an image you like, click it, and then click the
Find Similar Clips button, the fourth button on the button drop-down menu, to
continue your search for images like the one you clicked. Clicking the Artistic
Style button presents images in the same style; clicking the Color & Shape
button finds images with the same shape or the same muted or bright colors.
You can also click a keyword in the list to see images of a similar description.

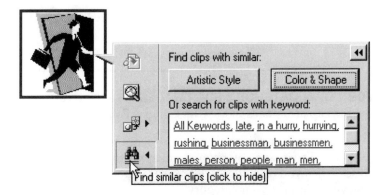

Organizing and Managing Images in the Clip Gallery

If you expect to spend a lot of time in the Clip Gallery, you may as well organize the
images so that you can find them more easily. To do so, you can place images in
new categories, load the Favorites category with the images you use often, create a
category of your own for images, and even attach a new keyword to an image to
make finding it easier.

*Clip art images can appear in more than one category. The images you see in the Clip
Gallery are actually pointers to folder locations where the images are stored. When you
move or copy an image to a new category, all you are doing is moving or copying the
instructions that Word uses to get the clip art file from the CD or folder on your
computer where the file is located.*

PLACING IMAGES IN THE FAVORITES CATEGORY   When you come upon a clip
art image you are sure to use again, add it to the Favorites category. That way, you can
find it very quickly. The Favorites category appears at the top of the list of categories
that you see when you click the All Categories button or choose Insert | Picture | Clip

Art to open the Clip Gallery. Adding an image to the Favorites category does not remove it from the category in which it currently lies. All you do by adding it to the Favorites category is designate it as a "favorite" so you can find it quickly.

To place an image in the Favorites category, click it and then click the Add Clip To Favorites or Other Category button, the third button in the drop-down button menu. "Favorites" appears already in the Add Clip To The Following Category menu, so all you have to do is click the Add button.

CREATING YOUR OWN CATEGORY FOR IMAGES   Yes, you can create a new category for storing clip art images in the Clip Gallery. Follow these steps:

1. In the Clip Gallery, locate an image to represent the category on the All Categories list. The image you choose will appear in the All Categories list, the list you see when you click the All Categories button. It will appear along with the name you select for your category.

2. Right-click the image and choose Clip Properties from the menu. You will see the Clip Properties dialog box.

3. Click the Categories tab.

4. Click the New Category button.

5. In the New Category dialog box, enter a name for the category and click OK.

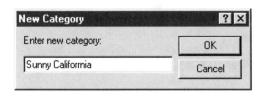

6. Click OK in the Clip Properties dialog box.

To rename a category, right-click it in the Categories list, choose Rename Category from the menu, and enter a new name in the Rename Category dialog box. To delete a category, right-click it and choose Delete. Images are not deleted when you delete a category—only the category itself is deleted.

ADDING IMAGES TO AND REMOVING IMAGES FROM CATEGORIES   Follow these steps to add an image to or remove an image from a category:

1. Right-click the image and choose Clip Properties to open the Clip Properties dialog box.

2. Click the Categories tab. A check mark appears beside the names of categories in which the image appears.

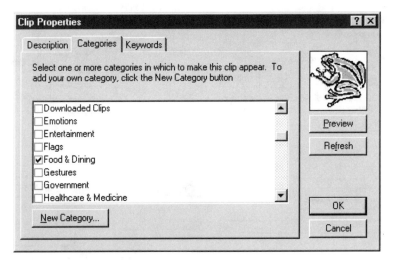

3. Remove check marks to remove the image from categories, or click the check boxes next to the names of categories in which you want the image to appear.

4. Click OK.

The fastest way to add a clip art image to a category is to select the image and click the Add Clip to Favorites or Other Category button. When the menu appears, click the down arrow to see the list of categories, and then click the category where you want the image to appear.

ATTACHING A NEW KEYWORD TO AN IMAGE   Microsoft has attached several keywords to each image in the Clip Gallery. As you know, you can enter a keyword in the Search For Clips text box to look for images. Suppose you bring one of your own images into the Clip Gallery. How will you find it? One way is to attach a few keywords to your image so you can search for it by way of the Search For Clips text box. Follow these steps:

1. Right-click the image that needs a keyword or two and choose Clip Properties from the menu.

2. Click the Keywords tab in the Clip Properties dialog box. The Keywords tab lists words that have already been attached to the image.

3. Click the New Keyword button, type a keyword in the Enter New Keyword text box, and click OK.

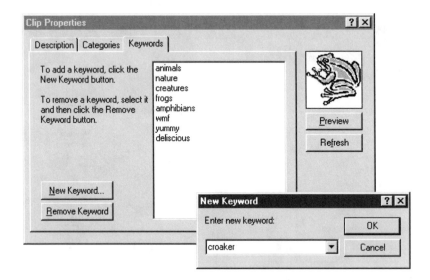

4. Add as many keywords as you like (or remove keywords for that matter by clicking the Remove Keyword button) and then click OK.

Putting Your Own Images in the Clip Gallery

If you spend any time in the Clip Gallery, you'll soon realize that it is a very convenient device for finding and organizing clip art images. Here's some good news: You can store your own clip art images in the Clip Gallery. Instead of having to fumble around in your computer to find a clip art or graphic image, you can get it by way of the Clip Gallery.

Take note of where on your computer, on a CD, or on a zip drive the graphic image you want to store in the Clip Gallery is located, and then follow these steps to hang it in the Clip Gallery:

1. Choose Insert | Picture | Clip Art to open the Clip Gallery.

2. Click the Import Clips button. You see the Add Clip to Clip Gallery dialog box shown in Figure 13-2.

3. Find and select the graphic or clip art file you want to bring into the Clip Gallery.

4. Under Clip Import Option, decide how you want to handle the graphic or clip art file:

- **Copy Into Clip Gallery**   Makes a copy of the file and stores it in the C:\Windows\Application Data\Microsoft\Media Catalog folder. This option wastes disk space if the file is already stored on your hard disk. By making a copy, however, you retain the original and always know where to find it if you need it.

- **Move Into Clip Gallery**   Moves the file into the C:\Windows\Application Data\Microsoft\Media Catalog folder. This option saves disk space. On the other hand, if you need the file someday, you aren't likely to find it in the folder to which the Clip Gallery copies it.

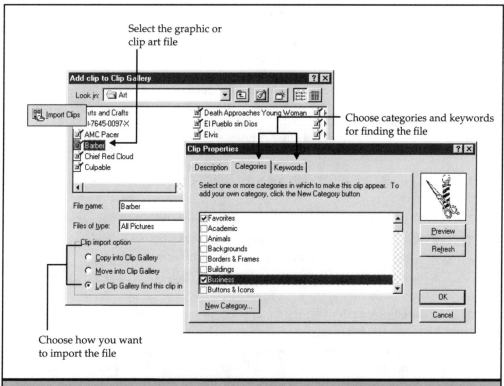

Figure 13-2.   *You can put your favorite clip art images in the Clip Gallery to make finding and inserting them easier*

■ **Let Clip Gallery Find This Clip In Its Current Folder Or Volume**   Leaves the file where it is. With this option, the Clip Gallery summons your file from its current location when you call upon it.

Caution   *The Let Clip Gallery Find This Clip In Its Current Folder Or Volume option is the best choice, since it saves on disk space and always allows you to keep your file where you are used to finding it. However, to make use of this option, you must never move your file from the folder in which it now resides. If you move your file, the Clip Gallery won't know where to find it.*

5. Click the Import button. You will see the Clip Properties dialog box shown in Figure 13-2.

6. On the Categories and Keywords tabs, assign categories and keywords to your new graphic image. The previous section in this chapter describes the Clip Properties dialog box in detail.

7. Click OK.

Going Online to Search for Clip Art

As long as your computer is connected to the Internet, you can go online and scavenge clip art images, pictures, sound, and videos from "Clip Gallery Live," Microsoft's online repository of clip art. The images are free as long as you agree not to sell them, transmit them on video, use them to endorse a product, or otherwise use them in a libelous or unlawful manner. (I'm getting this from the end-user license agreement you have to accept to download the clip art.)

Follow these steps to download clip art images and import them into the Clip Gallery:

1. Choose Insert | Picture | Clip Art to open the Clip Gallery dialog box, if necessary.

2. Click the Clips Online button. Your Web browser starts and appears onscreen.

3. Click the Connect button, if necessary, to go on the Internet. Soon you'll arrive at the "Clip Gallery Live," the Clip Gallery's online home page.

4. Click the Accept button. You come to the Clip Gallery Live Web page shown in Figure 13-3.

5. Click the Clip Art tab to search for clip art, or the Pictures tab to search for pictures.

6. To conduct a search, either enter a word that describes the kind of art you are looking for in the Search Clips By Keyword box and click the Go button, or open the Browse Clips By Category drop-down list and select a category. You'll see thumbnail images of the clip art you can download.

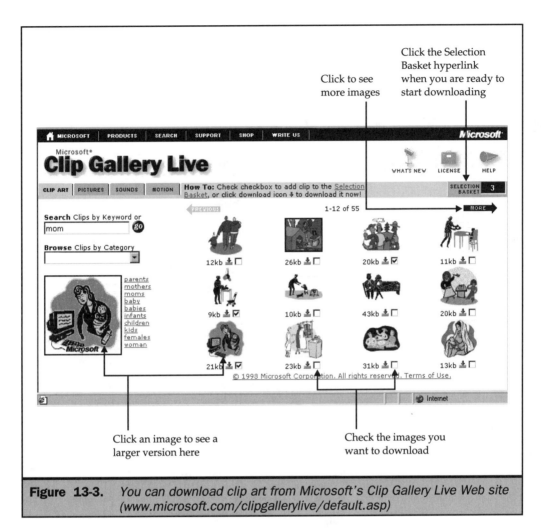

Click to see more images

Click the Selection Basket hyperlink when you are ready to start downloading

Click an image to see a larger version here

Check the images you want to download

Figure 13-3. *You can download clip art from Microsoft's Clip Gallery Live Web site (www.microsoft.com/clipgallerylive/default.asp)*

7. Click the check box beside each image you want to download.

You can click an image to see its enlarged version in the box on the left side of the Web page. The "Selection Basket" counter in the upper-right corner tells you how many images you have chosen to download to your computer. Click the More button to see another page of images or your browser's Back button to return to a page you saw before.

> **Tip** *Click the down arrow beside a check box to download an image right away.*

8. When you are ready to download images, click the Selection Basket hyperlink. You will see a page with all the images you chose to download. You can uncheck boxes if you change your mind about downloading images.

9. Click the Download hyperlink to download the images to your computer. A Web page tells you how many images you chose and how long it will take to download them.

10. Click the Download Now hyperlink to download the images. The images you chose to download appear in the Clip Gallery dialog box.

 Clip art downloaded from the Internet is placed in the Download Clips category of the Clip Gallery dialog box. However, you can move the images to other categories. See "Organizing and Managing Images in the Clip Gallery," earlier in this chapter.

Inserting a Graphic File in a Document

For all I know, you have accumulated hundreds of graphic files and you want to use them in your documents in lieu of Word's clip art. Table 13-1 lists the graphic file

File Extension	Format	Bitmap/Vector
BMP	Windows Paint	Bitmap
CDR	CorelDRAW	Vector
CGM	Computer Graphics Metafile	Vector
EMF	Enhanced Metafile	Vector
EPS	Encapsulated PostScript	Vector
FPX	FashPix	Bitmap
GIF	Graphics Interchange Format	Bitmap
JPG	Interchange Format	Bitmap
PCD	Kodak Photo CD	Bitmap
PCT	Macintosh PICT	Vector
PCX	PC Paintbrush	Bitmap
PNG	Portable Network Graphics	Bitmap
TIF	Tagged Image File Format	Bitmap
WMF	Windows Metafile	Vector
WPG	WordPerfect Graphics	Vector

Table 13-1. *Graphic File Formats You Can Use in Word Documents*

formats that are compatible with Word. You can bring a graphic into a Word document as long as it is in one of the formats in Table 13-1. Rather than study the table closely, however, I suggest trying to import the file. If Word chokes on it, the file isn't one that Word can work with.

 Earlier in this chapter, "Putting Your Own Images in the Microsoft Clip Gallery" explains how you can use the Microsoft Clip Gallery to manage your own graphics along with the clip art images that come with Word.

Follow these steps to copy a graphic file directly into a Word document:

1. Choose Insert | Picture | From File or click the Insert Picture button on the Picture toolbar.
2. In the Insert Picture dialog box, find the folder where you keep your graphic files. If necessary, click the down arrow beside the View button in the Insert Picture dialog box and choose Preview to see what files look like before you insert them.

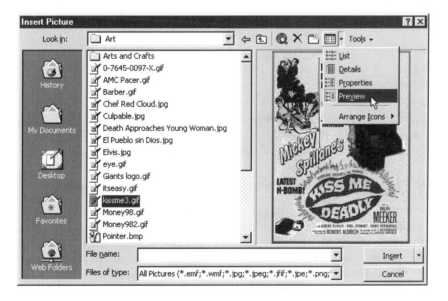

3. Select a file and click the Insert button.

When you import a graphic, it arrives as an inline graphic and can't be moved. You can change that, however, by displaying the Picture toolbar, clicking the Text Wrapping button on the toolbar, and choosing Behind Text or In Front of Text. Later in this chapter, "Manipulating Art, Text Boxes, Shapes, and Other So-Called Objects" explains how to move graphics and position them on the page.

Bitmap and Vector Graphics

All graphic images fall in either the bitmap or vector category. A *bitmap graphic* is composed of thousands upon thousands of tiny dots called *pixels* that, taken together, form an image (the term "pixel" comes from "picture image"). A *vector graphic* is drawn with the aid of computer instructions that describe the shape and dimension of each line, curve, circle, and so on.

As far as Word documents are concerned, the difference between the two formats is that vector graphics do not distort when you enlarge or shrink them, whereas bitmap graphics loose resolution when their size is changed. Furthermore, vector images do not require near as much disk space as bitmap graphics. Drop a few bitmap graphics in a Word document and soon you are dealing with a document that is 500KB or 750KB in size.

Images you create yourself with the tools on the Drawing toolbar are vector graphics. The clip art images in the Microsoft Clip Gallery are vector graphics, too. To get technical about it, they are Windows metafile (.WMF) graphics. Stick with the images in the Clip Gallery and you won't have to worry about documents growing too large or whether images can be shrunk or enlarged without distorting them.

Tip *You can tell Word to go directly to the folder where you keep graphics whenever you click the Insert Picture button or choose Insert | Picture | From File. To do so, choose Tools | Options and click the File Locations tab in the Options dialog box. Then select Clipart Pictures on the File Types list, click the Modify button, and, in the Modify Location dialog box, find and select the folder where you keep art. After you click OK, the Location list in the Options dialog box shows the folder you chose.*

Changing the Appearance of an Image or Graphic

Every clip art image or graphic in a Word document can be a collaboration, not the work of a single artist. By clicking an image, displaying the Picture toolbar, and clicking the Image Control, More Contrast, Less Contrast, More Brightness, and Less Brightness buttons, you can collaborate with the original artist and create something new. Figure 13-4 shows an image that has been made over several times with tools on the Picture toolbar. Click an image and play with these buttons on the Picture toolbar to change its appearance:

■ **Image Control Button**   The Grayscale and Black & White options on the Image Control menu are for rendering a color image in shades of gray or black and white. The Watermark option creates a transparent image. Watermarks are meant to appear in the background behind text and other images.

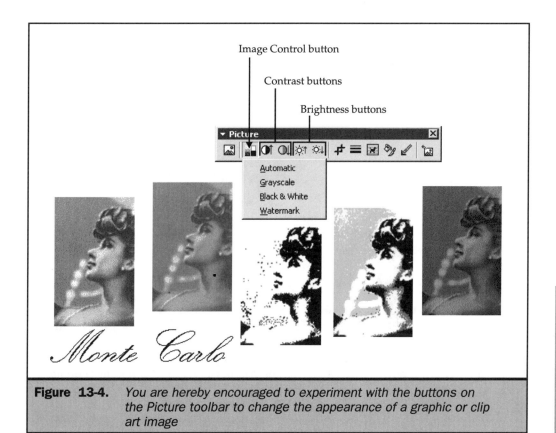

Figure 13-4.   *You are hereby encouraged to experiment with the buttons on the Picture toolbar to change the appearance of a graphic or clip art image*

- ■ **More Contrast and Less Contrast Buttons**   Enhance or mute the difference between light and dark colors or shades.

- ■ **More Brightness and Less Brightness Buttons**   Make an image brighter or more somber.

Note   *See "Changing the Size and Shape of Objects," later in this chapter, to learn how to stretch, scrunch, or miniaturize a clip art image.*

The Format Picture dialog box also offers a Brightness command, Contrast command, and means of rendering a graphic as a black-and-white, grayscale, or watermark image. Either right-click the picture and choose Format Picture from the shortcut menu or choose Format | Picture to open the Format Picture dialog box. Commands for changing the appearance of an image are found under Image Control on the Picture tab. It might interest you to know that clicking a Brightness or Contrast button on the Picture toolbar changes the Brightness or Contrast setting by 3 percent.

Image control		
Color:	Grayscale ▼	
Brightness:	◀ ▢ ▶	50 % ⬍
Contrast:	◀ ▢ ▶	32 % ⬍

   If you regret torturing a graphic out of shape and want your original graphic back, select your graphic by clicking it, click the Image Control button on the Picture toolbar, and choose Automatic from the drop-down menu.

Cropping Off Part of an Image

"Cropping" means to cut off part of a clip art image or graphic. I'm afraid you can't use Word's cropping tool like a pair of scissors or an X-ACTO knife to cut zigzag around the edges of a graphic or clip art image or cut a hole in the middle. You can, however, cut strips from the side, top, or bottom. Here, the cropping tool was used to cut off all but the heads of different images, and then the heads were laid over another clip art image to make for a very strange group picture.

To crop off part of a graphic or clip art image, click the image to select it, and then click the Crop button on the Picture toolbar. Two corner angles appear on the end of the pointer. Move the pointer over a selection hand (a square at the corner or side of the image), and click and drag. Dashed lines show what will be left of your image when you finish cropping it. Release the mouse button when only the portion of the image that you want is inside the dashed lines.

PROFESSIONAL-LOOKING
DOCUMENTS WITH
WORD 2000

Tip *Depending on whether pictures in your document "snap to the grid," cropping a picture with precision can be difficult. As "Positioning Objects on the Page" explains later in this chapter, the grid is a set of invisible horizontal and vertical lines on which graphics and other objects are aligned. When objects snap to the grid, aligning them is easier because they always stick to the gridlines, but moving them and cropping them with precision is more difficult. If you need to shave off a small part of a picture but are having trouble doing it, hold down the ALT key as you drag the Cropping tool. By holding down the ALT key, you can crop off the parts of a picture that fall between gridlines.*

You can also crop an image in the Format Picture dialog box, although the only reason to do that is to crop an image by the same amount on all sides or, better yet, increase the distance between the image and its border on all sides. By entering negative numbers in the Crop From boxes, you can increase the distance between an image and the border that surrounds it. To reach the Format Picture dialog box, click the image and choose Format | Picture, or right-click and choose Format Picture. Go to the Picture tab to enter the negative numbers in the Crop From boxes.

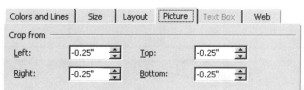

Decorating Pages with Watermarks

According to the Microsoft Corporation, a *watermark* is a faint image that appears behind the text in the same place on each page. As papermakers know, a watermark is really an image impressed in the paper that appears when you hold the paper to the light. A Word watermark is not impressed in the paper, but it's the closest thing to watermarks you can get in the debased digital world in which we live.

Figure 13-5 shows an example of a watermark. Odd as it may seem, watermarks are actually part of the page header. To create a watermark, you choose View | Header and Footer, click in the Header box, and then import the clip art image. Because the clip art image is technically part of the header, it appears on every page, as a header does. In its wisdom, Word recognizes that a clip art image introduced as part of the header is a watermark, and the program dims the image to keep it from obscuring the text.

LEARN BY EXAMPLE

To see what a watermark looks like firsthand, open the 13-4 Watermarks document on the companion CD.

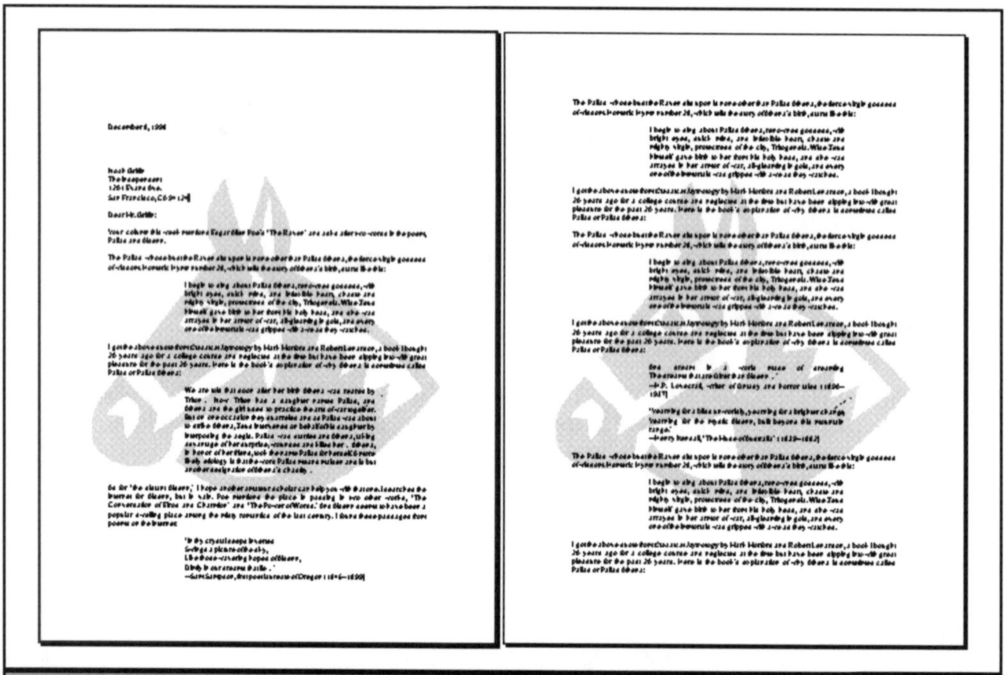

Figure 13-5. *Watermarks are technically part of the page header, so they appear on every page in the same location*

Follow these steps to decorate a document with a watermark:

1. Click the Zoom menu down arrow and choose 50% from the drop-down menu. At 50 percent, you can see how well an image fits on the page.

2. Choose View | Header and Footer. You see the Header box for entering headers.

3. Insert the clip art image or graphic. See "Getting Images from Microsoft's Clip Gallery" and "Inserting a Graphic" earlier in this chapter. Be sure to insert a dark image. Light-colored images can hardly be seen on the page as watermarks.

4. Drag the image out of the Header box and into the middle of the page. Enlarge or shrink the image as need be. Later in this chapter, "Manipulating Art, Text Boxes, Shapes, and Other So-Called Objects" explains how to move and change the size of clip art images. Click the Close button the Header and Footer toolbar.

Note
To reposition the watermark or change its hue, you have to choose View | Header and Footer first. Without choosing that command, you can't get at the watermark. Earlier in this chapter, "Changing the Appearance of an Image or Graphic" explains how to change the contrast or brightness of an image. Click the More Brightness button on the Picture toolbar to make a watermark less opaque.

Tip
To place a watermark in the very center of the page, right-click the watermark and choose Format Picture. On the Layout tab of the Format Picture dialog box, click the Advanced button, and then click the Picture Position tab in the Advanced Layout dialog box. Under Horizontal, click the Alignment option button, and choose Centered and Page from the Relative To drop-down lists. Under Vertical, click the Alignment button and choose Centered and Page again. Then click OK twice to return to your document.

PROFESSIONAL-LOOKING DOCUMENTS WITH WORD 2000

Putting a Text Box on the Page

Text boxes are one of the best things going in Word 2000. Think of a text box as a page within a page. Almost everything that can be done to a page—putting borders around it, formatting text in different ways—can be done inside a text box. After you drop a text box on the page, you can move it very easily from place to place. Typically, text boxes are used to make boxed announcements like the one on the left side of Figure 13-6. However, with a little imagination you can use them in all kinds of interesting ways. That's a text box on the right side of Figure 13-6, too, but I removed the border and the "fill"—the color inside the box—so that the clip art image of the frog can show through the text box.

These pages explain how to insert a text box, change the direction of text in a text box, and make text flow from text box to text box. Later in this chapter, "Manipulating Art, Text Boxes, Shapes, and Other So-Called Objects" explains how to change the borders of a text box, change its fill color, move it around on the page, wrap text around it, and change its size.

Announcing a
**FROG JUMPING
CONTEST**
~~Calaveras County~~
July 5-7

Announcing a
**FROG JUMPING
CONTEST**
~~Calaveras County~~
July 5-7

Figure 13-6.   *A typical text box with borders and a color background (left) and a text box without borders superimposed on a clip art image (right)*

Inserting a Text Box

To put a text box on the page, either choose Insert | Text Box or click the Text Box button on the Drawing toolbar. The pointer turns into a cross. Click where you want one corner of the box to be and drag toward its opposite corner. Lines appear as you draw the box. Release the mouse button when the box is the right size.

Remember these little tricks when you draw text boxes:

- Hold down the SHIFT key as you draw the box to make a perfect square.
- Hold down the CTRL and SHIFT keys to draw a perfect square in an outward direction starting in the middle.

After you have created your text box, click inside it and start typing to enter the text. Everything you ever learned about text formatting applies to the text in a text box as well. Click the Align Left or Align Center button on the Formatting toolbar to left-align or center text, for example. Or drag Indent markers on the ruler to indent the text. By the way, you can select text that you have already entered and click the Text Box button or choose Insert | Text Box to place the text in a text box.

To remove a text box, select it and press the DELETE key. Be careful, however, because deleting a text box deletes all the text inside it as well. Copy the text inside the text box to the Clipboard before you delete the text box if you want to preserve the text.

Selecting a text box can be problematic. See "Selecting Objects So You Can Manipulate Them," later in this chapter.

Changing the Internal Margins of a Text Box

Unless you change the internal measurements, words in a text box lie .1 inch from the left and right sides, and .5 inch from the top and bottom. Suppose you want text to come closer to or move further from the sides of a text box. Follow these steps to change the internal margins of a text box:

1. Either right-click the side of a text box and choose Format Text Box on the menu or select the text box and choose Format | Text Box. You will see the Format Text Box dialog box.

2. Click the Text Box tab.

3. Change the Internal Margin settings. The only way to change these settings is to visit the Format Text box dialog box. Drag the sides of a text box to change the internal margins and you will drag in vain.

Colors and Lines	Size	Layout	Picture	Text Box	Web

Internal margin

Left: `0.5"`   Top: `0.75"`

Right: `0.25"`   Bottom: `0.75"`

Changing the Direction of the Text

On the Text Box toolbar is a button called Change Text Direction. Select a text box, click the button, and all the words in the text box change direction, as shown in Figure 13-7. Keep clicking the button until the text turns in the direction you want it to turn. You don't have to select any words or letters before clicking the button. All you have to do is select the text box, choose View | Toolbars | Text Box if necessary, and start clicking the Change Text Direction button on the Text Box toolbar.

By the way, when you turn text on its side, the buttons on the Formatting toolbar that pertain to arranging text also turn on their sides. If you have trouble reading the buttons, lean far to the left or right, cock your head, and squint.

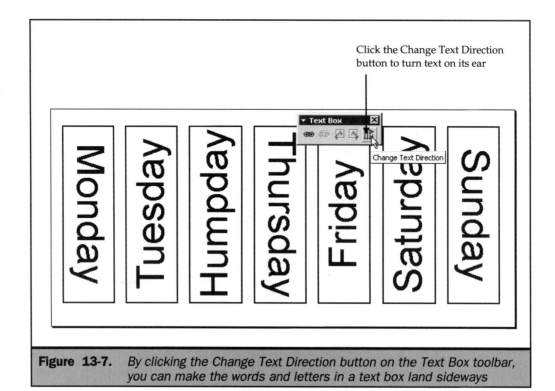

Click the Change Text Direction
button to turn text on its ear

Figure 13-7. *By clicking the Change Text Direction button on the Text Box toolbar, you can make the words and letters in a text box land sideways*

Linking Text Boxes So That Text Passes from Box to Box

With the right amount of foresight and planning, you can link text boxes so that text passes from box to box as each box is filled. You need to plan ahead, however, because you can't link text boxes into which text has already been typed. To link text boxes, write the text first, then insert each text box in the chain, pour the text in the first box, and tell Word where to make text go as each box is filled up.

Figure 13-8 shows an example of text boxes that have been linked. When you add a word or two to the first box, text is pushed into the second and subsequent text boxes. Delete words in a box and text is pulled from subsequent boxes. Linked text boxes are especially useful in newsletters and brochures when an article on page 1, for example, is continued on page 6. As long as the text boxes on page 1 and 6 are linked, text passes directly from page 1 to 6 as the box on page 1 fills up. Many people prefer to create columns by linking text boxes because the Format | Columns command, the usual way to lay out columns, doesn't permit text to jump long distances.

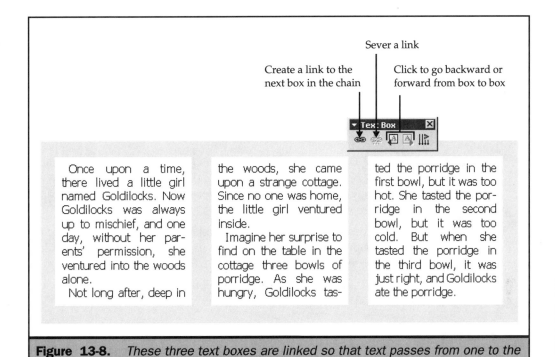

Sever a link

Create a link to the
next box in the chain

Click to go backward or
forward from box to box

Tex: Box

Once upon a time, there lived a little girl named Goldilocks. Now Goldilocks was always up to mischief, and one day, without her parents' permission, she ventured into the woods alone.
   Not long after, deep in

the woods, she came upon a strange cottage. Since no one was home, the little girl ventured inside.
   Imagine her surprise to find on the table in the cottage three bowls of porridge. As she was hungry, Goldilocks tas-

ted the porridge in the first bowl, but it was too hot. She tasted the porridge in the second bowl, but it was too cold. But when she tasted the porridge in the third bowl, it was just right, and Goldilocks ate the porridge.

Figure 13-8.   *These three text boxes are linked so that text passes from one to the next as each is filled up*

To make text pass between text boxes, click the sender text box to select it, click the Create Text Box Link button on the Text Box toolbar, and click inside the receiver text box. Here are the specifics of linking text boxes:

1. Type the text and proofread it. Editing text after it has been put in text boxes is difficult, so edit the text first.

2. Insert all the text boxes you will need (see "Inserting a Text Box," earlier in this chapter).

3. Cut or copy the text, click in the first text box, and click the Paste button or choose Edit | Paste. Now all the text is in the first text box. Don't worry about the text not fitting in the first text box—you will take care of that shortly.

4. Click the first text box in the chain to select it.

5. Display the Text Box toolbar and click the Create Text Box Link button. The pointer changes into a pitcher with an arrow on it.

6. Move the pitcher over the next text box in the chain, and click when the pitcher turns into a pouring pitcher. Text passes into the text box.

Press the ESC key if you find yourself with a full pitcher but nowhere to pour it. In other words, if you click the Create Text Box Link button but forget which text box is next in the chain, press ESC so you can start all over.

7. Select the text box that you just poured text into and repeat steps 5 and 6 to enter text into the subsequent text boxes.

Don't forget these amenities as you work with linked text boxes:

■ **Going from Text Box to Text Box**   To travel from box to box in the chain, click the Previous Text Box or Next Text Box button on the Text Box toolbar. By clicking these buttons, you don't have to scroll from page to page when far-flung text boxes are located on different pages.

■ **Keeping Text from Passing to the Next Box**   To keep text from going to the next text box in the chain, select the text box and click the Break Forward Link button. Text boxes subsequent to the one you selected are emptied.

■ **Selecting All the Text**   To select all the text in all the boxes in the chain, click in any box and press CTRL-A.

Introducing a New Text Box in the Middle of a Chain

Suppose you made a planning error, and after all the text boxes have been linked, you realize that a new text box needs to be inserted in the middle of the chain. Follow these steps to introduce a new text box:

1. Create the new text box.

2. Select the text box in the chain that is to go before the new text box and click the Break Forward Link button on the Text Box toolbar. All text is removed from text boxes that are subsequent to the text box you selected in this step.

3. With the text box you selected in step 2 still selected, click the Create Text Box Link button. The pointer turns into a pitcher.

4. Click inside the new text box you created in step 1. Now text passes to this text box. Your next task is to link the new text box to the rest of the chain.

5. Select your new text box, click the Create Text Link button, and click the text box that is to go after the one you created. By doing so, you connect your new text box to the boxes in the second half of the chain.

Drawing Lines and Shapes

Whether you know it or not, Word 2000 comes with a drawing program with which you can create your own images. These pages explain how to use the drawing program to embellish a document with lines and shapes. For that matter, you can amuse yourself on a rainy afternoon with the drawing program. Read on to find out how you can use the tools on the Drawing toolbar to draw curved and straight lines, arrows, freeform lines, ovals, rectangles, and all manner of shapes. This illustration shows the various and sundry things you can draw.

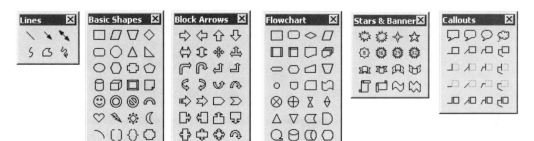

Drawing Lines and Arrows

Drawing a line can be as easy or as difficult as you want it to be. To draw a straight line, all you have to do is click the Line button on the Drawing toolbar and start dragging. You can also draw curves, freeform lines, and arrows, and you can choose a thickness for your line or a dashed or dotted line as well. Better read on.

Later in this chapter, "When Objects Overlap: Choosing Which Appears Above the Other" explains how to make a line appear in front of or behind text boxes, clip art images, and other so-called objects.

Drawing and Editing Straight Lines

To draw a straight line, click the Line button on the Drawing toolbar and drag onscreen where you want the line to appear. A square selection handle appears on either end of the line after you draw it. By dragging the selection handles, you can change the length or angle of a line after you've drawn it.

You can't change anything about a line until you select it. To select a line, gently move the pointer over it and click when you see the four-headed arrow. The selection handles appear after you've selected a line.

To move a line or adjust its length or angle, select it and do the following:

- **Change the Angle of a Line** Drag a selection handle up, down, or sideways. A dashed line shows where the line will be when you release the mouse button.

- **Change the Length** Drag a selection handle outward and release the mouse button when the dashed line is the right length.

- **Move a Line** Move the pointer over the line and click when you see the four-headed arrow. Then drag the line to a new location.

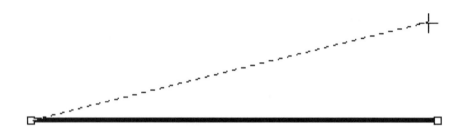

Pressing Keys to Draw Lines Across the Page

Here's a little trick for drawing a line that stretches across the page: Press the hyphen, asterisk, underline, equals, or tilde key three times and then press ENTER. As this illustration shows, Word draws a line from margin to margin.

Hyphen (-)

Asterisk (*)

Underline (_)

Equals (=)

Tilde (~)

To remove a line that was drawn this way, very carefully select it by clicking in the margin to its left and then press the DELETE key.

Choosing a Line Type, Width, and Color for Lines

To begin with, lines are .75 points wide, black, and not dotted or dashed, but you can change them by clicking buttons on the Drawing toolbar. Select a line and follow these instructions to change it to a dotted or dashed line, change its width, or change its color:

- ■ **Line Type**   Click the Dash Style button on the Drawing toolbar and choose a line type from the pop-up menu.

- ■ **Width**   Click the Line Style button and choose a point size for your line. To make the line wider than 6 points, click the More Lines option, and go to the Format AutoShape dialog box. In the Weight text box, enter a point size of your choice.

- ■ **Color**   Click the down arrow beside the Line Color button and choose a color from the pop-up menu.

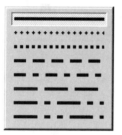 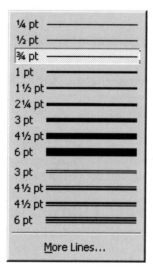 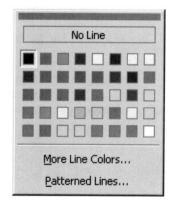

Drawing an Arrow

The rules for drawing arrows and lines, changing their width, and changing their color and dash style are the same. The only difference is that you draw an arrow by clicking the Arrow button on the Drawing toolbar instead of the Line button.

Select the arrow and follow these instructions to change the style of the arrowhead, attach an arrowhead to both or either side of the arrow, or change the size of the arrowhead:

- ■ **Changing the Style of the Arrowhead**   Click the Arrow Style button on the Drawing toolbar and choose a style from the pop-up menu.

- ■ **Deciding Which End the Arrowheads Go On**   Click the Arrow Style button on the Drawing toolbar and choose an option to put arrowheads on both or either side of the arrow. If the arrow style you want isn't on the menu, choose the More Arrows option to open the Format AutoShape dialog box. Under Arrows, choose a Begin Style option and End Style option. Choose No Arrow to keep an arrowhead from appearing on either side of the line.

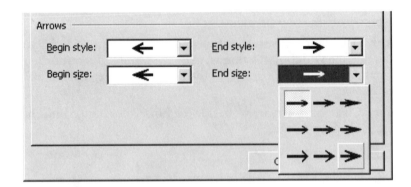

- **Changing the Size of the Arrowheads**   Click the Arrow Style button on the Drawing toolbar and choose More Arrows or right-click and choose Format AutoShape. In the Format AutoShape dialog box, choose a Begin Size and End Size option.

   To attach an arrowhead to a line you have already drawn, select the line, click the Arrow Style button on the Drawing toolbar, and choose an arrow option.

Drawing and Editing Arcs and Curved Lines

Before you attempt to draw curved lines or arcs, you should know that drawing curved lines falls in the "more trouble than it's worth" category. It can be done, but not very elegantly. You can spare yourself a lot of trouble by choosing an AutoShape and manipulating it instead of drawing curves and arcs on your own. Editing a curve or arc is especially difficult.

CREATING THE CURVED LINE OR ARC   Click the Curve button to draw a curved line or arc. To find and select the Curved button, click the AutoShapes button on the Drawing toolbar, choose Lines on the pop-up menu, and click the Curve button on the submenu. Drag onscreen to draw a curved line. As you do so, take note of these important facts:

- **Drawing Curves in the Line**   As you draw, click when you want to draw a curve in the line. Word enters a *point* on the line each time you click. Very shortly, you will learn how to view the points on a line and edit a line by dragging or removing its points. This illustration shows where I clicked to draw a curved line. Each black square on the line is a point.

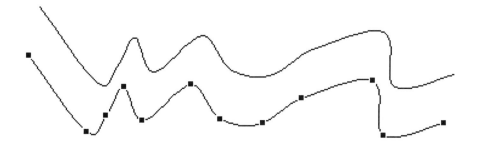

- **Ending the Curved Line**   Double-click when you want to stop drawing. When you double-click, selection handles appear around the extremities of the line you drew. You'll see eight selection handles, not the two you get when you draw a straight line.

> **Note** *A curved line or arc is an object. Techniques for moving objects, changing their size, and making them appear above or below other objects are explained in the second half of this chapter. See "Manipulating Art, Text Boxes, Shapes, and Other So-Called Objects."*

DRAWING A CLOSED SHAPE   To draw a closed shape with no beginning or end, double-click to end the curved line. Then right-click immediately and choose Close Curve from the shortcut menu. Word draws a straight line from the point you clicked to the start of the line.

DRAWING AN ARC   An arc is simply a line with one curve in it. To draw an arc, click the Curve button and draw a straight line. Then click the line to select it, right-click, and choose Edit Points on the menu. Next, move the pointer over the line where you want the apex of the arc to be, click, and drag to turn the line into an arc. Word places a point on the line at the apex of the arc. Drag the point, if necessary, to change the arc's appearance.

EDITING CURVED LINES AND ARCS   To change the shape of a curved line or arc, click to select it, and then right-click and choose Edit Points. Points appear on the line and show where each curve in the line is located. To make a curve sharper or smoother, drag its point.

If you have a lot of time on your hands, you can right-click a curved line while its points are on display and choose options from the shortcut menu to do the following:

- **Removing a Curve**   Right-click a point and choose Delete Point from the menu.
- **Adding a Curve**   Right-click where you want the curve to go, choose Add Point from the menu, and drag the point on the line.

- **Turning a Curve into a Straight Line**   Right-click between two points and choose Straight Segment from the menu. To turn a straight line into a curve, choose Curved Segment from the menu.

- **Removing Part of a Line**   Right-click between two points and choose Delete Segment from the menu.

- **Opening a Closed Shape**   Right-click a point and choose Open Curve from the menu.

- **Changing the Curve Type**   Right-click a point and choose Smooth Point, Straight Point, or Corner Point to make a curve steeper or smoother. A blue line appears across the point. Drag an end of the line to change the angle of the curve.

To select a curved line—or any object for that matter—move the pointer over it and click when you see the four-headed arrow. You can tell when a curved line has been selected because its eight selection handles appear.

Freeform Drawing

So you want to play Etch-A-Sketch® on your computer? Bully for you. Here's how to do it:

1. Click the AutoShapes button on the Drawing toolbar, choose Lines on the pop-up menu, and click either the Freeform or Scribble button. The Freeform tool draws smoother lines than the Scribble tool.

2. Start drawing.

3. Double-click when you have finished drawing your line.

Eight selection handles instead of the usual two appear around a freeform line when you have finished drawing it. Your freeform line, for better or worse, is an object. Later in this chapter, "Manipulating Art, Text Boxes, Shapes, and Other So-Called Objects" explains how to move objects and change their sizes and shapes.

Shapes, Shapes, and More Shapes

Besides drawing lines and arrows, you can draw shapes and what Word calls *autoshapes* with the tools on the Drawing toolbar. The Drawing toolbar offers about 60 different shapes and autoshapes. Apart from the rectangle and oval, you can draw octagons and various other "-agons," arrows, stars, and banners. Click the AutoShapes button on the Drawing toolbar and rest the pointer on the Basic Shapes, Block Arrows, Flowchart, Stars and Banners, and Callouts options on the menu to view the submenus and see all the autoshapes you can draw.

Follow these steps to draw a shape or autoshape:

1. Click the Oval or Rectangle button on the Drawing toolbar to draw an oval or rectangle; otherwise, click the AutoShapes button, click a menu name, and choose a shape from the submenu. The cursor changes into a cross.

2. Click onscreen and drag to draw the shape. It appears before your eyes.

Tip   *Hold down the SHIFT key as you draw the autoshape if you want it to retain its symmetry.*

3. Release the mouse button. Selection handles appear around the shape or autoshape so you can move it or change its size. The next section in this chapter explains all the different ways to manipulate an object.

A yellow diamond, sometimes two or three, appears on some autoshapes. By dragging the diamond, you can change the symmetry of the autoshape. Figure 13-9, for example, shows the same autoshape—the Quad Arrow Callout on the Block Arrows submenu—twisted into four different shapes. Notice where the diamonds are. By dragging a diamond even a very short distance, you can do a lot to change the symmetry of an autoshape.

Tip   *To exchange one autoshape for another, select it, click the Draw button on the Drawing toolbar, choose Change AutoShape on the menu, choose an AutoShape submenu, and select a substitute on the submenu.*

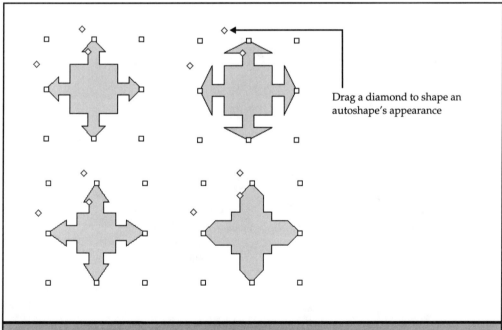

Drag a diamond to shape an autoshape's appearance

Figure 13-9.   *By dragging the diamonds on an autoshape, you can change its appearance slightly or not so slightly*

Manipulating Art, Text Boxes, Shapes, and Other So-Called Objects

After you insert a clip art image, graphic, autoshape, shape, line, text box, WordArt image, or chart in a document, it becomes what Word 2000 calls an "object." Figure 13-10 shows eight objects. The techniques for manipulating objects like these are the same whether you are dealing with a graphic, text box, line, or shape. To use objects successfully in a document, you have to know how to position them on the page. You also have to know to make them fit beside other objects and text.

Including a few so-called objects on pages is probably the best way to make a document look more sophisticated. But manipulating objects can be troublesome if you don't know how Word handles objects or how to use the commands for working with objects. On the following pages are instructions for doing these tasks with objects:

- **Selecting**   Before you can do anything to objects, you have to select them.
- **Positioning**   Drag an object to move it on the page. However, positioning objects is not as simple as that because objects can move with the text to which they are attached or be "locked" so that they don't move on the page. Word offers many commands for positioning, aligning, and distributing objects on a page.

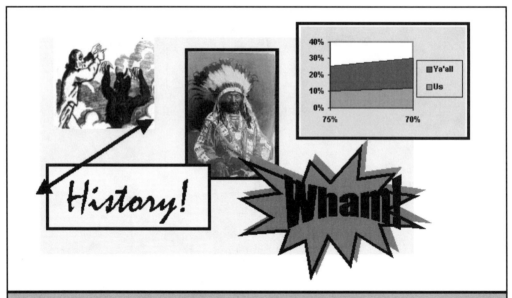

Figure 13-10.   *Examples of objects: clip art, a graphic, a chart, a text box, a line, an autoshape, and a WordArt image. Behind all these objects is yet another object—a rectangle*

- **Changing Size and Shape**   You can enlarge, shrink, stretch, and scrunch objects.

- **Rotating and Flipping**   Readers turn their heads when they see an object that has been flipped or rotated. You can rotate and flip shapes, autoshapes, lines, and WordArt images.

- **Applying Borders and Fills**   A border has been placed around all the objects in Figure 13-10 except one, the graphic in the upper-left corner. Putting borders on objects makes them stand out. You can also fill some kinds of objects with a color or pattern.

- **Using a Shadow or Third Dimension**   On the Drawing toolbar there are special commands for making an object cast a shadow or appear in three dimensions.

- **Overlapping**   Making an object appear above or behind another object is a tricky task. In Figure 13-10, for example *Wham!* (a WordArt image) overlaps an autoshape, which in turn overlaps a graphic. Word offers several confusing commands for "layering" objects on the page.

- **Grouping**   To make working with several different objects at the same time easier, you can "group" them so that they become a single object. After objects have been grouped, manipulating them—manipulating it, I should say—is easier.

- **Wrapping Text**   When text runs beside an object, the text can appear behind the object, in front of it, or be wrapped around it. Word offers many artful ways to wrap text.

Word only permits you to work on graphics, text boxes, and other objects in Page Layout view. In Normal view, you can't see objects. If the graphics in your document mysteriously disappear, don't panic. Click the Print Layout button or choose View | Print Layout instead.

By the way, if you spend any time whatsoever manipulating objects, you will soon learn how important the Draw menu and its submenus are. As shown in Figure 13-11, to open the Draw menu, click the Draw button on the Drawing toolbar (if you don't see the Drawing toolbar, choose View | Toolbars | Drawing or click the Drawing button on the Formatting toolbar). On the Draw menu, the Order, Nudge, Align or Distribute, Rotate or Flip, and Text Wrapping submenus can be turned into floating toolbars, as Figure 13-11 shows. To turn a submenu into a toolbar and make options easier to choose, drag the gray line at the top of the submenu onto the screen. You often have to experiment with commands on the Draw submenus. You can save time by giving the commands from toolbars instead of submenus.

LEARN BY EXAMPLE
The 13-1 Lines and Objects document on the companion CD offers a bunch of different objects that you can experiment with as you read the following pages.

PROFESSIONAL-LOOKING DOCUMENTS WITH WORD 2000

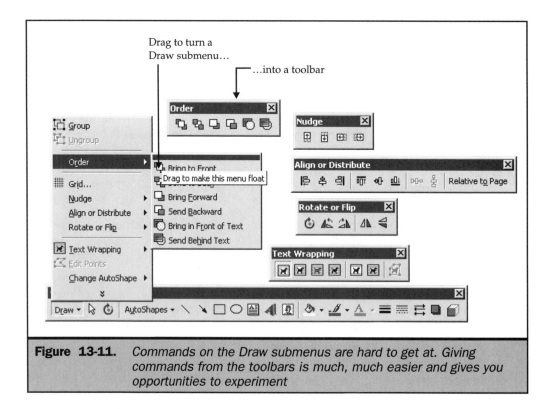

Figure 13-11. *Commands on the Draw submenus are hard to get at. Giving commands from the toolbars is much, much easier and gives you opportunities to experiment*

Selecting Objects So You Can Manipulate Them

Before you can move or change the border of a graphic, text box, or other object, you have to select it. To select an object, simply move the pointer over it, wait till you see the four-headed arrow, and click. Sometimes, to align or decorate several objects at once, you have to select more than one object at the same time. To select two or more objects:

- SHIFT-click them. In other words, hold down the SHIFT key as you click the objects.
- Click the Select Objects button on the Drawing toolbar, click on one side of the objects you want to select, and drag the cursor across the objects. A box with dotted lines appears. All objects inside the dotted lines are selected when you release the mouse button.

You can tell when an object or objects have been selected because small square selection handles appear. As the next illustration shows, objects have eight selection handles each; a line has two selection handles. On rectangular objects, the selection handles appear on the corners and sides. On irregularly shaped objects like the autoshape shown here, handles appear on the corners and sides of the object's outermost extremities. Use selection handles to change an object's shape.

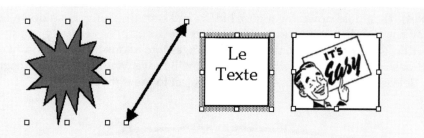

PROFESSIONAL-LOOKING
DOCUMENTS WITH
WORD 2000

 Selecting a text box can be tricky. When you click inside a text box, the selection handles appear but the box isn't really selected—you have simply clicked in the box and can start typing or editing text. To select a text box in order to manipulate it, move the pointer over the perimeter of the text box and click when you see a four-headed arrow. Instead of diagonal lines around the perimeter of the box, you'll see crosshatches when a text box has been selected.

Positioning Objects on the Page

Word offers about a dozen commands for positioning objects on the page. Get to know these commands and you can lay out pages quickly. Herewith are instructions for doing these tasks:

- **Moving Objects**   Move objects either by dragging them or by entering measurements in the Advanced Layout dialog box.

- **Aligning Objects**   Objects can be lined up with one another or with a page border.

- **Distributing Objects**   Distribute objects on the page so that the same amount of space appears between each one.

- **Snapping Objects to Word's Grid**   Snap objects to the grid to make aligning them easier.

- **Making Sure Objects Stay in the Right Place**   Lock an object so it stays in the same place on the page no matter where the paragraph to which it is attached moves.

LEARN BY EXAMPLE
To try your hand at positioning graphics, open the 13-3 Graphics document on the companion CD.

Moving Objects

The easiest way to position an object is to simply drag it. To do so, move the pointer over the object and click when you see the four-headed arrow (click the perimeter of text boxes). Then hold down the mouse button and start dragging. Hold down the SHIFT key has you drag to move an object either horizontally or vertically in a straight line. As this illustration shows, the pointer changes into a four-headed arrow and a dot-and-dash outline appears where the object will move when you release the mouse button. Release it when you have moved the object to the right place.

Tip
When you insert or move an object, Word attaches it to the nearest paragraph. You can tell which paragraph an object is attached to by clicking the Show/Hide ¶ button. An anchor appears next to the paragraph to which the object is attached. Choose Tools | Options, click the View tab in the Options dialog box, and check the Object Anchors button if you want to see the anchors at all times.

Another, more complicated way to position objects is to enter measurements on the Picture Position tab of the Advanced Layout dialog box shown in Figure 13-12. If you are dealing with the Alignment settings in the dialog box (not Absolute Position settings), the Horizontal and Vertical settings work like so:

■ Horizontal settings determine the left-to-right position of the object with respect to the left or right edge of the page, left or right side of the margin, left or right side of the column (if the text runs in columns), or the left or right side of a character.

■ Vertical settings determine the up-and-down position of the object with respect to the top or bottom of the page, the top or bottom margin, or the top or bottom of the paragraph to which the object is anchored.

If you are dealing with Absolute Position settings in the Advanced Layout dialog box, the Horizontal and Vertical settings all work with respect to the top or left side of a part of the layout:

■ Horizontal settings determine the exact position of the object from the left edge of the page, the left margin, the left side of the column (if the text runs in columns), or the left side of a character.

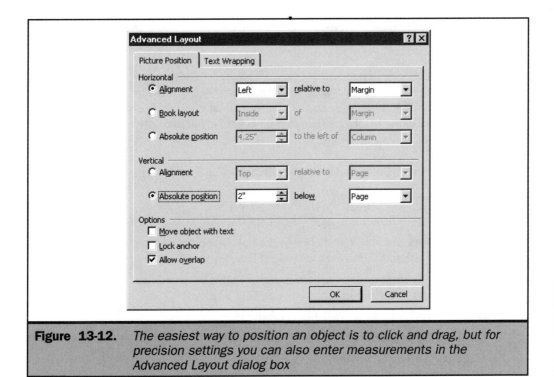

Figure 13-12.   *The easiest way to position an object is to click and drag, but for precision settings you can also enter measurements in the Advanced Layout dialog box*

■ Vertical settings determine the exact position of the object from the top of the page, the top margin, the top of the paragraph, or the top of a line.

The Book Layout options are for placing objects on or in the margin in double-sided, bound documents in which text will be printed on both sides of the page:

■ **Inside Page**   Places the object in the inside margin next to the binding.

■ **Outside Page**   Places the object in the margin furthest from the binding.

■ **Inside Margin**   Places the object flush with the inside margin next to the binding.

■ **Outside Margin**   Places the object flush with the outside margin furthest from the binding.

You can combine Alignment and Absolute Position settings. For example, suppose you are laying out a catalog with three graphics per page. You want the graphics to line up with the left margin and be, respectively, 2 inches, 4 inches, and 6 inches from the top of the page. In that case, you would choose the settings shown in Figure 13-12 for

the first graphic on the page: Alignment Left Relative To Margin, Absolute Position 2"
Below Page.

Only use the Advanced Layout dialog box if you are working on a catalog or brochure in which objects such as graphics have to line up at precise distances from a margin or page edge. As "Tricks for Aligning and Distributing Objects" explains shortly, Word offers easier ways of lining up objects than the Advanced Layout dialog box. To make objects line up, use an Align command.

To get to the Picture Position tab in the Advanced Layout dialog box:

1. Click to select the object.
2. Do one of the following to open the Format dialog box:
   - Right-click the object and choose the Format command on the shortcut menu—Format Picture, Format Text Box, Format AutoShape, and so on.
   - Choose Format on the main menu and then choose the last Format menu command—Format Picture, Format Text Box, and so on.
   - Click the Format Picture button on the Picture toolbar.
3. Click the Layout tab in the Format dialog box.
4. Click the Advanced button.
5. Click the Picture Position tab.

Figure 13-13 shows a page with text boxes that were positioned using the Horizontal and Vertical Alignment options in the Advanced Layout dialog box (see Figure 13-12). Each text box lists the Alignment options that I chose for it. Figure 13-14 shows a graphic that was positioned using Absolute Position settings. The horizontal arrows show Horizontal Absolute Position distances between the left margin, left side of the page, and left side of the column, respectively. The vertical arrows show the Vertical Absolute Position distances between the top margin, top of the page, and top of the paragraph, respectively.

Nudging an Object into the Right Position

If you can't quite fit an object in the right place, try using a Nudge command. Nudge commands move objects ever so slightly upward, downward, to the left, or to the right. Select the object, click the Draw button on the Drawing toolbar, choose Nudge, and then choose Up, Down, Left, or Right. Keep pressing F4 (the Repeat command) until the object looks just so.

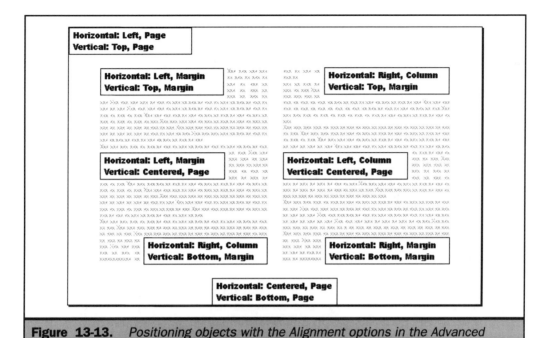

Figure 13-13.   *Positioning objects with the Alignment options in the Advanced Layout dialog box.*

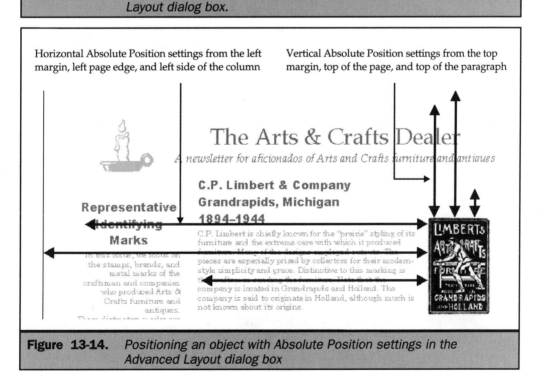

Figure 13-14.   *Positioning an object with Absolute Position settings in the Advanced Layout dialog box*

Copying Objects

The standard techniques for copying blocks of text also work for copying objects. You can cut and paste objects by moving them to the Clipboard, or you can hold down the CTRL key and drag an object to make a second copy. If you opt for the drag method of copying, don't start dragging until you see the plus sign (+) next to the pointer.

 To copy a shape in a straight line horizontally or vertically, hold down the CTRL and SHIFT keys while you drag.

Tricks for Aligning and Distributing Objects

When several objects appear on the same page, you can make the page look tidier by aligning the objects or by distributing them so that they lie an equal distance from one another. Word offers special commands for doing these tasks—and the aligning and distributing commands are easy to execute. What's more, you can fool with Word's drawing grid to make lining up objects easier. Read on.

ALIGNING OBJECTS   Suppose you are working on an album or yearbook and you need to paste several photos in a row or column. Obviously, lining up the photos neatly on the page makes a good impression. To line up several objects, select them and choose a command from the Draw | Align or Distribute menu on the Drawing toolbar.

Figure 13-15 shows the Draw | Align or Distribute menu. When you choose an Align command, you have the option of aligning objects with respect to one another or aligning them with respect to the page. In Figure 13-15, the ovals—there are three to a set—are aligned with respect to one another; the black cartoon figures are lined up with respect to the page:

- **With One Another**   As the dotted lines in Figure 13-15 show, objects can line up along their left or right edges, their top or bottom edges, or down the center either vertically or horizontally.

- **With the Page**   The objects are placed against a page edge, down the center of the page, or through the middle of the page.

Follow these steps to line up objects on the page:

1. Select the objects you want to align. To do so, SHIFT-click them.

2. Click Draw on the Drawing toolbar and choose the Align or Distribute command on the menu. You will see a menu of choices, as shown in Figure 13-15.

3. Click Relative to Page if you want to align the objects with respect to the page—or make sure the command is not checked if you want to line up objects with respect to each other. (If you click Relative to Page, repeat step 2 to see the menu choices again.)

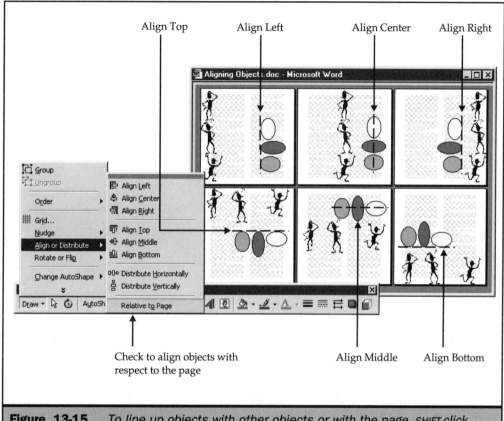

Align Top   Align Left   Align Center   Align Right

Check to align objects with respect to the page

Align Middle   Align Bottom

Figure 13-15.   *To line up objects with other objects or with the page, SHIFT-click them. Then click Draw on the Drawing toolbar, choose Align or Distribute, and choose an Align command. To line up objects with respect to the page, choose Relative to Page as well*

4. Choose an Align command—Left, Center, Right, Top, Middle, or Bottom. Figure 13-15 shows how these commands align objects. You can also click a button on the Align or Distribute toolbar if you displayed it (drag the gray line at the top of the Align or Distribute submenu to display it).

5. If necessary, drag the objects on the page. That's right—drag them. After you give an Align command, the objects are still selected. As such, you can drag to adjust their positions.

Tip   *The Nudge commands on the Draw menu (and Nudge toolbar) can be very useful for making adjustments. Click the Draw button, choose Nudge, and click the Up, Down, Left, or Right button to move the object ever so slightly.*

DISTRIBUTING OBJECTS SO THEY ARE EQUIDISTANT   The Draw | Align or Distribute submenu on the Drawing toolbar (see Figure 13-15) offers two more handy commands for laying out objects on the page—Distribute Horizontally and Distribute Vertically. These commands arrange objects on the page so that the same amount of space appears between each one. Rather than go to the trouble of pushing and pulling objects until they are distributed evenly, you can simply select the objects and choose a Distribute command.

In this illustration, the same amount of horizontal (side-to-side) space appears between movie posters. Distributing objects like these on your own, perhaps by entering measurements in the Advanced Layout dialog box (see Figure 13-12), is a waste of time when you can use a Distribute command.

To distribute objects evenly, SHIFT-click each object to select it, click Draw on the Drawing toolbar, choose Align or Distribute, and choose Distribute Horizontally to align objects across the page or Distribute Vertically to align objects up and down the page.

   Make sure Relative To Page is not selected on the Align or Distribute menu. Checking that command only makes mincemeat out of the objects on the page.

MAKING OBJECTS "SNAP TO THE GRID"   If your work calls for you to line up objects with precision, you should know about the drawing grid. The *grid* is an invisible set of horizontal and vertical lines to which objects can cling when you move them on the page. Objects that cling to the grid line up squarely with one another because their edges lie on the same horizontal and vertical lines—in other words, on the gridlines. However, making objects snap to the grid also has its drawbacks. When you move objects onscreen, they slide from gridline to gridline, so you can't place an object between gridlines.

Tip   *Whether objects "snap to the grid" or not, you can press the ALT key as you draw or drag an object to override whichever setting is chosen in the Drawing Grid dialog box. For example, if you checked Snap Objects To Grid, press the ALT key as you drag objects to keep them from clinging to the gridlines; to make objects cling to gridlines if you chose not to do that in the Drawing Grid dialog box, press the ALT key as you drag or draw objects.*

To make objects lie squarely on the grid, open the Drawing Grid dialog box and check the Snap Objects To Grid check box. Figure 13-16 shows the Drawing Grid dialog box. To open it, click the Draw button on the Drawing toolbar and choose Grid. When you drag or draw an object that "snaps to the grid," it moves jerkily by increments instead of smoothly across the page because it sticks to gridlines as it is drawn or moved.

Aside from the Snap Objects To Grid check box, other options in the Drawing Grid dialog box are:

- **Snap Objects To Other Objects**   As an aid to aligning objects, this places objects so that their edges line up with gridlines.

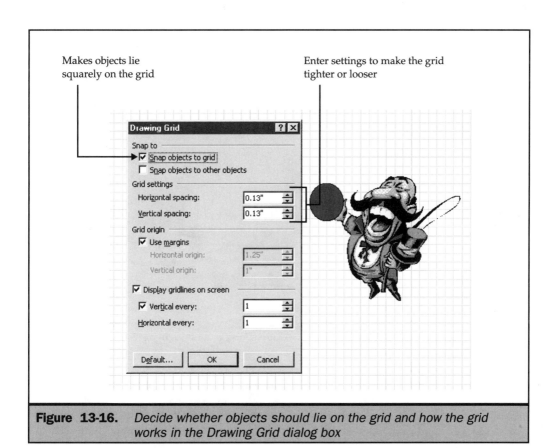

Figure 13-16.   *Decide whether objects should lie on the grid and how the grid works in the Drawing Grid dialog box*

PROFESSIONAL-LOOKING DOCUMENTS WITH WORD 2000

- **Grid Settings**   Enter Horizontal and Vertical Spacing settings here to make the grid tighter or looser. Gridlines can be drawn in increments of 0.1 (a tenth of an inch) to 22 inches. A loose grid makes lining up objects easier but tends to make the page look blocky and rigid because you can't place objects between gridlines.

- **Grid Origin**   Determines the grid's starting point in the upper-left corner of the page. Change the settings here if you often place objects in the margins.

- **Display Gridlines On Screen**   Shows the gridlines onscreen (see Figure 13-16). Enter Vertical and Horizontal settings to tell Word how many gridlines to show.

Changing the Size and Shape of Objects

To change the size or shape of a clip art image, graphic, text box, shape, or other object, either eyeball it and drag a selection handle; or go to the Format dialog box and make entries there. Selection handles are the squares that appear on an object after you select it. With the "eyeball it" method, click the object and drag a selection handle:

- Drag a corner selection handle to maintain the object's original scale—that is, to make the object larger or smaller but keep its proportions.

- Drag a selection handle on the side to stretch or compress an object.

This illustration shows the difference between dragging a corner handle to maintain the scale of an object and dragging a side handle to throw the object out of whack, which can make for interesting effects and give readers the impression that they are looking in a funhouse mirror:

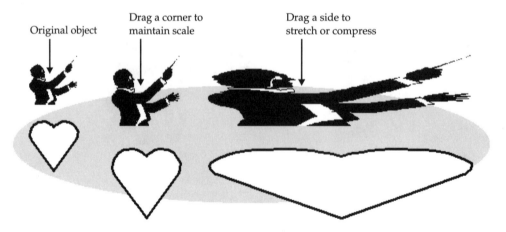

Try holding down the CTRL key as you drag a selection handle—instead of altering one side of the object, you alter the side you are dragging as well as its opposite side.

The only reason to use the Format dialog box to change the size of objects is to give objects a uniform size. In a catalog, icon library, or brochure, for example, objects need to be the same size, or at least the same width or height, so that they are displayed the same way. You can give objects a uniform appearance by following these steps:

1. SHIFT-click to select the objects that are to be the same or a similar size.

2. Right-click an object and choose Format, choose Format and then the last command on the Format menu, or click the Format Object button on the Picture toolbar.

3. Click the Size tab in the Format dialog box.

4. Under Size And Rotate (not Scale), enter a measurement in the Height or Width box or in both boxes and click OK.

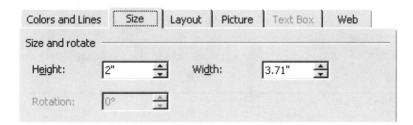

 *You can enter measurements in centimeters, points, or picas in the boxes by typing **cm**, **pt**, or **pi** after your entry. Word converts the centimeters, points, or picas to inches (or the default measurement you chose on the General tab of the Options dialog box).*

The objects you selected grow or shrink to the same degree. You can adjust their height and width by dragging a selection handle on an object. Since the objects are still selected, dragging a handle on one object changes the size of the others as well.

Caution *If an object or two is out of step with the others and did not change size correctly, its aspect ratio was not locked. Locking an object's aspect ratio tells Word to maintain the object's scale when you change its size. To remedy the problem, click the Undo button, right-click the object that didn't change size correctly, click the Lock Aspect Ratio check box on the Size tab, and click OK. Then repeat steps 1 through 4 above.*

The original height and width of graphics and clip art images is listed on the bottom of the Size tab in the Format dialog box. To return a graphic or clip art image to its original size, select it and either click the Reset button on the Size tab or click the Reset Picture button on the Picture toolbar.

Making Sure Objects Appear on the Right Page

When you insert or move an object, Word attaches it to the nearest paragraph. That's fine. Now the object will move whenever the paragraph to which it is attached is moved. But suppose you want an object to stay in one location? In newsletters, sometimes a graphic or text box needs to stay on the middle of the page. Consider the chart in Figure 13-17. It is formatted to stay in the middle of the page, so it can't move up or down the page when the paragraph that refers to it moves. However, if the paragraph that refers to it moves to the next page, it must move there as well so that readers can find it on the same page as its reference paragraph, and when it lands on the next page it must land squarely in the middle of that page, too.

To make an object stay in the same location on the pages to which it is moved, lock its anchor by following these steps:

1. Click the object to select it.

2. Place the object where you want it to be on the page (see "Moving Objects" earlier in this chapter if you need help).

3. Make sure the object is attached to the right paragraph—the one with which it will move from page to page. To do so, click the Show/Hide ¶ button. As Figure 13-17 shows, an anchor appears next to the paragraph that the object is

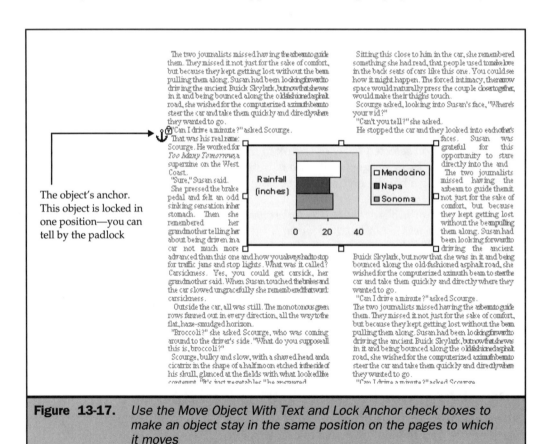

Figure 13-17. *Use the Move Object With Text and Lock Anchor check boxes to make an object stay in the same position on the pages to which it moves*

attached to. If necessary, drag the anchor up or down the screen to attach the object to the paragraph that refers to the object (you can't move the anchor if a padlock appears beside it). If the object is to stay on the first page of a newsletter, for example, drag the anchor beside the newsletter title.

| **Tip** | *You can make the anchor appear without pressing the Show/Hide ¶ button. Choose Tools | Options, click the View tab in the Options dialog box, and check the Object Anchors check box.* |

4. Open the Format dialog box. To do so, right-click the object and choose Format (the last command on the shortcut menu); choose Format on the menu bar and then the last command on the Format menu; or click the Format button on the Picture toolbar (these commands and buttons change names, depending on the kind of object you are working with). You will see the Format dialog box.

5. Click Layout tab.

6. Click the Advanced button and then click the Picture Position tab in the Advanced Layout dialog box.

7. Uncheck the Move Object With Text check box and check the Lock Anchor check box.

```
Options ─────────────────────────────────────
    ☐ Move object with text
    ☑ Lock anchor
    ☑ Allow overlap
```

8. Choose the Absolute Position option button under Horizontal and Vertical, and choose Page as the Absolution Position option in the To The Left Of and the Below drop-down menus.

9. Click OK.

As Figure 13-17 shows, you can tell when an object has been "locked" because a small padlock appears beside the anchor when you press the Show/Hide ¶ button. To "unlock" an object, return to the Advanced Layout dialog box and uncheck the Lock Anchor check box.

Rotating and Flipping Objects

Rotating and flipping objects—that is, changing their orientation—is a neat way to make a layout look more sophisticated. As Figure 13-18 demonstrates, you can rotate and flip these kinds of objects: lines, WordArt, shapes, and autoshapes. For the record, you can also flip the words inside a text box, but that involves flipping the text itself, not the text box, a topic covered under "Putting a Text Box on the Page," earlier in this chapter.

To flip or rotate an object, select it and do one of the following:

- **Roll Your Own** Click the Free Rotate button on the Drawing toolbar. Green rotation handles appear on the corners of the object you selected. Move the pointer over a green handle, and when the pointer changes to a semi-circle, click and drag to rotate the object.

- **Choose a Rotate or Flip Command** On the Drawing toolbar, choose Draw | Rotate or Flip, and then choose a Rotate or Flip command on the submenu. You can also click buttons on the Rotate or Flip toolbar if you've displayed it (drag the gray line at the top of the Rotate or Flip submenu to do so).

Tip *On the Size tab in the Format dialog box is a Rotation box for rotating objects to specific degrees—45°, 90°, 111°, whatever. Presumably, this box is for rotating several objects to the same degree, but you don't really need it. To rotate different objects to the same degree, SHIFT-click to select each object and then choose a rotate or flip command or click the Free Rotate button and drag a rotation handle. The objects rotate or flip in unison.*

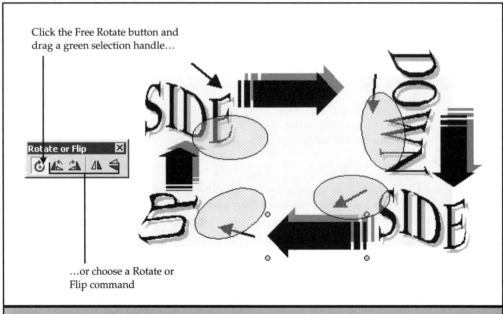

Click the Free Rotate button and drag a green selection handle…

…or choose a Rotate or Flip command

Figure 13-18. *Readers turn their heads when lines, WordArt, shapes, and autoshapes are flipped or rotated*

Putting Borders and "Fills" on Objects

One of the best and easiest ways to decorate a page is to place borders around graphics, clip art images, text boxes, shapes, autoshapes, and other objects. And "filling in" the space inside an object isn't a bad idea, either. You can fill certain kinds of objects with a color or pattern. This illustration shows a few of the different borders and so-called fills you can put around or in an object. Read on to find out how to handle borders and fills.

Putting a Border Around an Object

The first step in putting a border around an object is to select it. After that, you can fashion a border either by clicking buttons on the Drawing or Picture toolbar or by opening the Format dialog box and choosing options there, as shown in Figure 13-19. The Format dialog box offers many combinations of choices, but the toolbars are hard to beat if you want to experiment by quickly clicking this and that until the border comes out right.

   To open the Format dialog box, right-click the object and choose Format, the last command on the shortcut menu; choose Format on the main menu and then the last Format menu command; or click the Format button on the Picture toolbar (the Format commands and buttons change names depending on the kind of object you selected). In the Format dialog box, choose the Colors and Lines tab to fashion a border.

PROFESSIONAL-LOOKING DOCUMENTS WITH WORD 2000

Designating a Design for All the Objects You Will Work With

A command on the Draw menu called Set AutoShape Defaults makes putting borders and fills on shapes and autoshapes a lot easier. To use this command, select an object with a border and fill that you want for the majority of the shapes and autoshapes you will work with. Then choose the Set AutoShape Default command on the Draw menu (this menu is located on the Drawing toolbar). When you create a new shape or autoshape, it is given the same border and fill as the object that you chose as your official default object.

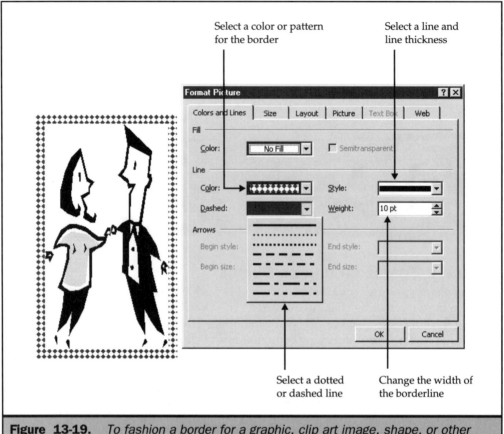

Select a color or pattern for the border

Select a line and line thickness

Select a dotted or dashed line

Change the width of the borderline

Figure 13-19. *To fashion a border for a graphic, clip art image, shape, or other object, either click buttons on the Drawing or Picture toolbar or make choices in the Format dialog box*

Tip   *The fastest way to get to the Colors and Lines tab is to click the Line Style button on the Drawing toolbar and choose More Lines on the pop-up menu.*

Putting borders on objects is easier than it looks. Have fun experimenting with these options:

- **Line Styles and Thicknesses**   Click either the Line Style button on the Drawing or Picture toolbar or the Style drop-down menu in the Format dialog box and choose a line. To toy with the thickness of lines, go to the Format dialog box and change the measurement in the Weight box.

- **Dashed Lines**   Either click the Dash Style button on the Drawing toolbar and choose a line from the menu, or choose a line from the Dashed menu in the Format dialog box.

- **Border Colors and Patterns**   Either click the down arrow beside the Line Color button on the Drawing toolbar and choose a color, or do the same from the Color drop-down menu in the Format dialog box.

  At the bottom of the Line Color and Color menus are options called More Colors and Patterned Lines. The first merely offers more colors. Choose Patterned Lines to open a dialog box and choose, instead of a border line, a border pattern like the one on the picture in Figure 13-19. You can even choose colors for the foreground and background of the pattern.

Tip   *The stripe on the Line Color button shows the color you selected last. To apply that color again, simply click the Line Color button.*

To remove a border, either click the arrow beside the Line Color button on the Drawing toolbar and choose No Line, or go to the Colors and Lines tab in the Format dialog box and choose No Color from the Color menu.

Unfortunately, Word makes it well-nigh impossible to draw a border on one, two, or three sides of an object. You can draw borders with the Line tool on the Drawing toolbar (see "Drawing Lines and Arrows," earlier in this chapter). Or, if your object happens to be a text box, try removing the border lines and then using the Tables and Borders toolbar to draw borders inside the boundaries of the text box.

Filling an Object with a Color or Pattern

Text boxes, autoshapes, and shapes are empty when you put them on the page, but you can fill them with a color, pattern, or even a picture. You can also put colors and patterns in certain kinds of graphics and clip art images—vector graphics and clip art images, to be exact. Word uses a peculiar term to describe the colors and patterns in objects: *fill*, as in "landfill."

The simplest way to fill an object with a color is to select it, click the Fill Color arrow on the Drawing toolbar to open the Color menu, and choose a color, as shown in Figure 13-20. (Fans of the Format dialog box will be glad to know that the Color menu is also available there on the Colors and Lines tab.)

If the color you crave is not on the Color menu, click More Fill Colors. That takes you to the Colors dialog box with its two self-explanatory tabs for choosing various colors. As Figure 13-20 shows, colors you choose in the Colors dialog box are placed on the Color menu so you can choose them in the future from the Color menu without having to revisit the Colors dialog box.

Tip   *The chief advantage of clicking More Fill Colors and going to the Colors dialog box is being able to choose semitransparent colors. To do so, choose a color and then check the Semitransparent check box (you will find it in the lower-left corner of the dialog box). Semitransparent colors are especially useful in text boxes, because the text shows through the semitransparent color and can be read easily.*

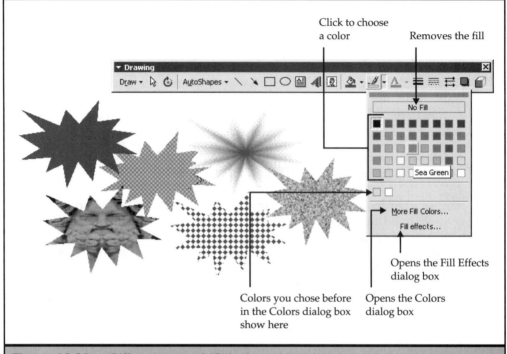

Figure 13-20. *Different ways of "filling" an object (clockwise from upper-left): a color, a semitransparent color, a gradient (two-color from center), a texture (granite), a pattern (solid diamond), and a picture*

If a pattern or unusual background is what you want, click the arrow on the Fill Color button and choose Fill Effects on the Color menu. Doing so opens the Fill Effects dialog box. As you entertain yourself with the options on these tabs, keep your eye on the Sample box in the lower-right corner—it shows what you have chosen or created:

- ■ **Gradient** For one- or two-color shading. You can choose between various shading styles.

- ■ **Texture** Offers 24 patterns meant to simulate various surfaces. The choices include Granite, Recycled Paper, and Pink Tissue Paper. Be sure to use the scroll bar to see all the choices.

- ■ **Pattern** Presents numerous patterns, including Zig Zag, Small Confetti, and Checker Board. Experiment with foreground and background colors for the pattern you chose by making choices from the Foreground and Background menus.

- ■ **Picture** Lets you fit a picture inside a shape, autoshape, or text box. Click the Select Picture button, find and click a picture file in the Select Picture dialog box, and click OK.

PROFESSIONAL-LOOKING
DOCUMENTS WITH
WORD 2000

Tip   *As Figure 13-20 demonstrates, fills and patterns often look better when border lines are not drawn around the object. To remove a border, click the arrow beside the Line Color button on the Drawing toolbar and choose No Line on the pop-up menu.*

Putting a Shadow or Third Dimension on an Object

Yet another way to play interior decorator with your Word documents is to give text boxes, shapes, autoshapes, WordArt, or clip art images a shadow or third-dimension. Figure 13-21 illustrates a few of the many, many ways to play with the Shadow and 3-D settings.

To call attention to an object on the page by making it cast a shadow or by giving it another dimension, start by selecting the object. Then click either the Shadow or 3-D button on the Drawing toolbar to open the Shadow or 3-D menu and make a choice. As Figure 13-21 shows, the choices on the Shadow and 3-D menus are many.

If you want to get down and dirty with Shadow or 3-D effects, click the Shadow Settings or 3-D Settings button to display the Shadow Settings or 3-D Settings toolbar. As Figure 13-21 shows, these toolbars offer numerous commands for tweaking

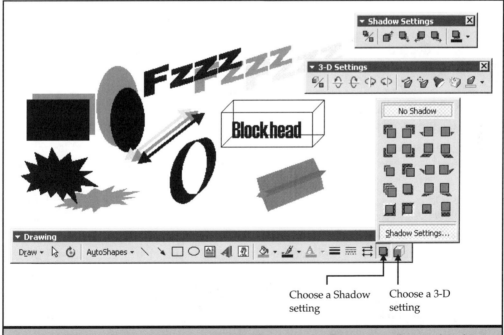

Choose a Shadow setting

Choose a 3-D setting

Figure 13-21.   *Click the Shadow or 3-D button on the Drawing toolbar and make a choice from the menu to make objects cast shadows or appear in three dimensions*

shadows and 3-D effects. Experiment at will. In the time it would take me to explain what these buttons do, you will have found one you like.

To remove a shadow from an object, click the No Shadow button on the Shadow menu. To remove the third-dimension from a object, click the No 3-D button on the 3-D menu.

LEARN BY EXAMPLE
Open the 13-2 3D Shapes document on the companion CD if you want to experiment in the third dimension.

When Objects Overlap: Choosing Which Appears Above the Other

Objects inevitably overlap on a page that is crowded with text, text boxes, graphics, shapes, and autoshapes. For that matter, a page on which objects deliberately overlap looks interesting and is attractive to readers. But when objects overlap, how do you tell Word to put one object in front of or behind another? And how do you tell Word to put text in front of or behind objects?

Unfortunately, when you start overlapping text and objects you run into one of the most difficult concepts in Microsoft Word: *layers,* sometimes known as *drawing layers.* Whether an object appears above or behind another object, or above or behind the text on the page, depends on which layer it resides on. Objects can lie on three of the four layers. From top to bottom, the layers are:

- **Foreground Layer**   The topmost layer. Objects on this layer obscure, or block out, objects and text in the layers below. When you bring an object into a document, it lands by default on the foreground layer.

- **Text Layer**   The text you type in a Word document goes on the text layer. This layer is reserved for text only. Objects placed on the foreground layer obscure the text; objects on the background layer appear behind the text.

- **Background Layer**   Objects on this layer appear behind the text and behind objects placed on the foreground layer.

- **Header/Footer Layer**   The bottommost layer. This layer is for watermarks (see "Decorating Pages with Watermarks," earlier in this chapter). Objects on the header/footer layer appear behind all other objects as well as the text on the page. You cannot use the Order commands (described shortly) to move an object on the header/footer layer up the stack. These objects remain permanently on the bottommost header/footer layer.

In this illustration, the objects are—from left to right—on the foreground layer, background layer, and header/footer layer. Notice how the object on the foreground layer obscures the text, but the text, which is on the text layer, obscures objects on the background and header/footer layer:

Layers seem simple enough on the surface, but the layers concept gets more complicated when objects reside on the same layer. Consider this illustration, in which all the objects reside on the background layer. These objects overlap. In a case like this, how do you tell Word to put one object in front of or behind another?

Word has a special set of commands called Order commands for changing the layer on which objects reside and determining which object in a group on the same layer overlaps the others. To bring an object forward or backward in a stack, select it and do either of the following:

- Right-click, choose Order on the shortcut menu, and then choose an Order command.

- Click the Draw button on the Drawing toolbar, choose Order, and then choose an Order command, as shown in Figure 13-22.

Tip   *Selecting an object on the background layer is nearly impossible if the object is obscured by text unless you click the Select Objects button on the Drawing toolbar first. To select an object on the background layer, click the Select Objects button and then click the object.*

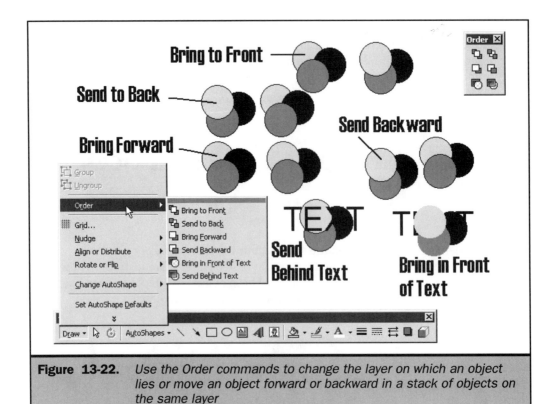

Figure 13-22. *Use the Order commands to change the layer on which an object lies or move an object forward or backward in a stack of objects on the same layer*

The commands on the Order menu (and buttons on the Order toolbar) are explained in Table 13-2 and outlined in Figure 13-22. In the figure, the overlapping circles demonstrate what happens when you choose an Order command. The first four Order commands affect objects that reside on the same layer; the last two commands are for moving objects to a different layer.

The Order commands can be confusing. Maybe the easiest way to handle them is to select an object, display the Order toolbar (by dragging the gray line at the top of the Order menu to make the commands "float"), and start clicking buttons on the Order toolbar. Keep clicking until the object lands on the right layer.

Two Word features can make arranging objects in layers still more confusing: transparent colors and wrapping. Where normally an object on the foreground layer obscures the text, text shows through the object if the object has been filled with a transparent color or has no fill (see "Putting Borders and Fills on Objects," earlier in this chapter, if you don't know what a fill is). As for wrapping, which is explained

Command	What It Does
Bring to Front	For objects on the same layer, moves the object to the top of the stack. For example, if three objects on the foreground layer overlap, this command moves the selected object in front of the other two.
Send to Back	For objects on the same layer, moves the object to the bottom of the stack.
Bring Forward	For objects on the same layer, moves the object higher in the stack. For example, if three objects on the foreground layer overlap and you use this command on the bottommost object, the object moves from the bottommost to the middle position.
Send Backward	For objects on the same layer, moves the object lower in the stack.
Bring in Front of Text	Moves the object from the background layer to the foreground layer, where it obscures the text (and it also obscures objects on the background layer).
Send Behind Text	Moves the object from the foreground layer to the background layer, where it appears behind the text (and behind objects on the foreground layer).

Table 13-2. *Order Menu (and Order Toolbar) Commands*

shortly, many users get confused when they see text wrapped around an object, and to keep text from wrapping, they attempt to move the object to the background layer. But that has no effect whatsoever. You have to choose a new wrapping style instead (see "Wrapping Text around an Object," later in this chapter).

If, try as you might, you can't get one object to overlap another, the objects are on different layers. One is on the foreground layer and the other is on the background layer. Click the Draw button on the Drawing toolbar, choose Order, and select either Bring in Front of Text or Send Behind Text to place both objects on the same layer.

Grouping Objects to Make Working with Them Easier

Consider the lines, clip art, and text boxes in Figure 13-23. If I wanted to move these objects to the side, down the page, to another page, or to another document, I would have to laboriously move them one at a time—I would, if it weren't for the Group command.

The Group command assembles different objects into a single object to make moving, copying, and reshaping objects easier. In the figure, you can see all the objects being moved at once up the page. To use the Group command, select the objects that you want to "group" by SHIFT–clicking them or by drawing a box around them with the Select Objects pointer on the Drawing toolbar. Then do either of the following:

■ Click the Draw button on the Drawing toolbar and choose Group, as shown in Figure 13-23.

■ Right-click one of the objects you selected and choose Grouping | Group.

After objects are grouped, they form a single object with the eight selection handles. Now you can use the standard techniques to move or resize all the objects at once.

Tip   *To add an object to a group, select the object and the grouped objects by SHIFT-clicking, and then choose the Group command.*

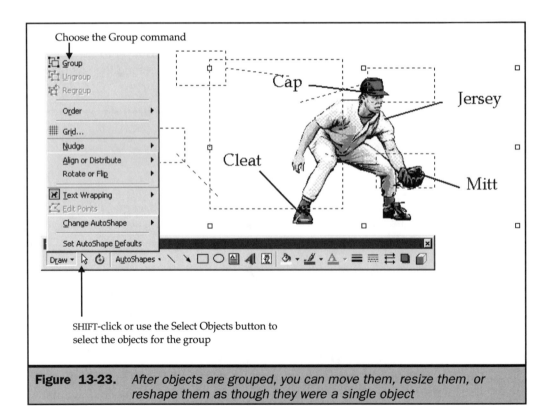

Figure 13-23.   *After objects are grouped, you can move them, resize them, or reshape them as though they were a single object*

What are the Ungroup and Regroup commands on the Draw menu and shortcut menu for? To "ungroup" an object and break it into its components parts and perhaps to fiddle with one of the objects in the group, select the object and choose the Ungroup command. Word remembers which objects were in a group after you ungroup it. To reassemble the objects in a group, click an object that was formerly in the group and then choose the Regroup command. You might be interested to know that clip art images are composed of many different parts that have been grouped, as this illustration demonstrates:

PROFESSIONAL-LOOKING
DOCUMENTS WITH
WORD 2000

The Group command is a great way to enlarge or shrink different objects to the same degree. After objects have been grouped and made one object, drag a selection handle to enlarge or shrink all of them at once.

Wrapping Text Around an Object

Word offers many elegant ways to wrap text around a clip art image, graphic, shape, autoshape, text box, or other object. In fact, wrapping text around an object is probably the best way to present a sophisticated layout with a minimum amount of work. All you have to do is choose a wrapping style, tell Word around which side of the object to wrap the text, and there you have it—a sophisticated looking page.

Choosing How and Where to Wrap Text

Figure 13-24 demonstrates the 15 different ways to wrap text around an object. Follow these steps to tell Word how and where to wrap text:

1. Select the object you intend to wrap the text around.

2. Open the Format dialog box: Right-click and choose Format, choose Format and the last command on the Format menu, or click the Format Picture button on the Picture toolbar.

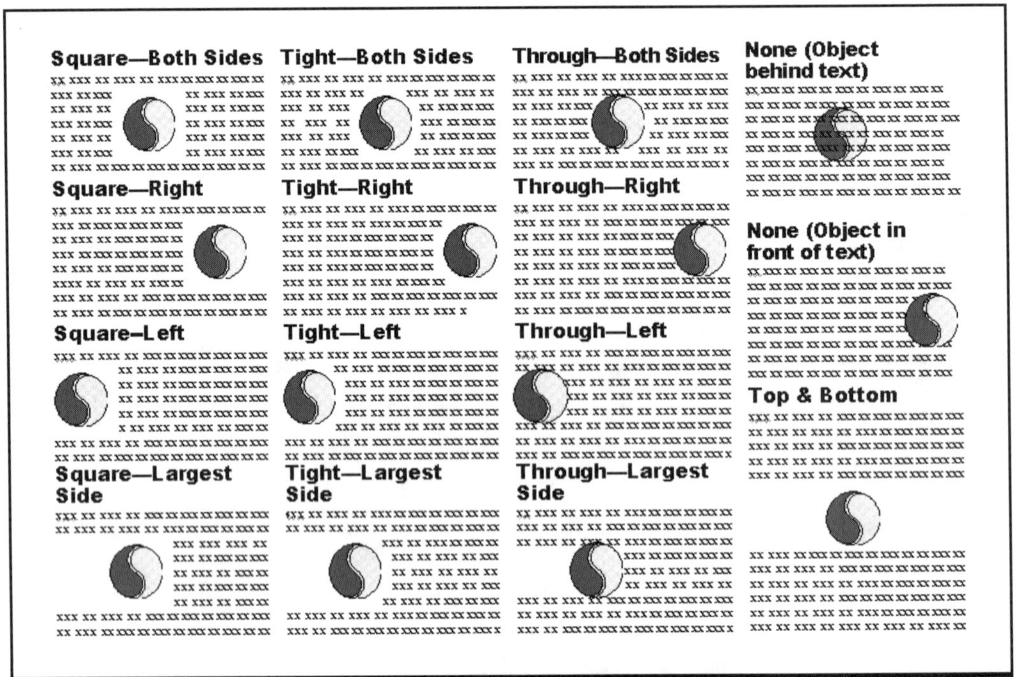

Square—Both Sides   Tight—Both Sides   Through—Both Sides   None (Object behind text)

Square—Right   Tight—Right   Through—Right   None (Object in front of text)

Square—Left   Tight—Left   Through—Left   Top & Bottom

Square—Largest Side   Tight—Largest Side   Through—Largest Side

Figure 13-24. *The fifteen ways to wrap text. With the None and Top & Bottom wrapping styles, text isn't wrapped around the sides of the object, so Wrap To options are not available with those styles*

3. Click the Layout tab in the Format dialog box, as shown Figure 13-25.

4. Choose a Wrapping Style and Horizontal Alignment option. For a Top And Bottom or Largest Side wrap, click the Advanced button to go to the Advanced Layout dialog box and choose options there (see Figure 13-25).

5. Click OK to return to your document.

Caution *At least .6 inches of space is needed to wrap text around the side of an object. In other words, you can't wrap text if there isn't .6 inches of space between the side of the object and the margin or column. Furthermore, wrapped text looks better when it has been hyphenated. With hyphens, the text can get closer to the object. And if you are working in columns, try justifying the text to make the letters line up cleanly with the columns as well as the objects.*

After you experiment with the wrapping options (see Figure 13-25), you soon learn what they do. In fact, to quickly experiment with text wrapping, select an object and then click the different Text Wrapping buttons on the Picture toolbar.

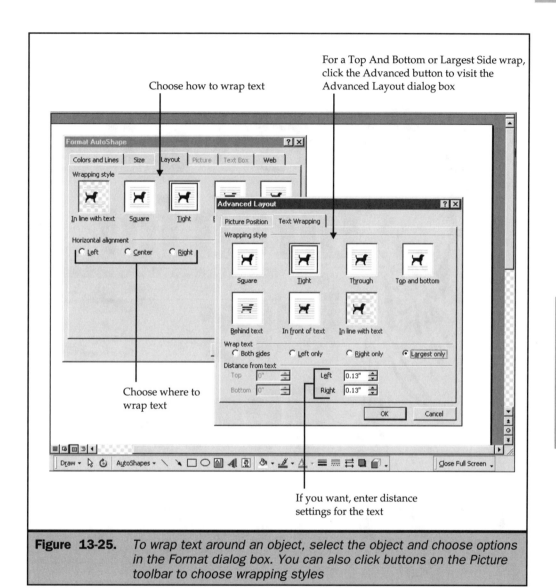

Choose how to wrap text

For a Top And Bottom or Largest Side wrap, click the Advanced button to visit the Advanced Layout dialog box

Choose where to wrap text

If you want, enter distance settings for the text

PROFESSIONAL-LOOKING
DOCUMENTS WITH
WORD 2000

Figure 13-25.   *To wrap text around an object, select the object and choose options in the Format dialog box. You can also click buttons on the Picture toolbar to choose wrapping styles*

Bringing the Text Closer to or Further from an Object

If you want to adjust the distance between the text and the object, make entries in the Distance From Text boxes—Top, Bottom, Left, and Right—in the Advanced Layout dialog box (see Figure 13-25). With the Tight and Through wrapping styles, you can tell Word precisely how close to wrap the text by dragging the wrap points. Figure 13-26 shows *wrap points,* the square, black selection handles. A dotted line runs between all the wrap points.

Figure 13-26. *To bring text closer to an object, click the Text Wrapping button on the Picture toolbar and choose Edit Wrap Points. Then start dragging wrap points*

To move text closer to an object:

1. Select the object.

2. Choose a large Zoom percentage. In Figure 13-26, for example, I choose 500% from the Zoom menu. Enlarging your view of the screen makes it easier to work with wrap points.

3. Click the Text Wrapping button on the Picture toolbar and choose Edit Wrap Points, as shown in Figure 13-26.

4. Carefully drag the wrap points away from or toward the object to draw the text closer or to push it further away.

Exam | MOUS Exam Objectives Explored in Chapter 13

Objective	Heading	Practice File
Use the drawing toolbar	"Drawing Lines and Shapes"	13-1 Lines and Objects
Insert graphics into a document (Word Art, Clip Art, images)	"Handling Graphics and Clip Art in documents"	
Create watermarks*	"Decorating Pages with Watermarks"	13-4 Watermarks
Delete and position graphics*	"Positioning Objects on the Page"	13-3 Graphics
Add bitmapped graphics*	"Handling Graphics and Clip Art in Documents"	
Use advanced text alignment features with graphics	"Wrapping Text around an object"	

* Denotes an Expert exam objective.

Top 10

Ten Tricks for Handling Clip Art, Text Boxes, and Other Objects

Here are a handful of tricks for handling objects such as clip art and text boxes. Use these tricks and you can impress your impressionable friends.

1. MAKE TEXT APPEAR IN FRONT OF A GRAPHIC OR CLIP ART IMAGE.

Follow these steps to make words and letters appear over a clip art image or graphic:

1. Create a text box and enter the words in the text box.

2. Drag the text box on top of the image.

3. With the text box still selected, click the arrow beside the Fill Color button on the Drawing toolbar and choose No Fill from the pop-up menu.

4. Click the arrow beside the Line Color button on the Drawing toolbar and choose No Line from the pop-up menu.

5. If the image appears in front of the words, right-click the image, click Order on the menu, and choose Send Behind Text on the submenu.

6. If the image still appears in front of the words, right-click it again, click Order on the menu, and choose Send to Back or Send Backward on the submenu.

A dark image can obscure the words. To fix that problem, display the Picture toolbar and experiment with the Image Control, Contrast, and Brightness buttons to make the image less opaque (see "Changing the Appearance of an Image or Graphic" earlier in this chapter). Or else change the color of the words to white, yellow, or a light color (see "Changing the Color of Text" in Chapter 7).

2. USE THE ALIGN OR DISTRIBUTE COMMANDS TO LAY OUT OBJECTS ON THE PAGE.

Making text boxes, clip art images, graphics, or shapes line up on the page can be difficult if you do the task on your own. You have to drag the objects here and there and rely on your eyesight to line them up. Placing the same amount of empty space between objects is nearly impossible if you do it yourself, especially if you are dealing with several objects at once.

Instead of relying on your eyesight and your skill at dragging objects, use the Align or Distribute commands to make objects line up or lie evenly across the page. SHIFT-click to select the objects, display the Drawing toolbar, click the Draw button on the toolbar, choose Align or Distribute, and select an Align command or Distribute command. See "Positioning Objects on the Page," earlier in this chapter, for all the details.

3. CHANGE THE SIZE OF SEVERAL OBJECTS AT THE SAME TIME.

Sometimes several objects need to be enlarged or shrunk by the same degree. Maybe several shapes are too small or several clip art images are too large. You can change the size of several objects at once by SHIFT-clicking to select all of them and then dragging the corner selection handle of one object in the bunch. All the objects change size—and by the same degree.

4. USE THE CROPPING TOOL TO MOVE BORDERS AWAY FROM A CLIP ART

IMAGE.   Strange as it seems, the only way to increase the distance between a clip art image or graphic and its borders is to use the Cropping tool on the Picture toolbar. Normally, this tool is used to cut off parts of an image, but if you drag away from the image instead of toward its center, you put more space between the image and its borders. Better yet, right-click the image, choose Format Picture, click the Picture tab in the Format Picture dialog box, and enter equal measurements in the four Crop From boxes: Left, Right, Top, and Bottom. By doing so, you increase the distance between the image and the border on all sides by an equal amount of space.

5. MOVE OBJECTS IN STRAIGHT LINES.   When you are trying to align objects,

being able to move them either horizontally or vertically in a straight line helps a lot. Hold down the SHIFT key has you drag to move an object either horizontally or vertically in a straight line. To copy a shape in a straight line horizontally or vertically, hold down the CTRL and SHIFT keys while you drag.

6. MAKE USE OF THE CTRL AND SHIFT KEY TO DRAW SYMMETRICAL

OBJECTS.   Hold down the SHIFT key to draw a perfect circle, square, square text box, or autoshape. Hold down the CTRL and SHIFT keys to draw a perfect circle, square, or square text box in an outward direction starting in the middle. To draw an object from the center outward, hold down the CTRL key as you draw it.

7. PUT YOUR FAVORITE GRAPHICS IN THE FAVORITES CATEGORY OF THE

CLIP GALLERY DIALOG BOX.   When you find a clip art image you like in the Clip Gallery, add it to the Favorites category. That way, you can find it again. To add an image to the Favorites category, click it, click the Add Clip to Favorites or Other Category button, and then click Add in the Add Clip to the Following Category dialog box. Earlier in this chapter, "Putting Your Own Images in the Clip Gallery" explains how you can access the clip art that you have collected by way of the Clip Gallery. You can put your own images in the Favorites category, too.

8. RESET A PICTURE TO ITS ORIGINAL DIMENSIONS.   The original height and

width of graphics and clip art images is listed on the bottom of the Size tab in the Format dialog box. If you tug a graphic or clip art image out of shape and want to return it to its original size, select it, right-click, and choose Format from the shortcut menu. Then, in the Format dialog box, click the Size tab. At the bottom of the Size tab, under the words "Original Size," is the height and width of the object before you started fooling with it. Click the Reset button to restore the object to its original size. You can also click the Reset Picture button on the Picture toolbar to restore a graphic to its original dimensions.

9. DRAW BORDERS ON ONE, TWO, OR THREE SIDES OF A TEXT BOX.   Yes, it can be done. You can put borders on one, two or three sides of a text box. To do so, remove the borders from the text box (see "Putting a Border Around an Object," earlier in this chapter). With that done, select the text box and display the Tables and Border toolbar. Use the Border drop-down menu on the toolbar to place borders on one, two, or three sides of the text box.

10. USE TEXT BOXES AND LINES TO ANNOTATE A FIGURE.   Sure, you can click the AutoShapes button on the Drawing toolbar, choose Callouts on the pop-up menu, and choose a callout to annotate a figure, but the callouts on the menu are unwieldy and hard to manage. You can't change the width of the line or remove the box that goes around the callout text. A better way to annotate a figure is to create a text box for the annotation and draw a line from the text box to the part of the figure that the text box refers to. The text box method gives you more freedom to experiment with annotations. You can remove the box that goes around the text, change the width of the line, or put an arrow on the line if you want to.

To remove borders from a text box, select the text box, click the arrow beside the Line Color button on the Drawing toolbar, and choose No Line from the pop-up menu. To change the width of a line, select the line, click the Line Style button on the Drawing toolbar, and choose a line width.

Chapter 14

Constructing
the Perfect Table

The best way to present a bunch of data at one time is to present it in a table. Provided the row labels and column headings are descriptive, looking up information in a table is the fastest and easiest way to find it. And tables impose order on chaos. What used to be a knotty lump of nondescript data can be turned into an orderly statement of fact if the data is presented in a table. No report is complete without one or two of them.

Microsoft Word 2000 devotes an entire menu to creating and formatting tables—the Table menu. On the Table menu are numerous commands for handling tables. Read on to find out how to create tables, enter the text, lay out a table, format a table, prettify a table, do the math, turn a list into a table, and use tables as a means of laying out text in columns. At the end of this section, for you and you alone, are ten tricks for handling tables.

What You Should Know Before You Begin

Before you can start creating tables in Word 2000, you need to know table terminology. Figure 14-1 shows the various parts of a table. Here is what the terms mean:

- **Borders** The lines that mark where columns and rows are, as well as the extremities of the table. Borders are different from gridlines. When you first create a table, you will see gridlines, not borders. You decide what your table borders will look like.

- **Cell** The box that is formed where each column and row intersect. Each cell holds one data item. The table in Figure 14-1 comprises 20 cells (5 rows × 4 columns).

- **Gridlines** Gray lines that show where columns and rows are. Gridlines help you see where one row or column ends and the other begins. Until you format a table and give it borders, gridlines show where the columns and rows are, but in a table with borders, the borderlines cover the gridlines. In Figure 14-1,

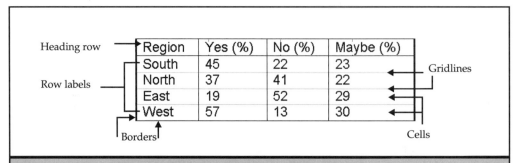

Region	Yes (%)	No (%)	Maybe (%)
South	45	22	23
North	37	41	22
East	19	52	29
West	57	13	30

Figure 14-1. *Every table has columns, rows, and cells, and most include a heading row as well*

borders have been drawn on the columns but not the rows, and gridlines show where rows begin and end. To see or turn off the gridlines, choose Table | Show Gridlines or Table | Hide Gridlines.

- **Heading Row**   The row at the top of the table that describes what is in the columns below. In Figure 14-1, the heading row includes four entries: "Region," "Yes (%)," "No (%)," and "Maybe (%)." You can tell Word to make the heading row appear again on the next page when a table breaks across two pages. Some tables have two or even three heading rows.

- **Row Labels**   The entries in the first column of a table that describe what kind of data is in each row. The table in Figure 14-1 includes four row labels: "South," "North," "East," and "West."

To help create and format tables, Word offers the Tables and Borders toolbar (click the Tables and Borders button on the Standard toolbar to display it). Between the Tables and Borders toolbar and the shortcut menu commands for dealing with tables, you can conveniently do most of the work without having to open the cumbersome Table menu on the menu bar.

Note   *Tables can be as fancy or bare as you want them to be. Don't worry about tables' appearance, however, because you can rely on the Table | Table AutoFormat command to do all the formatting for you. See "Letting the Table AutoFormat Command Do the Work," later in this chapter.*

Creating a Table

Word gives you no less than three different ways to create a table, and you can also turn a list into a table as long as you format the list properly. These pages explain how to create a table, move around in a table, enter the text and numbers, and enter data from an Excel worksheet into a Word table.

When you create a table, you can tell Word to include umpteen rows and many, many columns. But sometimes starting with only one row works best. As you enter data, you can add rows as you need them. To add a new row to a table as you enter data, press the TAB key when you have finished entering data in the last column of the last row. Pressing TAB when the cursor is in the last column of the last row adds another row to the table.

The Three Ways to Create a Table

Choose your weapon when you want to create a table. You can create a bare-bones table with the Insert Table button on the Standard toolbar, choose the Table | Insert | Table command to take advantage of one or two refinements in the Insert Table dialog box, or draw a table with the Draw Table button on the Tables and Borders toolbar. Better read on.

Starting with the Insert Table Button

The fastest way to create a table is to click the Insert Table button on the Standard toolbar. Click the button and you'll see an empty table grid, but by moving the pointer onto the grid and dragging sideways and downward, you can tell Word how many rows and columns to put in the table. Click when the bottom of the menu lists the number of rows and columns you want. Here, a table four rows long and nine columns wide is being created:

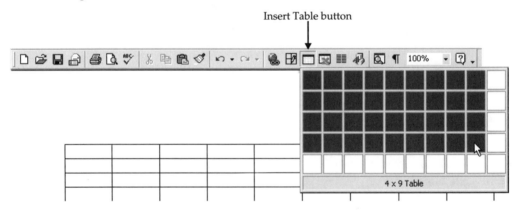

Insert Table button

4 x 9 Table

Your new table fills the page from margin to margin. Each column is the same width. Later in this chapter, "Changing the Layout of a Table" explains how to change the size of a table, its rows, and its columns.

Click in the first column, first row of a table and press ENTER to insert a blank line above the table. In a document with a table and nothing more, you can get trapped in the table unless you know to press ENTER in the first cell. Pressing ENTER inserts a blank line so you can do other things in the document besides fooling with a table.

Starting with the Table I Insert I Table Command

By starting with the Table I Insert I Table Command, you can have a say over how wide the columns are and whether the table stretches from margin to margin or occupies less space on the page. Follow these steps to create a table starting with the Table I Insert I Table command:

1. Click where you want the table to be.

2. Choose Table I Insert I Table or click the Insert Table button on the Tables and Borders toolbar. You'll see the Insert Table dialog box shown in Figure 14-2.

3. Under Table Size, enter how many columns and rows you want.

4. Under AutoFit Behavior, choose how wide to make the column and the table:

   ■ **Fixed Column Width**   Enter a measurement to make all columns the same width. Choosing Auto in the text box creates a table with columns of equal size that goes from margin to margin (choosing Auto is tantamount to choosing the AutoFit To Window option).

   ■ **AutoFit To Contents**   Choosing this option makes each column wide enough to accommodate its widest entry. You will get very narrow columns to begin with. As you enter data, Word adjusts the size of columns and rows to make rows and columns roughly the same size.

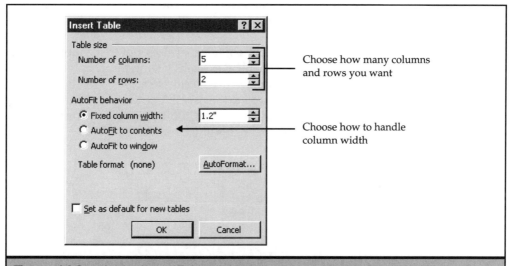

Figure 14-2.   *In the Insert Table dialog box, you can decide for yourself how wide columns are and how wide the table is*

Many people find it hard to enter data in a table that was created with the AutoFit to Contents option because row and column boundaries shift continuously as you enter data when this option is turned on. However, you can always enter the data and apply the AutoFit To Contents command later. To do so, click your table and choose Table | AutoFit | AutoFit to Contents.

■ **AutoFit To Window**   This option, which is used for creating Web pages, makes the table fill the window when the table is shown in Web Layout view or seen through a Web browser. As Chapter 16 explains, you can use tables as a means of laying out Web pages.

5. Click OK.

Clicking the AutoFormat button in the Insert Table dialog box (see Figure 14-2) takes you to the Table AutoFormat dialog box, where you can choose a table design for your table. However, I suggest entering the data before you choose a table design. Entering data in a bare-bones table is easier than entering data in a table that is all gussied up. See "Letting the Table AutoFormat Command Do the Work," later in this chapter.

Drawing a Table

The third way to create a table is to sketch it. Choose Table | Draw Table or click the Draw Table button on the Tables and Borders toolbar. The pointer changes to a pencil (and the Tables and Borders toolbar appears if you chose Table | Draw Table). Start by dragging the pencil across the screen to create the outer boundaries of the table. Then fill in the columns and rows. If you make a mistake, click the Eraser button on the Tables and Borders toolbar and rub out your mistake with the new pointer, which looks like an eraser.

Using the pencil is a great way to draw cells of unusual sizes, not to mention diagonal lines. As "Merging and Splitting Cells and Tables" explains later in this chapter, you can use the Split Cells and Merge Cells commands to make cells of various sizes, but those commands are downright unwieldy compared to the pencil. Use the pencil and eraser (along with the Distribute Rows Evenly and Distribute Columns Evenly commands) to create forms and elaborate tables like the one in this illustration.

	1	2	3	4	5	6	7	8	9	
Giants	2	0	4	1	0	3	2	1	3	15
Dodgers	0	0	0	0	0	0	0	0	0	0

Welcome to Pac Bell Park

Turning a List into a Table—and Vice Versa

Let me guess: You turned to this page in the book from "Writing a Form Letter" or "Printing Labels for Mass-Mailings" in Chapter 20. You want to generate form letters or print labels, but your names and addresses are in list form, not in table form, so you can't use them in their present condition to write form letters or generate the mailing labels. Don't worry about a thing. These pages explain how to turn a list into a table and how to turn a table into a list.

Turning a List into a Table

In order to turn a list into a table, all of the components of the list—also known as the fields—must be separated by tab spaces or commas. For example, Figure 14-3 shows identical address lists in which the following components have been separated, first by tab spaces and then by commas: first name, last name, street number and name, city, state, zip code. To turn a list into a table, Word looks for tab spaces or commas, and the program separates data into columns according to the location of the tab spaces or commas.

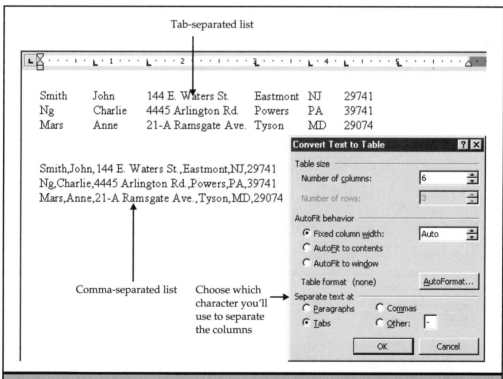

Figure 14-3.   *As long as the components of the list are separated from one another by tab spaces or commas, Word can turn a list into a table*

This illustration shows what a tab-separated list looks like after it has been turned into a table. A *tab-separated list* (also known as a *tab-delimited list*) is one in which the components are separated by tab spaces. In a *comma-separated list* (also known as a *comma-delimited list*), the components are separated by commas. Notice where the tab stops on the ruler are in this illustration. The column boundaries are drawn at the tab stops.

Smith	John	144 E. Waters St.	Eastmont	NJ	29741
Ng	Charlie	4445 Arlington Rd.	Powers	PA	39741
Mars	Anne	21-A Ramsgate Ave.	Tyson	MD	29074

Smith	John	144 E. Waters St.	Eastmont	NJ	29741
Ng	Charlie	4445 Arlington Rd.	Powers	PA	39741
Mars	Anne	21-A Ramsgate Ave.	Tyson	MD	29074

Tip   *Separating list components by tab spaces is preferable to separating them by commas. As the previous illustration shows, the tab spaces hint at where text will fall after it is turned into a table. With commas, it is hard to tell where the columns will begin and end after the list has been turned into a table.*

Editing a list so that each component is separated by a tab space or comma seems easy enough. All you have to do is go through the list and enter the commas or tab spaces. However, to convert the list to a table, you have to watch out for something else: Each line must have the same number of components. Watch what happens to this list when it is turned into a table. The extra component in the second address, a post office box number, throws the table out of whack.

W. Watts	111 E. Lyle St.	Tibideaux	WA	92014
E. Ryne	21 Ruth St.	P.O. Box 221	Myla	OR	94871
T. Muñoz	76 Lawn St.	Rapt	WA	92079

W. Watts	111 E. Lyle St.	Tibideaux	WA	92014	
E. Ryne	21 Ruth St.	P.O. Box 221	Myla	OR	94871
T. Muñoz	76 Lawn St.	Rapt	WA	92079	

You couldn't use this table to generate form letters or mailing labels, since the columns contain different kinds of data. Therefore, make sure each line includes the same number of components, even if it means editing P.O. boxes out of the list, removing titles, or adding another component to some entries to equal out the number of entries.

Follow these steps to turn a list into a table after you have done all the preliminary work:

1. Select the list.

2. Choose Table I Convert I Text to Table. You see the Convert Text to Table dialog box shown in Figure 14-3.

3. Under Separate Text At, choose the Tabs or Commas option, depending on which you used to separate the components on the list.

4. Under AutoFit Behavior, choose how wide to make the columns and the table (see "The Three Ways to Create a Table" earlier in this chapter to find out what these options do).

5. Click OK.

Turning a Table into a List

Turning a table into a list is quite easy. Follow these steps:

1. Click anywhere in the table.

2. Choose Table I Convert I Table to Text. You will see the Convert Table To Text dialog box.

3. Chose Paragraph Marks to put the data in each cell on its own line; choose Tabs, Commas, or enter a punctuation mark of your choice in the Other box to leave each table row on its own line, but separate the data in each column by a tab, comma, or other punctuation mark.

4. Click OK.

Entering the Text and Numbers

After you create your table, start entering the data. Table 14-1 lists keyboard shortcuts you can use to move from cell to cell. As cells fill with data, text moves to the second and subsequent lines in cells. Remember: When you have reached the last cell in a table, you can press TAB to attach another row to the table and continue to enter data.

Press	To Go Here
TAB or →	Next column in the row
SHIFT-TAB or SHIFT-←	Previous column in the row
↓	Row below
↑	Row above
ALT-HOME	Start of row
ALT-END	End of row
ALT-PGUP	Top of column
ALT-PGDN	Bottom of column

Table 14-1.   *Getting Around in Word Tables*

Making a Table Fit on One Page

Tables, like waistlines, have a tendency to grow wider, and when they do, right-hand columns fall off the page. Here is some advice for trimming tables so they stay on one page:

■ **Shrink the Font Size**   Shrinking the font size makes columns narrower and packs more columns onto the page.

■ **Tilt the Heading Row on Its Ear**   In a top-heavy table in which the heading row cells contain text, and the cells below contain numbers, you can make the entire table narrower by changing the orientation of the text in the heading row cells (see "Turning Text Sideways in Tables," later in this chapter). Compare the first table in this illustration to the second table. They present the same data, but one is slimmer than the other.

Timmy	Jeremy	Buster	Davey	Tommy
4	1	8	3	6
3	9	7	4	2
1	4	4	1	4
6	7	8	4	6

Timmy	Jeremy	Buster	Davey	Tommy
4	1	8	3	6
3	9	7	4	2
1	4	4	1	4
6	7	8	4	6

■ **Try Combining Columns**   Sometimes you can put data that might normally be in two columns into one column and thereby make a table one column narrower. Consider the tables in this illustration. Both present the same data, but the second table is narrower, and readers can still find the keyboard shortcut in the second table because the italicized text shows them where to look. By the way, a table with only a word or two in some columns and reams of text in the other, like the first table shown here, looks awkward. Combining columns, as was done in the second table, is a great way to prevent this problem.

Command	Explanation	Keyboard Shortcut
Table | Select Table	Selects the entire table so that you can format it, for example, or change fonts throughout.	Alt+5

Command	Explanation
Table | Select Table	Selects the entire table so that you can format it, for example, or change fonts throughout. *Keyboard shortcut:* Alt+5

■ **Change the Page Orientation**   If worse comes to worst, you can always present the table on a landscape page (see "Changing the Size and Orientation of Pages" in Chapter 9). Obviously, more columns can fit on a landscape page than a portrait page. However, the table has to appear on a page by itself if you go this route, and you will have to create a new section for the landscape table as well (see "Section Breaks for Changing Layouts" in Chapter 9).

Chances are, if your table can't fit on one page, presenting the information in a table is not the best option. Try presenting it in bulleted or numbered lists. Or present the information in short paragraphs under small fourth- or fifth-level headings. In my editing days, I edited the work of more than one author with table-itis, a peculiar affliction that causes authors to want to stuff everything into a table ("I see my book as this gigantic matrix of information," an author told me). However, looking up information in row after row and column after column of a large table is harder than looking up information in a well-crafted list or a handful of pages with descriptive headings.

PROFESSIONAL-LOOKING DOCUMENTS WITH WORD 2000

Tip   *You can number cells by selecting them and clicking the Numbering button on the Formatting toolbar. Chapter 10 explains all the different ways to number items, including table cells. To remove numbers from a table, select the cells and click the Numbering button again.*

Sorting, or Reordering, a Table

To *sort* a table means to rearrange the data in one column so that it falls in alphabetical, numerical, or by-date order in one column. Sorting makes entering data easier. Instead of entering names in alphabetical order, for example, you can enter them at random and then sort the table to arrange the names in one column in alphabetical order. Instead of putting an address list in zip code order, you can tell Word to do it. What's more, Word 2000 makes all the sorting decisions for you. For example, you don't have to know or decide whether San Jose, California comes before or after San José, Costa Rica in an alphabetical list of city names because Word decides for you.

LEARN BY EXAMPLE
Open the 14-1 Revise Table document on the companion CD to try your hand at sorting a table.

EXAMPLES

Tables can be sorted in ascending or descending order:

- **Ascending Sort**   Arranges text in alphabetical order from A to Z, numbers from smallest to largest, and dates from earliest in time to latest in time.

- **Descending Sort**   Arranges text from Z to A, numbers from largest to smallest, and dates from latest in time to earliest.

Caution

Be sure to sort a table before you format it. When you sort, the rows in the table are rearranged, and the rearranged rows carry their borders and shading with them. The heavy border around row 8 might be out of place when row 8 becomes row 2.

The fastest way to sort a table is to click in the column by which the table is to be sorted and then click the Sort Ascending or Sort Descending button on the Tables and Borders toolbar. The first of these tables, for example, has been sorted in ascending order on the Date of Birth column; the second has been sorted in descending order on the Zip Code column.

First Name	Initial	Last Name	Date of Birth	Zip Code
Walter	B.	Johnson	11/19/46	94112
Hiram	I.	Johnson	12/19/47	94124
Jenny	X.	Abiqui	8/14/53	94111
Ralph	D.	Meeker	1/4/56	94111
Hester	T.	Scopus	7/31/58	94113
Susan	B.	Johnson	10/14/76	94127

First Name	Initial	Last Name	Date of Birth	Zip Code
Susan	B.	Johnson	10/14/76	94127
Hiram	I.	Johnson	12/19/47	94124
Hester	T.	Scopus	7/31/58	94113
Walter	B.	Johnson	11/19/46	94112
Jenny	X.	Abiqui	8/14/53	94111
Ralph	D.	Meeker	1/4/56	94111

Notice that each line in the table remains intact when it is moved elsewhere. The information about Walter B. Johnson, for example, remains the same no matter where sorting moves him in the table. Notice as well that Word recognizes the heading row and does not sort names or numbers in the heading row; "Date of Birth" and "Zip Code" stay at the top of the columns to which they belong.

Sorting a table by clicking a column and then clicking a Sort button works fine under these conditions:

■ Identical information does not appear in the same column. Notice the three Johnsons in the sample table in the previous illustration. Word can't accurately sort the table by the Last Name column because it can't tell which Johnson goes first.

■ The table has a heading row. As you know, Word ignores the first row in a table when you click a Sort button to sort a table. If the first row presents information, not column descriptions, the information in the first row is not sorted.

Follow these steps to sort a table when identical information appears in the column where the sorting takes place:

1. Click in the column that you want to sort.
2. Choose Table | Sort. You will see the Sort dialog box shown in Figure 14-4. The name of the column you selected in step 1 appears in the first Sort By box (if you don't see the column name, click the Header Row option button at the bottom of the dialog box).
3. If necessary, open the first Type drop-down menu and choose Text, Number, or Date to describe what kind of data you are dealing with.
4. Select the Ascending or Descending option button to declare whether you want an ascending or descending sort.
5. In the first Then By drop-down menu, choose the tiebreaker column. In Figure 14-4, for example, First Name is the tiebreaker column. If two names in the Last Name column are alike, Word looks to the First Name column to break the tie and place one name before another in the table.
6. Repeat steps 3 and 4 for the Then By column, if necessary.
7. Choose a second Then By column to break ties in the third Then By drop-down menu. In Figure 14-4, for example, Initial is chosen in the second Then By box.
8. Click OK.

To sort a table without a heading row, click in the column that you want to sort on and choose Table | Sort. Instead of column names, you'll see column numbers in the Sort dialog box (see Figure 14-4). Make sure the appropriate column number appears in

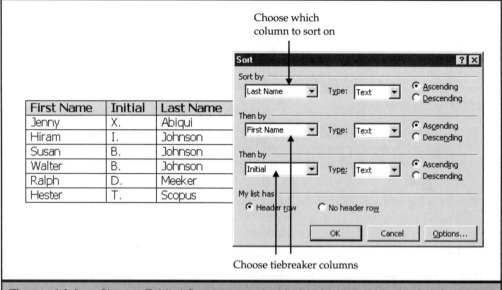

First Name	Initial	Last Name
Jenny	X.	Abiqui
Hiram	I.	Johnson
Susan	B.	Johnson
Walter	B.	Johnson
Ralph	D.	Meeker
Hester	T.	Scopus

Figure 14-4.   *Choose Table | Sort to sort a table in which the same information is found in some columns. In this table, the Johnsons have been sorted in the right order*

the first Sort By drop-down list, make sure the No Header Row option button is selected, and click OK.

Suppose a table has two or more descriptive rows at the top. How can you keep them from being sorted? Click the first cell in the table below the descriptive rows at the top, press F8 (or double-click EXT on the Status bar), and then click the last cell in the table. By doing so, you will select all the rows except the descriptive rows at the top of the table. Choose Table | Sort, select which column you want to sort on in the first Sort By drop-down menu, and click OK.

Changing the Layout of a Table

Most tables need an overhaul or two before you are done with them. A row or column needs to be added or deleted. Data in one column needs to go to another. The ceiling on one row is too low and the ceiling on another is too high. Read on to find out how to insert and delete rows and columns, rearrange rows and columns, and change column widths and row heights. You will also find instructions here for selecting, merging, and splitting rows and columns.

These pages explain how to draw the boundaries, columns, and rows in a table. If you came here to learn how to spruce up a table, see "Decorating a Table with Borders, Shading, and Color," later in this chapter.

LEARN BY EXAMPLE
Open the 14-2 Modify Table document on the companion CD if you want to experiment with the commands for modifying tables.

Selecting Parts of a Table

Before you can insert or delete columns, rows, and cells; change their size; draw borders around them; or change their coloring; you have to select them. Unfortunately, selecting parts of a table is one of those tasks for which there are so many techniques that you can't remember any of them. Scour Table 14-2 to find a handful of selection techniques that suit you. By learning the speediest ways to select parts of a table, you can make your work go that much faster.

To Select	Do This
Cells	
One cell	Move the pointer to the lower-left corner and click when you see the black arrow *or* Choose Table | Select | Cell
Several cells in a row or column	Drag the pointer across the cells *or* Hold down the SHIFT key and click arrow keys
Rows	
One row	Click to the left of the row *or* Click in the first or last cell in the row and press ALT-SHIFT-END or ALT-SHIFT-HOME, respectively
Several rows	Click to the left of the first row to select it and then drag downward *or* Drag to select one cell in each row you want to select, and then choose Table | Select | Row

Table 14-2. *Techniques for Selecting Parts of Tables*

To Select	Do This
Columns	
One column	Move the pointer on top of the column and click when you see the black arrow *or* Hold down the ALT key and click the column *or* Choose Table I Select I Column
Several columns	Move the pointer on top of a column, click when you see the black arrow, and drag to the left or right *or* Drag to select one cell in each column you want to select, and then choose Table I Select I Column
Rows and Columns	
Block of cells	Drag across the cells *or* Click one cell and SHIFT-click another *or* Click one cell, press F8 or double-click EXT on the Status bar, and click another cell *or* Hold down the SHIFT key and click arrow keys
Entire Table	
Whole shebang	Triple-click to the left of the table *or* Press ALT-5 (the 5 on the numeric keypad) *or* Choose Table I Select I Table

Table 14-2.   *Techniques for Selecting Parts of Tables (continued)*

Inserting and Deleting Rows, Columns, and Cells

The first step in deleting or inserting rows, columns, or cells is to select them. Selecting a row, column, or cell in order to insert a row, column, or cell seems odd, but by selecting, you tell Word what you want to insert. After you make a selection, the Insert Table button on the Standard toolbar changes names and is called the Insert Rows, Insert Columns, or Insert Cells button. Right-click after you make a selection and you get commands on the shortcut menu that pertain to the thing you selected. Notice the different Insert and Delete commands on these shortcut menus.

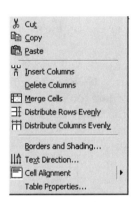
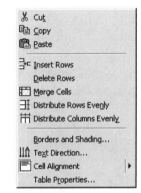

Inserting Rows and Columns

Follow these steps to insert a row or column:

1. In your table, select the number of rows or columns you want to insert:

   - The new row or rows will appear above the row or rows you select.
   - The new column or columns will appear to the left of the column or columns you select.

2. Give the command to insert the rows or columns:

   - Right-click and choose Insert Rows or Insert Columns.
   - Choose Table | Insert and then either the Rows Above (or Rows Below) or Columns to the Left (or Columns to the Right) command.
   - Click the Insert Rows or Insert Columns button on the Standard toolbar (you will find the button where the Insert Table button used to be).
   - Click the arrow beside the Table Insert button on the Tables and Borders toolbar and choose the appropriate command.

To insert a new row at the end of a table, put the cursor in the last cell and press TAB. To insert a new column on the right side of a table, select the rightmost column and choose Table | Insert | Columns to the Right. You can also very, very carefully move the pointer over the upper-right corner of the table. When you see the black arrow, move the pointer slightly to the right and click. Then click the Insert Columns button on the Standard toolbar.

Inserting Cells

Follow these steps to insert cells in a table:

1. Select the number of cells you want to insert. By your choice, the new cells will either shift existing cells to the right or downward.

2. Click the Insert Cells button on the Standard toolbar (you will find it where the Insert Table button used to be), choose Table | Insert | Cells, or click the arrow beside the Table Insert button on the Tables and Borders toolbar and choose Insert Cells on the drop-down menu. You will see the Insert Cells dialog box.

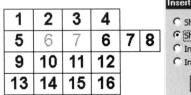
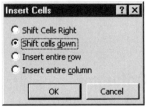

3. Choose Shift Cells Right or Shift Cells Down and click OK.

Deleting Rows, Columns, and Cells

Deleting rows, columns, and cells isn't as simple as selecting them and clicking the DELETE key. Do that and you'll delete the data in the rows, columns, and cells you selected, not the rows, columns, and cells. Follow these steps to delete rows, columns, or cells:

1. Select the rows, columns, or cells you want to delete.

2. Give the Delete command:

   ■ Right-click and choose Delete.

   ■ Choose Table | Delete and, on the submenu, Columns, Rows, or Cells.

In the case of cells, you'll see the Delete Cells dialog box. Choose Shift Cells Left or Shift Cells Up and click OK.

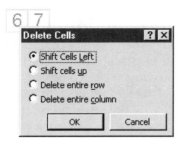

 To delete an entire table, click it and choose Table | Delete | Table.

Rearranging Rows and Columns

The usual copy-and-paste and cut-and-paste rules apply to tables as well as text. You can copy or move text from cell to cell, row to row, or column to column by dragging and dropping it or cutting and pasting it. However, I'll bet you came here to learn how to move or copy an entire row or column from one place in a table to another:

1. Select the row(s) or column(s) you want to move or copy. Be sure to select entire rows or columns. The surest way to do that is to select rows by clicking to their left and columns by clicking directly above them when you see the black down-pointing arrow.

2. Click the Cut or Copy button, press CTRL-X or CTRL-C, or right-click and choose Cut or Copy from the shortcut menu. The rows or columns are moved to the Clipboard.

3. Tell Word where to move or copy the rows or columns:

   - **Rows** Select the row directly below where the row or rows will be moved or copied.

   - **Columns** Select the column to the right of where the column or columns will go.

4. Click the Paste button, right-click and choose Paste, choose Edit | Paste, or press CTRL-V.

You can also move columns and rows by dragging and dropping them. Be sure to select entire rows or columns when you drag and drop.

 A convenient way to move rows is to switch to Outline view, click in the row you want to move, and click the Move Up or Move Down button on the Outlining toolbar as many times as necessary to move the row where you want it to be.

PROFESSIONAL-LOOKING DOCUMENTS WITH WORD 2000

Changing the Size of Rows and Columns

In a generic table—the kind you get before you start fooling with the commands for formatting tables—each row is 2 points higher than the tallest letter in the row. Depending on which option you chose when you created your table, columns either stretch from margin to margin or are wide enough to accommodate their widest entry.

Usually, you have to wrestle with the rows and columns in a table to make the table look just right. These pages explain how to change the height of rows and width of columns with the numerous techniques that Word offers for doing those tasks.

Two Quick Ways to Resize a Table

Before you start wrestling with your table to give it the right shape and size, check out these commands. They change the overall layout and size of a table and are worth trying out before the wrestling match truly begins.

- **Choose Table | AutoFit | AutoFit To Contents** This command analyzes the table and endeavors to tailor rows and columns so that rows are roughly the same size and columns are roughly the same size. The table stretches from margin to margin with this option. Choose it when you are done entering data in a table, since columns and rows continuously change positions when this option is on, and that makes entering data difficult. You can also right-click a table and choose AutoFit | AutoFit to Contents to give this command.

- **Drag the Lower-Left Corner of the Table** Click in the table to select it, and then drag the square in the lower-left corner. Dashed lines show what shape the table will be when you release the mouse button. Release it when the table is the size and shape you want.

State	Tribes	Population
Arizona	Apache, Hopi, Navajo, Papago, Pima, Yavapai	203,527
Colorado	Ute	27,776
New Mexico	Apache, Navajo, Pueblo	134,335
Utah	Goshute, Navajo, Southern Paiute, Ute	24,283

Changing Row Size

To change the size of rows, you can drag them one at a time, go to the Row tab of the Table Properties dialog box and flail away, or use the very convenient Distribute Rows Evenly command:

■ **Distribute Rows Evenly Command**   Shrink the rows, make one row the size you want for all the rows, and then select the rows whose size you want to change and click the Distribute Rows Evenly button on the Tables and Borders toolbar, as shown in Figure 14-5. This command makes each row as tall as the tallest row in the group of rows you selected. For example, if one row in the group you selected is 1 inch tall and the rest are .5 inch tall, all rows are made 1 inch tall. You can also right-click the rows and choose the command from the shortcut menu or choose Table | AutoFit | Distribute Rows Evenly.

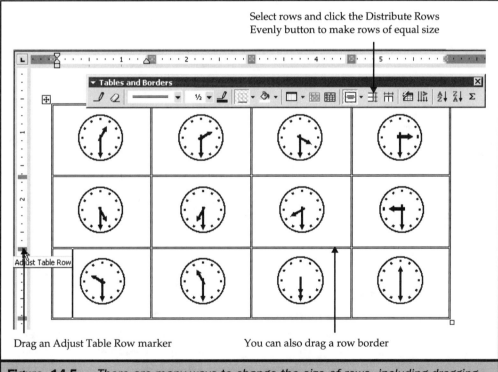

Select rows and click the Distribute Rows Evenly button to make rows of equal size

Drag an Adjust Table Row marker   You can also drag a row border

Figure 14-5.   *There are many ways to change the size of rows, including dragging an Adjust Table Row marker or selecting rows and clicking the Distribute Rows Evenly button*

- **One Row at a Time by Dragging**   Move the mouse pointer over the bottom boundary of the row whose size you want to change. When you see the double arrow, click and start dragging up or down. You can also drag the Adjust Table Row marker on the vertical ruler, as shown in Figure 4-5.

- **Entering Measurements in the Table Properties Dialog Box**   Select more than one row to change the height of several rows if need be and then choose Table | Properties. Then click the Row tab and enter a measurement in the Specify Height box. From the Row Height Is drop-down menu, choose At Least to allow the row to increase in height if you enter a graphic or character taller than the measurement in the Specify Height box; choose Exactly to make the row stay the same height no matter what. You can click the Previous Row or Next Row button to specify measurements for other rows if you didn't select several rows to begin with.

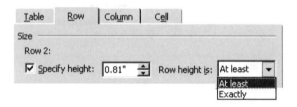

Changing Column Size

Changing the size of columns is similar to changing the size of rows in that you can distribute them evenly across the page, drag their boundaries to change their size, or enter exact measurements in the Table Properties dialog box:

- **Distribute Columns Evenly Command**   Select the columns whose size you want to change and click the Distribute Columns Evenly button on the Tables and Borders toolbar, as shown in Figure 14-6. This command makes each column you choose the same width. To decide the width of the columns, Word takes the average width of the columns you selected and applies it to all the columns. You can also choose this command by right-clicking or by choosing Table | AutoFit | Distribute Columns Evenly.

- **One Column at a Time by Dragging**   Either drag a Move Table Column marker on the horizontal ruler, as shown in Figure 14-6, or move the pointer over a column boundary, click when you see the two-headed arrow, and start dragging.

- **Entering Measurements in the Table Properties Dialog Box**   Select more than one column to change the size of several columns if you want and then choose Table | Properties. In the Table Properties dialog box, click the Column tab, check the Preferred Width check box, and enter a measurement in the Preferred

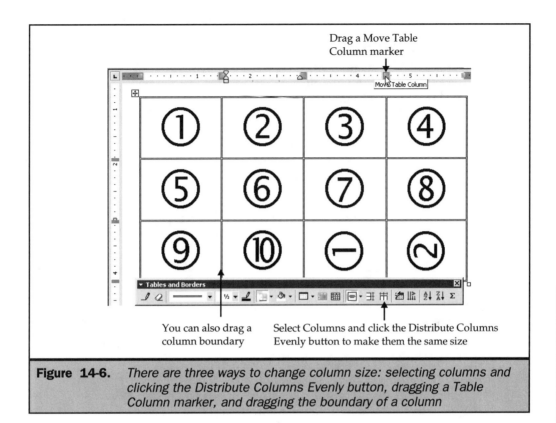

Figure 14-6. *There are three ways to change column size: selecting columns and clicking the Distribute Columns Evenly button, dragging a Table Column marker, and dragging the boundary of a column*

Width box. You can click the Previous Column or Next Column button to enter measurements for other columns as well.

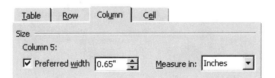

Merging and Splitting Cells and Tables

Merging cells means to join several different cells so that they form a single cell. *Splitting* cells means to divide one cell or more than one cell into several different cells. As shown in Figure 14-7, you can merge or split cells when you are laying out a table and you need to get away from the traditional row-column structure or you are using the Table menu commands to draw a fill-in form.

Adjusting the Internal Cell Margins

Each table cell is like a miniature page in that is has a left, right, top, and bottom margin. The left and right cell margins are .08 inch; the top and bottom margins are 1 point if your text is 12-points high and more than 1 point if you are working in a larger font size. Except when a table or cell has thick borders, the cell margins are fine. A thick border, however, can impose on the margin and come too close to the text.

Follow these steps to adjust the internal margins of table cells to move text further from or closer to the row and column borders:

1. Select the cells whose margin you want to adjust if you want to adjust the margins in a few cells. To adjust the internal margins throughout a table, simply click in the table.

2. Choose Table | Table Properties. You will see the Table Properties dialog box.

3. Either adjust cell margins throughout the table or adjust margins in the cells you selected in step 1, if you selected cells in step 1:

   ■ **Cell Margins Throughout the Table** Click the Table tab and then click the Options button. Enter Top, Bottom, Left, and Right measurements in the Table Options dialog box and click OK.

   ■ **Cell Margins in the Cells You Selected** Click the Cell tab and then click the Options button. In the Cell Options dialog box, enter Top, Bottom, Left, and Right measurements and click OK.

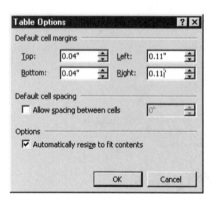 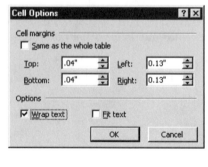

4. Click OK to close the Table Properties dialog box.

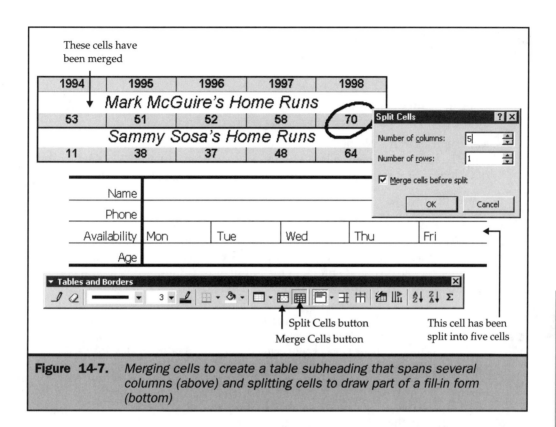

These cells have been merged

Figure 14-7. *Merging cells to create a table subheading that spans several columns (above) and splitting cells to draw part of a fill-in form (bottom)*

Tip *You can use the Split Cells and Merge Cells commands to reconfigure a table. Suppose, for example, that you created too many columns. Select all the columns, merge them, and then split them again, but this time enter the number of columns you really need in the Number of Columns box in the Split Cells dialog box (see Figure 14-7).*

Merging Cells in a Table

Follow these steps to merge cells:

1. Select the cells you want to merge.
2. Click the Merge Cells button on the Tables and Borders toolbar, right-click and choose Merge Cells, or choose Table | Merge Cells.

If the cells you merged held data, the data from each cell is now in its own paragraph inside the new cell.

Splitting Cells in a Table

Follow these steps to split a cell or cells into several different cells:

1. Select the cell or cells you want to split.

2. Click the Split Cells button, right-click and choose Split Cells, or choose Table | Split Cells. The Split Cells dialog box appears (see Figure 14-7).

3. Make entries in the Number Of Columns and Number Of Rows boxes to describe how many new cells you want. For example, entering **3** in the Number of Columns box and **3** in the Number of Rows box creates 9 new cells.

4. Click OK.

Unchecking the Merge Cells Before Split check box tells Word to enter the same number of new cells inside each cell you selected, not a certain number of cells in the sum of the cells you selected. For example, if you select two cells, uncheck the Merge Cells Before Split check box, and enter **4** in the Number of Columns box, you'll get eight new cells—two each inside the four cells you selected.

A fast way to split cells is to use the Draw Table tool. Click the Draw Table button on the Tables and Borders toolbar or choose Table | Draw Table. Using the pencil pointer, simply draw lines on your table to split cells. If you make a mistake, click the Eraser button and rub out the lines you drew.

Splitting a Table

To split a table, select the row that is to be the first row in the new table and choose Table | Split Table. Sorry, you can't split a table down the middle. You can, however, select the columns that will form the new table, cut them to the Clipboard, and paste them elsewhere to create a new colony of your old table, so to speak.

To merge two tables, simply delete the blank spaces that appear between them.

Aligning and Reorienting Text in Columns and Rows

After you have entered the data in a table, you can start making it presentable. These pages explain how to align data in columns and rows and how to change the orientation of text so that it lies sideways. You will also find instructions here for lining up numbers in columns on the decimal point.

Centering, Aligning, and Justifying the Text

Figure 14-8 shows the nine ways you can align the text in columns and rows. No doubt you are already familiar with the Align Left, Center, and Align Right buttons on the

Formatting toolbar for aligning text. Clicking those buttons aligns text in columns. To align text in rows across the top, the middle, or the bottom, click an Align button on the Tables and Borders toolbar, as shown in Figure 14-8.

Select cells, entire rows, or entire columns, and follow these instructions to change the alignment of the text:

- Click an Align button on the Formatting toolbar if you are aligning text in columns.
- Click the arrow beside the Align button on the Tables and Borders toolbar and click a button (see Figure 14-8).
- Right-click, choose Cell Alignment, and click a button on the drop-down menu.

Experiment freely with the Alignment commands until the text in your table is easy to read and understand.

Turning Text Sideways in Tables

As "Making a Table Fit on One Page" explained earlier in this chapter, turning the text in the heading row on its side is one way to squeeze more columns onto a page. And

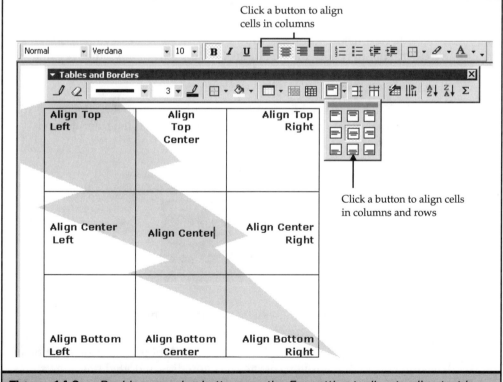

Figure 14-8. *Besides pressing buttons on the Formatting toolbar to align text in columns, you can take advantage of the Top, Center, and Bottom commands to align text across rows*

text turned sideways looks neat, too. To turn text on its ear, select the cells whose text needs a turn and click the Change Text Direction button on the Tables and Borders toolbar. Keep clicking the button until the text turns the direction you want it to turn.

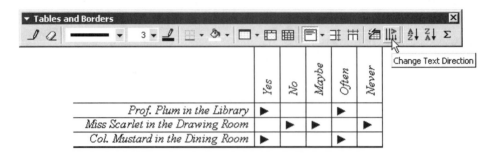

Lining Up Numbers on the Decimal

"Changing the Tab Settings" in Chapter 8 explains how to align text on the decimal point by changing tab settings on the ruler. Using the same techniques in a table, you can align numbers in a column on the decimal point as well. Follow these steps to align the numbers in a column on the decimal point.

1. Select the cells whose numbers you want to align on the decimal point. Be careful not to choose the text in the heading row or any other cell that contains text. Text appears to the left of the decimal point if you accidentally include a cell with text in it.

2. Click the Tab button on the left side of the ruler as many times as necessary to see the Decimal Tab symbol (choose View | Ruler if the ruler doesn't appear onscreen).

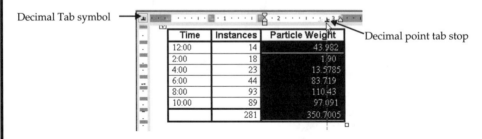

3. Click on the ruler where you want the decimal point to be in the cells. The decimal point tab stop symbol appears on the ruler.

4. Drag the decimal point tab stop symbol left or right to adjust the position of the numbers in the cells you selected. As you drag, a dotted line shows how the numbers will line up.

Handling Table Headers and Page Breaks in Tables

A table that begins on one page and ends on the next presents a problem or two. Readers who turn to the second page that the table is on need to know what they are reading, and they can't do that unless they can see the heading row, the row at the top of the table whose headings describe what is in the body of the table. What's more, a table that breaks off in the middle of a row is awkward indeed. Consider the table shown in this illustration. Readers have to turn the page backward and forward once or twice to make any sense of this table.

2:15 p.m.	Evinces a marked swelling around the tibia that is not typical of the disease and is likely to have been caused by	Temperature: Normal Pulse: 122 Bandaged the knee

	overexposure to heat. Moreover, the patient expresses discomfort when walking. He reports difficulty in bending his ankle and knee.	and the patient's shin too.

These pages explain how to make the heading row or heading rows appear on the following page when a table breaks across pages and how to make sure a table breaks cleanly in a row.

Repeating Heading Row of a Long Table on the Next Page

To make the heading row appear at the top of the table on each page that the table appears on, click in the heading row and choose Table | Heading Rows Repeat. If your table has two or more heading rows, select all or part of them before choosing Table | Heading Rows Repeat. You can also repeat the heading rows on subsequent pages by selecting the heading rows, choosing Table | Table Properties, clicking the Row tab in the Tables Properties dialog box, and checking the Repeat As Header Row At The Top Of Each Page check box.

 You can only see table headings on subsequent pages in Print Layout view.

Making Sure a Table Breaks Cleanly

When a row is more than two lines long, Word cuts it across the middle if half of it falls on one page and the other half falls on the other. However, you can tell Word not to break a row in the middle but move it instead to the next page if it straddles two pages. Follow these steps to keep a row or rows from breaking across pages:

1. Select the row or rows that you do not want to straddle pages.

2. Choose Tables | Tables Properties.

3. Click the Row tab in the Table Properties dialog box.

4. Under Options, uncheck the Allow Row To Break Across Pages check box and click OK.

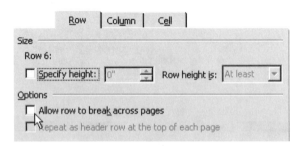

As a desperate measure, you can also force a table to break in a certain row by clicking in the row and pressing CTRL-ENTER. However, heading rows do not appear at the top of the next page when you break a table this way. And by introducing a hard page break, you run the risk of putting a lot of blank space at the bottom of the page, since Word has to move the second part of the table to the next page right away.

Decorating a Table with Borders, Shading, and Color

Before you learn anything about dressing up a table, you should know that Word 2000 offers a special command for doing the job. Instead of drawing the borderlines, shading parts of the table, or sprinkling color on a table yourself, you can tell Word to do it for you. These pages explain how to decorate a table on your own, or with Word's help.

Letting the Table AutoFormat Command Do the Work

Half the commands on the Table menu have to do with formatting tables, but here's a little secret: You don't really have to learn the table-formatting commands. Instead, you can let Word do the job—and a very good job, too—of formatting your table. Follow these steps to choose a prefabricated format for your table:

1. Click anywhere in the table.

2. Click the Table AutoFormat button on the Tables and Borders toolbar or choose Table | Table AutoFormat. You will see the Table AutoFormat dialog box shown in Figure 14-9.

3. Choose a format from the Formats list. Try clicking five, six, or seven formats until you find the one you like. The Preview box shows what your choice looks like.

4. Under Formats To Apply in the bottom of the dialog box, check and uncheck options to alter the table design and choose different borders, shading, and font colors.

5. Under Apply Special Formats To, check and uncheck options and watch what happens in the Preview box. Experiment until the table meets your high expectations.

6. Click OK.

 Tip

In a document with more than one table, the tables should be laid out the same way for consistency's sake. Take note of the format you choose in the Table AutoFormat dialog box so you can apply it again to the next table. You can always click in a table and choose Table | Table AutoFormat or click the Table AutoFormat button to choose a different format.

Putting Borders, Shading, and Color on a Table

Usually, you have to tinker with borders, shades, and colors until you find the right look for your table. To help you tinker, Word offers two means of attaching borders,

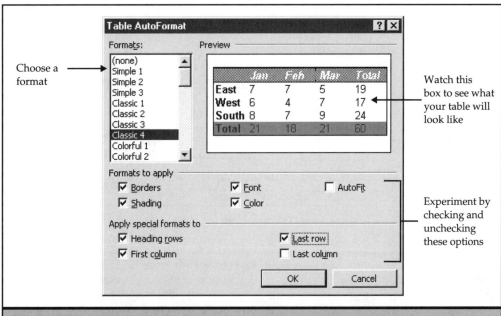

Figure 14-9. *By choosing a format in the Table AutoFormat dialog box, you can save yourself the trouble of formatting the table on your own*

shading, and color to a table or to parts of a table: the Borders and Shading dialog box and the Tables and Borders toolbar, shown in Figure 14-10. However you decide to decorate your table, start by selecting the part of the table you want to decorate. Then do the following to change your table's appearance:

- Click a down arrow or button on the Tables and Borders toolbar and make a selection. (You can click the Tables and Borders button on the Standard toolbar to display the Tables and Borders toolbar).

- Right-click and choose Borders and Shading to open the Borders and Shading dialog box and go to work there. You can also choose Format | Borders and Shading to open this dialog box.

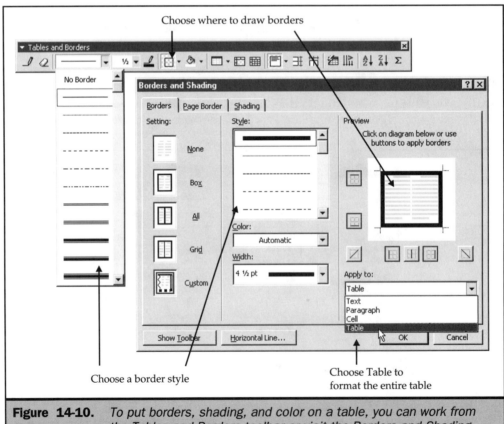

Figure 14-10.   To put borders, shading, and color on a table, you can work from the Tables and Borders toolbar or visit the Borders and Shading dialog box

By starting from the Borders tab of the Borders and Shading dialog box, you can apply different borders to different parts of a table or to the table itself. Choose Table from the Apply To menu to work on an entire table. Under Settings, choose Grid to draw borders on the perimeter of the cell block you chose, All to draw borders on the perimeter and interior cells, or Custom to draw different borders on different parts of the cell block.

Drawing Borders on a Table

To draw borders around or inside parts of a table, select the part of the table that needs borders. Then do either of the following:

■ **On the Borders Tab of the Borders and Shading Dialog Box**   (See Figure 14-10.) From the Style menu, choose what kind of border you want; from the Color menu, choose a color for the borderlines; from the Width menu, choose how thick to make the borderline; in the Preview box, either click border buttons or click on the box itself to tell Word where to draw the borders.

■ **From the Tables and Borders Toolbar**   Open the Line Style drop-down menu and choose what kind of border you want (see Figure 14-10); open the Line Weight drop-menu and choose how thick a border you want; and open the Border drop-down menu and click a button to tell Word where to draw the borders. You can also choose a color for borderlines from the Border Color drop-down menu.

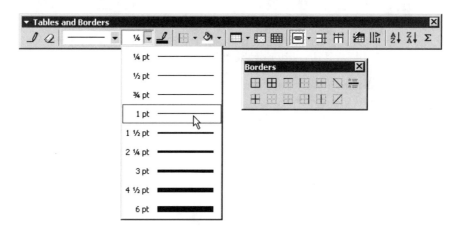

Shading and Coloring Parts of a Table

Select the part of your table that needs a color or gray shade and follow these instructions to paint your table:

- **On the Shading Tab of the Borders and Shading Dialog Box** Under Fill, choose a color or gray shade. You can click the More Color button to see more color choices.

- **From the Tables and Borders Toolbar** Click the down arrow to open the Fill drop-down menu and make a color or gray shade choice. You can click More Fill Colors at the bottom of the menu to see more color choices.

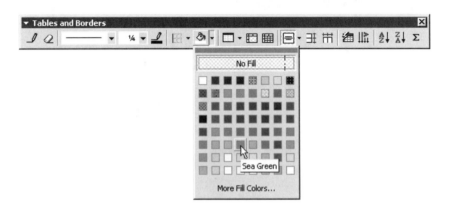

Centering and Indenting Tables on the Page

New tables line up along the left margin of the page, but that doesn't mean you can't center them or indent them from the left margin. To change the position of a table on the page, click the table and do either of the following:

- **Drag the Table to a New Position** Move the pointer over the small selection handle beyond the upper-left corner of the table, click, and start dragging. Dashed lines show where the table will go when you release the mouse button. To move the table in a straight line, hold down the SHIFT key as you drag.

Country	Elvis Sightings
United States	1,146
Canada	312
England	947
France	194

- **Change Alignments or Indentations in the Table Properties Dialog Box** Choose Table | Table Properties and click the Table tab in the Table Properties dialog box, as shown in Figure 14-11. Then either click the Center or Right option under Alignment to align the table with respect to the left and right margin, or enter a measurement in the Indent From Left text box to indent the table from the left margin.

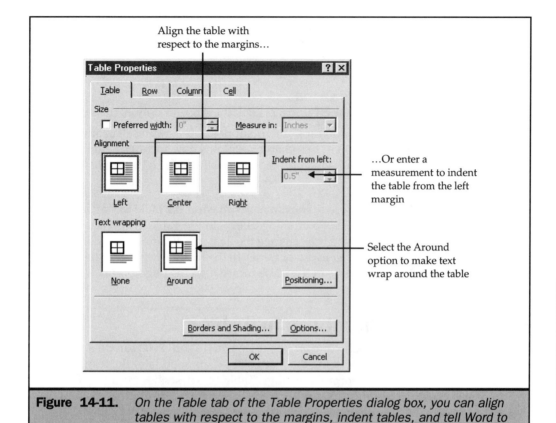

Figure 14-11.   *On the Table tab of the Table Properties dialog box, you can align tables with respect to the margins, indent tables, and tell Word to wrap text around tables*

Wrapping Text Around a Table

Besides wrapping text around clip art images, text boxes, and other objects (a subject of Chapter 13), you can wrap text around a table. Wrapping text around a table relieves you from having to cite a table by number or name in the text, since the table appears beside the text and readers know precisely which table you are referring to.

As these figures show, the number of Elvis sightings cannot be linked to population, since even countries with relatively small populations report Elvis sightings in large numbers. What, then, can we conclude from these statistics? Well, for one, we may conclude that countries where

Country	Elvis Sightings
United States	1,146
Canada	312
England	947
France	194

the so-called King's music was popular evince a marked rise in Elvis sightings. Many Elvis fans can be found in England, for example, which accounts for that

Follow these steps to wrap text around a table:

1. Click the table to select it.
2. Choose Table | Table Properties. You will see the Table Properties dialog box shown in Figure 14-11.
3. Under Text Wrapping on the Table tab, click the Around option; then click OK.
4. Move the table into the paragraph that is supposed to wrap itself around the table. The previous section in this chapter explains how to move a table. To do so, click the selection handle beyond the upper-left corner of the table and start dragging.

If you think text comes too close to the table or you want the table to stay in the same location on the page, click the Positioning button in the Table Properties dialog box. In the Table Positioning dialog box, change the Distance From Surrounding Text measurements to move text further away or closer to the table. Unchecking the Move With Text check box keeps the table in the same location on the page.

Crunching the Numbers in Tables

Don't waste time doing the math yourself in a table when Word 2000 can do it for you. Besides saving you the trouble of doing the math, the program updates the results of formulas as the numbers in the formulas change. Table 14-3 describes the math functions you can use to construct formulas in tables. Word is not a spreadsheet program, and if you want to do serious number-crunching you should do it in Excel or Lotus 1-2-3, but you can compute simple formulas in tables. These pages explain basic techniques for computing in tables, the pitfalls of doing the math in a table, and how to do fancy math calculations so that the results are accurate.

Function	What It Does
AVERAGE	Obtains the average of the values in the cells
COUNT	Returns the number of cells
MAX	Returns the largest value
MIN	Returns the smallest value
PRODUCT	Multiplies the values in the cells
SUM	Totals the values in the cells

Table 14-3.   *Math Functions for Use in Tables*

Note | *Later in this chapter, "Calling On Excel 2000 to Construct Worksheet Tables" explains how you can get Excel's help to do math in tables without leaving Word.*

LEARN BY EXAMPLE
On the 14-3 Calculations document on the companion CD is a table you can use to practice crunching numbers.

The Basics: Entering Formulas in Tables

Follow these basic steps to do a math calculation in a table:

1. Click in the cell that is to show the results of the calculation.

2. Choose Table | Formula. You will see the Formula dialog box shown in Figure 14-12. To begin with, Word enters the SUM function and makes an educated guess as to which cells you want to total. In parentheses, you'll see either the argument ABOVE, which means to total all the cells above the cell you are working in, or the argument LEFT, which means to total all the cells to the left of the cell you are working in.

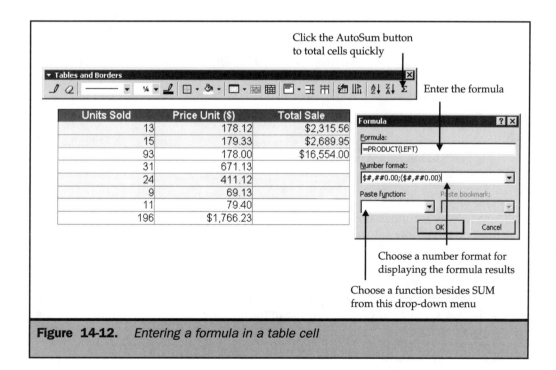

Figure 14-12. *Entering a formula in a table cell*

Tip   *The fastest way to total cells in a table is to click in the cell where the total is to appear and then click the AutoSum button on the Tables and Borders toolbar (see Figure 14-12). Usually, Word guesses correctly that you want to total the cells above the cell you are working in or the cells to the left of the cell you are working in and all is well.*

3. Construct the formula in the Formula box.

To do so, start by clicking to the right of the equals sign (=) and entering the correct function. Table 14-3 lists the functions you can use. To enter a function name, open the Paste Function drop-down menu and choose a function.

In the parentheses after the function, indicate where, relative to the cell you are working in, the cells you want to calculate can be found. You can enter **left**, **right**, **above**, or **below** (you can enter the word in upper- or lowercase letters). In Figure 14-12, LEFT has been entered because the formula multiplies the numbers in the two cells to the left of the formula cell. Later in this chapter, "Entering Complex Arguments in Formulas" explains other ways to indicate which cells to compute in a formula.

If necessary, delete the SUM function and its parentheses that appeared when you opened the Formula dialog box.

Caution   *Do not delete the equal sign in the Formula text box or enter any numbers, symbols, or text before the equal sign. Delete the equal sign and the formula will not compute—period.*

4. From the Number Format drop-down menu, choose a number format for displaying the results of the calculation. Table 14-4 describes the different number formats.

Tip   *You can invent a number format of your own by entering zeroes in the Number Format text box. Enter **0.0**, for example, to display numbers to one decimal place. Enter **0.00000** to display numbers to five decimal places.*

5. Click OK.

The results of formulas are shown in fields. "All About Fields" in Chapter 23 explains fields. For now, all you need to know is that you can change the numbers in the cells to which a formula refers and update the results of the formula so it is accurate. To update a formula, select the results of the formula and press F9 or right-click and choose Update Field from the shortcut menu. If you see field codes instead of formula results after you enter a formula, do the following to see the results: Choose Tools | Options, click the View tab in the Options dialog box, and uncheck the Field Codes check box.

Format	Example	Description
#,##0	4,321	Does not display decimals. Displays zero if the number is less than one.
#,##0.00	4,321.00	Displays numbers to two decimal places. Displays zero on the left side of the decimal point if the number is less than one (0.21).
$#,##0.00; ($#,##0.00)	$4,321.00 ($4,321.00)	Includes the dollar sign in the results and displays the number to two decimal places (see Figure 14-12). Negative numbers are enclosed in parentheses.
0	4321	Makes sure at least one positive digit is displayed even if the formula results are less than one (0.21 is displayed as 0).
0%	4321%	Displays the results as a percentage.
0.00	4321.00	Makes sure that at least one positive digit and two decimals are displayed in the formula results.
0.00%	4321.00%	Display the results as a percentage to two decimal places.

Table 14-4. *Formats for Displaying Formula Results*

Making Sure Your Calculations Are Accurate

The problem with performing math in tables is that Word computes the wrong numbers if you are not careful. Unless you instruct it otherwise, Word computes the numbers in cells adjacent to the cell in which the formula is located (Word computes the cells to the LEFT, RIGHT, ABOVE, or BELOW). Sometimes that renders the formula inaccurate. In this illustration, for example, formulas in the Total Pts. column are supposed to add the number of first half points and second half points in the third and fourth column. However, Word includes the numbers in the second column, Ranking, in the calculations and the results in the fifth column are not correct. The totals in the fifth column should be 4, 2, and 3 respectively.

Team	Ranking	1st Half Pts.	2nd Half Pts.	Total Pts.
Old Goats	1	2	2	5
Possums	3	1	1	5
Wombats	2	1	2	5

Even stranger, Word includes text in a calculation if the text happens to include a number. Failing to take account of numbers in heading rows and row labels is the chief cause of mathematical errors in Word tables. In this table, for example, the heading row includes numbers (1, 2, 3, and 4), and those numbers are computed in the formulas in the last row. The 4th Qtr. total should be 5, but Word counts the 4 in "4th Qtr." and the total is 9 instead.

Company	1st Qtr	2nd Qtr.	3rd Qtr.	4th Qtr.
Robco	1.5	2	1	1
Dunmen	1	1.5	1.5	1.5
Pilfer	2	1.75	2	1
XS Steel	1	1	2.5	1.5
Totals	6.5	8.25	10	9

Here's a little trick for getting around the problem of computing the wrong cells in a formula: Enter a blank row or column where you want Word to stop computing the values in cells. In this illustration, for example, a blank row has been inserted between the heading row (1st Qtr., 2nd Qtr., and so on) and the next row. Now the calculations in the total row are correct because Word calculates the values in adjacent cells. The program does not look beyond the blank row for values to calculate.

Company	1st Qtr	2nd Qtr.	3rd Qtr.	4th Qtr.
Robco	1.5	2	1	1
Dunmen	1	1.5	1.5	1.5
Pilfer	2	1.75	2	1
XS Steel	1	1	2.5	1.5
Totals	5.5	6.25	7	5

Entering Complex Arguments and Formulas

In the Formula dialog box (see Figure 14-12), the part of the formula that appears in parentheses is called the argument. The *argument* lists the cells that are computed by the function. As you know if you read the last handful of pages, Word uses the cells to the left, to the right, above, or below the formula cell as the argument.

Under these circumstances, however, you can't use the LEFT, RIGHT, ABOVE, or BELOW argument in a formula and obtain an accurate result:

■ The cells you want to compute are not adjacent to the formula cell.

■ The cells you want to compute are adjacent, but not all of them are valid for making calculations (see the previous section of this chapter for a torturously detailed explanation of this particular problem).

■ The cells occupy more than one row or column.

Under these circumstances, the only way to enter the argument is to use cell addresses. Each cell in a table has an address, as shown at the top of Figure 14-13. Rows are numbered 1, 2, 3, and so on; columns are assigned the letters A, B, C, and so on; each cell's address comes from its row number and column letter. Hence the address of the first cell in a table is A1. In Figure 14-13, cells E2, E3, E4, and E5 are being entered as the argument. The total of the numbers in the four cells will appear in cell E6, which lists the total profits in the 4th quarter.

To enter cell addresses as the argument, choose Table | Formula as you normally would. In the Formula dialog box (see Figure 14-13), list the cell addresses between parentheses, and separate each cell address by a comma (just a comma, not a comma and a blank space).

Caution *If you insert a new row or column in your table, cell addresses are rendered invalid and you have to re-enter arguments so they refer to the correct cells. Sorry, Word is not a spreadsheet program. Cell references are not updated as you insert new columns and rows.*

After you know about cell addresses, you can start using conventional operators to add (+), subtract (–), multiply (*), and divide (/) the numbers in cells. For example, =A4+A5 adds the numbers in those cells. The formula =E5/4 divides the number in cell E5 by 4. Just be sure to enter the equal sign in front of your homemade formula. Without it, Word stubbornly refuses to do any calculations.

PROFESSIONAL-LOOKING DOCUMENTS WITH WORD 2000

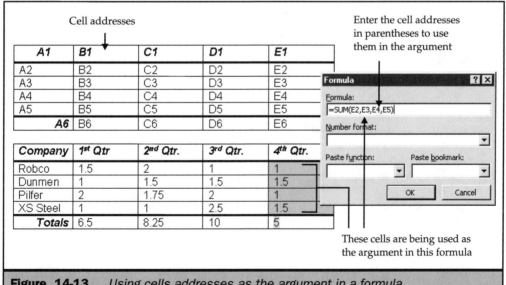

Figure 14-13.   *Using cells addresses as the argument in a formula*

Referring to Far-Flung Tables in Formulas

Suppose you want to refer to a cell in another table in a formula. It can be done. To do it, select the cell and bookmark it. With the cell selected, choose Insert | Bookmark, enter a descriptive name in the Bookmark Name text box (bookmarks can't start with numbers or include blank spaces), click the Add button, and click OK. In the Formula dialog box, open the Paste Bookmark drop-down menu and enter the bookmark as part of the formula. Here, the tax amount and the rakeoff amount are being subtracted from the sum of the numbers in cell D1 and D4 to arrive at the profit amount.

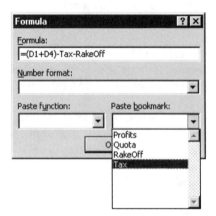

Calling On Excel 2000 to Construct Worksheet Tables

Excel 2000 fans who saw the last handful of pages in this book about performing calculations in tables probably shook their heads and thought, "Too bad you can't simply do these calculations in Excel." Well, you can do table calculations in Excel. By clicking the Insert Microsoft Excel Worksheet button on the Standard toolbar, you can call upon every Excel command the program has to offer. These pages explain how to create an Excel worksheet in Word 2000, import a worksheet from Excel, and change the look of a table you constructed from an Excel worksheet.

To create a standard Word table from the data in an Excel worksheet, select the data in the worksheet, copy it to the Clipboard, and paste it in a Word document. You will get a standard Word table. The Excel menus and buttons aren't available for manipulating the data in the table.

LEARN BY EXAMPLE
Open the 14-4 Excel Table document on the companion CD to see exactly what an Excel worksheet looks like in a Word document.

Creating an Excel Worksheet in a Word Document

It turns out that Word and Excel are joined at the hip. With a click of the Insert Microsoft Excel Worksheet button on the Standard toolbar, you can place an Excel worksheet in a Word document. The worksheet is embedded in your Word document. Whenever you click the worksheet, Excel buttons and tools appear onscreen instead of Word buttons and tools.

Follow these steps to place an Excel worksheet in a Word document:

1. Click the Insert Microsoft Excel Worksheet button. A grid appears so you can choose the number of rows and columns you want.

2. Move the cursor onto the grid and click to order a certain number of rows and columns. The bottom of the drop-down menu tells how many rows and columns you'll get when you click. After you click, an Excel worksheet appears onscreen. Look around and you will see that Excel menus, Excel buttons, and the Excel formula bar appear as well, as shown in Figure 14-14.

3. Enter data in your worksheet and do all the things you love to do so much in Excel. You can call on all of the Excel commands as you work.

4. Click outside the worksheet when you are done.

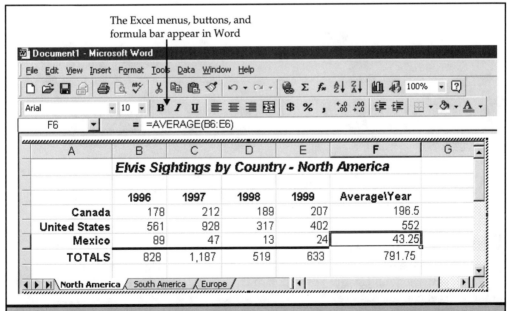

Figure 14-14.   *Click the Insert Microsoft Excel Worksheet button on Word's Standard toolbar to place a worksheet in a Word document*

The worksheet is embedded in your document. When you want to work on it again, double-click it to see the worksheet rows and columns as well as the Excel menus and toolbars.

Click the worksheet when you want to move it onscreen. You will see the selection handles. An Excel worksheet, at least a worksheet in a Word document, is an object. As such, you can move it or change its size. See "Manipulating Art, Text Boxes, Shapes, and Other So-Called Objects" in Chapter 13.

Importing an Excel Worksheet into a Word Table

If the Excel worksheet you need for your Word document has already been formulated and filled with data, you can bring the worksheet straight into Word. To do so, copy the columns and rows in the worksheet that you need, click in your Word document, and choose Edit | Paste Special to open the Paste Special dialog box. In the As box, click Microsoft Excel Worksheet Object and click OK.

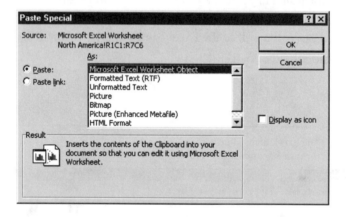

"Linking Documents So That Text Is Copied Automatically" in Chapter 2 explains how you can create a link between an Excel worksheet and a Word document so that changes made to the worksheet are made automatically in the Word document as well.

The worksheet is embedded in the Word document. When you need to fool with the numbers, double-click the worksheet. You will see Excel menus and buttons where Word menus and buttons used to be. Go to it.

Modifying a Worksheet

Being able to make mathematical calculations in an Excel worksheet is well and good, but when you are done you are left with a drab-looking table. Fortunately, you can call on these Excel commands to embellish your worksheet:

- **Drawing Borders on Worksheets** Select the cells on which you want to place borders. Then click the down arrow beside the Borders button on the Formatting toolbar and choose a border. Usually, you have to wrestle with the Borders buttons until you come up with borders you like.

- **Decorating Worksheets with Colors** Select the cells, click the down arrow beside the Fill Color button, and choose a color from the drop-down menu. Choose No Fill from the drop-down menu to remove a color.

Tip

The fastest way to adorn a worksheet is to let Excel do it. Select the cells in your worksheet and choose Format | AutoFormat. In the AutoFormat dialog box, choose a worksheet design that tickles your fancy. While you're at it, click the Options button and play around with the Formats To Apply check boxes until you construct a worksheet design that suits you.

MOUS Exam Objectives Explored in Chapter 14

Objective	Heading	Practice File
Create and format tables	"Creating a Table"	
Revise tables	"Sorting, or Reordering, a Table"	14-1 Revise Table
Modify table structure (merge cells, change height and width)	"Changing the Layout of a Table"	14-2 Modify Table
Rotate text in a table	"Turning Text Sideways in Tables"	
Embed worksheets in a table*	"Creating an Excel Worksheet in a Word Document"	
Perform calculations in a table*	"Crunching the Numbers in Tables"	14-3 Calculations
Modify worksheets in a table*	"Modifying a Worksheet"	14-4 Excel Table
Link Excel data as a table*	"Importing an Excel Worksheet into a Word Table"	

* Denotes an Expert exam objective.

Ten Tips for Handling Tables

It so happens I have a lot of experience constructing and deconstructing tables. Here are ten tips and tricks that have served me in good stead.

1. ENTER THE TEXT AND NUMBERS BEFORE YOU START FORMATTING.

Before you decorate a table with fancy borders and various colors or gray shades, enter the data. You will save a lot of time that way. When you try to enter data in a table that is already dressed up, the fancy formats get in the way. Besides, if form follows function, entering the data is a prerequisite, since you have to see what's in the table before you can decide how to format it.

2. SPLIT THE SCREEN TO SEE THE TABLE HEADINGS.

Past row 10 or so in a long table, it's hard to tell which row you are in. You can fix that problem, however, by splitting the screen. Split the screen so that you can see the heading rows at the top of the table no matter which row you are working on. "Splitting the Screen" in Chapter 6 explains how to do it, but here are shorthand instructions in case you are in too much of a hurry to visit Chapter 6:

1. Choose Window | Split. A gray line appears across the middle of the screen.
2. Scroll to the top of the screen so that the gray line appears below the heading row—the row at the top of the table that describes what is in the columns below—and then click. Now you will be able to see the heading row wherever you go in the table.
3. In the bottom half of the screen, use the scroll bars to go to the bottom of the table.
4. Start entering the data. The heading row shows precisely which column to enter it in.

Rank	Name	County	State	Yes	No
1.	Claris	Rosemund	CO	x	
2.	Retsh	Pitsmine	NM		x
32.	Hectane	Dulord	MO		x
33.	DuLeen	Riverside	CA		x
34.	Ng	Meetch	WA	x	
35.					

3. DRAW ON TABLES TO HIGHLIGHT THE IMPORTANT STUFF.

By "draw" I mean use the Oval button or Draw button on the Drawing toolbar to circle or point to important places in a table. "Drawing Lines and Shapes" in Chapter 13 explains the many lines and shapes you can draw. "When Objects Overlap: Choosing Which Appears Above the Other" in the same chapter explains how to make the lines appear on top of the table where they can be seen. While you're in Chapter 13, check out "Changing the Size and Shape of Objects" and "Rotating and Flipping Objects" to learn how to make the line or circle on your table look just right.

1994	1995	1996	1997	1998
Mark McGuire's Home Runs				
53	51	52	58	70

4. USE THE TABLE | TABLE AUTOFORMAT COMMAND TO DECORATE

TABLES.   Some people go to school for years to learn how to format tables. They spend many hours playing with the commands for drawing borders on tables. They learn the numerous and sundry ways to slap gray shades and color on tables. Other people, however, simply rely on the Table | Table AutoFormat command. And these people get very nice tables with hardly any effort. See "Letting the Table AutoFormat Command Do the Work," earlier in this chapter, if formatting a table with minimum effort appeals to you.

5. LEARN THE WAYS TO MAKE A TABLE FIT ON A SINGLE PAGE.   About
a fourth of the way into this chapter, "Making a Table Fit on One Page" offers four techniques for making a table fit on one page. Tables have a habit of getting wider, but with the four techniques explained there and listed here you can keep tables from growing too wide:

- Shrink the font size
- Turn the heading row on its ear
- Try combining columns
- Change the page orientation

6. RIGHT-CLICK TO GIVE COMMANDS IN TABLES.   All the great word
processors, the ones who can whip up a table faster than a chef can whip up a soufflé, right-click to give commands in tables. Try selecting a row or two and right-clicking the rows to see the advantages of right-clicking: The menu presents commands for inserting and deleting rows. Select a column and right-click, on the other hand, and you get commands for inserting and deleting columns. Almost anything you can do from the Table menu on the main menu bar can be done faster by right-clicking.

7. TAKE ADVANTAGE OF THE DISTRIBUTE COMMANDS.   Rather than tug at
row borders and column borders to make them the right size, get used to using the Distribute Rows Evenly and Distribute Columns Evenly commands. As "Changing the Size of Rows and Columns" explains earlier in this chapter, the commands do the following:

- **Distribute Rows Evenly**   Makes each row as tall as the tallest row in the group of rows you selected. All you have to do to make rows a uniform size is shrink them, make one the right size, select all the rows, and give the Distribute Rows Evenly command. You'll end up with rows of the same size.

■ **Distribute Columns Evenly**   Makes each column you choose the same width. To determine the width of the columns, Word takes the average width of the columns you selected and applies it to all the columns.

8. TAKE ADVANTAGE OF THE ALIGN COMMANDS.   As "Centering, Aligning, and Justifying the Text" explains earlier in this chapter, Word offers no less than nine different ways to align data in table cells. And experimenting with the nine different ways is easy. All you have to do is select the cells, click the arrow next to the Align button on the Tables and Borders toolbar, and choose one of the nine options.

9. USE THE OPTIONAL HYPHEN TO FIX SPACING PROBLEMS.   "Hyphenating Text" in Chapter 7 explains how you can insert an optional hyphen to break a word and make part of it go to the next line. In table cells, long words can create awkward white spaces, but you can fix that problem by pressing CTRL-hyphen (the hyphen next to the 0, not the one on the numeric keypad) to insert a hyphen and break the word to remove the white space.

10. PRESS ENTER IN THE FIRST CELL TO PUT A BLANK LINE ABOVE A

TABLE.   Here's a little trick that prevents claustrophobia: Click in the first cell in a table, to the left of text if any text is in the first cell, and press ENTER. Doing so enters a blank line above the table.

This little trick seems hardly worth mentioning or remembering until the day you open a new document, create a new table in the document, and want to write a line or two above the table. Unless you know this little trick, you won't be able to do that. You will be trapped inside your table. You will start to feel itchy and begin suffering from claustrophobia.

Chapter 15

Working on Newsletters, Brochures, and Forms

his brief chapter explains a few tried-and-true techniques for creating
newsletters, brochures, and forms. You will find instructions here for running
text in newspaper-style columns as well as other kinds of columns; and, you'll
find ways to put different kinds of drop capital letters at the start of articles. These
pages explain numerous ways to decorate page margins—with clip art, pull quotes,
and side headings, for example. This chapter also explains how to create a fill-in paper
form and, last but not least, ten easy techniques for sprucing up a document.

Drop Caps for Marking the Start of Articles

A *drop cap*, also known as a *drop capital letter*, is a large letter that drops three or four
lines into the text. Drop caps appear at the start of chapters and articles, but with a little
imagination, you can find more uses for drop caps. In Figure 15-1, for example, a drop
cap is used to identify the song titles on the A side of a homemade cassette tape. Notice
as well in the figure that you can "drop" more than one letter at a time.

Follow these steps to create a drop cap:

1. Click anywhere in the paragraph whose first letter will "drop." The letter that
   needs dropping should already have been typed.

2. Choose Format | Drop Cap. You will see the Drop Cap dialog box shown in
   Figure 15-2.

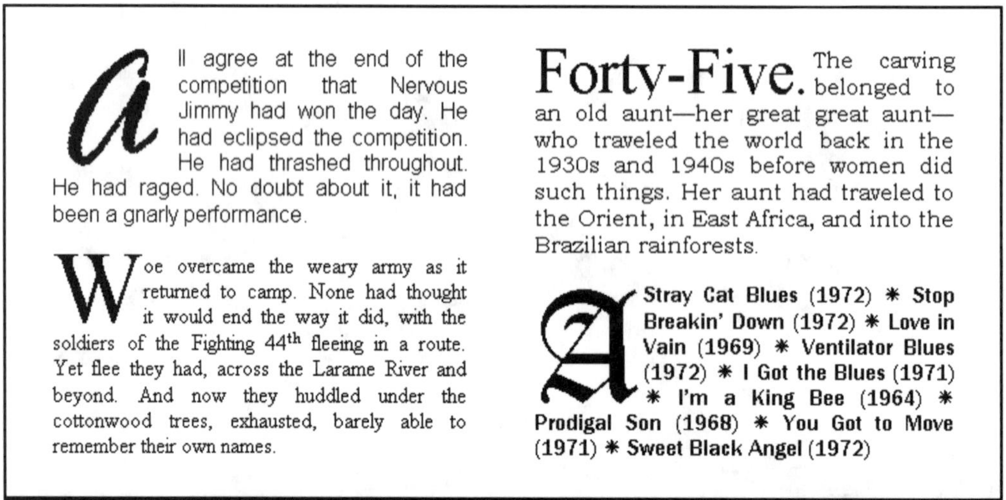

*a*ll agree at the end of the competition that Nervous Jimmy had won the day. He had eclipsed the competition. He had thrashed throughout. He had raged. No doubt about it, it had been a gnarly performance.

*W*oe overcame the weary army as it returned to camp. None had thought it would end the way it did, with the soldiers of the Fighting 44th fleeing in a route. Yet flee they had, across the Larame River and beyond. And now they huddled under the cottonwood trees, exhausted, barely able to remember their own names.

Forty-Five. The carving belonged to an old aunt—her great great aunt—who traveled the world back in the 1930s and 1940s before women did such things. Her aunt had traveled to the Orient, in East Africa, and into the Brazilian rainforests.

A Stray Cat Blues (1972) ✻ Stop Breakin' Down (1972) ✻ Love in Vain (1969) ✻ Ventilator Blues (1972) ✻ I Got the Blues (1971) ✻ I'm a King Bee (1964) ✻ Prodigal Son (1968) ✻ You Got to Move (1971) ✻ Sweet Black Angel (1972)

Figure 15-1. *Typically, drop caps appear at the start of articles and chapters, but you can also find other uses for them*

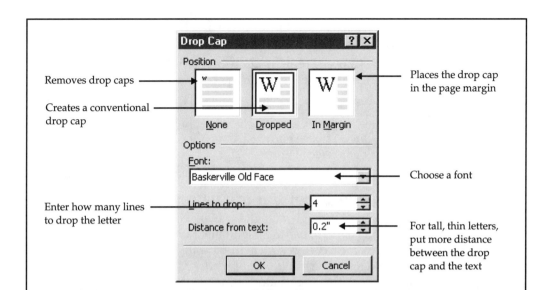

Removes drop caps

Creates a conventional drop cap

Places the drop cap in the page margin

Choose a font

Enter how many lines to drop the letter

For tall, thin letters, put more distance between the drop cap and the text

Figure 15-2. *Describe the drop capital letter that you want in the Drop Cap dialog box*

3. Under Position, choose Dropped or In Margin. The In Margin option puts the drop cap in the margin beside the paragraph (and looks kind of odd, I think). Use the None option to remove a drop cap.

4. Choose a font for the drop cap from the Front drop-down list. Choose a font that is different from the font in the rest of the paragraph to make the drop cap stand out. And don't worry about choosing the right font. Shortly I'll show you a quick way to change the font of a drop cap.

5. In the Lines To Drop text box, enter how many lines you want the drop capital letter to occupy.

Tip *If the letter being dropped is an H, I, M, N, U, or a number whose right side stands straight up, enter .2 or .3 in the Distance From Text box. Without a bit of space between the drop cap and the letter or number, the text comes too close to the drop cap.*

6. Click OK to close the Drop Cap dialog box.

The drop cap appears in a frame, a container for text. Like text boxes, you can drag frames to change their size and position, but don't bother dragging the frame to alter your drop capital letter. Follow these instructions to change its appearance or get rid of it altogether:

- ■ **Changing the Font**   Drag across the drop cap to select it and choose a new font from the Font drop-down menu on the Formatting toolbar.

- ■ **Changing the Size**   Choose Format | Drop Cap and, in the Drop Cap dialog box (see Figure 15-2), make a new entry in the Lines To Drop text box.

- ■ **Using Words for Drop Caps**   Click in the frame to the right of the drop cap and start typing.

- ■ **Removing a Drop Cap**   Choose Format | Drop Cap and click the None option in the Drop Cap dialog box (see Figure 15-2).

Stand-Up Letters and Other Variations on the Drop Cap

The next time you are paging through a fat glossy magazine with pictures of scrawny women modeling clothes, pause for a moment to look at the start of the articles. Chances are, the articles begin with a drop capital letter or a stand-up letter. Instead of dropping into the text, a *stand-up letter* rises above the first paragraph in an article, as shown in this illustration.

*H*ello and welcome to Reno, the biggest little city
in the world, gateway to the state of Nevada...

Personally, I like stand-up letters better than drop caps, but creating a stand-up letter isn't simply a matter of selecting the first letter and giving it a larger font size. Do that and Word puts extra space between the first and second line in the paragraph (the program does that because it is supposed to adjust line spacing to accommodate tall characters, but why it puts extra space between the first and second lines I do not know). To create a stand-up letter, you have to put the letter in a text box, tell Word not to wrap text around the text box, and move the letters in the first word to the right to make room for the stand-up letter.

Follow these steps to create a stand-up letter for the first paragraph in an article:

1. Delete the first letter in the first word of the article. You will make the letter you delete the stand-up letter.

2. Create a text box and type the stand-up letter in the text box. "Putting a Text Box on the Page" in Chapter 13 explains text boxes. Increase the font size of the letter to make it a stand-up letter. With that done, shrink the text box so it is small enough to hold the letter without cutting off part of the letter. "Changing the Size and Shape of Objects" in Chapter 13 explains how to make a text box larger or smaller.

3. Drag the text box into the first paragraph, roughly where you want the stand-up letter to be. Text in the paragraph moves to the right to accommodate the text box, but you will fix that in the next step.

4. Choose Format | Text Box, click the Layout tab in the Format Text Box dialog box, choose the Behind Text option, and click OK. Now the start of the first line overlaps the text box.

5. Click in the first line of the paragraph, press the HOME key to move the cursor to the start of the paragraph, and press the SPACEBAR as many times as necessary to move the text in the first line to the right of the stand-up letter.

6. Move the pointer to the top of the stand-up letter, and when you see the four-headed arrow, click to select the text box that holds the stand-up letter. In the next step, you will adjust the position of the stand-up letter.

7. Move the pointer over the side of the text box, and when you see the four-headed arrow, click and drag the text box to adjust its position. You might have to perform this step several times to make the stand-up letter fit beside the rest of the word at the start of the paragraph.

*H*ello and welcome to Reno, the biggest little city
in the world, gateway to the state of Nevada…

8. Finally, to remove the borders around the text box so that nobody knows the text box is there, choose Format | Text Box, click the Colors and Lines tab in the Format Text Box dialog box, open the Color drop-down list (the one under Line, not Fill), choose No Line, and click OK. You can also remove the borders from a text box by clicking the arrow beside the Line Color button on the Drawing toolbar and choosing No Line from the pop-up menu.

Although you removed the borders around the text box, you can still adjust its position and in so doing adjust the position of the stand-up letter. To adjust the position of the text box, carefully move the pointer over the stand-up letter, click when you see the four-headed arrow, and start dragging.

In the Clip Gallery are many letters you can use as drop caps or stand-up letters. "Getting Images from Microsoft's Clip Gallery" in Chapter 13 explains how to import a clip art image (in the Microsoft Clip Gallery dialog box, type **alphabet** in the Search For Clips text box to find letters). In this illustration, I used a clip art image of the letter "S" as a drop cap.

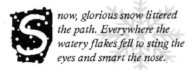

*S*now, glorious snow littered
the path. Everywhere the
watery flakes fell to sting the
eyes and smart the nose.

Putting Text in Columns

Probably the easiest way to prove your word-processing prowess is to run text in newspaper-style columns. Columns look great and you can pack a lot of words in columns. However, before you get too excited at the prospect of running text in columns, be sure to read "Comparing the Ways to Lay Out Text in Columns," the next section in this chapter. Newspaper-style columns, the kind you get when you choose the Format | Columns command, are not the only kind of columns you can create in Word 2000. In fact, often the best way to present text in columns is by using a table or several text boxes.

These pages investigate the different ways to create columns, how to lay out newspaper-style columns on the page, and how to adjust the position and size of columns. You will also learn how to break a column in the middle and how to make a headline straddle columns. Also in this section of the book are instructions for laying out columns in tables and text boxes.

Write and edit the text before you lay it out in columns. Make sure all spelling, grammatical, and questions of clarity have been taken care of. Editing text after it has been laid out in columns is difficult and should be avoided.

Laying Out Text in Newspaper-Style Columns

The fastest way to lay out newspaper-style columns is to make use of the Columns button on the Standard toolbar, but if you want to be thorough about it, use the Format | Columns command. With the Columns button, you get generic columns of equal size. With the Format | Columns command, you can tinker with the width of columns, adjust the amount of space between columns, and draw lines between columns. Columns must be at least .5 inch wide. At most, 9 columns can appear on a portrait page and 15 can appear on a landscape page with a .5-inch left and right margin.

Note　*Where the cursor is located and whether you have selected text matters a lot when you create columns. Before you give the command to put text in columns, select the text if you want to "columnize" text you have already written. Otherwise, if you simply click in the text and give the Format | Columns command, you have the option of columnizing all the text in the document, all the text in the section that the cursor is in, or all the text from the position of the cursor to the end of the document. With the Columns button, all the text in the section is "columnized," or, if the document has not been divided into sections, all the text from the cursor position to the end of the document is turned into columns.*

Comparing the Ways to Lay Out Text in Columns

Word offers three ways to lay out text in columns: the Format | Columns command (or Columns button), text boxes, and tables.

Choose the Format | Columns command and you'll get newspaper-style columns, also known as "snaking columns." As this illustration shows, text winds from column to column in newspaper-style columns. When text reaches the bottom of one column, it "snakes" to the top of the next column.

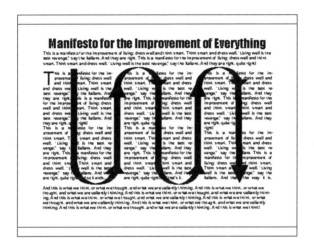

Newspaper-style columns are fine for simple newsletters and multicolumn brochures. Drawing lines between columns is easy with the Format | Columns command. And changing the width and length of columns is easy, too. However, newspaper-style columns present more than a few layout problems:

- The columns occupy the width of the page. Reserving a third of the page for normal text and the other two-thirds for newspaper-style columns is impossible. With newspaper-style columns, it's the width of the page or nothing at all.

- For practical purposes, you can't present one article in one column and another article in another column because text "snakes" from column to column. Unless the article in the left-hand column ends precisely at the bottom of the left-hand column, text from the first article floods the next column and pushes the second article down the page.

- Because columns "snake," you can't present the first half of an article on one page, break it off, and continue the article on another page. When text in a column reaches the bottom of the page, it goes directly to the next page. You can't make text jump two pages or three pages deeper into a document.

- Word creates a new section for newspaper-style columns, which can be a real bother in a document with headers and footers that change from section to section. "Section Breaks for Changing Layouts" in Chapter 9 explains sections.

In my experience, newspaper-style columns are fine when they are confined to a single page. As the previous illustration shows, two or three columns on a page with normal text above and normal text below looks very good and presents hardly any layout problems. But if you want to do any serious layout work in columns, you need to think about text boxes as a means of presenting text in columns.

Laying out columns in text boxes is more difficult than laying out newspaper-style columns, but text boxes solve all the problems caused by newspaper-style columns. As this illustration shows, you can present one article on the left side of the page and a second article on the right side of the page. Instead of text snaking from column to column, you can make text go wherever you please when it reaches the end of a column. In an 8-page brochure, for example, an article can start on page 1 and finish on page 8. Later in this chapter, "Using Text Boxes to Present Text in Columns" explains the ins and outs of laying out columns in text boxes.

The last way to present text in columns is to lay out the columns in a two-, three-, or four-column table. Go this route when the entries in the columns have to refer to one another. In a résumé, for example, entries in the first column (the job title column, for example) refer to entries in the second column (the job description column). If you tried to lay out a résumé with the Format | Columns command, you would be asking for trouble. Because text snakes from column to column, lining up entries in the first and second column would be a monumental chore. A better way to lay out a résumé is to create a two-column table and then erase the table boundaries so that no one knows the columns were laid out in a table, as was done in this illustration. Later in this chapter, "Using Tables to Present Text in Columns" explains how easy it is to lay out columns in a table.

John Harqueford   411 E. Fordham Pl. , New York, NY 38790 (888)555-1212 john@email.com

Résumé

Job Title	Description
Poacher *4/98–11/99*	Poached exotic animals from important places without anybody knowing it. Duties included locating animals to poach and then poaching them. Developed advanced poaching procedures pursuant to my duties as a poacher.
Roustabout *12/97–2/98*	Rousted around and did various things. Was voted Roustabout of the Year by my peers in the Society of Roustabouts. Developed rousting procedures pursuant to my duties as a roustabout.

Creating Generic Columns with the Columns Button

Follow these steps to create columns of equal size with the Columns button on the Standard toolbar:

1. Select the text if you have written text that you want to put in columns. Without selecting text, Word "columnizes" all the text in the section that the cursor is in, or, if your document has not been divided into sections, all text from the position of the cursor to the end of the document.

2. Click the Columns button on the Standard toolbar.

3. Drag the cursor over the number of columns you want and click. To get five or six columns, keep dragging the mouse toward the right.

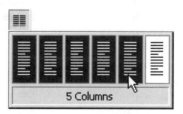

5 Columns

Word switches to Print Layout view if you weren't already in Print Layout view and there you have it—columns of equal size. To determine how wide to make the columns, Word notes the amount of horizontal space between the left and right margin, sets aside

.5 inch of space for the area between columns, and divides remaining space by the number of columns you asked for.

Newspaper-style columns only appear in Print Layout view. If you can't see the columns, click the Print Layout View button or choose View | Print Layout to switch to Print Layout view.

LEARN BY EXAMPLE
Open the 15-1 Columns document on the companion CD if you want practice editing text in columns and revising the structure of columns.

Laying Out and Adjusting Columns with the Format | Columns Command

Follow these steps to use the Format | Columns command to lay out columns or adjust columns you have already created:

1. Select the text you want to columnize if you've already written it; otherwise, place the cursor in a section you want to columnize or place the cursor at the position where columns are to begin appearing. If you want to adjust a column layout, click in a column.

2. Choose Format | Columns to open the Columns dialog box, shown in Figure 15-3.

3. Either enter the number of columns you want in the Number Of Columns box or click a Presets option box to choose a predesigned column layout of one, two, or three columns. Notice that three of the Presets options offer columns of unequal size.

4. Check the Line Between check box if you want lines to appear between columns. Unfortunately, you can only place lines between all the columns, not between a select one or two.

5. Adjust the width of columns and the amount of space between columns. As you do so, watch the Preview box to see the effects of your choices. Be prepared to wrestle with the Width and Spacing option boxes, since Word adjusts width and spacing settings as you make entries in the Width and Spacing boxes.

For columns of unequal size, uncheck the Equal Column Width check box.

■ **Adjusting the Width of Columns**   For each column, enter a number in the Width box to tell Word how wide to make the column. Click the down arrow on the scroll bar, if necessary, to get to the fourth, fifth, or sixth column.

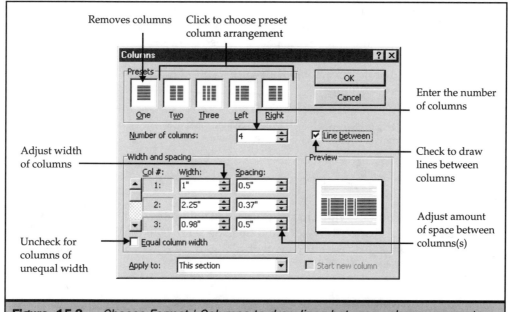

Removes columns

Click to choose preset column arrangement

Enter the number of columns

Adjust width of columns

Check to draw lines between columns

Adjust amount of space between columns(s)

Uncheck for columns of unequal width

Figure 15-3.   *Choose Format | Columns to draw lines between columns or create columns of different widths*

- **Adjusting the Amount of Space Between Columns**   For each column, enter a number in the Spacing box to tell Word how much space to put between it and the column to its right.

6. In the Apply To drop-down list, tell Word to "columnize" the section that the cursor is in, the remainder of the document, the entire document, or text you selected.

7. Click OK.

Text in columns, especially narrow columns, looks better when it is hyphenated and justified. To justify text, select it and click the Justify button on the Formatting toolbar. "Hyphenating Text" in Chapter 7 explains hyphenation techniques.

Changing the Width of Newspaper-Style Columns

To change the width of newspaper-style columns, either drag column markers on the ruler or open the Columns dialog box (see Figure 15-3) and make adjustments there. If your columns are the same size, you have to choose Format | Columns to make adjustments in the Columns dialog box. You can't adjust the width of columns on the ruler if the columns are of equal size.

■ **Changing Column Width with the Ruler** Drag the Move Column marker on the ruler to change a column's width (choose View | Ruler if you don't see the ruler). To adjust the amount of space between columns, move the pointer over the tiny white line on the left or right side of the Move Column marker. When you see the double arrows and the words "Left Margin" or "Right Margin," click and start dragging.

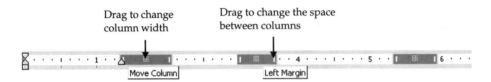

■ **Changing Column Width in the Columns Dialog Box** Choose Format | Columns and change the Width and Spacing settings in the Columns dialog box. Watch the Preview box as you go along to see what your choices mean in real terms.

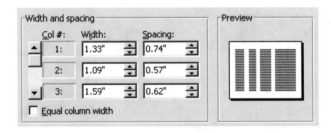

To make all columns the same width (if they are not all the same width already), choose Format | Columns and check the Equal Column Width check box in the Columns dialog box (see Figure 15-3). You can also click the Columns button and choose the number of columns you already have from the drop-down menu to get columns of equal size.

Techniques for Working with Newspaper-Style Columns

Making newspaper-style columns fit a page isn't easy. Here are a few techniques for taming columns so that they land where you want them to land on the page:

■ **Moving Text to the Next Column** Word fills columns whether you like it or not, but you can leave empty space at the bottom of a column and move text directly to the next column if you want. To do so, move the insertion point to the start of the line that you want to move to the next column and either press CTRL-SHIFT-ENTER or choose Insert | Break and click the Column Break option button in the Break dialog box, as shown in Figure 15-4.

To remove a column break, click the Show/Hide ¶ button to see where the break is, click the break with the mouse, and then press the DELETE key.

Tip   *As Figure 15-4 shows, another way to move text to the next column is to insert a text box, clip art image, or other object at the bottom of the column and tell Word to wrap the text around the object such that the text moves to the next column. See "Wrapping Text Around an Object" near the end of Chapter 13.*

■ **Making Columns the Same Length**   Unless text fills the entire page, columns are different lengths. However, you can make all the columns on a page the same length by confining them to a section. Click at the end of the text in the last column, choose Insert | Break, and click the Continuous option button on the Break dialog box (see Figure 15-4). By creating a new section, you confine columns to the same section and make columns the same length.

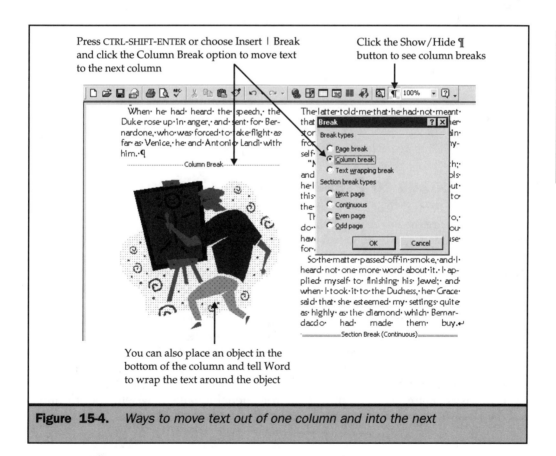

Press CTRL-SHIFT-ENTER or choose Insert | Break and click the Column Break option to move text to the next column

Click the Show/Hide ¶ button to see column breaks

You can also place an object in the bottom of the column and tell Word to wrap the text around the object

Figure 15-4.   *Ways to move text out of one column and into the next*

■ **Changing the Number of Columns** Before you can change the number of columns, you have to select all the columns, which is tricky. To select all the columns, click at the start of the first column, press F8, and then click at the end of the last column. With all columns selected, either click the Columns button on the Standard toolbar and choose the number of columns you want from the drop-down list, or choose Format | Columns and choose the number of columns you want in the Columns dialog box (see Figure 15-3).

■ **Drawing Lines Between Columns** For full-length lines between columns, choose Format | Columns and check the Line Between check box in the Columns dialog box (see Figure 15-3). For horizontal lines or lines that run partway down a column, you have to draw the lines yourself with the tools on the Drawing toolbar. See "Drawing Lines and Shapes" in Chapter 13.

To see precisely where columns begin and end without having to draw lines between them, choose Tools | Options, click the View tab in the Options dialog box, and click the Text Boundaries check box under Print And Web Layout Options.

■ **Removing Columns** Click in the columns, choose Format | Columns, and choose the One option under Presets in the Columns dialog box (see Figure 15-3).

LEARN BY EXAMPLE
Open the 15-2 Column Balance document on the companion CD if you want to try your hand at balancing the length of columns on the page

Using Text Boxes to Present Text in Columns

Earlier in this chapter, "Comparing the Ways to Lay Out Text in Columns" explains that text boxes are the better way to lay out text in columns. A certain amount of expertise is needed, however, to run columns in text boxes. See "Putting a Text Box on the Page" in Chapter 13 if you want to try out the text box method of laying out text in columns. That section of Chapter 13 explains how to create a text box and link text boxes so that text can pass from box to box. See "Positioning Objects on the Page" in Chapter 13 to learn how to place text boxes on the page.

With the text box method of laying out columns, you can create a text box for each column you need. Then simply link the text boxes so that text can pass from column to column. For example, text can pass from a text box on the left side of page 1 to a text box on the top of page 8. Needless to say, laying out columns in this manner requires foresight and planning, not to mention an advanced understanding of Word 2000, but the rewards are many. You end up with a professional-looking newsletter or brochure, not the fill-in-the-numbers columns you get with the Format | Columns command.

Headlines and Pull-Quotes for Newspaper-Style Columns

As this illustration shows, headlines can straddle newspaper-style columns, and so can pull-quote boxes. A *pull-quote* is a quote from an article that is meant to entice readers. The trick to formatting headlines and pull-quotes is to put the headlines or quotes in text boxes, wrap the text around the text boxes, and then remove the borders from the text boxes. In this illustration, one text box holds the headline and another holds the pull-quote. Notice how text wraps around the sides of the headline and pull-quote.

Follow these steps to create a headline or pull-quote for newspaper-style columns:

1. Create a text box and type the headline or pull-quote text in the box. "Putting a Text Box on the Page" in Chapter 13 explains text boxes.

2. Drag the text box onto the newspaper-style columns where you want the headline or pull-quote to be. "Positioning Objects on the Page" in Chapter 13 explains how to move a text box.

3. Choose Format | Text Box to open the Format Text Box dialog box. In this dialog box, you will tell Word to wrap text around the text box, lock the text box so it doesn't move on the page, and remove the borders from the text box.

4. Click the Layout tab.

5. Under Wrapping Style, click the Tight option.

6. Click the Advanced button to open the Advanced Layout dialog box.

7. Click the Picture Position tab, and, under Horizontal, select the Absolute Position option button and choose Page from the To The Left Of drop-down list; under Vertical, select the Absolute Position option button and choose Page from the Below drop-down menu. "Positioning Objects on the Page" in Chapter 13 explains all the options on the Picture Position tab.

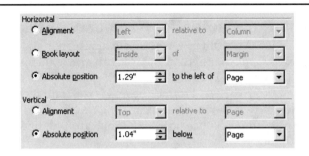

8. Click OK to return to the Format Text Box dialog box.

9. Click the Colors and Lines tab, and, under Line, open the Color drop-down list and choose No Line.

10. Click OK.

You can adjust the size and position of the text box. To do so, click inside it to make the selection handles appear. Then drag a selection handle to change the size of the box or move the pointer over the perimeter, wait till you see the four-headed arrow, and click and drag to change the text box's position.

Most of what you need to know to lay out text in columns is explained in detail in Chapter 13. Here are a few tips and tricks to make laying out columns in text boxes faster and easier:

■ **Making Columns the Same Size**   Rather than creating several text boxes that are the same size, create one text box and copy it. To copy a text box, select it, hold down the CTRL key, and then drag the copy away from the original. Suppose you need to shrink or enlarge your text boxes. Rather than changing their size one at a time and risk ending up with text boxes that are no longer the same size, SHIFT-click to select all the text boxes and then change the size of one box. As you change the size of one text box, all the others change size as well, as shown in this illustration.

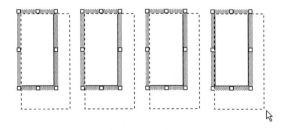

■ **Aligning Columns**   The Align and Distribute commands can be very handy
when you want to align text boxes or distribute them equally across the page.
SHIFT-click to select the text boxes, click the Draw button on the Drawing
toolbar, click the Align or Distribute command, and choose an Align option
or a Distribute option. "Positioning Objects on the Page" in Chapter 13 explains
these commands in detail.

■ **Locking Columns So They Don't Move**   Obviously, if text boxes slide
from page to page, your newsletter or brochure soon turns to mincemeat. See
"Making Sure Objects Appear on the Right Page" in Chapter 13 to make sure
text boxes don't slide from page to page.

Using Tables to Present Text in Columns

Earlier in this chapter, "Comparing the Ways to Lay Out Text in Columns" explains
why laying out columns in tables is absolutely necessary if one column has to refer to
another. By laying out columns in tables, you can make certain that entries in the
different columns line up correctly with one another. This schedule, for example,
shows text in three columns, but the schedule really was laid out in a three-column
table. Because the table borders have been removed, only people in the know can tell
that these three columns are really a table.

Time	Speaker	Topic
9:30–10:30	Dr. Jacques Arnoux	"*Madame Bovary* and Feminist Theory" Explores feminist themes in *Madame Bovary*, the first feminist novel. Describes the plight of women in rural 19th Century France.
11:00–12:30	Louis Colet, M.A. Dr. Bouvard Picochet	"The Seduction of Flaubert" Examines Flaubert's fascination with things Eastern. Compares his Egyptian notebooks to the two works his trips to the East inspired: *Salammbô* and *Hérodias*.

Chapter 14 is devoted to all the different ways of laying out and formatting a
table. After you have entered the text, be sure to remove the table borders so that
no one knows how the columns were really made. To remove the borders, choose
Table | Select | Table, click the down arrow beside the Border button on the Tables
and Borders toolbar, and click the No Border button on the drop-down menu.

Creating a Side Heading or Margin Note

As Figure 15-5 shows, a *side heading* is a heading that perches to the left of the text
instead of above the text. A margin note, like a side heading, perches in the margin,
but it offers a bit of extra commentary on the text. Side headings and margin notes are
elegant and easy to create as long as you know how text boxes work. "Putting a Text
Box on the Page" in Chapter 13 explains text boxes. The trick to making a side heading
or margin note is to make sure that the heading or note does not fall into the bottom
margin when the paragraph to which it refers appears near the bottom of a page.

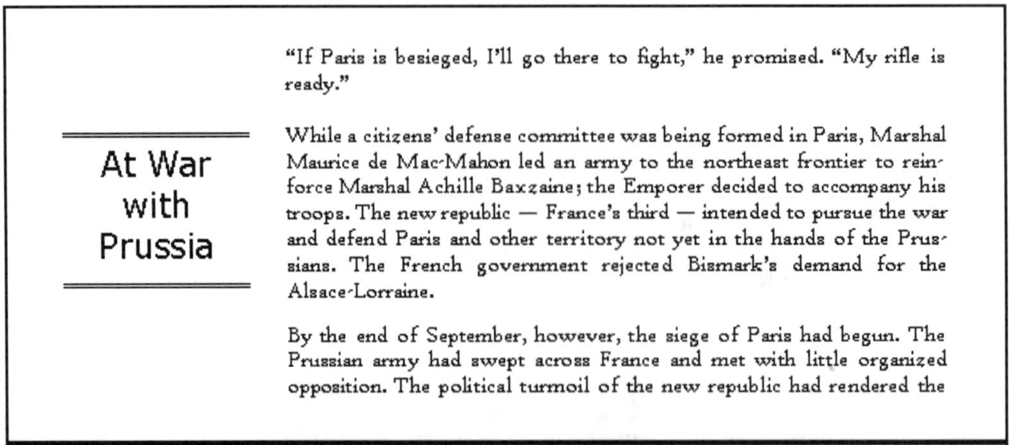

"If Paris is besieged, I'll go there to fight," he promised. "My rifle is
ready."

At War with Prussia

While a citizens' defense committee was being formed in Paris, Marshal
Maurice de Mac-Mahon led an army to the northeast frontier to rein-
force Marshal Achille Baxzaine; the Emporer decided to accompany his
troops. The new republic — France's third — intended to pursue the war
and defend Paris and other territory not yet in the hands of the Prus-
sians. The French government rejected Bismark's demand for the
Alsace-Lorraine.

By the end of September, however, the siege of Paris had begun. The
Prussian army had swept across France and met with little organized
opposition. The political turmoil of the new republic had rendered the

Figure 15-5.   *Side headings look elegant and are easy to create as long as you understand how text boxes work*

Tip   *If you intend to use side headings and margin notes throughout a document, make sure the left margin is wide enough to accommodate them. See "Setting the Margins" in Chapter 9.*

Follow these steps to create a side heading or margin note, decorate it with a line or two, and make sure that it doesn't scrape the bottom of the page when the paragraph to which it refers appears near the bottom of the page:

1. Create a text box beside the paragraph that the heading or note refers to. As long as you place the text box beside the appropriate paragraph, the text box will be attached to the paragraph and will move along with it if the paragraph gets moved in the course of editing.

2. Enter the heading or note in the text box. You can format the heading or note by changing its font, boldfacing it, or centering it, for example.

3. Remove the borders from the text box. To do so, click the down arrow beside the Line Color button on the Drawing toolbar and choose No Line from the pop-up menu. You can click the Drawing button on the Standard toolbar to display the Drawing toolbar.

4. To enter a decorative line above and below the heading or note (if decorating is one of your hobbies), start by displaying the Tables and Borders toolbar (click the Tables and Borders button on the Standard toolbar). Then choose a line from the Line Style menu, choose a thickness from the Line Weight drop-down menu, click the down arrow beside the Borders button, and click the Top Border and then the Bottom Border button.

5. Click in the paragraph directly to the right of the side heading or note. In the next step, you will make sure that all the text in this paragraph always appears

on the same page, and in so doing you will make sure that the side heading or note does not fall into the bottom margin.

6. Choose Format | Paragraph, click the Line and Page Breaks tab in the Paragraph dialog box, check the Keep Lines Together check box, and click OK.

Note   *In Chapter 7, "Creating a "Hanging Heading" explains another way to make use of the margin—by creating a heading that appears to hang, or stick into, the left margin of the page. "Numbering the Pages" in Chapter 9 explains how to put page numbers in the left or right margin.*

Creating a Fill-In Form

A fill-in form is really only a table that has been decorated to look like a form. By making use of the border and fill commands on the Table menu and Table and Borders toolbar, by merging cells and splitting cells, you can whip up a fill-in form like the one in Figure 15-6. See "Decorating a Table with Borders, Shading, and Color" in Chapter 14 to learn the Table techniques for creating fill-in forms.

The Rug Repairers
4127 - 23rd Street
San Demas, CA 94114

SERVICE ORDER

Name:		Date In:
Address:		
City:		Ready By:
State:	Zip:	
Home Phone:		Order Taken By:
Work Phone:		

Item	Price	Description
		Subtotal
		Tax
		Total Estimate

Figure 15-6. *To create fill-in forms like this one, use the commands on the Table menu and the Tables and Borders toolbar*

The Draw Table tool on the Tables and Borders toolbar comes in very handy when you are constructing fill-in forms. Use the tool to draw vertical lines on the form and split cells.

The fill-in form shown in Figure 15-6 is really three separate tables. The tables have been merged so that you can't tell where one ends and the other begins. Notice how different borders and shading are used to distinguish one part of the form from another.

"Creating and Using an Online Data-Entry Form" in Chapter 24 explains how to create an electronic form—a form with drop-down lists and menus that data-entry clerks can use to enter data.

MOUS Exam Objectives Explored in Chapter 15

Objective	Heading	Practice File
Create and use newspaper columns	"Laying Out Newspaper-Style Columns"	15-1 Columns
Revise column structure	"Laying Out Newspaper-Style Columns"	
Balance column length*	"Laying Out Newspaper-Style Columns"	15-2 Column Balance

* Denotes an Expert exam objective.

Top 10 — Ten Ways to Make a Document Livelier

Documents don't have to be dull in appearance. You can spice them up with the techniques described here. Here are the ten best and simplest ways to make a document livelier. Some of the techniques listed here are explained in detail in other chapters, but they are listed here nonetheless as part of my nation-wide campaign to keep word processed documents from looking so dull.

1. INCLUDE CLIP ART IN YOUR DOCUMENT. As "Handling Graphics and Clip Art in Documents" in Chapter 13 explains, dropping a clip art image in a document is pretty simple. And you don't have to tell anyone where the clip art image came from, either. Probably one or two naïve readers will think you created it yourself.

2. CREATE A WATERMARK FOR THE PAGES. A watermark is a faint image that appears behind the text. "Decorating Pages with Watermarks" in Chapter 13 explains how you can make the same faint watermark image appear on every page in a document or section of a document.

3. WRAP TEXT IN UNUSUAL WAYS. Probably the easiest way to impress the impressionable is to wrap text around a clip art image or text box. A square, tight wrap looks especially good and breaks up the page nicely. See "Wrapping Text Around an Object" in Chapter 13 for all the details.

4. PLACE A BORDER AROUND THE PAGES. By placing a border around the page, you can frame it very nicely. The title page of a document is an ideal candidate for a page border. And putting a border around the first page of a document is very easy. See "Decorating a Page with a Border" in Chapter 9.

5. SPLASH COLORS ON YOUR DOCUMENT. If you have a color printer, you have a golden opportunity to dress up your pages in color. Word offers numerous ways to splash color on a document. You can print text in color, put a color background behind text boxes, and draw lines in color.

6. TAKE ADVANTAGE OF WORDART. WordArt is a little-used feature of Word, and that's a shame, because WordArt images make good headlines and can do a lot to enliven a document. "WordArt for Bending, Spindling, and Mutilating Text" in Chapter 7 explains WordArt.

Try using a WordArt image

7. DRAW LINES BELOW HEADERS AND ABOVE FOOTERS.   Personally, I think no header should appear at the top of a page unless a line is drawn below it. And no footer should appear at the bottom of the page unless a line is drawn above it. The lines separate headers and footers from the main text and help frame the page. "Headers and Footers for Different Pages and Sections" in Chapter 9 explains how to draw lines above footers and below headers.

8. BREAK TEXT INTO COLUMNS.   Columns are wonderful indeed, as this chapter has argued so eloquently. Use the Format | Columns command to lay out newspaper-style columns on a single page. For sophisticated columns, lay out the columns in text boxes. For documents such as résumés and schedules in which text in each column has to line up correctly, lay out the columns in tables.

9. THROW IN A DROP CAP.   The start of this chapter explains precisely how easy it is to put a drop cap at the beginning of an article or chapter. Pound for pound, drop caps are the easiest layout trick there is in Word.

10. MAKE USE OF WORD'S "TEXT EFFECTS."   The "text effects" in the Font dialog box are very good for headings. Experiment with the Shadow, Outline, Emboss, and Engrave effects to see what happens. "Playing with Word's 'Text Effects'" in Chapter 7 explains text effects in detail.

The
Complete
Reference

Part IV

**Developing Web Pages
with Word 2000**

The Complete Reference

Word 2000

Chapter 16

Building a Basic Web Page

This and the following chapter explain how to construct Web pages with Microsoft Word 2000. Word wasn't designed for creating Web pages, as you know. Still, the program is pretty good at creating simple Web pages, and you only have to learn a few new skills to create a Web page with Word if you already know your way around the program. What's more, converting Word documents into Web pages is pretty easy.

This chapter explains what you need to know to create Web pages and Web sites with Word. It covers laying out Web pages, inserting hyperlinks to connect your pages with the World Wide Web, decorating Web pages, including frames in Web pages, and uploading Web pages to an Internet service provider (ISP). At the end of this chapter is a list of ten places you can go on the Internet to find free clip art and Web art.

What You Need to Know Before You Begin

Before you learn anything about creating a Web page with Word 2000, you should know that Word is not primarily a program for creating Web pages. The Web pages that you can create with Word are utilitarian and do a good job if you want to post a simple page on the company Intranet or create an appealing page for friends, like-minded hobbyists, and aficionados. However, if you want to engage in selling on the Web, or if you want to promote a business, your pages should have a professional look. Would you shop in a store whose windows were cluttered with junk? Probably not. You need the help of a pro if you want to do business on the Web.

> **Tip** *The best way to find someone to handle Web pages if you need the help of a pro is to surf the Web and find a Web page you like. At the bottom of most Web pages is the e-mail address of the Webmaster, the person responsible for maintaining a Web page. Contact the Webmaster and see if he or she can develop a Web page for you.*

Finding the Right Internet Service Provider

Before you create a Web page, give a thought to how you will put it on the Internet—or *post* it, as they say in Cyberspeak. You need more than an e-mail account with an Internet service provider (ISP) to post a Web page. You need what is called a *full-service account*. These days, some ISPs offer their e-mail subscribers the opportunity to post Web pages. If your e-mail provider does not offer this service, you need to find a provider that does.

The best way to find a reliable ISP is to ask someone who already posts pages on the Internet. That way, you benefit from someone else's research and experience. Lacking that method, try looking in the Yellow Pages under "Internet" (my Yellow Pages lists eight pages of Internet service providers). Another way to find an ISP is to look in the classified advertisements of the local newspaper.

*Yet another way to find an ISP is to go to **www.thelist.com**. There you will find a complete listing of the nearly 5,500 ISPs in the U.S. and Canada.*

Which ISP should you choose? Telephone companies such as PacBel, AT&T, and Sprint offer ISP services, as do large independents such as Netcom and Sprynet. Then there are the "mom and pop" ISPs that offer local and regional service. As you shop for an ISP, get answers to these questions:

- *Can I dial in without having to call a long-distance number?*   When you go on the Internet, the modem in your computer calls the ISP's computers. If that telephone call is a long-distance call, going on the Internet becomes an expensive proposition because you have to pay long-distance rates each time you go on the Internet. National ISPs such as those run by the major telephone companies offer regional phone numbers that you can call no matter where you travel. If you travel a lot and have to connect a laptop computer to the Internet from various cities and regions, consider signing on with an ISP that offers what are called "points of presence," or simply POPs, the regional telephone numbers you can dial to connect to an ISP.

- *What is the set-up fee?*   Most ISPs charge a one-time set-up or enrollment fee. Depending on how many ISPs are located in your area and how stiff the competition among ISPs is, fees vary from no charge at all to $30.

- *What is the monthly service charge?*   Monthly service charges range from $15 to $30 for people who use relatively slow 14.4kbs, 28.8kbs, or 56kbs modems to dial the ISP. Companies that require the faster digital services of an ISDN, ADSL, or T1 line might have to pay double or many times more the going rate of $15 to $30 per month.

- *How many hours of monthly online time are included in the monthly fee?*   Not so long ago, ISPs and online service providers such as America Online (AOL) charged by the hour to go online. Nowadays, most ISPs charge a flat monthly rate to go online for as many hours as you want. Still, find out if the ISP whose services you are considering charges a flat rate or a by-the-hour rate. That way, you will know what to expect from your first bill.

- *How much storage space am I allowed for the Web pages I want to post on the Internet?*   When you post a page on the Internet, you store your page with an ISP. Most ISPs allow from 1 to 2MB to as much as 50MB of file storage space. Storage limitations aren't usually a problem for the average Word user, however, since the Web sites you can create with Word rarely exceed 1MB in size.

- *Do you offer technical help?*   Typically, ISPs that charge a low monthly rate do not offer very much technical assistance to customers, but even if you go with an expensive ISP, find out how long the company takes to reply to e-mail queries for technical assistance. Find out as well if the ISP maintains a telephone line that you can call if you forget your password or can't go online to ask for help. By the way, queries as to what to do about smoke coming from a modem should be directed to the local fire department, which is obliged to respond faster than an ISP.

Note *At two sites on the Web, geocities.com and tripod.com, you can post Web sites for free. The hitch, however, is that you have to post advertisements on your Web site.*

Doing the Preliminary Work

Before you create any Web pages, create the following new folders on your C: drive:

- A folder for storing Web pages. Give the folder a descriptive name such as "My Web Site." The folder will be your working folder and will help you stay organized during the project.

- A folder for storing completed pages. Inside the "My Web Site" folder, create another folder called "Web Upload" (or something similar) for storing the final files that you will upload to your ISP.

- A folder for castoffs. When you have finished building your site, you will put all the files you no longer need in the Castoff folder in case you really do need them.

The Three Fast Ways to Create Web Pages

As long as you thoughtfully applied styles to your Word 2000 document, you can turn it into a Web page simply by saving it as a Web page. To save files as Web pages, Word looks at the styles and assigns specific HTML (Hypertext Markup Language) codes to each style. Hypertext markup language is the "mother tongue" of the World Wide Web. Its codes tell Web browsers, the software that is used for surfing the Web, how to read pages and display them on computer screens.

However, certain elements of a Word document either cannot be translated into HTML codes or can't be translated entirely. Table 16-1 lists the elements that cannot appear on a Web page or are altered when they appear on a Web page. If you want to turn a Word document into a Web page, be sure to read Table 16-1 to find out whether any elements in your document cannot make the transition.

Besides turning a common Word document into a Web page, you can create Web pages from scratch from a template. And by using a wizard, you can create new Web pages as well as bring Web pages into a multipage Web site. Better read on.

Feature	What Happens in HTML	Explanation
Charts, Equations, and OLE objects	Modified	OLE objects are converted to .GIF images.
Comments	Deleted	All comments made with the Insert | Comment command are lost.
Drop Caps	Deleted	However, you can substitute a graphic or .GIF image.
Fields	Modified	The value of the Date field is retained but is no longer updated.
Font attributes (italic, bold, strikethrough, and underline)	Unaffected	Some of the esoteric underline attributes are converted to solid underlines.
Font Sizes	Modified	The font size closest to the font size in use is applied to the text.
Footnotes and endnotes	Deleted	These do not translate to HTML.
Headers and footers	Deleted	Headers and footers have no role on a Web page.
Highlighting	Deleted	You can't highlight text on a Web page.
Margins	Deleted	The BLOCKQUOTE tag and tables are good substitutes.
Newspaper-style columns	Deleted	Use a table as a substitute
Page borders	Deleted	Substitute other graphic elements such as horizontal rules, banners, and frames.
Page numbering	Deleted	Web pages are usually named, not numbered.

Table 16-1. *How Document Elements Make the Transition to HTML*

Feature	What Happens in HTML	Explanation
Shapes and AutoShapes	Modified	Early versions of some browsers cannot display shapes.
Styles	Modified	The basic styles are retained but the complicated styles cannot make the transition.
Tables	Modified	Many basic attributes must be "remodeled."
Text Effects	Deleted	The effect is lost but the letters themselves remain.

Table 16-1.   *How Document Elements Make the Transition to HTML* (continued)

Creating a Web Page from a Word Document

Create a new folder for your new Web page if you haven't already done so and then follow these steps to turn a Word document into a Web page:

1. Choose View | Web Layout or click the Web Layout View button to see what your document will look like on a Web browser.

2. Choose File | Save As Web Page.

3. In the Save As dialog box shown in Figure 16-1, find and select the folder where you will store the page.

4. Click the Change Title button, enter a name in the Set Page Title dialog box, and click OK. A visitor who comes to your Web page will see the title you enter on the title bar at the very top of his or her browser.

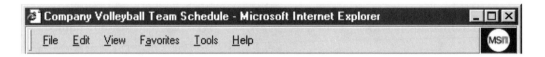

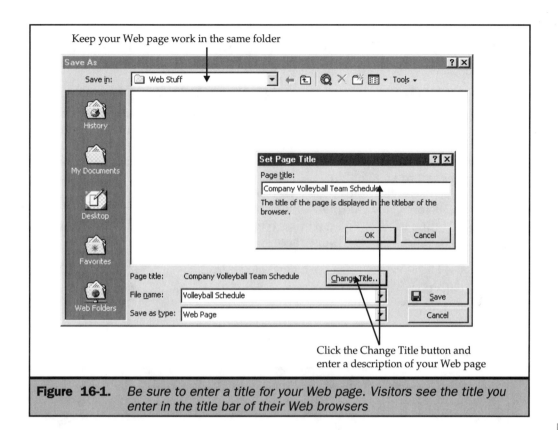

Keep your Web page work in the same folder

Click the Change Title button and
enter a description of your Web page

Figure 16-1. *Be sure to enter a title for your Web page. Visitors see the title you
enter in the title bar of their Web browsers*

 *Choose a descriptive name for the title. Lycos, Yahoo, and other search engines keep careful
track of the words on Web pages, and the word or words that are given a lot of weight are
the ones in the page title. If you enter **Madagascar** in the title, for example, a Web surfer
who enters they keyword **Madagascar** in order to conduct a search of the Web is more
likely to find your page than he or she is if you enter **Greenland** for the title.*

5. Click the Save button. The page appears in Web Layout view so you can see
   roughly what it will look like to visitors on the Internet.

 *You can always change the title of a Web page by choosing File | Properties, clicking the
Summary tab in the Properties dialog box, and entering a new title in the Title box.*

Creating a Web Page with a Template or Wizard

Turning a file into a Web page is easy enough, but if you want a professional-looking
Web page, create a Web Page with a template or wizard. With a template, you get your
choice of several different generic Web pages that you can embellish to your heart's

content. With the Web Page Wizard, you can create new Web pages and even create a Web site by bringing in Web pages you've already created. Wizards and templates are excellent ways to create Web pages without going to a lot of trouble.

Creating a Web Site with the Web Page Wizard

When you create a Web page with the wizard, you will see a series of dialog boxes, answer the questions in the dialog boxes, and end up with a Web site that includes several different Web pages, as shown in Figure 16-2. The hyperlinks that the visitors to your site click to go from page to page are already set up. All you do is enter the text or copy and paste it from other files.

Use the Web Page Wizard to create a Web site when the site is to comprise more than one page. Before you create the Web site, be sure to create a folder on your computer for storing its files. You can bring Web pages you have already created into a site with the Web Page Wizard. Follow these steps to create a Web site with the wizard:

1. Choose File | New to open the New dialog box.

2. Click the Web Pages tab. On the tab you can choose from several templates for creating Web pages as well as the Web Page Wizard.

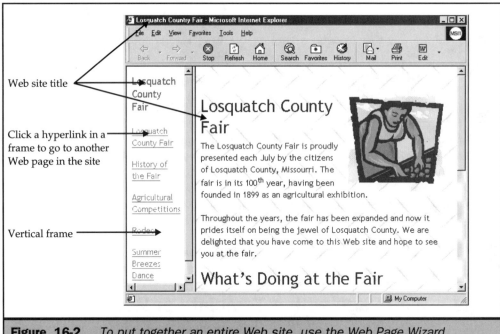

Figure 16-2.   *To put together an entire Web site, use the Web Page Wizard*

3. Double-click the Web Page Wizard icon and wait while the first of seven Web Page Wizard dialog boxes appears onscreen. During the next few minutes, you will enter a title for your Web page, decide how users will get from place to place on your Web site, perhaps add pages to the Web site, organize the pages, and choose a "visual theme"—a look for the site.

4. Click the Next button.

5. Enter a title for the site. As Figure 16-2 shows, the title you enter will appear at the top of your site's table of contents pages, so choose a title carefully. What's more, visitors to your site will see the title you enter on the title bar of their Web browsers.

6. Click the Browse button to open the Copy dialog box, find the folder you created to hold your Web site, double-click the folder, and click the Open button. Back in the dialog box, the name and path to the folder appears in the Web Site Location box.

7. Click the Next button.

8. Choose the kind of frame you want, Vertical or Horizontal, or choose Separate Page for displaying hyperlinks; then click Next.

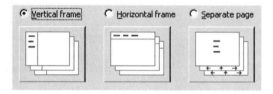

Note *Later in this chapter, "Dividing a Web Page into Frames" describes frames in enormous detail.*

The Navigation dialog box, an important one, is for determining how visitors to your site get from page to page. With the Vertical Frame option, hyperlinks for getting around appear in a frame on the left side of the screen (see Figure 16-2); with the Horizontal Frame option, hyperlinks appear along the top of the screen; and with the Separate Page option, they appear on a page all their own. The Separate Page option is for antiquated browsers that can't display frames. These days, most browsers can handle frames with no trouble at all.

9. Click the Next button to move to the Add Pages dialog box. To begin with, Word gives you three Web pages. This is where you decide how many Web pages your site needs and whether you want to bring pages you already created into the site.

Tip *How many pages does a Web site need? Most Web site developers believe that no page should be so long you have to scroll a long way to get to the bottom of it. Instead of creating a long page, create two short ones.*

10. Add pages to or remove pages from your Web site:

   ■ **Adding Pages to the Site**   Click the Add New Page button to add a generic page to the site. If you want to add a Web page you already created, click the Add Existing File button, find and select the page in the Open dialog box, and click the Open button. To add a page from a Web page template, click the Add Template Page button, choose the template in the Web Page Templates dialog box, and click OK. Word opens to a sample template page so you can see what the Web page templates look like (the next section in this chapter describes the templates in detail).

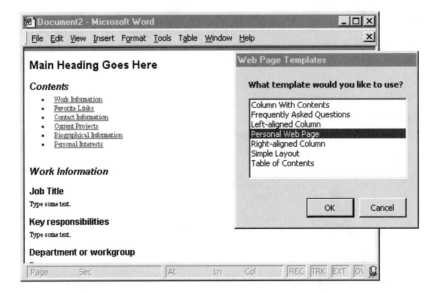

   ■ **Removing Pages from the Site**   Click the page in the Current Pages In Web Site box and then click the Remove Page button.

11. Click the Next button. You will see the Organize Pages dialog box.

12. If necessary, change the position of the Web pages by clicking a page and then clicking the Move Up or Move Down button; then click Next. The page at the top of the list will be the first page on your Web site.

Click a page and then click the Rename button to rename it. The names you enter will appear in the navigation frame. By clicking a page name in a frame, visitors can go to another Web page.

13. Make sure the Add A Visual Theme option button is selected, and then click the Browse Themes button. You'll see the Theme dialog box shown in Figure 16-3. This is where you choose a look for your Web site. By choosing a theme, you save yourself the trouble of decorating the Web site yourself.

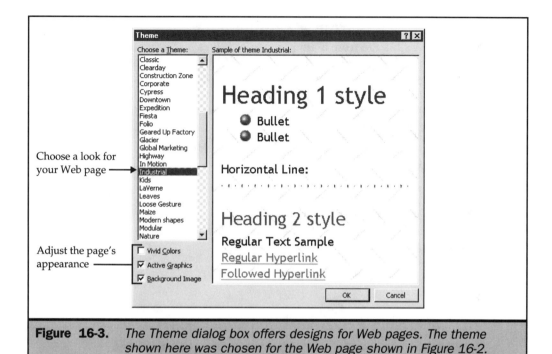

Figure 16-3. *The Theme dialog box offers designs for Web pages. The theme shown here was chosen for the Web page shown in Figure 16-2.*

14. In the Choose A Theme box, select the theme that tickles your fancy; check or uncheck the Vivid Colors, Active Graphics, and Background Image check boxes in the lower-left corner of the Theme dialog box; and click OK.

   ■ **Vivid Colors**   Makes Web page elements stand out by giving them brighter colors.

   ■ **Active Graphics**   Makes graphics on the Web page move (only available in certain templates).

   ■ **Background Image**   Add or removes the background design on the page.

15. Click Next to go to the Finish dialog box. Now is your chance to click the Back button to return to the dialog boxes and change your mind. Speak now or forever hold your peace.

16. Click the Finish button.

In a moment or two, you will see the first page of your Web site. If you pulled generic pages into the site, you have some work to do. Enter your own text in place of the generic text on the Web pages. You can always copy and paste text from other files and call on all the Word formatting commands. Change fonts and font sizes if you want. And if you want to include clip art or pictures, be my guest.

DEVELOPING WEB PAGES WITH WORD 2000

Creating a Web Page from a Template

When you create a Web page from a template, Word does all the layout work for you. All you have to do is fill in the text and, in the case of a couple of templates, import the clip art. Follow these steps to create a Web page from a template:

1. With Word running, choose File | New. You will see the New dialog box.

2. Click the Web Pages tab.

3. Click an icon and look in the Preview box to see what kind of Web page you can create with it.

4. Click OK when you've found the Web page you want.

As Figure 16-4 shows, you get a sample Web page with placeholder text and a placeholder graphic. Start entering your own text and importing your own graphics to make this page come alive.

Figure 16-4.   *When you create a Web page with a template, you get generic text and sometimes a placeholder graphic*

Seeing What Your Page Looks Like in a Browser

Choose File | Web Page Preview to see what your page looks like in the Internet Explorer Web browser. Once you choose the command, Internet Explorer opens and you see your page in all its glory, typos and all. Turn back a few pages to Figure 16-2 to see what a Web page created in Word looks like in the Internet Explorer browser.

Before you start marveling at how similar Web pages look in Word and in a browser, one or two words are in order. Unfortunately, not all browsers are the same when it comes to displaying Web pages. Internet Explorer and Netscape Navigator, the two most popular browsers, are alike in some ways, but each offers different features and capabilities. Usually, professional Web page designers target a particular browser when they do their work, but they nonetheless test their Web pages in Internet Explorer and Netscape Navigator. You are wise to test your Web pages in both browsers to see what they look like.

Tables as an Aid to Laying Out Web Pages

A great way to arrange text and objects on a Web page is to create a table, put objects and text into the table cells, and make sure that the AutoFit To Window option is turned on. By using a table to lay out text, you make putting text and objects in the right places easier. By applying the AutoFit To Window option, you make sure that your Web page fills the screen when people see it in their browsers.

Figure 16-5 demonstrates how the AutoFit To Window option works. Notice how the table cells—and consequently the text inside the cells—change shape to accommodate the different-size browser window. No matter which browser displays this Web page, all the content will be seen. Notice as well how tables can serve as a means of laying out text and graphics on the Web page. If I removed the boundaries of these tables, you would never know a table was used to lay out this Web page. You would think I was some kind of layout genius.

Follow these steps to activate the AutoFit To Window feature and make a Web table automatically fit the Web browser window:

1. Click anywhere in the table.
2. Choose Table | AutoFit | AutoFit To Window.

Chapter 14 explains how to make a table in Word 2000, change the size of the columns and rows, and insert the text. Here are a few tricks for laying out Web pages in tables:

■ **Use the Pencil Tool on the Tables and Borders Toolbar**   The Pencil tool is an excellent means of creating asymmetrical tables, since you can use it to split

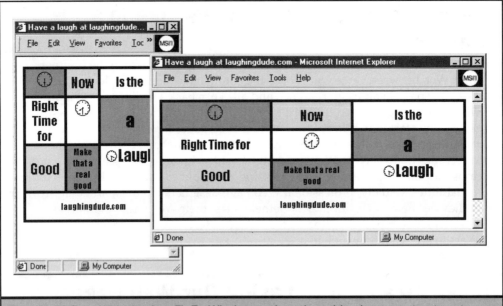

Figure 16-5. With the AutoFit To Window option, the table changes structure to accommodate the browser window

cells. The Eraser tool can also be useful. Use it to rub out the border between two cells and thereby merge cells.

■ **Leave a Few Empty Cells** Be sure to leave some cells empty to create white space on your Web page. Without the white space, a Web page soon gets too crowded and is hard to read.

■ **Remove Table Borders to Give Tables a "Floating Effect"** Remove the table borders when you are done laying out your Web page. That way, the graphics and text will appear to float on the page and only the cognoscenti will know that the layout looks so skillful because it was done with a table. To remove table borders, choose Table | Select | Table, click the down arrow beside the Border button on the Tables and Borders toolbar, and click the No Border button.

■ **Take Advantage of the Shading and Color Commands** Don't forget the shading and coloring commands. You can use them to decorate part of a table—part of a Web page, I mean. "Decorating a Table with Borders, Shading, and Color" in Chapter 14 describes the shading and color commands.

Hyperlinking Your Page to the Internet

A *hyperlink* is an electronic shortcut between two Web pages or two documents. You know when you have encountered a hyperlink on a Web page or Word document because the pointer changes into a hand. By clicking when the hand appears, you go to a different Web page or document.

These pages explain how to include hyperlinks on a Web page. Creating hyperlinks takes only a few steps and is easy to do. Read on to find out how to link to other places on a Web page, to other pages on your own Web site, and to other Web sites on the Internet.

Creating a Hyperlink to a Page on the Internet

Hyperlinks are the coolest thing about the Web. In fact, surfing the Web from hyperlink to hyperlink is what the Web is all about, because hyperlinks turn the Web into an adventure. Word offers a bunch of nice shortcuts for entering the address of the site with which you want to link. Follow these steps to link a Web page you created to another site on the Internet:

1. Select a word, phrase, or graphic to serve as the hyperlink. When visitors to your Web page click the words or graphic, they will go to another site on the Internet.

2. Choose Insert | Hyperlink, press CTRL-K, or right-click the word or graphic you selected and choose Hyperlink from the shortcut menu. You will see the Insert Hyperlink dialog box shown in Figure 16-6.

Note *Each page on the Internet has an address, also known as a URL, or uniform resource locator. You can tell the address of a Web page by looking in the Address box in the Web browser.*

3. Make sure that the Existing File Or Web Page button is selected. This button is located on in the upper-left corner of the dialog box.

4. Choose one of the following techniques for entering the address of the site that your hyperlink goes to. Some of the buttons in the dialog box are for inserting hyperlinks that go to other pages in your Web site, not pages on the Internet.

   ■ **Type The File Or Web Page Name**   Enter the address of the Web page, if you happen to know it, in this text box.

   ■ **Browsed Pages Button**   Click this button, scroll through the list of pages you visited in the last 90 days, and click the page's address if you happen to remember it. (Kind of scary how your computer keeps track of all the sites you visited. The addresses of these sites are kept in the C:\Windows\Temporary Internet Files folder and its subfolders.)

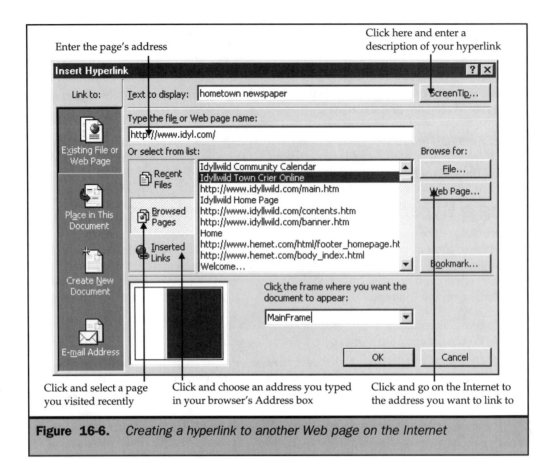

Enter the page's address

Click here and enter a
description of your hyperlink

Click and select a page
you visited recently

Click and choose an address you typed
in your browser's Address box

Click and go on the Internet to
the address you want to link to

Figure 16-6. *Creating a hyperlink to another Web page on the Internet*

- **Inserted Links Button** Click this button and choose the address of a Web site that you typed recently into the Address box of your Web browser. This list is considerably shorter than the others.

- **Web Page Button** Click this button to go on the Internet and find the page you want to link to. When you arrive at the page, its name appears in the Type The File Or Web Page Name text box.

5. Click the ScreenTip button and enter a phrase or a short sentence in the Set Hyperlink ScreenTip dialog box that describes the who, the what, or the where of your hyperlink. When a visitor moves the pointer over the hyperlink you are creating, he or she will see the text you enter. The brief description will help the viewer decide whether or not the Web site that the hyperlink goes to is worth visiting. Without the ScreenTip, visitors see a cryptic path name instead of a tidy description.

The Town Crier, newspaper of Idyllwild
California

checking up on my <u>hometown newspaper</u>, I happened to notice

6. If you want the page to which you are linking to appear in a frame instead of occupying the whole screen, choose the frame you want the page to appear in from the drop-down list at the bottom of the dialog box.

7. Click OK to insert the hyperlink.

To remove a hyperlink, right-click it and choose Hyperlink | Remove Hyperlink on the shortcut menu. You can also select the hyperlink (right-click it and choose Hyperlink | Select Hyperlink to do so), choose Insert | Hyperlink, and click the Remove Hyperlink button in the Edit Hyperlink dialog box.

You can also insert a hyperlink merely by typing its address and pressing the SPACEBAR. Word is trained to recognize common parts of Internet addresses—the at symbol (@), the letters "www" followed by a period, and the letters "http://". When you type these letters and press the SPACEBAR you get a hyperlink. If you prefer not to enter hyperlinks automatically, choose Tools | AutoCorrect, click the AutoFormat As You Type tab, and uncheck the Internet And Network Paths With Hyperlinks check box.

Editing and Maintaining Hyperlinks

Hyperlinks can be troublesome if you need to edit or alter them. After all, if you click a hyperlink and try to delete characters or add a word or two, Word thinks you want to activate the hyperlink and you end up being pushed onto the Internet.

To edit or maintain a hyperlink, right-click it and then choose Hyperlink on the shortcut menu. You will see a handful of commands that can be very useful for dealing with hyperlinks. Here's what you can do starting from the Hyperlink submenu:

- **Change the Destination of a Hyperlink**   Click the Edit Hyperlink command to open the Edit Hyperlink dialog box, where you can choose a new destination for the hyperlink. The Edit Hyperlink dialog box looks and works exactly like the Insert Hyperlink dialog box (see Figure 16-6).

- **Change the Text of a Hyperlink**   Click the Edit Hyperlink command and, in the Edit Hyperlink dialog box, enter a new word or two in the Text To Display text box.

- **Select a Hyperlink Without Activating It**   Click the Select Hyperlink command. The words in the hyperlink are highlighted. Now you can change fonts, for example, or italicize the words in the link.

- **Copy a Hyperlink**   Click the Copy Hyperlink command. The hyperlink is copied to the Clipboard. You can paste it elsewhere.

Inserting a Hyperlink to Another Place in Your Web Site

Creating a hyperlink to a different place on the same Web page or to a different page in your Web site is easy. It's easy, I should say, as long as the destination of the hyperlink has been assigned a heading style or been bookmarked. If the graphic or text to which you want to make a hyperlink is not a heading, select the graphic or text and create a bookmark around it (see "Bookmarks for Getting Around" in Chapter 2).

Keeping all your Web site files and graphics in the same working folder is especially important when you insert hyperlinks. Unless two pages that are linked together are in the same folder, the link will not work after you upload your Web pages to your ISP.

Follow these steps to insert a hyperlink to a different page or to a different location on the same page:

1. Select the words, phrase, or graphic that will form the hyperlink. If necessary, type a new phrase or enter a graphic. Type the word or phrase in a frame if a frame is where you want the link to appear.

2. Choose Insert | Hyperlink, press CTRL-K, or right-click the word or graphic you selected and choose Hyperlink from the shortcut menu. The Insert Hyperlink dialog box appears (see Figure 16-6).

3. Create the link to a place on the same Web page or to a different Web page on your site:

   ■ **To a Different Web Page on Your Site**   Click the Exiting File or Web Page icon under Link To, and then click the File button. In the Link to File dialog box, find and select the name of the Web page you want to link to. Then click OK.

   ■ **To a Location on the Same Web Page**   Click the Place In This Document icon under Link To. A list of headings and bookmarks on your Web page appears in the Insert Hyperlink dialog box (click the plus signs next to the words "Headings" and "Bookmarks" to see all the headings and bookmarks). Then click a heading or bookmark.

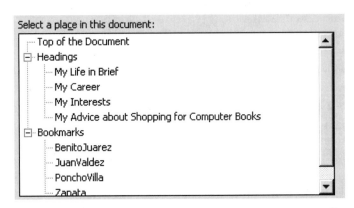

4. Click the ScreenTip button and enter a brief description of the hyperlink. Anyone who points to the link will see the description you enter in a pop-up box.

5. From the Click The Frame drop-down list at the bottom of the Insert Hyperlink dialog box, choose a frame if you have carved your Web page into frames and you want the page to which you are linking to appear in a frame, not in its own window.

6. Click OK to insert the hyperlink.

Changing the Look of the Web Pages

Word offers two ways to change the look of a Web page. You can choose a color, background pattern, or picture, or you can visit the Theme dialog box and select a full-blown design for the various elements—the headings, bulleted items, and hyperlinks, for example. Read on to see how to turn a simple Web page into a high-fashion boutique.

Decorating Pages with a Background Color, Texture, or Picture

To spruce up a Web page by giving it a color background, a texture background, or a picture background, start by choosing Format | Background. You will see the Color Palette menu. From here you can take off and do some serious interior decorating:

- **Color Background**   Click a color on the Color Palette menu. If none of the colors tickle your fancy, click More Colors at the bottom of the menu and select a color in the Colors dialog box.

- **Texture Background**   Choose Fill Effects at the bottom of the Color Palette menu, click the Texture tab, and choose a texture. Be sure to scroll to the bottom of the list. Word offers 24 textures in all.

Contrast is everything on a computer monitor. Some of the textures in the Fill Effects dialog box are too busy to do any good as Web Page backgrounds. Graphics and text can get lost in a background that is too fanciful or busy.

■ **Picture Background**   Choose Fill Effects at the bottom of the Color Palette menu. As shown in Figure 16-7, click the Picture tab in the Fill Effects dialog box, and click the Select Picture button. In the Select Picture dialog box, locate and select the picture file to use as a background on your Web page, and then click the Insert button. Click OK in the Fill Effects dialog box. You can use .BMP, .GIF, .JPG, or any other Windows–compatible graphic file as a background.

Caution   *A picture can require many hundreds or thousands of kilobytes. Therefore, pictures can take a long time to download and be seen in a browser.*

If you regret choosing a background for your Web page and you want to start all over, choose Format | Background and click the No Fill button on the Color Palette. By the way, the Clip Gallery offers a category called Web Backgrounds that you can use to decorate Web pages. "Handling Graphics and Clip Art in Documents" in Chapter 13 explains the Clip Gallery.

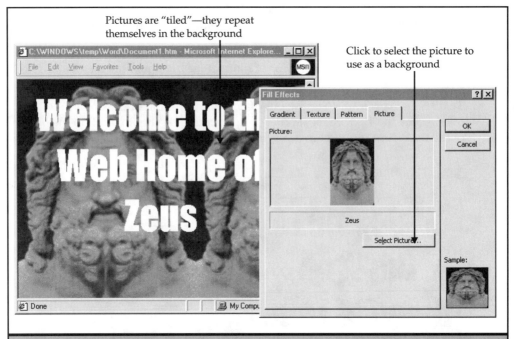

Figure 16-7.   *Besides colors and themes, you can use a picture or clip art image as the background of a Web page*

Choosing a Background Theme for Your Web Page

A background theme is a "ready-to-wear" design. When you choose a background theme, all elements of the Web page are overhauled—the headings, bulleted items, and the background as well. If you created your Web site with the help of the Web Page Wizard, you already know about themes, since the Web Page Wizard gives you the opportunity to choose a theme as you create Web pages.

Insert the Office 2000 CD-ROM into your computer and follow these steps to choose a theme for your Web page:

1. Choose Format | Theme. The Theme dialog box appears (see Figure 16-3).

2. Under Choose A Theme, click a few theme names until you find a theme you like. Theme samples appear on the right side of the dialog box.

3. When you have found your theme, you can tweak it to your liking by checking or unchecking the three check boxes at the bottom of the Theme dialog box:

   ■ **Vivid Colors** Offers muted or vibrant variations of graphic elements in the theme.

   ■ **Active Graphics** Turns off and on the .GIF animations or animated cartoons in the theme, if the theme includes animations.

   ■ **Background Image** Removes or restores the page background.

4. Click OK to apply the new theme to your Web page.

Dividing a Web Page into Frames

A *frame* is a separate window that appears to the side of a Web page. These days, most Web sites include a frame for navigation purposes. By clicking hyperlinks in the frame, you can go from page to page in the Web site. The frame is always there, lurking on the side or top of the screen so you can click a hyperlink and quickly go elsewhere. Think of a frame as a signpost that is always there for the people who visit your Web site to see. By clicking a destination on the sign, they can travel somewhere else.

These pages explain how to create a frame for your Web site, change the location of the frame, place headings in a frame, adjust the size of frames, and remove frames.

Adding a Frame to a Web Site

When you create a frame, you create a new file as well. The new file comprises your original file and the new frame. Follow these steps to add a frame to a Web site:

1. Either choose View | Toolbars Frames or right-click a toolbar and choose Frames to display the Frames toolbar shown in Figure 16-8.

2. Depending on where you want the frame to appear, click a button on the Frames toolbar: New Frame Left, New Frame Right, New Frame Above, or

New Frame Below. Figure 16-8 shows an unlikely Web site in which all four frames are used. Usually, the frame appears either on the left or above.

Note *When you create a frame, you create a new Web page. Notice in the title bar that the Web page now has a generic name—Document1, for example.*

3. Choose File | Save or click the Save button, enter a descriptive name for your new Web page in the Save As dialog box, click the Change Title button and enter a title for the Web page, click OK, and click Save. Be sure to save the new file in the folder with the rest of your Web stuff.

When you want to work the Web page, open it under its new name, but when you want to see the Web page as well as its frame, open the file you named and saved in step 3. The frame file you created always shows the changes you made to the original file.

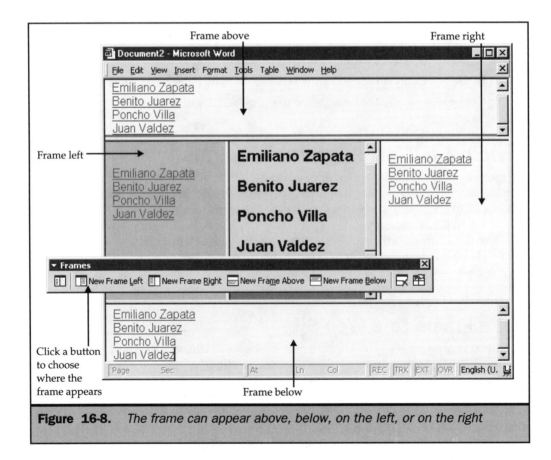

Figure 16-8. *The frame can appear above, below, on the left, or on the right*

Deleting a Frame

To delete a frame, click it and then click the Delete Frame button on the Frames toolbar or choose Format | Frames | Delete Frame. If you made entries in the frame, Word asks you to save the contents of the frame before you delete it. Save the contents in your Castoffs folder in case you regret deleting the frame and need it later. You can't delete a frame until you have saved its contents first. Nor can you choose Edit | Undo to undo the Delete command after the frame is dead and gone.

Entering Hyperlinks and Other Stuff in a Frame

A frame is simply a narrower version of a Web page. As such, you can put company logos, pithy sayings, or whatnot in a frame. You can also change the background color or enter hyperlinks to other parts of your Web site or to sites on the Internet. Go to it,

Generating a Table of Contents for a Frame

As long as the headings on your Web page were assigned heading styles (Chapter 12 describes styles), you can generate a table of contents (TOC) from the headings and place it in a frame. Visitors to your Web site can click hyperlinks in the table of contents frame and go immediately to the headings on your Web page.

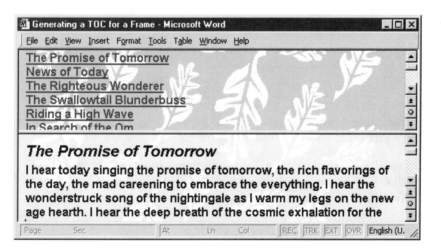

To generate a table of contents, click in the main page and then click the Table of Contents In Frame button on the Frames toolbar. Whether you like it or not, a new frame with the table of contents appears on the left side of the screen. To put the table of contents in the frame where you want it to go, select the table of contents, click the Cut button on the Standard toolbar, and paste the table of contents in the frame where you want it to appear. If necessary, click the frame you created when you generated the table of contents and then click the Delete Frame button on the Frames toolbar to remove the frame.

but remember that a frame takes up valuable space onscreen. Don't allow entries in the frame to get in the way of the main page.

Handling Frame Borders and Frame Size

To adjust the size of a frame, click its border and drag the border up or down or left or right. Beyond that, you can open the Frame Properties dialog box and fool with the options there to tell Word how to handle frame borders. To open the Frame Properties dialog box, click in the frame and then click the Frame Properties button on the Frames toolbar or choose Format | Frames | Frame Properties.

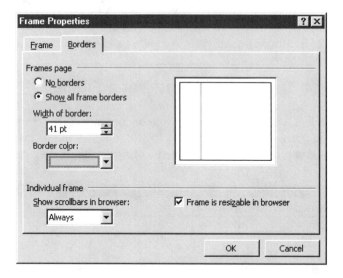

Take advantage of these options on the Borders tab in the Frame Properties dialog box to tell Word how to handle frame borders:

- **Frames Page**   Click the No Borders option if you want to remove the frame border. This option is for using frames like table cells as a layout tool for decorating Web pages.

- **Width Of Border**   Enter a measurement to adjust the width of the border itself (not the size of the frame).

- **Border Color**   Choose a color from the drop-down menu if you want to get away from the standard gray border.

- **Show Scrollbars In Browser**   By default, scroll bars only appear if the contents of the frame cannot be seen all at once in the browser window. However, you can choose Always to make the scroll bars appear whether or not all the contents can be seen, or Never to prevent scroll bars from appearing.

- **Frame Is Resizable In Browser**   Make sure this check box is checked so that the frame size is flexible and can change size as the browser window changes size.

Uploading Your Web Pages to an ISP

Uploading means to send Web pages across the phone lines to an Internet service provider so the pages can be made available on the Web. ISPs store Web pages on a dedicated computer called a *server*. As the start of this chapter explained, you need an account with an ISP or an online service like America Online in order to post pages on the Web. The following pages explain how to upload your files by using the Web Publishing Wizard.

Before you start uploading your Web pages, you need to know the following:

- Your user name or user ID (the part of your e-mail address that appears before the at symbol, @).
- The password you use to log in.
- The URL (uniform resource locator) address of your Web site.
- The name of your Internet service provider's Web server and the path for uploading files to your ISP's Web server.

Tip   *If you are unsure in any way, shape, or form what you need to do to upload Web pages, call your ISP. Any ISP worth the name is required to help its customers upload pages to the Internet.*

Follow these steps to upload Web pages to your ISP with the Web Publishing Wizard:

1. Dial up your ISP on the Internet.
2. Click the Start button and choose Programs | Accessories | Internet Tools | Web Publishing Wizard.
3. Click Next in the first wizard dialog box.
4. In the Select A File Or Folder dialog box, click the Browse Folders button if you are uploading files to your Web site for the first time; if you changed some of your Web pages, choose Browse Files to upload just a few files
5. In the Browse dialog box, find the folder or file on your computer that you want to upload and double-click it. You will be returned to the Select A File Or Folder dialog window. The name of the folder or file appears in the File Or Folder Name box.

Note   *Make sure the Include Subfolders box is checked if you are uploading your site for the first time or you are uploading new pages with graphics subfolders.*

6. Click the Next button. You see the Name The Web Server dialog box.
7. Type the name of your ISP in the Descriptive Name box and click the Next button.

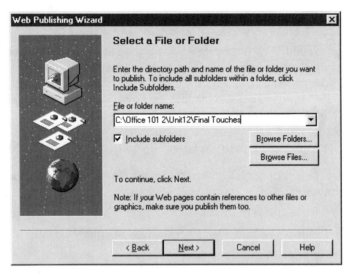

8. In the Specify The URL And Directory Window dialog box, type the address to which you are supposed to upload Web pages in the URL or Internet Address box. Only your ISP knows for sure what the address is, but you probably type something like **ftp.***YourISPName*.

9. Type in the name of the directory on your computer that contains your final Web site files.

10. Click the Next button.

11. In the Connect dialog box, enter your User ID and password, and click Connect to go on the Internet.

Shortly, you'll see the Publishing Files window and its familiar image of paper files being tossed form place to place. As long as the Web Publishing Wizard doesn't encounter any glitches, a dialog box tells you, "Web Publishing Wizard has successfully published your files to the Web server."

Exam # MOUS Exam Objectives Explored in Chapter 16

Objective	Heading	Practice File
Use Web Page Preview	"Seeing What Your Web Page Looks Like in a Browser"	
Save as Web Page	"Creating a Web Page from a Word Document"	
Create a hyperlink	"Hyperlinking Your Page to the Internet"	

* Denotes an Expert exam objective.

Ten Places on the Internet to Get Free Clip Art and Web Art

Hey buddy? Want some free clip art? Want some .GIF animations you can stick on your Web pages? Here are ten places on the Web where you can get clip art and Web art for free.

1. BARRY'S CLIPART SERVER   Besides the art, you will find a FAQ (frequently asked questions) page devoted to helping newcomers construct Web pages.
Address: **www.barrysclipart.com**

2. BIGNOSEBIRD.COM   This site claims to be "The strangest name in Web authoring resources." Here you will find free graphics, scripts, MIDI files, and tutorials.
Address: **bignosebird.com**

3. CLIPARTCONNECTION   A very crowded Web page with all kinds of free stuff divided into many categories. You will find many links here to other sites that offer free art.
Address: **clipartconnection.com**

4. DHD PHOTO GALLERY   Lots of free photos categorized very tidily into many categories.
Address: **http://www.hd.org/Damon/photos**

5. ECLIPSED DIGITAL   This site is the starting point for going to three animation sites that offer 19,000 files altogether: Animation Factory, Animation Artists, and Gifartist.com.
Address: **www.eclipsed.com**

6. EQUIZOTIC   A specialty clip art and background graphics site that offers images of horses, horses, and more horses! For the horsey set.
Address: **www.equizotic.com/free.html**

7. THE INTERNATIONAL CLIP ART SITE   Presents links to numerous clip art sites throughout the world. Interestingly, the sites are categorized by country. An enterprising person with a lot of time on his or her hands could do a comparison of clip art from different nations by starting from this site.
Address: **clipart.tudogs.com**

8. PAMBYTES FREE WEB GRAPHICS   Offers freeware images of all kinds for use in the development of commercial Web sites and personal Web sites. Be sure to visit the tutorial that explains adding text to buttons.
Address: **www.tgn.net/~pambytes**

9. REALLYBIG.COM   Features many content areas with over 3000 resources for Web site builders, from beginners to experienced. Categories include clip art, backgrounds, icons, CGI, animation, counters, fonts, WYSIWYG editors, HTML, Java, buttons, photos, and other subjects.
Address: **reallybig.com**

10. THE WEBSITE LUNATIC   The Grand Central Station of clip art! Here you will find links to some of the coolest clip art, animations, and graphics on the Web. The site is updated often and includes a "Site of the Day."
Address: **http://www.biginfo.net/clipart.html**

The
Complete
Reference

Chapter 17

Creating Fancy
Web Pages

A Web page doesn't have to be drab looking. With a tweak here and a tweak there, you can turn a plain Web page into a colorful place that attracts Web surfers. To that end, this chapter offers a half-dozen techniques for making Web pages livelier. You will find instructions for putting dividers and banners on Web pages, laying down a bit of scrolling marquee text on the page, and presenting images in thumbnails. Also in this chapter is advice for turning a Web page into a multimedia carnival with video and sound. Finally, this chapter offers a brief tutorial in the Hypertext Markup Language (HTML) and explains how you can make sure your Web pages get "found" by people searching the Internet.

Ways to Spruce Up a Web Page

Think of the World Wide Web as desktop publishing on steroids. On the Web, everyone can be a publisher, art director, writer, and editor. Word offers many tools for turning a humdrum Web page into a page that attracts people's attention. On these pages are instructions for drawing rules on Web pages, putting marquee text on a page, and including a banner or two.

Be sure to read "Changing the Look of the Web Pages" in Chapter 16. It explains how to change the background color of a page or give it a predesigned "theme."

Putting a Web Divider across the Page

Take a look at most Web pages on the Internet and you will find one or two Web dividers that separate one part of a page from another. Web dividers are a great way to distinguish one subject from the next on a page. When a viewer sees the horizontal line, he or she knows that the Web page is entering a new area of interest. On some sites, Web dividers are color-coded so that viewers know, for example, that part of a Web page pertains to instructional material and another part lists Web addresses or hyperlinks. Figure 17-1 shows examples of Web dividers.

Follow these steps to insert a Web divider:

1. Click on your Web page roughly where you want the horizontal line to go. Make sure there is space on the page for a Web divider.

2. Choose Insert | Picture | Clip Art. You will see the Clip Gallery dialog box.

Note *"Handling Graphics and Clip Art in Documents" in Chapter 13 describes the Clip Gallery in detail.*

3. Scroll to the bottom of the dialog box and click the Web Dividers icon. A dialog box appears with the 60 Web dividers that Word offers. You can also reach this dialog box by choosing Format | Borders and Shading, clicking the Borders tab

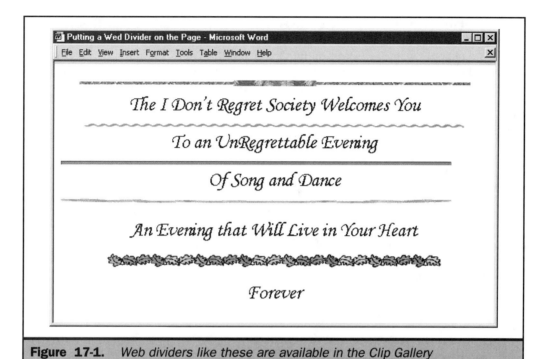

Figure 17-1.   *Web dividers like these are available in the Clip Gallery*

in the Borders and Shading dialog box, and clicking the Horizontal Line button. However, if you go this route, the dialog box is called Horizontal Line.

4. Find the Web divider you like, click it, and click the Insert Clip button.

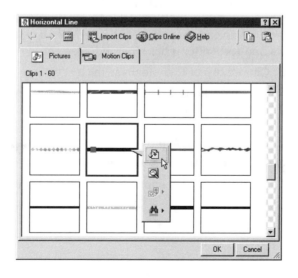

Most of the Web dividers are centered on the Web page, but some are flush with the left side of the page. All adjust their size as the browser window in which they are displayed changes size. See "Positioning Objects on the Page" in Chapter 13 if you want to change the position of a Web divider, and "Changing the Size and Shape of Objects" in the same chapter if you want to change the divider's size and shape.

If you get bored with the Web dividers in the Clip Gallery dialog box, you can make your own by calling on the tools on the Drawing toolbar. See "Drawing Lines and Shapes," also in lucky Chapter 13.

Scrolling Text for a Marquee Effect

Have you ever seen a Web page with scrolling text that marches across the page over and over and over again? You can put scrolling text on your Web pages as well, although I should warn you that not all browsers can display scrolling text. Only Internet Explorer 3.0 and above can display such text. You can't see scrolling text in any version of Netscape Navigator.

Follow these steps to make text scroll on a Web page:

1. Click on your Web page where you want the scrolling text to appear.

2. Display the Web Tools toolbar. To do so, choose View | Toolbars | Web Tools or right-click a toolbar and choose Web tools.

3. Click the Scrolling Text button, the rightmost button on the toolbar. You see the Scrolling Text dialog box shown in Figure 17-2.

4. Choose options and enter text in the dialog box to tell Word what the text is and how to make it scroll. The Preview box shows what your scrolling text looks like and how it will behave onscreen.

   ■ **Behavior**   Choose Scroll, the default option, to make text emerge one character at a time and cross the screen; choose Slide to make text cease scrolling after it appears onscreen; or choose Alternate to make text appear to rock back and forth after it has emerged onscreen.

   ■ **Direction**   Choose Left or Right to make the text emerge from the left or right.

   ■ **Background Color**   Choose Auto to make text scroll on the screen without appearing in a box. If you choose a color, the text appears in a box—a box the color you chose.

   ■ **Loop**   Choose a number to tell Word how many times to make the text scroll, or choose Infinite to make it scroll until the cows come home.

   ■ **Speed**   Adjust the slider to change the speed at which text appears onscreen.

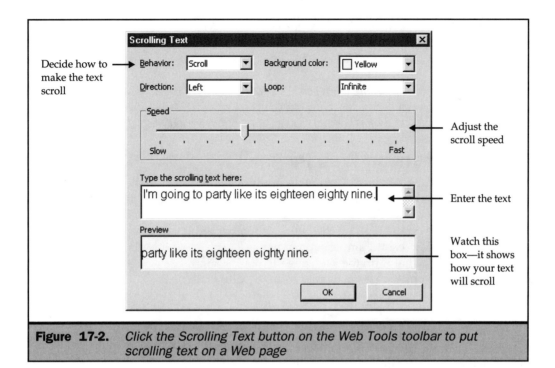

Figure 17-2.   *Click the Scrolling Text button on the Web Tools toolbar to put scrolling text on a Web page*

- **Type The Scrolling Text Here**   Type the text in this box. Make sure your message contains less than 30 words. Long messages take a long time to download. Besides, by making your message longer than 30 words, you will try people's patience.

5. Click OK.

Scrolling text appears in a frame (the kind of frame that drop caps appear in, not a Web page frame). Follow these instructions to alter the scrolling text:

- **Editing the Text and Altering Its Behavior Onscreen**   Double-click the scrolling text to make the Scrolling Text dialog box appear (see Figure 17-2). In the dialog box, choose options or enter text to change the scrolling text.

- **Changing the Size or Location of the Scrolling Text**   Click the Design Mode button on the Web Tools toolbar to see the scroll frame, and then drag a black selection handle to change the size of the frame or drag the frame to move it elsewhere. Click the Exit Design Mode button to make the text scroll again.

- **Changing the Font and Font Size of Characters**   Click on the text and then choose a new font and font size from the Font and Font Size menus on the Formatting toolbar.

DEVELOPING WEB PAGES
WITH WORD 2000

■ **Deleting the Scrolling Text**   Click the Design Mode button on the Web Tools toolbar to see the scroll frame, and then click the scroll frame and press the DELETE key.

Scrolling text is a nuisance when you are working on a Web page. To keep the text from distracting you while you are laying out your Web page, right-click it and choose Stop on the shortcut menu. Right-click and choose Play when you want the text to scroll again.

Including Banners on Web Pages

As Figure 17-3 shows, a *banner* is a large decorative graphic found at the top or in the margin of a Web page. On commercial Web sites, banners often serve as mini-billboards. Importing a banner from the Clip Gallery is easy, and you can also fashion your own banners by calling on the tools on the Drawing toolbar or by using another graphics program such as Microsoft Paint. Use a banner as a headline that calls attention to itself and that describes what is on the Web page.

Follow these steps to insert a banner from the Clip Gallery:

1. Click where you want the banner to go.

2. Choose Insert | Picture | Clip Art.

3. Scroll to the bottom of the Insert Clip Gallery dialog box and click the Web Banners icon. You will see various Web banners.

4. Click the banner you want and then click the Insert Clip button.

Figure 17-3.   *Examples of banners, the decorative graphics you can put on Web pages*

"Changing the Size and Shape of Objects" in Chapter 13 explains how to change a banner's size and shape. "Positioning Objects on the Page" in the same chapter explains how to move a banner.

If you think that the banners in the Clip Gallery are kind of drab, you can find more banners by clicking the Clips Online button in on Clip Gallery dialog box and going online to get clip art (see "Going Online to Search for Clip Art" in Chapter 13). When you arrive at the Clip Gallery Live Web site, enter **banner** as the keyword.

Check out "Ten Places on the Internet to Get Free Clip Art and Web Art" at the end of Chapter 16 for more sources of banners. You can also find banners on the many clip art CD-ROMs that are for sale in computer stores.

Including Thumbnail Images on Pages

As Figure 17-4 shows, a *thumbnail* is a smaller "preview" of a larger graphics or photo image. When you click a thumbnail, you'll go to another Web page where the graphic you clicked on is shown at full size. A thumbnail image is really a hyperlink.

A Photographer's Thumbnail Journey

Click on a thumbnail image below to see the full size version

Sunrise/Moonset

Death Valley Shadows

Grace Cathedral

Hearst Castle

Japanese Village

Japanese Temple

Photo Sketch

Date Palms

Birds of Paradise

Figure 17-4. *With thumbnails, visitors can choose which graphic or photo they want to see*

Thumbnails can be very useful on Web sites because you can fit many on the page, they give an idea of the many graphics that are available on the site, they give visitors a choice of what to see, and they download faster than full-size graphics.

Do the following to put thumbnail images on a Web page:

1. Create a smaller version of each graphic or photo that you want to present as a thumbnail. Make sure your images are large enough that visitors can tell what they are but not so large that they occupy too much space on the screen. See "Changing the Size and Shape of Objects" in Chapter 13 if you need help. When you choose File | Save As to save the smaller version of your graphic and photo under a different name, put a "T" after the name so you know that the image is thumbnail size.

2. Create a Web page or different Web pages for the large-size graphics or photos.

3. Lay out the thumbnail images on a Web page. The easiest way to lay out thumbnails is to do so in a table. See "Tables as an Aid to Laying Out Web Pages" in Chapter 16. You can also use the Align and Distribute commands on the Drawing toolbar to make sure the thumbnails are aligned and distributed correctly on the Web page. See "Positioning Objects on the Page" in Chapter 13.

4. Create a hyperlink from each thumbnail image to the Web page where its larger relative is. See "Inserting a Hyperlink to Another Place in Your Web Site" in Chapter 16.

Jazzing Up a Web Site with Sound and Multimedia

Multimedia is one of those buzzwords that pops up when computer people start talking. Technically, the term refers to a CD-ROM or Web site that presents material in more than one medium. For example, a CD-ROM about music with essays about composers and recordings of the composers' work is a multimedia CD-ROM. Similarly, a Web site that presents text, pictures, video, and sound is considered a multimedia Web site.

A Web site that presents material in more than one medium can be a very interesting place to visit, but you have to take into consideration one or two things before you dabble in multimedia. First, multimedia places demands on visitors' computer hardware. Not all computers have speakers for playing sound. Not all computers have video cards and can play video. Second, video files, sound files, and .GIF animation files can be very large and take a long time to download. For that reason, visitors to a site can grow impatient and move on before the multimedia files have finished downloading.

*Visit the Macromedia site at **www.macromedia.com** for examples of multimedia files that Web sites can play back.*

These pages explain how to play background music for visitors who come to your Web site and how to include a video clip on your Web site.

Adding Background Sound to a Web Page

Playing background sounds or music for visitors to a Web site is kind of neat, but care should be taken about the size of the sound file and the annoyance factor. A poor-quality sound clip that repeats itself over and over causes visitors to flee a site in nothing flat. You can use these types of sound files on a Web page created with Word: .WAV, .MID, .AU, .AIF, .RMI, .SND, and .MP2.

That a sound file or other multimedia file can perform well on your computer is no guarantee that it will play satisfactorily on the Internet. Always test a multimedia file online before you make it part of a Web site.

Follow these steps to make background sounds or background music for a Web site:

1. Put the cursor in the upper-left corner of your Web page. That way, if you need to remove or alter the sound later, you will know to look for it in the upper-left corner.

2. Display the Web Tools toolbar. To do so, choose View | Toolbars | Web Tools.

3. Click the Sound button, the second button from the right on the Web Tools toolbar. The Background Sound dialog box shown in Figure 17-5 appears.

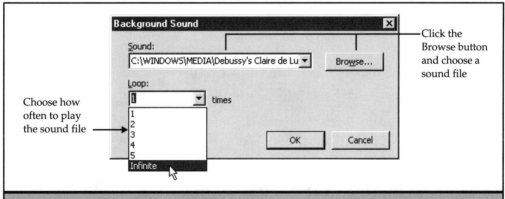

Figure 17-5. *Including a sound file in a document is easy, but make sure you choose one that won't annoy visitors to your Web site*

4. Click the Browse button. The Open File dialog box opens to the C:\Windows\Media folder. Windows stashes its own sound files in this folder.

5. Either select a file in the Media folder and click Open, or locate another sound file in the File Open dialog box, select it, and click Open to return to the Background Sound dialog box.

6. From the Loop drop-down list, either choose the number of times to play the file or choose Infinite to play it over and over and over and over again.

7. Click OK and the sound starts playing.

Suppose you want to change sounds or change the number of times the sound plays in a row? For that matter, suppose you want to stop playing the sound altogether? Better follow these steps:

1. Click the Design Mode button, the leftmost button on the Web Tools toolbar. The sound stops playing and a rectangle with a speaker in it appears to show where the sound file has been embedded in your Web page. You will have to look pretty closely to find the rectangle and speaker if you didn't follow my advice and stick the sound file in the upper-left corner of your Web page.

Pure Rockin' Sounds

2. Click the rectangle with the speaker in it.

3. With the black selection handles showing and the sound box selected, either alter the sound or silence it:

   - **Change the Sound** Click the Sound button on the Web Tools toolbar. You will see the Background Sound dialog box (see Figure 17-5). Choose a new sound or a new Loop option and click OK.

   - **Stop Playing the Sound** Press the DELETE key. The sound box is removed from your Web page along with the sound file.

4. Click the Exit Design Mode button on the Web Tools toolbar.

By the way, you can also insert a sound clip from the Clip Gallery. To do so, choose Insert | Picture | Clip Art, click the Sounds tab in the Clip Gallery dialog box, and choose a sound.

Including a Video Clip on a Web Page

Including a video clip on a Web page adds to the WOW factor, but video clips are not just large, they are huge. A mere five seconds of video requires a 100KB file (and that's without any sound). Whether a visitor to your site will wait long enough for the video file to download depends on how badly he or she wants to see the video. You can include these types of video files on a Web page: .AVI, .MOV, .MOVIE, .MPG, .MPEG, and .QT.

Tip *Here's a traffic advisory for the Internet: Take the alternate route and use Apple Corporation's QuickTime video .MOV files instead of Microsoft's .AVI files. The .MOV format is the standard on the Internet. More people can play .MOV video clips.*

Follow these basic instructions to attach a video clip to a Web page:

1. Click on your Web page roughly where you want the video clip to go.
2. Choose View | Toolbars | Web Tools to display the Web Tools toolbar.
3. Click the Movie button, the third button from the right on the Web Tools toolbar. You will see the Movie Clip dialog box shown in Figure 17-6.
4. Click the Browse button and, in the File Open dialog box, locate the video file, select it, and click the Open button. If you are looking for a video file you inserted recently, you might be able to find it by clicking the down arrow next to the Movie text box.

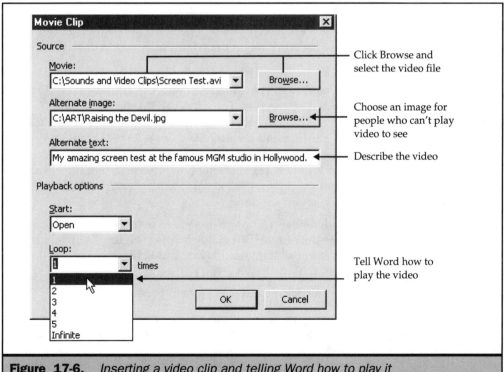

Figure 17-6. *Inserting a video clip and telling Word how to play it*

5. Click the Browse button next to the Alternative Image text box, and, in the File Open dialog box, find a graphic image to appear in place of the video clip if the video clip cannot be played. Not everyone can play video clips on their computer. By choosing an alternative image, you make sure that your Web page doesn't show a gaping hole to those who come to your page and are unable to see the video.

6. In the Alternate Text text box, type a few enticing words to describe your video clip. The words will appear on the Web page as the video clip is downloading. Try to write something that will encourage visitors to stick around while the video clip downloads.

7. Choose Playback options:

   ■ **Start** Choose Open to start downloading the video clip as soon as the Web page is opened; Mouse-Over to start downloading the video when the visitor moves his or her mouse pointer over the movie; or Both to play the video when the Web page opens and again when the visitor moves his or her pointer over the movie.

   ■ **Loop** Select the number of times to play the video or choose Infinite to play it continuously.

8. Click OK.

The video clip starts playing. Very likely, you will need to change the size of the video screen and perhaps move it elsewhere on the page. Follow these instructions to do so:

■ **Change the Size and Position of the Video Screen** Click the Design Mode button, the leftmost button on the Web Tools toolbar. To change the size of the screen, drag a corner handle (not a side handle, since that changes the proportions of the video screen and distorts the video). To change the position of the screen, drag it elsewhere. You might have to right-click, choose Format control, and click the In Front Of Text option on the Layout tab of the Format Control dialog box to get the screen to move on your Web page. Click the Exit Design mode button when you are done.

■ **Choose a Different Video File or Change the Video Settings** Double-click the video clip. You'll see the Movie Clip dialog box (see Figure 17-6), where you can change video clips or chose different Playback options.

■ **Remove the Video from the Page** Click the Design Mode button on the Web Tools toolbar, click the video screen to select it, and press the DELETE key.

You can also go to the Clip Gallery to insert a video clip. Choose Insert | Picture | Clip Art, click the Motion Clips tab in the Clip Gallery dialog box, select the clip you want, and click the Insert Clip button.

Coding Web Pages on Your Own

Word 2000 goes a long way to help you make a basic but appealing Web page. However, you may decide to learn Hypertext Markup Language (HTML) tags and code parts of your Web pages on your own. The tags tell Web browsers how to display the content of Web pages. Knowing a few important HTML tags and how to apply them can help you make your site a better one. Maintaining a site is certainly easier if you know a few HTML tags.

I hope that learning about HTML tags will encourage you to explore Web page development on your own a bit more. As the start of Chapter 16 points out, Word 2000 is not really a Web development tool, but it can be a starting point for learning how to develop Web pages. These pages give you a basic introduction to HTML tags. After briefly describing the most important HTML tags, I'll explain how you can view the styles yourself and enter HTML tags directly into Web pages.

 Caution   *When you turn a Word document into a Web page, the program inserts all kinds of needless HTML code. Literally, you will find 90 lines of miscellaneous proprietary gunk for every one line of content. When you want to study the codes, look at sites that weren't produced in Word.*

Understanding HTML Tags

HTML is not so much a programming language as it is a set of desktop publishing style tags. The tags tell Web browsers how to display the content of Web pages. For example, tags tell the browser to display text in boldface, make a table, display a graphic, or to fetch a page in Cyberspace.

When a browser sees the HTML angle brackets, it knows that the brackets contain instructions for displaying text, photographs, or multimedia. Most style tags are found in sets, with an opening tag and a closing tag. The closing tag begins with a forward slash. This illustration shows the opening and closing tag of the TITLE style.

Viewing the HTML Tags at a Web Site

The next time you are surfing the Internet, choose View | Source to open the Notepad so you can see the HTML tags and codes that were used to construct the site.

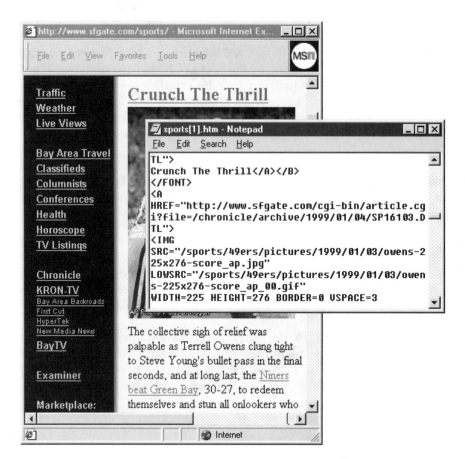

What you'll see seems like a daunting array of gibberish at first, but look closer. Scroll down the page and try to find a headline or something else you recognize from the Web page. Notice the angle brackets (<>) that hold the HTML tags, attributes, and values inside them. At the top of the Notepad window, you will find the HTML, HEAD, and META tags (discussed shortly), that are at the top of every Web page. The more you look at HTML codes and tags, the more familiar they become.

Tags Found on Every Web Page

As Figure 17-7 shows, a handful of required HTML style tags are found on every Web page. Required tags tell the browser what follows:

HTML Style Tag	Purpose
<HTML> </HTML>	Announces to the browser that the contents of the file can be read by it. These tags are the first and last tags placed on every Web page.
<HEAD> </HEAD>	Contains technical information such as TITLE tags, META tags, and, optionally, JavaScript code. The content between the HEAD tags is invisible to viewers and is only seen by the browser.
<TITLE> </TITLE>	Marks what appears in the title bar at the top of every browser.
<META>	Marks the starting point for keywords and phrases that describe the Web site. The keywords and phrases help search engines index the contents of Web pages. There is no closing META tag.
<BODY> </BODY>	Tells the browser where to start displaying the visible content of the Web file.

Within the opening BODY tag are many attributes whose job is to give color instructions to the browser. These attributes are placed within the BODY tag, so they do not need angle brackets. Color instruction attributes are as follows:

HTML Color Attribute	Purpose
BGCOLOR=color	Determines the background color of the file. There are 256 possible colors that can be displayed on your page.
BACKGROUND=*background*.gif	Lists the name of the GIF graphic file that appears in the background of the Web page.
TEXT=*color*	Determines the color of the text. (To change the color of individual letters, words, or paragraphs, use the <FONT COLOR="#*color*"> </FONT> tags.)

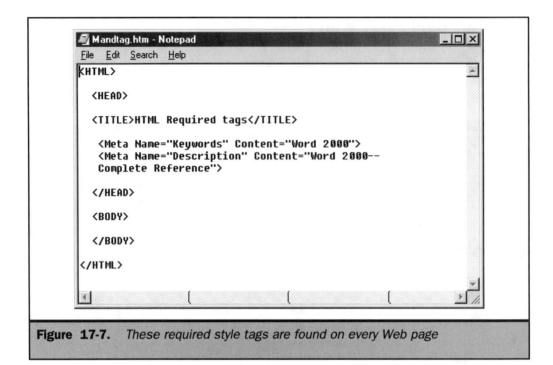

Figure 17-7.   *These required style tags are found on every Web page*

HTML Color Attribute	Purpose
ALINK=*color*	Determines the color of the active hyperlink. The active color is the temporary color of the hyperlink as you click on it with the mouse.
LINK=*color*	Determines the color of an unvisited hyperlink on a browser. Typically, the LINK attribute is dark blue.
VLINK=*color*	Determines the color of a hyperlink that has already been visited. This attribute is usually displayed as violet.

Line Spacing Tags

The following HTML tags are found after the opening BODY tag. They serve to break up the content by placing empty lines between lines of text.

HTML Tag	Purpose
<P> </P>	The PARAGRAPH tag creates a double-line break between lines of text or images. Only one <P> tag can be used to create horizontal space between paragraphs or images. For multiple line spaces between paragraphs, use the tag. The closing </P> is optional.
 	The BREAK tag creates a single line break. The rest of the line continues on the next line below, starting at the left margin. Two BREAK tags are the equivalent of one PARAGRAPH tag. You can use as many BREAK tags as you wish to create more horizontal space on a Web page.

Heading Tags

As Figure 17-8 shows, heading tags mark the headings on a Web page. Heading tags boldface the text and make it larger as well. You can combine other tags with the heading tags to italicize or underline text, for example. A double-line space appears after the heading tag.

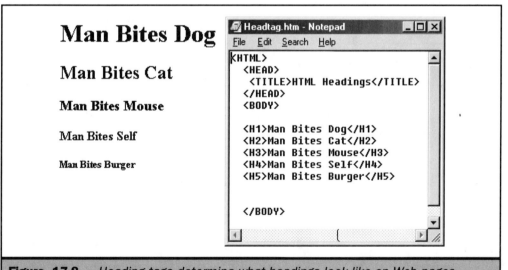

Figure 17-8.   *Heading tags determine what headings look like on Web pages*

Font Attribute Tags

To control the appearance of text on a Web page, use font attribute tags. You can combine style tags, by the way, to boldface and underline and italicize text, for example. These tags change the size and look of the text.

HTML Style Tag	Purpose
<FONT SIZE= > </FONT>	Changes the font size of text
<FONT COLOR="#"> </FONT>	Assigns a color to text
<B> </B>	Boldfaces the text
<I> </I>	Italicizes the text
<U> </U>	Underlines the text

List Tags

Two kinds of list tags are available for creating lists: the ORDERED LIST (OL) tag and the UNORDERED LIST (UL) tag. Use ORDERED LIST tags for numbered lists and the UNORDERED LIST tags for bulleted lists and other lists in which items are not numbered. Figure 17-9 shows an ordered list and an unordered list and how the lists are coded. The <OL> or <UL> tag appears at the top of the list. The code <LI> precedes the list items. When the list is complete, the <\OL> or <\UL> tag appears.

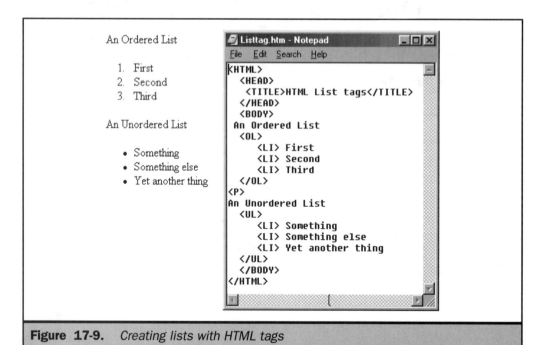

Figure 17-9.   *Creating lists with HTML tags*

Using the Visual Studio to Modify HTML Tags

Word offers a Web development tool called the Visual Studio for modifying HTML tags. As Figure 17-10 shows, Visual Studio shows all the HTML tags on a Web page. These are the same codes you see when you choose View | Source in a Web browser. In the Visual Studio window, you can type HTML tags and thereby modify a Web page without fooling around in Word.

Visual Studio is a simplified version of Script Editor, a comprehensive Web development tool that was created for the professional market. Script Editor is not covered in this book. To open Script Editor, click the Microsoft Script Editor button on the Web Tools toolbar.

Choose View | HTML Source to open your Web page in the Visual Studio window. The left side of the window shows how a browser sees your Web page with its HTML tags, attributes, values, and content. Notice that the HTML tags are colored brown and have blue brackets. The tag attributes appear in red, their values are blue, and the body text is black. On the right side, Project Explorer lists every file you have opened in Visual Studio. The files are listed in alphabetical order.

To edit a file, click on its icon in the Project Explorer and then click again on the second icon that drops down below it. As soon as you click, the file appears in the main

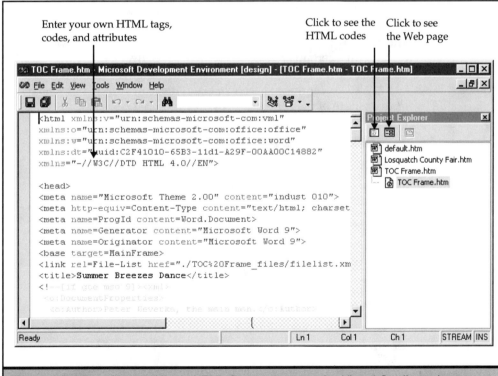

Figure 17-10.   *Choose View | HTML Source to open the Visual Studio and enter HTML codes*

window. Then click in the area where you want to place your new HTML tags or new content and either type in the new tags or contents or paste them in. When you are done, be sure to choose File | Save or click the Save button to make your changes appear on your Web page.

Helping Your Site Get "Found" in Web Searches

At present there are an estimated 350 million Web pages and that number is growing by the day. With so many Web pages on the Internet, how can you keep your site from getting lost in the shuffle? One way is to enter descriptive META tags so that search engines are more likely to find your site. As I explained earlier in this chapter, a META tag is an HTML code that contains keywords and a very brief summary of the Web site. When search engines such as Lycos and Webcrawler index Web pages, they use the META tags they find as a means of categorizing the site. By including descriptive META tags on your site, you increase the chances of your Web site being found in a Web search.

Note *Earlier in this chapter, "Understanding HTML Tags" explains what HTML tags are.*

The META tags that Word 2000 inserts in a Web page are not the type of META tags that describe a Web site to a search engine. To lure search engines to your site, you have to enter META tags on your own. As you do so, enter the keywords that a person searching the Internet would enter if he or she were looking for a site like the one you've created. The keywords go in a certain area of the HTML code between the HEAD tags.

This illustration shows how I would construct the META tags for a Web site that promoted this book. A Web surfer doesn't see what is in the META tags, but search engines read it and make note of the META tags as they index sites.

```
meta.htm - Notepad
File   Edit   Search   Help

<HTML>
  <HEAD>
   <TITLE>Word2000--Complete Reference Home Page</TITLE>

   <Meta Name="Keywords" Content ="Word 2000, Microsoft Office 2000,
    computer reference books, computer books, Osborne McGraw-Hill,
    Peter Weverka, David A. Reid">

   <Meta Name="Description" Content="Word2000--Complete Reference,
    the number one selling computer reference book in the history
    of publishing. Honest.">

  </HEAD>

     <BODY>
     <CENTER>
     <H1>
     Welcome to the Word2000--Complete Reference Home Page!
     </H1>
     </CENTER>
     </BODY>
</HTML>
```

As the illustration shows, the first META tag, the keywords tag, contains all of the words, pairs of words, and short phrases that people searching the Internet are likely to enter if they want to find the site in question. You can list as many keywords as you want, but try to stick to keywords that describe your site.

When you enter keywords, include a few misspellings. That way, if someone searching the Internet enters a typo as a keyword or enters a misspelling because he or she isn't sure how to spell a word, your site will come up in the search.

The second META tag, the description tag, is a short sentence that describes the Web site. This short description is the one that appears on the "Results" page after you conduct a search of the Web. At one time or another you have probably seen gibberish where a site description should be on the "Results" page. Gibberish appears when a Web site developer forgets to put a META description tag on his or her Web page. If there is no description META tag, the search engine displays the first words that it finds on the body of the Web page.

Follow these steps to enter META tag descriptions on your Web page:

1. Choose View | HTML Source to open your Web page in the Visual Studio window. The previous section of this chapter describes the Visual Studio window.

2. Using the previous illustration as your guide, find the META tag, enter keywords to describe your site, and enter a one- or two-sentence description of your site.

3. Click the Save button to save the descriptions as part of your Web page.

4. Click the Close button to close the Visual Studio window.

DEVELOPING WEB PAGES WITH WORD 2000

The Complete Reference

Word 2000

Part V

Using Word 2000 at the Office

The Complete Reference

Word 2000

Chapter 18

Tools for Reports, Manuals, and Scholarly Papers

This chapter is hereby devoted to anyone who has had to delve into the realm of the unknown and write a report about it. Writing reports, manuals, and scholarly papers is not easy. You have to explore uncharted territory. You have to contemplate the ineffable. And you have to write bibliographies and footnotes and maybe an index, too. Word 2000 cannot help you explore uncharted territory, but the program can take the sting out of it.

This chapter explains how to handle footnotes and endnotes, generate a table of contents, generate a caption table, write automatic captions for figures and tables, index a document, and include cross-references in documents.

Handling Footnotes and Endnotes

Footnotes are references, explanations, or comments that appear along the bottom of a page. *Endnotes* are the same as footnotes except they appear at the end of chapters. When you write footnotes and endnotes, you still have to list authors, their works, the dates their works were published, and the rest of the scholarly hoopla, but at least you don't have to worry about formatting, deleting, moving, or numbering the notes. Word handles that for you. When you delete a note or add a note, all notes are renumbered.

Unless you tell Word to put footnotes below the last line of text on the page, footnotes appear directly above the bottom margin. On a page with footers, footnotes fall between the footer and the text. Word numbers footnotes with Arabic numerals and endnotes with lowercase Roman numerals, although you can change that. Endnotes appear at the end of the document, after the final line of text, but you can place them at the end of sections if you so choose. A document can have both endnotes and footnotes.

These pages explain how to write footnotes and endnotes, move and delete the notes, change the look and numbering scheme of notes, change notes' position, and decide how to separate the notes from other text on the page.

LEARN BY EXAMPLE
Open the 18-2 Notes document on the companion CD if you want to try entering, moving, and deleting footnotes and endnotes.

The Basics: Writing a Footnote or Endnote

As the next handful of pages will make painfully clear, you can do a lot to fool with the look and numbering scheme of footnotes and endnotes. But if you are content with standard notes, you've got it made. You can simply use the note conventions that Word provides. Follow these basic steps to insert a footnote or endnote in a document:

1. Click where you want the *note citation*—a number in the case of footnotes, a lowercase Roman numeral in the case of endnotes—to appear.

2. Choose Insert | Footnote. You will see the Footnote and Endnote dialog box shown in Figure 18-1.

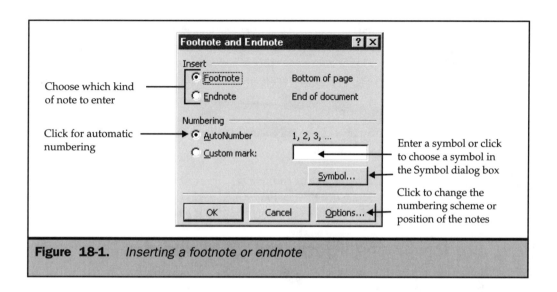

Figure 18-1.   *Inserting a footnote or endnote*

3. Click the Footnote option button to enter a footnote or the Endnote option button to enter an endnote.

4. Make sure the AutoNumber option button is selected. Later in this chapter, "Choosing a Numbering Scheme or Reference Scheme for Notes" explains how to choose a new numbering scheme or use symbols as note citations.

5. Click OK.

What you'll see next depends on whether you are in Normal view or Page Layout view. In Normal view you'll see the notes box, as shown at the top of the following illustration. In Page Layout view, you'll go to the bottom of the page or the end of the document or section, where, beside the number or roman numeral, you can type the footnote or endnote, as shown in the following illustration. If notes have already been entered, they appear beside the note you are about to enter.

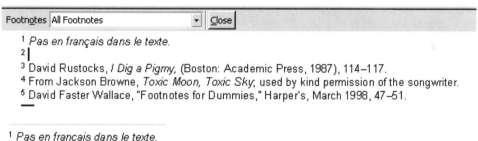

In Normal view, drag the boundary line between the notes box and the rest of the page. Drag up or down to make more room to see notes. If your document has footnotes and endnotes and you want to see one or the other, click the arrow in the notes box to open the Footnotes or Endnotes drop-down menu and choose All Footnotes or All Endnotes.

6. Type the footnote or endnote.

7. Click the Close button if you are in Normal view to leave the notes box. In Print Layout view, scroll up the page.

  The fastest way to insert a footnote or endnote is to press ALT-CTRL-F (for footnotes) or ALT-CTRL-E (for endnotes). With this technique, you bypass the Footnote and Endnote dialog box and go straight to the place where footnotes or endnotes are entered.

Editing and Reviewing Footnotes and Endnotes

Word offers a bunch of different techniques for reading, reviewing, and perhaps editing the footnotes and endnotes you have entered. Follow these instructions to ride herd on the footnotes and endnotes in your document:

- **Reading a Note As You Review the Text**   To read a note in the text without having to open the notes box or scroll to the bottom of a page or end of a document, move the pointer over the note citation. A box appears with the text of the note.

> David Rustocks, I Dig a Pigmy, (Boston: Academic Press, 1987), 114-117.

Jonathan Swift's giants were allegorical, not metaphorical.[3]

- **Double-Clicking to Read or Edit a Note**   To get to a note so you can read and perhaps edit it, double-click its note citation. In Normal view, you will see the notes box, where you can read and edit the notes. In Page Layout view, you can scroll to the bottom of the page, end of the section, or end of the document, where you can read and edit the notes.

- **Keeping the Notes Box Open for Reading and Editing Notes**   In Normal view, you can keep the notes box open on the bottom of the screen and always see the notes that are on the page you are working on. To do so, choose View | Footnotes or else hold down the SHIFT key and drag the split box, the small horizontal slot at the top of the vertical scroll bar, down the screen.

  Besides clicking, you can press F6 in Normal view to quickly go back and forth between a citation number on the page and the notes box on the bottom of the screen.

Citing the Same Note More Than Once

Anything can happen in the world of academics (anything can happen on paper, anyhow), and it might happen that you need to cite the same footnote or endnote more than once. Suppose a word of wisdom on page 8 needs to cite a footnote that already appears on page 2. You can always enter the same note twice, once on page 2 and once on page 8, but you can also follow these steps to cite a note that was cited earlier in your document:

1. Click where the note citation is to appear and choose Insert | Cross-Reference. You will see the Cross-Reference dialog box.

2. Choose Footnote or Endnote from the Reference Type drop-down list. A list of the footnotes or endnotes in your document appears in the Cross-Reference dialog box.

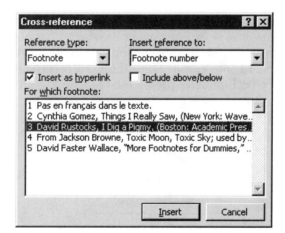

3. Select the footnote or endnote you want to cite a second time and click the Insert button.

4. Click the Close button to return to your document. The note is not superscripted like the other footnotes or endnotes, but you can fix that.

5. Select the note. To do so, carefully drag the mouse over it.

6. From the Style menu on the Formatting toolbar, choose Footnote Reference or Endnote Reference.

- **Going to a Specific Note in the Text**   Choose Edit | Go To or press CTRL-G to open the Find and Replace dialog box. On the Go To Tab, choose Footnote or Endnote, and then enter a note number and click the Go To button.

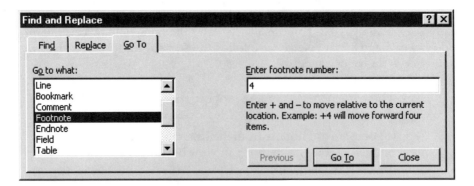

- **Going from Note to Note in the Text**   Click the Select Browse Object button and then click the Browse by Footnote or Browse by Endnote button on the menu. You'll go to the next footnote or endnote in the document. To skip merrily from note to note, click the blue double arrows on either side of the Select Browse Object button (or press CTRL-PAGE UP or CTRL-PAGE DOWN).

Moving and Deleting Footnotes and Endnotes

Maybe the best thing about footnotes and endnotes is being able to delete and move them with no trouble at all. When you delete a note, Word renumbers both the note citations in the text and the notes themselves. Likewise, if you move a note to the other side of another note, note citations and the notes themselves are renumbered so that they are in the right order.

- **Moving Notes**   Select the note's citation in the text and either cut and paste or drag it to a new location. To select a note citation, carefully drag over it with the mouse. When you move a citation, the note at the bottom of the page or end of the document moves as well if that is necessary.

- **Deleting Notes**   Select the note's citation and press the DELETE key. Notes are also renumbered when you delete one.

Exchanging Footnotes for Endnotes and Vice Versa

Fickle scholars will be glad to know that you can turn all footnotes into endnotes and all endnotes into footnotes. Follow these steps to switch notes:

1. Choose Insert | Footnote to open the Footnote and Endnote dialog box (see Figure 18-1).
2. Click the Options button. You will see the Note Options dialog box.
3. Click the Convert button. The Convert Notes dialog box appears.

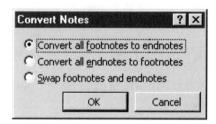

4. Choose an option and click OK twice to return to the Footnote and Endnote dialog box.
5. Click Close (if you click OK you will enter a note in your document).

Suppose you want to turn a single footnote into an endnote or a single endnote into a footnote. To do so, locate the note in question (not its citation), right-click the note, and choose Convert To Endnote or Convert To Footnote on the shortcut menu.

Tip   *To delete all the footnotes or endnotes in a document, choose Edit | Replace to open the Find and Replace dialog box. Click in the Find What box, click the More button if necessary, and then click the Special button and choose Footnote Mark (^f) or Endnote Mark (^e) from the pop-up menu. Then leave the Replace With box empty and click the Replace All button. I recommend saving a second copy of your document before you try this trick. You might need your footnotes or endnotes and regret deleting them.*

Choosing a Numbering Scheme or Reference Scheme for Notes

Until or unless you fool with the default settings, footnotes and endnotes are numbered continuously. Footnotes are numbered with Arabic numerals and endnotes with lowercase Roman numerals. You can, however, use alternative numbering schemes, use a symbol for the note citation, or number the notes beginning with each page or each section. Better read on.

Changing the Numbering Scheme for Notes

Follow these steps to choose a numbering scheme of your own for footnotes and endnotes:

1. Choose Insert | Footnote to open the Footnote and Endnote dialog box (see Figure 18-1).
2. Click the Options button. You will see the Note Options dialog box shown in Figure 18-2.
3. Click the All Endnotes or All Footnotes tab, if necessary.

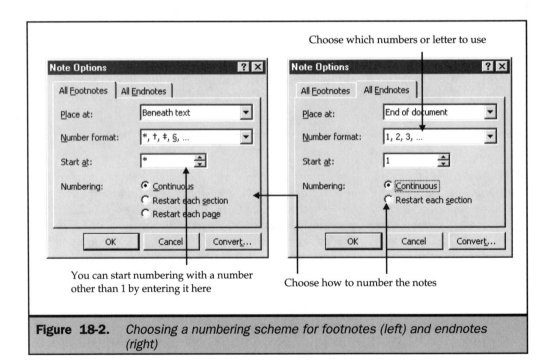

Figure 18-2.   *Choosing a numbering scheme for footnotes (left) and endnotes (right)*

4. Choose numbering options on the All Footnotes or All Endnotes tab:

- **Number Format**   Choose Arabic numerals, letters, Roman numerals, or a series of common footnote symbols.

- **Start At**   Normally, notes start with 1, a, A, i, I, or the asterisk, but you can start with another number or letter by entering it or clicking the up arrow in this box.

- **Numbering**   Choose how the notes are numbered. You can start numbering anew at each section or (in the case of footnotes) on each page.

5. Click OK to return to the Footnote and Endnote dialog box.

6. Click Close (if you click OK, you insert a note).

Using Your Own Symbol for the Note Citation

I don't recommend using your own symbol for the note citation. If you are fonder of symbols than numbers and you want to use a symbol for note citations, the Number Format drop-down list in the Note Options dialog box (see Figure 18-2) offers symbols—the asterisk, dagger, double dagger, and others. Choose the symbols in the dialog box, because if you enter symbols on your own, Word cannot renumber your footnotes or endnotes as you insert or delete them. Word can't make sure you enter the same symbol twice, either. Besides, if you use your own symbols, you have to enter a symbol on your own each time you enter a footnote or endnote. Still, I guess you could enter a symbol on your own if you wanted to be cute or you wanted to find out how daffy a document you could make.

To use your own symbol as a note citation, click where the citation will go and choose Insert | Footnote. In the Footnote and Endnote dialog box (see Figure 18-1), click the Custom Mark option and either enter the symbol or click the Symbol button and choose your symbol in the Symbol dialog box ("Entering Symbols and Foreign Characters" in Chapter 2 explains the dialog box). Then click OK and type the footnote or endnote.

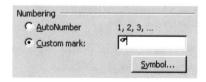

Changing the Location of Footnotes and Endnotes

Unless you change settings, footnotes appear on the bottom of the page, right above the footer. Endnotes appear at the end of the document after the final line of text. If these locations don't agree with you, you can change them. Footnotes can appear after the last line of text on the page and endnotes can appear at the end of each section instead of the end of the document. Follow these steps to change the location of notes:

1. Choose Insert | Footnote to open the Footnote and Endnote dialog box (see Figure 18-1)

2. Click the Options button to open the Note Options dialog box (see Figure 18-2).

3. Click the All Footnotes tab or All Endnotes tab, depending on which type of note you are dealing with.

4. Choose an option from the Place At drop-down list.

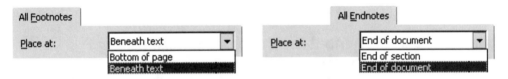

5. Click OK to return to the Footnote and Endnote dialog box.

6. Click Close (if you click OK you'll insert a new note).

You can only see the location of notes on the page in Page Layout view. In Normal view, notes appear in the notes box.

Changing the Appearance of Footnotes and Endnotes

To change the type size, font, distance by which note citations are superscripted, or otherwise change the appearance of footnotes and endnotes, you need to modify the footnote and endnote styles. Chapter 12 explains styles and how to modify them. By changing styles, you will make sure that all the citations and notes in your document keep the same appearance.

Alter these styles if you want to change the appearance of footnotes and endnotes:

■ **Footnote Text**   Text in footnotes is 10 points high and takes the default font.

■ **Footnote Reference**   Citation notes are superscripted and take the default font.

■ **Endnote Text**   Text in endnotes is 10 points high and takes the default font.

■ **Endnote Reference**   Citation notes are superscripted and take the default font.

Right-click a footnote or endnote and choose Style from the shortcut menu to get to the Style dialog box, where you can click the Modify button to modify a style. See "Modifying a Style" in Chapter 12.

Dealing with Note Separators

A *note separator* is the line that marks where the main text ends and the footnotes or endnotes begin. By default, the note separator is a 2-inch horizontal line, as shown in Figure 18-3. If the notes are too numerous or too long to fit on a single page, Word scoots them to the next page and draws a *note continuation separator* over the notes, as shown in Figure 18-3. At 6 inches, a note continuation separator is longer than a note separator. If you so desire, you can also handle long notes by entering a *note continuation notice*, a brief reminder that notes continue on the next page, as shown in Figure 18-3. You must type the note continuation notice yourself.

All changes to note separators have to be made in Normal view, not Page Layout view. Switch to Normal view, choose View | Footnotes to see the notes box, and follow these steps to alter the separators or enter a continuation notice:

■ **Change the Note Separator**   Choose Note Separator on the drop-down menu. You'll see the separator line. Using keys on the keyboard such as the hyphen

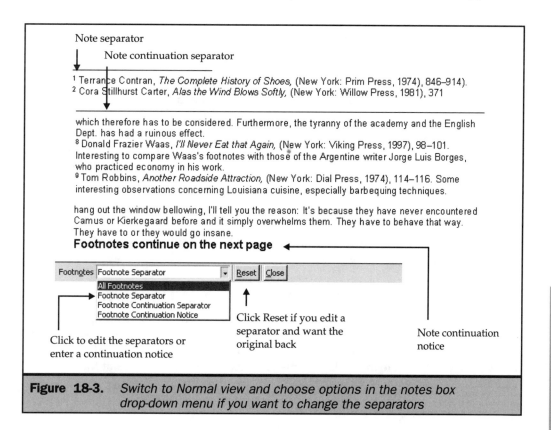

Figure 18-3.   *Switch to Normal view and choose options in the notes box drop-down menu if you want to change the separators*

USING WORD 2000
AT THE OFFICE

or equal key, you can draw a new line. Backspace to erase the line that is already there.

■ **Change the Note Continuation Separator** Choose Note Continuation Separator on the drop-down menu and use the keys on the keyboard to draw this line, too. ("Pressing Keys to Draw Lines across the Page" in Chapter 13 explains how to draw long lines by pressing keys. Look under "Drawing Lines and Arrows" in that chapter.)

■ **Enter a Note Continuation Notice** Choose Note Continuation Notice and type a brief notice to the effect that footnotes or endnotes continue on the next page.

Choose an option on the drop-down menu and click the Reset button on the notes box to start using a default separator again or to delete the note continuation notice.

Generating a Table of Contents

Every reference work of any length needs a table of contents (TOC) so readers can find what they need to find in the work. To generate a TOC, you start by deciding which headings to include. Any heading that has been assigned a style can be included in a TOC without any trouble whatsoever. And if you need to include the odd heading or paragraph, you can mark it for inclusion in the TOC as well. After you have decided what goes in the TOC, you generate it. These pages explain how to make sure the right headings go in the TOC, generate it, and update it.

Later in this chapter, "Compiling a Caption Table for Figures, Equations, Tables, and More" explains how to generate a table of the figures, graphs, tables, and what-all in a document.

LEARN BY EXAMPLE
Open the 18-1 TOC sample document on the CD if you want practice making table of contents entries and generating a TOC.

Deciding What to Include in the Table of Contents

Practically speaking, you must have assigned headings styles to the headings in your document in order to generate a table of contents (TOC). As I will explain shortly, you can mark entries for the TOC one at a time, but you may as well type the TOC as do that. Before you generate the table of contents, make sure that the parts of the document that you want to include in the TOC are ready to go:

- Headings assigned a Heading style from the Style menu can be included in a TOC. Make sure the headings in your document have been assigned heading styles. Chapter 12 explains styles.

- Paragraphs to which you assigned a particular style can also be included in a TOC. For example, suppose you are writing the definitive work about the history of comedy in the United States and your little masterpiece includes profiles of comedians. As long as you created a style called Comedian Profile, for example, and assigned the style to each heading that introduces the profile of a comedian, you can include Comedian Profile headings in your TOC (see "Creating Your Own Styles" in Chapter 12). In fact, as this illustration shows, you can generate a TOC with only headings assigned a particular style.

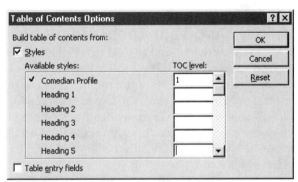

- You can make the TOC refer to the odd paragraph, illustration, photograph, or whatever in a document by marking it with the TC (table of contents) field. Use this technique to include oddball items in the TOC. See "Marking TOC Entries with the TC Field," in the next section of this chapter.

Marking TOC Entries with the TC Field

When you want the table of contents to refer to a particular place in a document, not to all paragraphs assigned the same style, follow these steps to mark that place with a TC (table of contents) field:

1. If you can, select the text that you want to include in the TOC. You'll save a little time that way, but if you can't select text because the text you want to put in the TOC doesn't appear in the document, simply click in the heading or paragraph you want to refer to.

2. Press ALT-SHIFT-O. You'll see the Mark Table of Contents Entry dialog box. If you selected text in step 1, it appears in the Entry box.

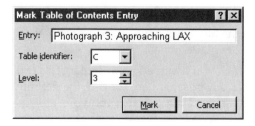

3. Either enter text in the Entry box or edit the text that is there. What appears in the Entry box will appear in your table of contents. You can format the text by

Making Sure Your Table of Contents Is a Useful One

Many people are tempted to load down the table of contents with every heading in the document, but putting too many headings in a TOC defeats the purpose of having a table of contents. After all, the purpose of a TOC is to help people look up information. In a TOC that is many pages long, looking up information is difficult, because you have to read many headings before you can find the one you are looking for. In this book, for example, only the first- and second-level headings appear in the TOC. If I included every heading, this book's TOC would be twice as long as it is now.

On more piece of advice about TOCs: Put the TOC in its own section at the start of the document, number the TOC pages with Roman numerals, and start numbering the pages with Arabic numerals after the TOC ends and the document begins in earnest. If you don't follow my advice, your TOC will appear on page 2 or 3, and the first heading that the TOC refers to will not be on page 1, but on page 4 or 5, for example. Using Roman numerals for the TOC and Arabic numerals for the rest of the material is the convention in book publishing. Study the start of this book, for example, and you will see that the table of contents (and title pages and Introduction) are numbered in lowercase Roman numerals. You won't see an Arabic page 1 in this book until you get to the meaty stuff.

Refer to these sections in Chapter 9 to format the TOC and number its pages:

- "Section Breaks for Changing Layouts" explains how to create a new section for the TOC.

- "Headers and Footers for Different Pages and Sections" explains how to change the page-numbering scheme from section to section.

- "Numbering the Pages" explains how to number pages with Roman numerals.

selecting it and pressing the boldface (CTRL-B), italic (CTRL-I), or underline (CTRL-U) keyboard shortcut.

4. Make sure C (for Contents) appears in the Table Identifier box.

5. In the Level box, enter a number to tell Word how to treat the entry when you generate the table of contents. For example, 1 tells Word to treat the entry like a first-level heading and give it top priority. A 3 places the entry with the third-level headings.

6. Click the Mark button.

You'll see a TC (table of contents) field code in your document ("All About Fields" in Chapter 23 explains fields in detail). From here, you can scroll to another part of your document and enter another TOC field entry, or you can click Close in the dialog box and be done with it. Click the Show/Hide ¶ on the Standard toolbar to hide the ugly field codes and be able to see your document better.

Generating the Table of Contents

With the preliminary work done, you can generate your table of contents. You've made sure that headings were assigned the right style. You've marked oddball TOC entries, if there are any, with the TC field. You've created a new section for your TOC and used Roman numerals to number its pages. You've entered and centered the words **Table of Contents** at the top of the page. Follow these steps to generate the table of contents:

1. Click where you want the first TOC entry to go and choose Insert | Index and Tables.

2. Click the Table of Contents tab, as shown in Figure 18-4.

3. From the Formats drop-down menu, choose a TOC design. Watch the Print Preview box to see what your design looks like.

4. In the Show Levels box, tell Word how deep the TOC should be. Entering **2**, for example, puts only headings assigned the Heading 1 and Heading 2 style in the TOC, as well as headings and paragraphs assigned to outline levels 1 and 2.

Note   *"Choosing an Outline Level for Paragraphs" in Chapter 8 explains what outline levels are. When you create a new style, assign it an outline level of 1, 2, or 3 if you intend to use paragraphs assigned to the style in TOCs. A paragraph assigned outline level 1, for example, is treated like a Heading 1 heading in tables of contents, outlines, and the document map.*

5. Choose a tab leader, decide whether to show page numbers and whether to right-align page numbers, and keep your eye on the Print Preview box as you

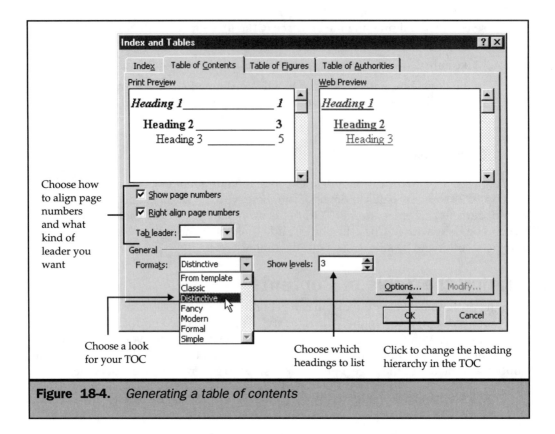

Figure 18-4.   *Generating a table of contents*

do so. A *tab leader* is a punctuation mark that appears between the heading
reference and the page number in a TOC.

6. Click OK, or read on if you want to change the rank of headings in the TOC or
   include TOC entries you made with the TC field code.

Suppose you used the Heading 1 style for the title of your work and the Heading 2
style for the first-level heads. In that case, you must exclude Heading 1 entries from the
TOC and put Heading 2 entries where Heading 1 entries would normally go. Suppose
your document includes many different styles you created on your own, some of
which you want for the TOC. How do you tell Word to rank those styles with the first-,
second-, or third-level headings in the TOC?

To change the structure of a TOC or include entries you made with the TC field
code, click the Options button in the Index and Tables dialog box (see Figure 18-4). You
will see the Table of Contents Options dialog box shown in Figure 18-5. This dialog box
lists all styles in use in your document. Follow these instructions in the Table of
Contents Options dialog box to change the contents of the TOC:

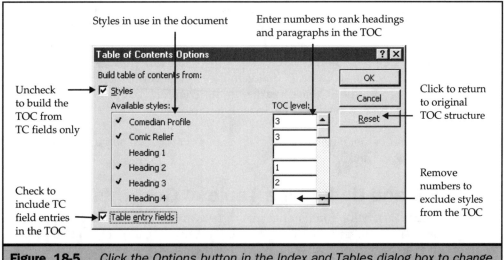

Styles in use in the document

Enter numbers to rank headings and paragraphs in the TOC

Uncheck to build the TOC from TC fields only

Click to return to original TOC structure

Remove numbers to exclude styles from the TOC

Check to include TC field entries in the TOC

Figure 18-5. *Click the Options button in the Index and Tables dialog box to change the rank of headings, include styles, or include TC fields in the table of contents*

■ **Changing the Rank of a Style in the TOC** Enter a number in the TOC Level box. The higher the number, the more prominent the heading in the TOC. You can delete the numbers that are already there and enter new ranking numbers.

The Tables of Contents as a Means of Getting Around

Tables of contents are "live," or "hot," to use two popular buzzwords. Click an entry in a TOC and you'll go several pages ahead to the heading that the entry refers to. Clicking a TOC entry also brings out the Web toolbar. To go back to the TOC after you have clicked a TOC entry, click the Back button on the toolbar (or press ALT-←). "Using Links to Turn a Manual into an Online Help Program" in Chapter 24 explains how you can use TOCs along with hyperlinks and cross-references to turn a Word document into an online Help file.

- **Excluding a Style from the TOC**   Remove the number from the TOC Level box. Headings and paragraphs assigned to the style in question do not appear in the TOC.

- **Including TC Fields in the TOC**   Check the Table Entry Fields check box to include entries marked with TC fields in the table of contents (see "Marking TOC Entries with the TC Field" earlier in this chapter). To construct a TOC from TC fields only, uncheck the Styles check box.

Click the Reset button if you get tangled up and want to start all over again with the default styles and rankings.

Regenerating and Updating a Table of Contents

A table of contents is a field. You'll notice that right away as soon as you create it. Each entry and page number in the TOC is linked to a heading or paragraph in your document and can be updated as you make editorial changes. Follow these instructions to update a TOC and regenerate it in case you want to change the TOC's formats or heading levels:

- **Regenerating a TOC to Change Its Look or Headings**   Move the pointer to the left of the TOC and click to select it. Then choose Insert | Index and Tables and choose new table of contents options (see the previous section in this chapter). Click Yes when Word asks if you want to replace the TOC.

- **Updating a TOC So the Headings and Page Numbers Are Accurate**   Move the pointer to the left of the TOC and click to select it. Then either press F9 or right-click and choose Update Field. A dialog box asks if you want to update the page numbers or the page numbers and the TOC entries. Click either option and click OK. The only reason to update the page numbers only is to save time if yours is a huge, huge document.

Be sure to update the table of contents before you print a document so that the TOC is accurate. To be absolutely sure the TOC is updated, you can tell Word to update all fields before printing a document. To do so, choose Tools | Options, click the Print tab in the Options dialog box, and check the Update Fields check box.

Changing the Look of a TOC on Your Own

As you know, Word gives you many options for choosing a table of contents design. In the Index and Tables dialog box (see Figure 18-4), you can choose from several different formats on the Formats drop-down menu. But if none of the formats suits you, you are hereby invited to take on the task of designing table of contents styles on your own.

To create a new TOC style, choose Insert | Index and Tables, make sure the From Template choice appears in the Formats drop-down menu, and click the Modify button. You will see the Style dialog box with its list of all the TOC styles in the template you are using. Choose a style, click the Modify button, and go to it. See "Modifying a Style" in Chapter 12 if you need any help.

Compiling a Caption Table for Figures, Equations, Tables, and More

Occasionally, at the start of a scholarly paper, besides a table of contents, you'll find a table of figure captions, equation captions, or table captions similar to the one in this illustration. The table serves as a secondary table of contents to help scholars find their way around a work. The entries in the table come from captions—table captions, equation captions, graph captions, and so on—found throughout the document.

Table 1: Incidences of Elvis Sightings in Tennessee _____ *1*
Table 2: Rainfall by County in Tennessee _____ *5*
Table 3: U.S. Iguana Production 1999 _____ *8*
Table 4: Incidences of Andrew Jackson Sightings in Tennessee _____ *9*
Table 5: Swallowtail Births per 1000 _____ *15*

These pages explain how to compile caption tables like these automatically. Read on to find out how to mark entries for the table, generate the table, and update it. If you came here directly from the previous section in this chapter about generating a table of contents, much of what follows will seem familiar. Expect to experience acute déjà vu.

Marking Entries for the Caption Table

In order to compile a table, you must have marked the captions. Word offers three methods for marking the figure captions, equation captions, table captions, graph captions, and what-all captions so they can be thrown together in a table:

- **Use the Insert | Caption Command** When you use the Insert | Caption command to put captions on tables, figures, equations, graphs, or whatever, Word can compile the captions into a table very easily. The program recognizes all captions made with this command. See "Captions for Figures, Equations, Tables, and More," the next section in this chapter, to learn about the Insert | Caption command.

- **Create a Style for the Captions You Want to Compile in the Table** If you decide to create a special caption style, make sure that you apply the style to each caption that you want to compile in the table. Chapter 12 explains how to create and apply styles.

■ **Use the TC (Table of Contents) Field to Mark Each Caption** Go this route if your figures, equations, tables, or whatever do not have captions. When you mark an entry with a TC field, you enter a caption. When the table is compiled, your caption appears in the table.

Chapter 12 explains styles and the next section in this chapter describes the Insert | Caption command. Follow these steps to mark captions for the table with a TC (table of contents) field:

1. Click the table caption, graph caption, or whatever. If the item you want to compile in a table doesn't have a caption, click the part of it that you want the page number in the table to refer to.

2. Press ALT-SHIFT-O to display the Mark Table of Contents Entry dialog box.

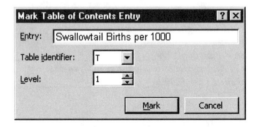

3. Type a caption in the Entry box. The caption you type will appear in the caption table, so type the entry carefully. You can format the text by selecting it and pressing the boldface (CTRL-B), italic (CTRL-I), or underline (CTRL-U) keyboard shortcut.

4. Choose an identifier from the Table Identifier drop-down list. The letter "C" is reserved for table of contents entries, so don't use it. I recommend choosing the first letter of the thing you want to compile in a table: "F" for Figures, "T" for Tables, for example.

Be sure to remember the identifier you select and be sure to select the right identifier if you intend to compile more than one caption table by entering TC fields. Later, when you compile the table, you will be asked for the identifier you choose now. When you compile the table, Word lists all captions given the same identifier, so if you accidentally give the wrong identifier, your table will not include the caption you enter now.

5. Leave the 1 in the Level box. All entries in a caption table have the same level.

6. Click the Mark button.

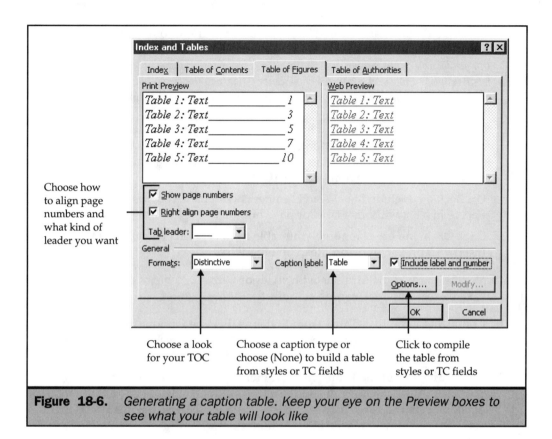

Choose how to align page numbers and what kind of leader you want

Choose a look for your TOC

Choose a caption type or choose (None) to build a table from styles or TC fields

Click to compile the table from styles or TC fields

Figure 18-6. *Generating a caption table. Keep your eye on the Preview boxes to see what your table will look like*

A TC (table of contents) field code appears in your document ("All About Fields" in Chapter 23 explains fields codes). At this point you can either scroll to another part of the document that needs a TC field entry or you can click Close in the dialog box. Click the Show/Hide ¶ button on the Standard toolbar to remove field codes from the screen.

Generating the Caption Table

Follow these steps to generate the caption table after you have marked all the captions in the document:

1. Choose Insert | Index and Tables to open the Index and Tables dialog box.

2. Click the Table of Figures tab shown in Figure 18-6.

3. From the Caption Label drop-down list, choose the type of caption you are dealing with if you marked captions with the Insert | Caption command; choose (None) if you marked captions with styles or TC field entries.

4. From the Formats drop-down list, choose a format for your caption table.

If your document has a table of contents as well as a caption table, choose the same format for the caption table and the tables of contents. That way the two tables, appearing one after the other, won't look jarringly dissimilar and cause readers to blink in dismay.

5. Choose a tab leader, choose whether to show page numbers, and whether to right-align page numbers, and keep your eye on the Preview boxes as you do so. A *tab leader* is a punctuation mark that appears between the heading reference and the page number in a TOC.

6. Uncheck the Include Label And Number check box if you want the text to appear in a list without a label or page number.

7. Click OK if you are compiling your table from captions you entered with the Insert | Caption command. Read on otherwise.

People who marked the captions with styles or with TC (table of contents) fields need to take these additional steps to compile the table:

- **Compiling a Caption Table from Styles** Click the Options button, and, in the Table of Figures Options dialog box, check the Style check box and choose the style with which you marked captions from the Style drop-down list.

- **Compiling a Caption Table from TC Fields** Click the Options button and then check the Table Entry Fields check box in the Table of Figures Options dialog box. In the Table Identifier drop-down list, choose the identifier letter you chose when you marked the caption entries.

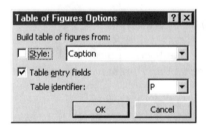

If you can't remember the identifier letter you chose when you marked the captions with TC field codes, press ESC to leave the Index and Tables dialog box and return to your document. Then press the Show/Hide ¶ button to see the field codes, scroll to a caption you entered with a TC field code, and look for the capital letter in the field code. The capital letter is the letter identifier. In this code, for example, "P" is the identifier: {TC "View of Lake Amoe" \f P \l "12"}.

Updating, Regenerating, and Changing the Look of a Caption Table

Sorry to make you jump and turn to another part of this book, but the very same techniques that are used to update, regenerate, and change the look of a caption table work as well on a table of contents. Turn a few pages backward to "Regenerating and Updating a Table of Contents" and "Changing the Look of a TOC on Your Own" to learn how to update, regenerate, and change the look of a caption table.

Captions for Figures, Equations, Tables, and More

In manuals and reports, sometimes the figures, tables, and equations are numbered for reference purposes. In the book you are reading, for example, figure captions are numbered so that readers know precisely which figure is being referred to. The problem with numbering captions is that you have to be careful to number them correctly and you occasionally have to renumber them when a figure gets deleted or you insert a new figure before others you have already inserted.

To make numbering captions easier, Word offers the Insert | Captions command. As you enter new captions and remove old ones, the captions are renumbered. You don't have to worry whether the captions are in the correct numerical order. What's more, using the Insert | Caption command makes generating a caption table very easy, as the last section in this chapter explained.

Word offers built-in figure, equation, and table captions, and you can devise your own caption labels for illustrations, photographs, or whatever. Read on to find out how to enter captions, edit and delete them, and devise your own caption labels.

Entering a Caption

Follow these steps to slap a numbered caption on a figure, equation, table, or other item:

1. Click the item that needs a caption.

2. Choose Insert | Caption. You'll see the Caption dialog box shown in Figure 18-7.

3. In the Caption box, enter your caption. Notice that you can't change the item number, since Word numbers items automatically. You can put a colon (:), period, or other punctuation mark after the item number if you want. If you do so, however, make sure you do it consistently for every item you enter a caption for. In other words, if you put a colon after the number, do so throughout your document.

USING WORD 2000 AT THE OFFICE

Enter the caption   Choose which kind of item you are dealing with

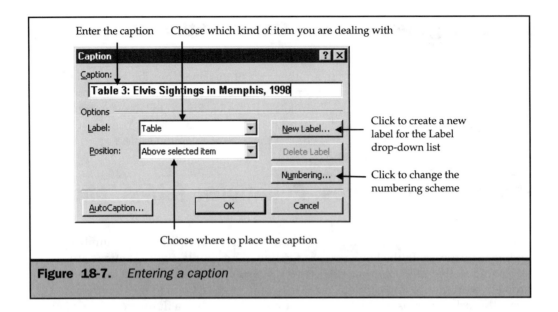

Click to create a new label for the Label drop-down list

Click to change the numbering scheme

Choose where to place the caption

Figure 18-7.   *Entering a caption*

4. From the Label drop-down menu, choose which type of item you are dealing with—an equation, figure, table, or other item. See "Devising Your Own Caption Label" if the item you want to caption is not on the list.

5. From the Position drop-down menu, choose whether to put the caption above or below the item. Again, be sure to choose the same option consistently. Captions should appear in the same place relative to figures, tables, equations, and other items throughout a document.

6. Click OK, or else read on if you want to change caption numbering schemes or make chapter numbers a part of caption numbers.

Captions are numbered using Arabic numerals, but you can change that if you want. You can use letters or Roman numerals. And you can also attach chapter numbers to caption numbers so that items are numbered, for example, 1-1, 1-2, 1-3, and so on in Chapter 1. However, to include chapter numbers in caption numbers, you must have divided your document into sections and made chapter numbers part of the page-numbering scheme in your documents (see "Headers and Footers for Different Sections and Pages" in Chapter 9 and "Choosing a Heading-Numbering Scheme" in Chapter 10).

In the Captions dialog box (see Figure 18-7), click the Numbering button to change the numbering scheme. You see the Caption Numbering dialog box. Follow these instructions to change the way that captions are numbered:

- **Using Letters or Roman Numerals** Choose a new numbering scheme from the Format drop-down list.

- **Including the Chapter Number in the Caption Number** Check the Include Chapter Number check box, make sure Heading 1 appears in the Charter Starts With Style drop-down list, and choose a punctuation mark to separate the chapter number from the caption number in the Use Separator drop-down list.

Devising Your Own Caption Label

When you choose Insert | Caption and open the Caption dialog box, you'll find three labels with which to caption items in a document: Equation, Figure, and Table. But suppose you want to write captions for illustrations or maps or joke boxes or photographs? Follow these steps to devise your own label for captions:

1. Choose Insert | Caption to open the Captions dialog box (see Figure 18-7) if you have not already done so.

2. Click the New Label button. You will see the New Label dialog box.

3. Enter a label in the Label box and click OK.

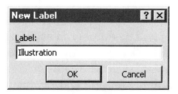

If you need to delete a label you created yourself, select it in the Label drop-down list and click the Delete Label button. You can't delete the Equation, Figure, or Table label, the three labels that Word devised for you.

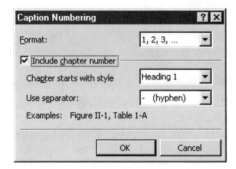

Editing Captions

Don't worry about caption numbers if you delete or move a caption because Word handles the renumbering for you. The caption number in a caption is a field. As such, it can be updated automatically as long as you tell Word to update the fields. To update a single caption number, click to select it and then press F9 or right-click and choose Update Fields. However, the surest way to update caption numbers is to select the entire document and press F9. Doing so updates all the fields in the document, including the caption numbers.

Caution   *Be careful when you move a caption that you move the item that it refers to as well. For example, select a table and its caption before you move the table elsewhere.*

Apart from the label and caption number, you can edit text in captions to your heart's content. Whatever you do, don't edit the label. Even if you change a figure label in your document into an illustration label by deleting the word "Figure" and entering the word "Illustration" in its place, Word will think it is dealing with an figure label. When Word numbers captions, it numbers them in sequence, so the figure label you turned into an illustration label will be numbered as though it was a figure. If you mistakenly used the wrong label in a caption, don't delete the caption label and enter a new caption label yourself. Instead, select the caption, choose Insert | Caption to open the Caption dialog box (see Figure 18-7), and choose a new label from the Label drop-down list.

Changing the Look of Captions

To my mind, captions look kind of bulky. Word uses the default font and the boldface style for captions, but you can change the look of captions if you so desire. To do so, modify the Caption style, the style that Word applies automatically to captions that you enter with the Insert | Caption command. See "Modifying a Style" in Chapter 12 to learn how to modify s style.

Indexing a Document

A good index is a thing of beauty. No reference work or manual is complete without an index that readers can refer to when they want to look up information. Besides the table of contents, the only way to find anything in a long document is to look in the index. These pages explain how to mark words and phrases in a document for inclusion in the index, how to generate an index form the words or phrases you marked, and how to compile an index. You will also find advice here for editing an index.

LEARN BY EXAMPLE
Open the 18-4 Index document on the companion CD to try your hand at entering index entries and generating an index.

What You Need to Know Before You Begin

As shown in Figure 18-8, Word offers four different ways to make entries in an index: a cross-reference, a main entry, a subentry, and sub-subentry. Look closely at the figure and you will also see that index entries can refer to a single page or a *page range*—two, three, or many more pages in a row. To wit, Word offers these ways to make an index entry:

■ **Main Entry** The standard index entry. All entries begin with a main entry.

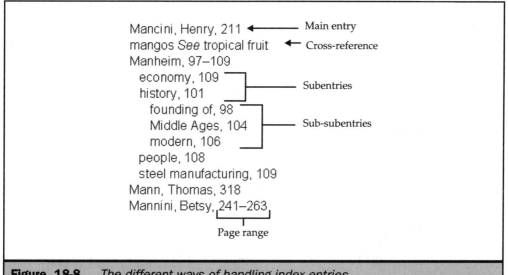

Figure 18-8.   *The different ways of handling index entries*

- **Cross-Reference**   Refers the reader to another entry in the index. Cross-references are preceded by the word "See."

- **Subentry**   An entry that is subordinate to a main entry. A subentry is indented a bit further than the main entry. A subentry is a subtopic of the main entry.

- **Sub-Subentry**   An entry that is subordinate to a subentry (as well as the subentry's main entry). A sub-subentry is indented further than a subentry. A subentry is a sub-subtopic of the main entry.

- **Page Range**   Instead of a single page number, you can cite a page range in an index entry to show that more than one page is devoted to a topic.

When you mark index entries by means of a concordance file (explained shortly), you can't cite page ranges in index entries or cross-reference another topic without including a page number in the cross-reference.

The Two Ways to Mark Words and Phrases for the Index

Word offers two ways to mark the words and phrases in a document for the index: by marking them one at a time in the Mark Index Entry dialog box or by creating a *concordance file* and marking the entries all at once. The concordance file method makes for a quick-and-dirty index that isn't much use to anyone. However, if your index is strictly for show, if you are slaving away in a cubicle somewhere to produce a document that hardly anyone is going to read anyway, you may as well generate your index with a concordance file. You will save time that way. Read on to learn the two ways to mark the index entries.

Marking Index Entries One at a Time

With the one-at-a-time method of marking index entries, you open the Mark Index Entry dialog box, put the box in a corner of the screen, read the document carefully, and mark index entries as you go along. Some people prefer to mark index entries as they proofread a document. Do the following for each part of your document that you want the index to refer to:

1. Click a part of your document that you want to cite with an index entry. If a word or phrase can be used as the index entry itself, select the word or phrase. By doing so, you save a little time in step 3.

2. Press ALT-SHIFT-X. The Mark Index Entry dialog box shown in Figure 18-9 appears.

3. Enter your index entry in the top of the dialog box:

   - **Main Entry**   Enter the main entry. Every entry needs a main entry. The word or phrase you selected in step 1, if you selected a word or phrase, appears in the Main Entry box. Edit the word or phrase or keep it. What you enter in the Main Entry box appears in the index.

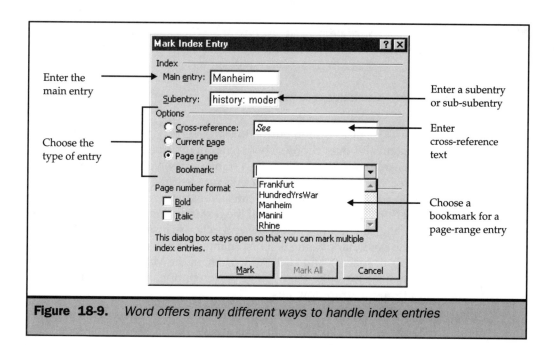

Figure 18-9.   *Word offers many different ways to handle index entries*

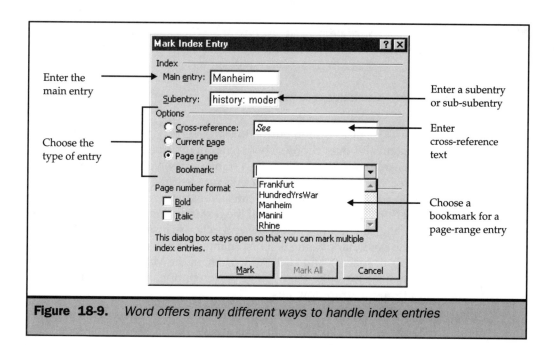

Tip   *As you mark index entries, ask yourself how you would search for information in an index if you came to your document for the first time. Try to imagine how others will look up information in your document and enter the index entries accordingly.*

■ **Subentry**   Enter subentry or sub-subentry text, or leave the box blank if this entry does not have a subentry. To enter a sub-subentry (Figure 18-8 shows exactly what a sub-subentry is), type a colon (:) and then type the sub-subentry (see Figure 18-9). The text you type will appear in the index, so spell the words carefully.

Caution   *If you need to enter a colon (:) as part of an index entry, precede the colon with a backslash (\). Word needs the colon for constructing sub-subentries, so unless you enter the backslash, Word thinks you are entering a sub-subentry. Word enters the backslash for you automatically if you select text with a colon before pressing ALT-SHIFT-X to open the Mark Index Entry dialog box.*

4. Under Options, decide how to handle the page-number reference that follows the index entry:

■ **Cross-Reference**   Type a main entry's name in this box after the word "See" if you want the main entry to refer to another entry in the index. What you type in this box appears in the index.

Word does not double-check entries that you type in the Cross-Reference text box. You have to make sure on your own that the main entry you enter in the box is really in your index.

- **Current Page**   Click this option button if your index entry cites a single page in the document.

- **Page Range**   Click this option button to cite several pages in a row in your document, and then choose a bookmark name from the Bookmark drop-down list. In order to create a page-range entry, you must create a bookmark for the page range ("Bookmarks for Getting Around" in Chapter 2 explains bookmarks in detail). To create a bookmark, click outside the Mark Index Entry dialog box, select all the text in the page range (click at the start of the range and SHIFT-click at the end), choose Insert | Bookmark, type a name in the Bookmark Name text box (names cannot start with a number or include blank spaces), and click Add. Then, in the Mark Entry dialog box, click the down arrow in the Page Range option button, and choose the bookmark from the drop-down list.

5. Click the Bold or Italic check box if you want to boldface or italicize the page number or range in the index entry. By convention, the page or page range where a topic is explained in the most depth is boldfaced or italicized in some indexes. In other indexes, a page in which a figure or illustration appears is boldfaced or italicized.

6. Click the Mark button to mark the entry for inclusion in the index.

Note
If you selected a word in step 1, you can click the Mark All button to mark each instance of the word in your document for inclusion in the index. Sounds nice, but this option can be troublesome. You never really know how or where a word is used in a document. By citing every instance of a word, you run the risk of burdening your index with entries that aren't really important enough to be in an index. If you click the Mark All button, make sure the word you selected appears only in a few choice places in your document.

Tuck the Mark Index Entry dialog box in a corner and use it again when you find the next item in your document that bears mentioning in the index. All the field codes, including index field codes, appear in your document after you click the Mark button to enter the first index entry. You can click the Show/Hide ¶ button on the Standard toolbar to hide the ugly field codes again.

Marking Index Entries with a Concordance File

The other way to mark words and phrases for the index is to construct a concordance file. A few pages back I vilified this method of generating indexes. The problem with the concordance file method is that you don't get to review the index entries as you mark them. You simply create a table with words and phrases to look for and tell Word to blindly include an index entry for each word or phrase in the table.

This illustration shows a concordance file, a two-column table with words to look for in the document and their corresponding index entries. The words in the left-hand column of the table are the ones Word searches for. When it finds a word that is listed in the left-hand column, it records the corresponding text in the right-hand column as the index entry along with the page number on which the word is found. For example, upon finding "dirigible" in the left-hand column of the concordance file table shown here, Word enters "zeppelins, 6" (or some other page number) in the index. With the concordance file method of indexing, you can't include page ranges for entries or enter a cross-reference without a page number appearing beside the cross-reference, which looks kind of ridiculous.

dirigible	zeppelins
Mancini	Mancini, Henry
Eagle Steel Works	Manheim:steel manufacturing
Manini	Manini, Betsy
mangos	tropical fruit:history of
whirligig	merry-go-round
subinfeudation	land tenure:history of

Do the following if you opt for the concordance file method of marking entries for an index in spite of my prohibitions:

1. Start a new Word document.

2. Create a two-column table. Chapter 14 describes how to create tables.

3. In the left-hand column, type text from your document that you want Word to find for the index. What you enter in the left-hand column is not the index entry itself—just the topic of the entry. For example, to make an index entry on Thomas Mann, type **Mann** in the left-hand column to tell Word to look for all occurrences of that name.

Caution   *To be indexed, words in your document must be exact matches of the words in the left-hand column. For example, if you type* **eagle steel works** *in the left-hand column of the concordance file table but the name is "Eagle Steel Works" (with each word capitalized) in your document, the topic won't be indexed because Word won't recognize it.*

4. In the right-hand column, type the index entries. For example, to create an index entry called "Mann, Thomas," type **Mann, Thomas**. You can create subentries by using a colon (:). For example, to make "Mann, Thomas, early life" a subentry of "Mann, Thomas," enter **Mann, Thomas:early life**.

> **Tip** *A fast way to create a concordance file is to open the document with the text you are indexing along with the concordance file, choose Window | Arrange All to put both documents onscreen at once, and copy text from the document to the left-hand column of the concordance file.*

5. Save the concordance file when you are finished entering the words and phrases to look for in the left-hand column and the index entries in the right-hand column. Your next step is to use the concordance file to mark index entries in your document.

6. Open the document that needs indexing.

7. Choose Insert | Index and Tables and click the Index tab in the Index and Tables dialog box.

8. Click the AutoMark button. You will see the Open Index AutoMark File dialog box.

9. Find the concordance file, select it, and click the Open button.

Throughout your document, field codes appear where the concordance file marked entries for the index. Hide the ugly field codes by clicking the Show/Hide ¶ button.

Generating the Index

After you have marked the index entries, you can generate the index. Word indexes are run out in newspaper-style columns. The program creates a new section for the index. Follow these steps to generate an index:

1. Choose Insert | Index and Tables and click the Index tab. You'll see the Index and Tables dialog box shown in Figure 18-10.

2. From the Formats drop-down menu, choose a format for your index. Watch the Preview box as you make this and other choices in the dialog box to see what your index will look like.

3. Under Type, click the Run-In option instead of the Indented option if you want subentries and sub-subentries to appear directly below main entries instead of being indented.

4. Choose the number of columns for your index in the Columns box. If you want more than 2 columns, choose the Run-In option so the columns don't crowd one another.

5. Fiddle with these options in the bottom of the dialog box:

   - **Right Align Page Numbers**   Check this box if you want numbers to appears below one another instead of beside index entries.

   - **Tab Leader**   Choose a leader to go between the index entry and the page number if you don't like the leader in the format you chose in step 2.

6. Click OK.

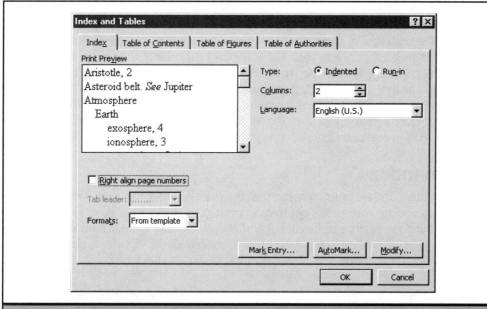

Figure 18-10. *Choose a format and tinker with the appearance of the index before clicking OK to generate it*

Note

If you are adventurous and want to develop index styles of your own, click the Modify button in the Index and Tables dialog box. That will take you to the Style dialog box, where you can click a style, click the Modify button, and devise a look for the index on your own. Chapter 12 explains how to modify a style. The Index 1 style governs main entries, the Index 2 style subentries, and the Index 3 style sub-subentries. The rest of the styles are for sub-sub-subentries and their subordinates, which I don't explore in this book in order to preserve your sanity.

Editing an Index

Be sure to proofread your index after you generate it. Index entries are not kept in the index itself, but in field codes throughout the document, so finding and repairing an index entry that was misspelled or doesn't belong can be difficult. As shown in the following illustration, index entries are enclosed in braces and quotation marks and are preceded by the letters "XE" (for Index Entry). The text of the index entry appears inside the quotation marks. This entry includes a subentry, the words "early life," which appear after the colon.

{·XE·"Sinatra,·Frank:early·life"·}

To edit an index, start by clicking the Show/Hide¶ button on the Standard toolbar to see the field codes in your document. Then look for the entry that needs correcting or deleting. The easiest way to do that is to choose Edit | Find (or press CTRL-F), enter the word in the index that needs your attention, and click the Find Next button as many times as necessary to find the word. The Find command finds index entries as well as words—as long as you click the Show/Hide¶ button.

After you find the entry, either delete it and re-enter it, or simply type the correct spelling inside the quotation marks in the XE field code. Just make sure you don't delete the quotation marks or insert extra spaces where they don't belong.

Updating an Index

From time to time, update your index so that the page number references are accurate. And be sure to update your index before you print your document. To update an index, click it and press F9 or right-click it and choose Update Field. To be absolutely sure your index is up to date before you print it, choose Tools | Options, click the Print tab in the Options dialog box, and check the Update Fields check box.

Including Cross-References in Documents

Cross-references are one of my favorite Word 2000 features. As you know if you have spent any time in this book, I am a firm believer in cross-references. Why repeat yourself when you can send the reader to another place in a document or book where he or she can learn all the details?

Word cross-references can refer readers to book pages, headings, numbered items such as footnotes and numbers in figure and table captions, and bookmarked items. Best of all, Word double-checks cross-references to make sure all are accurate. If you delete the heading to which a cross-reference refers, Word tells you about it when you update the cross-references in your document. If your cross-reference points to an item on page 26 but the item is moved to page 32, the cross-reference is still valid. It tells readers to go to page 32. You can even turn cross-references into hyperlinks and click a cross-reference to go straight to the thing the cross-reference refers to.

LEARN BY EXAMPLE
Check out the 18-3 Cross-References document on the companion CD. It shows how cross-references work.

Inserting a Cross-Reference

Before you insert a cross-reference, make sure the thing you want to refer to is really there. Word can cross-reference the following items automatically:

- Headings that have been assigned a built-in heading style. Chapter 12 explains styles.

- Bookmarks you inserted with the Insert | Bookmark command. Insert a bookmark in a paragraph if you want to refer to the paragraph. See "Bookmarks for Getting Around" in Chapter 2.

- Footnotes and endnotes. See "Handling Footnotes and Endnotes" at the start of this chapter.

- Equations, tables, and figures whose captions are numbered. See "Captions for Figures, Equations, Tables, and More," earlier in this chapter.

Secure in the notion that the thing you want to refer to is indeed in your document, follow these steps to insert a cross-reference:

1. Type the cross-reference text. What you type depends on which kind of cross-reference you intend to make:

   - **To a Numbered Item**   Type something like this: **To find out more concerning this grave dilemma, turn to page**. Or type: **To see an example of this problem, turn to**. Be sure to put a blank space after the word "page" or the words "turn to" to make room, respectively in this example, for the page number or table caption you are cross-referencing.

   - **To a Heading**   Type something like this: **To discover more about these discoveries, turn to "**. In this case, don't leave a blank space after the quotation mark, because the heading you will refer to comes right after the quotation mark.

2. Choose Insert | Cross-Reference to open the Cross-Reference dialog box shown in Figure 18-11.

3. In the Reference Type drop-down list, choose what the cross-reference refers to.

4. Make a choice in the Insert Reference To drop-down list. What appears on the list depends on what you chose in step 3.

5. Uncheck the Insert As Hyperlink check box if you don't want the cross-reference to double as a hyperlink.

6. Check the Include Above/Below check box if you want the word "above" or "below" to be part of the cross-reference. For example, the cross-reference could read, "See footnote 1 below." (This option isn't available for all cross-references.)

7. In the For Which box, click on the item that the cross-reference refers to—a bookmark, heading, footnote, caption, or whatever.

8. Click the Insert button and then the Close button to return to your document.

9. Finish writing the cross-reference text, if necessary.

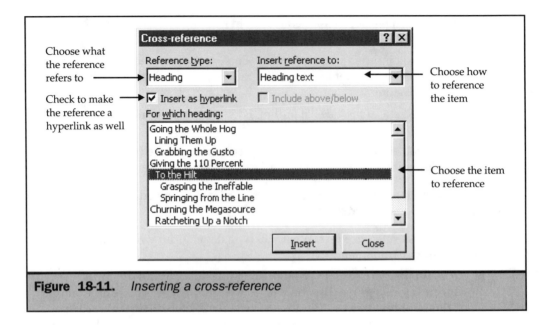

Choose what
the reference
refers to ⟶

Check to make
the reference a
hyperlink as well

Choose how
to reference
the item

Choose the item
to reference

Figure 18-11.   *Inserting a cross-reference*

Making Sure Cross-References Are Up to Date

As pages get added or deleted from a document, page numbers in cross-references
need to be updated. Since cross-references are usually found throughout a document,
the best way to update them is to select the document and update them all at once. To
do so, choose Edit | Select All (or press CTRL-A) and then either press F9 or right-click
and choose Update Field from the shortcut menu.

Fixing Errant Cross-References

The great drawback of including cross-references in a document is that the cross-reference
really has to be there. If you tell readers to go somewhere in a document and the thing
isn't there, readers tell you where to go instead of the other way around. Fortunately,
Word alerts you when a cross-reference has gone astray. Delete the heading, caption,
footnote, endnote, or bookmark to which a cross-reference refers and you get the error
message shown in this illustration.

Error! Reference source not found.

To fix errors like those, you have to find them first. After you update the
cross-references in a long document, choose the Edit | Find command (or press CTRL-F)

to open the Find and Replace dialog box, enter **Error!** In the Find What box, and click the Find Next button. In this way, locate all errant cross-references and repair them one at a time. To repair an errant cross-reference, select it, choose Insert | Cross-Reference, and insert the cross-reference again, but correctly this time.

Putting Charts in Documents

A report without a chart or two isn't really a report. To help you draw charts, Word offers a tool called Microsoft Graph. These pages explain how to create a chart, enter the data in a chart, and dress up a chart in fanciful colors. You will also find instructions here for importing chart data from an Excel worksheet.

LEARN BY EXAMPLE
Open the 18-5 Charts practice document on the companion CD to try your hand at tinkering with charts.

Creating the Chart and Entering the Data

Each chart is constructed from data of some kind—Elvis sightings in four cities, monthly rainfall in Barstow, annual sales posted by different department stores. The first step in creating a chart is to enter the data so that Microsoft Graph knows how wide or tall or thick to make the pie slices or bars or columns in the chart. Follow these steps to start the Microsoft Graph program and enter the data for the chart:

1. Click where you want the chart to appear in your document and choose Insert | Picture | Chart. The Microsoft Graph program opens.

   Notice that a new set of buttons appears on the Standard toolbar and that some of the menu names have changed. You might not know it, but you have opened a new program—Microsoft Graph. A datasheet and sample chart constructed from the surrogate data on the datasheet appear onscreen.

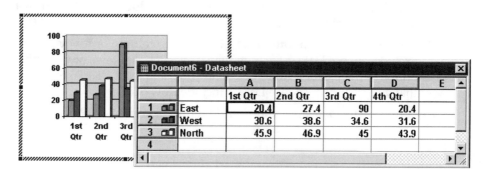

Tip *The datasheet is unwieldy and hard to use. By far the easiest way to enter the data for a chart is to start with a table (Chapter 14 explains how to create and enter data in a table). After you have entered the data in the table, select the table (choose Table | Select | Table) and choose Insert | Picture | Chart. The chart arrives onscreen fully clothed and looking like a chart. All the data is already entered in the datasheet. When you return to your Word document, delete the table. Doing so has no effect on the chart.*

2. Enter the data you want to plot in the chart in the datasheet. For now, don't worry about whether data appears in the right place on the chart. Later, I will show you how to rearrange the various parts of a chart. As you enter the data, observe these technicalities:

   ■ **Entering the Numbers**   Click in a cell—the place where a column and row intersect—and enter data or descriptive labels.

   ■ **Formatting Numbers**   Select numbers in the datasheet and click a Style button on the Formatting toolbar (Currency Style, Percent Style, or Comma Style) to change number formats. To increase or decrease the number of decimal places in a number, click the Increase Decimal or Decrease Decimal button.

   ■ **Changing the Width of Columns**   If a row isn't wide enough to show data, you'll see number signs (#####) instead of data. To make a column wider, move to the top row of the datasheet, place the cursor between letters, and click and drag toward the right when you see the two-headed arrow.

   ■ **Deleting Data, Columns, and Rows**   Drag across data and then press the DELETE key to delete data. To delete an entire row or column, right-click its number or letter in the datasheet and choose Delete from the shortcut menu.

   ■ **Inserting a Column or Row**   Right-click a column letter and choose Insert to insert a new column to the left of the column you right-clicked. Right-click a row number and choose Insert to insert a new row—the row appears above the row whose number you clicked.

   ■ **Enlarging the Datasheet**   Move the pointer to the lower-right corner of the datasheet and start dragging when you see the double-headed arrow to make the datasheet larger.

   ■ **Excluding Data from the Chart**   Click in the column or row you want to exclude, choose Data | Exclude Row/Col, click the Rows or Columns option button in the Exclude Row/Col dialog box, and click OK. To reinclude a row that you excluded, choose Data | Include Row/Col.

3. Click outside the datasheet and chart to return to your Word document.

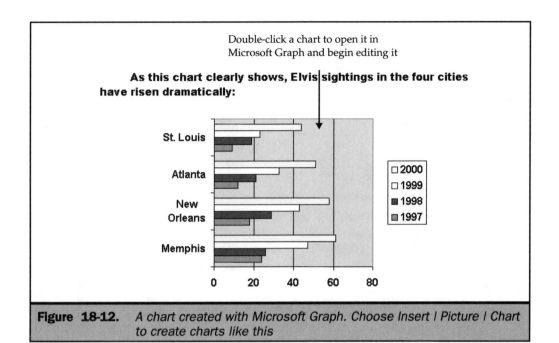

Double-click a chart to open it in
Microsoft Graph and begin editing it

Figure 18-12. *A chart created with Microsoft Graph. Choose Insert I Picture I Chart to create charts like this*

As shown in Figure 18-12, you can view your new chart in all its glory in your Word document. Double-click a chart to open it in Microsoft Graph so you can edit it. A chart, like a text box or clip art image, is an object. As such, you can move it to a new position onscreen or drag one of its selection handles to change its size (see "Manipulating Art, Text Boxes, Shapes, and Other So-Called Objects" in Chapter 13).

Changing the Chart's Layout

Getting it right the first time isn't easy when you are dealing with charts. Fortunately, the Microsoft Graph program offers about a hundred different ways to tinker with charts' appearance and change the way that charts are laid out. To tinker with charts, either click buttons on the Standard toolbar or choose Chart I Chart Options to open the Chart Options dialog box shown in Figure 18-13. As you experiment with the different settings in the dialog box, watch the graph—the dialog box shows your graph and how it is affected by the settings you choose. Double-click your chart to open it in the Microsoft Graph program and follow these instructions to make your chart just so.

USING WORD 2000
AT THE OFFICE

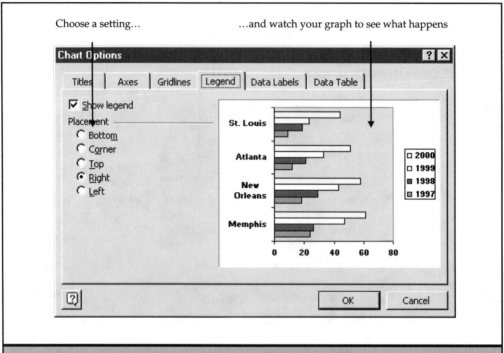

Figure 18-13. *What's that chart in the Chart Options dialog box? Why, it's none other than the chart you are working on*

CHOOSING A NEW CHART TYPE   Click the down arrow beside the Chart Type button and choose a new type of chart from the drop-down menu. The program offers 18 kinds of charts, including bar charts, area charts, column charts, and spider charts. Experiment with the different charts until you find one you like.

 Click the View Datasheet button to remove the datasheet from the screen and be able to see the chart better. Click the button again if you need to see the datasheet and edit the data from which the chart is plotted.

CHANGING THE COLUMN DATA SERIES ORIENTATION   Click the By Column or By Row button on the Standard toolbar to reorient the graph and change which data appears in the legend and how values and categories are plotted. You can also choose Chart | Chart Options and play with the values on the Axes tab of the Chart Options dialog box.

Bringing Data from an Excel Worksheet into the Datasheet

People who use Excel to manage data will be glad to know that you can import data from an Excel worksheet into the datasheet and thereby spare yourself the trouble of entering data for a graph all over again. Follow these steps to use data from an Excel worksheet to plot a graph in Microsoft Graph:

1. Open the Excel worksheet and take note of which data from the worksheet you want to import. Later, you will be asked to name the worksheet you want to import and list the range of cells you want to import as well.

2. Click in the datasheet, press CTRL-A to select the data, and press the DELETE key to delete the sample data in the worksheet.

3. With the cursor in the upper-left corner of the datasheet, choose Edit | Import File or click the Import File button on the Standard toolbar. You'll see the Import File dialog box.

4. Locate the Excel file you want to import, select it, and click the Open button. You'll see the Import Data Options dialog box.

5. Choose the worksheet whose data you want to import, and, additionally if you want to import data from specific cells, click the Range option button and enter the cell range in the in the text box.

6. Click OK.

It's very likely that you'll have to delete a few columns and rows after you import the worksheet. See "Creating the Chart and Entering the Data," the previous section in this chapter.

DISPLAYING OR NOT DISPLAYING THE GRIDLINES Gridlines are lines on the graph that mark value amounts. Click the Category Axis Gridlines and Value Axis Gridlines buttons on the Standard toolbar to see or display gridlines. You can also choose Chart | Chart Options, click the Gridlines tab, and check or uncheck the boxes to decide where the gridlines fall.

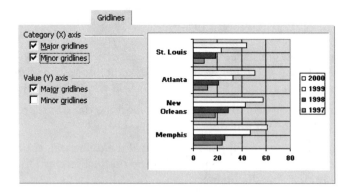

HANDLING LEGENDS, TITLES, AND LABELS Click the Legend button on the Standard toolbar to display or hide the *legend*, the box on the graph that describes what is being plotted on the graph. To enter category and value names on your chart, choose Chart | Chart Options, click the Titles tab, and enter the names. Click the Legend tab and choose an option button to tell Microsoft Graph where in relation to your chart to place the Legend box (see Figure 18-13)

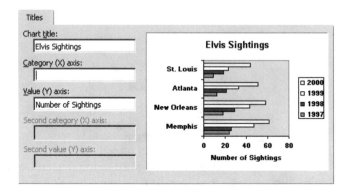

Click the Data Labels tab in the Chart Options dialog box and click one or two Show option buttons to make data labels appear right on the graph as well as on the sides of the graph.

CHANGING THE APPEARANCE OF THE CHART A chart is composed of different areas—the category axis and chart area, among others. The Chart Objects drop-down menu on the Standard toolbar lists all the areas. Try moving the pointer over the different parts of the chart—pop-up boxes list the parts of the chart as you move the pointer around. Follow these steps to change an area's background colors, font settings, or borders:

1. Click the part of the chart that needs changing. Black selection handles appear on the part of the chart you clicked.

2. Either double-click the chart or click the Format button on the Standard toolbar (the button changes names, depending on which part of the chart you selected.). The Format dialog box appears so you can choose new borders, fonts, or whatever for your chart.

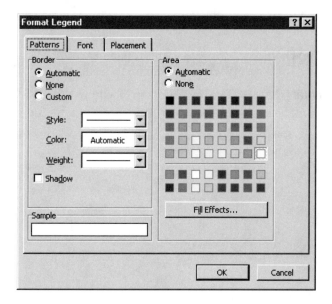

3. Visit the different tabs in the Format dialog box to change settings and then click OK.

If necessary, choose Edit | Undo and start all over if your changes to the chart didn't work out. Usually, you have to wrestle with Format dialog boxes for five minutes or so before the chart starts smelling like a rose.

Tip   *The legend, plot area, and chart title on a chart are objects in their own right. As such, you can drag to move them in the chart area. To move an object, click to select it. When you see the black selection handles, start dragging. A dotted line shows where the object will land when you release the mouse button.*

USING WORD 2000 AT THE OFFICE

Exam	**MOUS Exam Objectives Explored in Chapter 18**

Objective	Heading	Practice File
Create and modify a table of contents*	"Generating a Table of Contents"	18-1 TOC
Create or revise footnotes and endnotes*	"Handling Footnotes and Endnotes"	18-2 Notes
Create cross-references*	"Including Cross-References in Documents"	18-3 Cross-References
Create and modify an index*	"Indexing a Document"	18-4 Index
Import data into charts*	"Bringing Data from an Excel Worksheet into the Datasheet"	
Create and modify charts*	"Putting Charts in Documents"	18-5 Charts

* Denotes an Expert exam objective.

Chapter 19

Working on Team Projects

This chapter explains how you can get the help of Word 2000 to complete projects that you undertake with other people and large, unwieldy projects that you undertake on your own. Because so many people are connected to private networks and the Internet, a lot of work is collaborative. You write it and send it to someone else. That someone rewrites it and sends it to someone else again. These pages explain how to use Track Changes and Comments to make sure that collaborative efforts go smoothly. You will also find instructions for using the very valuable Outline feature to organize your work and the sometimes-but-not-always valuable Master Document feature for organizing big, big jobs.

Keeping Track of Revisions to Documents

At some point or other you must have written a document, given it to others to revise, and discovered upon its return that the changes made to it were so all-encompassing as to make the document unrecognizable. Collaborating with others on a document can be like playing Telephone, the children's game in which one child whispers a word to another, who whispers it to another, until after four or five transactions the original word turns into something completely different.

To keep track of revisions to documents, review revisions, and perhaps reverse them, Word offers the Tools | Track Changes command. When you activate this command, all changes made to a document are marked in different colors, with one color for each person who works on the document. A line is drawn through crossed-out words, additions are underlined, and a vertical line in the left margin shows where revisions were made to the original copy. You can even tell Word to mark where formatting changes were made.

Figure 19-1 shows what the revision marks look like. As you review a document, you can accept or reject the changes that were made to it by right-clicking, clicking buttons on the Reviewing toolbar, or clicking buttons in the Accept or Reject Changes dialog box. By moving the pointer over a revision, you can see who made it and when it was made. You can also compare or merge the first draft of a document to a subsequent draft to see where revisions were made to the original.

Read on to find out how you can track changes as you revise a document, accept or reject revisions, and fiddle with the way that revisions are marked onscreen.

"Saving (and Opening) Different Versions of a Document" in Chapter 22 explains another way to track revisions to a document—by saving different versions of it.

LEARN BY EXAMPLE
On the companion CD is a document called 19-4 Track Changes that you can open if you want to see how revision marks work.

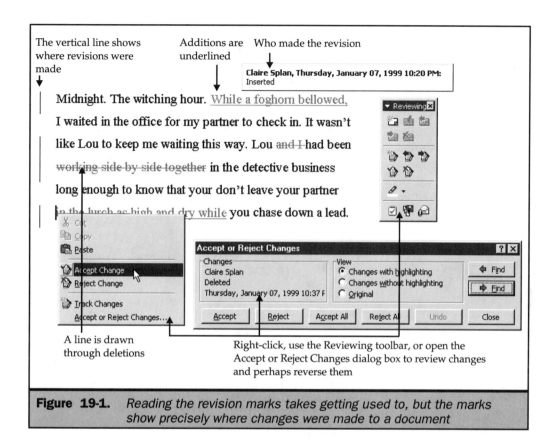

The vertical line shows where revisions were made

Additions are underlined

Who made the revision

Claire Splan, Thursday, January 07, 1999 10:20 PM:
Inserted

Midnight. The witching hour. While a foghorn bellowed,

I waited in the office for my partner to check in. It wasn't

like Lou to keep me waiting this way. Lou ~~and I~~ had been

~~working side by side together~~ in the detective business

long enough to know that your don't leave your partner

~~in the lurch as high and dry~~ while you chase down a lead.

▼ Reviewing

Cut
Copy
Paste
Accept Change
Reject Change
Track Changes
Accept or Reject Changes...

Accept or Reject Changes   ? X
Changes
Claire Splan
Deleted
Thursday, January 07, 1999 10:37 P

View
◉ Changes with highlighting
○ Changes without highlighting
○ Original

← Find
→ Find

Accept   Reject   Accept All   Reject All   Undo   Close

A line is drawn through deletions

Right-click, use the Reviewing toolbar, or open the Accept or Reject Changes dialog box to review changes and perhaps reverse them

Figure 19-1.   *Reading the revision marks takes getting used to, but the marks show precisely where changes were made to a document*

Tracking Revisions to a Document

Word offers no less than three different ways to track the changes that are made or were made to the original copy of a document. You can track the changes as you go along, compare the original copy to an edited copy to see where the edited copy differs from the original, or merge the original copy with a revised edition to make revision marks appear in the original. No matter which technique you choose, you end up with a document with revision marks that show precisely where changes were made to the original. Later, you can accept or reject the revisions.

- **Tracking Changes as You Make Them**   Revision marks appear as you delete text and make additions. The marks appear in the document as you work.

- **Comparing the Edited Document to the Original**   Instead of being distracted by revision marks, simply make editorial changes to the original copy. When you are done, choose Tools | Track Changes | Compare Documents, compare the edited copy to the original, and see on the edited copy where all revisions were made to the original. The original document is not changed.

Making Sure Revisions to a Document Are Tracked

Before you send out a document for others to review and change, you can choose Tools | Protect Document to make sure that all revisions to the document are tracked with revision marks. In a document that has been protected this way, reviewers cannot accept or reject revisions. Reviewers can't turn off the revision marking. All additions, deletions, and formatting changes are tracked whether the reviser likes it or not.

Follow these steps to make sure all revisions to a document are tracked:

1. Choose Tools | Protect Document. You will see the Protect Document dialog box.

2. Click the Track Changes option button.

3. Enter a password in the Password text box if you want to keep others from turning off the protection mechanism. Without the password, someone in the know can choose Tools | Unprotect Document and revise the document without the revisions being tracked. Passwords are case-sensitive, so be careful which password you enter. Enter the password in all lowercase letters, for example, and you will have to do the same when you turn off the protection mechanism.

4. Click OK. If you entered a password, you have to enter it again in the Confirm Password dialog box.

Choose Tools | Unprotect Document if you decide that the protection mechanism isn't necessary. If you attached a password to your document, you'll see the Unprotect Document dialog box. Enter the password and click OK.

- **Merging the Original with Edited Versions**   To see what others have done to the original document, choose Tools | Merge Documents to merge edited versions of the document with the original. Revision marks appear in the original document. Merge the original with edited versions when you want to see what more than one reviewer did to the original.

Later in this chapter, "Telling Word How to Mark Revisions" explains how to choose a color for marking revisions and how to choose for yourself which markings are used to show revisions.

Tracking Changes as You Make Them

To track changes that you make to a document as you make them, simply tell Word to start tracking changes. Word offers no less than four ways to do it:

- Double-click the TRK button on the Status bar.
- Click the Track Changes button on the Reviewing toolbar.
- Press CTRL-SHIFT-E.
- Choose Tools | Track Changes | Highlight Changes (or right-click the TRK button and choose Highlight Changes). In the Highlight Changes dialog box, check Track Changes While Editing and click OK.

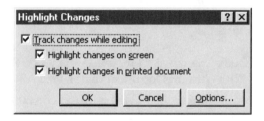

You can track revisions in a document without being distracted by the revision marks. To do so, open the Highlight Changes dialog box (choose Tools | Track Changes | Highlight Changes) and uncheck the Highlight Changes On Screen check box. When you want to see the revisions you have made, open the dialog box and check the Highlight Changes On Screen check box.

Each person who revises a document is automatically given a different display color. Additions appear in the display color, as do deletions. You can also tell Word to track formatting changes as well as changes to text (see "Telling Word How to Mark Revisions" later in this chapter). Try moving the pointer over a revision—your name and the time and date of the revision appear in a pop-up box. If the wrong name appears, choose Tools | Options, click the User Information tab in the Options dialog box, and enter your name.

> Betsy Manini, Thursday, February 11, 1999 9:45 AM:
> Inserted

~~HIX HICKS~~ NIX STICKS PIX

To quickly make an editorial change without it being recorded by revision marks, double-click the TRK button on the Status bar to turn off the revision marks. Then make your editorial change and double-click TRK again.

Comparing the Edited Document to the Original

Even if someone edited your document without turning on the revision marks, you can compare the original to the edited version to see where revisions were made and display revision marks in the edited copy. After the comparison is made, text that was added to or deleted from the original document is marked in the edited copy. Follow these steps to find out where the edited copy of a document and the original differ:

1. Open the edited copy of the document.

In order to compare the edited copy with the original, the edited copy cannot contain any revision marks. If revision marks show in the edited copy, accept all revisions. To do so, choose Tools | Track Changes | Accept or Reject Changes, click the Accept All button in the Accept or Reject Changes dialog box, and click Yes when Word asks if you want to accept all revisions. Then click the Close button in the Accept or Reject Changes dialog box and save the document.

2. Choose Tools | Track Changes | Compare Documents. You will see the Select File to Compare With Current Document dialog box.
3. Locate the original of the document, select it, and click the Open button.

Revision marks appear in the edited document. Lines are drawn through text that was deleted from the original, additions to the original are underlined, and all changes are displayed in color.

You can compare two versions of a document that you saved with the File | Versions command. To do so, however, you have to save and rename the earlier version of the document. Display the earlier version of the document, choose File | Save As, save the version under its own name, and then run the document comparison.

Merging the Original Copy with Edited Versions

Suppose you write the first draft of a document and give copies to several people for editing. When the copies are returned and you need to find out what each reviser did to the original, merge the original with the descendant copies. After the merge is complete, revision marks appear in the original document to show where revisers made additions and deletions in the text.

In order to merge an original document with its descendants, revision marks must be showing in the descendant copies. Open each descendant copy and make sure revision marks are showing. If someone forgot to track revisions in a descendant copy, compare the original to the descendant copy to make revisions marks show in the descendant. The previous section in this chapter explains how to compare the original of a document with a descendant copy.

Follow these steps to merge an original document with its descendant copies and thereby find out how revisers changed the original copy:

1. Open the clean, pristine original copy of the document.
2. Choose Tools | Merge Documents. You will see the Select File to Merge into Current Document dialog box.
3. Find and select the descendant copy you want to merge with the original, and then click the Open button.
4. Repeat steps 2 and 3 for each descendant copy you want to merge with the original.

In the original copy, changes made by the different revisers appear in different colors, lines are drawn through deletions, and additions are underlined.

When you merge an original document with it descendant copies, comments made by revisers also show up in the original. Later in this chapter, "Commenting on a Document" explains how comments work.

Reviewing, Accepting, and Rejecting Revisions

Reviewing revision marks and accepting or rejecting the changes that other people propose can be a daunting task. Especially if you are looking at a document with many revision marks, trying to see what will be left after revisions are accepted or rejected is difficult. Can you tell at a glance what will be left of the paragraph shown in this illustration if all the revisions are accepted? Turn this page upside-down to find out.

> | **About** ~~this situation, let me say this about that, and that is that, well, we are doing our best under~~ the ~~problem~~<u>circumstances to resolve this, and so</u>all I'<u>ll</u> can tell you is~~say this about that:~~ ~~W~~<u>we</u>'re <u>trying</u> ~~to solve it.~~

About the problem, all I can tell you is we're trying to solve it.

In my experience, the best way to handle revisions is to right-click the ones you want to reject and choose Reject Change from the shortcut menu. Keep the revisions you like, and when you finish reviewing the document, accept all the revisions (I'll show you how shortly). Here are techniques and tricks for reviewing, accepting, or rejecting revisions:

- **Accepting or Rejecting Revisions in a Block of Text**   Select the text and click the Accept Change or Reject Change button on the Reviewing toolbar.

- **Reviewing Revisions One at a Time with the Reviewing Toolbar**   Click the Previous Change or Next Change button on the Reviewing toolbar. Word highlights a revision. Click the Accept Change or Reject Change button to accept or reject it.

- **Reviewing Revisions One at a Time in the Accept or Reject Changes Dialog Box**   Choose Tools | Accept or Reject Changes (or right-click the TRK button and choose Accept or Reject Changes). You will see the Accept or Reject Changes dialog box shown in Figure 19-2. Click a Find button and then click the Accept or Reject button to accept or reject the revision that Word highlights. As Figure 19-2 shows, you can click a View button to see your document with

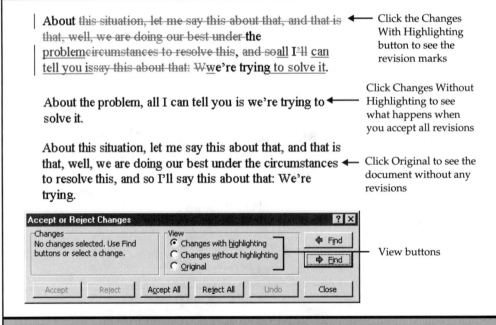

Figure 19-2.   *Click a View button in the Accept or Reject dialog box to see what your document looks like with revision marks (top), with revisions accepted (middle), and with revisions rejected (bottom)*

revision marks (Changes With Highlighting), with all revisions accepted (Changes Without Highlighting), and with all revisions rejected (Original).

■ **Accepting or Rejecting All Revisions at Once**   Click the Accept All or Reject All button in the Accept or Reject Changes dialog box (see Figure 19-2), and then click Yes when you are asked if you really want to accept or reject all the revisions in the document. To open the Accept or Reject changes dialog box, right-click the TRK button on the Status bar and choose Accept or Reject Changes.

Be sure to proofread your document carefully after you accept or reject revisions. Unfortunately, tracking changes with the Tools | Track Changes command introduces extra blank spaces, run-in words, misspellings, and various other errata.

Telling Word How to Mark Revisions

Unless you decide otherwise, inserted text is underlined, deleted text is crossed out, a vertical line appears in the left margin when revision marks are made, and changes made by each reviser appear in a different color. If these settings don't suit you, you can change them by going to the Track Changes tab in the Options dialog box. To get there, right-click the TRK button and choose Options or choose Tools | Options and click the Track Changes tab in the Options dialog box, as shown in Figure 19-3.

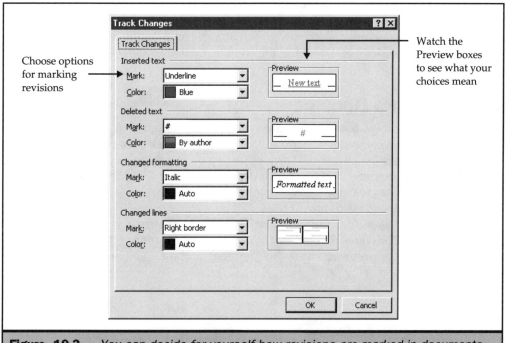

Figure 19-3.   *You can decide for yourself how revisions are marked in documents*

These options are self-explanatory, I think. Keep your eye on the Preview boxes to see what your choices do to revision marks. The only odd option is the Mark option under Changed Formatting. Choose a Mark option besides (None) and Word marks formatting changes to the document as well as text changes. Go ahead and choose a color beside the one that Word assigned you for revision marks, but be careful not to choose a color that was assigned to someone else. If you do, no one will be able to tell which revisions are yours and which are someone else's without pointing to a revision mark and reading the pop-up box.

Ways to Critique Others' Work

In prehistoric times, critiquing other people's work meant scribbling illegibly in the margin of a page, or—it seems fantastic to us now—actually visiting someone in an office to talk face to face about a project! Then came the sticky note, a small yellow piece of paper that could be scribbled on and stuck to the corner of a page. In the early days of computer networks, attempts were made to send sticky notes over the cable wires, but those early experiments gummed up the wires and failed dismally. Now, in the era of the network and the Internet, new ways have been devised for critiquing others' work and collaborating with others. New, exciting ways! It is now possible to collaborate for weeks, months, or even years with other people without even knowing what they look like! Science marches on! These pages explain three techniques for critiquing others' work and collaborating with others: commenting on a document, making notes with hidden text, and highlighting text.

Commenting on a Document

A *comment* is a note to yourself or to someone else that is attached to a document but isn't printed. Insert a comment to remind yourself to do a task or to critique another's writing. Comments do not upset the formatting of a page, so you can sprinkle as many comments as you want in a document. Comments aren't printed, either, unless you tell Word to print them, so you don't have to worry about embarrassing yourself in print with a sharp-edged, barbed comment.

This illustration shows what a comment looks like in the text. Comments are highlighted. When you move the pointer over a comment, a pop-up box appears, you'll see the name of the person who wrote the comment, and the comment itself.

> **Joanne Cuthbertson:**
> Kind of far-fetched, don't you think?

Here's the plan: I xerox it and fax it to you. Then you xerox the fax. Send the xerox of the fax to Marsha, but send the fax itself to Dave. Have Dave scan the fax and xerox the scan. He can then send it to Illya. Do you think this will work?

Read on to find out how to insert a comment, insert a voice comment, review comments, delete and move them, prevent others from changing comments, and print comments.

LEARN BY EXAMPLE
Open the 19-3 Comments sample document on the CD to learn about comments.

Inserting and Recording Comments

Follow these steps to insert a comment:

1. Select the word or sentence that needs criticizing or praising.

2. Choose Insert | Comment or click the Insert Comment button on the Reviewing toolbar. The so-called Comment pane appears at the bottom of the screen. Other comments, if any have been made, appear in the Comment pane. The comments are numbered. Beside each comment are the initials of the person who wrote it. Click and drag the boundary of the Comment pane if you need more room to read comments.

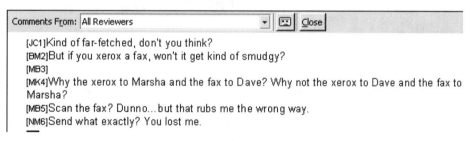

3. Type your comment.

4. Click the Close button, click the Edit Comment button on the Reviewing toolbar, or double-click the boundary of the Comment pane to close the Comment pane.

As long as your machine is capable of recording sound and, more importantly, the people who need to hear your voice comment are capable of playing sound on their computers, you can record a voice comment. To do so, select the part of the document that deserves a comment, choose Insert | Comment, and click the Insert Sound Object button in the Comment pane. When the Sound Object dialog box appears, record your voice comment and type a word or two of text as well. Then click the Close button to close the Comment pane. Tell your friends and co-workers whose computers can play sound to double-click the loud speaker icon in the Comment pane to hear your comment.

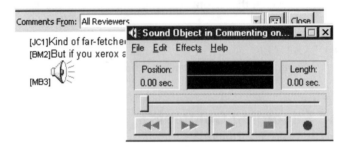

If someone else's name appears in the pop-up box when you record a comment, choose Tools | Options, click the User Information tab in the Options dialog box, and enter your name in the Name text box.

Allowing Reviewers to Comment on but Not Revise Documents

Word offers a command with which you can pass around a document and allow others to comment on it but not change it. To welcome others' comments but prohibit their editorial changes, choose Tools | Protect Document and click the Comments option button in the Protect Document dialog box. If you want, enter a password in the Password dialog box to keep someone from unprotecting the document. Without the password, all you have to do to make editorial changes is choose Tools | Unprotect Document. Passwords are case-sensitive, so remember the combination of upper- and lowercase letters you enter as well as the password name. When you choose Tools | Unprotect Document to allow editorial changes in the document, Word asks you to enter the password again.

Reviewing the Comments in a Document

The easiest way to review the comments in a document is to move the pointer over a comment and read the pop-up box. (If you don't see a pop-up box and you can't see the yellow highlights that show where comments are located, choose Tools | Options, click the View tab in the Options dialog box, and check the ScreenTips check box.) However, to add wealth to riches, Word offers numerous other ways to review comments:

■ **Read (and Edit) Comments in the Comment Pane**   To open the Comment pane and read the comments (and edit them as well), choose View | Comments or click the Edit Comments button on the Reviewing toolbar. The Comment pane opens. Scroll through the comments. When you click a comment, the top half of the window scrolls to the comment you clicked. You may have to drag the boundary of the Comment pane up the screen to read all the comments. To read comments from a particular reviewer, click the down arrow beside the Comment From text box and choose a name.

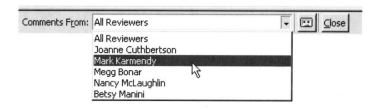

If a comment is worthy of belonging in the document itself, you can copy or move it into the document. Either drag the comment from the Comment pane into the document or cut and paste it there.

■ **Skip from Comment to Comment**   Click the Previous Comment or Next Comment button on the Reviewing toolbar. You can also click the Select Browse Object button, choose Browse by Comment on the pop-up menu, and then click the double arrows above and below the Select Browse Object button to skip backward or forward from comment to comment.

■ **Find Comments from a Particular Reviewer**   Besides choosing a reviewer's name in the Comments pane, you can choose Edit | Go To (or press CTRL-G) to locate comments from a reviewer. On the Go To tab of the Find and Replace dialog box, choose Comment in the Go To What menu, choose the reviewer's name from the Enter Reviewer's Name drop-down list, and start clicking the Previous or Next button.

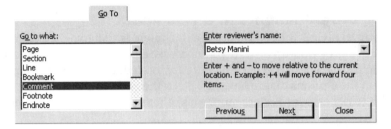

Deleting Comments

Forget the Comment pane when you want to delete a comment. To delete a comment, you have to go to the main text and click its marker, the initials and number enclosed in square brackets. Choose View | Comments or click the Show/Hide ¶ button to see the markers, click the one you want to delete, and then do one of the following:

- Click the Delete Comment button on the Reviewing toolbar.
- Right-click and choose Delete Comment.
- Press either the DELETE or BACKSPACE key twice.

To delete all the comments in a document, click the Show/Hide ¶ button to see the markers, move the cursor to the top of the document, and choose Edit | Replace to open the Find and Replace dialog box. With the cursor in the Find What box, click the Special button (you might have to click the More button first) and choose Comment Mark (^a) from the pop-up menu. Then glance at the Replace With box to make sure it is empty and click the Replace All button.

Printing the Comments in a Document

Normally, comments are not printed along with the rest of the document, but you can tell Word to print them. Initials of people who entered comments and comment numbers are printed as well. Word also lists the page numbers on which comments are found. Follow these steps to print the comments in a document:

1. Choose File | Print or press CTRL-P to open the Print dialog box.

2. Either print the comments by themselves or print the document and the comments:

- **Printing Only the Comments** Choose Comments from the Print What drop-down menu and click OK.

- **Printing the Document and the Comments** Click the Options button. On the Print tab of the Options dialog box, look under Include With Document and check the Comments check box. Click OK twice. The comments are printed on a separate page at the end of the document.

Highlighting the Important Text

Another way to point out parts of a document that need attention is to highlight them. Click the down arrow beside the Highlight button on the Formatting toolbar or Reviewing toolbar and you will see a drop-down menu of 15 colors you can use for highlighting text. Highlighting is the digital equivalent of those fat felt pens that sleepy college students drag across the pages of the books that they may or may not actually be reading.

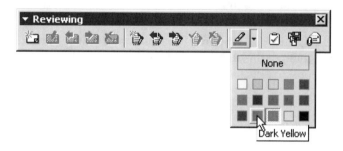

Highlighting is strictly for use online. Highlight parts of a document so you can return to them later. Color-code headings that pertain to certain topics. You can think of many uses for highlighting. These pages explain how to highlight text and how to remove the highlighting when you print a document.

Highlighting Text in a Document

Here are the two ways to highlight text:

- Click the down arrow beside the Highlight button on the Formatting toolbar or Reviewing toolbar and choose a color from the drop-down menu. Notice how the stripe along the bottom of the Highlight button changes colors and the pointer changes into a fat crayon. Drag the crayon pointer across the text you want to highlight. Click the Highlight button again or press ESC to put the fat crayon back in the crayon box.

- Select the text you want to highlight, click the down arrow beside the Highlight button, and choose a color. The text is highlighted with the color you chose.

 The stripe along the bottom of the Highlight button shows the last color you chose. To apply that color again, simply click the button without opening the drop-down menu.

Removing the Highlights

Whatever you do, do not print a document with text that has been highlighted. The highlights look awful on the printed page. Here are two strategies for removing the highlights:

■ **Removing All the Highlights in a Document** If you are done reviewing a document, you may as well remove all the highlights. To do so, choose Edit | Select All or press CTRL-A to select the entire document, click the down arrow beside the Highlight button, and choose None from the drop-down menu.

■ **Removing Highlights Temporarily While You Print a Document** To temporarily remove the highlights while you print a document, choose Tools | Options and click the View tab in the Options dialog box. Under Show, find the Highlight check box and uncheck it. Then print your document. When you want to see the highlights again, return to the View tab and check the Highlight check box.

Instead of strolling through a long document to find highlights, you can call upon the Edit | Find command to find them. Choose Edit | Find or press CTRL-F, click the Format button in the Find and Replace dialog box (you might have to click the More button to get to it), choose Highlight on the pop-up menu, and click Find Next repeatedly to find all the places where you highlighted text.

Making Notes with Hidden Text

I'm not exactly sure what hidden text is for. The text is not truly hidden, since all you have to do to see it is click the Show/Hide ¶ button. Hidden text is not printed, so you can use it to comment or make notes on a document, but the Insert | Comment command is better for doing that because comments are easy to find, whereas hidden text is nearly impossible to find unless you know where it is.

This illustration shows what hidden text looks like. A dotted underline appears under the text. Except for its being hidden, hidden text can be edited or formatted like other text. Maybe the purpose of hidden text is to describe the subliminal messages in advertisements.

Summer's·here·and·that·means·bathing·suit·time·again·and·you·put·on·
weight·since·last·summer,·I·bet.··Why·not·come·visit·us·at·the·Union·
Street·Health·Center?·You'll·meet·lots·of·friendly·people.··Come·on.··
You've·got·nothing·to·lose·—·nothing·but·a·few·pounds,·that·is.¶

Here is how to handle hidden text:

- **Entering Hidden Text** Select the text first if you have already written it, and then either press CTRL-SHIFT-H or choose Format | Font and check the Hidden check box in the Font dialog box. Start typing. The text doesn't appear onscreen. To enter normal text again, either press CTRL-SHIFT-H a second time or revisit the Font dialog box and uncheck the Hidden check box.

- **Viewing Hidden Text** Click the Show/Hide ¶ button on the Standard toolbar or press CTRL-SHIFT-*. Click the button or press the shortcut key combination again to hide the text.

- **Printing Hidden Text** Choose File | Print, click the Options button in the Print dialog box, look under Include With Document on the Print tab of the Options dialog box, and check the Hidden Text check box. The hidden text is printed along with the rest of your document. Don't forget to revisit the Options dialog box and uncheck the Hidden Text check box to keep hidden text from being printed in the future.

Organizing Your Work with Outlines

In a long report or manual, you can save a lot of time you would otherwise spend organizing your work by starting from an outline. In Outline view, you can see all the headings in a document, the major headings, the major and minor headings, or the headings in a particular section. Outline view shows how the different parts of a document fit together. And if something is amiss, if the parts don't fit together, you can rearrange them in Outline view. You can simultaneously move headings and the text underneath headings to new places in a document. Outline view is quite simply the easiest way to move text from place to place and stay organized.

These pages explain what is one of the most valuable features of Word 2000. You'll learn how to create an outline, view your outline in different ways, move headings and text throughout a document, promote and demote headings, edit text in Outline view, and arrange the headings in alphabetical order.

LEARN BY EXAMPLE
Open the 19-1 Outline document on the companion CD to get some practical experience with outlines.

Outline View: The Big Picture

In order to do any work in Outline view, you must have applied Heading styles from the Style menu to the headings in your document. Either that, or you must be working with styles that have been assigned outline levels higher than Body Text. "Choosing an Outline Level for Paragraphs" in Chapter 8 explains how to assign different outline levels to paragraphs. Chapter 12 explains styles, including how to apply Heading styles from the Style menu.

To switch to Outline view:

- Click the Outline View button in the lower-left corner of the screen.
- Choose View | Outline.
- Press ALT-CTRL-O.

 To see a document in Outline view and Normal view at the same time, split the screen and switch to Normal view on one side of the screen. See "Splitting the Screen" in Chapter 6.

Figure 19-4 shows two of the many different ways to examine a document in Outline view. In both outlines, headings assigned Headings styles are shown. In the outline at the top of the figure, however, the Show Heading 1 button on the Outlining toolbar has been clicked, so only first-level headings are shown. In the second outline, the Show Heading 2 button has been clicked, so first- and second-level headings appear. By clicking Show Heading buttons 1 through 7, you tell Word button which headings to display in Outline view, and in so doing you can tell whether your document needs reorganizing.

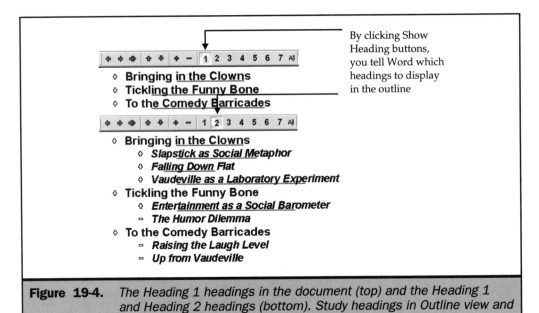

Figure 19-4.   *The Heading 1 headings in the document (top) and the Heading 1 and Heading 2 headings (bottom). Study headings in Outline view and you can tell whether your document is well organized*

Suppose you need to examine the headings in a certain part of your document. You can do that without displaying all the headings, as this illustration shows. Here, the third-level headings are on display in one part of a document but not in the other parts.

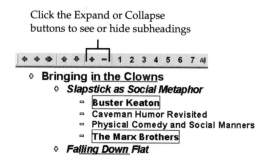

Click the Expand or Collapse
buttons to see or hide subheadings

And if Outline view reveals that a document is not well organized? In that case, you can reorganize it without leaving Outline view:

- Edit the headings. Delete words and enter new ones. Go ahead. No one is going to bite you. Outline view is the best place to edit headings, since you can see all or several of them at once.

- Click the Promote or Demote button on the Outlining toolbar to change a heading's heading-level assignment. Instead of choosing another Heading style from the Style menu, you can simply click the Promote or Demote button.

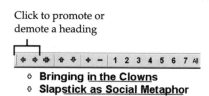

Click to promote or
demote a heading

- Click the Move Up or Move Down button to move headings—as well as their subheadings and the text beneath them—forward or backward in the document. In Outline view, you can move entire sections of a document in a second or two without resorting to the Cut and Paste commands.

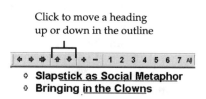

Click to move a heading
up or down in the outline

"Printing an Outline" in Chapter 5 explains how to print outlines.

Getting the Right View of Your Outline

Outline view presents many different ways of looking at the headings in a document as well as the first line in body text paragraphs. Here are different ways of examining your document in Outline view:

- **Viewing Headings Up to a Certain Level**   Click Show Heading button 1 through 7 on the Outlining toolbar to see first- through seventh-level headings in a document. All headings are shown with this technique. Very likely, you have to scroll through the document to read all the headings. You can also press ALT-1 through ALT-7 to view headings at different levels.

- **Viewing All the Headings**   Click the All button on the Outlining toolbar (or press ALT-SHIFT-A). Click the button once and all text is shown, but click it a second time and only headings appear onscreen.

- **Drilling Down to Examine Subheadings in Part of a Document**   Either click the plus sign (+) next to a heading or click to the left of a heading to select it, and then click the Expand button (or press ALT-+) to see the subheadings. If no subheadings are found under a heading, a minus sign instead of a plus sign appears beside the heading in Outline view.

  A plus sign next to a heading means   ✛ Bringing in the Clowns
  subheadings are found below the heading   ✛ Tickling the Funny Bone

- **Hiding Subheadings in Part of a Document**   Click to the left of a heading to select it, and then click the Collapse button on the Outlining toolbar.

Click the Show Formatting button to see headings in their native formats. Click the button again and the headings appear as plain text.

 Double-click the plus sign next to a heading to display all subheadings underneath it, or, if the subheadings are already displayed, to hide all subheadings underneath it.

Moving Headings—and Text—in a Document

Outline view is the most convenient place to move headings forward or backward in a document. Instead of the messy Cut and Paste commands, you can simply click buttons on the Outlining toolbar. The text under a heading moves along with the heading when the heading is moved elsewhere. Starting in Outline view, follow these steps to move a heading in a document:

1. Click the heading you want to move.

2. Tell Word whether you want to move subheadings (if there are any) below the heading:

   ■ To move the subheadings along with the heading, click the Collapse button to fold the subheadings into the heading. As long as no subheadings are displayed beneath the heading, the subheadings move along with the heading.

   ■ To move the heading independently of its subheadings, click the Expand button to display the subheadings. If subheadings are displayed beneath the heading, only the heading moves.

3. Click the Move Up or Move Down button as many times as necessary to move the heading where you want it to go.

Rearranging, Promoting, and Demoting Headings

When a heading needs to be promoted or demoted or needs to be turned into text, click it and call on the three buttons on the left side of the Outlining toolbar. By clicking one of the three buttons, you can turn a Heading 2 heading into a Heading 1 or Heading 3 heading, for example.

Whether subheadings are promoted or demoted along with a heading depends on whether the subheadings appear in Outline view. When subheadings appear below a heading, the heading is promoted or demoted independently of the heading. But when the subheadings do not appear onscreen, they are promoted or demoted to the same degree as the heading. To promote or demote subheadings along with the heading, click the heading then click the Collapse button on the Outlining toolbar to fold the subheadings into the heading. Click the Expand button to display the subheadings if you want to promote or demote the heading independently of its subordinates.

Arranging Headings in Alphabetical Order

Here's a little trick for arranging the first-level headings in a document in alphabetical order. Switch to Outline view and click the Show Heading 1 button on the Outlining toolbar. Then choose Table | Sort and click OK in the Sort Text dialog box.

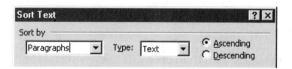

Text and subheadings underneath the first-level headings are moved right along with the headings themselves. "Alphabetizing and Sorting Lists" in Chapter 10 explains all the vagaries of the Sort Text dialog box.

Select a heading and follow these instructions to promote or demote a heading:

- **Promote It** Click the Promote button on the Outlining toolbar as many times as necessary to move it up the ladder
- **Demote It** Click the Demote button once, twice, or several times
- **Turn It into Text** Click the Demote to Body Text button

You can also promote or demote headings by clicking them and then choosing a style from the Style menu on the Formatting toolbar.

Master Documents for Organizing Big Jobs

A document longer than 50 pages, especially if it includes a graphic or two, can get very unwieldy. Searching for text in a document like that can take forever. In Page Layout view, paginating a document that long takes a while, too. To make handling long documents easier and to make working on team projects in which several people work on the same document go more smoothly, Word offers the master document. A *master document* is a set of subdocuments that have been organized under one umbrella document.

With a master document, you can work in the master document or one of the subdocuments. Work done in a subdocument is recorded in the master document as well. Likewise, work done in the master document is saved in the subdocument. The master document arrangement makes long documents easier to work with. What's more, everything that you can do in Outline view to organize or rearrange a document can be done in a master document, so a master document also gives you all the advantages of working in Outline view.

So much for the good news about master documents. I would be remiss if I didn't tell you that master documents tax the memory resources of your computer and have been known to stop working or work sluggishly. Word newsgroups are full of complaints about master documents. This book's technical editor remarks, "Word sometimes completely and irrecoverably corrupts the master document and all of the subdocuments." A couple years ago, while doing some contract work for a company, I sat in the cubicle next to someone who made the mistake of using a master document to organize a long company manual. I can still hear the poor woman groaning while her computer failed time and time again. If you decide to use a master document, do so with these reservations:

- Do not track revisions with the Tools | Track Changes command. Between tracking revisions and handling subdocuments, your computer's memory resources will be hammered.
- Make sure everyone who works on the project, if more than one person will work on it, uses the same template.

- Turn off the Allow Fast Saves feature. As "Telling Word How to Save Documents" in Chapter 22 explains, Word actually keeps a document in two separate files when the feature is turned on. The two-file arrangement makes saving documents go faster, but it also increases the size of documents and makes sharing documents more problematic. To turn off the Allow Fast Saves feature, choose Tools | Options, click the Save tab in the Options dialog box, and uncheck the Allow Fast Saves check box.

- Do not put any graphics, sound files, or other memory-intensive items in the document until you are nearly done with the project.

- Create a new folder for your document and subdocuments and do not under any circumstances move documents out of the folder.

Frankly, my experiences with master documents have been so bad I cannot recommend using the feature, but it's too early to tell whether master documents in Word 2000 have been improved. Anyone who reads this and goes on to try master documents is invited to send me an e-mail message at **Peter_Weverka@msn.com**. I would like to know about your experience with the feature and whether you recommend using it.

Anyhow, the word "complete" is in the title of this book, so I am obliged to cover master documents. Read on to find out how to assemble documents into a master document, create a master document from scratch, work with master documents, and lock master documents so that others cannot edit them.

Knowing how to work in Outline view is a prerequisite for working with master documents. Don't bother creating a master document unless you are familiar with the buttons on the Outline toolbar.

LEARN BY EXAMPLE
The 19-2 Master document on the companion CD demonstrates how master documents work.

Creating a Master Document

How you create a master document depends on whether you create it from scratch or assemble documents you have already created in a master document. Read on to explore the two ways to create a master document.

Make sure all subdocuments are kept in the same folder. That way, Word can find them easily. If you are just starting your master document, create a new folder for storing its subdocuments.

Creating a Master Document from Scratch When You Start a Project

To create a master document from scratch, write an outline of your new project in Outline view. Then divide the headings equally into subdocuments. Follow these steps to create a master document and its subdocuments:

1. Create a new document and save it in the folder you created for your master document.

2. Choose View | Outline to switch to Outline view.

3. Enter the headings for your project. As you do so, open the Style menu and assign Heading styles to your headings. Be sure to assign at least a few headings to the Heading 1 style. Later, you will divide the document into subdocuments where the Heading 1 styles are.

4. Click the plus sign beside the first Heading 1 heading in the document. By clicking the plus sign, you select the heading and all of its subheadings.

5. Click the Create Subdocument button on the Outlining toolbar. You will find this button on the right side of the toolbar. A box appears around the headings in the subdocument and a subdocument icon appears in the upper-left corner of the box.

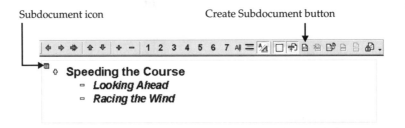

6. Select the set of headings and click the Create Subdocument button again to create a second subdocument. In this way, divide the master documents into subdocuments of roughly the same size.

7. Save your master document.

Word saves all subdocuments when you save the master. To name the subdocuments, Word takes the name of the first heading.

Assembling Documents for a Master Document

Perhaps you started your project before you decided to manage it by way of a master document. In that case, you have to assemble documents from different places and bind them together as a master document. Do so by following these steps:

1. Create a new document and save it in the folder you created especially for your new master document.

2. Choose View | Outline to switch to Outline view.

3. Click the Insert Subdocument button to open the Insert Subdocument dialog box.

4. Locate and select the document that will be the first in the master document and click the Open button.

5. Repeat steps 3 and 4 until you have loaded down your master document with subdocuments.

When you assemble documents for a master document, the subdocuments keep their original names.

Working on the Master and Its Subdocuments

When the time comes to start work on a master document, you can begin with a subdocument or open the master. Either way, the work you do is recorded in the master document. Open a subdocument and you won't notice any differences between working in a subdocument and a document that doesn't have a master. But if you open the master document, you might be surprised to see your screen looking like Figure 19-5.

When you open a master document, the first thing you see are hyperlinks that you can click to open subdocuments and start your work there. Notice that each hyperlink lists the path to a subdocument. Very convenient indeed. By clicking a hyperlink, you can open a subdocument and start working. On the other hand, if you want to stay in the master document, you can stay put and do your work there by clicking the Expand Subdocuments button on the Outlining toolbar (or by pressing CTRL-\). You will see the document in Outline view. Switch to Normal view or Page Layout view and get to work.

Reorganizing the Master Document

You are invited to use all the buttons on the Outline toolbar to organize your master document (earlier in this chapter, "Organizing Your Work with Outlines" explains the buttons). For example, you can move headings and subheadings to and fro by clicking the Move Up and Move Down buttons. And you can promote or demote headings by clicking the Promote and Demote buttons.

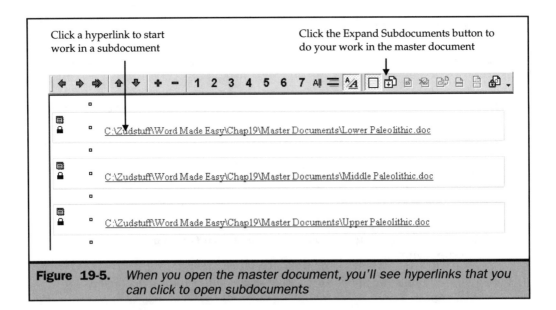

Click a hyperlink to start
work in a subdocument

Click the Expand Subdocuments button to
do your work in the master document

C:\Zudstuff\Word Made Easy\Chap19\Master Documents\Lower Paleolithic.doc

C:\Zudstuff\Word Made Easy\Chap19\Master Documents\Middle Paleolithic.doc

C:\Zudstuff\Word Made Easy\Chap19\Master Documents\Upper Paleolithic.doc

Figure 19-5.   *When you open the master document, you'll see hyperlinks that you
can click to open subdocuments*

*Unless you want to split a subdocument in two, click the 1 button on the Master
Document toolbar when you are working with subdocuments. Seeing only the first-level
headings makes moving, merging, and removing subdocuments easier.*

Apart from the buttons on the Outlining toolbar, here are instructions for handling
subdocuments in a master document:

- **Dividing a Subdocument in Two**   Click the first heading in the subdocument
  and then click the Expand button to see all the headings. With that done, click
  the heading that you want to be the first in the new subdocument and click the
  Split Subdocument button.

- **Merging Subdocuments**   Move the subdocuments so that they are next to
  each other in the master document. Then hold down the SHIFT key and click
  each subdocument's subdocument icon to select both subdocuments. Finally,
  click the Merge Subdocument button.

- **Moving Subdocuments**   Click the subdocument icon of the subdocument you
  want to move and drag it up or down the screen to move it. Make sure when
  you do this that you don't drop the subdocument inside another subdocument.

- **Removing a Subdocument**   Click the subdocument icon and then click the
  Remove Subdocument button. Removing a subdocument does not delete it.
  You can still find and open the subdocument under its own name.

■ **Locking a Subdocument So It Can't Be Edited**   When you lock a subdocument, no one can read or alter it without visiting the master document and unlocking it. To lock a subdocument, click it and then click the Lock Document button, the last button on the Outlining toolbar. To unlock it, click the Lock Document button again. A padlock appears beside subdocuments that have been locked, showing a picture of a padlock next to their names:

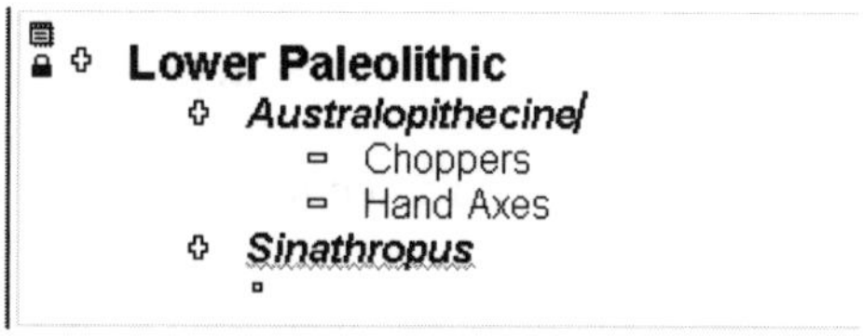

> **Lower Paleolithic**
> > *Australopithecine*
> > > □ Choppers
> > > □ Hand Axes
> > *Sinathropus*
> > > □

Exam | MOUS Exam Objectives Explored in Chapter 19

Objective	Heading	Practice File
Highlight text in a document	"Highlighting the Important Text"	
Work with master documents and subdocuments*	"Master Documents for Organizing Big Jobs"	19-2 Master
Insert comments*	"Commenting on a Document"	19-3 Comments
Track changes to a document*	"Keeping Track of Revisions to Documents"	19-4 Track Changes

* Denotes an Expert exam objective.

Top **Ten Tips for Sharing Documents with Others**

Sharing documents with other people presents several problems, some of which can grow into big problems if you are not careful. Following are ten tips for sharing documents with others. Take these tips into consideration when you collaborate on a document.

1. MAKE SURE EVERYONE IS USING THE SAME TEMPLATE.   When people who work at different computers collaborate on a document, problems with styles can arise if the template on which the document was founded is not loaded on each computer. As you know if you read Chapter 12, every Word document is grounded in a template. When you choose a style from the Style menu, you in effect ask the template to format a part of your document. If everyone who collaborates on a document asks a different template to format their document, you'll get different formats. Headings change appearance. Indents change. New fonts appear. Lists are not formatted the same way. The document you gave to somebody else to work on comes back looking like an impostor.

When you pass along a document to your collaborator, make sure that he or she also has the template with which you created the document. For that matter, when someone hands you a document, make sure you also get the template with which the document was created. And that brings us to Tip #2 in the list....

2. ATTACH THE TEMPLATE FOR THE SHARED DOCUMENT TO THE DOCUMENT.   When you get a template from someone else, load it on your computer and attach the template to the document you want to collaborate on. "Applying Styles *En Masse* with the Templates and Add-Ins Command" in Chapter 12 explains how to attach a template to a document. Load your template in the C:\Windows Application Data\Microsoft\Templates folder.

If your computer is connected to a network workgroup, you can share templates over the network with others. Tell your network administrator that you want to be able to share a template with other members of your workgroup and ask the administrator which folder shared templates are stored in. Then do the following in your computer to tell Word where to find the template you need to work with:

1. Choose Tools | Options.
2. Click the File Locations tab in the Options dialog box.
3. Under File Types, select Workgroup Templates, and then click the Modify button. You see the Modify Location dialog box.
4. Find the folder on your network where the workgroup templates are located. You can get the name of the folder from the network administrator.
5. Click OK and then click OK again in the Options dialog box.

After all collaborators have attached the right template for the document they are sharing, they can rest assured that no formats will change when the document is passed from collaborator to collaborator. Well, they can rest assured except for a couple of minor details, which brings up Tip #3.

3. TELL WORD NOT TO ASSIGN STYLES AUTOMATICALLY. Word 2000 assigns styles to certain paragraphs automatically. If you format a paragraph a certain way, Word may decide that you need a style and assign a style for you. Automatic style assignments are fine and dandy when you are working on your own, but they can wreak havoc when a document is shared with others. An automatic style gets assigned here, another gets created there, and pretty soon you are looking at a crazy quilt of a document.

Follow these steps to tell Word not to assign styles automatically:

1. Choose Tools | AutoCorrect to open the AutoCorrect dialog box.
2. Click the AutoFormat As You Type tab.
3. Under Automatically As You Type, uncheck the Define Styles Based On Your Formatting check box.
4. Under Apply As You Type, uncheck the Headings check box.
5. Click OK.

4. TURN OFF THE FAST-SAVING MECHANISM. As "Telling Word How to Save Documents" explains in Chapter 22, the Allow Fast Saves feature makes it possible to save documents as you work. That's nice except for one thing: Word does not save recent changes in the document file, but in a separate file so that updates can be made faster. When you pass a document to someone else and the fast-saving mechanism is in effect, you really pass two files to someone else. Passing along two files instead of one can be confusing to the computer that receives the document. Microsoft recommends turning off the Allow Fast Saves option when you finish working on a document or give it to someone else. To turn it off, choose Tools | Options, click the Save tab in the Options dialog box, and uncheck the Allow Fast Saves check box.

5. USE COMMON FONTS THAT ARE FOUND ON EVERYONE'S COMPUTER.
Fonts can be a problem when you share documents because the same fonts are not available on all computers. To get around the font problem, use common fonts such as Arial and Times Roman for early drafts of your work. When the time comes to get the document ready for a presentation, give it to one person to put the finishing touches on. Let the last person who handles the document apply the fancy fonts. You will waste your time if you apply fancy fonts in the early stages because the fancy fonts are likely to disappear when they travel to other people's computers.

6. TAKE PAPER SIZE INTO ACCOUNT. Recently I designed a template for an international company with offices in Europe and the United States. Because Europeans and North Americans have different paper standards, I had to design two templates, one for 210 × 297-millimeter (A4) paper and one for 8½ × 11-inch paper. Paper sizes effect layouts. If you are collaborating with others across international borders, take paper size into account. You may have to create two documents, one for your paper standard and one for theirs.

7. SEE IF YOU CAN GET EVERYONE TO USE THE SAME VERSION OF WORD.

I realize that asking all collaborators to use Word 2000 is asking a lot. Upgrades can be expensive. Learning the new version of a computer program creates a certain amount of anxiety and takes time. Still, you'll save a lot of trouble if all collaborators use Word 2000. Some formats are lost when a Word 2000 document is saved as a Word 97 or Word 95 document.

8. DO NOT TRADE VERSIONS OF DOCUMENTS.

As "Saving (and Opening) Different Versions of a Document" explains in Chapter 22, Word offers a very nice feature whereby different versions of a document can be saved and kept on hand in case they are needed. You might be tempted to pass along versions of a document to others, but don't do it. Others may open different versions of the document and pretty soon you won't know which version is which.

Before you pass along a document for which you've created different versions, open the version that you want to pass along. Then choose File | Save As and save the version under its own name.

9. USE DOCUMENT SUMMARIES TO DESCRIBE WORK DONE TO A DOCUMENT.

When a document gets passed here, there, and everywhere, knowing who worked on it and what was done to it can be difficult. To describe the work that was done, instruct everyone who handles the document to choose File | Properties and jot a note or two in the Comments box on the Summary tab of the Properties dialog box. By reading the notes, you can see what the different collaborators did to the document.

10. CREATE FOLDERS FOR ORGANIZING THE PROJECT.

Nothing gets out of hand faster than a project in which you collaborate with many people. Create folders for different drafts of the work. Save versions of the work from different collaborators in different folders. And make sure you always know which version of the document is the most up to date and represents the fruition of everyone's labor.

The Complete Reference

Word 2000

Chapter 20

Churning Out Form Letters, Mass-Mailing Labels, and Lists

605

This chapter describes *mail-merging*, Microsoft's term for generating form letters, labels, and envelopes for mass-mailings. No doubt you've received form letters in the mail. And you've seen your name on a printed mailing label, too. Large companies generate form letters and mailing labels by taking names and addresses from databases and plugging those names and addresses into form letters or printing them on mailing labels. You can do the same in Word 2000. You can plug names and addresses from your own tables and address lists into form letters and mailing labels. In your own small way, you can be a junk mailer.

Be sure to read the first section in this chapter, "Mail-Merging: The Big Picture," if you are new to mail-merging. It explains how Word gathers names and addresses for the mail-merge and what mail-merging entails. You'll also find out how to generate form letters, mailing labels, envelopes for mass-mailings, and lists in this chapter. Toward the end of the chapter are advanced techniques for sorting and querying data before you mail-merge it. You will also find a list of ten common mail-merge problems and advice for solving them at the end of the chapter.

Mail-Merging: The Big Picture

"Mail-merges," as they are known in Word 2000, are deceptively simple. In fact, if it weren't for the many dialog boxes that Word throws in the way to be helpful, you would see right away how mail-merging works. *Mail-merging* means to plug data from an address table into a form letter, address label, or list. The details of mail-merging are described throughout this chapter. These pages describe the three basics steps of mail-merging. To start a mail-merge, choose Tools | Mail Merge and go to work in the Mail Merge Helper dialog box shown in Figure 20-1.

Note *To generate mailing labels and form letters, you have to know two terms from the dreary world of databases: field and record. A field is one category of information. A record comprises all the data about one person or thing. It helps to think of fields and records in terms of the rows and columns in a table: Each row in a table is a record, since it lists what is known about one person or thing; each record is divided into several fields, or categories, of information, in the same way that each row is divided into columns.*

1. MAIN DOCUMENT For the main document, the one in which the merging takes place, you can create a new document or use an existing one. In the case of labels and envelopes, you'll tell Word what size labels or envelopes you intend to print on. In the case of form letters and catalogs, you will write the text of the letter or catalog in the main document.

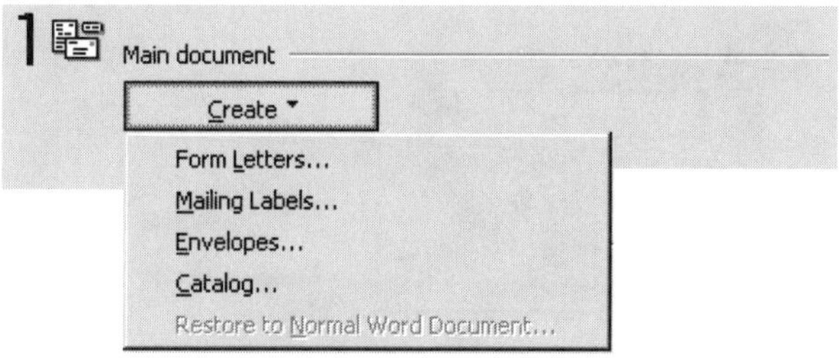

2. DATA SOURCE   The *data source*, as it is known, is where the names and addresses for the mailing labels, envelopes, or form letters come from. The data source can be a table in a Word document, an Excel worksheet, a database table, or the address book or contact list where you store your addresses. You can also choose Create Data Source to create a data source—that is, create a table of names and addresses—if you have not already done so.

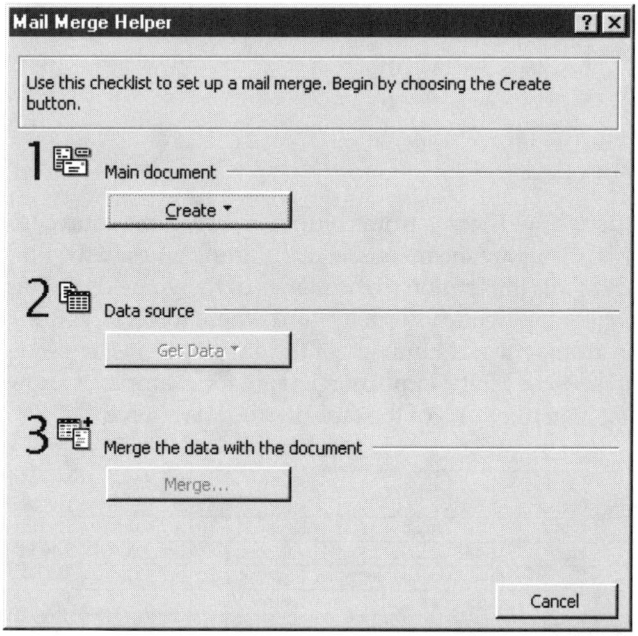

Figure 20-1.   *All mail-merges begin in the Mail Merge Helper dialog box*

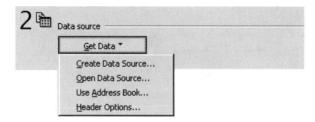

After you create or declare the data source, you insert the *merge fields*, the different pieces of the address or list, in the main document. By inserting merge fields, you tell Word where to plug information from the data source into the main document. You also tell Word which data to take from the data source. You don't have to include all the information in a data source in the labels, form letters, or envelopes. This illustration shows merge fields in the address and salutation of a form letter. Notice the chevrons (« ») that appear on either side of merge field names.

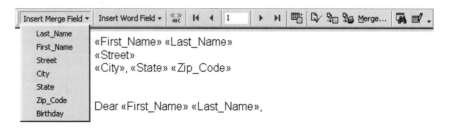

The names of merge fields come from column names in the source table where the addresses are stored. Compare the merge field/column names in the first row of the source table shown in this illustration to the names of merge fields in the previous illustration. The names are identical. To tell Word where to get data from the source document—that is, from which column to get the data—you insert a merge field/column name. When Word sees the First_Name merge field, for example, it knows to insert a first name from the First Name column of the table in the data source.

Last Name	First Name	Street	City	State	Zip Code	Birthday
Maves	Carlos	11 Guy St.	Reek	NV	89201	February 28
Creed	Hank	443 Oak St.	Atherton	CA	93874	July 31
Weiss	Shirley	441 Second St.	Poltroon	ID	49301	May 4
Smith	Jane	121 First St.	Colma	CA	94044	January 10
Daws	Leon	13 Spruce St.	Colma	CA	94044	April 1
Ng	Winston	1444 Unger Ave.	Colma	CA	94404	November 12

3. MERGE THE DATA WITH THE DOCUMENT   *Merging* is when you generate the form letters, mailing labels, envelopes, or list. During the merge, Word takes data from the data source and plugs it into appropriate places in the main document. After the merge, you can save the letters, labels, envelopes, or list in a document or send the data straight to the printer. By clicking the Query Options button in the Mail Merge Helper, you can sort the letters, labels, or envelopes as you merge the source document and main document. You can even query the data source to exclude certain addresses or merge only a select few.

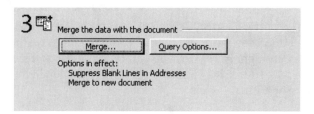

Preparing the Data Source

Before you attempt to generate form letters, address labels, or envelopes for mass-mailing, make sure that the data source is in good working order. The data source is the file where the address information is kept. The data source can be a Word table, database, address book, or contacts list. And Word offers a special dialog box for creating a data source from scratch. Read on to find out how to prepare the data source for a mail-merge.

After you create the data source, do not move it to a different folder or rearrange the merge field/columns. If you do so, the main document can't read the data source correctly and you can't complete the mail-merge.

Using a Word Table as the Data Source

In my experience, the easiest type of data source to manage is a Word table. Either create an address table from scratch or copy a table you have already created and save the table by itself in a document. Save the table under a name you will recognize. When you merge the data source table with the main document, you will be asked to locate and select the document that holds your addresses.

To use a Word table as the data source, the table must meet these standards:

- A descriptive heading must appear across the top of each column. The row of descriptive headings across the top of a table is called the *header row*, or sometimes the *heading row*. As the previous section in this chapter explained, the names in the header row double as merge field names when you insert merge fields in the main document.

- No text can appear above the table in the document. To be on the safe side, save the table in a document by itself.

Note　*See "Turning a List into a Table—and Vice Versa" in Chapter 14 to learn how to turn an address list into a table that can be used in mail-merges. Chapter 14 explains tables in excruciating detail.*

Constructing the Data Source in the Mail Merge Helper

The Mail Merge Helper offers a special mechanism for creating the data source from scratch. Personally, I don't see the advantage of using it, since creating and entering the data in a table is easy enough. However, you can follow these steps in the Mail Merge Helper to create the data source if you find yourself without one when you want to generate form letters or address labels:

1. Choose Tools | Mail Merge to open the Mail Merge Helper dialog box (see Figure 20-1), click the Create button, choose what you need the data source for, and click Active Window.

2. Click the Get Data button and choose Create Data Source from the drop-down menu. You will see the Create Data Source dialog box shown in Figure 20-2. This is where you tell Word which merge fields to include in the data source

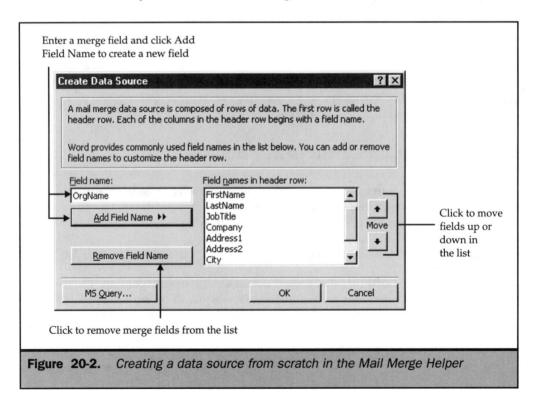

Figure 20-2. *Creating a data source from scratch in the Mail Merge Helper*

table. A set of generic merge field names already appears in the Field Names In Header Row box. You can keep those names, remove them, or add names of your own to the list.

3. Click each field you don't need in the Field Names In Header Row list and click the Remove Field Name button. Almost every address data source needs the FirstName, LastName, Address1, City, State, and PostalCode merge fields. Keep them and drop as many of the others as you deem necessary.

4. To create a merge field of your own, type its name in the Field Name text box and click the Add Field Name button. Perhaps you need a Birthday field or an Organization Name (OrgName) field. Merge field names cannot include spaces or start with numbers.

5. Select a field name and click a Move button to move the name higher or lower on the list.

6. Arrange the field names in the Field Names In Header Row box in the order in which they will appear in your form letter. To do so, highlight a field and click one of the Move buttons to move the field to the right place.

7. Click OK to close the Create Data Source dialog box.

8. In the Save As dialog box, enter a name for the source document, and click the Save button.

9. Click the Edit Data Source button. You'll see the Data Form dialog box.

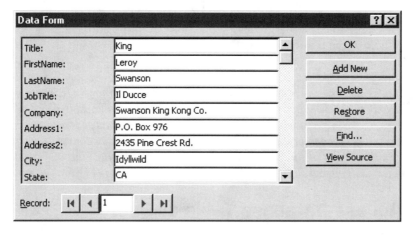

10. Enter the source data next to the names of the merge fields.

11. Click Add New when you are done entering information for each addressee.

12. Click OK when you have entered the information concerning all the addressees.

13. Save your source data document.

Using an Address Book as the Data Source

Most people maintain an address book of some kind on their computers for storing the addresses and phone numbers of friends and co-workers. You can use those addresses for mass-mailings and form letters. To do so, follow these steps:

1. Choose Tools | Mail Merge to open the Mail Merge Helper dialog box (see Figure 20-1), click the Create button to open the drop-down menu, choose what you need the data source for, and click Active Window.

2. Click the Get Data button and choose Use Address Book. You'll see the Use Address Book dialog box.

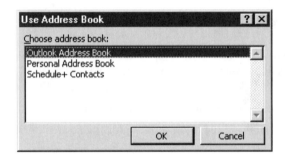

3. Choose which address book you want to get names and addresses from and click OK. You'll see the Confirm Data Source dialog box.

4. Click OK again. The merge fields you chose from the address book are made available in the main document.

Typically, some addresses in an address book are incomplete. In my address book, for example, some names are accompanied only by a telephone number, while other names come with all kinds of information—pager numbers, Bahamian addresses, Web site addresses. The problem with using an address book as the data source in a mail-merge is that many names do not include address information. See "Customizing Merges with Word Fields" later in this chapter to learn how you can exclude incomplete addresses from form letters and address labels with the Skip Record If field.

Using an Access Database Table or Query as the Data Source

If you happen to know your way around database programs such as Access, you also know that a database table is the best place to store addresses because you can query a database table to drudge up only the records you need. People who know their way round Access will be glad to know that you can use an Access database table or Access query as the data source for a mail-merge by following these steps:

1. In the Mail Merge Helper dialog box (see Figure 20-1), click the Get Data button and choose Open Data Source. You will see the Open Data Source dialog box.
2. From the Files Of Type drop-down menu, choose MS Access Databases.
3. Find and select the Access file with the table or query you want to use as the data source.
4. Click the Open button. You'll see the Confirm Data Source dialog box.
5. Select MS Access Databases via DDE and click OK. The Microsoft Access dialog box appears.
6. Click the Tables or Queries tab and do the following to use an Access table or query as the data source:

   - **Tables Tab** Select a table and click OK. Word retrieves the records in the table whenever you use the table as a data source.

   - **Queries Tab** Select the query you want as the data source. To use the query results as they stand now for your mail-merge, uncheck the Link To Query check box. Check the Link To Query check box if you want Access to conduct a new query and produce the results for the mail-merge each time you perform a mail-merge. Click OK.

Caution *Don't move or delete the query or the Access file if you check the Link To Query check box in the Microsoft Access dialog box. Do so and your source document will no longer function in the mail-merge.*

EXAMPLES

LEARN BY EXAMPLE
Open the 20-2 Alternative Data Source document on the companion CD if you want to see how to gather data from an Access query for a mail-merge.

Writing a Form Letter

Now that you know how to prepare the data source, you are ready to write and generate form letters. A *form letter* is a near-identical letter sent to numerous people. Only the particulars of each recipient are different—the recipient's name, the recipient's address, and perhaps one or two identifying facts about the recipient. Figure 20-3 shows a form letter in which recipients' birthdays and nicknames are mentioned as well as their names and addresses:

- The data source, shown at the top of the figure, includes a "Birthday" and "Nickname" merge field/column.

- In the bottom of the figure, on the left side, is the form letter with the merge fields showing. Notice that the merge field names are identical to the names in the header row of the data source.

- In the bottom of the figure, on the right side, is the form letter after it has been merged with the data source. Notice how the recipient's name, address, birthday, and nickname plugs into the form letter after the merge is complete.

LEARN BY EXAMPLE
Open the 20-1 Form Letter document on the companion CD if you want to try your hand at generating a form letter.

Follow these steps to create and generate form letters:

1. Open the document with the text of the letter if you have already written the letter. If you're starting from scratch, create a new document.

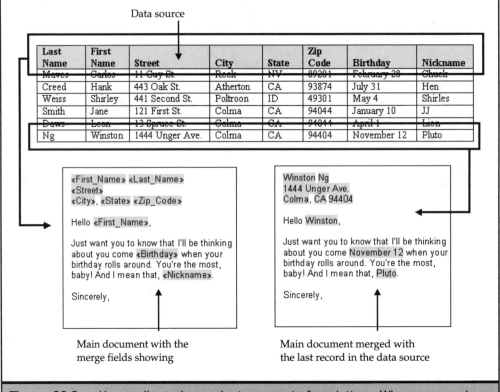

Figure 20-3.   *How mail-merging works to generate form letters. When you are done, you'll have one form letter for each row, or record, in the data source*

2. Choose Tools I Mail Merge. The Mail Merge Helper dialog box appears (see Figure 20-1).

3. Under Main Document, click the Create button and choose Form Letters from the drop-down menu. A dialog box asks if you want to use the document you are looking at as the form letter or create a new document for the form letter. In step 1, you either created a new document or opened the document you intend to use for form letters, so you can click the Active Window button.

4. Click the Active Window button.

5. Under Data Source, click the Get Data button and choose one of these three options on the drop-down menu to tell Word where to get the name and address information for the form letters:

   ■ **Create Data Source**   Click this option to enter the names and addresses for the data source now. Earlier in this chapter, "Constructing the Data Source in the Mail Merge Helper" explains what to do if you haven't entered the names and addresses yet and you want to do so in the Mail Merge Helper.

   ■ **Open Data Source**   Click this option if the names and addresses are stored in a Word table, Access database table, or Access query. See "Using a Word Table as the Data Source" and "Using an Access Database Table or Query as the Data Source," earlier in this chapter.

   ■ **Use Address Book**   Click this option to get the names and addresses from an address book or Outlook 2000 Contact List. See "Using an Address Book as the Data Source," earlier in this chapter.

   What happens next depends on which option you chose. Eventually, however, a message box informs you that the time has come to enter merge fields in the main document.

6. Click the Edit Main Document button in the message box to go into the main document and insert the merge fields. When you return to your document, the Mail Merge toolbar appears onscreen.

7. Compose the form letter and, as you do so, insert the merge fields by choosing their names from the Insert Merge Field drop-down menu, as shown in Figure 20-4. Insert a merge field in the form letter wherever information about a recipient is required.

Caution   *In the main document, be careful when entering blank spaces and punctuation marks around merge fields. A blank space, for example, goes between the FirstName and LastName field in the address. Enter a comma or colon after the LastName field in the salutation. You can always click the View Merged Data button on the Mail Merge toolbar to see whether punctuation marks and blank spaces will appear correctly after the form letters are printed.*

USING WORD 2000 AT THE OFFICE

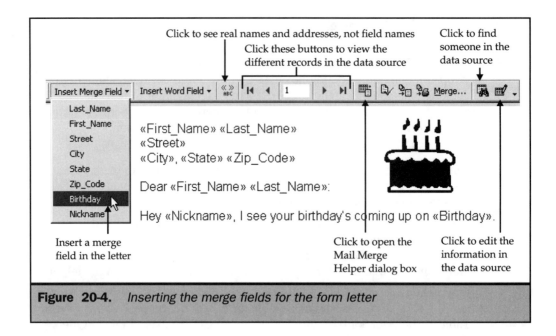

Figure 20-4. *Inserting the merge fields for the form letter*

8. Save your document when you are done writing it and entering the merge fields.

9. Click the Merge button on the Mail Merge toolbar to merge the main document and data source and generate the form letters. See "Merging the Main Document and Data Source," later in this chapter.

A handful of buttons on the Mail Merge toolbar come in handy when the need arises to do these tasks:

■ **Seeing What the Letters Will Look Like When They Are Printed**   From time to time as you insert merge fields, click the View Merged Data button on the Mail Merge toolbar to see what your letter will look like when you print it. Clicking the button makes real names and addresses instead of merge field names appear onscreen. Click the button a second time to see the merge field names again.

> Hey «Nickname», I see your birthday's coming up on «Birthday».
>
> Hey Pluto, I see your birthday's coming up on November 12.

■ **Seeing to Whom the Letters Will Be Sent**   Click the View Merged Data button and then click a Record button or enter a record number in the Go To Record box to see the names and addresses of all the people to whom the letters will be sent.

- **Finding a Recipient in the Data Source**   You can search the data source file by clicking the Find Record button. In the Find in Field dialog box, choose a field from the In Field drop-down list, and then enter a word or two in the Find What text box to describe what you are looking for.

- **Editing Information in the Data Source**   Suppose you click the View Merged Data button to see names and addresses, and you notice that information in the data source needs editing. Click the Edit Data Source button (or press ALT-SHIFT-E). In the Data Form dialog box, enter the correct data and click OK.

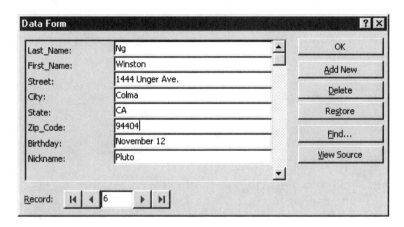

Customizing a Form Letter with Word Fields

Next to the Insert Merge Field drop-down menu on the Mail Merge toolbar is another drop-down menu called Insert Word Field. By including Word fields in a form letter, you can customize it. Instead of churning out the same form letter for everyone, you can include a sentence here and there in some of the letters when the letters are merged. Or you can arrange it so that some recipients receive one letter and others receive a slightly different letter.

Two fields on the Insert Word Field drop-down menu are useful for writing form letters: If...Then...Else and Skip Record If.

Use the If...Then...Else field to enter one sentence or another in the form letters. Here, you'll see the dialog box that appears when you choose If...Then...Else on the Insert Word Field drop-down menu. Choose a field name, a comparison operator, and a value. In this illustration, high school graduates who have an A in the Grade_Avg (Grade Average) field are told one thing in the form letters, and graduates whose grade point averages are lower than A are told something else. Choose an option on the Comparison drop-down menu and enter a value in the Compare To text box to tell Word which recipients receive which sentence on their form letters.

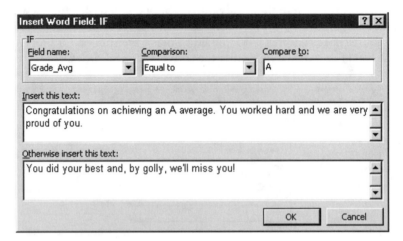

Use the Skip Record If field to keep incomplete addresses from being generated in form letters and mailing labels. If the data source does not list a street, city, state, or postal code, no form letter can be delivered. This illustration shows the dialog box that you get when you choose Skip Record If from the Insert Word Field drop-down menu. By choosing the Street, City, State, or Postal Code field in the dialog box and choosing Is Blank from the Comparison drop-down menu, you prevent form letters from being generated for people whose complete addresses are not listed in the data source.

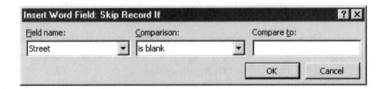

Printing Labels for Mass-Mailings

As long as you know how data sources work (see "Preparing the Data Source" earlier in this chapter), you can generate labels for mass-mailings. To generate the labels, you get the names and addresses of recipients from the data source. Figure 20-5 shows how mail-merges work to generate labels:

■ **Address information comes from the data source.** In Figure 20-5, five merge field/column names from the data source are used to produce the labels. Two merge field/column names in the data source, "Birthday" and "Nickname," are not used.

■ **Select merge field/column names from the data source.** In the bottom of the figure, on the left side, is the dialog box where you tell Word which merge field/column names from the data source to put on the labels. Notice that the merge field names are identical to five of the seven names in the header row of the data source.

■ **Merge the main document and data source to generate the labels.** In the bottom of the figure, on the right side, is one of the labels that was generated when the main document and data source were merged. Notice how the recipient's first name, last name, street, city, state, and ZIP code fit on the label after the merge is complete.

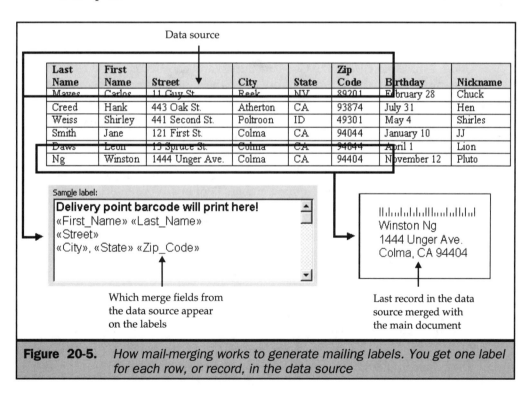

Figure 20-5.   *How mail-merging works to generate mailing labels. You get one label for each row, or record, in the data source*

"Printing a Single Label or Sheet of Labels with the Same Address" in Chapter 5 explains how to print one or two labels at a time.

LEARN BY EXAMPLE
Check out the 20-3 Labels document on the companion CD if you want to see how to generate labels in Word.

Before you print labels, take note of what brand labels you have and what size your labels are. Word asks for that information when you generate labels. The program needs to know what size your labels are so it can place the labels correctly on the label sheet. Follow these steps to generate labels for a mass-mailing:

1. Create a new document.

2. Choose Tools | Mail Merge. The Mail Merge Helper dialog box appears (see Figure 20-1).

3. Click the Create button and choose Mailing Labels from the drop-down menu. Word asks if you want to create a new document. That isn't necessary, since you just created one.

4. Click the Active Window button.

5. Under Data Source, click the Get Data button and choose an option from the drop-down menu to tell Word where to get the name and address information for the labels:

   ■ **Create Data Source**   Click this option if you need to enter the names and addresses now. See "Constructing the Data Source in the Mail Merge Helper" in this chapter to learn how to enter the names and addresses.

   ■ **Open Data Source**   Click this option if the names and addresses for the labels have already been entered and are kept in a Word table, Access database table, or Access query. See "Using a Word Table as the Data Source" and "Using an Access Database Table or Query as the Data Source," earlier in this chapter.

   ■ **Use Address Book**   Click this option to get the names and addresses from the address book or Outlook 2000 Contact List. See "Using an Address Book as the Data Source," earlier in this chapter.

   When you return to the Mail Merge Helper dialog box, a message box announces that you need to set up your main document.

6. Click the Set Up Main Document button. You'll see the Label Options dialog box, where you describe the labels you will print your names and addresses on.

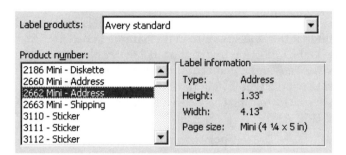

7. Choose an option from the Label Products and the Product Number drop-down lists to describe the labels you will print on. The Label Information box clearly shows what size label you are choosing.

Choose Other on the Label Products drop-down list if you can't find your brand of labels, and then try to find a product number that matches the labels you have. If you are desperate, you can click the New Label button and describe your labels in the New Custom dialog box.

8. Click OK. You'll see the Create Labels dialog box shown in Figure 20-6.

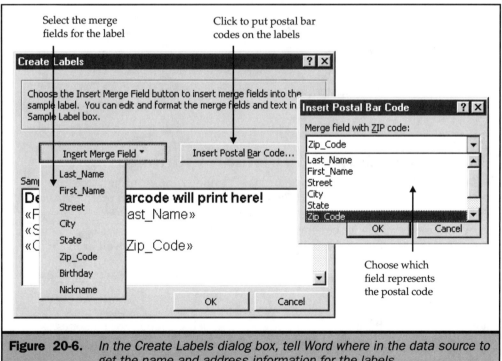

Figure 20-6.   *In the Create Labels dialog box, tell Word where in the data source to get the name and address information for the labels*

9. As shown in Figure 20-6, click the Insert Merge Field button and insert each merge field that the labels require in the Sample Label box. Press ENTER to move the cursor to the following line in the label, enter blank spaces where blank spaces are needed, and enter a comma where it is required. If your labels are addressed to people who live in the United States, for example, enter a comma and a blank space after the City merge field, as shown in this illustration.

> **Delivery point barcode will print here!**
> «First_Name» «Last_Name»
> «Street»
> «City», «State» «Zip_Code»

 Be sure to enter blank spaces between fields and all the necessary punctuation marks. After you generate the labels, you can't return to the Create Labels dialog box and rearrange fields. No, you have to start all over again and generate the labels a second time if you make mistake.

10. Click the Insert Postal Bar Code button and, in the Insert Postal Bar Code dialog box (see Figure 20-6), open the drop-down menu and choose the field in the data source where postal codes or ZIP codes are kept. From the second drop-down menu, you can also choose the field where street addresses are stored if your labels are for a mailing in the United States. Click OK to return to the Create Labels dialog box.

11. Click OK. You return to the Mail Merge Helper dialog box.

12. Merge the main document and data source to generate the form letters. See "Merging the Main Document and Data Source," later in this chapter.

Printing Envelopes for Mass-Mailings

The procedure for printing envelopes for mass-mailings and printing labels for mass-mailings are nearly the same. (The previous section in this chapter, "Printing Labels for Mass-Mailings," explains how to print labels.) The difference between the two procedures is that, with envelopes, you are asked which size envelope you will print on instead of which size label you will print on. Of course, the other major difference between printing labels and envelopes for mass-mailings is that printing the envelopes is much, much harder. Unless you have a sophisticated printer, you have to feed the envelopes to the printer one at a time, which is a tedious job if your mass-mailing is truly a mass-mailing and not a puny mailing. An easier way to send out letters is to print the addresses on labels and attach the labels to envelopes.

> **Note**   *See "Making Sure the Return Address is Printed" later in this chapter to learn how to handle the return address on the envelopes. "Printing Addresses and Return Addresses on Envelopes" in Chapter 5 explains how to print a single envelope.*

Refer to the previous section in this chapter for details about merging the data source and envelopes. Choose Tools | Mail Merge to begin. In the Mail Merge Helper dialog box, click the Create button and choose Envelopes from the drop-down list. After you tell Word where the data source is and click the Set Up Main Document button, you'll see the Envelope Options dialog box shown in Figure 20-7.

Do the following in the Envelope Options dialog box to tell Word about your envelopes:

- ■ **Describing the Size of the Envelope**   Choose an option from the Envelope Size drop-down menu.

- ■ **Printing Bar Codes and FIM-A Codes**   Click the check boxes to print delivery point bar codes and facing identification marks on the envelopes. These marks help the postal service deliver letters faster.

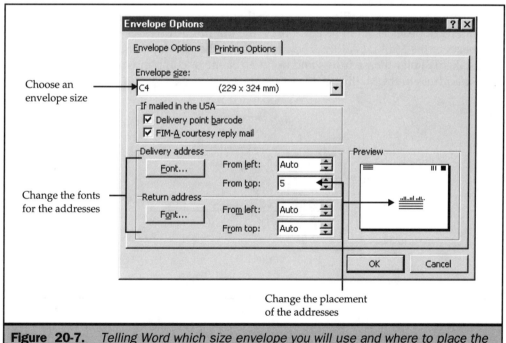

Figure 20-7.   *Telling Word which size envelope you will use and where to place the addresses*

- **Changing the Font of Addresses**   Click a Font button to open the Envelope Address dialog box and choose a new font and font size for the address or return address.

- **Choosing the Position of Addresses**   Change the From Left or From Top settings to alter the position of the address or return address. The Preview box shows where the addresses go when you move them.

After you click OK in the Envelope Options dialog box, you'll see the Envelope Address dialog box. This dialog box is the spitting image of the Create Labels dialog box shown in Figure 20-6. Refer to Figure 20-6 and steps 9 through 12 in the previous section of this chapter if you need help placing merge fields in the Envelope Address dialog box.

Making Sure the Return Address Is Printed

The return address that Word prints on envelopes comes from the Mailing Address box on the User Information tab in the Options dialog box. To get there, choose Tools | Options and click the User Information tab. Before you print envelopes for a mass-mailing, make sure that the address you want to appear on your envelopes is listed in its entirety on the Mailing Address text box. Whatever appears in the Mailing Address box appears on the envelopes. Some people mistakenly enter their address and not their name or company name along with their address in the Mailing Address text box.

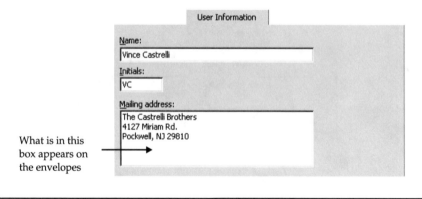

What is in this
box appears on
the envelopes

Mail-Merging to Print a List

Click the Create button in the Mail Merge Helper dialog box and you will see four options: Form Letters, Mailing Labels, Envelopes, and Catalog. The Catalog option is for printing a list with data from a database source. The advantage of mail-merging to create lists is that the lists are easier to update. After the data source is updated, you can simply re-generate the list without having to format it, make new entries, or delete out-of-date entries. A company phone list like the one in Figure 20-8 is an ideal candidate for a mail-merge. Instead of editing the list whenever a new employee arrives or an old employee moves on, you can simply update the list from a data source and be done with it.

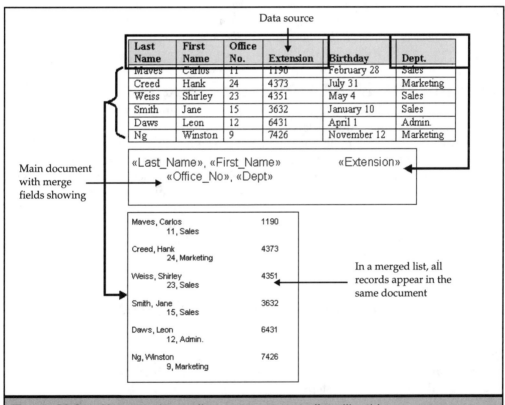

Figure 20-8. *You can also mail-merge to generate lists like this company phone list*

The procedure for mail-merging with the Catalog option to generate a list is nearly the same as mail-merging to generate form letters (see "Writing a Form Letter," earlier in this chapter). The only differences between the two procedures are these:

- The entire list appears on the same page or pages. When you mail-merge a form letter, you get a different page for every addressee.

- You can't enter the accompanying text until the merge is complete. In the company phone list shown in Figure 20-8, for example, you have to wait until you mail-merge the list to enter headings such as "Name" and "Phone Extension." If you enter headings in the main document, they will appear over and over again when the list is merged.

See "Merging Some of the Records in the Data Source," later in this chapter, to learn how you can keep some names off the list. When you mail-merge to generate a list, you don't have to include all the information in the data source.

Merging the Main Document and Data Source

The final step in mail-merging is to merge the main document and the data source to generate the form letters, address labels, envelopes, or list. These pages explain the various ways to merge the main document and the data source. Instead of merging all the records in the data source with the main document, you can merge a select few records by querying the data source. For example, you could merge only the records of people who live in a single ZIP code. Or you could merge only the records of people who live in Montana and Idaho. Besides querying, you can sort the records as well so that your labels or form letters are arranged in alphabetical or ZIP-code order.

Read on to find out how to do a basic merge, query the data source before the mail-merge, sort the data source before the merge-merge, and check for errors in the mail-merge.

Merging the Main Document with All the Records in the Data Source

Unless you decide to check for errors in the mail-merge, query the data source, or sort the data source before the mail-merge, mail-merging is an uncomplicated matter. All you have to do is follow these steps:

1. Open the Merge dialog box shown in Figure 20-9. To do so, either click the Merge button in the Mail Merge Helper dialog box (see Figure 20-1) or click the Merge button on the Mail Merge toolbar.

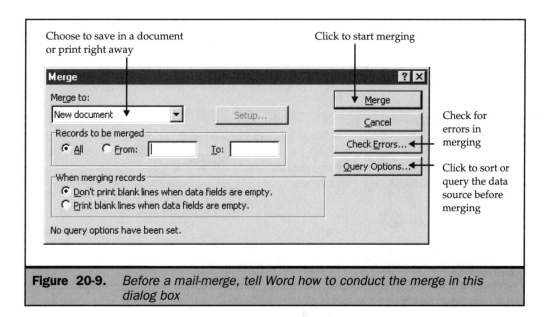

Figure 20-9. *Before a mail-merge, tell Word how to conduct the merge in this dialog box*

2. From the Merge To drop-down menu, choose New Document or Printer:

■ **Saving the Form Letters, Labels, or Envelopes in a New Document** Choose New Document to make all the letters, labels, or envelopes appear in a new document. In the case of form letters, you can scroll through the document and type a sentence or two in certain letters to give them the personal touch. Choose this option if you want to save your form letters, labels, or envelopes in a document so you can generate them on a later day.

■ **Printing the Form Letters, Labels, or Envelopes Right Away** Choose Printer to mail-merge and send the letters, labels, or envelopes straight to the printer. You save disk space with this option, as Word doesn't put the stuff in a new document before printing begins.

3. If you are mail-merging to create labels, make sure that a check appears in the Don't Print Blank Lines When Data Fields Are Empty check box. Without the check mark, Word leaves ugly empty spaces in labels where information for a field isn't available, as shown here.

Carlos Maves
P.O. Box 976
11 Guy St.
Reek, NV 87481

Hank Creed

443 Oak St.
Atherton, CA 94044

Shirley Weiss

441 Second St.
Poltroon, ID 81074

USING WORD 2000 AT THE OFFICE

4. Click the Merge button. Your form letters, labels, or envelopes start to print or appear in a new document, depending on which option you chose in step 2.

You can mail-merge without visiting the Merge dialog box. To do so, click the Merge to New Document or Merge to Printer button on the Mail Merge toolbar.

Whether you merge to a new document or merge to the printer, be sure to save the main document after the merge. That way, you can generate your mailing labels, form letters, envelopes, or list again by opening the main document, clicking the Merge button on the Mail Merge toolbar, and making selections in the Merge dialog box (see Figure 20-9). As long as the data source is still intact, you can get up-to-date addresses from the data source.

Testing for Errors in a Mail-Merge

Word offers the Checking and Reporting Errors dialog box for testing the accuracy of a mail-merge before you run it. All errors in mail-merges are caused by changes in the data source. If you move the data source file to a different folder, delete the data source file, remove information from the data source that is needed in the main document, or even do so little as rearrange the merge fields/columns in the data source file, the mail-merge will be unsuccessful. By checking for errors beforehand, you can find out whether your mail-merge will really do its job.

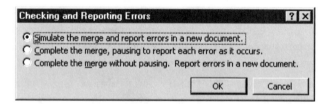

To test for errors in a mail-merge, either click the Check for Errors button on the Mail Merge toolbar or click the Check Errors button in the Merge dialog box (see Figure 20-9). You'll see the Checking and Reporting Errors dialog box. The dialog box offers three options for checking for errors, two of which in my opinion are useless:

■ **Simulate The Merge And Report Errors In A New Document**   Does not undertake the mail-merge, but pretends to and reports errors if any are found. This option is highly recommended.

- **Complete The Merge, Pausing To Report Each Error As It Occurs**
  Merges the main document and data source. If errors are found, you get the
  chance to correct them in a dialog box as the mail-merge
  takes place.

- **Complete The Merge Without Pausing. Report Errors In A New
  Document**   Merges the main document and data source. Records that
  could not be merged are listed in a document by number. Don't bother with
  this one, since handling records by record number is very difficult if you
  are dealing with a data source with more than a few records.

If Word finds an error, you'll see a dialog box similar to the ones shown in this
illustration. Some dialog boxes offer the opportunity to fix errors. In the Invalid
Merge Field dialog box, for example, you can click the Remove Field button to
remove a field from the main document or choose a new field from the data source
in place of the field that could not be merged successfully. Probably the best way to
handle errors when they are found is to return to the main document if you can
and rethink your form letter, mailing labels, or envelopes. Mail-merges should go
smoothly. Start all over if the error-checking mechanism encounters an error.

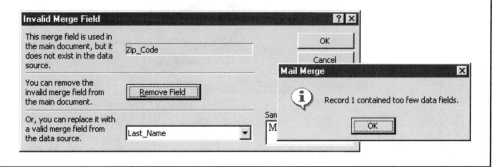

Sorting, or Reordering, the Records in the Data Source

Sorting means to rearrange data in alphabetical, numerical, or chronological order (by
date). Sorting makes reading and interpreting a list easier. As for mailing labels, form
letters, and envelopes, the best reason to sort them has to do with bulk-mailing. To
send letters in bulk and be eligible for lower postage rates, the United States Post Office
wants the letters to be bundled by ZIP code. Bundling letters by ZIP code can take
hours—unless you sort the addresses in the data source. Sort the addresses in
numerical order by ZIP code and your mailing labels, form letters, or envelopes are
arranged by ZIP code.

Information from the data source can be sorted in ascending or descending order:

- **Ascending Sort**   Arranges text in alphabetical order from A to Z, numbers from smallest to largest, and dates from earliest in time to latest in time.
- **Descending Sort**   Arranges text from Z to A, numbers from largest to smallest, and dates from latest in time to earliest.

Follow these steps to sort records from the data source as you merge the data source and the main document:

1. If you are looking at the Mail Merge Helper dialog box, click the Query Options button; if you are staring at the Merge dialog box, click the Query Options button there. (To open the Merge dialog box, click the Merge button on the Mail Merge toolbar.)

2. Click the Sort Records tab in the Query Options dialog box.

3. From the Sort By drop-down menu, choose the merge field/column by which to sort the data. Here, for example, the data is being sorted by the Last Name field.

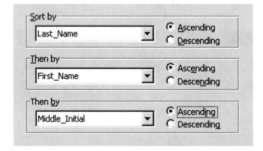

4. Next to the Sort By menu, click the Ascending or Descending option button to declare whether you want an ascending or descending sort.

5. In the first Then By drop-down menu, choose the tie-breaker merge field/column, if necessary. In a merge field/column with last names, for example, common last names such as Martinez and Smith are sure to appear more than once. By making First Name the tie-breaker merge field/column, you tell Word to look to the First Name merge field/column to break the tie and place one name before the other.

6. Repeat steps 4 and 5 for the second Then By column, if necessary.

7. Click OK to return to the Merge dialog box or Mail Merge Helper dialog box and start the mail-merge.

Merging Records by the Number

As long as you know that the record numbers in the data source or the data source is small enough that you can count records on your fingers and toes, you can print records by number. Records are numbered sequentially in the data source starting at 1 with the first record. To mail-merge a particular record or handful of records, enter the beginning and ending record numbers in the Merge dialog box. Being able to print records by number is convenient when one label or form letter needs reprinting because you can simply enter its number in the From and To box.

How can you tell a record's number? If the data source is a Word table, select the entire first column except for the merge field/column name at top and click the Numbering button on the Formatting toolbar. The records are numbered. What's more, the numbers do not appear on labels, form letters, or envelopes after a mail-merge.

If the data source is an Access database table or query, you can number the records there by creating an AutoNumber field that numbers each record. See the Help program in Access if numbering records this way excites you.

Word offers a field that you can stick in the main document to number records. From the Insert Word Field drop-down menu on the Mail Merge toolbar, select the Merge Record # field. The problem with numbering records in the data source this way, however, is that a record number appears on the label, form letter, envelope, or list—it appears where you put the Merge Record # field in the main document. Unless, for example, you can tuck the record number in a corner of the form letter where no one will notice it, numbering records with the Merge Record # field doesn't offer any real advantages because you get unsightly numbers on your labels and form letters.

Merging Some of the Records in the Data Source

Before you merge the main document and the data source, you can tell Word to merge only a few select records from the data source with the main document. Suppose you want to send a form letter or print mailing labels for people in one ZIP code. Or send a form letter to people in two states, not to everyone whose address is listed in the data source. Pulling a few select records from the data source is called *querying*.

Follow these steps to query the data source before you merge records in the data source with the main document:

1. If you are starting from the Mail Merge Helper dialog box, click the Query Options button; if you are starting at the Merge dialog box, click the Query Options button there. (Click the Merge button on the Mail Merge toolbar to open the Merge dialog box.)

2. Click the Filter Records tab in the Query Options dialog box, as shown in Figure 20-10. On this tab, you can construct a query that tells Word which records to take from the data source. The query in Figure 20-10 finds San Francisco addresses (in ZIP codes 94101 through 94199) as well as addresses in the four satellite cities to the south of San Francisco. Each criterion in the query—there are six in the figure—is called a *rule*.

3. On the Filter Records tab, choose a field, choose a comparison operator, and enter a value to describe the records in the data source that you want to merge with the main document. You can enter one or as many as six rules. Table 20-1 describes the comparison operators and how you can use them to construct rules in a query.

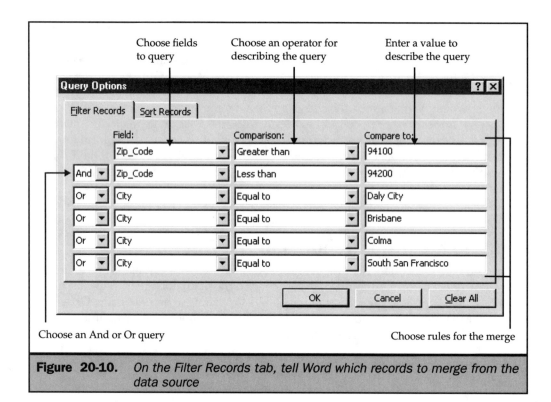

Figure 20-10. On the Filter Records tab, tell Word which records to merge from the data source

Comparison Operator	Explanation	Example
Equal To	Merges records that match the Compare To value.	*City* **is equal to** *Boston* merges addresses of Bostonians.
Not Equal To	Excludes records that match the Compare To value.	*State* **is not equal to** *Utah* excludes addresses in Utah from the merge.
Less Than	Merges records whose values are smaller than the Compare To value.	*Elvis_Sightings* **is less than** *200*.
Greater Than	Merges records whose values are larger than the Compare To value.	*Income* **is greater than** *30,000*.
Less Than or Equal To	Merges records whose values are smaller than or the same as the Compare To value.	*Zip_Code* **is less than or equal to** *94149*.
Greater Than or Equal To	Merges records whose values are larger than or the same as the Compare To value.	*Annual_Rainfall* **is greater than or equal to 25**.
Is Blank	Merges records when no value appears in the field.	*Bill_Paid* **is blank** merges records in which no entry was made in the Bill_Paid field.
Is Not Blank	Merges records when a value appears in the field.	*Country* **is not blank** merges records in which a country is found in the Country field.

Table 20-1.   *Comparison Operators for Use in Constructing Query Rules*

4. If you enter more than one rule, choose And or Or from the drop-down list to describe how the next rule you enter modifies the one above it:

■ **And**   Narrows the number of records that are merged to those described by the rule you enter in combination with the rule above. In this illustration, for example, the two rules tell Word to merge only the records of people who live in San Francisco *and* whose income is greater than or equal to $35,000. The address of a San Franciscan whose income is less than $35,000 is not merged. To be merged, a record has to satisfy both rules.

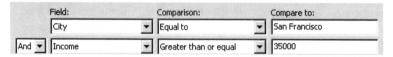

- **Or**   Broadens the number of records that are merged to include records described by the rule. In this illustration, for example, the two rules tell Word to merge the records of anyone who lives in Los Angeles *or* San Francisco. To be merged, a record only has to satisfy one of the rules, not both.

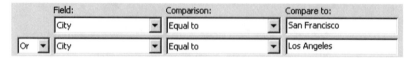

5. Click OK to return to the Merge dialog box or Mail Merge Helper dialog box and start the mail-merge.

Exam | MOUS Exam Objectives Explored in Chapter 20

Objective	Heading	Practice File
Create main document*	"Writing a Form Letter"	20-1 Form Letter
Create data source*	"Preparing the Data Source"	
Merge main document and data source*	"Merging the Main Document and the Data Source"	
Sort records to be merged*	"Sorting, or Reordering, the Records in the Data Source"	
Merge a document using alternate data sources*	"Using an Address Book as the Data Source" and "Using an Access Database Table or Query as the Data Source"	20-2 Alternative Data Source
Generate labels*	"Printing Labels for Mass Mailings"	20-3 Labels

* Denotes an Expert exam objective.

Ten Mail-Merge Problems and How to Solve Them

After going to all the trouble of setting up a mail-merge, finding out that it doesn't work is a drag. Here are ten mail-merge problems and advice for solving them.

1. WORD TELLS ME THAT IT CAN'T LOCATE THE DATA SOURCE WHEN I OPEN MY DOCUMENT.

Word says this because the data source has been moved from its original location. If you know where the data source file was moved, click the Find Data Source button in the dialog box and locate the data source in the Open Data Source dialog box. Click the Options button if the data source no longer exists or you want to make the document into a normal document that isn't tied to a data source. In the Next dialog box, choose Remove Data/Header Source if the data source doesn't exist or Remove All Merge Info to turn your document into a normal Word document.

> **Microsoft Word** [X]
>
> (?) Form Letters is a mail merge main document. Word cannot find its data source, Data Source.
>
> [Find Data Source...]   [Options...]

2. I WANT TO USE MY FORM LETTER LIKE A REGULAR LETTER.

You can sever the tie between the main document and the data source and use a form letter as a normal Word document. To do so, choose Tools | Mail Merge, click the Create button in the Mail Merge Helper dialog box, and choose Restore to Normal Word Document from the drop-down menu. Merge fields remain in the document, but they don't mean anything and are not tied to the data source. Delete them.

3. I HITCHED MY MAIN DOCUMENT TO THE WRONG DATA SOURCE.

Unfortunately, solving this problem isn't simply a matter of choosing a new data source with the same merge field/columns as the original data source. Word makes the connection between merge fields in the main document and the data source not by name, but by location. Suppose, for example, that you ask Word to insert names from the Last Name merge field/column in the data source and Last Name is the first merge field/column. Really, you are asking Word to get data from the first field/column, not the one named "Last Name."

The upshot of all this technical mumbo-jumbo, unfortunately, is that you have to start all over. If your main document's job is to generate labels or envelopes, start from the very beginning. If you are working on a form letter, sever the tie between your document and the data source, delete all the merge fields in the main document, establish a connection with a new data source, and re-enter the merge fields. To disconnect the main document from its data source, choose Tools | Mail Merge, click the Create button in the Mail Merge

Helper dialog box, and choose Restore To Normal Word Document. Then, with the Mail Merge Helper dialog box still open, take it from the top.

4. SOME OF THE ADDRESSES IN MY FORM LETTERS AND LABELS ARE WRONG.
If you notice that data in a mail-merge is incorrect, you can change it without opening the data source and changing it there. To do so, either click the Edit Data Source button on the Mail Merge toolbar or, in the Mail Merge Helper dialog box, click the Edit button under Data Source and choose the name of the data source document from the drop-down menu. You'll see the Data Form dialog box. To find the record that needs changing, either click the Record buttons or click the Find button and enter information for the search in the Find in Field dialog box. Click OK when you have entered the right information.

Editing information in the Data Form dialog box in no way alters the information in the data source. The data source stays the same no matter what you do in the Data Form dialog box. To update the information once and for all, open the data source and edit it there.

5. I NEED TO CHANGE THE SIZE OF THE MAILING LABELS I USE.
Unfortunately, the only way to change the size of mailing labels (or envelopes) after the mail-merge is complete is to start all over. That's right—take it from the top. Choose Tools | Mail Merge and set up the whole shebang, but this time choose the right size mailing label.

6. I GET A "RECORD CONTAINED TOO FEW DATA FIELDS" ERROR MESSAGE.
This cryptic message appears when you or someone else either rearranged the merge field/columns or removed a merge field/column in the data source. The data source is a fragile thing. Tamper with it and mail-merging doesn't work. To fix this problem, open the data source and make sure that the merge fields/columns you need for your mail-merge are there. Then open the main document, delete the merge fields, and re-enter them.

7. WHEN I PRINT, I SEE MERGE FIELDS INSTEAD OF DATA.
That happens because someone told Word to display fields codes when printing. To fix the problem, choose Tools | Options, click the Print tab in the Options dialog box, and uncheck the Field Codes check box. Back in the main document, click the Merge to Printer button on the Mail Merge toolbar to print the form letters, labels, or envelopes with the addresses showing.

8. BLANK LINES APPEAR IN MY ADDRESS LABELS.
You see blank lines because you forgot to check the Don't Print Blank Lines When Data Fields Are Empty check box in the Merge dialog box (see Figure 20-9). Go back to the main document,

click the Merge button on the Mail Merge toolbar to see the Merge dialog box, and click the check box this time around.

9. I WANT TO PRINT ONE OR TWO FORM LETTERS ONLY, BUT I CAN'T GET WORD TO DO IT.

When you merge form letters to a new document, you get a large document in which the letters are divided into sections. Printing a letter here or there in the middle of the new document can be difficult because sections throw the page numbers out of whack. To print a particular letter, find and click it in the new document. Then glance at the Status bar to see which section you are in. If the Status bar reads "Sec 5," for example, you know to print section 5. Choose File | Print to open the Print dialog box, click in the Pages text box, and enter **s** followed by the section number. For example, to print the letter in section 5, enter **s5**. Then click OK to print the letter.

"Printing Parts or Copies of a Document" in Chapter 5 explains how to print more than one section at a time.

10. THE MERGED STUFF IN MY FORM LETTERS IS FORMATTED DIFFERENTLY THAN THE LETTER TEXT.

Looks like you formatted the text but scrupulously avoided formatting the merge fields. You needn't be so careful. Except for typing inside the chevrons (« ») that appear on either side of merge fields, you can format a merge field any way you want. Change the field's font or font size. Indent it. Apply a style to a merge field. When the form letter, label, envelope, or list is printed, the text will show the formats.

The
Complete
Reference

Chapter 21

Word 2000 for Legal Professionals

Of all the chapters in this book, this one hits home the most for me, because I used to be a "legal professional." Not that I was a lawyer or even officially a legal secretary, but I used to work in law offices and I typed many a pleading in my day. As a matter of fact, the first document I ever typed on a word processor was a legal document, a pleading in a divorce case, if I remember correctly. I typed it on a now-extinct word processing program called XYZWrite. Those were the days!

This chapter explains how to get the help of Word 2000 to prepare a pleading, number the paragraphs and lines in a document to legal specifications, insert citations in a document, and generate a table of authorities. By the way, not all the tasks described in this chapter are for legal professionals only. For example, everyone is invited to number the paragraphs and lines in their documents.

Creating and Modifying a Legal Pleading Template

Courts, especially supreme courts and courts of appeals, are very fussy about the pleadings that are brought before them. Some courts want pleadings to be double-spaced. Some want pleadings to be printed on letter-size rather than legal-size paper. Kind of ironic, I think, that courts will accept a poorly argued pleading before they will accept a pleading that is not laid out correctly.

To make sure pleadings are laid out correctly, Word offers the Pleading Wizard (hard to imagine a wizard pleading, but I suppose it's possible). Use the Pleading Wizard to create a template for the pleadings that you submit to a particular court. As you know if you read Chapter 1 of this book, a template is a special kind of file that is used as the starting point for creating Word documents. As you create your pleading template, the wizard asks you whether the court wants single- or double-spaced text, what kinds of borders to put on the pages, what kind of caption box the court requires, and a host of other questions.

When you are done, you have a template that you can use whenever you need to submit a pleading to a particular court. The template takes care of the layout decisions. It knows whether to double- or single-space lines and what kind of borders to use, for example. All you have to do is type the pleading itself. Of course, you can always alter the layout in a document you created from a template. But the template is an excellent starting point and a good guarantor that your pleading is being laid out correctly.

These pages explain how to create a pleading template to the specifications of a particular court of law. You will also learn how to modify your template in case you didn't get the layout specifications right the first time around.

Note   *Later in this chapter, "Preparing a Pleading" explains how to create a pleading document from a template you created.*

Creating a Legal Pleading Template

When you are done creating your pleading template, it will appear on the Legal Pleadings tab of the New dialog box. The Legal Pleadings tab shown in this illustration presents three templates—one for the California Supreme Court, one for the Kangaroo Court, and one for the U.S. Superior Court. By double-clicking a template you created, you can start preparing a pleading for a particular court.

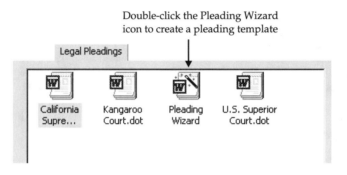

Double-click the Pleading Wizard icon to create a pleading template

> *Get a copy of a court document that was submitted to the court for which you are creating a template. You definitely need a sample court document to work from. That way, you can study the document as you create your template and be sure to make the right layout choices.*

Meanwhile, to create a pleading template, choose File | New, click the Legal Pleadings tab in the New dialog box, and double-click the Pleading Wizard icon. As shown in Figure 21-1, you'll see the first of ten Legal Pleading Wizard dialog boxes. To create your template, visit each Pleading Wizard dialog box: Choose Task, Court Name, Page Layout, and so on. Either click a dialog box name or click the Next or Back button to go from dialog box to dialog box. The following pages explain the decisions you have to make along the way.

> **Note**   *Don't worry about getting it right the first time. As "Modifying a Pleading Template" explains later in this chapter, it's never too late to refine a pleading template.*

CHOOSE TASK   Make sure the first option, Create A New Pleading Template For Another Court, is selected and click the Next button. The second option is for modifying a template you already created and the third is for writing a pleading.

COURT NAME   Enter the name of the court as it should appear at the top of the pleading. If the court name needs to appear in uppercase letters, enter it in uppercase. Examine a document that was submitted to the court and then click the Left, Center, or

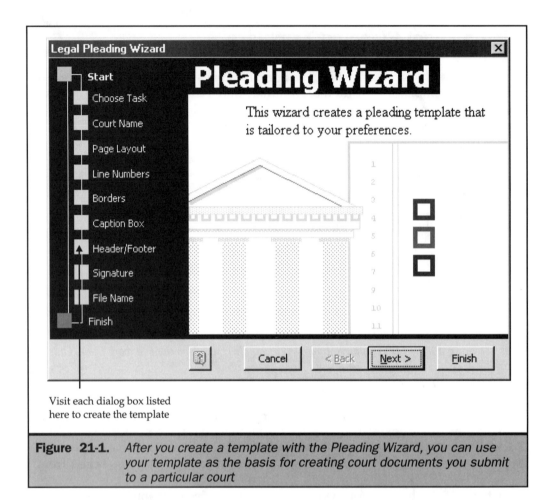

Visit each dialog box listed
here to create the template

Figure 21-1. *After you create a template with the Pleading Wizard, you can use
your template as the basis for creating court documents you submit
to a particular court*

Right option button to left-align, center, or right-align the court's name. The name is
aligned with respect to the left and right margins of the document.

PAGE LAYOUT Higher courts are especially fussy about page layouts. Study a court
document and fill in this dialog box accordingly. Be very careful about entering a
number in the Lines Per Page box (I suggest counting the number of lines on a court
document in order to enter the number correctly). How many lines appear on each
page depends on whether the pleading is double-spaced and which size paper it is
printed on. Word does not change the Lines Per Page default number as you select
Line Spacing and Paper Size options.

LINE NUMBERS   Decide whether to include or omit line numbers in the Line Numbers dialog box. If you click the Yes option button to include line numbers, do the following in the Line Numbers dialog box:

- **Start Pleading At Line**   Enter which line is numbered first. In some court documents, the caption box information (the court name, names of parties to the case, and so on) are not numbered and numbering begins at the first line of the pleading itself.

- **Line Numbers Start At**   Enter the number at which Word should start counting lines, usually 1.

- **Show Line Numbers In Increments Of**   Choose One to number each line or Two to number every second line.

   Later in this chapter, "Numbering the Lines in a Document" explains all the line-numbering options that Word offers.

BORDERS   Stare at your sample pleading, notice whether borders appear on the pages, and choose options in the Borders dialog box. The sample page shows precisely what your choices mean.

CAPTION BOX   The *caption box* in a pleading lists the parties to the case. Take a hard look at the options in the Caption box dialog box and choose the one that matches the caption box in your sample pleading.

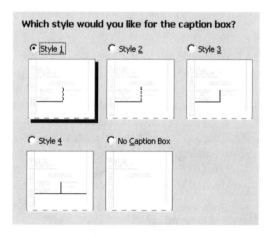

HEADER/FOOTER   The name "header" in this dialog box is kind of misleading. Check or uncheck the first two check boxes to tell the wizard whether firm names, attorney names, and the judge's name need to appear above the caption box at the top of the pleading, as shown in this illustration. The names do not appear at the top of every page like a typical document header.

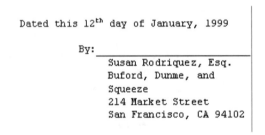

```
1  ‖ Buford, Dunme, and Squeeze              Judge Rutherford P. Anhale
   ‖ 214 Market Street
2  ‖ San Francisco, CA 94102
```

The three check boxes at the bottom of the Header/Footer dialog box are truly for footers. Check them if a pleading summary, name and address, and page number need to appear at the bottom of each page in the pleading.

SIGNATURE   A *signature block* is a space for an attorney who has submitted a pleading to sign his or her name, as shown in the illustration. Choose options in this dialog box to decide whether to include the signature block, place the firm's name and address in the signature block, and include the date in the signature block.

```
          Dated this 12ᵗʰ day of January, 1999

                 By: _____
                        Susan Rodriquez, Esq.
                        Buford, Dunme, and
                        Squeeze
                        214 Market Street
                        San Francisco, CA 94102
```

FILE NAME   The wizard suggests naming the template after the court name, but very likely a shorter name is more appropriate. The name you enter here will appear on a template icon in the Legal Pleadings tab of the New dialog box. Enter a short, descriptive name that clearly identifies which court the pleadings you create with your new template are meant for.

When you click the Finish button, Word saves the template you created. Then it shows you the Legal Pleading Wizard dialog box in case you want to prepare a pleading with the template you just finished creating. Click Cancel for now. See "Preparing a Pleading," later in this chapter, if you indeed want to type a pleading at this time.

Modifying a Pleading Template

If your pleading template needs adjusting here and there, choose File | New, click the Legal Pleadings tab in the New dialog box, and double-click the Pleading Wizard icon. When the Pleading Wizard opens, click Next to go to the Choose Task dialog box shown in Figure 21-2. In the dialog box, click the Modify The Pleading Template For The Court

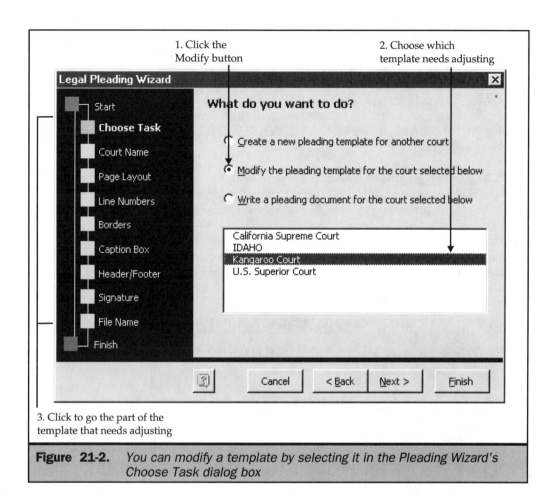

Figure 21-2. *You can modify a template by selecting it in the Pleading Wizard's Choose Task dialog box*

Selected Below option button, select the court whose template needs adjusting, and click the Next button. After that, either click the Next button until you reach the dialog box where you can make your adjustment, or click a dialog box name on the left side of the Pleading Wizard dialog box. The previous section in this chapter explains what the dialog boxes are and how you can use them to construct a pleading template.

Preparing a Pleading

After you have created a pleading template, you can use it to start work on a pleading. To do so, choose File | New, click the Legal Pleadings tab in the New dialog box, click the template named after the court to which you will submit the pleading, and click

OK. You'll see the first Legal Pleading Wizard dialog box. Clicking Next as you go along, visit each wizard dialog box—Parties, Names, and so on—to enter the particulars of your pleading. Then type the pleading itself.

PARTIES Depending on what the pleading is all about, choose an option to describe the parties to the case. Click the Debtor option button if your pleading is a decree of dissolution, for example. If you aren't an attorney, you might need to consult one before choosing the correct option button.

NAMES Enter the name or names of the parties to the case. If a party is listed in the Address book on your computer, you can click the Address Book button and choose a name from the Address book rather than enter the name yourself.

TITLES & CASE NO. Enter the case number, the number of firms who are filing the pleading, and a title for the pleading. The pleading summary is optional. It appears in the footer if your template calls for a pleading summary in the footer. The case number and title of the pleading appear to the right of the caption box.

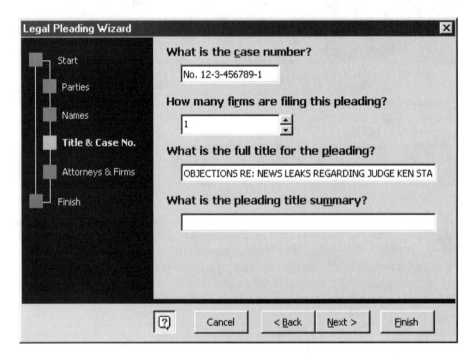

ATTORNEYS & FIRMS Enter the names of the attorney or attorneys who are filing the pleading and the name and address of the law firm they represent. Click the Include For check box if you want an "Attorney's for" line to appear on the pleading.

The Legal Pleading Toolbar

As you work on a document you created with a pleading template, you can call on the buttons on the Legal Pleading toolbar. The toolbar, which is named after the template from which you created your pleading, offers these buttons:

- **Block Quotation**   Indents a paragraph by .5 inch from the left and right margins.

- **Single Spacing, 1.5 Spacing, Double Spacing**   Changes the line spacing of text.

- **Table of Authorities**   Opens the Table of Authorities dialog box so you can mark a citation, or generate a table of authorities (a list of the rules, cases, statutes, regulations, and so on, cited in a legal document). See "Marking Citations for a Table of Authorities" and "Generating a Table of Authorities," later in this chapter.

Be sure to choose the right option from the drop-down list. Your choice should match the one you made in the Parties dialog box.

When you click the Finish button, Word creates a pleading document from your template. Boilerplate text from the template appears in the document, as do the attorney names and addresses you entered in the Pleading Wizard dialog boxes. Start typing away.

Numbering the Lines in a Document

In legal pleadings and certain kinds of literary and religious texts, the lines are numbered so that readers can refer to specific lines or go to a line quickly. Numbering the lines in a Word document is easy. You can number all the lines, number lines in a particular section, and number the lines continuously or starting anew on each page. Lines can only be seen in Print Layout view, so switch to Page Layout view and follow these steps to number lines:

1. Click in a section to number the lines in a particular section of a document; otherwise click wherever you want.

2. Choose File | Page Setup.

3. Click the Layout tab in the Page Setup dialog box.

4. Click the Line Numbers button. You'll see the Line Numbers dialog box shown in Figure 21-3.

5. Check the Add Line Numbering check box.

6. Choose options in the dialog box:

- ■ **Start At** Lines are numbered starting with 1, but if for some reason you want to begin with another number, enter it in this text box.

- ■ **From Text** Line numbers appear .25 inch to the left of the left margin of the page, but you can move them further away or closer to the text by entering a number in this text box.

- ■ **Count By** All lines are numbered, but by entering a number here you can make numbers appear at an interval. For example, entering **10** makes numbers appear at intervals of 10 (10, 20, 30).

- ■ **Numbering** Tell Word how to number the lines. You can number lines beginning anew at the start of each page or section, or number lines consecutively throughout a document.

7. Click OK twice to return to your document.

If your document is divided into sections and you want to number lines in other sections as well, click in the other sections and number them. You can do that very quickly by clicking in another section and pressing F4 or choosing Edit | Repeat Page Setup straight-away after you number the lines in one section.

To remove line numbers, click in a section, choose File | Page Setup, click the Layout tab in the Page Setup dialog box, click the Line Numbers button, and uncheck the Add Line Numbering check box in the Line Numbers dialog box (see Figure 21-3).

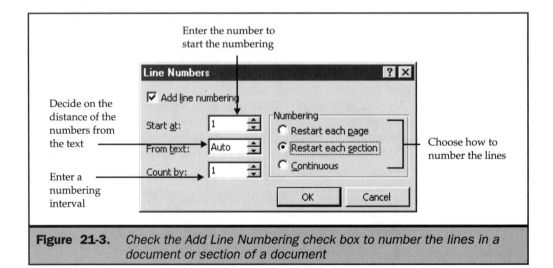

Figure 21-3. *Check the Add Line Numbering check box to number the lines in a document or section of a document*

Preventing Certain Lines from Being Numbered

Follow these steps to keep a handful of lines in the middle of a document or section from being numbered:

1. Select the lines that don't require numbers.
2. Choose Format | Paragraph to open the Paragraph dialog box.
3. Click the Line and Page Breaks tab.
4. Check the Suppress Line Numbers check box and click OK.

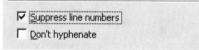

Numbering Paragraphs in the Text

In some kinds of legal contracts and technical documents, paragraphs are supposed to be numbered in sequence. To spare yourself the trouble of numbering the paragraphs yourself, you can take advantage of paragraph-numbering schemes in the Bullets and Numbering dialog box. Paragraph numbers work like the numbers in numbered lists. When you remove a paragraph or enter a new one, the paragraphs are renumbered.

Figure 21-4 shows two of three numbering schemes that Word offers. In the first, paragraphs are numbered in outline form, and in the second, each paragraph is assigned from one to nine numbers, depending on how deep it is in the hierarchy. The third paragraph-numbering scheme is more of a "bulleting scheme," with each paragraph in the hierarchy assigned a different bullet, not a number. You can create your own paragraph-numbering schemes, too. Read on.

Numbering the Paragraphs

Follow these steps to number paragraphs:

1. Select the paragraphs that you want to number. Be sure not to select any headings.
2. Choose Format | Bullets and Numbering.
3. As shown in Figure 21-5, click the Outline Numbered tab.
4. Choose one of the three paragraph-numbering options in the top half of the dialog box (the four options in the bottom half are for numbering headings, not paragraphs).

1) King
    a) Knave
    b) Jester
2) Queen
    a) Prince
    b) Princess
        i) Lady in Waiting
        ii) Garment Bag Carrier
3) Duke
4) Duchess
5) Marquis
    a) Marquise
        i) Earl
        ii) Earlene
        iii) Count (I'd hate to be the one who
           has to account for the Count).
        iv) Countess
6) Viscount
7) Viscountess
	1. King
	    1.1. Knave
	    1.2. Jester
	2. Queen
	    2.1. Prince
	    2.2. Princess
	        2.2.1. Lady in Waiting
	        2.2.2. Garment Bag Carrier
	3. Duke
	4. Duchess
	5. Marquis
	    5.1. Marquise
	        5.1.1. Earl
	        5.1.2. Earlene
	        5.1.3. Count (I'd hate to be the one
	             who has to account for the Count).
	        5.1.4. Countess
	6. Viscount
	7. Viscountess

Figure 21-4. *Two methods of numbering paragraphs: in outline form (left) and in numerical sequence (right)*

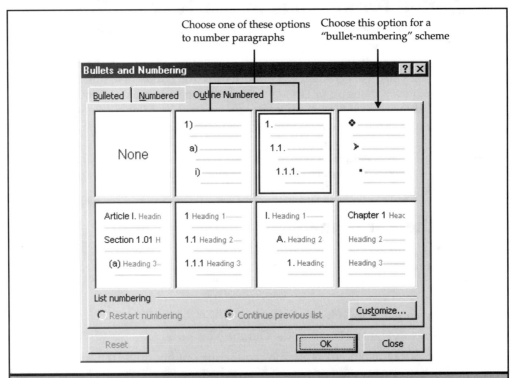

Figure 21-5. *Click an option in the top half the Outline Numbered tab to number paragraphs. The None option is for removing numbers*

> **Tip** *For legal-style paragraph numbering, click one of the numbering schemes, and then click the Customize button. In the Customize Outline Numbered List dialog box, click the More button if necessary, and then check the Legal Style Numbering check box. You will find the check box at the bottom of the dialog box below the Preview box.*

    5. Click OK.

In your document, all paragraphs are numbered 1, 2, 3, 4, and so on. To make a paragraph subordinate to another paragraph in the numbering hierarchy, click the subordinate paragraph and then click the Increase Indent button on the Formatting toolbar or press CTRL-M. The subordinate paragraph is given a lower outline-level number. In effect, increasing or decreasing the indentation of a paragraph tells Word how important the paragraph is. By clicking the Increase Indent and Decrease Indent buttons, you can assign different level numbers to paragraphs.

Follow these instructions to remove paragraph numbers, start numbering anew, or pick up the numbering sequence where you left off:

■ **Removing Numbers from Paragraphs** Select the paragraphs whose numbers you want to remove and click the Numbering button on the Formatting toolbar. After you remove numbers, paragraphs that were subordinate in the list are still indented. If necessary, click those paragraphs and start clicking the Decrease Indent button to remove their indentation.

■ **Resuming the Numbers** Select the next batch of paragraphs that need numbers and click the Numbering button on the Formatting toolbar.

■ **Restarting a New List at 1** Select the next batch of paragraphs and choose Format | Bullets and Numbering. On the Outline Numbered tab, click the paragraph-numbering scheme you have been using, click the Restart Numbering option button, and click OK.

> **Note** *Yes, you can devise a paragraph-numbering scheme of your own. See "Altering a Numbering Scheme" in Chapter 10. The instructions there, which apply to headings, also apply to paragraph numbers.*

Creating a Table of Authorities

In plaintiff versus defendant cases, attorneys cite precedent cases to make their arguments, and those cases have to be assembled in a table of authorities. A *table of authorities* is a list of the cases, statutes, and regulations cited in a legal document. These pages explain how to mark citations in a legal document so you can assemble them in a table of authorities. You'll also learn how to generate a table of authorities from the citations you've marked.

Entering Citations for the Table of Authorities

Follow these steps to mark citations in a legal document so you can compile them later in a table of authorities:

1. Select a citation you want for the table.

2. Either press ALT-SHIFT-I or click the Table Of Authorities button on the Legal Pleading toolbar and then click the Mark Citation button in the Table of Authorities dialog box. You will see the Mark Citation dialog box shown in Figure 21-6. The citation appears in the Selected Text box.

3. If necessary, edit the citation in the Selected Text box. When you generate the table, you can either list long citations from the Selected Text box or short citations from the Short Citation box.

4. In the Category drop-down list, choose a category that describes the case being cited. When you generate a table of authorities, you can generate tables in a single category or all the categories.

Tip
If no category adequately describes the case being cited, click the Category button in the Mark Citation dialog box. In the Edit Category dialog box, choose a number at the bottom of the Category list, and then enter a new category name in the Replace With text box and click the Replace button. Then click OK. Back in the Mark Citation dialog box, your new category appears on the Category drop-down list.

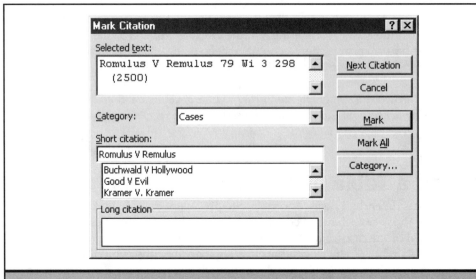

Figure 21-6. *By marking the citations in a legal document, you can compile them in a table of authorities*

5. In the Short Citation box, edit the citation. You can generate a table of authorities with short citations or long citations, so edit the citation carefully.

6. Click the Mark or Mark All button:

   ■ **Mark** Marks the citation for inclusion in the table of authorities. Other instances of this citation are not marked.

   ■ **Mark All** Marks all instances of the citation throughout the document.

7. Click the Close button.

In your document, you'll see a field code where you marked the citation. You can remove those ugly field codes from the screen by clicking the Show/Hide ¶ button on the Standard toolbar. Word uses the field codes to generate the table of authorities.

 Besides scouring a legal document on your own for citations, you can click the Next Citation button in the Mark Citation dialog box (see Figure 21-6). When you click this button, Word scrolls to legalese such as re and V in the document in case you want to mark it, too, for the table of authorities.

Generating the Table of Authorities

After you have picked through the document and marked all the citations, you can generate the table of authorities. Click where you want the table to appear and follow these steps to generate it:

1. Either choose Insert | Index and Tables and click the Table of Authorities tab in the Index and Tables dialog box, or click the Table of Authorities button on the Legal Pleading toolbar. You'll see the Table of Authorities tab shown in Figure 21-7.

2. In the Formats drop-down list, choose a format for the table. The Print Preview box shows exactly what you are choosing. Be sure to scroll down the box and take a good look.

3. In the Category drop-down list, choose All or a single category to tell Word how large a table to generate.

4. Leave the check mark in the Use Passim box if you want more than five references to the same citation to be cited with the word "passim" instead of a page number. In the glorious Latin language, "passim" means "scattered." In legal documents, the word refers to citations that appear throughout a document.

5. Leave the check mark in the Keep Original Formatting text box if you want to retain the original formatting of long citations in the table. You can uncheck this box if you want the table of authorities to show only short citations.

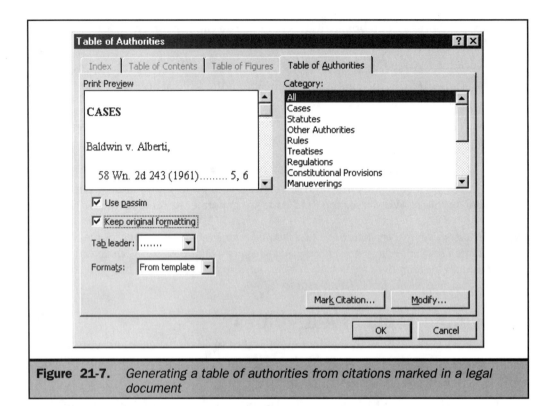

Figure 21-7. *Generating a table of authorities from citations marked in a legal document*

6. Choose a tab leader from the Tab leader drop-down list if the one you see in the Print Preview box doesn't suit you.

7. Click OK to generate the table of authorities.

To update a table of authorities after you mark new citations or edit the document, move the pointer to the left of the table and click to select it. Then either right-click and choose Update Field or press F9.

The Complete Reference

Word
2000

Part VI

Getting More Out of Word 2000

Chapter 22

Managing Your
Documents Better

657

This chapter explains how to organize and manage your documents and folders. It offers strategies for storing your work on disk, explains how to back up documents in Word 2000, and explores all the different ways to save documents in the background. On the subject of saving, you'll also learn how to save different versions of the same document and to save documents so they can be opened in other word processing programs. This chapter also presents techniques for protecting documents against unwanted changes and finding lost documents. Finally, at the end of this chapter are ten techniques for handling and preventing computer crashes.

Devising a Strategy to Store Your Work on Disk

The surest way to keep from losing documents is to store them carefully in the first place. When you create and save a document, Word 2000 asks which folder to save it in. Make sure, before you save a new document, that a folder is ready and waiting to receive it—a folder with a descriptive name that is located in a prominent place on your computer.

Many people mistakenly believe that Word documents must be stored deep in the computer along with the Word program files, but you can store Word documents anywhere you want on a computer. And you should store them in folders that are easy to find. I keep all my Word documents, for example, in a folder on the C drive that I named starting with the letters "AAA." The letters "AAA" place my most important folder at the top of the list of folders in the Open dialog box where I can find it easily. You are advised to devise a strategy of your own for storing Word documents where you can find them easily.

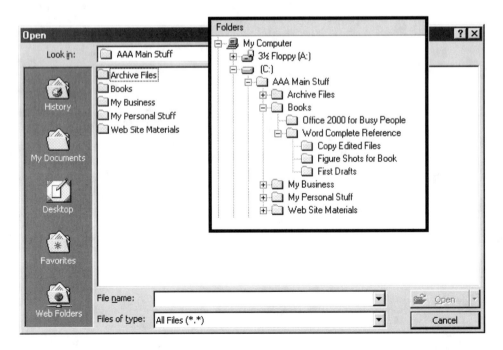

Read on to find out how to create a folder in Word for storing files and how to choose the default folder, the one that appears first thing in the Open and Save As dialog box when you choose File | Open or File | Save As.

Creating the Folders You Need

The best way to create a new folder is to do so with Windows Explorer or My Computer, the two Windows programs whose job is to organize and manage files. In Windows Explorer and My Computer, you can see the grand scheme. You can make better choices about where to place your new folder in the folder hierarchy. However, you can create a new folder in Word by following these steps:

1. Choose File | Open or File | Save As. You will see either the Open dialog box shown in Figure 22-1 or the Save As dialog box. The dialog boxes are identical except that one is for opening files and the other is for saving them.

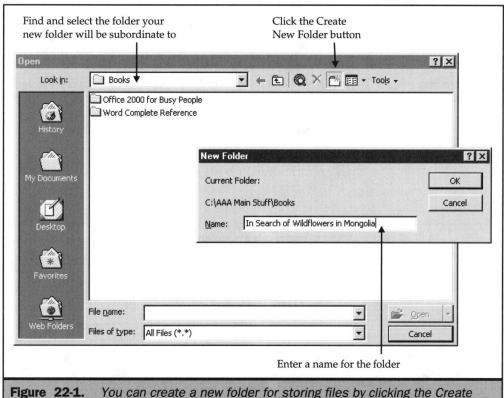

Figure 22-1. *You can create a new folder for storing files by clicking the Create New Folder button in the Open or Save As dialog box*

2. In the dialog box, find and select the folder that you want your new folder to be subordinate to. To put the new folder at the top of the C drive, open the Look In drop-down list and choose (C:).

3. Click the Create New Folder button. You'll see the New Folder dialog box shown in Figure 22-1. Notice that the dialog box lists the path to your new folder.

4. Enter a descriptive name for your new folder and click OK. Your new folder appears in the Look In box.

5. Click Cancel to close the Open dialog box or Save As dialog box.

Choosing a Default Folder Apart from "My Documents"

Word is very fond of the My Documents folder. Choose File | Open to open a document and you'll see the contents of the My Documents folder in the Open dialog box. You'll see the My Documents folder, I should say, until you open a document in another folder. Then the Open dialog box shows the contents of the last folder you visited in order to open a document.

My Documents is the default folder because the makers of Word expect you to keep the documents you are working on at present in the My Documents folder. The idea is for you to move documents to other folders when you finish working on them. Suppose, however, that you keep documents that need the most attention in a particular folder on your computer. You can make that folder the default folder that appears first thing when you choose File | Open. Follow these steps to tell Word which folder to display by default in the Open dialog box:

1. Choose Tools | Options to open the Options dialog box.

2. Click the File Locations tab. This tab lists the default locations of documents, templates, and files that pertain to Word.

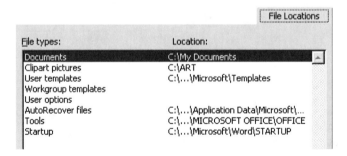

3. Under File Types, click Documents.

4. Click the Modify button. You will see the Modify Location dialog box.

5. Locate and select the folder that you want to appear by default in the Open dialog box. Make sure the name of the folder appears in the Look In box.

6. Click OK. On the File Locations tab, the name and location of your new default folder appears in the Location column.

7. Click the OK button.

Backing Up Your Work

Backing up a document means to make a second copy in case the original meets with an unfortunate accident. Unless you had the foresight to back up important documents, the documents are lost if they are damaged. If your computer breaks down, a virus ruins your computer, or your computer is stolen, you are out of luck unless you made backup copies of important documents.

Unfortunately, you can't back up Word documents to a floppy disk or zip disk with Word 2000. A backup copy that Word makes is stored in the same folder as the original. True, you can open the backup copy if the original gets damaged, but your computer must be alive and well for you to open the backup copy. Backup copies stored on a dead or stolen computer are not worth very much. To be absolutely safe, make backup copies of your important documents to floppy disks or zip disks.

Note   *Use the Windows programs Windows Explorer or My Computer to copy documents to floppy disks or zip disks. If your machine runs Windows 98, you can also back up documents with Backup, a utility the program that comes with Windows 98. Click the Start button and choose Programs | Accessories | System Tools | Backup to see if the Backup program is for you.*

Backup copies of Word documents have the .WBK (Word backup) file extension and are kept in the same folder as original copies. To name a backup document, Word attaches the words "Backup of" to the document's name, as shown in Figure 22-2. A backup copy is made each time you the save the original. However, the backup copy is not the same as the currently saved version of its original—the backup copy represents the version of the document as of the time you most recently saved it. If your computer fails and you can't open the original, you can open the backup copy and obtain a fairly up-to-date version of your document.

Caution   *Backup copies eat up a lot of disk space because two copies of each Word document are stored on disk. If you're running low on disk space, don't make backup copies with Word. Back up your documents to floppy disks or zip disks instead.*

Follow these steps to tell Word to make backup copies of documents:

1. Choose Tools | Options to open the Options dialog box.

2. Click the Save tab.

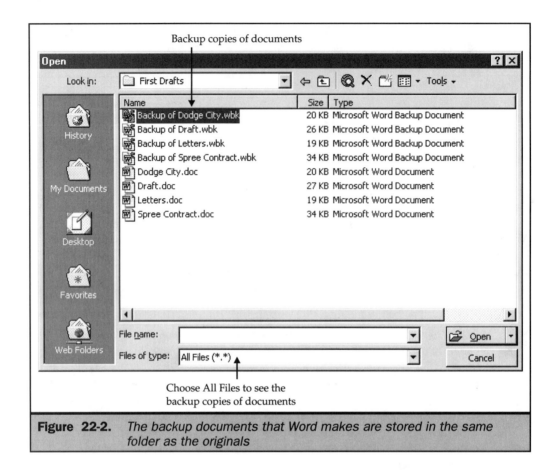

Backup copies of documents

Choose All Files to see the
backup copies of documents

Figure 22-2. *The backup documents that Word makes are stored in the same folder as the originals*

3. Check the Always Create Backup Copy check box and click OK. You can't create backup copies automatically and also "allow fast saves." The next section in this chapter explains fast saves.

To open the backup copy of a document, choose File | Open, locate the folder where the backup copy and original are kept, and choose All Files from the Files Of Type drop-down list, if necessary, to see the backup copies. Then click a backup copy and click the Open button.

Tip *By saving a document twice in succession, you can render the backup copy identical to the original. The previously saved version, not the saved version, of your document is kept in the backup document, so by saving twice you place the latest edition of the document in the backup copy.*

Strategies for Saving Documents

Everybody knows that you click the Save button, choose File | Save, or press CTRL-S to save a document. But that isn't the whole story. As Figure 22-3 shows, Word offers many ways to save documents in the background and in different formats. You can save different versions of a document as well. These pages explain how to save different versions of the same document, save a document under a different name, and save documents in different formats. You will also find out how to decide which strategy for saving files in the background is best for you.

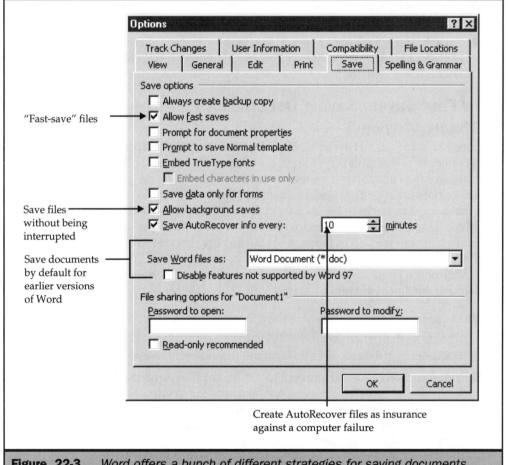

"Fast-save" files

Save files without being interrupted

Save documents by default for earlier versions of Word

Create AutoRecover files as insurance against a computer failure

Figure 22-3.   *Word offers a bunch of different strategies for saving documents*

Telling Word How to Save Documents

On the Save tab of the Options dialog box (see Figure 22-3) are three options for saving documents in the background: Allow Fast Saves, Allow Background Saves, and Save AutoRecover Info Every *X* Minutes. To visit the Save tab of the Options dialog box, choose Tools | Options and click the Save tab, or choose File | Save As, click the Tools button in the Save As dialog box, and choose General Options from the drop-down menu. The three options are described in detail in the pages that follow:

- **Allow Fast Saves** Supposedly speeds up the saving mechanism, but increases the size of documents and presents other disadvantages.

- **Allow Background Saves** Lets you keep working on a document while the computer saves it to the hard disk.

- **Save AutoRecover Info Every *X* Minutes** Creates a second, temporary copy of your document that opens automatically when you restart your computer after it hangs or fails.

Allow Fast Saves: Saving Documents Faster (In Theory, Anyway)

It's strange how the Allow Fast Saves check box is checked by default, yet the option doesn't offer many real advantages. In fact, the Allow Fast Saves option presents more disadvantages than advantages. I suggest unchecking it. When the option is selected, Word does not save recent changes in the document file, but in a separate file, the idea being that a smaller, separate file is faster to update than the document file itself. Everything is done behind the scenes so you never know there is a separate file. Eventually, changes tracked in the separate file are incorporated in the document file when either the separate file grows too large or you uncheck the Allow Fast Saves option, which Microsoft recommends doing when you are finished working on a document.

Here are the disadvantages of "fast-saving":

- Documents are larger. They require more disk space for storing and take longer to send over networks and the Internet.

- Documents put more of a strain on the computer's memory.

- You can't convert the document to a different file format without causing all kinds of problems for the person who opens the document in another word processor or computer program. Very likely, the other word processor or computer program doesn't know what to make of the two-file system and garbles the document accordingly.

- Sharing the document with others is problematic, since you are dealing behind the scenes with two files, the document file and the file in which changes to the document are stored.

- You can't save the document over a network connection.
- The chances of recovering a document after a computer or hard-drive problem are dramatically reduced.

The list of advantages is considerably shorter. In fact, the list extends to one item:

- A document with many graphics and other memory-intensive items does not take as long to save.

 Even if you decide to "fast-save" documents, be sure to uncheck the Allow Fast Saves check box in the Options dialog box (see Figure 22-3) when you finish working on a document, when you give a document to someone else to work on, or when you engage in a memory-intensive activity such as generating an index or table of contents.

Allow Background Saves: Saving Documents as You Work on Them

Check this option and you can continue to work while the hard disk on your computer grinds away and Word saves your document on disk. In theory you have to wait for Word to finish saving a document before you can start working again if this option is not checked, but computers are so fast these days it doesn't really matter whether this option is turned on. Might as well leave it on. Only uncheck it if your computer is running very low on memory.

Save AutoRecover Info Every *X* Minutes: Recovering Documents After a Crash

When the Save AutoRecover Info Every *X* Minutes check box is checked—and you should definitely check it—Word creates a temporary copy of your document every few minutes (you decide how many minutes by entering a number in the Minutes box). If your computer crashes or a power failure occurs while you are working on a document, all is not lost because you can open the AutoRecover edition of your document, the one that Word had in reserve when the computer died. The AutoRecover document probably isn't entirely up to date, but it is as up to date as of the number of minutes you entered in the Minutes box.

After you get your computer up and running again and start Word, AutoRecover copies of the documents that were open when the crash or power failure occurred appear onscreen. The word "Recovered" in parentheses appears in the title bar after the name of the document that was recovered.

At this point, click the Save button or press CTRL-S and do either of the following in the Save As dialog box:

■ **Keep Two Copies of the Recovered Document**   Enter a new name for the recovered document in the File Name box and click the Save button. This way, you get two copies of the document. You can compare the recovered file to the original to see which is more up to date and which, therefore, needs deleting.

■ **Keep the Recovered Document, Not the Original**   Click the Save button and then click Yes when Word asks if you want to replace your original file with its AutoRecover copy. Go this route if you know that the AutoRecover copy is more up to date than the one that is stored on disk.

If the AutoRecover document doesn't appear when you start your computer, go to the folder where it is kept and open it from there. You will find AutoRecover copies of documents in the C:\Windows\Application Data\Microsoft\Word folder, or, if you run Windows NT, the C:\Windows\Profiles*username*\Application Data\Microsoft\ Word folder.

Changing the Folder Where AutoRecover Documents Are Stored

AutoRecover copies of the documents you are working on are kept in the C:\Windows\Application Data\Microsoft\Word folder (on Windows NT 4 and later computers and computers in which more than one profile is in use, the files are stored in the C:\Windows\Profiles*username*\Application Data\Microsoft\ Word folder). In the event of a crash, you can always go to the AutoRecover folder and look for your wounded document there.

Follow these steps to change the location of the AutoRecover folder if you want to keep the temporary documents in a more accessible location:

1. Choose Tools | Options and click the File Locations tab in the Options dialog box.

2. Under File Types, click AutoRecover Files.

3. Click the Modify button.

4. In the Modify Location dialog box, find and select the folder that you want to store AutoRecover files in, and then click OK.

5. Click OK in the Options dialog box.

Saving (and Opening) Different Versions of a Document

In a long document that drags on and on and requires many drafts, sometimes saving different drafts is useful. If you need to retrieve a paragraph or two that got dropped from an earlier draft, you can do so. You can even abandon later drafts and start all over with an earlier draft. For long projects that require many drafts, Word offers the File | Versions command. This command makes it easy to save different versions of the same document and, better yet, retrieve an earlier version. These pages explain how to save versions of a document, open a version, and save a version in a new file.

EXAMPLES

LEARN BY EXAMPLE
Open the 22-1 Versions practice document on the companion CD to practice handling different versions of a document.

Saving a Version of a Document

Follow these steps to save different versions of a document as it evolves:

1. Choose File | Versions. You will see the dialog box shown in Figure 22-4. The dialog box lists earlier versions of the document (if any), who saved the different versions, and comments describing what is found in earlier versions.

2. Click the Save Now button. The Save Version box appears so you can enter a comment or two to describe this version of the document.

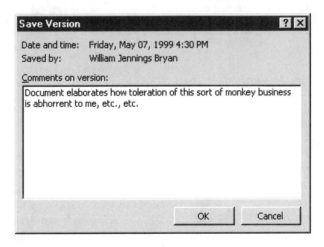

3. Enter a descriptive comment and click OK. The first few words of what you write will appear in the Comments column of the Versions In dialog box (see Figure 22-4).

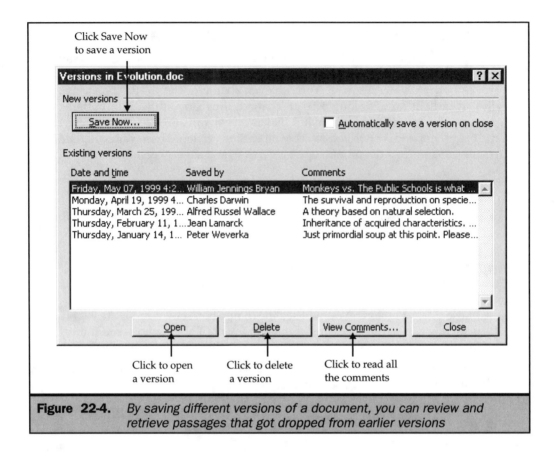

Figure 22-4. *By saving different versions of a document, you can review and retrieve passages that got dropped from earlier versions*

4. Click Close in the Versions In dialog box.

Click a version and then click the Delete button in the Versions In dialog box if you no longer require the services of an earlier version of a document.

Many people are tempted to click the Automatically Save A Version On Close check box in the Versions In dialog box, but I don't recommend it. Clicking this check box tells Word to save a new version each time you close your document. However, you can't enter comments to describe the version when you save a version this way. You end up with a bunch of dated versions in the Versions In dialog box, none of which is easy to distinguish from the other because the words "Automatic version" appear in the Comments column where normally a description of the version would appear.

Opening an Earlier Version of a Document

Go to work on your document as though no version were attached to it, but when you want to see an earlier version, choose File | Versions. The Versions In dialog box appears (see Figure 22-4) and you see the list of all the versions. Click a version and then click the Open button to open it. If necessary, click a version and then click the View Comments button if you aren't sure which version is which.

The version opens in its own window onscreen. To switch between the version and the latest draft, either click in a different window or choose a name from the Window menu. Click the Close button in the version window to remove the version from the screen.

If a version of a document deserves to be a document in its own right, open it and choose File | Save As and save it under its own name. The next section in this chapter provides all the details.

Saving a Document Under a New Name

As long as you know your way around the Save As dialog box, saving a document under a different name is easy. All you have to do is choose File | Save As, enter a new name in the File Name text box, perhaps select a new folder to store your newly named document in, and click OK. You'll end up with two documents, your original and the one you just named.

Another way to save a document under a new name is to open a copy of the original. Choose File | Open, locate and select the document that needs copying, click the down arrow beside the Open button, and choose Open As Copy from the drop-down menu. A file named after the original with the words "Copy of" opens onscreen.

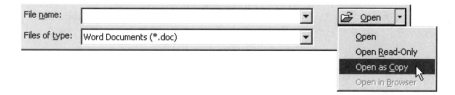

"Opening Documents" in Chapter 1 explains all the buttons and tools in the Save As and Open dialog box. The dialog boxes offer the same tools and buttons.

Saving Documents in Different Formats So Others Can Use Them

Not everyone is a proud owner of Microsoft Word 2000. Before you pass along a document to someone who uses another version of Word or another word processor altogether, save your document so that the other person can open and make good use of it. Read on to learn how to save a document so it can be opened in another word processing program or an earlier version of Word.

Saving a Word document in a different format for use in another word processor is like translating texts between foreign languages—something always gets lost in the translation. Proofread documents carefully after they are opened in the other word processing program. Typically, symbols and special characters get lost or mistranslated. Fancy formats such as text boxes and columns may not make it to the other side at all.

Saving Documents for Use in Other Word Processors

To save a copy of a document for use with another word processing program, open the document and choose File | Save As to open the Save As dialog box. Then, from the Save As Type drop-down list, choose the name of the word processing program to which the file needs translating, and click the Save button. Word is on speaking terms with Write, WordPerfect, and Works. You will find their names on the Save As Type drop-down list.

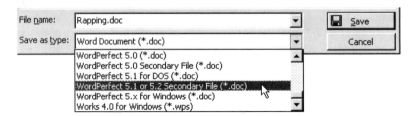

And if the word processing program you need isn't on the list? Then you have to speak Esperanto and rely on one of the following plain-text file formats. From best choice to worst, save your Word document in one of these formats so it can be opened in another word processor:

■ **Rich Text Format (.RTF)**   Saves formats along with text. Microsoft and Microsoft-compatible programs can read and display .RTF files. This is the first choice for making the conversion because formats are retained.

■ **Text with Layout (.TXT)**   Strives to maintain layouts by inserting blank spaces to approximate indentations, for example. This format preserves some formatting.

■ **Text Only (.TXT)**   Saves text but not formats. A last resort. Use this one only if none of the others work.

■ **MS-DOS Text Only (.TXT)**   Same as Text Only, but for use with non-Windows-based programs.

One way to get around the problem of not being able to export a document to another word processor is to find out if the other word processor can import WordPerfect files. If it can, save your Word document as a WordPerfect file, and then use the other word processor to open the WordPerfect file.

Saving Documents for Use in Earlier Versions of Word

People with Word 97 can open Word 2000 documents without the documents having to be converted to a different format. However, formats that are new in Word 2000 are replaced by their Word 97 equivalents or near-equivalents in Word 97, and advanced formats in the Word 2000 document are lost.

To convert a document so it can be opened in Word 95 or Word 6, make a copy of the document. Then open the copy, choose File | Save As to open the Save As dialog box, choose Word 6.0/95 (*.DOC) on the Save As Type drop-down menu, click the Save button, and click Yes when Word asks if you want to replace the existing file. For every document element that will be lost in the conversion, Word asks you again whether you want to convert the document. Keep clicking Yes. You can always go back to the original Word 2000 document as long as you made a copy of it.

Saving Documents for Word 97 or Word 6.0/95 by Default

If you are way ahead of the pack and you always have to save Word 2000 documents in a different format so that co-workers can open them, make the different format the default format for saving documents. That way, you don't have to choose a new format whenever you pass off a file to a co-worker. To change the default file format, choose Tools | Options and click the Save tab in the Options dialog box (see Figure 22-3). Then choose a different Word file format as the format with which your Word documents are saved:

- **Saving Documents for Word 97**   Check the Disable Features Not Supported by Word 97 check box. Page layout formats, table layout formats, and other formats in your Word 2000 documents that aren't found in Word 97 are converted to formats that are found in Word 97, so advanced formats are lost. (To learn which formats are lost, open the Help program, click the Answer Wizard, type **What happens when I turn off features not supported by Word 97?**, and click the Search button.)

- **Saving Documents for Word 95 and Word 6**   Choose Word 6.0/95 on the Save Word Files As drop-down list.

After your co-workers get their copies of Word 2000, be sure to return to the Options dialog box and make Word 2000 the default file format. To do so, choose Word Document in the Save Word Files As drop-down list and uncheck the Disable Features Not Supported by Word 97 check box.

Protecting Documents Against Undue Tampering

Before you make a document available over a network or otherwise give co-workers a chance to tamper with it, you can do one or two things to make sure that your document doesn't get turned into mincemeat. These pages explain how to retain control over documents by clamping passwords on them and designating them as "read-only." Along with Windows, Word 2000 offers four ways to protect documents against tampering:

- **A Password Is Required to Open the Document**   Without the password, no one can open the document. See "Clamping a Password on a Document."

- **A Password Is Required to Edit the Document**   Anyone can open and read the document. To make editorial changes and save them in the document, however, you must know the password. People who don't know the password can save their editorial changes by saving the document under a new name. See "Clamping a Password on a Document."

- **Others Are Asked to Read But Not Edit the Document**   When others open the document, a dialog box asks them to please open the document in such a way that they can read it but make no editorial changes without saving the document under a new name. However, others can ignore the request. They can open the document and make as many editorial changes as they want. See "Protecting Documents by Giving them Read-Only Status."

- **Others Can Read the Document But Make No Edits Without Saving the Document Under a New Name**   Others can open the document and read it, but if they make editorial changes and try to save them, they see the Save As dialog box. At that point, others can save their editorial changes in a new document or abandon the enterprise. The original document remains intact. See "Protecting Documents by Giving them Read-Only Status."

> **Note**   *Chapter 19 explains how you can use the Tools | Protect Document command to make sure that editorial changes to a document do not go unnoticed. "Keeping Track of Revisions to Documents" describes how to make sure that all editorial changes to a document are tracked with revision marks; "Commenting on a Document" describes how you can allow reviewers to comment on but not revise a document.*

Clamping a Password on a Document

To make absolutely certain that only the select few can open or make changes to a document, you can clamp a password on it. People who do not have the password are either barred from opening the document or barred from making editorial changes to it, depending on which kind of password you give your document:

- **Password to Open**   Anyone who tries to open the document sees the Password dialog box and has to enter the password correctly before the document can be opened. Fail to enter the password correctly and you cannot open the document no matter what.

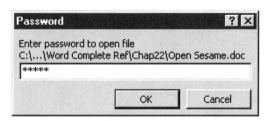

- **Password to Modify** Anyone who tries to open the document sees the Password dialog box. People who enter the password correctly can open the document, make editorial changes, and save the changes in the document. People who don't have the password can click the Read Only button to see the document. However, if they make editorial changes and try to save them, they see the Save As dialog box and have to save the document under a new name to record their editorial changes in a new document.

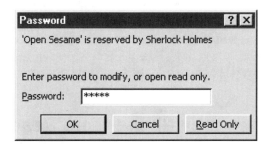

Follow these steps to clamp a password on a document:

1. Open the document that needs a password and choose Tools | Options.

2. Click the Save tab in the Options dialog box.

3. Under File Sharing Options For, enter the password. Passwords can be 15 characters long. If you include upper- and lowercase letters in your password, remember them well because passwords are case-sensitive. You have to enter upper- and lowercase letters exactly as you enter them now when you try to open your document. Asterisks instead of letters appear in the text box when you enter the password.

   - **Password To Open** Enter the password here if you want to keep others from opening the document without a password.

   - **Password To Modify** Enter the password here to keep only the select few from making editorial changes to the document.

File sharing options for "Open Sesame"
Password to open: Password to modify:
*****   *****

 It goes without saying, but you must never forget a password. Forget the password and you can't open or modify the document, much less remove the password. Here's a trick for devising a password that you are not likely to forget and someone else is not likely to discover: Pick your favorite foreign city and spell it backwards. If I needed a password for my documents, it would be **ezneriF***.*

4. Click OK in the Options dialog box. You'll see the Confirm Password dialog box.

5. Enter your password exactly as you entered it before and click OK.

6. Click the Save button or press CTRL-S to activate the password.

Suppose you decide to remove or change a password. Open the document in question, choose Tools | Options, click the Save tab in the Options dialog box, and follow these instructions:

■ **Removing the Password**   Delete the asterisks in the Password To Open or Password To Modify text box and click OK.

■ **Changing the Password**   Delete the asterisks in the Password To Open or Password To Modify text box and enter a new password. Then click OK, reproduce your new password in the Confirm Password dialog box, and click OK again.

Protecting Documents by Giving them Read-Only Status

A *read-only* document is one that can be read onscreen but not changed in any way, shape, or form. In order to record editorial changes you've made to a read-only document, you have to save the document under a new name. The read-only document remains in the pristine condition it was in when you opened it.

The previous section in this chapter explains how you can clamp a password to modify on a document and require others who do not have the password to open the document as a read-only file. Here are two more strategies for giving a document read-only status:

■ **Recommend That the Document Be Opened as Read-Only**   Anyone who opens the document sees a dialog box that suggests opening the document as read-only. By clicking Yes, the person opens the document as a read-only file. By clicking No, the person opens the document as a normal file. This strategy counts on the user's discretion to treat the document as a read-only file. Nothing prevents others from opening the document and making changes to it.

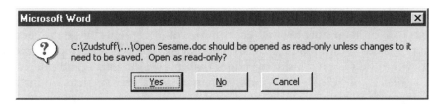

■ **Make the Document a Read-Only File**   Everyone can open the document, but if they make editorial changes and try to save them, they must save the document under a new name. The words "Read-Only" in parentheses appear in the title bar when you are dealing with a read-only file.

To recommend that a document be opened as read-only, open the document, choose Tools | Options, and click the Save tab in the Options dialog box. Then, under File Sharing Options For, check the Read-Only Recommended check box. You must save your document before it acquires read-only status.

To turn a document into a full-fledged read-only file, leave Word and open either of the Windows programs for managing files, Windows Explorer or My Computer. Then locate your document in one of those programs, select it, and choose File | Properties. In the Properties dialog box, click the General tab, and then check the Read-Only check box.

Remember how to get to the Properties dialog box in My Computer or Windows Explorer. You can choose File | Properties in a Word document to open the Properties dialog box, but you can't change the read-only status of a document in the Properties dialog box in Word. To change a document's read-only status, you have to start from Windows Explorer or My Computer and choose File | Properties.

Finding a Lost Document

Occasionally a document gets lost. You don't remember its name. You remember its name but you don't know which folder you put it in. You remember part of its name and a sentence you typed in it, but that's all. Word 2000 offers a special dialog box for looking for stray documents. You can search by filename, by a modification date, by file size, and a host of other criteria. These pages explain how to search for missing documents in Word and how to enter descriptions of documents in the Properties dialog box to make finding missing documents easier. You will also find instructions for using Windows' search tools in the pages that follow. Personally, I think searching for missing files is much easier in Windows than in Word, so I've included instructions for searching with Windows, too.

Entering Document Summaries to Find and Identify Documents

Especially if documents are strewn across a network, anybody who has to handle a hundred or more documents owes it to him- or herself to enter descriptions of documents in the Properties dialog box. Choose File | Properties to open the Properties dialog box. Descriptions you enter help identify documents and they can also be used as an aid in searching for stray documents. Figure 22-5 shows the Summary tab of the

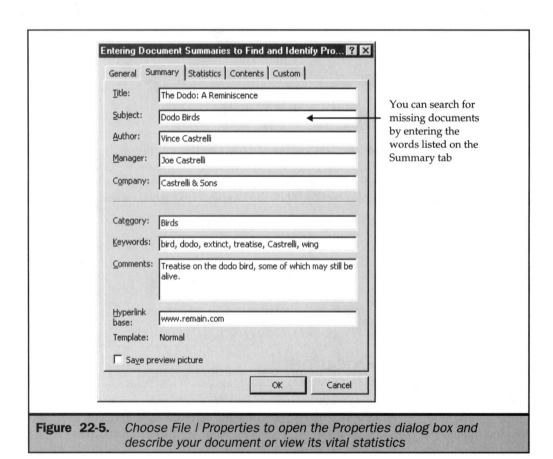

Figure 22-5. *Choose File | Properties to open the Properties dialog box and describe your document or view its vital statistics*

Properties dialog box. As the next section in this chapter explains, you can search for stray documents by title, subject, author, manager, company—in short, you can look for identifying words that you entered in the text boxes on the Summary tab.

In sum, the Properties dialog box offers these tabs:

- **General**   Basic information about the document such as when it was created, its size, and when it was last modified and accessed. You can use this information when searching for a document.

- **Summary**   As shown in Figure 22-5, the identifying characteristics of the document. The author name and company name are entered for you. Enter the rest of the information on your own.

- **Statistics**   Vital statistics about the document, including the number of pages, total editing time, and the name of the person who last saved the document. This information can also be used in searches.

Statistics:	Statistic name	Value
	Pages:	4
	Paragraphs:	62
	Lines:	127
	Words:	919
	Characters:	4306
	Characters (with spaces):	5169

- **Contents**   A list of the headings to which you assigned heading styles—Heading 1, Heading 2, and so on—in the document. To make the list appear, click the Save Preview Picture check box on the Summary tab.

- **Custom**   For further describing the document. Choose a category in the name box, choose what type of category it is on the Type drop-down list (Text, Date, Number, or Yes or No), and enter a description in the Value box. You can create your own categories by entering their names in the Name box and clicking the Add button after you have chosen a type and entered a value. Click the Link To Content check box and choose a bookmark name from the Source drop-down list to use a changeable bookmark reference in your document as a document description.

Document properties can be printed. Choose File | Print to open the Print dialog box, choose Document Properties on the Find What drop-down list, and click OK.

If identifying and describing documents in the Properties dialog box is important to you, you can tell Word to display the Properties dialog box whenever a document is saved for the first time. To do so, choose Tools | Options, click the Save tab in the Options dialog box (see Figure 22-3), and check the Prompt For Document Properties check box.

Getting the Statistics on a Document

Instead of going to the trouble to open the Properties dialog box to see statistics about a document, you can simply choose Tools | Word Count. The Word Count dialog box tells you how many pages, words, characters, and what-all are in your document. Be sure to check the Include Footnotes And Endnotes check box if you are being paid by the word to write your document. That way, you can inflate the word count.

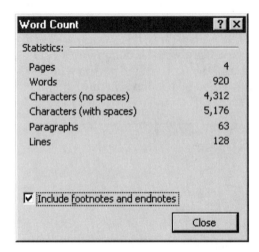

By the way, the Tools | Word Count command forces Word to count all the pages in a document. Sometimes Word is slow about doing that, but you can crack the whip by choosing Tools | Word Count. In a long document, for example, the number of pages in the document doesn't appear right away when you click the Insert Number of Pages button on the Header and Footer toolbar. But you can make the number of pages appear by choosing Tools | Word Count. The number of pages in the document is listed correctly as well on the Status bar when you choose Tools | Word Count.

Finding a Lost Document with Word 2000

Whether or not you entered descriptions of your document in the Properties dialog box (see Figure 22-5), you can still use the Find dialog box to search for stray documents, although your searches will be more fruitful if you entered document properties. To start searching for a document, chose File | Open, click the Tools button in the Open dialog box, and choose Find from the drop-down menu. You'll see the Find dialog box shown in Figure 22-6. An ugly, complicated-looking dialog box, is it not?

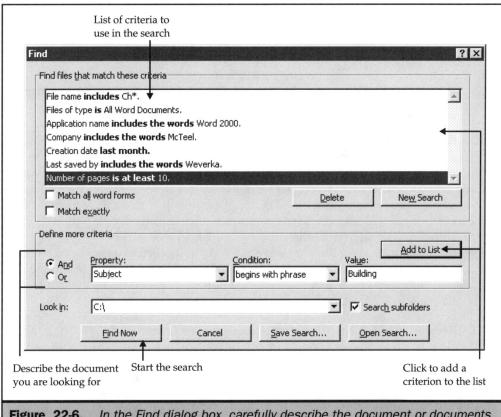

List of criteria to
use in the search

Figure 22-6.   *In the Find dialog box, carefully describe the document or documents
you are looking for*

Describe the document   Start the search
you are looking for

Click to add a
criterion to the list

Note   *Later in this chapter, "Finding a Lost Document with Windows 98" describes how to
find documents with Widows' search tools. The Windows search tools are easier to use
and more productive, especially if you didn't enter document properties to describe your
document in the Properties dialog box.*

Describing the document you are searching for in the Find dialog box is like
searching the Internet: The more criteria you enter to describe your document, the
more likely you are to find it *and* the more likely you are to make a mistake and enter a
wrong criterion. To see your way out of the Catch-22 situation, only enter criteria for
the search that you know to be true. Don't enter many criteria simply because you can
do so in the Find dialog box.

TELLING WORD WHERE TO LOOK   Especially if you are looking on a network, you
can make the search go much, much faster by carefully making a choice in the Look In

box. As best you can, choose the folder or drive where the document is likely to be found. Be sure to check the Search Subfolders button to look in the folder's subfolders as well.

To enter a folder in the Look In box, click Cancel to return to the Open dialog box, find and select the folder there, click the Tools button, and choose Find from the drop-down list to return to the Find dialog box.

DESCRIBING THE LOST DOCUMENT   Start by describing the lost document. From the Property drop-down menu, choose a document property from the Properties drop-down list, choose a condition that describes what you know about the property from the Condition list, and, if necessary, enter a value to further describe the property in the Value text box. Then click the Add to List button. Your search criterion appears in the list at the top of the Find dialog box. Click a criterion and then click the Delete button if you need to remove a criterion from the list.

Describe as many criteria this way as you can. As you describe each additional criterion, click the And option button if you want the document you are describing to meet all the conditions you list, or the Or option button if the search can meet any of the conditions.

MATCHING WORD FORMS   If your search criteria includes words, check the Match Exactly check box if you want to take upper- and lowercase letters into account and require words to match the case of the words you entered. Check the Match All Word Forms if you want a little leeway, so that entering "Script" as a Keyword property, for example, finds "Scripts" and "Scripted" as well.

CONDUCTING THE SEARCH   When you have described the document and are ready to start searching for it, click the Find Now button. If Word can find the document you are looking for, you'll see its name in the Open dialog box. Click the name and click the Open button to open your document.

If Word couldn't locate the document, click the Tools button and choose Find from the drop-down menu to return to the Find dialog box. Then either remove a criteria or two, or add a criteria or two, and start the search again. Click the New Search button to start with a blank slate.

Finding a Lost Document with Windows 98

As I mentioned earlier in this chapter, I think the Windows search tools are far easier to use than the ones that are found in Word 2000. The Word 2000 Find command relies on document properties, but you needn't have entered those to conduct a search in Windows. Follow these steps to look for a document in Windows:

1. Click the Start button, click Find on the Start menu, and click the Files or Folders command. The Find dialog box shown in Figure 22-7 appears. In the figure, a search has already been conducted and the results show at the bottom

Enter the
search criteria

Choose where
to search

Click to start
the search

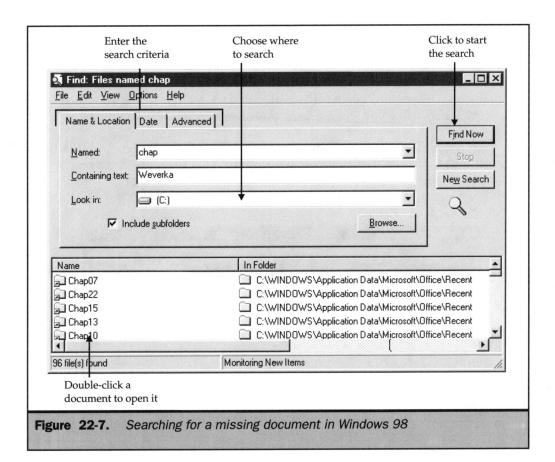

Double-click a
document to open it

Figure 22-7.   *Searching for a missing document in Windows 98*

of the Find dialog box. As you enter criteria for your search, enter what you
know about the missing document. You don't have to fill in all the tabs in the
Find dialog box.

2. On the Name & Location tab, enter what you know about the document's name
   and tell Windows where to look. You can enter a part of the name—you don't
   have to enter all of it. To tell Windows where to look for the document, click the
   Browse button and select a folder in the Browse for Folder dialog box.

3. On the Date tab, describe when the document was last saved, when it was
   created, or when it was last accessed.

4. On the Advanced tab, open the Of Type drop-down menu and choose
   Microsoft Word Document. If you know roughly how big your document is,
   enter the number in kilobytes.

5. Click the Find Now button. If Windows can find your document, it is listed at
   the bottom of the dialog box.

6. Double-click a document to open it.

Saving Search Criteria So You Can Run Searches Again

After you laboriously construct criteria for conducting a search, you may as well save it in case you have to run the same search later. To do so, click the Save Search button while your criteria are listed at the top of the Find dialog box. You'll see the Save Search dialog box. Enter a descriptive name for the search criteria and click OK.

To run a search whose criteria you saved, open the File dialog box and click the Open Search button. In the Open Search dialog box, click the name of the search you want to run and click the Open button. Back in the Find dialog box, click the Find Now button to run your search.

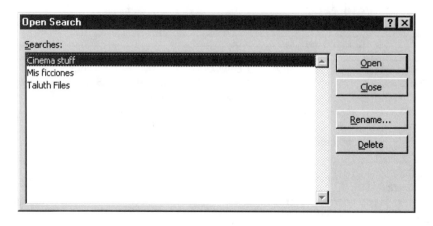

MOUS Exam Objectives Explored in Chapter 22

Objective	Heading	Practice File
Create multiple versions of a document*	"Saving (and Opening) Different Versions of a Document"	22-1 Versions
Protect documents*	"Protecting Documents Against Undue Tampering"	

* Denotes an Expert exam objective.

Top
10

Ten Techniques for Handling Computer Crashes and Other Untoward Events

When a computer crashes or a power failure occurs, it can be disconcerting, especially if you are working on an important document. Here are some tried-and-true techniques for preventing crashes, recovering from crashes, and steeling yourself and your computer against crashes.

1. WHEN YOU CAN, ALWAYS SHUT DOWN YOUR COMPUTER PROPERLY.

Everybody knows the routine for shutting down properly: Click the Start button, choose Shut Down, click the Shut Down option button in the Shut Down Windows dialog box, and click OK. If you don't shut down properly, you run the risk of damaging your hard disk and the files that happened to be stored on the part of your hard disk that was damaged. Shutting down properly is the first defense against damaging your computer.

And if your computer freezes and you can't shut down properly…

2. PRESS CTRL-ALT-DEL WHEN YOUR COMPUTER HANGS OR FREEZES. It

happens. Sometimes the computer freezes and refuses to do anything more. And then you can't shut down the proper way and you have to resort to this technique to make your computer start working again:

1. Press CTRL-ALT-DEL. With luck, the Close Program dialog box appears.

2. Click the name of the program that is "not responding." You will see the words "not responding" after the program's name.

3. Click the End Task button. Again with luck, the program that made your computer hang closes and you can get back to work. Save all open documents, close all programs, and restart your computer.

4. If your computer still doesn't respond, press CTRL-ALT-DEL again. With luck, your computer shuts down and restarts.

5. If you continue to suffer bad luck, turn off the computer's power switch and wait a full minute before turning your computer on again. If you turn it on before the platters stop spinning, you could harm the hard disk.

Windows runs the ScanDisk utility when you turn your computer back on to see if any damage was done to the hard disk. That's quite all right.

3. ALWAYS BACK UP IMPORTANT DOCUMENTS. As long as you back up

important documents, you don't have to worry too much about system crashes and files being corrupted. Earlier in this chapter, "Backing Up Your Work" explores all the nuances of backing up Word documents.

4. INVEST IN A SURGE PROTECTOR. Especially if you live in the southern United States or another lush semitropical zone where thunderstorms occur frequently, you need a surge protector, a device that protects computers again electrical surges. An electrical surge can do serious damage to a computer, but a surge protector provides an alternative path to electricity when it rises above the normal level on the power line.

5. GET ANTI-VIRUS SOFTWARE. To tell the truth, I don't know what to make of the virus scare. Everyone thinks viruses are a grave danger, but I wonder sometimes if damage from viruses is exaggerated. Anyhow, I am hereby passing along the standard gratuitous advice about being careful to avoid viruses. In Word, macros can carry viruses, so you should be careful about opening documents that include macros. And you should buy anti-virus software for your computer if you often receive files over the Internet.

   If you think your computer has been struck by a virus, you may want to visit **www.microsoft.com/ msoffice**, the Office 2000 Web site, and check for updates concerning viruses. When you're done, go to the Computer Virus Myths site at **www.kumite.com/myths/ home.htm**, where you can read about virus hoaxes and virus hoaxsters.

6. WHAT TO DO WHEN WORD SAYS THE "FILE IS IN USE." When a document isn't closed properly or your computer gets momentarily confused by competing demands, you may see a message that says the "file is in use" when you try to open a document. The file, however, isn't really in use, and you know that but the computer doesn't.

   If you are working at home and your computer isn't connected to a network, the only thing you can do to remedy the problem is close all documents, shut down your computer, and restart your computer. Doing so removes from the computer's memory all vestiges of the document that was supposed to be open, and you can open the document.

   If you are working at an office and your computer is connected to a network, the file-sharing properties of your documents probably have not been set up correctly. Ask the network administrator to solve the problem for you.

7. CHECK THE SAVE AUTORECOVER INFO EVERY *X* MINUTES CHECK BOX IN THE OPTIONS DIALOG BOX. Earlier in this chapter, "Telling Word How to Save Documents" explains what the Save AutoRecover Info Every X Minutes check box on the Save tab of the Options dialog box does. When the check box is selected, Word creates a second, temporary copy of your document every certain number of minutes. The temporary copy opens onscreen automatically when you restart your computer after your computer hangs or fails. Be sure to select this very valuable option.

8. RECOVER THE TEXT FROM A DAMAGED DOCUMENT. Even if a document is in shambles, you can try this technique to recover the text inside it:

   1. Choose Tools | Options and click the General tab in the Options dialog box.

2. Check the Confirm Conversion At Open check box and click OK.

3. Choose File | Open to see the Open dialog box.

4. In the Files Of Type drop-down list, choose Recover Text From Any File.

5. Find and select the text that needs rescuing and click the Open button. The document opens as a text-only file. Select the text you need and copy it to a safe place.

9. RUN DISK CLEANUP TO MAKE YOUR COMPUTER WORK FASTER.   The Windows 98 Disk Cleanup utility removes the files that clutter the hard disk so that your system can run better. Follow these steps to run Disk Cleanup:

1. Click the Start button and choose Programs | Accessories | System Tools | Disk Cleanup.

2. Make sure Temporary Internet Files and Temporary Files are checked in the Disk Cleanup dialog box.

3. Click OK and then click Yes.

10. RUN SCANDISK TO CHECK FOR AND REPAIR ERRORS TO THE HARD DISK.   The Windows 98 ScanDisk utility is designed to check the hard disk for damage. Run the utility program if your computer fails frequently, if you see "bad sector" or "unable to read" errors, or if you get a bunch of gibberish after you open a file. Follow these steps to run ScanDisk:

1. Click the Start button and choose Programs | Accessories | System Tools | ScanDisk.

2. Choose a disk to check.

3. Choose to run a Standard test.

4. Click the Start button.

The
Complete
Reference

Word
2000

Chapter 23

Your Own Customized
Word 2000

This chapter takes on a subject which inspires more trepidation in most people than is really necessary—it explains how to customize Word 2000. As this chapter will demonstrate, customizing Word is not as hard as it seems. Perhaps you've noticed the little arrow on the right side of the toolbars. Merely by clicking that arrow and making a choice or two, you can add buttons to or remove buttons from a toolbar. You can also devise your own toolbars, menus, and keyboard shortcuts for the commands that take up most of your time.

This chapter explains how to customize the Normal template and how to customize toolbars, menus, and keypresses. You will also learn how macros can save you from doing tedious tasks and how to manipulate fields to take the drudgery out of word processing.

Choosing Default Settings for the Normal Template

Most documents are created with the Normal template. When you click the New button, press CTRL-N, or choose File | New and select the Blank Document icon to create a new document, your document arrives with all the default settings in the Normal template. Because so much work is done in documents created with the Normal template, Word offers Default buttons in many dialog boxes for choosing your own Normal template default settings. To change the default font in the Normal template, for example, choose a font in the Font dialog box and then click the Default button.

Table 23-1 lists the location of all the dialog boxes with Default buttons. The table explains how to reach each dialog box and the default settings you can make in the Normal template. If you know your way around Word, by all means make your favorite settings a part of the Normal template. That way, you can get off to a good start when you click the New button or press CTRL-N to create a new document.

Dialog Box	How To Open It	Default Settings
Page Setup	File	Page Setup	Margin size, paper size and orientation, paper tray for printing
Date and Time	Insert	Date and Time	Formats for displaying the date or date and time
Font	Format	Font	Font, font style, font size, kerning
Language	Tools	Language	Set Language	Language in use

Table 23-1.   *Dialog Boxes Where You Can Choose Default Settings for the Normal Template*

Tip

On the Save tab of the Options dialog box is a check box called Prompt To Save Normal Template. If that check box is selected, a dialog box appears when you close Word after making changes to the Normal template. In the dialog box, click Yes to keep the changes you made to the template or click No to abandon them. Activate the Prompt To Save Normal Template check box if you want the chance to reconsider changes you make to the Normal template before you close Word. To reach the Save tab of the Options dialog box, choose Tools | Options and click the Save tab.

Customizing the Menus, Toolbars, and Keyboard Shortcuts

You are hereby invited to play cosmetic surgeon with Word 2000. The program makes rearranging the menus, toolbars, and keyboard shortcuts fairly simple. And if you go overboard and make a hash of your menus, toolbars, or keyboard shortcuts, you can get the originals back. These pages explain how to change the face of Word. Here, you'll learn how to set up your own menus, change the Word menus, invent your own toolbars, and alter the Word toolbars. You will also find instructions here for creating your own keyboard shortcuts.

Caution

If you share your computer with others, be sure to get their permission before you start tinkering with toolbars and menus. You are liable to change a toolbar or menu that someone else relies on and thereby lose a friend for life.

Templates and Customizations

Where changes to menus, toolbars, and keyboard shortcuts appear depends on which template you are working in when you start customizing. If you are working on a document based on the Normal template, your customizations will appear wherever you go in Word. But if you are working in a document based on a template other than the Normal template, your customizations show up only when you work in documents based on the template you were working in when you customized menus, toolbars, and keyboard shortcuts.

To make universal changes to Word's menus, toolbars, and keyboard shortcuts, start by clicking the New button or pressing CTRL-N in order to work on a Normal template document. Otherwise, if the customizations you propose to make will be useful only in documents based on a particular template, open a document in the template and start customizing.

By the way, all is not lost if you alter a toolbar in one template but wish you had altered it in another as well, because you can use the Organizer to copy toolbars from template to template. See "Assembling Styles from Different Templates" in Chapter 12.

Setting Up Your Own Menus

Set up your own menus to remove unneeded commands from menus, place the commands you use most often on a single menu, or gather commands for a specific task in one place. Commands aren't the only items you can put on a menu, by the way. You can also put macros, fonts, AutoText entries, styles, and hyperlinks on a menu. What's more, you can customize shortcut menus as well as the menus on the menu bar. A shortcut menu is one you see when you right-click text or part of the screen.

Whatever you want to do to your menus, start by choosing Tools | Customize or right-clicking a toolbar and choosing Customize. You'll see the Customize dialog box shown in Figure 23-1. This dialog box is the starting point for removing commands from menus, adding commands to menus, creating new menus, rearranging menus, redecorating menus, and restoring a menu to its original state. The Customize dialog box is a curious thing. While it is open, you can drag menus and menu commands to new places, drag menu commands off menus, and do a lot of other things to menus. As soon as you close the dialog box, menus work in the usual way.

All Word commands are listed on the Commands tab of the Customize dialog box. The details of customizing menus are described in the pages that follow. Here are

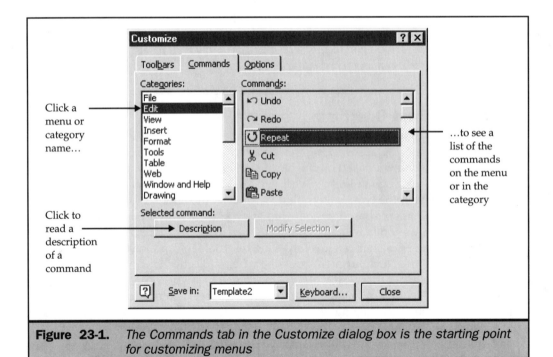

Figure 23-1.   *The Commands tab in the Customize dialog box is the starting point for customizing menus*

instructions for finding your way around the Commands tab on the Customize
dialog box:

■ **Locating Menu Commands** Before you can add a command to a menu, you
have to find and select it in the Commands dialog box. To do so, click a name in
the Categories list, read the list of commands in the Commands box, and select
a command name. The first eight names in the Categories list happen to be the
names of menus on the menu bar. Click a menu name in the Categories box and
you'll see the names of commands on the menu whose name you clicked. In
Figure 23-1, for example, the Edit category has been clicked, so you can see the
commands on the Edit menu. You can click the All Commands category to see
an alphabetical list of all the commands in Word.

■ **Learning What a Command Is** A command name often doesn't reveal what a
command does. When that is the case, click the command and then click the
Description button to read an explanation of the command.

■ **Adding Macros, Fonts, AutoText Entries, and Styles to Menus** Near the
bottom of the Categories list are categories named Macros, Fonts, AutoText,
and Styles. Click these categories when you want to add a macro, font,
AutoText entry, or style to a menu.

■ **Rearranging the Menus** Also near the bottom of the Categories list is a
category called Built-In Menus. Click it when you want to add a menu—File,
Edit, View, and so on—to a toolbar or create a second version of a menu. Yes,
you can place menus on toolbars.

■ **Creating a New Menu** At the bottom of the Categories list is a category called
New Menu. Click it when you want to create a new menu of your own.

Spend any time on the Commands tab in the Customize dialog box and you will
soon realize that Word offers many commands. Commands on all menus and submenus
are found in the Customize dialog box. Word offers about 500 commands in all. I suggest
scrolling through the list and looking at a few of them. Some of these commands are
very nice indeed and deserve to be placed on menus.

Customizing the Shortcut Menus

The Customize dialog box is also the starting point for customizing a shortcut menu. However, instead of going to the Commands tab, click the Toolbars tab, and then select Shortcut Menus on the Toolbars list. The Shortcut Menus toolbar appears onscreen. Click the Text, Table, or Draw button to open a drop-down list of shortcut menus. Select the shortcut menu you want to customize. After the shortcut menu is displayed onscreen, you can change or rearrange its menu commands.

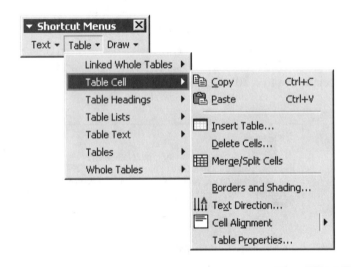

Removing Commands from a Menu

As far as I know, you may use Word strictly to write letters to friends, in which case you don't need nine-tenths of the commands on the Word menus. For you, Word offers two techniques for removing commands from menus and shortcut menus:

- Press ALT-CTRL-HYPHEN and select the menu command you want to remove. As soon as you choose this command, the pointer changes into an ominous-looking black bar. With the black bar showing, click the command you want to remove as though you were selecting it. Press ESC if you pressed ALT-CTRL-HYPHEN accidentally and you want the ominous pointer to go away.

- Choose Tools | Customize to open the Customize dialog box (see Figure 23-1). While the dialog box is open, move the pointer out of the dialog box, open the menu with the command you want to remove, and click the command. Then either right-click the command and choose Delete from the shortcut menu or click the Modify Selection button in the Customize dialog box and choose

Delete from the pop-up menu. You can also simply drag the menu command off the menu.

 See "Restoring a Menu (or the Menu Bar) to Its Original State" later in this chapter, if you regret removing a command from a menu.

Adding Commands, Styles, Macros, Fonts, and AutoText Entries to Menus

Follow these steps to place a command, style, macro, font, or AutoText entry on a menu:

1. Choose Tools | Customize to open the Customize dialog box.

2. On the Commands tab, locate the command you want to place on a menu, as shown in Figure 23-2. To do so, choose a category in the Categories list and then click the command in the Commands list. Click Macros, Fonts, AutoText, or

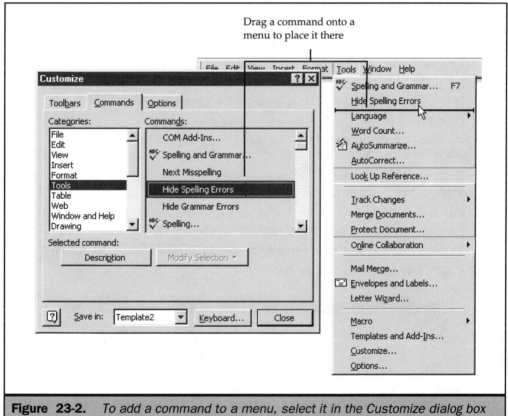

Figure 23-2. *To add a command to a menu, select it in the Customize dialog box and drag it onto a menu*

Styles at the bottom of the Categories list if you want to add one of those items to a menu.

3. In the Commands list, click the command, macro, or whatnot that you want to add to a menu, drag it out of the Customize dialog box, drag it over the name of the menu or shortcut menu you want to place it on, and drag the command to the place on the menu where you want the command to go.

As shown in Figure 23-2, a black line shows where the command will appear on the menu when you release the mouse button. The previous section in this chapter explains how to remove a command from a menu, in case you regret putting it there.

Later in this chapter, "Making Menus and Toolbars Easier to Read and Understand" explains how to handle hot keys in menu commands and how to decorate commands with images.

Creating Your Own Menu

Follow these steps to create your own menu and place it on the menu bar or a toolbar:

1. If you are placing the menu on a toolbar, display the toolbar.

2. Choose Tools | Customize to open the Customize dialog box (see Figure 23-2).

3. On the Commands tab, scroll to the bottom of the Categories list and click New Menu. The name New Menu appears in the Commands list.

4. Click New Menu in the Commands list and drag if off the Customize dialog box and onto the menu bar or toolbar where you want your new menu to be. A thick black line shows where the menu will land when you release the mouse button.

5. Release the mouse button. The name "New Menu" appears on the menu bar or toolbar. Not much of a menu name, is it?

6. Either right-click your new menu or click the Modify Selection button in the Customize dialog box. A menu appears for managing menus.

7. In the Name text box, type a name for your menu, and then press ENTER.

8. Click Close in the Customize dialog box.

The previous section in this chapter explains how to put items on a menu. To delete a menu you created, choose Tools | Customize to open the Customize dialog box, and then either right-click the menu and choose Delete or click the Modify Selection button and choose Delete.

Restoring a Menu (or the Menu Bar) to Its Original State

All right, you went to a bunch of trouble to change the menus around, and now you regret it. Or, worse yet, you accidentally dragged one of the names—File, Edit, View, and so on—from the menu bar. Scary when that happens, isn't it? Choose Tools | Customize to open the Customize dialog box, click the Commands tab (see Figure 23-2), and follow these instructions to restore a menu or the menu bar to its original state:

- **Restoring a Word Menu to Its Original State**   Click the menu in question, click the Modify Selection button in the Customize toolbar, and choose Reset from the pop-up menu.

- **Putting a Word Menu Back on the Menu Bar**   Scroll in the Categories list and click the next-to-last item, Built-In Menus. The Commands list shows Word menu names on the menu bar in their rightful order. Click the menu that needs restoring, drag it out of the Customize dialog box, and place it on the menu bar.

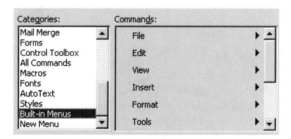

To get back the original shortcut menus, choose Tools | Customize and click the Toolbars tab in the Customize dialog box. In the Toolbars list, check the Shortcut Menus check box. Then click the Reset button.

Creating Your Own Toolbars and Toolbar Buttons

The starting point for constructing your own toolbars or making Word's toolbars work more efficiently is the Customize dialog box shown in Figure 23-3. As long as the Customize dialog box is open, you can drag buttons from toolbar to toolbar, put new buttons on toolbars, or create new toolbars. To get to the Customize dialog box, choose Tools | Customize or right-click a toolbar and choose Customize. The Toolbars tab lists each toolbar. If you created toolbars of your own, their names appear at the bottom of

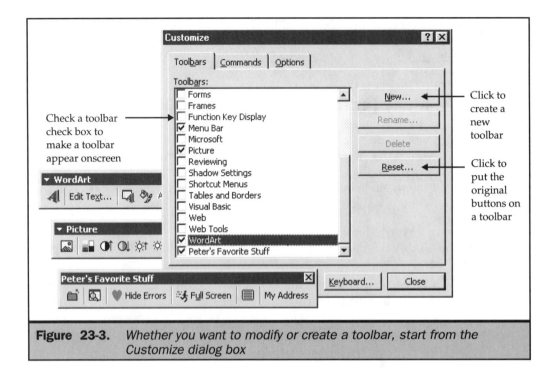

Figure 23-3. *Whether you want to modify or create a toolbar, start from the Customize dialog box*

the list. By clicking a toolbar check box, you can make a toolbar appear onscreen without leaving the Customize dialog box.

Read on to find out the fast way to remove or add toolbar buttons and the slow but thorough way to add or remove toolbar buttons. You will also find out how to create your own toolbars, restore a Word toolbar to its original condition, and create a hyperlink button for a toolbar.

 "Getting to Know the Toolbars" in Chapter 1 explains how to display toolbars and arrange them onscreen.

The Fast Way to Add and Remove Toolbar Buttons

The More Buttons button, a minuscule arrow, appears on toolbars when they are docked along the top or bottom of the window. (To dock a toolbar, double-click its title bar.) The More Buttons button is easy to miss, but look closely and you will see it on the right side of toolbars, as shown in Figure 23-4.

When you click the More Buttons button, you'll see the Add or Remove Buttons button (refer to Figure 23-4). Click it and you'll see a drop-down menu that lists the buttons on the toolbar. By checking or unchecking buttons on the drop-down menu,

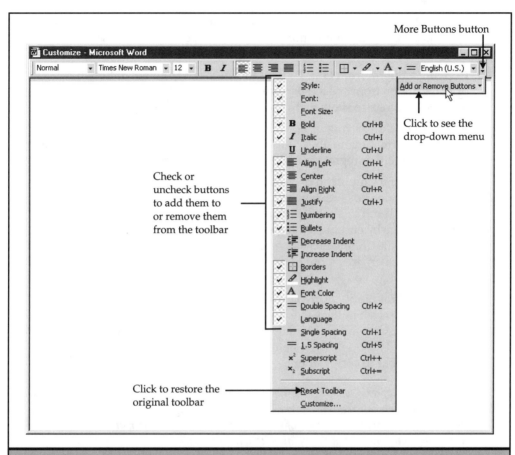

Figure 23-4. *Click the More Buttons button (the tiny arrow) to add or remove
toolbar buttons without having to go to the Customize dialog box*

you can add buttons to or remove buttons from the toolbar. Click the Reset Toolbar
button if you go overboard and remove too many buttons

The Thorough Way to Add and Remove Toolbar Buttons

Clicking the More Buttons button is the fast way to add buttons to or remove buttons
from a toolbar. But suppose you want to gather toolbar buttons from far and wide for a
toolbar. In that case, choose Tools | Customize, click the Toolbars tab in the Customize
dialog box (see Figure 23-3), check the names of the toolbars to display the ones you
want to work with, and follow these instructions:

■ **Moving a Button from One Toolbar to Another**   Drag the button between
    toolbars. That's right—simply click the button you want to move and drag it to the

other toolbar. A black line shows where the button will appear when you release the mouse button. Be careful not to release the mouse button too soon, or you'll remove the button from the toolbar instead of moving it.

- **Copying a Button from One Toolbar to Another**   Hold down the CTRL key and drag the button from one toolbar to another. As you drag, a cross appears below the mouse pointer to show that you are copying the toolbar button, not moving it.

- **Removing a Button from a Toolbar**   Right-click the button and choose Delete from the shortcut menu. (See "Restoring a Toolbar to Its Original State," later in this chapter, if you regret removing the toolbar button.)

- **Putting a Menu Command on a Toolbar**   Click the Commands tab in the Customize dialog box (see Figure 23-2). As "Setting Up Your Own Menus" explained earlier in this chapter, you can find any Word command on the Commands tab by clicking a category in the Categories list and then clicking a command in the Commands list. After you have found the command you want to place on a toolbar, drag it out of the Customize dialog box and onto the toolbar. Drag it as though you were moving a button from one toolbar to another.

- **Putting Macros, Fonts, AutoText Entries, and Styles on a Toolbar**   Click the Commands tab in the Customize dialog box (see Figure 23-2), scroll to the bottom of the Categories list, and click Macros, Fonts, AutoText, or Styles. In the Commands list, select the item you want to place on a toolbar and drag it onto the toolbar to copy it there.

Note   *Later in this chapter, "Making Menus and Toolbars Easier to Read and Understand" explains how you can rename toolbar buttons, place images on toolbar buttons, and place lines on toolbars to divide one set of buttons from another. Earlier in this chapter, "Creating Your Own Menu" explains how to put a menu on a toolbar.*

Creating Your Own Toolbar

Follow these steps to create a toolbar of your own and fill it with your favorite buttons and commands:

1. Choose Tools | Customize or right-click a toolbar and choose Customize.

2. Click the Toolbars tab in the Customize dialog box.

3. Click the New button. You will see the New Toolbar dialog box.

4. Enter a descriptive name for your toolbar. The name will appear in the title bar.

5. In the Make Toolbar Available To drop-down menu, choose which template to keep your toolbar in. As the start of this chapter explained, toolbars that you create for the Normal template are available no matter where you go in Word. Choose a template other than Normal and your toolbar will be available only in the template you chose.

6. Click OK. A puny toolbar appears onscreen.

7. Move or copy toolbar buttons onto your new toolbar, or place commands or menus on the toolbar. The previous section in this chapter explains how to load buttons on a toolbar. Simply drag the buttons or commands onto your new toolbar and watch it grow longer.

To delete a toolbar you created, choose Tools | Customize, click the toolbar's name on the Toolbars tab in the Customize dialog box (see Figure 23-3), and click the Delete button. Click the Rename button in the Customize dialog box to give a toolbar a new name. You can't delete or change the name of a Word toolbar. Only toolbars you invented yourself can be deleted or renamed.

Creating a Hyperlink Toolbar Button

Here's a neat little trick: You can put a hyperlink button on a toolbar and by so doing be able to click the button and go straight to another document or a site on the Internet. A hyperlink is an electronic shortcut between two documents or two Web sites. Follow these steps to put a hyperlink button on a toolbar:

1. Choose Tools | Customize to display the Customize dialog box (see Figure 23-3) and put a button on the toolbar. Which button you put on doesn't matter. After you turn the button into a hyperlink, your button will change functionality. In fact, you might name the button after the document or Web site which the link will go to.

2. Right-click your new button and choose Assign Hyperlink | Open. You will see the Assign Hyperlink: Open dialog box.

3. Either enter the address of the Web page or document you want to link to or choose it in the dialog box. "Creating a Hyperlink to a Page on the Internet" in Chapter 16 explains how to use this dialog box to create a hyperlink to Web site. "Including Hyperlinks in Documents" in Chapter 24 explains how to link to another Word document.

To remove the hyperlink from a button, right-click it while the Customize dialog box is open and choose Edit Hyperlink | Remove Link. Right-click and choose Edit Hyperlink | Open to establish a new link for the button.

Restoring a Toolbar to Its Original State

Don't despair if you make hash of a toolbar, because you can make the original reappear. Use either of these techniques to restore a toolbar to its original state:

- Click the More Buttons button (the tiny arrow on the right side of the toolbar), click Add or Remove Buttons, and choose Reset Toolbar from the drop-down menu (see Figure 23-4).

- Choose Tools | Customize, click the Toolbars tab in the Customize dialog box (see Figure 23-3), click the name of the toolbar that needs restoring, and click the Reset button.

Making Menus and Toolbars Easier to Read and Understand

Take a close look at the Word menus and toolbars and you will see that the Microsoft Corporation has gone to great lengths to make the menus and toolbars in Word easy to read and understand. Each button is dressed in a distinctive image that hints at what it is used for. Menu names are descriptive. Hot keys, the underlined letters in menu and command names, were chosen carefully. On menus, thin lines called separators divide similar commands into groups. Separators also appear on toolbars, where they distinguish one set of buttons from another.

These pages explain how you can make the menus and toolbars you create easier to read and understand. Read on to learn how to rearrange commands on menus and buttons on toolbars, change the names of buttons and menus, decorate buttons with images, and draw separator lines on menus and toolbars.

Rearranging Buttons and Commands on Toolbars and Menus

As long as the Customize dialog box is open, you can drag items on menus and buttons on toolbars wherever you want. Drag a menu item up or down the list of commands. Drag a toolbar button from side to side on the toolbar. Choose Tools | Customize to open the Customize dialog box.

As you drag a button or command name, a gray box appears below the pointer, and a black line shows where the menu command or toolbar button will land when you release the mouse button. Release it when the command name or button is in the right spot.

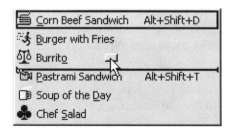

Changing the Names of Buttons and Menus

To change the name of a menu or button, choose Tools | Customize or right-click a toolbar and choose Customize to open the Customize dialog box. Then click the menu or button that needs a new name and either click the Modify Selection button on the Commands tab in the Customize dialog box or right-click. You'll see a menu of commands for handling names and images on buttons and toolbars. Enter a new name in the Name text box.

As you know, each menu name and command name includes a hot key, an underlined letter that you can press in combination with the ALT key to give a command or open a menu. To tell Word which letter is the hot key, place an ampersand (&) before the hot key letter. In the previous illustration, for example, the "L" in "Luncheon" is the hot key. Here, the "C," "B," and "o" in "Corned Beef Sandwich," "Burger with Fries," and "Burrito" are the hot keys.

Be sure to choose a shortcut key that isn't taken already by another command name. Choose a conspicuous letter. Usually, that means the first letter, but if the first letter is taken, choose a long vowel or notable consonant.

Choosing or Creating Images for Toolbar Buttons and Menu Commands

Images appear on toolbar buttons when you borrow or take buttons from other toolbars. Images also appear when you put certain commands on toolbars. Not all commands, however, are attached to an image. Sometimes when you put a command from the Commands tab of the Customize dialog box on a toolbar, only a name appears on the toolbar. However, you can decorate a toolbar button (or command name on a menu as well) with an image by following these instructions.

1. Choose Tools | Customize to open the Customize dialog box.
2. Display the toolbar or menu whose button or command needs a change of image.

3. Right-click the button or command. By choosing options on the shortcut menu, you can do the following to your button or menu command:

■ **Choose an Image from the Change Button Image Drop-Down Menu**   Click the Change Button Image option and choose an image from the drop-down menu. Please don't choose the smiley face, however. Seeing that particular cliché on a toolbar button is depressing.

■ **Draw an Image**   If you are artistically inclined and accustomed to working in bitmaps, click the Edit Image option. You'll see the Button Editor dialog box shown in Figure 23-5. By choosing colors and clicking on the bitmap, you can construct an image. Click a Move button to nudge your image leftward, rightward, upward, or downward. Click Erase and click on the bitmap where you want gray to appear on the button.

■ **Borrow a Button Image from Elsewhere**   To obtain an image from another button, right-click the other button and choose Copy Button Image from the shortcut menu. Then right-click the toolbar button or menu command that needs an image and choose Paste Button Image.

You can always right-click a button and choose Reset Button image to see the original image—the one that appeared on the toolbar button or menu command before you started tinkering.

Also on the shortcut menu are four obscure options for displaying text, the image, or the text and the image on toolbar buttons and menus:

■ **Displaying Only the Image**   Check the Default Style option.

■ **Displaying Only the Text**   Check the Text Only (Always) option.

■ **Displaying Only the Text (Not the Image As Well) on Menus**   Check the Text Only (In Menus) option.

■ **Displaying Both the Image and the Text**   Check the Image and Text option.

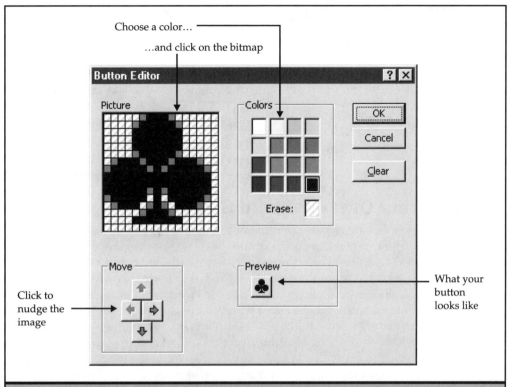

Figure 23-5. *Bit by bit, you can construct an image for a toolbar button or menu command in the Button Editor dialog box*

Drawing Separators for Menu Items and Toolbar Buttons

A *separator* is a faint line on a toolbar or menu that distinguishes one set of buttons or menu commands from the next. Draw a separator line to make it clear to users where one set of buttons or commands ends and another begins. Open the Customize dialog box (choose Tools | Customize) and follow these instructions to put a separator on a toolbar or menu:

- **Placing a Separator on a Toolbar** Click the toolbar button that is to be to the right of the separator and drag the button ever so slightly to the right. Do this correctly and the separator line appears. To remove a separator, click the button to its right and drag the button ever so slightly to the left.

- **Placing a Separator on a Menu** Click to open the menu, right-click the menu option that is to appear below the separator, and check Begin A Group on the drop-down menu. To remove a separator, right-click the menu option below the separator and uncheck the Begin A Group option on the drop-down menu.

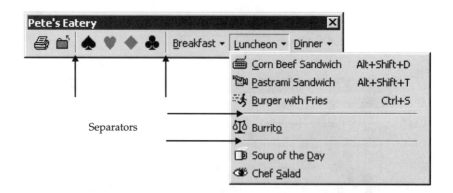

Separators

Designating Your Own Keyboard Shortcuts

Keyboard shortcuts, as long as you can remember them, are great. Instead of opening a menu and choosing a command, you can simply press two or three keys at the same time and be done with it. Word offers numerous keyboard shortcuts for giving commands, but if your favorite command doesn't have a shortcut key, you can make one. You can make your own keyboard shortcuts for Word commands, macros, styles, fonts, AutoText entries, and symbols. Don't worry about causing chaos with keyboard shortcuts; you can always restore the original shortcuts by clicking the Reset All button in the Customize Keyboard dialog box (more on that subject shortly).

Note *As "Templates and Customizations" explained earlier in this chapter, keyboard customizations made to the Normal template apply in every document, no matter which template it was made with. Customizations made to a particular template, however, apply only to documents made with the template.*

Follow these steps to create a keyboard shortcut for a command, style, macro, or whatnot that you are tired of having to deal with by using conventional commands:

1. Choose Tools | Customize or right-click a toolbar and choose Customize.

2. Click the Commands tab in the Customize dialog box.

3. Click the Keyboard button to open the Customize Keyboard dialog box shown in Figure 23-6. The Categories box lists menu names and, at the bottom, the Macros, Font, AutoText, Style, and Common Symbols category.

4. Click a category in the Categories box, and then click the item in the Commands box that needs a keyboard shortcut. Yes, the commands in the Commands box are hard to understand, but if you look closely you will see that the first word in each command is a menu name and the second word happens to be a command found on the menu. If a keyboard shortcut has already been assigned to a command, the shortcut is listed in the Current Keys box.

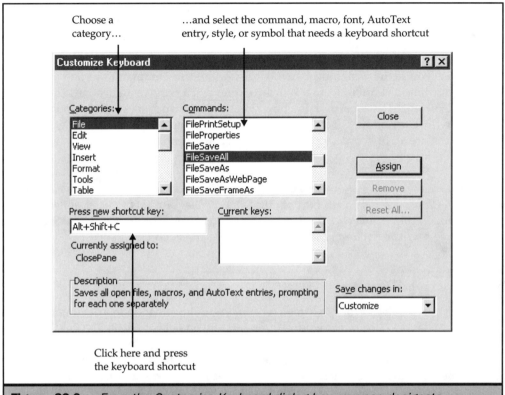

Figure 23-6. *From the Customize Keyboard dialog box, you can designate keyboard shortcuts for commands, macros, fonts, AutoText entries, styles, and symbols*

5. Click in the Press New Shortcut Key box and press the keyboard shortcut you want for the command. Press the actual keys. For example, if the shortcut you want is CTRL-F12, press the CTRL key and the F12 key—don't type out **C-t-r-l-f-1-2**.

The words "Currently Assigned To" and a command name appear if the keys you pressed have been assigned to another command. However, you can override the other keyboard assignment by entering a keyboard assignment of your own.

6. Click the Assign button.

7. Click Close in the Customize Keyboard dialog box and click Close again in the Customize dialog box.

Suppose you regret assigning a keyboard shortcut to a command or you want to remove a keyboard shortcut from a Word command. To remove a keyboard shortcut, open the Customize Keyboard dialog box, find the command, select the keyboard shortcut in the Current Keys box, and click the Remove button. Click the Reset All button to restore all of Word's keyboard shortcuts and render the keyboard shortcuts you devised invalid.

The easiest way to assign a keyboard shortcut to a symbol is to start in the Symbol dialog box. Choose Insert | Symbol to open the Symbol dialog box, find the symbol that needs a shortcut, click it, and click the Shortcut Key button. You'll see the Customize Shortcut dialog box, where you can enter a shortcut key for the symbol.

All About Fields

A *field* is a code that tells Word to enter a certain type of information in a document. Instead of updating a document yourself, you can rely on fields to do it. The field code gets the information from Word or from the computer's clock and plugs the information directly into the document. Most people are intimidated by fields without realizing that they use fields all the time. When you click the Insert Page Number button on the Header and Footer toolbar, for example, you insert a PAGE field in your document. The PAGE

Printing a List of Word's Keyboard Shortcuts

Before you assign new keyboard shortcuts, perhaps you would like to see a list of all the keyboard shortcuts. That way, you can find an obscure keyboard shortcut that isn't used often and put it to good use.

To see and print a list of commands and their keyboard shortcuts, choose Tools | Macro | Macros (or press ALT-F8) to open the Macros dialog box. In the Macros In menu, choose Word Commands. You will see a list of Word's macros. Either type **ListCommands** in the Macro Name box or scroll down the list of macro names and click ListCommands. Click the Run button. Click OK in the List Commands dialog box to choose the Current Menu and Keyboard Settings. A Word document with command names, their keyboard assignments, and their menu locations appears on screen. Click the Print button to print the document.

field asks Word for the number of each page and inserts that number in the appropriate place. When you choose Insert | Date and Time, choose a date, and tell Word to revise the date you entered automatically, you insert a TIME field in your document. The TIME field asks the clock on your computer for the date and time and enters that information in your document.

Figure 23-7 shows the Field dialog box. Choose Insert | Field to open the dialog box, click a few categories, note the field names, and you'll soon realize that Word enters many of these fields on its own behind the scenes when you choose certain commands. However, you can enter fields on your own from the Field dialog box, as the following pages show.

These pages explain what the different fields are. You will also learn how to update fields to make them accurately show the information they are meant to show and how to display fields or field codes in documents. These pages explain how to lock fields so the field data does not change and unlink fields to turn field data into normal data. You will also learn how to modify fields with switches. Meanwhile, Table 23-2 describes the field categories in the Field dialog box and the various kinds of fields you can place in documents.

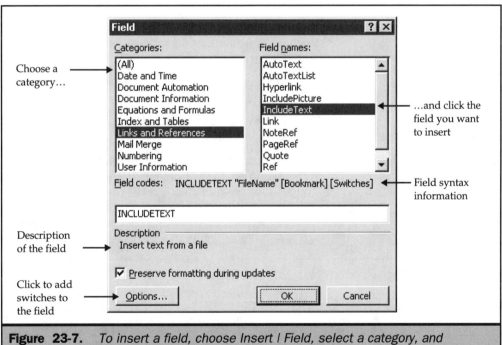

Figure 23-7. *To insert a field, choose Insert | Field, select a category, and double-click a field name*

Category	Types of Fields
Date and Time	Fields for entering the date and time, as well as the dates and times your document was created, last printed, last saved, and worked on.
Document Automation	Advanced fields for use with macros for comparing values, evaluating arguments, moving the insertion point, and running macros.
Document Information	Fields for reporting statistics about the document, including its size and number of words, as well as information you enter in the Properties dialog box (choose File | Properties).
Equations and Formulas	Fields for calculating formulas and inserting special characters.
Index and Tables	Fields for an inserting index, table of contents, table of figures, or table of authorities entries, as discussed in Chapter 18.
Links and References	Fields for getting information from elsewhere in a document, from other documents, and from AutoText entries.
Mail Merge	Fields for generating mailing labels and form letters, as discussed in Chapter 22.
Numbering	Fields for numbering items, such as pages and items in lists and outlines.
User Information	Fields for inserting data from the User Information tab in the Options dialog box (choose Tools | Options and click the User Information tab).

Table 23-2.   *Field Categories*

Inserting a Field in a Document

To insert a field in a document, choose Insert | Field, choose a category in the Field dialog box (see Figure 23-7), select a field, and click OK. True, fields have cryptic names, but you can click the question mark in the dialog box and then click a field name to find out precisely what a field does, as the sidebar explains. A description of the field you choose also appears in the dialog box.

Finding Out Precisely What a Field Does

As you know if you read Chapter 4, you can click the question mark button in the upper-right corner of a dialog box and then click a dialog box option to find out what the option does. However, the question mark button in the Field dialog box does more than that when you click a field name. Instead of the short explanation you usually get, the Help program window opens with a detailed explanation of the field whose name you clicked. Read the description to find out what the field does and which switches you can use to modify the field.

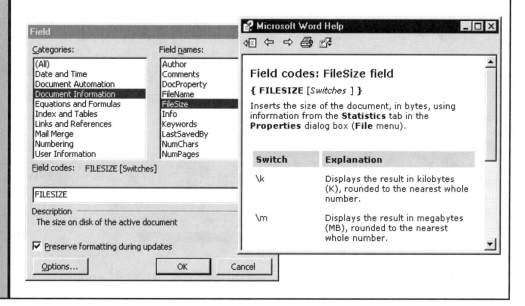

Caution *Make sure a check mark appears in the Preserve Formatting During Updates check box if you want to be able to format the field code results in your document. Field code results can be formatted like normal text. You can boldface them or change their fonts, for example, as long as you didn't remove the check mark from the Preserve Formatting During Updates check box. Word puts the MERGEFORMAT switch in fields whose formatting is preserved.*

If you are feeling adventurous or you are a fan of fields, you can attach switches to your fields. A *switch* is an instruction that modifies, formats, or prevents changes to the results of a field code. Each field offers its own set of switches. Think of switches as enhancements to field codes that make them work more efficiently. You can tell whether switches are available to a field by glancing at the syntax line directly below the Categories box in the Field dialog box (see Figure 23-7).

To attach switches to a field, choose the field in the Field dialog box and then click the Options button. You'll see the Field Options dialog box shown in Figure 23-8. Click a switch and then click the Add to Field button to include a switch in the field code. The Field Options dialog box describes which switches are available for the field and what the switches do. Again, you can click the question mark button and click a field in the Field dialog box to get a detailed description of the switches you can use with a field. Generally, switches fall into two categories:

- **General Switches**   Change the look of field results or lock field results to keep them from changing.

- **Field-Specific Switches**   Do any number of things, depending on the field you are working with. Click a switch and read its description in the Field Options dialog box.

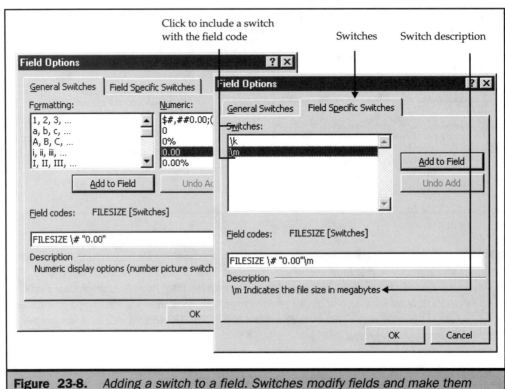

Figure 23-8.   *Adding a switch to a field. Switches modify fields and make them work more efficiently*

Ways of Displaying Fields and Field Results

Unless you change the default setting, field results and not field codes appear in the text. What's more, fields are shaded so that you can tell when you are dealing with a field (the shading is strictly to help you recognize fields and it isn't printed). However, you can decide for yourself how to display fields by choosing Tools | Options and clicking the View tab in the Options dialog box, as shown in Figure 23-9. The View tab offers these ways of displaying fields:

- **Showing the Fields, Not the Field Results**   Click the Field Codes check box.

- **Showing the Field Results, Not the Fields**   Open the Field Shading drop-down list and choose Never.

- **Shading the Field Results Onscreen**   Choose Always from the Field Shading drop-down list.

- **Shading the Field Results When Fields Are Selected**   Choose When Selected from the Field Shading drop-down list.

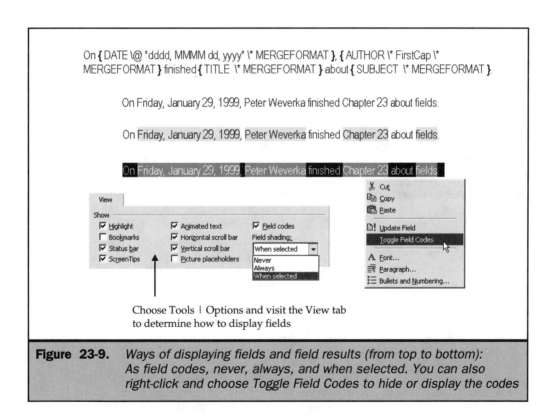

Choose Tools | Options and visit the View tab
to determine how to display fields

Figure 23-9.   *Ways of displaying fields and field results (from top to bottom): As field codes, never, always, and when selected. You can also right-click and choose Toggle Field Codes to hide or display the codes*

Another way to handle fields is to right-click a field whose code or results you want to see and choose Toggle Field Codes on the shortcut menu.

Managing and Caring for Fields

Fields, like furry creatures, need managing and caring for. These pages explain how to update the fields in a document, lock fields so that they aren't updated, and unlink fields so that they display raw data, not field results. You will also find instructions here for going from field to field.

Updating the Fields

A field is current as of the moment you enter it. However, if a field has to do with time or a date or a document statistic, it soon becomes outdated. Word offers these techniques for updating fields:

- **Updating Fields One at a Time**   Right-click the field and choose Update Field from the shortcut menu. You can also click a field and press F9 to update it.

- **Updating All the Fields**   Press CTRL-A or choose Edit | Select All to select the entire document, and then press F9 or right-click and choose Update Field to update all the fields in a document.

- **Updating the Fields Before You Print**   Choose Tools | Options, click the Print tab in the Options dialog box, and check the Update Fields check box. (Check the Field Codes check box if you want to print the codes instead of the field code results.)

Locking, Unlocking, and Unlinking Fields

Locking a field means to prevent a field from being updated and make it stay the same no matter what. A locked field retains its connection to the document or clock. You can unlock it and in so doing update the field. *Unlinking* a field means to sever the connection between the field and the document or clock. An unlinked field ceases to be a field. You can't update it anymore.

Follow these instructions to lock, unlock, and unlink a field:

- **Locking a Field**   Click or select the field and press CTRL-F11. Locked fields look the same as normal, unlocked fields. You can tell when a field is locked because Word won't let you update it. Right-click on a locked field and the Update Field option on the shortcut menu will be grayed out.

- **Unlocking a Field**   Click or select the field and press CTRL-SHIFT-F11. Unlocking a field does not update it. Press F9 or right-click and choose Update Field to update the field you unlocked.

- **Unlinking a Field**   Click or select the field and press CTRL-SHIFT-F9. Unlink a field when you want to copy or move it to another document. Unless you unlink first, the field codes will have nothing to refer to in the other document and the data will not transfer successfully. Fields that have been unlinked lose their status as fields. They become normal text and are not shaded. If the field you unlinked happened to be a hypertext field, the blue characters and underlines remain. Use the Font Color button and Underline button on the Formatting toolbar to remove the blue text and underlines.

Unlinking is especially useful with tables of contents. After you generate a table of contents, you can unlink it and move or copy the table of contents to another document.

Traveling from Field to Field

When you want to find a particular field in a document, take advantage of these techniques:

- Press F11 to go forward from field to field or SHIFT-F11 to go backward.

- Click the Select Browse Object button and choose Browse By Field. See "Using the Select Browse Object Button to Get Around" in Chapter 2 for details.

- Choose Edit | Go To, choose Field from the Go To What list in the Find and Replace dialog box, choose a field name from the Enter Field Name drop-down list, and click Next or Previous. "Going from Place to Place with the Go To Command" in Chapter 2 explains the command in detail.

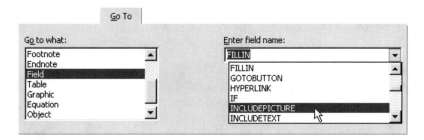

Working with Macros

A *macro* is a sequence of computer instructions recorded and saved under a name. When the macro is activated, Word carries out the instructions in the macro. Macros help automate repetitive and complex tasks. Instead of having to enter the commands yourself, the macro does it for you. And the macro does it far faster than you could do it on your own. These pages explain how macros work and how to record a macro. You will also learn how to run and edit macros.

How Macros Work

Any task that you have to do repeatedly, even a simple task like boldfacing or indenting text, is a candidate for a macro. Macros can be as complex or a simple as you want them to be. You can devise a macro that formats paragraphs or a macro that gathers information from other documents, formats the information in a table, and tabulates the data in various columns. Recording the second macro is considerably more difficult than the first, but the benefits of the second macro are greater as well.

The easiest way to create a macro is to turn on the macro recorder and choose the commands and enter the keystrokes that you have to do repeatedly. Word stores the commands and keystrokes as Visual Basic commands. *Visual Basic* is Word's programming language. All commands, macro and otherwise, are recorded in Visual Basic. In a way, you play the role of programmer when you record a macro. Your keystrokes and command choices are bundled into a new command—a macro command that you can call on the same way you call on the commands on the Word menus.

After you record a macro, you can run it by choosing it in the Macro dialog box. For that matter, you can place your macro on a toolbar or assign it a keyboard shortcut. Word offers special buttons in the Record Macro dialog box for placing macros on toolbars and providing keyboard shortcuts for macros.

If you know your way around the Visual Basic programming language, you can develop macros in the Microsoft Visual Basic Editor without setting foot in Word. This book explains a few procedures in the Visual Basic Editor, but this book is not a developer's guide and it can't cover the Visual Basic Editor in any detail. I only want you to know that the Visual Basic Editor, a complex program, is there in case macros interest you, or you want to develop around Word 2000.

Recording a Macro

Word offers the macro recorder for recording macros. The recorder was modeled after a tape recorder (the cursor even looks like a cassette tape while the macro is being recorded). You turn on the macro recorder, choose commands, and turn off the macro recorder. All commands that you choose while the macro recorder is on are made part of the macro. When you run the macro, Word gives all the commands you gave when you recorded the macro in the first place. Herewith are the ground rules for recording macros and instructions for recording macros.

Ground Rules for Recording Macros

As you record your macro, observe these rules:

- You can use the mouse to select menu commands, but not to select text. If the action you are recording in a macro requires you to select text, select the text by pressing keys, not by dragging the mouse. See "Selecting Blocks of Text" in Chapter 3 to learn all the ways to select text. Remember: You can select text by pressing F8 and then pressing a keyboard shortcut for moving the cursor. For example, press F8 and then END to select text from the position of the cursor to the end of the line.

■ If your macro calls for the cursor to move to a specific place in a document, enter a bookmark in that place so you can move the cursor there. "Bookmarks for Getting Around" in Chapter 2 explains bookmarks.

■ If you intend to choose the Edit | Find or Edit | Replace command in a macro, open the Find dialog box before you start recording the macro and click the More button to display all the find-and-replace options. Make sure All is chosen in the Search drop-down menu as well.

■ When you visit a dialog box, Word records the option or options you choose as well as all the settings in the dialog box. For example, if you visit the Font dialog box and choose 10 points on the Font Size list, Word duly records the 10-point font size in the macro, but it also records the Arial font in the macro if Arial happens to be the font that is chosen in the Font dialog box. The moral: Take account of all the settings in a dialog box when you visit it while recording a macro.

■ In dialog boxes with tabs, you cannot click tabs to switch from tab to tab and choose commands. Instead, click OK to close the dialog box, then reopen it, click a different tab, choose a command on the tab, and close the dialog box again.

■ Toggle commands that you can switch on and off have no place in macros, since Word can't know when the macro starts running, whether the command is on or off. Don't choose View | Ruler or double-click the TRK button on the Status bar, for example, while recording a macro.

■ Like styles and AutoText entries, macros are stored as part of a template. Before you start recording a macro, Word asks if you want to store the macro in the Normal template or in the template you are working in. If you want to save your macro in a particular template, open a document with the template before you record the macro. (You can copy macros from template to template. See "Assembling Styles from Different Templates" in Chapter 12.)

Recording a Macro

Now that you know the ground rules, follow these steps to record a macro:

1. Open a document in a template other than Normal if you want to store the macro in another template.

2. Double-click the REC button on the Status bar or choose Tools | Macro | Record New Macro. You see the Record Macro dialog box shown in Figure 23-10.

3. In the Macro Name text box, enter a name for the Macro. A macro name cannot start with a number or include blank spaces.

4. Describe the macro in the Description box. You can read the description you enter in the Macros dialog box when the time comes to run the macro.

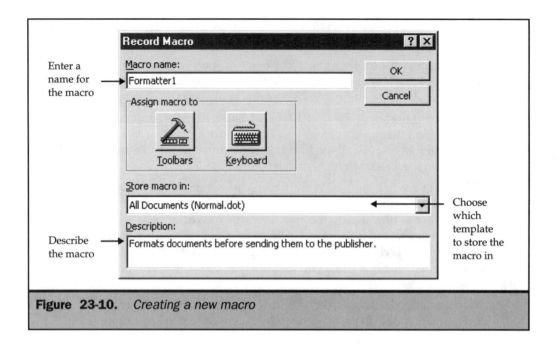

Figure 23-10. *Creating a new macro*

5. In the Store Macro In drop-down list, make sure the name of the template you want to store the macro with is listed.

Note *Click the Toolbars button in the Record Macro dialog box if you want to create a toolbar button for the macro. See "Creating Your Own Toolbars and Toolbar Buttons" earlier in this chapter. Click the Keyboard button to assign a keyboard shortcut to the macro. See "Designating Your Own Keyboard Shortcuts" earlier in this chapter. You can wait until later to put a button for your macro on a toolbar or create a keyboard shortcut for your macro.*

6. Click OK. You'll see the Stop Recording toolbar and a mini-cassette tape appears below the pointer.

7. Very carefully enter the commands and do everything else that your macro requires. Click the Pause button if you need to stop recording for a moment. Click the Resume Recorder button (it is located where the Pause button used to be) when you are ready to start recording the macro again.

8. Click the Stop Recording button on the toolbar or double-click REC on the Status bar when you are done recording the macro.

You can press the BACKSPACE or DELETE key to correct typing mistakes while you record your macro. The deletions merely become part of the macro, but because macros work so much faster than humans, the extra keypresses don't slow the macro by a noticeable amount of time.

Running a Macro

As know if you read the last page or so, you can place a macro on a toolbar button or assign a keyboard shortcut to a macro. However, if your macro has not been turned into a toolbar button or keyboard shortcut, you can still run it by following these simple steps:

1. Choose Tools | Macro | Macros or press ALT-F8. You see the Macros dialog box shown in Figure 23-11.

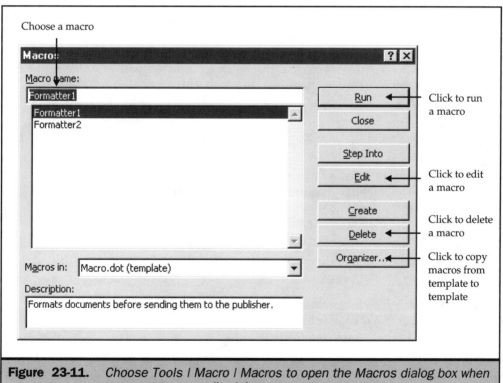

Figure 23-11. *Choose Tools | Macro | Macros to open the Macros dialog box when you want to run, edit, delete, or rename a macro*

2. Click the name of the macro you want to run. If you don't see its name, open the Macros In drop-down list and choose either another template or All Active Templates And Documents, which lists all macros you created for the Normal template as well as all other templates.

3. Click the Run button.

Suppose your macro is a long one and you want to stop it from running. To do so, press CTRL-BREAK (on most keyboards the BREAK key is found along with the PAUSE key to the right of the F, or Function, keys).

Word's Automatic Macros

Word offers five automatic macros that run at certain times when you use Word. Create your own macro and name it with one of the five names on the following list to make Word work your way. As long as you name your macro with one of these names, it runs automatically:

■ **AutoExec**   Runs when you start Word. Use this macro to impose your favorite screen settings on the program or to open the last document you worked on, for example.

■ **AutoNew**   Runs when you create a new document in a particular template. Use this macro to create a header or footer with your name in it, for example. You can create one AutoNew macro for each template.

■ **AutoOpen**   Runs when you open a document based on a particular template. Use this macro, for example, to change printer settings and be able to send a document to a different printer. You can create one AutoOpen macro for each template.

■ **AutoClose**   Runs when you close a document that is based on the template in which you stored the macro. Use this macro, for example, to reverse changes you made to screen settings. You can have one AutoClose macro for each template you work with.

■ **AutoExit**   Runs when you shut down Word. Use this macro to do the chores you need to do when you are finished word processing—back up documents, for example.

Remember which template you store the AutoNew, AutoOpen, and AutoClose macros in. Many a Word user has saved these macros in the wrong template and wondered why the macros didn't work.

Editing a Macro

Editing a macro entails opening the Visual Basic Editor and editing Visual Basic codes, which is not for the faint of heart. If your macro is an uncomplicated one, you are better off re-recording it. As I mentioned a few pages back, this book is not a developer's guide, so it can't go into the details of using the Visual Basic Editor. However, the following pages explain the basics of reading a macro in the Visual Basic Editor, deleting parts of a macro, and copying part of a macro to another macro.

Follow these steps to view a macro in the Visual Basic Editor:

1. Choose Tools | Macro | Macros or press ALT-F8 to open the Macros dialog box (see Figure 23-11).

2. Select the macro that needs editing.

3. Click the Edit button. You'll see the Visual Basic Editor window, shown in Figure 23-12.

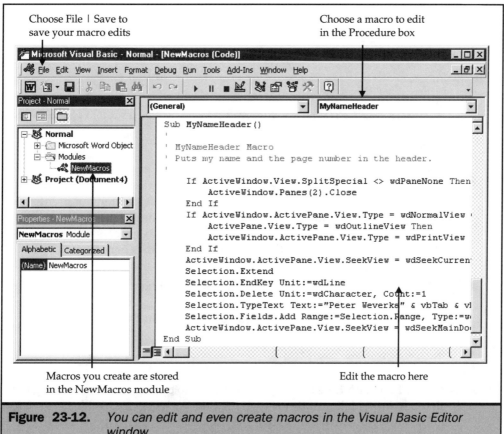

Figure 23-12.   *You can edit and even create macros in the Visual Basic Editor window*

The name of the macro you select appears in the Procedure box. By choosing a different macro name in the Procedure box or scrolling in the Code window, you can see the Visual Basic codes in each macro you've created. Word saves macros in modules. As the upper-left corner of Figure 23-12 shows, macros you create are stored in the NewMacros module.

Those are computer codes in the Code window. Scary, aren't they? You will find one line of code for each command in the macro. Edit computer codes the same way that you edit text in a document. For example, click to the left of a line to select it and then press DELETE to delete a line. Or type in the Code window to add commands or change the text that the macro enters in documents.

Reading a Macro in the Code Window

Before you can do any editing in the Visual Basic Editor, you have to know how to read the codes in the Code window. Observe these attributes of the Code window:

- **Sub and End Sub Lines**   A macro begins with the Sub line and ends with the End Sub line.

```
Sub InsertPageCentral()
'
' InsertPageCentral Macro
' Puts the page number at the bottom of the page, in the center
'
    Selection.Sections(1).Footers(1).PageNumbers.Add PageNumberAlignment:=
        wdAlignPageNumberCenter, FirstPage:=True
End Sub
```

- **Apostrophes (') at the Beginning of Lines**   Word ignores lines that begin with an apostrophe ('). Begin a line with an apostrophe to enter a descriptive comment in the Code window or enter a blank line. The descriptive line you enter in the Record Macro dialog box (see Figure 23-10) appears near the top of the macro after an apostrophe. Enter blank lines and lines of commentary to make macros easier to read and understand.

- **Text Is Enclosed in Double Quotation Marks (")**   Text that is typed in as part of the macro is enclosed in double quotation marks ("). To edit the text in a macro, edit the text between double quotation marks in the Code window.

```
Selection.TypeText Text:="And now for something completely different"
```

- **With and End With Lines**   Codes that pertain to choices made in a dialog box begin with the With line and end with the End With line. In this illustration, for example, the With line tells you that the choices that follow were made in the Font dialog box. The End With line shows where the dialog box was closed.

```
With Selection.Font
        .Name = "Courier New"
        .Size = 12
End With
```

- **All Dialog Box Options Are Recorded**   Even if you select only a single option in a dialog box, the macro records all the options in the dialog box. A visit to the Font dialog box, for example, adds 23 lines to a macro—one line for every option in the dialog box. However, you can edit out lines that your macro does not require. For the previous illustration, for example, I removed 21 of the 23 lines.

Deleting Parts of a Macro

Delete part of a macro when you want to remove a command or command sequence. For that matter, you may delete parts of a macro if they are unnecessary. Deleting unnecessary lines makes a macro easier to read and run faster. As I mentioned in the previous section of this chapter, a visit to a dialog box such as the Font dialog box adds many lines to a macro, most of which are unnecessary. Your macro only requires the lines that pertain to changing settings.

To delete part of a macro, delete the lines as though they were text in a Word document: Click or click and drag in the left margin and then press the DELETE key. The Edit | Undo Delete command (press CTRL-Z) is also available in the Visual Basic Editor in case you regret deleting macro lines.

Copying One Macro into Another

Perhaps a command sequence in one macro can be recycled and used in one or two other macros. To copy part of a macro into another macro:

1. Select the parts that can be copied in the Code window. You can copy them the same way you copy text in a Word document.

2. Choose Edit | Copy.

3. Find the other macro in the Visual Basic Editor. To do so, either choose the macro's name from the Procedure drop-down menu (see Figure 23-12) or, if the macro is in a different template, open a document in the other template, choose Tools | Macro | Macros, select the macro, and click the Edit button to return to the Visual Basic Editor.

4. Click where you want the command sequence to go and choose Edit | Paste.

Deleting, Renaming, and Copying Macros

Unfortunately, copying macros isn't as easy as one, two, three, because macros are kept in what Word calls *modules*. For each template in which you create new macros, Word creates a module called NewMacros. Macros you create are kept in the NewMacros module. In order to copy macros from template to template, you have to copy the whole module. You can't copy a single macro. As a consolation, however, deleting and renaming macros is pretty easy. Read on to find out how to delete, rename, and copy macros.

LEARN BY EXAMPLE

Open the "23-1 Macros" practice document on the companion CD if you would like practice deleting, renaming, and copying macros.

DELETING A MACRO   Choose Tools | Macro | Macros or press ALT-F8 to open the Macros dialog box (see Figure 23-11). If necessary, choose Normal.dot from the Macros In drop-down list to find the macro you want to delete (if you can't find your macro, open a document in the template in which your macro is stored before you try to delete a macro). Then click the macro that needs deleting, click the Delete button, and click Yes when Word asks if you really want to do it.

RENAMING A MACRO   Choose Tools | Macro | Macros or press ALT-F8 to open the Macros dialog box (see Figure 23-11), click the macro that needs renaming, and click the Edit button. The Visual Basic Editor window opens (see Figure 23-12). On first line of the macro, to the left of the parentheses, is the macro's name. Delete the name and enter a new one. Remember: Macro names cannot start with a number or include blank spaces. Then choose File | Save.

COPYING MACROS FROM ONE TEMPLATE TO ANOTHER   Follow these steps to copy macros from one template to another:

1. Open a document in the template whose macros need copying.

2. Choose Tools | Macro | Macros, and click the Organizer button. You'll see the Organizer dialog box. The box on the left lists macro modules in the template you are currently working in.

3. Click the NewMacros module on the left side of the dialog box to select it, or else click another module if you have added a second macro module to the template and you want to copy its modules.

4. Click the Close File button on the right side of the dialog box, click the Open File button, and, in the Open dialog box, find and select the template to which you will copy the macros, and click the Open button. The name of the "copied

to" template appears on the right side of the Organizer dialog box, as does a list of the macro modules in the template.

 If the template to which you want to copy the macros also has a NewMacros module, rename the NewMacros module in the "copied from" template on the left side of the dialog box. To do so, click NewMacros on the left side of the dialog box, click the Rename button, and enter a new name in the Rename dialog box. Renaming the NewMacros module this way creates a second copy of the NewMacros module in the "copied from" template. The NewMacros module remains intact in the "copied from" template.

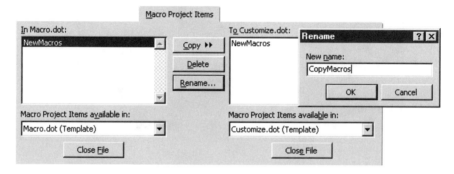

5. Click the Copy button.

6. Click the Close button to close the Organizer dialog box.

MOUS Exam Objectives Explored in Chapter 23

Objective	Heading	Practice File
Insert a field	"Inserting a Field in a Document"	
Create, apply, and edit macros	"Working with Macros"	
Copy, rename, and delete macros	"Deleting, Renaming, and Copying Macros"	23-1 Macros
Customize toolbars	"Creating Your Own Toolbars and Toolbar Buttons"	

The Complete Reference

Word 2000

Chapter 24

Working with Online and Multimedia Documents

T his chapter looks to the future and explains how to make Word 2000 documents that need never be printed. For years, pundits have been predicting a paperless office where paper is obsolete and all documents are read on computer screens. It could happen here!

In this chapter, you will learn a few simple techniques for decorating documents that will be shown online but not printed. This chapter also explains how to create an online data-entry form—an electronic version of a paper form that makes entering data easier. You'll also learn how to place hyperlinks in documents to connect them to other documents or to sites on the Internet. For the budding ingenue, this chapter describes how to include sound and video in Word documents. Finally, the end of this chapter offers ten Windows techniques that all Word users should know.

Creating Online Documents in Word

An *online document* is one that is meant to be seen on computer screens but not printed. Not that you can't print an online document. You can print one, but the background designs and text animations don't show up on paper. To create an online document, do all your work in Web Layout view so you can see what others will see when they view it. These pages explain how to apply background colors and themes to an online document. You will also learn how to animate text.

 Make sure others know to switch to Web Layout view to see your online documents. Backgrounds and text animations can't be seen in Normal or Print Layout view.

Changing the Background Color on the Pages

Decorating the pages of a document with a background color, texture, picture, or clip art image is pretty simple. But remember that a loud or dark background is a distraction. Choose a light color or subtle texture for the background. Or, if you opt for a dark background, be prepared to change the color of the text to white or a light color so that it can be read more easily.

Click the Web Layout View button or choose View | Web Layout to switch to Web Layout view and then follow these instructions to give the pages in your document a background color, a texture, or a picture background:

■ **Color Background** Choose Format | Background and choose a color from the color palette. If none of the 40 choices suits you, click More Colors at the bottom of the menu and select a color in the Colors dialog box.

- **Texture Background** Choose Format | Background and click Fill Effects at the bottom of the Color Palette menu. You'll see the Fill Effects dialog box shown in Figure 24-1. Click the Texture tab and choose a texture. Be sure to scroll to the bottom of the list and examine all the different textures. (You can use a gradient or a pattern from the Fill Effects dialog box if you want to, but I think gradients and patterns do not make good backgrounds. You may well think differently, however. Or, as the Apple Corporation so ungrammatically puts it, you may "think different.")

Tip *Three effects in the Font dialog box work very nicely with texture backgrounds in online documents: Emboss, Engrave, and Shadow. Choose Format | Font to open the Font dialog box.*

- **Picture Background** Choose Format | Background, click the Fill Effects option at the bottom of the color palette, and click the Picture tab in the Fill Effects dialog box. From there, click the Select Picture button. In the Select Picture dialog box, locate and select the picture file to use as a background,

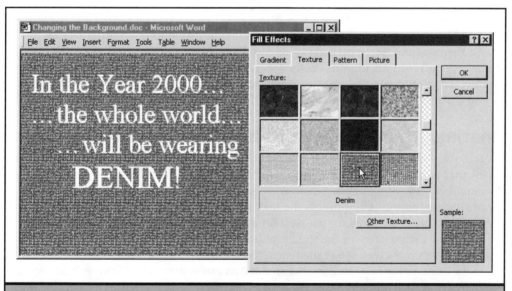

Figure 24-1. *In the Fill Effects dialog box, you can choose texture, gradient, pattern, or picture backgrounds for online documents*

and then click the Insert button. You can use any Windows-compatible graphic file as a background. The picture appears on the page in the form of tiles.

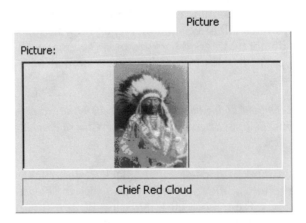

To remove the background from an online document, choose Format | Background and click the No Fill button on the color palette.

Choosing a Theme for the Pages

"Choosing a Background Theme for Your Web Page" in Chapter 16 explains exactly what a theme is and how you can use one to decorate the background of a Web page or the pages in a Word document. Themes were designed for Web pages, but that doesn't mean you can't use one to decorate an online document. Choose Format | Theme and choose a design in the Theme dialog box to decorate your pages with a theme.

"Animating" Headline Text in an Online Document

Tucked away in an obscure corner of the Font dialog box is a set of *animations*—special effects that you can apply to headlines and other prominent text in a document. Personally, I find animations annoying, especially the "blinking background," which simply highlights and unhighlights the text. However, the animations are eye-catchers and they are good for amusing yourself on a rainy day.

Figure 24-2 shows two of the six animations that you can use to breathe life into a headline. To animate text, select the text, choose Format | Font, click the Text Effects tab in the Font dialog box, and choose an Animations option. The Preview box shows precisely what each animation option does.

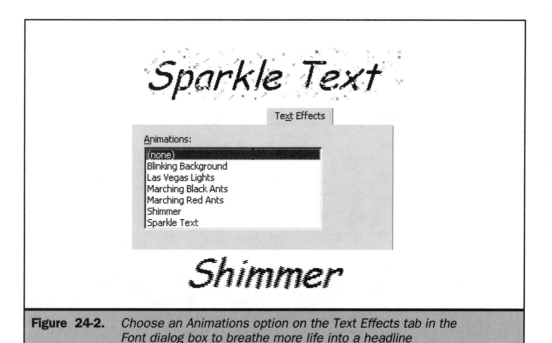

Figure 24-2.   *Choose an Animations option on the Text Effects tab in the Font dialog box to breathe more life into a headline*

Creating and Using an Online Data-Entry Form

A *form* is a means of collecting information. Most forms are paper forms. You fill them out, hand them to a clerk, and they are filed away for safekeeping. An online form works the same way, except instead of entering every piece of information, you can choose it from drop-down lists or check boxes. Online forms make it easier for data-entry clerks to enter data because the clerks don't have to type in every piece of information. And they make data-entries more accurate, too, because you can arrange the form so that only entries of a certain type or size can be made in certain places. In some respects, an online form has more in common with a dialog box than a paper form.

Figure 24-3 shows part of an online data-entry form for recording information that was gathered in a survey about software use. To enter data on this form, the data-entry clerk has only to choose options from drop-down menus, click check boxes, and enter the occasional name or ZIP code in a text box. In the case of the ZIP code text field, the clerk can only enter five numbers (the number of digits in an abbreviated ZIP code), which helps ensure that the ZIP code is entered accurately. If the clerk had to type all this information, it would take him or her longer. Furthermore, the chances of entering the

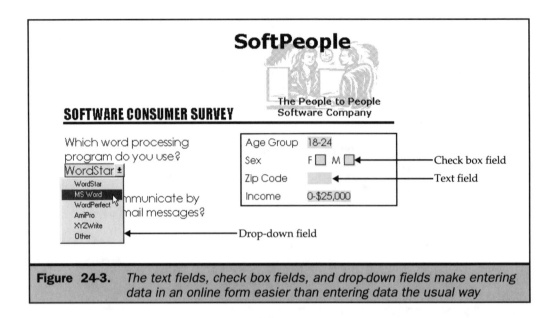

Figure 24-3. *The text fields, check box fields, and drop-down fields make entering data in an online form easier than entering data the usual way*

data inaccurately would increase, because the clerk might misspell a word. You can even provide Help instructions for data-entry clerks to help them enter information accurately.

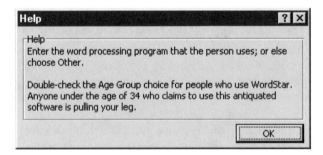

An online form is really a template. After you have created the data-entry form template, open a new document based on the form template, and then fill in the form. These pages explain how to create an online data-entry template and enter the text fields, check box fields, and drop-down fields. You will also learn how to lock a form so that entries can be made only in the fields, the shaded areas where the data is entered, not the other parts of the form. These pages also explain how to include help instructions, make calculations on forms, and fill in a form.

LEARN BY EXAMPLE
*The 24-2 Online Forms practice document on the companion CD offers an online
data-entry form that you can use to experiment with forms.*

Designing the Form Template and Entering the Form Fields

The first step in creating an online form is to lay it out and save it as a template. Or, if you've already created a paper form, you can use the paper form for your online data-entry form by saving it as a template. You can call on all the commands in Word to lay out the form. The commands on the Table menu are especially useful for aligning the different parts of the form (Chapter 14 explains tables). Drop in a clip art image or two if you intend to print the forms after you fill them in. Except for the form fields— the text fields, check box fields, and drop-down fields for entering the data—an online form is no different than a Word document. Be sure to leave blank spaces for the text, check box, and drop-down fields.

*"Creating a Fill-In Form" in Chapter 15 explains how to draw up a paper form.
Many of the techniques for creating a paper form work as well for laying out an
online data-entry form.*

The pages that follow explain how to enter the text fields, check box fields, and drop-down fields in a form. When the form is complete (or perhaps before the form is complete so you don't lose your work in the event of a computer failure), save your form as a template by following these steps:

1. Choose File | Save (or choose File | Save As if you created your online form from a paper form).

2. In the Save As dialog box, open the Save As Type drop-down menu and choose Document Template (*.dot) from the drop-down list. The Save In box lists the folder where you store templates.

3. Enter a descriptive name for the online form template in the File Name box and click OK.

Entering the Text Fields

A *text field* is a place on a form for typing in words, numbers, a date, the current time or date, or the results of a calculation. To enter a text field, click where you want the text field to go, display the Forms toolbar, and click the Text Form Field button on the Forms toolbar. A gray shade appears on the form (click the Form Field Shading button on the

Forms toolbar if you don't see the gray shade). Don't worry about the gray shade only being a few characters long. When you enter data in the text field, the field grows longer.

Unless you visit the Text Form Field Options dialog box and make changes there, the text field you created accommodates text—not numbers, a date, or a calculation—and can be any number of characters long. However, by clicking the Form Field Options button on the Forms toolbar or double-clicking the text field, you can open the Text Form Fields Options dialog box and change settings for the text field.

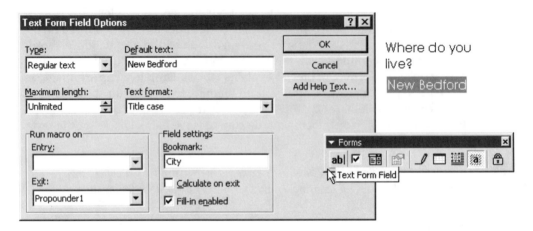

The Text form Field Options dialog box offers these settings:

- **Type**   Choose an option from the drop-down list to describe the type of data that will be entered in the field: Regular Text, Number, Data, Current Date, Current Time, or Calculation. Your choice is important for making sure data is entered accurately, because entry clerks can't enter text, for example, if you choose the Number option.

- **Maximum Length**   Choose Unlimited or enter the maximum number of characters that can be entered in the field. Your choice here is also important for entering data accurately, since you can prevent too many characters from being entered in the field accidentally. If the field is for entering two-character state abbreviations, for example, enter **2** to keep entry clerks from entering more than two characters.

- **Default**   Either leave the box blank or enter the text, date, or number that will be entered the majority of the time. By entering default text or a default number, you spare the entry clerk from having to enter it. If you enter default text or a default number, however, be sure to tell data clerks that they can override the default entry and enter something else.

- **Format**   Choose a format for entering text, a number, or a date.

Note   *To make a calculation on an online data form, place the fields whose numbers will be calculated in a table. Then open the Text Form Field Options dialog box, choose Calculation from the Type drop-down list and enter the formula for the calculation in the Expression box. "Crunching the Numbers in Tables" in Chapter 14 explains how to enter formulas in tables.*

Entering the Check Box Fields

A *check box field* is a place on a form that you can place a check mark to show agreement or disagreement. Use check boxes in surveys when respondents can choose more than one answer. Like a check box in a Word dialog box, more than one check box can be selected on a form.

To place a check box on a form, click where you want it to go, display the Forms toolbar, and click the Check Box Form Field button. A gray-shaded box appears (click the Form Field Options button on the Forms toolbar if you don't see the gray shade). Unless you change the default settings, check boxes are 10-points high and are not checked by default, but you can change those settings either by double-clicking the

---

Macros and Bookmarks for Form Fields

Each Form Field dialog box includes menus for running macros and marking fields with bookmarks. Here is what the options do:

- **Run Macro On Entry and Run Macro On Exit**   Choose a macro from the drop-down list to make a macro run when the data-entry clerk either clicks in the field to enter it or leaves the field by clicking elsewhere or pressing TAB. Choose an Exit macro, for example, to move the cursor automatically to another field in the data form. Or choose an Entry macro to perform a data calculation that bears on what the clerk is supposed to enter in the field. Chapter 23 explains macros.

- **Bookmark**   Enter a bookmark name if you want to use the field entry in a macro. You can then use the bookmark name to refer to the field. Word automatically assigns a bookmark name to each field, but enter your own to keep them straight if you intend to use them in macros.

check box or clicking the Form Field Options button on the Forms toolbar. You will see the Check Box Form Field Options dialog box. Change settings there and click OK.

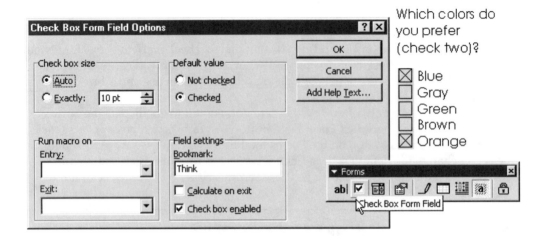

Entering the Drop-Down Fields

A *drop-down field,* like a drop-down list in a Word dialog box, offers several different choices. Use drop-down fields when a finite number of choices are available. All that data-entry clerks have to do is click the down arrow to open the drop-down field and make a choice. Or, if the first option in the field happens to be the right one, they can bypass the drop-down field and go to the next part of the form.

Follow these steps to place a drop-down field on a form:

1. Click where you want the field to go, display the Forms toolbar, and click the Drop-Down Form Field button. You'll see a gray shade where the drop-down field will go (click the Form Field Shading button on the Forms toolbar if you don't see the gray shade).

2. Either double-click the gray shade or click the Form Field Options button on the Forms toolbar. You'll see the Drop-Down Form Field Options dialog box.

GETTING MORE OUT OF
WORD 2000

Enter a list item and
click the Add button

Click a move button to change
an item's location on the list

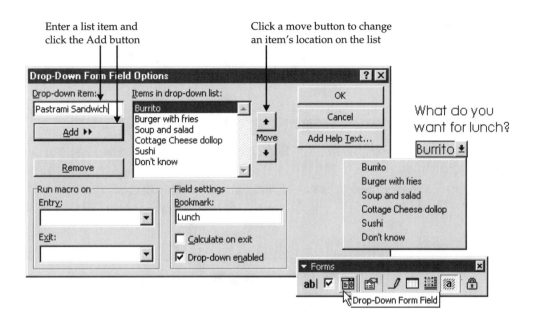

3. Type each entry for the drop-down list and click the Add button. To arrange
   options on the list, click an option and then click the Move button.

The topmost option on the list is the default choice—the one that is selected if the
data-entry clerk does not open the list and make a different choice.

*Click the Protect Form button on the Forms toolbar to be able to see the down arrow and
open the drop-down list. In order to start editing the form again or open the Drop-Down
Form Field Options dialog box, you have to click the button a second time to
"unprotect" the form. Later in this chapter, "Protecting a Form So No One Tampers
With It" explains how to click the Protect Form button to keep others from changing the
text in the form.*

Providing Help Instructions for Form Fields

Especially if someone else will enter data on the forms, you owe it to yourself to enter
help text to explain exactly what goes in each field. When users press F1 while the

cursor is in a form field, they'll see a Help box like the one in Figure 24-4. Meanwhile, the Status bar at the bottom of the screen also offers a brief explanation of the form field, as shown in Figure 24-4.

To enter instructions for a Help box or the Status bar, either double-click a form field or click it and then click the Form Field Options button on the Forms toolbar. In the Form Field Options dialog box, click the Add Help Text button. The Form Field Help Text dialog box appears (see Figure 24-4). Enter the help instructions:

- **Instructions for the Help Box** Enter the instructions on the Help Key (F1) tab and click OK.

- **Instructions for the Status Bar** Enter the instructions on the Status Bar tab and click OK.

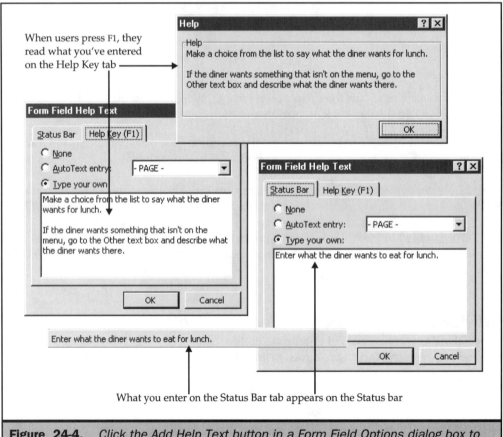

Figure 24-4. *Click the Add Help Text button in a Form Field Options dialog box to go to the Form Field Help Text dialog box and enter help instructions*

To allow data-entry people to change part of a form but not another part, divide the document into sections. Then choose Tools | Protect Document, click the Sections button in the Protect Document dialog box, and, in the Section Protection dialog box, put check marks next to each section that you want to protect. Unprotected sections can be changed; sections you checked off cannot be changed. "Section Breaks for Changing Layouts" in Chapter 9 explains sections.

Entering the Data on a Form

When your new form is laid out and protected, you can start entering data. To do so, open a document based on the form and get to work. Choose File | New, click the name of the template you created, and click the OK button. Then enter the data and save your form when you are done.

The Save tab in the Options dialog box offers a means of saving form data as a comma-separated list. Save the data this way in order to store it in a database. Choose Tools | Options, click the Save tab in the Options dialog box, and check the Save Data Only In Forms check box.

Including Hyperlinks in Documents

A *hyperlink* is an electronic shortcut from one place to another place in the same document, from one document to another document, or from one place to a site on the Internet. Clicking a hyperlink is the fastest way to go elsewhere. In Word documents, hyperlinks formed from text are blue and are underlined. Clip art images, shapes, text boxes, and other objects can also be hyperlinks. You can tell when you have encountered a hyperlink because the pointer changes into a gloved hand when it is moved over a link. Moreover, a yellow box tells you in so many words where the link takes you.

These pages explain how to make a hyperlink to a different spot in the same document or to another document, how to maintain hyperlinks, and how the Web toolbar can help you travel from link to link. You will also learn how to marshal various Word commands that pertain to hyperlinks in order to turn a manual into an online Help program.

"Creating a Hyperlink to a Page on the Internet" in Chapter 16 explains how to link to a Web site.

LEARN BY EXAMPLE
Open the 24-1 Hyperlink practice document on the companion CD if you want some practical experience with hyperlinks.

Making a Hyperlink to Another Document
or Part of a Document

Observe these rules about hyperlinking before you attempt to create a hyperlink from one document to another document or from one place in a document to another place:

- For a hyperlink to go from one place to another in the same document, the destination of the link must be marked with a bookmark or be a heading that has been assigned a heading style. Before you attempt to create the link, make sure the place you want to link to is bookmarked or has been assigned the Heading 1, Heading 2, or other Heading style.

- For a hyperlink to go to a particular place in another document, the place in the other document must be marked with a bookmark. Be sure to place a bookmark in the other document where you want the hyperlink to go. A hyperlink can go to the top of another document without a bookmark having to be in the other document.

- If you move or delete a document to which your document is hyperlinked, the hyperlink becomes invalid. It won't work. Likewise, a hyperlink fails if you remove a bookmark that is the destination of a hyperlink. Move or delete a document and you see the message box shown on the left side of this illustration; remove a bookmark and you merely see the Web toolbar when you click the hyperlink. (The next section in this chapter, "Editing and Maintaining Hyperlinks," explains what to do when a hyperlink fails.)

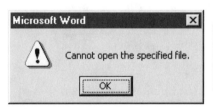

Chapter 12 explains styles, including Heading styles. See "Bookmarks for Getting Around" in Chapter 2 to learn about bookmarks.

Follow these steps to insert a hyperlink to a different document or to a different place in the same document:

1. Select the words, phrase, or graphic that will form the hyperlink.

2. Choose Insert | Hyperlink, press CTRL-K, or right-click the word or graphic you selected and choose Hyperlink from the shortcut menu. You'll see the Insert Hyperlink dialog box shown in Figure 24-5.

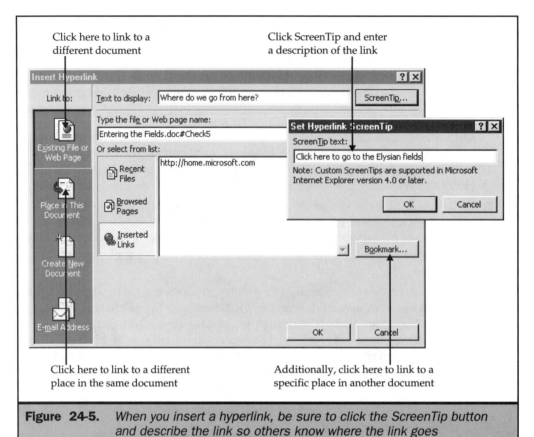

Click here to link to a
different document

Click ScreenTip and enter
a description of the link

Click here to link to a different
place in the same document

Additionally, click here to link to a
specific place in another document

Figure 24-5.   *When you insert a hyperlink, be sure to click the ScreenTip button
and describe the link so others know where the link goes*

3. Create the link to a different place in the same document, the top of a different
   document, or a particular place in a different document:

   ■ **To a Different Place in the Same Document**   Click the Place In This
   Document icon under Link To. A list of headings and bookmarks in your
   document appears in the Insert Hyperlink dialog box (click the plus signs
   next to the words "Headings" and "Bookmarks" to see all the headings and
   bookmarks). Then click the heading or bookmark that marks the destination
   of the hyperlink.

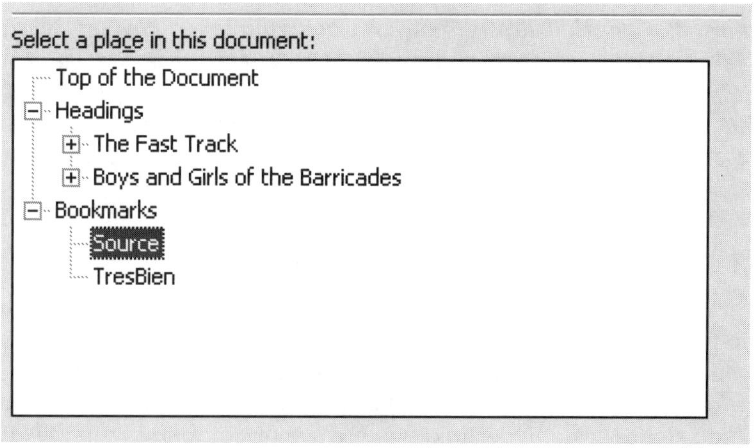

Select a place in this document:

- Top of the Document
- Headings
  - The Fast Track
  - Boys and Girls of the Barricades
- Bookmarks
  - Source
  - TresBien

- **To the Top of a Different Document**   Click the Existing File Or Web Page icon under Link To, and then click the File button. In the Link to File dialog box, find and select the name of the document you want to link to. Then click OK.

- **To a Particular Place in a Different Document**   Follow the instructions for linking to the top of a different document, and do the following besides: Click the Bookmark button, and, in the Select Place in Document dialog box, select a bookmark (click the plus sign next to the word "Bookmarks," if necessary, to see the bookmark names).

4. Click the ScreenTip button and enter a brief description of the hyperlink. Anyone who points to the link will see the description you enter in a pop-up box. If you forget to provide a description, the pop-up box shows the path to the link, a series of folder names followed by a filename.

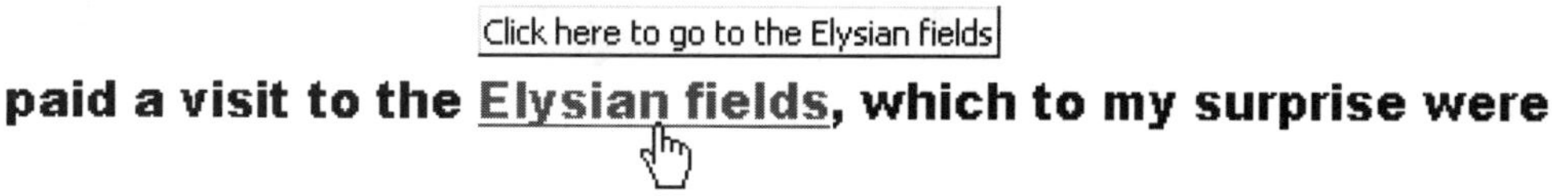

Click here to go to the Elysian fields

paid a visit to the Elysian fields, which to my surprise were

5. Click OK to insert the hyperlink.

Word inserts a hyperlink to a Web site (or what it thinks is a Web site) when you type any of the following characters and press the SPACEBAR: a character, the at symbol (@), and at least one other character; the letters "www" followed by a period; and the letters "http://". If you prefer not to enter hyperlinks automatically, choose Tools | AutoCorrect, click the AutoFormat As You Type tab, and uncheck the Internet And Network Paths With Hyperlinks check box.

Editing and Maintaining Hyperlinks

Hyperlinks are kind of hard to edit and maintain. After all, if you click a hyperlink in order, say, to type a word in the middle of the link, you activate the hyperlink. And selecting hyperlinks is kind of hard, too, since you can't drag across the link without activating it. The trick to editing and maintaining hyperlinks is to right-click instead of click. When you right-click a hyperlink, you see a shortcut menu with the Hyperlink option at the bottom. Click the Hyperlink option and you get a bunch of commands for handling hyperlinks.

For you and you only, here are some techniques for editing and maintaining hyperlinks:

- **Editing a Hyperlink** Right-click and choose Hyperlink | Edit Hyperlink. You will see the Edit Hyperlink dialog box, which looks and works exactly like the Insert Hyperlink dialog box (see Figure 24-5). Change the link destination, change the ScreenTip, or do what you will, and click OK.

- **Removing a Hyperlink** Right-click and choose Hyperlink | Remove Hyperlink. Removing a hyperlink does not delete the words or graphic that formed the link. Removing a link merely takes away the words' or graphic's hyperlink status.

- **Deleting a Hyperlink** Right-click, choose Hyperlink | Select Hyperlink to select the link, and press the DELETE key.

- **Selecting a Hyperlink So You Can Format It** Right-click and choose Hyperlink | Select Hyperlink. The link is highlighted. Now you can change its font or font size, for example.

- **Copying a Hyperlink** Right-click and choose Hyperlink | Copy Hyperlink. The link is copied to the Clipboard. Now you can paste it elsewhere.

The Web Toolbar for Going from Place to Place

As soon as you click a hyperlink and go elsewhere, the Web toolbar appears. The toolbar lists the name of the file you are in and offers a couple of buttons that are useful for going from place to place:

- **Back** Click to return to or backtrack through hyperlinks you have clicked.

- **Forward** Click to see hyperlinks you retreated from.

- **Show Only Web Toolbar** Removes all toolbars from the screen except the Web toolbar. Click this nifty button when you want to see more text onscreen. Click it a second time to see the other toolbars again.

- **Stop Current Jump** Click this button if you grow impatient waiting for another document to appear onscreen. Clicking the button tells Word not to open the hyperlinked document.

Back and Forward buttons   ─Stop Current Jump   Show Only Web Toolbar

Caution   *Do not use the Web toolbar to go on the Internet. True, the toolbar offers a Search the Web button and a Start Page button, but you are better off opening your Web browser and starting from there. I have found the Web toolbar to be very, very slow at finding and displaying Web pages. Use the Web toolbar strictly to move back and forth among documents on your computer.*

Using Links to Turn a Manual into an Online Help Program

With a little foresight and planning, you can take advantage of the numerous hyperlinking capabilities of Word to turn a manual into an online Help program. Design your Help program along these lines:

- Generate a "live" table of contents (TOC) that users can click to go to various Help topics. As "Generating a Table of Contents" explains in Chapter 18, you can click a TOC entry and go directly to the heading that the entry refers to when Word is in Web Layout view. In Web Layout view, TOC entries are blue and are underlined like hyperlinks. Tell the people who read your manual to switch to Web Layout view and click TOC entries to go the Help instructions they need.

- Cross-reference the different Help topics. As "Including Cross-References in Documents" in Chapter 18 explains, cross-references are "live" in that you can click a reference to go immediately to the thing that the reference refers to. Unlike TOC entries, however, cross-references are not underlined or blue in the text. Create a character style for hyperlinks that underlines them and turns them blue so that users of your Help program can recognize cross-references as items they can click for further information. Chapter 12 explains character styles.

■ Hyperlink terms in your manual to definitions in a glossary. Write a glossary and hyperlink each instance of a glossary word in the text to its definition in the glossary.

Be sure to explain to users of your online Help manual how they can use the Web toolbar to move back and forth among the different Help screens they view.

Note *If you want to get serious about making an online Help program, check out these software products: Robo-Help and Doc-to-Help. These programs are designed for creating online Help programs. Doc-to-Help, in fact, runs piggyback on Word, so you can install Doc-to-Help on your computer but run Word commands to devise a Help program in Doc-to-Help.*

Including Sound and Video in Documents

Was it only five years ago that "multimedia" was all the rage? A multimedia file is one that includes sound or video as well as text and pictures. Five years ago, entire books were published about multimedia (I edited one or two) and pundits heralded the arrival of the multimedia document, a document in which the viewer could read text, click sound icons to play sound files, or click video icons to see videos. The multimedia document didn't catch on quite like the pundits expected, chiefly because multimedia tends to make documents grow to large, unwieldy sizes.

These types of sound and video files can be imported into a Word 2000 document:

■ **Sound Files**   .WAV, .MID, .AU, .AIF, .RMI, .SND, and .MP2
■ **Video Files**   .AVI, .MOV, .MOVIE., .MPG, .MPEG, and .QT

Follow these steps to slip a sound file or video file into a Word document:

1. In My Computer or Windows Explorer, open the folder with the sound file or video clip that you want to put in your Word document, as shown in Figure 24-6.

2. Open the Word document that is to receive the sound or video file and place it side by side with the My Computer or Windows Explorer window.

3. Drag the sound file or video clip into the Word document. A mini-video screen or speaker icon appears on the page.

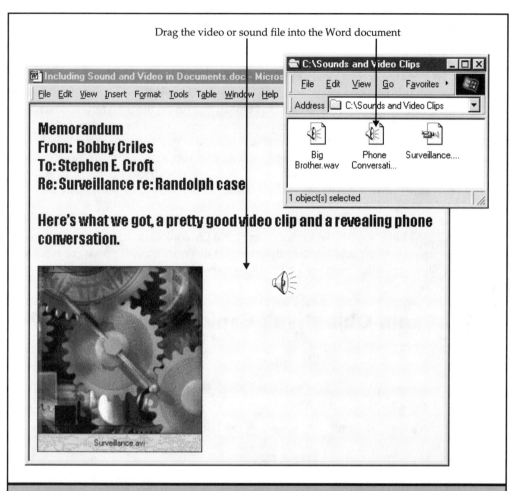

Figure 24-6.   *You can include a sound file or video clip in a document
by dragging it there*

Tell your audience that it can double-click the mini-video screen or speaker icon to
play the video or hear the sound file. The video or sound file is an embedded object, so
you need to tell the person who double-clicks the mini-video screen or speaker icon
that he or she must be running a computer that is capable of playing video and sound
in order to play the video or sound file.

Sending E-Mail Messages and Documents from Word

As long as you've installed Outlook 2000, you can send documents and e-mail messages over the Internet without leaving Word 2000. To send a document over the Internet, open the document you want to send and click the E-Mail button on the Standard toolbar. A space for entering address information appears at the top of the Word screen. In the To box, either enter the recipient's e-mail address or click the To icon to open the Select Recipients dialog box and choose names there. You can also send a copy of the document to a third party by entering an address in the Cc box. The document's name appears in the Subject box, but you can enter a different subject if you want. Finally, click the Send button.

Suppose you want to send a message along with your document. To do so, choose File | Send To | Mail Recipient (As Attachment). An Outlook message window appears. Enter the recipient's name and address information as you would if you were working in Outlook. Then enter the message and click the Send button.

Exam ▾ | MOUS Exam Objectives Explored in Chapter 24

Objective	Heading	Practice File
Create a hyperlink	"Including Hyperlinks in Documents"	24-1 Hyperlink
Create and modify a form*	"Designing the Form Template and Entering the Form Fields"	24-2 Online Forms
Create and modify a form control*	"Editing an Online Data-Entry Form"	
Send a Word document via e-mail	"Sending E-Mail Messages and Documents from Word"	

* Denotes an Expert exam objective.

Top 10

Ten Windows Techniques All Word Users Should Know

Whether you know it or not, you run two programs when you run Word 2000. Besides Word, you run the Windows operating system. Here are ten Windows techniques that can help make the time you spend in Word more productive. By the way, some of these techniques only work in Windows 98, not Windows 95.

1. LIST FILES IN DIFFERENT WAYS IN DIALOG BOXES. In the Open dialog box, Save As dialog box, and other dialog boxes where filenames are listed, you can view filenames in different ways by clicking the Views button or clicking the down arrow beside the Views button and making a choice from the drop-down menu. Either keep clicking the Views button to arrive at a new way of seeing the files or click the down arrow and choose one of these options from the menu:

- **List** Shows all the files in an alphabetical list. Choose this option when you know the name of the document you are looking for and you want to select it quickly.

- **Details** Shows files in an alphabetical list along with each file's size, its type (Microsoft Word Document, for example, or JPEG Image), and the date it was last modified. Choose this option when you are having trouble deciding which Word document to open.

- **Properties** Shows document properties for the file that is selected in the dialog box. Click a document and choose Properties from the Views drop-down menu to find out exactly what a document is. You'll see statistics about the document—the same statistics you get in the Properties dialog box when you choose File | Properties.

- **Preview** Shows a thumbnail image of the file that is selected in the dialog box. Click a document and choose Preview to find out for certain whether you want to open a document.

2. DISPLAY THE FILE EXTENSIONS IN DIALOG BOXES. A *file extension* is a three-letter designation at the end of a filename that describes what type of file the file is. Normally, file extensions do not appear in dialog boxes, but you can make them appear. Being able to see file extensions is an advantage when you work with different kinds of files. All you have to do is glance at the file extension to see what kind of file you are dealing with.

The following illustration lists some files with and without their file extensions:

ComRef Outline
Craigs List Interesting Jobs
Letter to Mom
Money Web Site
Osborne art
Other books by
Quevara's Variations

ComRef Outline.doc
Craigs List Interesting Jobs.doc
Letter to Mom.doc
Money Web Site.doc
Osborne art.doc
Other books by.doc
Quevara's Variations.doc

Follow these steps to see file extensions in the Open dialog box, Save As dialog box, and other dialog boxes where filenames are listed:

1. Click the Start button and choose Settings | Folder Options.
2. Click the View tab in the Folder Options dialog box.
3. Uncheck the Hide File Extensions For Known File Types check box and click OK.

3. OPEN DOCUMENTS FROM THE WINDOWS DOCUMENTS MENU.

Unquestionably the fastest way to open a document is to begin at the Windows Start menu. Click the Start button, choose Documents, and click the name of a file on the Documents menu. The Documents menu lists the last 15 files you worked on, be they Word documents or another kind of file. You can open Word and a Word document at the same time by clicking the name of a Word document on the Documents menu.

4. RECOVER FILES YOU DELETED ACCIDENTALLY.   Yes, you can make a Word document rise from the dead if you deleted it accidentally. To do so, go to the Windows desktop and double-click the Recycle Bin icon. In the Recycle Bin window, click the document that needs resuscitating and choose File | Restore.

5. PRESS CTRL-ALT-DEL WHEN THE COMPUTER FREEZES.   Every Windows user knows, or should know, to click the Start button and choose Shut Down before turning off the computer. But what if the computer freezes and you can't shut down properly? Follow these steps:

1. Press CTRL-ALT-DEL. The Close Program dialog box appears. It lists all programs that are running. The words "not responding" appear beside the name of the program that is making the computer freeze.
2. Click the name of the program that is "not responding" and click the End Task button. With luck, the program that made your computer freeze closes and you can get back to work.
3. Press CTRL-ALT-DEL again if your computer is still frozen. With luck, your computer shuts down and restarts.

Sometimes pressing CTRL-ALT-DEL doesn't shut down the computer. When that happens, turn off the computer's power switch, wait a minute for the computer's platters to stop spinning, and turn on your computer. Windows runs the ScanDisk utility to see if any damage was done to the hard disk. Get back to work.

6. REARRANGE THE NAMES ON THE PROGRAMS MENU. In Windows 98, you can rearrange the names on the Programs menu by clicking the icon beside a program's name and dragging it up or down the menu. Move "Microsoft Word" to a prominent place on the Programs menu where you can find it easily.

7. HIDE THE TASKBAR IF YOU WANT TO. The Taskbar takes up valuable space along the bottom of the screen, but you can do one or two things to handle the Taskbar:

- **Hiding the Taskbar** Move the pointer over the top of the Taskbar, and, when you see the double-headed arrow, click and drag the Taskbar below the bottom of the screen. To see the Taskbar again, move the pointer to the bottom of the screen, and, when you see the double-headed arrow, click and drag upward.

- **Automatically Hiding the Taskbar** With this technique, the Taskbar does not appear unless you move the pointer to the bottom of the screen. Click the Start button and choose Settings | Taskbar & Start Menu to open the Taskbar Properties dialog box. On the Taskbar Options tab, check the Auto Hide check box and click OK.

8. CHANGE THE SCREEN RESOLUTION. Depending on whether you are near-sighted or far-sighted, some screen resolutions are better than others. *Screen resolution* refers to how large or small things look on the screen. With a small screen resolution (640 by 480 pixels), everything looks larger, although the screen can seem cramped. With a large resolution (800 by 600 pixels), everything looks smaller but is easier to manage. Experiment with screen resolutions until you find a setting that suits you.

To change the screen resolution, right-click the desktop and choose Properties. In the Display Properties dialog box, click the Settings tab, and then drag the Screen Area slider to 640 by 480 pixels or 800 by 600 pixels (or 1,024 by 768 pixels on some machines). Then click OK.

9. RESET THE CLOCK, IF NECESSARY. You always know what time it is when you are running a Windows machine—all you have to do is look at the clock in the lower-right corner of the screen. And if you move the pointer over the clock, you can read the date and the day of the week. Making sure the clock tells accurate time is important not only for meeting appointments, but also for time- and date-stamping documents. When you save a document, Windows tells Word what time the document was saved. Documents are time-stamped and date-stamped so that you know which version of a document you are dealing with.

To reset the Windows clock or change the date, double-click the clock. You will see the Date/Time Properties dialog box. Change the date and time on the Date & Time tab and click OK.

10. CREATE DESKTOP SHORTCUT ICONS FOR YOUR FAVORITE DOCUMENTS.

All you have to do to open a document for which you've created a desktop shortcut icon is double-click. Create desktop shortcut icons for each document you go to often. The icons appear on the Windows desktop where you can find them in a hurry. To create a desktop shortcut icon, open Windows Explorer or My Computer and find the document, right-click it, and choose Send To | Desktop As Shortcut.

See ya later.   Till next time.   Bye, Reader.

The Complete Reference

Part VII

Appendixes

The
Complete
Reference

Appendix A

Installing Word 2000

This appendix describes how to install and reinstall Word 2000. It explains what to do before you start installing Word, how to install and reinstall Word, and how to reinstall Word to put more or fewer Office features on your computer.

The New Installation Technique

With Word 2000 and the other Office 2000 programs, Microsoft has introduced a new installation technique. Instead of installing Word and the various Office tools in their entirety, you install the essential parts of Word and the essential Office tools (I explain how in this appendix). Later, if you choose a Word command or Office tool that hasn't been installed on your computer, you'll see a message box like the ones shown in Figure A-1. The message box tells you in so many words that the command you chose has not been installed on your computer, but you can install it by clicking the OK button, the Install button, the Yes button, or whatever the button's name happens to be.

What the message box doesn't mention is that you need the Word 2000 CD or Office 2000 CD to install the command. Before clicking the OK, Install, or Yes button, put the Word 2000 CD or Office 2000 CD in your CD-ROM drive. When you click the button, Word copies program codes from the CD to your computer so that you can execute the command. The installation procedure takes only a few seconds. Without the CD, however, you can't install the program codes for the command you want.

Practically speaking, you need to keep the Word 2000 or Office 2000 CD at your side when you use Word. You need the CD in case Word encounters a command that it can't carry out. How to put this delicately? The new installation technique has made it fairly impossible to borrow a copy of Word or Office from someone else and install it

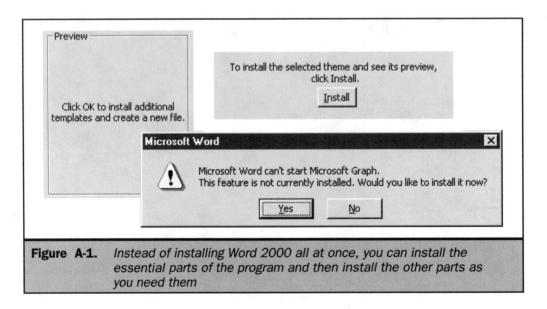

Figure A-1. *Instead of installing Word 2000 all at once, you can install the essential parts of the program and then install the other parts as you need them*

Be sure to tell data-entry clerks that they can press F1 or glance at the Status bar if they aren't sure what to enter in a form field.

Editing an Online Data-Entry Form

After you fill out a form or two, suppose you discover that your online form needs editing. In that case, open the form template and edit it. To open a template, choose File | Open. In the Open dialog box, choose All Word Documents from the Files Of Type drop-down list and find the folder where templates are stored. By default, Word keeps its templates in the C:\Windows\Application Data\Microsoft\Templates folder. However, if you or the person who saved the template first saved the template in a different folder, find it. In versions of Word prior to version 2000, templates were kept in the C:\Program Files\Microsoft Office\Templates folder, so you might find your form template there. When you have found the template, click it and then click the Open button.

While the form template is open, you can edit a form field by double-clicking it or clicking it and then clicking the Form Fields Option button on the Forms toolbar. You'll see the Form Field Options dialog box, where you can change settings to your heart's content.

Protecting a Form So No One Tampers With It

After you click the Protect Form button on the Forms toolbar, no one can change the form except by making entries in form fields. The form labels and explanatory text on the form are untouchable. The Protect Form button is designed to make it impossible for data-entry people to tamper with a form. All they can do is make entries in the fields.

A savvy person, however, could simply click the Protect Form button a second time to "unprotect" the form. When the button is not pressed down, you can change the form. To protect the form once and for all, choose Tools | Protect Document, click the Forms option button in the Protect Document dialog box, enter a password if you so desire, and click OK. Choose Tools | Unprotect Document if you want to be able to change the form. You will be asked for the password if you entered a password when you "protected" your document.

on your computer. Since you need the installation CD to run Word, you can't simply borrow Aunt Enid's copy of the program for a few days and load it on your computer. You can try your best to load all the Word 2000 and Office 2000 features that you need on your computer from the start (see "Custom Installation: Choosing Which Features to Install," later in this appendix), but installing all the features requires a lot of disk space and is not practical for most people.

Before You Install Word 2000

Before you install Word 2000, close all open programs. Microsoft also recommends backing up all your important files and documents before you install Word. While writing this book I installed and reinstalled Word many times and never lost a file or document, but I want you to know what Microsoft recommends.

Your computer must meet these requirements in order to install Word:

- An *x86*-compatible computer that meets minimum hardware requirements for Microsoft Windows 95, Windows 98, or Windows NT 4.0
- Windows or Windows NT
- A Pentium chip with 32MB or better (recommended)
- At least 280MB hard disk space
- A CD-ROM drive

If you run the Windows NT operating system, you must have installed Service Pack 3 or Service Pack 4 before you can run Word 2000 or another Office 2000 program. Follow these steps to find out which NT version you have and which Service Pack is installed: Click the Start button, choose Tools | Windows NT Diagnostics, and click the Version tab of the Windows NT Diagnostics dialog box. The Version tab lists the Windows NT version you are running and the most recent Windows NT Service Pack that is loaded on your system.

Installing Word 2000

Follow these steps to install Word 2000:

1. Close all open programs.
2. Put the CD in the CD-ROM drive. In a moment, you see the Welcome to the Microsoft Office (or Microsoft Word) 2000 Installation Wizard dialog box. Twiddle your thumbs while you wait for the Installation program to prepare to install Word.

APPENDIXES

> **Note**   *If you don't see the Welcome to the Microsoft Installation Wizard dialog box, follow these instructions to display it: Click the Start button and choose Settings | Control Panel. In the Control Panel window, double-click the Add/Remove Programs icon. In the Add/Remove Programs Properties dialog box, click the Install button. Click Next in the following dialog box, and then click the Finish button.*

3. Enter your name and other personal information, as well as the CD key (you will find this number in the Word 2000 or Office 2000 package). Then click Next. The User Name, Initial, and Organization information you enter here appears by default in many different places in Word and the other Office programs. For example, if you choose Insert | AutoText | Signature in Word, you can insert the name you enter in the User Name text box without having to type the name.

4. Read the user agreement, click the I Accept The Terms option button, and click the Next button.

   The next dialog box offers three installation choices (or two if an earlier version of Word or another office program is not already installed on your computer):

   ■ **Upgrade Now**   Removes previous versions of Office programs, including Word, and replaces them with the newest versions. You get roughly the same installation you had before, except newer editions of Word and the other Office programs are installed on your computer. If you click this button, the installation procedure begins right away.

   ■ **Typical**   The essential parts of Word and the other Office programs are installed on your computer. When you try to use a feature that hasn't been installed, you see a dialog box similar to the ones shown in Figure A-1 and you are given the chance to install the feature. I recommend choosing this option. As long as your Office 2000 or Word 2000 CD is handy, you can simply install features as you need them.

   ■ **Customize**   You pick and choose which parts of Word and the other Office programs to install on your computer. See "Custom Installation: Choosing Which Features to Install," the next section in this appendix.

5. Click an Installation button—Upgrade Now, Typical, or Customize.

6. Click Next in the following dialog box, which asks where on your computer to install Word and the other Office programs. Office programs are installed in the C:\Program Files\Microsoft Office folder.

The installation program starts installing Word and the other Office programs. The installation can take 20 to 30 minutes, depending on how many features need to be installed. If you decided to pick and choose which features to install, keep reading.

Custom Installation: Choosing Which Features to Install

In a Customize installation, you decide for yourself which Word 2000 or Office 2000 features to install on your computer. Figure A-2 shows the dialog box you see when you choose a Custom installation. To tell Word which features to install, click the plus sign next to Microsoft Word for Windows to see a list of features. Then, click the icon next to each feature and choose an option from the drop-down menu to decide how or whether to install it:

- **Run From My Computer**   Loads the feature onto your computer.
- **Run All From My Computer**   Loads all the features in a set of features on your computer. For example, if you click the icon beside Microsoft Word for Windows and choose Run All From My Computer, all the Word features are installed.

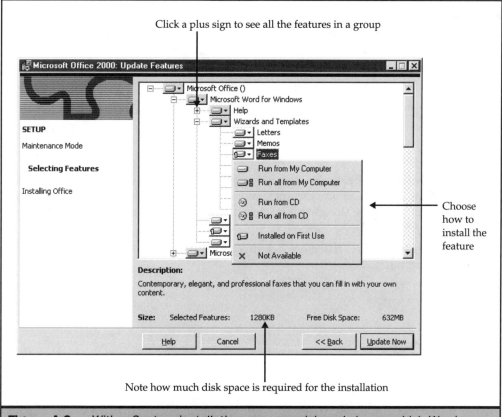

Figure A-2.   *With a Custom installation, you can pick and choose which Word features to install on your computer*

- **Run From CD**   Runs the feature from the Office or Word CD. This technique is not recommended, since running a program from a CD is markedly slower than running it from your hard drive.

- **Run All From CD**   Runs all the features in a set of features from the CD instead of from your hard drive. This technique is likewise not recommended.

- **Installed On First Use**   Does not install the feature on your computer, but gives the opportunity to install it when you choose it from a command menu or dialog box. When you try to activate the feature, you see a message box like the ones in Figure A-1.

 As you decide which features to install, be sure to take note of the Size figures at the bottom of the dialog box. The figures tell you how much disk space the features you are installing require and how much free disk space is on your computer.

Reinstalling (or Removing) Word 2000

Reinstall Word 2000 when you think the program files have been corrupted or you want to install or remove Word features from your computer. To reinstall Word, insert the CD in your CD-ROM drive. In a moment, you'll see a dialog box for reinstalling Word. Choose one of these options in the dialog box:

- **Repair Office**   Click this button to repeat the last installation you made of Word. All the features you chose the last time are reinstalled on your computer. (You can also activate this command in Word by choosing Help | Detect and Repair.)

- **Add Or Remove Features**   Click this button and you see the dialog box shown in Figure A-2, where you can pick and choose which features to install. See the previous section in this chapter to learn how to decide for yourself which Word features to install.

- **Remove Word (Or Office)**   Click this button to remove Word from your computer.

Appendix B

Becoming a Microsoft
Office User Specialist

The Microsoft Office User Specialist (MOUS) program is the best way for you to prove to yourself and to prospective employers that you have mastered one or more programs in the Microsoft Office 2000 suite. The program is a reliable way for you to measure your strengths and identify your weaknesses. And by following the prescribed coursework and preparing for the exam, you will improve your skills at using programs in the Office suite.

Three levels of MOUS certification are available:

- **Core**   Becoming a Microsoft Office User Specialist at the Core level indicates that you have a comprehensive understanding of the core computer tasks. This certification is available for Word, Excel, PowerPoint, Outlook, and Access.

- **Expert**   The holder of an Advanced certificate can handle more complex assignments. This certification is currently available for Word and Excel.

- **Master**   This is the highest level of certification. A Master is a person who has passed all five of the required exams in Word, Excel, PowerPoint, and Access.

How to Become Certified

To become a certified MOUS specialist in Word 2000, you need to prepare for the exam, register to take the test, take the test, and get your test results.

1. Prepare for the Exam

As you begin to prepare for MOUS certification in Word, figure out what parts of the program you know well and where you need to learn more. The skills you need to become a Microsoft Office User Specialist at the Core and Expert levels are listed in Appendix C of this book. You can also go to the MOUS Web site at **www.mous.net** to see a list of the skills.

MOUS exams are not multiple-choice exams or fill-in-the-blank exams. Instead, you are asked to perform assignments at a computer. For example, you might be asked to double-space a paragraph or create a form letter. To prepare for the exam, focus on Word tasks. Use the sample documents that come with this book to get hands-on practice in using Word. Don't bother memorizing information—doing so won't help you pass the test.

This book is a comprehensive reference to Microsoft Word. All tasks you can do in Word are explained in this book. Appendix C shows you where each course objective is covered in the book. At the end of most chapters is a table that tells you where MOUS exam objectives are covered. The self-test on the CD quizzes you on every skill set objective and activity. By taking the exam on the CD, you can find out how well you know Word and which areas you need to study more.

2. Register for the Test

All exams are administered by an Authorized Testing Center. To find the testing center nearest you, either phone 800-933-4493 or check the MOUS Web site at **www.mous.net**. Many testing centers require advance registration, but others accept walk-in candidates as well.

3. Take the Test

All the exams take an hour or less. You are judged on your ability to complete tasks and also on how long it takes you to complete tasks. As you take an exam, you can use the Help program, but doing so takes time and will detract from your test score.

Microsoft provides guidelines for taking MOUS exams. Here are some general tips for taking a MOUS exam:

- Carefully read the test instructions. When you begin a test, instructions are displayed at the bottom of the screen.

- Answer each question as if your work will be shown to the test exam administrator. Do nothing extra; do only what is requested.

- Since all questions have equal value, try to answer all of them, including the difficult questions.

- Pay close attention to how each question is worded. Responses must be precise. To answer a question correctly, you must do exactly as asked.

- Test scores are based on the end result, not on which technique was used to complete a task. Errant keystrokes and mouse-clicks do not count against your score as long as you achieve the correct result. The result is what counts.

- The overall test is timed. Spending a lot of time on a question doesn't matter as far as your test score is concerned, but taking too long on a question leaves less time for answering other questions.

- Answers are either right or wrong. You do not get credit for partial answers.

- If the message "method is not available" appears on the computer screen, try solving the problem a different way.

- IMPORTANT: Make sure you have entirely completed each question before clicking the Next Task button. After you click the Next Task button, you cannot return to that question. A question will be scored as wrong if it is not properly completed before moving to the next question.

Making Sure That a Question Is Properly Completed

To make sure that a question is properly completed, do the following:

- Close all dialog boxes, toolbars, Help windows, and menus.
- Make sure all of a task's steps are completed.

Don't do the following:

- Don't leave dialog boxes, toolbars, or menus open.
- Don't click the Next Task button until you have completely answered the question.
- Don't scroll in the question unless instructed to do so. Leave your answer visible.

4. Get Your Test Results

Each candidate sees his or her test results as soon as the test is completed. Test results are completely confidential. If you pass, you will receive a certificate by mail in four to six weeks. If you fail, you will be informed where you need to focus more attention. You can take the test as many times as you want. Refunds are not given if you don't pass the test; you must pay a new fee each time you take the test.

After you pass the test, you have recognized proof that you possess specific, relevant skills in Microsoft Word. A MOUS certificate is invaluable in the job market. The certificate proves to prospective employers that you have the skills to succeed.

The Complete Reference

Word 2000

Appendix C

MOUS Exam Objectives

The tables in this appendix are for Word users who are preparing for the Microsoft Office User Specialist (MOUS) exams in Microsoft Word 2000. In the tables, you will find cross-references to chapters and headings in the book where the exam objectives are explained. To prepare for a MOUS exam, read the list of objectives, and if you don't know an objective well, turn to the part of the book where it is explained.

At the end of most chapters in this book are tables that show where MOUS objectives are explained. You can also look at the end of chapters to find out where to go to learn more about a MOUS objective. If a practice document has been provided to help you master an objective, the practice document's name is also listed in the table at the end of the chapter.

Word 2000 Core Exam Objectives

Table C-1 lists the exam objectives that users must master to achieve Core status.

Exam Objective	Chapter	Look for This Heading
Working with Text		
Use the Undo, Redo, and Repeat command	2	"Repeating a Command or Text Entry" and "Undoing a Mistake—and Redoing What You Undid"
Apply font formats (Bold and Italic)	7	"Boldfacing, Italicizing, and Underlining Text"
Use the Overtype mode	2	"Typing Text and Erasing Mistakes"
Use the Spelling feature	11	"Correcting Your Spelling Errors"
Use the Thesaurus feature	11	"Choosing the Right Word with the Thesaurus"
Use the Grammar feature	11	"Correcting Grammatical Errors"
Insert page breaks	2	"Starting a New Paragraph, Line, or Page"
Highlight text in document	19	"Highlighting the Important Text"

Table C-1. *MOUS Objectives for the Core Exam*

Exam Objective	Chapter	Look for This Heading
Working with Text (continued)		
Insert and move text	3	"Moving and Copying Text"
Cut, Copy, Paste, and Paste Special using the Office Clipboard	3	"Copying and Moving Text with the Clipboard" and "Linking Documents So That Text Is Copied Automatically"
Copy formats using the Format Painter	12	"Applying Styles with the Format Painter"
Select and change font and font size	7	"Choosing a Font and Font Size for Text"
Find and replace text	6	"Conducting a Find and Replace Operation"
Apply character effects (superscript, subscript, strikethrough, small caps, and outline)	7	"Playing with Word's 'Text Effects'"
Insert date and time	6	"Quickly Entering the Date and Time" (under "Creating and Inserting AutoText Entries")
Insert symbols	2	"Inserting Symbols and Foreign Characters"
Create and apply frequently used text with AutoCorrect	6	"Entering Text and Graphics Quickly with the AutoCorrect Command"
Working with Paragraphs		
Align text in paragraphs (Center, Left, Right, and Justified)	8	"Aligning, Centering, and Justifying Text"
Add bullets and numbering	10	"The Bare-Bones Basics: Bulleted and Numbered Lists"
Set character, line, and paragraph spacing options	8	"Adjusting the Space Between Lines and Paragraphs"

Table C-1. *MOUS Objectives for the Core Exam* (continued)

Exam Objective	Chapter	Look for This Heading
Working with Paragraphs (continued)		
Apply borders and shading to paragraphs	7	"Putting Borders, Shading, and Color on Paragraphs"
Use indentation options (Left, Right, First Line, and Hanging Indent)	8	"Indenting Text on the Page"
Use the Tabs command (Center, Decimal, Left, and Right)	8	"Aligning Text with Tab Stops"
Create an outline-style numbered list	10	"Numbering the Headings and Chapters in a Document"
Set tabs with leaders	8	"Using Tab Stops to Create a Leader" (under "Adjusting and Removing Tab Stops")
Working with Documents		
Print a document	5	"Printing Documents"
Use print preview	5	"Examining a Document in the Print Preview Window"
Use Web page preview	16	"Seeing What Your Web Page Looks Like in a Browser"
Navigate through a document	2	"Moving Around in Long Documents"
Insert page numbers	9	"Numbering the Pages"
Set page orientation	9	"Creating a Landscape Document"
Set margins	9	"Setting the Margins"
Use Go To to locate specific elements in a document	2	"Going from Place to Place with the Go To Command"
Create and modify page numbers	9	"Numbering the Pages"
Create and modify headers and footers	9	"Putting Headers and Footers on Pages"

Table C-1. *MOUS Objectives for the Core Exam* (continued)

Exam Objective	Chapter	Look for This Heading
Working with Documents (continued)		
Align text vertically	9	"Aligning Text with Respect to the Top and Bottom of the Page"
Create and use newspaper columns	15	"Laying Out Text in Newspaper-Style Columns"
Revise column structure	15	"Laying Out Text in Newspaper-Style Columns"
Prepare and print envelopes and labels	5	"Printing Addresses and Return Addresses on Envelopes"
Apply styles	12	"Applying Styles in a Document"
Create sections with formatting that differs from other sections	9	"Section Breaks for Changing Layouts"
Use click and type	8	"Click and Type to Make Formatting Easier (Sort Of)"
Managing Files		
Use Save	1	"Saving and Naming Documents"
Locate and open an existing document	1	"Opening Documents"
Use Save As (different name, location, or format)	22	"Saving a Document Under a New Name"
Create a folder	22	"Creating the Folders You Need"
Create a new document using a wizard	1	"Creating a New Document"
Save as Web Page	16	"Creating a Web Page from a Word Document"
Use templates to create a new document	1	"Creating a New Document"
Create hyperlinks	16, 24	"Hyperlinking Your Page to the Internet" (16) and "Including Hyperlinks in Documents" (24)

Table C-1.   *MOUS Objectives for the Core Exam* (continued)

Exam Objective	Chapter	Look for This Heading
Managing Files (continued)		
Use Office Assistant	4	"The Office Assistant and What You Can Do About It"
Send a Word document via e-mail	24	"Sending E-Mail Messages and Documents from Word"
Using Tables		
Create and format tables	14	"The Three Ways to Create a Table"
Add borders and shading to tables	14	"Putting Border, Shading, and Color on a Table"
Revise tables (insert and delete rows and columns, change cell formats)	14	"Changing the Layout of a Table"
Modify table structure (merge cells, change height and width)	14	"Merging and Splitting Cells and Tables"
Rotate text in a table	14	"Turning Text Sideways in Tables"
Working with Pictures and Charts		
Use the Drawing toolbar	13	"Drawing Lines and Shapes"
Insert graphics into a document (WordArt, ClipArt, images)	13	"Handling Graphics and Clip Art in Documents"

Table C-1. *MOUS Objectives for the Core Exam* (continued)

Word 2000 Expert Exam Objectives

Candidates for Expert Specialist certificates must have mastered the exam objectives listed in Table C-2 as well as objectives listed in Table C-1.

Exam Objective	Chapter	Heading
Working with Paragraphs		
Apply paragraph and section shading	7	"Putting Borders, Shading, and Color on Paragraphs"
Use text flow options (Widows/Orphans options and keeping lines together)	8	"Controlling Where Text Falls on the Page"
Sort lists, paragraphs, tables	10, 14	"Alphabetizing and Sorting Lists" (10) and "Sorting, or Reordering, a Table" (14)
Working with Documents		
Create and modify page borders	9	"Decorating a Page with a Border"
Format first page differently than subsequent pages	9	"Headers and Footers for Different Pages and Sections"
Use bookmarks	2	"Bookmarks for Getting Around"
Create and edit styles	12	"Creating Your Own Styles"
Create watermarks	13	"Decorating Pages with Watermarks"
Use Find and Replace with formats, special characters, and non-printing elements	6	"Conducting a Find-and-Replace Operation"
Balance column length (using column breaks appropriately)	15	"Techniques for Working with Newspaper-Style Columns" (under "Laying Out Text in Newspaper-Style Columns")

Table C-2.   *MOUS Objectives for the Expert Exam*

APPENDIXES

Exam Objective	Chapter	Heading
Working with Documents (continued)		
Create or revise footnotes and endnotes	18	"Handling Footnotes and Endnotes"
Work with master documents and subdocuments	19	"Creating a Master Document"
Create and modify a table of contents	18	"Generating a Table of Contents"
Create cross-references	18	"Including Cross-References in Documents"
Create and modify an index	18	"Indexing a Document"
Using Tables		
Embed worksheets in a table	14	"Creating an Excel Worksheet in a Word Document"
Perform calculations in a table	14	"Crunching the Numbers in Tables"
Link Excel data as a table	14	"Importing an Excel Worksheet into a Word Table"
Modify worksheets in a table	14	"Modifying a Worksheet"
Working with Pictures and Charts		
Add bitmapped graphics	13	"Handling Graphics and Clip Art in Documents"
Delete and position graphics	13	"Positioning Graphics on the Page"
Create and modify charts	18	"Creating the Chart and Entering the Data"
Import data into charts	18	"Bringing Data from an Excel Worksheet into the Datasheet" (under "Creating the Chart and Entering the Data")

Table C-2.   *MOUS Objectives for the Expert Exam* (continued)

Exam Objective	Chapter	Heading
Using Mail Merge		
Create main document	20	"Writing a Form Letter"
Create data source	20	"Preparing the Data Source"
Sort records to be merged	20	"Sorting, or Reordering, the Records in the Data Source"
Merge main document and data source	20	"Merging the Main Document and the Data Source"
Generate labels	20	"Printing Labels for Mass Mailings"
Merge a document using alternate data sources	20	"Using an Address Book as the Data Source" and "Using an Access Database Table or Query as the Data Source"
Using Advanced Features		
Insert a field	23	"Inserting a Field in a Document"
Create, apply, and edit macros	23	"Working with Macros"
Copy, rename, and delete macros	23	"Deleting, Renaming, and Copying Macros"
Create and modify a form	24	"Designing the Form Template and Entering the Form Fields"
Create and modify a form control (e.g., add an item to a drop-down list)	24	"Editing an Online Data-Entry Form"
Use advanced text alignment features with graphics	13	"Wrapping Text around an Object"
Customize toolbars	23	"Creating Your Own Toolbars and Toolbar Buttons"

Table C-2.   *MOUS Objectives for the Expert Exam* (continued)

Exam Objective	Chapter	Heading
Workgroup Collaboration		
Insert comments	19	"Commenting on a Document"
Protect documents	22	"Protecting Documents against Undo Tampering"
Create multiple versions of a document	22	"Saving (and Opening) Different Versions of a Document"
Track changes to a document	19	"Keeping Track of Revisions to Documents"
Set default file location for workgroup templates	12	"Setting the Default File Location for Workgroup Templates" (under "Creating a Template from a Prototype Paragraph")

Table C-2. *MOUS Objectives for the Expert Exam* (continued)

The
Complete
Reference

Word
2000

Appendix D

What's On the CD

On the CD-ROM that comes with this book is a variety of tests that you can take to assess your skills with Microsoft Word 2000. By taking the tests, you can find out how well you know Word 2000 and where you need to learn more. Even if you are not interested in obtaining a MOUS certificate, the tests offer an excellent opportunity to test your Word skills and knowledge (Appendix B describes what the MOUS certification is).

Besides the tests, you will also find practice documents on the CD. Throughout this book are "Learn by Example" icons that describe the practice documents found on the CD. In this appendix are instructions for opening the practice documents on the CD or copying them to your computer so you can open them there.

How to Access the Tests and Practice Documents on the CD

Whether you want to take the tests or merely access the practice documents, follow these steps to start off:

1. Insert the CD into your CD-ROM drive.

2. Click the Start button and choose Programs | Windows Explorer.

3. In the Windows Explorer program, scroll to the bottom of the window on the left side of the screen and click the icon called Mousword (D:) (or Mousword [E:] if your CD-ROM is on the E drive).

The right side of the Windows Explorer screen shows two folders: MOUS Word Personal Testing Center and Practice Files.

Skip ahead to "Testing Your Ability with Word 2000" if you want to take a test. See "Making Use of the Practice Documents" to learn how to open the practice documents or copy them to your computer.

Setting Up to Take the Tests

The previous section in this chapter explains how to access the folders on the CD. Follow the steps in the previous section and then read on to find out how to take the tests.

1. Double-click the MOUS Word Personal Testing Center icon. You see several folders.

2. Double-click the Setup folder icon. Internet Explorer opens, and in a moment you see the Test Yourself window.

Caution   *Internet Explorer must be installed on your computer in order to take the test. If your browser is Netscape Navigator or if Internet Explorer has not been installed on your computer, you can install it by double-clicking the Internet Explorer 4 folder in the Windows Explorer window. You can also install Internet Explorer 5 on your computer by following the installation instructions in Appendix A.*

3. Click the Read button and very quickly read the End-User License Agreement. Then click the Back button to return to the Test Yourself window.

4. Click the Agree button. You see the Quick Start screen, which lists software requirements for running the tests.

5. Click the Next button at the top of the Quick Start screen. You land in the MOUS screen, which lists the two exams you can take (one for Core users and one for Expert users). You might have to scroll down the screen to see the testing options.

6. Click a check box to decide whether to take the Core or Expert exam and whether to take it from the CD or install the testing software on your computer. If you decide to install the tests on your hard dive, click either of the Install To Hard Drive check boxes. A File Download dialog box will ask where you want to install the testing software on your computer. However, you might as well take the exams from the CD. You will save disk space that way.

You see the Exam window. Read on.

Using this CD if Internet Explorer is not your default browser

If you have another browser set as your default, you must use Internet Explorer to run the Personal Testing Center software, but you do *not* have to establish IE as your default browser. Follow Steps 1–6 above, and when you come to the Quick Start screen, choose to install Internet Explorer 4.0.

Then, follow these simple steps below so that you can use this CD, no matter which browser you have as your default. Once you have installed Internet Explorer 4.0:

1. From your Windows 95 or Windows 98 start menu, chose Programs | Internet Explorer.

2. Once Internet Explorer is open, select File | Open from the IE toolbar, and choose Browse to locate the Personal Testing Center files and open them.

3. The Personal Testing Center files will be located under the letter of your CD drive, in the folder called Excel. Locate the file called exam.htm and double-click to begin the exam.

Note   *If your CD has two levels of MOUS Exams, you will need to click on two different exam.htm files to run both exams. One file will be in the folder called Expert; the other file will be in the folder called Proficient.*

The Three Types of Tests You Can Take

As the Exam window shows, you can take three types of exams: the Live exam, Practice exam, or Review exam. To decide which one you want to take, click an option button at the bottom of the Exam window and then click the Go button. You can also decide which areas you want to be tested on by unchecking Topic check boxes. Each test presents 100 questions concerning Word 2000. The exams are as follows:

- **Practice Exam**   Answers are not revealed right away. However, you can click the Answer button along the bottom of the screen to see the answer. And you can click the Answers In Depth hyperlink to see an explanation of the answer (you might have to scroll down the screen to see the Answers In Depth hyperlink). The Practice exam is not a timed test. When you are done with the Practice exam, click the Done icon to view the Assess Yourself evaluation page.

- **Live Exam**   The Live exam works like the Practice exam, except the test is timed. A clock appears on the left side of the screen. You are allotted 90 minutes to complete the test. When you have completed the exam, two scoring features are available: Assess Yourself and Benchmark Yourself.

- **Review Exam**   With the Review exam, you don't have the option of clicking the Answer button to find out what the answer to a question is. You don't need the Answer button, because answers appear at the bottom of the screen.

Scoring the TEST YOURSELF Personal Testing Center

Once you have completed a Practice or Live exam, click the Stop button. Then examine the Assess Yourself or Benchmark Yourself data to see how well you scored:

- **Assess Yourself**   Shows you how many questions you answered correctly in each subject area.

- **Benchmark Yourself**   Displays a bar graph that shows the percentage of correct answers in each subject area and lists the number of questions you answered correctly.

Making Use of the Practice Documents

Follow the directions under "How to Access the Tests and Practice Documents on the CD" at the start of this chapter. When you can see the MOUS Word Personal Testing Center and Practice Files folders in the Windows Explorer window, do either of the following to make use of the practice documents:

- **Copy the Practice Documents to Your Computer**   Drag the Practice Files folder over the (C:) drive icon on the left side of the Windows Explorer screen. By doing so, you create a new folder on your C drive called C:\Practice Files. You can open the practice documents from that folder.

■ **Open the Practice Documents on the CD**   Double-click the Practice Files folder. The list of practice documents appears on the right side of the Windows Explorer screen. Double-click a practice document to open it. You can make changes to practice documents, but you can't save the documents, since the documents have read-only status.

Tip   *I recommend copying the practice documents to your computer. You will find it easier to open them that way.*

Following is a list of the practice documents and the headings in this book under which they are found. Practice documents are named after chapters. For example, the 2-1 Navigate practice document is found in Chapter 2.

Practice Document	Section in This Book Where You Will Find the Practice Document
2-1 Navigate	"Moving Around in Long Documents"
2-2 Go To	"Going from Place to Place with the Go To Command"
2-3 Bookmarks	"Bookmarks for Getting Around"
3-1 Copying and Moving	"Moving and Copying Text"
5-1 Preview	"Previewing a Document Before You Print It"
5-2 Print	"Printing Documents"
5-3 Envelopes	"Printing Addresses and Return Addresses on Envelopes"
6-1 Find and Replace	"Finding and Replacing Text and Other Things"
6-2 AutoText Entries	"Ways to Enter Text Quickly"
7-1 Boldface, Italics, Underlines	"Boldfacing, Italicizing, and Underlining Text"
7-2 Fonts	"Choosing a Font and Font Size for Text"
7-3 Text Effects	"Playing with Word's Text Effects"
7-5 Shades	"Putting Borders, Shading, and Color on Paragraphs"
8-1 Aligning	"Aligning, Centering, and Justifying Text"
8-2 Indenting	"Indenting Text on the Page"
8-3 Setting Tabs	"Changing the Tab Settings"
8-4 Creating Leaders	"Using Tab Stops to Create a Leader"
8-5 Line Spacing	"Adjusting the Space Between Lines"

APPENDIXES

Practice Document	Section in This Book Where You Will Find the Practice Document
9-1 Margins	"Setting the Margins"
9-2 Sections	"Section Breaks for Changing Layouts"
9-3 Header and Footer	"Entering a Header or Footer" and "Numbering the Pages"
9-4 First Page Header	"Headers and Footers for Different Pages and Sections"
9-5 Odd and Even Headers	"Headers for Odd and Even-Numbered Pages"
9-6 Borders	"Decorating a Page with a Border"
9-7 Page Align	"Aligning Text with Respect to the Top and Bottom of the Page"
10-1 Sort	"Alphabetizing and Sorting Lists"
10-2 Bullets and Numbers	"The Bare-Bones Basics: Bulleted and Numbered Lists"
11-1 Spelling	"Correcting Your Spelling Errors"
11-2 Grammar	"Correcting Grammatical Errors"
12-1 Apply Styles	"Applying Styles in a Document"
12-2 Edit Styles	"Creating Your Own Styles"
13-1 Lines and Objects	"Drawing Lines and Shapes"
13-3 Graphics	"Positioning Objects on the Page"
13-4 Watermarks	"Decorating Pages with Watermarks"
14-1 Revise Table	"Sorting, or Reordering, a Table"
14-2 Modify Table	"Changing the Layout of a Table"
14-3 Calculations	"Crunching the Numbers in Tables"
14-4 Excel Table	"Modifying a Worksheet"
15-1 Columns	"Laying Out Newspaper-Style Columns"
15-2 Column Balance	"Laying Out Newspaper-Style Columns"
18-1 TOC	"Generating a Table of Contents"
18-2 Notes	"Handling Footnotes and Endnotes"

Practice Document	**Section in This Book Where You Will Find the Practice Document**
18-3 Cross-References	"Including Cross-References in Documents"
18-4 Index	"Indexing a Document"
18-5 Charts	"Putting Charts in Documents"
19-2 Master	"Master Documents for Organizing Big Jobs"
19-3 Comments	"Commenting on a Document"
19-4 Track Changes	"Keeping Track of Revisions to Documents"
20-1 Form Letter	"Writing a Form Letter"
20-2 Alternative Data Source	"Using an Address Book as the Data Source" and "Using an Access Database Table or Query as the Data Source"
20-3 Labels	"Printing Labels for Mass Mailings"
22-1 Versions	"Saving (and Opening) Different Versions of a Document"
23-1 Macros	"Deleting, Renaming, and Copying Macros"
24-1 Hyperlink	"Including Hyperlinks in Documents"
24-2 Online Forms	"Designing the Form Template and Entering the Form Fields"

Also on the CD are these support documents: Data Source, Lower Paleolithic, Middle Paleolithic, Neanderthal, Query, and Upper Paleolithic. Four of these documents are part of a master document. I've included Query, an Access file, so you can learn how to use addresses from Access to generate form letters and mailing labels.

APPENDIXES

The Complete Reference

Word 2000

Glossary

Word Processing
and Computer Terms

anchor: To fix an object relative to another object or part of a page so that the object stays in the same place on the page after the document is repaginated. To see where an object is anchored, press the Show/Hide ¶ button on the Standard toolbar and look for the anchor symbol. *See also* **object**.

applet: A small computer program that is designed to be run inside of another program.

application: Refers to commercial software programs such as Word 2000 and Excel 2000. By contrast, a *program* is a list of instruction codes designed to complete a certain task. Among high-end computer types, using the term "program" instead of "application" to describe applications such as Word is considered very bad etiquette.

ascender: In printer's terminology, the part of a lowercase letter, such as the stem of a "b" or "h," that rises above the body of the letter. Font size is measured from the top of the letter's highest ascender to the bottom of its lowest descender. *See also* **descender** and **font**.

autoshape: The lines, basic shapes, stars, callouts, and other forms that are available from the AutoShapes menu on the Drawing toolbar.

banner: A large decorative graphic found at the top or in the margin of a Web page.

baseline: In a line of text, the imaginary line that letters rest upon.

bitmap graphic: A graphic composed of many tiny dots called *pixels* that, taken together, form an image. Popular bitmap graphic formats include CompuServe Graphics Interchange Format (.GIF), JPEG Interchange Format (.JPEG), PC Paintbrush (.PCX), and Tagged Image File Format (.TIF). *See also* **vector graphic**.

browser: A computer program that connects to Web sites and displays Web pages. The most popular browsers are Internet Explorer and Netscape Navigator.

byte: The basic unit of computer data. Each byte comprises 8 bits and is the equivalent of a single character or digit. Disk space, memory, and file size are measure in bytes. *See also* **gigabyte**, **kilobyte**, and **megabyte**.

card: A circuit board or adapter that can be plugged into a computer to give it another function. For example, a sound card enables a computer to play sounds; a video card enables it to show video.

case: Refers to whether letters are UPPERCASE—that is, capitalized—or lowercase. The term dates from the days of lead type, when typesetters kept capital letters in the upper tray and lowercase letters in the lower tray.

CD-ROM: An optical disc that can store up to 1 gigabyte of data. CD-ROM drives are now standard equipment on computers. To install Word 2000 or Office 2000, a CD-ROM drive is required. The term stands for "Compact Disc Read-Only Memory."

cell: In a table, the box that is formed where each column and row intersect. Each cell holds one data item.

click: To press the left mouse button once. *See also* CTRL-**click**, **double-click**, **right-click**, and SHIFT-**click**.

clip art: An electronic graphic that can be inserted in a file. In Word, you can insert clip art from the Clip Art Gallery (choose Insert | Picture | Clip Art) or insert your own clip art (choose Insert | Picture | From File).

Clipboard: The holding tank where data that has been cut or copied from a document is stored. The Clipboard can hold 12 items. Graphics as well as text can be cut or copied to the Clipboard and pasted in a document.

comma-separated list: A list in which each component—name, city, and phone number, for example—is separated from the next by a comma. You can use the Table | Convert | Text to Table command to turn comma-separated lists into tables. Also called a "comma-delimited list." *See also* **tab-separated list**.

concordance file: For generating an ersatz index, a two-column Word 2000 table with all the words you want to include in the table. With a concordance file, you can generate an index without having to review each index reference.

content: The droll term that Web site developers use to describe what is presented on a Web site. The person responsible for writing the text on a site is sometimes called the "content provider."

CTRL-click: To hold down the CTRL key while clicking the left mouse button. CTRL-click to select several items at once.

curb-feeler: Before 1960, luxury cars were outfitted with curb-feelers. These antenna-like devices, attached to the right rear fender of cars, helped in parallel parking. When you backed too close to the curb, the curb-feeler scraped the cement and made a scratching noise. That's how you knew you were too close to the curb and should stop backing up lest you scrape your chrome bumper.

cursor: The blinking vertical line that shows where characters will appear when you start typing. To move the cursor elsewhere, click with the mouse. Also called the "insertion point."

default: Refers to the options that are already selected when you open a dialog box or are already in effect when you create a new document. In dialog boxes, default options are the ones that the makers of the program thought you were most likely to choose.

descender: The part of a lowercase letter, such as a "p" or "y," that sinks below the body of the letter. Font size is the distance between the lowest descender and highest ascender. *See also* **ascender** and **font**.

desktop publishing: Using specialized software to produce professional-quality documents for printing. Word 2000 has many desktop-publishing capabilities.

dingbat: A small picture, such as a star or arrow, that can be inserted in a document like a character. As with characters, you can change the size of dingbats by choosing a font size command.

directory: In the DOS operating system, files were stored in directories. In Windows, the folder has taken the place of the directory as the means of storing files.

disc: Refers to optical discs such as CD-ROM and DVD discs. The term "disk" refers to magnetic disks such as floppy disks.

document: A file created in Microsoft Word. In Word, files are called "documents."

double-click: To click twice with the left mouse button.

download: To transfer a copy of a file from a site on the Internet to a personal computer. *See also* **upload**.

drag: To hold down the left mouse button as you slide the mouse across your desk. Among other tasks, you can drag to select text and to move objects onscreen.

drag and drop: The fastest way to copy or move text. Select the text, hold down the left mouse button, drag the text to a new location, and release the mouse button.

drawing layer: *See* **layers**.

drive: At the top of the folder-and-file storage hierarchy, drives represent places on the computer where data is stored. Most computers have an A drive for floppy disks and a C drive for the hard disk.

drop cap: An ornamental first letter in an article or chapter, larger than the other letters in the paragraph, that drops three or four lines into the text. Also called a "drop capital letter." *See also* **stand-up letter**.

DVD: An improved CD-ROM disc that can hold 4.7 gigabytes or more of data, enough for a full-length movie. DVD discs cannot be played on CD-ROM drives. The term stands for "digital versatile disc" or, in some circles, "digital video disc."

FAQ (frequently asked questions): On a Web site, a page on which common questions are answered. Rhymes with "back."

field: In a database table or other table, one category of information. A field is the equivalent of a column in a table.

file extension: A three-letter file designation at the end of a filename that describes what type of file the file is. The extension comes after the filename and is separated from the filename by a period. Word files have the .DOC file extension.

file transfer protocol: *See* **ftp**.

fill: The color or gray shade inside a text box, shape, autoshape, or other object. You can change the fill color or gray shade inside some types of objects.

folder: In the Windows operating system, files are stored in folders and subfolders. Folders, in their turn, are kept on drives—the C drive, D drive, and so on. *See also* **drive**.

font: A type style. Word comes with many fonts. Their names are found on the Font menu and in the Font dialog box.

font size: The size of letters. Font size is measured in points. *See also* **points**.

footer: A line or more of text that appears at the bottom of pages and usually describes what is in the document. Often a page number appears in the footer. *See also* **header**.

forced page break: *See* **hard page break**.

frame: (1) Similar to a text box, a container for holding text. Page numbers are placed in frames when you enter them with the Insert | Page Numbers command. Drop capital letters also appear in frames. A frame is an object. As such, you can move it onscreen or change its size. (2) A part of a Web page, usually found on the left side or top, with hyperlinks that you can click to go from place to place on a Web site. *See also* **object** and **text box**.

ftp (file transfer protocol): The protocol, or rule, that governs how files are sent to an Internet service provider. An ftp site is a Web site that can receive Web pages for display on the Internet.

gigabyte (GB): Equals 2^{30} bytes, or roughly 1 billion bytes. Beyond the gigabyte is the terabyte (2^{40} bytes or roughly 1 trillion bytes) and the petabyte (2^{50} bytes or roughly 1 quadrillion bytes). *See also* **kilobyte** and **megabyte**.

grid: The invisible horizontal and vertical lines by which you can align objects such as text boxes, graphics, and shapes. If you so choose, you can make objects "snap to the grid" and thereby align or crop them with more precision. *See also* **object**.

gridlines: The gray lines that show where columns and rows are in a table. When you enter data in a table, gridlines help by showing where one row or column ends and the other begins. To see or turn off the gridlines, choose Table | Show Gridlines or Table | Hide Gridlines.

gutter: In a bound document, the part of the paper that is occupied by the binding. The term also refers to the empty space between newspaper-style columns.

handles: *See* **selection handles**.

hanging indent: A paragraph in which the first line appears to "hang" into the margin because the second and subsequent lines are indented. Word creates hanging indents when you click the Numbering or Bullets button to create a numbered or bulleted list. Also called an "outdent."

hard page break: Where the user instructs Word to end one page and begin another. Usually, with a soft page break, Word ends one page and begins the next as each page fills up. Press CTRL-ENTER to insert a hard page break. Also called a "forced page break" and a "manual page break."

header: A line or two that appears at the top of pages and describes what is in a document. *See also* **footer**.

heading row: In a table, the row at the top that describes what is in the columns below. You can tell Word to make the heading row appear again on the next page when a table breaks across two pages. A table can have more than one heading row. Also called a "header row."

home page: The first page, or introductory page, of a Web site. Usually the home page offers hyperlinks that you can click to go to other pages on the Web site. Also, in Internet Explorer, the first page you go to when you connect to the Internet.

hot key: The underlined letter in a command name. Press the hot key along with the ALT key to choose a menu command.

hyperlink: An electronic link between two documents or two addresses on the Internet. When you click a hyperlink, you go directly to another document or Web page. You can tell when the pointer has moved over a hyperlink because the pointer changes into a gloved hand.

Hypertext Markup Language (HTML): The formatting codes that browsers read in order to display Web pages on the Internet or on an intranet.

Internet: The "network of networks" that links computers. Web pages are displayed on the Internet, and e-mail can be sent across the Internet. The term is an abbreviation of "inter-network."

Internet service provider (ISP): A company that provides customers access to the Internet. Some ISPs also allow customers to post Web pages.

intranet: A private network, usually maintained by a company or institution, to which only employees or members have access. Web sites and Web pages can be posted on intranets as well as the Internet.

ISP: *See* **Internet service provider**.

K: *See* **kilobyte**.

KB: *See* **kilobyte**.

kerning: Moving pairs of letters closer together or farther apart. When large font sizes are used in headings, letters sometimes have to be kerned so they aren't jammed too close together or pushed to far apart.

keyword: For the purpose of searching the Internet or searching for instructions in a Help program, a word that describes what information is needed. If the keyword is found on a Web page or in a set of Help instructions, the Web page or set of instructions is named in the results of the search.

kilobyte (K, KB): Equals 2^{10} bytes, or roughly a thousand bytes. Storing one page of a Word 2000 document requires about 1 kilobyte of disk space. *See also* **byte**, **gigabyte**, and **megabyte**.

landscape page: A page turned on its side so that it is wider than it is tall. You can print landscape and portrait pages in Word 2000. *See also* **portrait page**.

layers: Whether an object appears above or behind another object, or above or behind the text on the page, depends on which layer it is on. From top to bottom, the layers are the foreground layer, text layer, background layer, and header/footer layer. To move an object from one layer to another, click the Draw button on the Drawing toolbar, choose Order, and then choose an Order command. *See also* **object**.

leader: A series of identical characters, usually periods, that lead the reader's eye from one place on the page to another. Leaders are often found in tables of contents. They are the periods between a table of contents entry and the page number it refers to.

leading: The vertical distance between two lines of type. Rhymes with "sledding." The term comes from the days of handset lead type when thin strips of lead were laid between rows of type in order to add space between the rows.

lowercase: *See* **case**.

macro: A set of command instructions recorded under a name. When a user executes the macro, the program carries out all the instructions.

mail-merge: Refers to merging an address list and letter text in order to generate form letters or mailing labels.

manual page break: *See* **hard page break**.

megabyte (MB): Equals 2^{20} bytes, or roughly 1 million bytes. Storing 500 pages in a Word 2000 document requires about 1 megabyte. *See also* **gigabyte** and **kilobyte**.

mirror margins: On a page spread, when margins on the left side of the gutter mirror those on the right side of the gutter. The left margin on the right-hand page and the right margin on the left-hand page, called the "outside margins," are the same width; the right margin on the left-hand page and the left margin on the right-hand page, called the "inside margins," are likewise the same width. *See also* **gutter** and **page spread**.

modem: The hardware device by which computers can transmit data over the telephone lines. You need a modem to travel the Internet or send e-mail messages. The term stands for "modulator-demodulator."

monospace font: A font in which each character occupies the same amount of horizontal space regardless of its width—a narrow letter, such as an "l," for example taking as much room as a wide letter like an "m." Courier is a monospace font. *See also* **proportional font.**

nested list: A list found inside of another list. Also called a "sublist."

nonbreaking hyphen: A hyphen you can enter to tell Word 2000 not to break a hyphenated phrase when it appears on the right side of a line and would normally be broken. Press CTRL-SHIFT-HYPHEN to enter a nonbreaking hyphen.

object: After a clip art image, graphic, autoshape, shape, line, text box, or WordArt image lands on the page, Word treats it as an object. The commands for manipulating objects—for positioning them, changing their size, and so on—are the same, no matter which type of object is being manipulated.

Office Assistant: The pesky animated figure that appears when you press F1 and sometimes appears without being invited when you do certain tasks. Type a question in the bubble caption above the Office Assistant and click the Search button to open the Help program and get advice about completing tasks.

OLE (Object Linking and Embedding): A standard by which data created in one file can be copied and displayed in another file. The copied data retains its connection to the source file, so that when the source file is edited, the editorial changes also appear in the copy.

orphan: In typesetter's terminology, when the first line of a paragraph appears by itself at the bottom of a page. To typesetters, an orphan is considered an eyesore and is to be avoided. *See also* **widow.**

outdent: *See* **hanging indent.**

overtype: To type over characters on the screen instead of pushing them aside. Normally, characters that are already onscreen move to the right as you enter new characters, but those characters are erased in overtype mode. Double-click the OVR button on the Status bar to switch to overtype mode. Also called "overwrite."

page spread: In a book or a bound document in which text is printed on both sides of the paper, the two pages that appear side by side when the book or Word document is opened. Even-numbered pages appear on the left side of the page spread; odd-numbered pages appear on the right side. You can create different headers and footers for odd-numbered and even-numbered pages on either side of a page spread.

patch: A fix-it file designed to correct a bug in a software program. Go to the Word Home Page (**www.microsoft.com/word/**) to find patches for repairing Word 2000 bugs.

path: A list of the successive folders in which a file is located. Also called the "pathname."

picas: A unit of measurement used by typesetters. One pica equals 1/6 of an inch.

point: As a verb, to move the mouse pointer over an object onscreen, a button, or a dialog box option. As a noun, a marker on a line that you can drag to change the line's shape, or a marker on the boundary of a clip art image that you can drag to alter the distance between surrounding text and the image.

points: The standard unit of measurement for type. One point equals 1/72 of an inch; letters that are 72-points high are 1-inch tall.

portrait page: The normal way to print pages, with the short ends of the page at the top and bottom and the long ends of the pages on the sides. *See also* **landscape page**.

post: To offer a Web page for viewing on the Internet. Also to send a message to a newsgroup on the Internet.

proportional font: A font in which each character has a different width depending on its size. By contrast, letters in monospace fonts are always the same width.

protocol: A computer standard or set of rules designed to permit computers to exchange data or connect to one another.

read-only: Refers to a document or file that can be read onscreen but not edited. You can make editorial changes to a read-only document, but to save your changes, you must save the document under a new name.

record: In a database table or other table, all the data that is recorded about one person or thing. A record is the equivalent of a row in a table. *See also* field.

right-click: To click with the right mouse button instead of the left mouse button. Right-click to see shortcut menus in Word.

sans-serif font: A plain font in which the characters do not have short ornamental lines (serifs) at the end. Sans-serif fonts are thought to be harder to read than serif fonts but are preferred in headings because they carry heavy type well. *Sans serif* means "without stroke" in French. *See also* **serif font**.

section: A formal break in a document where certain kinds of formats are introduced or a different size of paper is used.

Select Browse Object button: The round button in the lower-right corner of the Word screen. Click it (or press ALT-CTRL-HOME) and you'll see a menu for moving the cursor to different places in a document.

selection handles: The squares that appear on the periphery of an object when it is selected. By dragging a selection handle, you can change an object's size or shape. All objects except straight lines have eight selection handles; straight lines have two selection handles, one on either end. *See also* **object**.

serif font: A font with short, ornamental strokes on the ends of letters. Times New Roman is an example of a serif font. Serif fonts are considered easier to read and are often used for the main text, whereas sans-serif fonts are used in headings. *See also* **sans-serif font**.

shareware: Software that is offered for evaluation at no cost. Users of shareware are usually asked to pay a registration fee. Most shareware programs cease operating after a trial period if the registration fee is not paid.

SHIFT-click: To hold down the SHIFT key while clicking the mouse. SHIFT-click to select several items at once.

shortcut key: A key combination you press that gives a command right away. For example, press CTRL-S to save a document.

side heading: A heading that appears to the side of the text, in the left margin, instead of above the text.

soft page break: Where the page ends as one page fills up and another is needed, Word enters soft page breaks. By contrast, the user enters a hard page break to forcibly begin a new page before it is filled with text.

sort: To arrange text alphabetically from A to Z (or Z to A), numbers in order from smallest to largest (or largest to smallest), and dates in order from past to future (or future to past).

split: To divide a table cell into several cells.

split box: The small horizontal slot at the top of the vertical scroll bar that is used for splitting the Word screen. Move the pointer over the split box, and, when you see the two-headed arrow, click and drag to split the screen and view two parts of a document at the same time.

stand-up letter: A decorative letter, the first letter in an article, that is larger than the other letters. *See also* **drop cap**.

Status bar: The stripe along the bottom of the Word screen that shows what page the cursor is in, which section it is in, which page it is in, and where it is on the page. You can also click buttons on the Status bar to record a macro (REC), track revisions to documents (TRK), select text (EXT), and overwrite characters as you type in new ones (OVR). The right side of the status bar lists which language the cursor is in.

style: A collection of formatting commands that have been assembled under one name. Choose a style to format paragraphs and characters quickly.

sublist: A list that is found inside of another list. Also called a "nested list."

switch: An instruction that modifies, formats, or prevents changes to the results of a field code. The switch instruction, usually a character or a number, is preceded by a space and backslash (\).

tab-separated list: A list in which each component—first name, last name, and phone number, for example—is separated from the next by a tab space. Word can turn tab-separated lists into tables. Also called a "tab-delimited list." *See also* **comma-separated list**.

template: A special kind of file that is used as the starting point for creating other files. All Word documents are created from templates. Each template comes with many predefined styles. Template files have the .DOT file extension.

text box: A container for text. You can place text boxes anywhere on the page, put borders around them, and fill them with colors. A text box is an object. *See also* **object**.

TrueType font: A font whose letters look the same onscreen and on paper when they are printed. You can tell which fonts on the Font menu are TrueType fonts because the letters "TT" appears beside their names.

upload: To send Web pages across the Internet to an Internet service provider so that the Web pages can be displayed on the Internet.

uppercase: *See* **case**.

URL (uniform resource locator): A site address on the Internet. Every Web page has its own URL.

VBA: *See* **Visual Basic for Applications**.

vector graphic: A graphic that is drawn with the aid of computer instructions that describe the shape and dimension of each line, curve, circle, and so on. *See also* **bitmap graphic**.

View buttons: The Normal View, Web Layout View, Print Layout View, and Outline View buttons, located in the lower-left corner of the screen. Click the buttons to view Word documents in different ways.

Visual Basic for Applications (VBA): A computer programming language used for writing macros in Word 2000 and other Office 2000 programs.

Webmaster: The person responsible for maintaining a Web page. Usually, the Internet address of the Webmaster can be found on the home page of a Web site.

widow: In typesetter's terminology, when the last line of a paragraph appears by itself at the top of a page; also, when a short word or part of a word appears alone on the last line of a paragraph. *See also* **orphan**.

wildcard character: A character that represents characters in a search expression. For example, the asterisk (*) represents zero or more characters; the question mark (?) represents a group of characters.

wizard: In Microsoft programs, a series of dialog boxes in which the user makes choices in order to complete a task or set up a feature.

zooming: To make the Word 2000 screen look larger or smaller. Click the down arrow beside the Zoom box on the Standard toolbar and choose a Zoom percentage to zoom in or out.

Index

F

O

LICENSE AGREEMENT